Brando Unzipped

by Darwin Porter

ISBN 0-9748118-2-3
ALL RIGHTS RESERVED
Copyright 2005, Blood Moon Productions, Ltd.

Blood Moon Productions, Ltd.
302A West 12th Street, #358
New York, NY 10014
www.BloodMoonProductions.com
www.BrandoUnzipped.com

First Edition published December 2005
Cover design by Richard Leeds (www.bigwigdesign.com)
Photo and page layouts by Theodora Chowfatt
Corporate logo by Ed Husser

WHAT THE CRITICS SAID

"There has never been an actor like Marlon Brando. Impassioned, iconoclastic, imaginative, impulsive, indomitable, and, most of all, impossibly attractive. How well he knew it!

In an astonishing new biography, **Brando Unzipped***, veteran Hollywood reporter Darwin Porter paints an extraordinarily detailed portrait of Brando, particularly about his early years, that is as blunt, uncompromising and X-rated as the man himself.*

'I don't think I was constructed to be monogamous," Brando once declared. "I don't think it's in the nature of **any** *man to be monogamous. Sex is the primal force of our and every other species.'"*

Women's Weekly (Australia)

"The tempestuous affair with James Dean is just one of dozens of homosexual relationships, flings and one-night stands in which Brando indulged during a lifetime of sexual voraciousness, according to a shocking new book that is sparking a major reassessment of Brando's legacy as one of Hollywood's most macho lotharios."

Daily Express (London)

Chapter One

New York City, or so it is said, lived through its headiest days between 1943 and 1948, going from the black-out nights of World War II to the neon-lit, postwar years that would bring on America's greatest period of prosperity.

Facing a sultry, unusually hot May afternoon as his train from Chicago pulled into Penn Station in New York, Nebraska-born Marlon Brando stepped down onto the concrete. He knew that he was different from other actors arriving in New York, and he also knew that he wanted to be a contender. To call attention to himself, he wore a cherry-red fedora. In his own words, "I wanted to knock New York on its ass!"

At nineteen years of age, he was a virile, macho image who moved through the city with a panther's grace. The Army might have branded him 4F because of nearsightedness and a football knee injury, but the love-starved widows and girlfriends—all in Betty Grable Technicolor makeup—left behind by soldiers and sailors, knew what the military didn't: Marlon Brando was a perfect physical specimen.

He received immediate approval from New Yorkers when he stepped up to use the infamous urinals at Penn Station. The 4F homosexuals who cruised there gave him appreciative glances as he took a much-needed piss. The sex-hunters obviously wanted him, and he basked in both their attention and their hunger.

Checking his tousled hair in the bathroom mirror underneath the station, he decided to leave it deliberately disheveled. It added to his sexual allure. He could feel his heart beating with the raw magnetism of his own burgeoning youth.

Powerfully muscled shoulders and arms filled his white T-shirt, one size too small. His well-developed legs were encased in the tightest pair of blue jeans seen on the streets of New York in that era of baggy pants. Before leaving the Middle West, he'd washed his jeans a dozen times, letting them dry on his frame, until they showcased his genitals into a tight, provocative, and promising "package of goodies," as he called them.

31 years before *One-Eyed Jacks*

As he gathered up his lone suitcase, made of cowhide, his sweat wetted his T-shirt in half-moons around his armpits. He'd made the right decision to wear no underwear, as he didn't want anything to come between his jeans and his skin.

In the mirror, he checked what he called "my pearly whites." The face staring back at him was deliberately uncouth and just a bit hostile, as he knew how sexually magnetic that was to any horny woman or homosexual male who wanted to get plugged. Even after hours on the bus, away from the gym, his body was still rock hard, the creation of digging ditches and laying tiles under the hot sun of the Middle West.

Perhaps it's apocryphal, but Marlon was alleged to have given his last five dollars to a fat black shoeshine man, who'd ridden the train up from New Orleans. "What you doing in New York, Mr. Man?" the shoeblack supposedly asked.

"I'm here to have a hell of a time!" Marlon is alleged to have responded.

"Thanks for the tip, the biggest I ever got. I'm lucky to get a nickel." He looked Marlon up and down as if sizing him up, not able to place him. "Where you from?"

"Born in Rangoon," he lied. "My daddy had an overseas job there before the war."

"And where might this Rangoon be?" the shoeblack asked. "I don't rightly know."

"It's over there and down a bit," Marlon said.

"Ok, now I know where it is," the black said.

Waving him good-bye, Marlon wandered into the dying afternoon of a New York war year. He'd had his first conversation with a native, even though the man was from Louisiana.

Marlon sampled the local breezes—not as fresh as Nebraska, but the good air of a city at war in both the Pacific and the Atlantic. New Yorkers feared at any time they might come under aerial bombardment. With a sense of danger, he looked up at the clear sky, as if anticipating a squadron of Nazi bombers.

Arriving in town, he wanted to become the *enfant terrible* of this dynamic city that lived on the edge. His actress mother, Dorothy, whom he called "Dodie," had taught him what an *enfant terrible* was, and he wanted to become one.

Marlon Brando Sr. was back in Chicago, locked into a dull job at Calcium Carbonate, in which he earned one-thousand dollars a month, plus commissions. Marlon Jr. knew he'd never be controlled or dominated by his father ever again, once he'd "liberated" himself on the streets of New York.

As a send-off for his son from Chicago, Marlon Sr. said, "The theater? That's for faggots! It's not man's work. Just take a look at yourself in the mirror and ask yourself if someone would pay good money to see a shit-kicking Nebraska boy like you emote on the stage."

"Bud" was no longer the name for him. He'd outgrown that nickname applied at his birth on April 3, 1924, back in Omaha.

It was going to be Marlon from now on. In his hopes and dreams, he knew that the whole world would soon be familiar with the name Marlon. "No, that's not right," he said out loud, attracting the attention of two women shoppers. "No, not Marlon. The world will know me by only one name. BRANDO!"

And so it came to be.

* * *

His sister, Frances Brando, born a year and a half before Marlon, lived on a cul-de-sac on Patchin Place in Greenwich Village. An aspiring artist, she was in a deep depression, having heard from the War Department that her lover, a Navy pilot, had been shot down and was instantly killed. Marlon tried to cheer her up, but at the time she was inconsolable.

Escaping from her flat, he was "free at last." No military school, no critical father to chastise him. He could be a true bohemian and stay up all night if he wanted to. He recalled that one time, "the first night I got officially plastered in my whole life," he fell asleep in the bushes of Washington Square and woke up on the sidewalk, with men in briefcases stepping over him on their way to work.

He didn't want to become one of those dark-suited men with their briefcases. He tried the odd job here and there. A waiter in a spaghetti house on Bleeker Street. A sandwich man assisting a vendor on Fifth Avenue where Marlon claimed he made fifty tuna fish sandwiches in about one hour. A short order cook "frying juicy burgers" at a tourist trap hole-in-the-wall near Times Square. An elevator operator at Best's Department Store was followed by a brief stint as a lemonade salesman in Central Park. For three days he drove a truck in New Jersey before he crashed it.

3

Frances, Jocelyn, and Marlon in Evanston, Illinois

Mostly he was free to wander about, which is what he was doing on the day he discovered Life Cafeteria on Seventh Avenue South. It was a place where rubber-neckers from the Middle West, with tour guides in hand, ventured into the Village to "gape at the faggots and the bull dykes," who were on display through the cafeteria's picture windows that opened to the street. "I remember seeing these baboons on the sidewalk staring in at these young men and women ordering food and drink," Marlon later recalled. "The rednecks were pointing at the diners like animals in a zoo. I was immediately intrigued and ventured in. Before I left that afternoon, I discovered that many of the homosexual men were actually putting on a show for the jam." Jam was a code word for straights. "They were deliberately acting real effeminate as a fuck-you to the straights." He recalled that a table of men and women "quickly adopted me and made me feel like I belonged."

It made no difference to him what the patrons did in private. "All my life I've never been interested in someone else's sex life—only my own," Marlon said. "I became a regular patron. One of the waiters developed a crush on me and served me food even when I didn't have enough money to pay for it."

A regular patron of Life Cafeteria was a struggling young writer, Tennessee Williams, who also survived on the leanest of budgets. But the future Southern author and the actor "destined" to play Stanley Kowalski didn't meet until much later on the beach in Provincetown.

Not everyone rushed to accept this brash young man from Nebraska, who

4

wore his trademark red fedora for another year. On Patchin Place, the same street where he lived with Frances, the famous novelist and playwright, Djuana Barnes, maintained an apartment at No. 5.

Marlon had read her underground 1936 novel, *Nightwood*, a masterpiece of Modernist writing with its lesbian overtones. He felt he could just barge up to her second-floor studio and introduce himself in spite of the "Do Not Disturb" sign on her doorbell. Not knowing about Barnes' self-imposed exile, he met not the author but a burly, older women whom he later called "the Bitch of Buchenwald." He was chased down the stairs and into the street.

Receiving money from home, Marlon was free to enroll in the Dramatic Workshop at the New School for Social Research on West Twelfth Street. Since 1940 it had been turning out such graduates as Beatrice Arthur, Harry Belafonte, Shelley Winters, Rod Steiger, and ultimately Maureen Stapleton and Elaine Stritch. Even Tennessee Williams participated in a playwriting workshop here, an instructor warning him that his plays "are much too vulgar for stage presentation."

The acting courses were conceived by Erwin Piscator, disciple of Max Reinhardt, a refugee from the Third Reich and one of the most dynamic and creative forces on the contemporary stage. He was noted for his experimental stagecraft, which included bare sets and realistic acting. His left-wing ideology led to charges of Communism.

Piscator had created the celebrated Epic Theatre in Germany, but made a dangerous mistake in marrying Maria Ley, a Jewish ballet dancer from Vienna. Hearing of this, Hitler ordered the SS to arrest Piscator. The SS hauled in the wrong man. Before the mistake could be discovered, Piscator learned of the order of his arrest and somehow managed to escape to England where he, along with Maria, boarded a ship sailing for New York's harbor.

Marlon didn't take Piscator's classes all that seriously, often not showing up for them, and devoting himself to other classes such as yoga, dancing, and fencing. Walter Matthau, one of the graduates of the New School, mockingly called it the "Neurotic Workshop for Sexual Research." In his view, Marlon wanted to become an actor "so that he could get fucked from here to Timbuktu."

Behind Piscator's back, Marlon mocked his Teutonic mannerisms and speech, at one time pretending Piscator was Hitler, much to the howling amusement of Marlon's fellow Workshop students.

Erwin Piscator

Charles Chaplin and Albert Einstein

Piscator's heavy German accent made him easy for Marlon to caricature. The director's eyes were of the cold cobalt blue type that "dropped the gas pellets," and his mop of unruly hair was of a peculiar gray, like naval battleships were painted.

Marlon always showed up for class when a famous speaker appeared for talks, followed by a question-and-answer period. Paul Muni was a guest, later Sinclair Lewis and Paul Robeson, even Bertolt Brecht. Before he turned twenty, Marlon was meeting some of the cultural elite of America. The guest speakers had left-wing politics, or else they didn't get invited to the New School.

Through Piscator, Marlon one afternoon met Albert Einstein and would recall the meeting for the rest of his life. Einstein had lobbied the U.S. government to grant citizenship to Piscator.

Regrettably, Marlon was not in school the following week when Einstein reappeared to see Piscator. The scientist's guest was Charles Chaplin, whom Marlon viewed as the greatest artist of the cinema. Marlon frequently expressed regret that he did not get to meet Chaplin. However, he would have that dubious privilege--disastrously so--when The Little Tramp directed Marlon and Sophia Loren in *A Countess from Hong Kong*, released in 1967.

Marlon spoke frequently of his meeting with the great Einstein. Yet, strangely, he could not remember one single word of dialogue that took place between them. In later years, he claimed that "I have a great deal in common with Albert." When pressed to the exact nature of that shared identity, he said, "We've both fucked Marilyn Monroe, and I think he was a little better at it than I was."

One day Marlon strayed across the alleyway leaving Frances in her studio painting. The next day he announced he was moving in with a woman named Celia Webb. He later claimed falsely in his memoirs that over a candlelit supper by a fireplace in her one-room studio, he'd lost his virginity. That was a gross exaggeration, tantamount to his telling the shoeblack he'd been born in Rangoon. Marlon had long ago lost his virginity in Nebraska.

Celia was a window dresser for Macy's, and she was extremely small waisted and exotic looking, having arrived in New York from some South American country, perhaps Colombia. She was ten years older than Marlon and lived with her young son. Her husband was somewhere fighting on the battlefields of Europe, and she was "lonely and in need of a man," Marlon later recalled.

Celia would be the first in a long line of olive-skinned beauties with raven-black hair that Marlon would bed.

She was known around the village for her jungle-print dresses with plunging necklines that went all the way to her navel, almost unheard of in the mid-Forties. She slashed Victory Red lipstick across her rounded lips, and her ankle-strap high heels compensated for her shortness. Marlon remembered that she never wore underpants. While strolling the Village streets at night, and having a sudden need for Celia, he would take her into a dark alleyway and "bang her against a brick wall."

He bragged that in those days he walked around "in a state of perpetual erection." He would later tell best friend Carlo Fiore that Celia was a "sexual freak who liked it doggy fashion, often preferring penetration while she talked on the phone."

At one point Celia announced to Frances that her brother had proposed to her, but Marlon at the time was dating other women—and men—and had hardly settled down with one woman even as sexy as Celia.

When she lost her job as a window dresser and had to give up her apartment, Marlon eventually found another small studio for her on MacDougal Street in Greenwich Village.

Sometimes he'd show up at Village parties with another woman, even though Celia too would have been invited to the same gathering and was looking "love-starved and hungry for me," as he'd later remember. On those occasions, he would simply ignore Celia, pretending he didn't know her.

Their relationship would last on and off for several years. At the very moment of Marlon's greatest success in *A Streetcar Named Desire* on Broadway in 1948, Celia decided to give up her dream of marrying him. She departed for Paris. He would eventually follow her, but the relationship was never fully resumed, as Marlon discovered too many other distractions in Paris.

"I belong to the women of the world," Marlon would later tell Carlo Fiore. "Why shouldn't other women have a taste of me?"

In time, Marlon would summon Celia to live in Laurel Canyon in Hollywood—not as a lover but as his personal secretary. She'd try in vain to manage his messy business affairs.

* * *

Suddenly, Marlon was seen around the Village with an attractive woman named Caroline Burke. Born ten years before Marlon, she is credited with helping him "fine-tune" some of the subtleties of sexual intercourse with a woman.

Unlike Celia Webb, Caroline was Jewish, an intellectual, a theater-goer, an inveterate reader, a lover of classical music, and a collector of antiques.

As Marlon was to remember her, "She often wore some exotic perfume—Turkish, I think. I'm sure it was what dancing girls in the Harem wore when they shook their bellies in front of some horny Sultan. All I know is that every time she wore that perfume I got an immediate erection."

That Caroline was Jewish caused great admiration in Marlon. In spite of his growing up in an America riddled with prejudice, including anti-Semitism, he was a supporter of the Jewish people and their cultural accomplishments. That lack of prejudice also extended to blacks.

"He was a very liberal, very loving man," actress Elaine Stritch recalled, "at a time when there was much anti-black, anti-Jewish sentiment rampant even in the more educated enclaves of America."

In spite of all this admiration and that Turkish perfume, Caroline Burke had no sooner appeared on the radar screen than she disappeared from it.

* * *

While still operating an elevator at Best & Company, Marlon sought out another cafeteria in the Village when his favorite, Life, closed for vacation. He wandered into Hector's Cafeteria on Fourth Street and Seventh Avenue.

Sitting at the counter were two men with a seat between them. Since the only space available was that seat, Marlon, uninvited, sat down between them.

"I'm Norman Mailer," the man on Marlon's right said, extending his hand.

"And I'm James Baldwin," the black man on his left said, also extending his hand. "You can call me Jimmy."

In his memoirs, Marlon rather bizarrely claimed that Mailer was speaking with a Texas accent, claiming that he'd served in the Army and had told his fellow soldiers that he was from Texas to keep them from "beating up on a Jew boy."

Mailer, at least according to Marlon's account, still hadn't shaken that Texas accent. Actually, at the time of his meeting with Marlon, Mailer had yet to be drafted into the Army, whose experience would lead him to write one of the most memorable of all novels to come out of World War II, *The Naked and the Dead.*

"I grew up in Brooklyn," Mailer said. "So if you've got a problem with that, let's step outside and settle the score."

"No problem at all," Marlon said. "I'm from Nebraska. Have you got a problem with that?"

"I'm not sure that a place like Nebraska exists," Mailer said. "I think it's just a state of mind.

"If you're from Brooklyn, let's hear some Brooklyn talk," Marlon said.

"Fug you!" Mailer said in his best street-hood voice.

Over his bowl of soup, which cost twenty-five cents, Marlon learned that both Baldwin and Mailer were aspiring novelists. He liked Mailer but found him very macho, like a boxer who wanted to fist-fight you at the slightest provocation.

Marlon was more drawn to the black man on his left, who appeared far more sensitive. In spite of his ugly features, Baldwin possessed an inner beauty. Almost from the first encounter, Marlon concluded that Mailer was the most heterosexual man he was likely to meet in New York, whereas Baldwin was an obvious homosexual just emerging from the closet.

Marlon was later convinced that his initial opinion about Mailer and Baldwin was right on target. Years later, Baldwin recalled, hopefully with some accuracy, the first meeting of this unconventional and soon-to-be famous trio of rebels. Marlon had plopped himself down between the two men when they were

James Baldwin

engaged in an argument about race and sexuality.

"I have feelings of latent homosexuality," Mailer said. "Jimmy here has convinced me that I'm a latent homosexual. Even so, I chose to be heterosexual. What do you think of that?"

"To each his own," Marlon said, startled at the revelation and how quickly he'd entered another Greeenwich Village debate of the day.

"Norman feels that the issue of homosexuality is compounded by my blackness," Baldwin said.

"How so?" Marlon asked.

"I'm obsessed with black male sexuality," Mailer admitted. "You might say I'm romantically involved with the whole subject of blackness."

"Norman feels that the black male has the edge when it comes to sex," Baldwin said. "Want to chime in with your own opinion?"

"I really came in here for a cup of soup," Marlon said. "I don't want to get involved in any white boy/black boy kind of shit!"

In 1961 Baldwin would remember Marlon's dismissive comment when he wrote an article for *Esquire*. It was called "The Black Boy Looks at the White Boy," and in the piece he wrote about his relationship with Mailer.

"To me, the American Negro male is a walking, stalking phallic symbol," Mailer said. "I'm confused about the matter right now. But one day when I'm clear in the head, I'm going to write a piece about race relations. I'm going to call it *The White Negro*. Does that title excite you?"

"If you'll adapt it for the stage, I'll play the lead," Marlon said. "You see I'm an actor."

"Great!" Mailer said, rather dismissively. "So you're an actor. But what do you really do for a living?"

In the burgeoning friendship that soon developed between Marlon and Baldwin, the issue of race, at least according to Baldwin himself, never was an issue between them. "It just never came up," Baldwin claimed.

Later in life, in appraising Marlon, Baldwin said, "I had never met any  white man like Marlon. He was obviously immensely talented—a real creative force—and totally unconventional and independent, a beautiful cat. Race truly meant nothing to him. He was contemptuous of anyone who discriminated in any way. Very attractive to both women and men, he gave me the feeling that reports I was ugly had been much exaggerated."

During the days, and especially the nights, Baldwin introduced his new discovery to Harlem. The writer took Marlon to many of the

Norman Mailer

scenes of his own bleak and poverty-stricken childhood, showing him where he'd lived and played in the city dumps before going home hungry. He also took Marlon to the church where he'd become an evangelical minister at the age of fourteen. His 1953 novel, *Go Tell It On the Mountain*, documented these tortured early days.

Baldwin, the oldest of nine children, never knew his real father. His stepfather, a hard, cruel man who worked in a factory, had died in a mental hospital only months before Baldwin met Marlon.

He was sympathetic to the writer's early struggles, but mainly Marlon liked the Harlem jazz and the Harlem clubs to which Baldwin introduced him. By the time of Marlon's arrival in New York, the golden age of Harlem of the 20s and 30s had passed. It was the middle of a war, and clubs were still open but faced a dwindling number of whites who used to frequent their premises.

Baldwin told Marlon of such legendary night spots as the Cotton Club, and especially a place called "Hot Feet," where the entertainment was exotic and there were unlimited sexual possibilities. Cole Porter and Cary Grant were patrons, and a male madame, "La Rue La Rue," later arranged private rooms for the two celebrities with the more well-endowed performers. Brothels still flourished in Harlem, still catering to downtown whites who went north for "slumming."

At one "rent party," a free-for-all a tenant staged to raise money for his rent, Marlon was transfixed as he watched a piano player perform. Stripping to the buff, he inserted a lit candle, measuring twelve inches long, into his anal canal.

Marlon's favorite hangout became Lucky's Rendezvous at 773 St. Nicolas Avenue between 148th and 149th Streets. Lucky Roberts ruled the night, attracting a clientele of what one newspaper reviewer called "practitioners of what playwright Oscar Wilde called 'the higher philosophy.'" Lucky told the same newspaperman that he had no problems with his clients indulging in "same-sex hand-holding or gooey-eyed mooning."

It is not known for certain when the relationship between Baldwin and Marlon turned sexual. It perhaps occurred on the first night the author took his new friend to the notorious Mount Morris Baths at 1944 Madison Avenue, just below 125th Street. Opened in 1893, this was the oldest black bathhouse in the country. Although patronized by blacks, it also admitted white men, nearly all of whom were homosexual lured by the legendary tales of the endowments of black men.

Even when he wasn't with Baldwin, Marlon pursued Afro-Cuban music, and became a regular Wednesday night visitor to a club that staged a mambo contest. He was endlessly fascinated by the dance rhythms of New York's Puerto Rican colony.

From all reports, Baldwin was Marlon's first sexual experience with a black man. In his autobiography, Marlon admitted to having a sexual experience with Floretta, a nurse from Jamaica with what was known at the time as "bedroom eyes."

He said that it came as a surprise to him to discover that it was no different seducing a black woman than a white one, except in the sepia color of the skin, of course.

One night he bribed a musician with five dollars at a Harlem nightclub on 132nd Street to let him perform as a conga drummer. Later, he flirted outrageously with a beautiful "brown belle in a red satin dress slit up all the way to Honolulu."

When the beauty turned out to be the moll of a black gangster, Marlon, fearing he'd be knifed, ran all the way back to the Village.

* * *

Marlon's new acting teacher at the New School, Miss Stella Adler, made a grand entrance after all her pupils were seated. Barging into the room smoking a cigarette like Bette Davis, she was actually a cross between the devouring screen presence of Barbara Stanwyck and the steel magnolia aura of Margaret Sullavan. Stella was stunningly attired in a mink stole, red dress, and pink, spiked high heels. In all, she was a larger-than-life presence.

Sitting in stunned silence, Marlon found her entrance charismatic. In her early forties, she was a beautiful woman with soft blonde hair, steel-blue eyes,

Stella Adler

and a sharp, aquiline nose that she claimed made her look Jewish. Her appearance had sabotaged her attempt at a career in Hollywood.

Her mercurial reputation had preceded her entrance into the classroom.

Her father was Jacob Adler, one of the great stars of the American Yiddish Theater, and Stella herself had at the age of four in 1906 appeared on stage with her father's troupe. Her brother was the famous character actor, Luther Adler, and her husband the producer, Harold Clurman, who claimed that his wife's curly mouth was "the most sensual of any woman who had ever appeared on the stage."

Marlon was about to find out if that were true or not. He was immediately captivated by Stella. Or, as he put it to his sister, Frances, "I could have fucked her on the spot right in front of the class."

Harold Clurman

A passionate, expressive teacher, Stella in front of her class was volatile, often explosive. At one point, she fell on the floor in a fit of frenzy to illustrate a point in her lecture on Ibsen. She delivered "sermons" on acting like the most passionate of evangelists warning the faithful about the floodgates of Hell. As if watching a great moment in the the- ater, her workshop students were transfixed by her lectures which were more like performances than classroom studies. "She challenged the imagination," said student Shelley Winters, "and made us want to be bigger and greater than we are. Above all else, Stella never wanted us to bore an audience. That would be the greatest of all sins."

Stella had emerged from the Group Theater of the depression era. The avant-garde troupe was founded by Harold Clurman, Cheryl Crawford, and Lee Strasberg, who would later launch the Actors Studio. Playwrights such as William Saroyan and Clifford Odets came from the Group Theater, as did actor John Garfield, who would in the years ahead be offered the role of Stanley in *A Streetcar Named Desire*. Franchot Tone was a member, before going off to Hollywood and marrying Joan Crawford. The doomed Frances Farmer also electrified audiences in New York in the 1930s before heading for Hollywood.

Elia Kazan, who as a director would be a defining moment in Marlon's career, also emerged from the Group Theatre. The founding father of Method acting, of course, was Konstantin Stanislavsky of the Moscow Art Theatre. Group Theater members took Stanislavsky at his word: "The creativeness of the actor must come from within."

"The Method" of the Group Theatre changed acting in the American theater for all time. Up to then, acting had been stylized, artificial—external acting rather than internal. "The elocution was theatrical, the emotion unfelt until Stella came along," Marlon once said. "Through Stella, I, along with others, learned to truly experience the in-depth emotion of a character. The motivation came

Elia Kazan and Bobby Lewis
in *Waiting for Lefty*

from deep within our souls. After Stella, actors couldn't get away with that shit about putting their hand on their foreheads and sighing in pain to indicate despair, crap like that!"

In the middle of her lecture that day at the New School, Stella became aware of Marlon. All her other students were impeccably dressed, the young men in suits and ties. He showed up in a red fedora, dirty white T-shirt, threadbare jeans two sizes too small that showcased his genitals, and a three-day growth of beard.

"Mr. Vagabond," she said. "Please stand up. Do you have a name?"

"Marlon Brando!" he said, almost defiantly as if to challenge her.

"If there's a part for a bum I hear about, I'll recommend that you be cast."

Although dismissive of him at the time of their first encounter, because of his startlingly unkempt appearance, she quickly became his captive fan. Fellow student Gene Saks once said, "Stella was mesmerized by Brando, and he was completely captivated by her. It was a mutual admiration society."

After Marlon's first reading for her, Stella changed her opinion of her student almost at once. That night, she told her husband, Harold Clurman, that Marlon was "going to become the finest young actor on the American stage, far better than John Garfield." Since Marlon mumbled his reading before her, it is not entirely clear as to why she saw such great promise in her pupil.

In later years, she recalled the event. "The first day I saw Marlon, I knew he was a primitive genius. He was completely untrained, totally inexperienced, a vagabond who'd drifted in from the American plains but one of such visible magnetism I was physically aroused by his presence."

She had more to say. "In those days Marlon looked as if he might hump you at any moment like a beast in the field, and you knew you wouldn't resist. I predicted that women would swoon when he came out on the stage. I was one of the first among my peers to recognize his potent image as a male sex symbol. Ziegfeld was concerned with all those pretty girls being like a melody. But I knew that it was the woman who usually bought the tickets for theater. I also knew they'd pay good money to see Marlon. John Barrymore got it right. He once told me that every time he stuffed a big thick sock in his green tights, his female audiences doubled the line at the box office."

Marlon later confided to Frances. "I have found my mama. Stella will provide for all my needs."

Soon, much to the annoyance of her husband, Marlon appeared at the Adler apartment every night. Ostensibly, Stella had first brought Marlon home to meet her attractive teenage daughter, Ellen, but Marlon's interest seemed almost entirely focused on the mother, even though he later dated Ellen, presumably having an affair with her too.

One of the future founders of the Actors Studio, Robert Lewis, recalled

14

Before the broken nose

one night when he dropped off a script at Stella's. Marlon and his teacher were alone in her apartment. "He was stripped except for a pair of boxer underwear. He was sitting at Stella's feet, not having much to say but staring at her intently. She was smoking a cigarette while sprawled on the sofa in her nightgown. I just assumed they'd had sex earlier. I don't know where her daughter or husband were."

Upon seeing Lewis, Stella looked him over carefully. "Marlon and I are studying," she said. "Tonight I'm going to be a tasty overripe piece of cheese, and he's going to be a very hungry rat."

One evening Stella was sitting in a cafeteria with Marlon and two other students. Lewis was also at the table along with his pal, actor Burgess Meredith, who'd been rumored to have had an affair with Lauren Bacall before she'd gone off to Hollywood to meet her Bogie.

Meredith remembered that Marlon wasn't saying anything but was studying every move Stella made. Finally, annoyed with him, she said, "What in the hell are you up to? Do you want to become a Stella Adler male impersonator and take your act into clubs?"

"I like the way you smoke a cigarette," Marlon told his mentor. "You get carried away in conversation and carelessly drop the ashes on the table. You don't smoke a cigarette. You attack it."

Meredith was mildly surprised to hear Stella refer to Brando as "my puppy." "He did have a doglike devotion when he was in her presence," Meredith said. "I thought it was just the harmless crush of a teenage boy."

"Puppy," she said to Marlon, when he continued to stare at her, "are you listening to how I grow teeth?" To break the spell of his staring, she began to stare back at him. In front of Lewis and Meredith, she said, "What do you think of Marlon's face?" Although a question, she didn't expect an answer. "When he smiles, he shows all those shiny white teeth. Marlon's face seems to suggest that he has nothing to lose and everything to gain."

Theresa Helburn was a producer for the Theatre Guild and a key player in the stage career of Katharine Hepburn. Theresa was also a friend of Stella's, who introduced the producer to her protégé. At the time, Theresa was involved in the staging of her hit musical, *Oklahoma!* She gave him two tickets to see her show, and he later claimed "that's the first Broadway musical I'll ever go see—and the last!"

For years, Theresa "dined out" on her amusing story of Marlon's seduction of Stella. Theresa claimed that Stella herself revealed the details of Marlon's conquest of her.

It seemed that both Harold Clurman and daughter Ellen had left the Adler apartment without locking the door. On his nightly visit, Marlon knocked but there was no answer. He tried the doorknob, finding it open. Without knocking again, he entered the dimly lit apartment.

A light was coming from Stella's bedroom. He moved toward the light, pushing open the door to find Stella standing by the bed wearing "only her bloomers—no bra."

According to Theresa, "Stella was much too sophisticated to scream and cover up her breasts. She merely told Brando, 'I knew this was going to happen.'"

Slowly, according to Theresa, Marlon began to take off his T-shirt and jeans, revealing his young, muscled body. "There's nothing wrong with two actors being nude together," Marlon was alleged to have said. "It's part of my training. In our lifetime, full nudity will be sanctioned in the theater, and you know this to be true."

When Stella didn't say anything, but seemed mesmerized by his nudity, he went on. "Not only will actors of the future appear nude on the stage, they will also make love on the stage. In my lifetime, I will even seduce women on camera—that is, if I ever consent to make a movie. I need to learn how to act out the making of love on stage, which I know must be different from making love the real way. You are my teacher. It is your duty to show me the way."

Stella later confided to Theresa that she felt Marlon's seduction technique lines were the most original she'd ever heard.

"I guess you're going to take what you want," Stella told Marlon, "and I don't have any say in the matter."

"No!" he protested. "This is one scene where the teacher takes what she wants. I don't come to you. You come to me. Haven't you read the fucking script?"

"What script?" she asked. "There is no script."

"Teacher hasn't prepared her lesson," he mocked her.

"Stop it!" she shouted at him. "You're fucking up my mind. There's Harold. My daughter. I don't want this!"

"Then, why, I ask you, have you moved five steps closer in my direction?"

"I haven't taken one step, and you know that's true," she said.

"Cut the shit!" he said in a harsh, commanding voice. "We don't have all day. Harold and Ellen might return unexpectedly."

She moved toward him, standing awkwardly for a moment before letting her underwear fall to the floor.

In a low, sexy voice, he told her, "If you pretend I'm raping you, you'll have less guilt."

* * *

As a disciple of Stella Adler's, Marlon soon came into conflict with Lee Strasberg, her "blood enemy." Originally Strasberg and Stella worked in harmony at the Group Theatre.

Both of these acting teachers followed Stanislavsky's earlier teachings in which he claimed that an actor should "act from memory." For example, if the part called for an actor to show anguish, he should summon some personal tragedy from his own life to convey that pain on stage.

In 1934, Stella, along with Harold Clurman, journeyed to Paris to meet the great Stanislavsky and to study with him for five weeks. To her astonishment, she discovered that his earlier theories about Method acting had been severely altered. In his new teachings, Stanislavsky called for the actor to create his character by imagination rather than memory.

When Stella sailed back to New York with this new theory, Strasberg completely rejected "this revisionism,"

Lee Strasberg

17

clinging to the earlier lessons of his mentor. Students at the New School sharply divided into two warring camps, one led by Stella, the other by Strasberg.

"Your truth is in your imagination," Stella told her aspirant actors, including Marlon. In a dig at Strasberg, she said, "As for the rest, it's lice!"

The exact details may never be known, as there are too many conflicting versions. But the feud between Stella and Strasberg exploded into violence one afternoon in the hallway of the New School when she came upon her adversary. She was confrontational in nature and began to attack him verbally. At one point after an insulting remark he'd made, she slapped his face.

Instead of taking it like a gentleman, Strasberg was enraged and kicked her in the shin, knocking her down.

At this point, Marlon emerged in the hallway and rushed to Stella's rescue. He punched Strasberg in the face, bloodying his nose. Falling to the floor, the forty-two-year-old teacher was repeatedly kicked in the groin by Marlon, until two male students pulled him away. One of the actors claimed that Marlon was threatening to kill Strasberg if "he so much as laid a hand on Stella again."

The violence that occurred that afternoon would lead to a lifelong hatred of Marlon for Strasberg.

Marlon used the medium of his autobiography to strike back at Strasberg. Marlon wrote: "After I had some success, Lee Strasberg tried to take credit for teaching me how to act. He never taught me anything. He would have claimed credit for the sun and the moon if he believed he could get away with it."

Marlon denounced the head of the Actors Studio as "an ambitious, selfish man who exploited the people who attended the Actors Studio." He called Strasberg "tasteless and untalented."

The conflict bubbled over after the death of Marilyn Monroe. In her will, she left Strasberg in complete control of her estate. In time, that estate would earn millions of dollars in licensing fees for the use of Marilyn's image. The blonde goddess had wanted Strasberg to "distribute among my friends, colleagues, and those to whom I am devoted" the bulk of her estate.

Marlon was furious in October of 1999 when he learned that Christie's had auctioned the bulk of Marilyn's personal effects. In his will, read in 1982, Strasberg left Marilyn's effects to his wife, Anna, who had never met the star. Christie's auction brought $12.3 million.

This "greed" on the part of Strasberg wildly infuriated Marlon, who frequently throughout his life denounced his long-ago nemesis.

Marlon had been delighted when Strasberg lost the best supporting actor Oscar for *The Godfather, Part II*, in 1974 to his own protégé, Robert De Niro.

* * *

In August of 1943, all of Marlon's women and the odd boyfriend were put on hold, as if he were carefully storing them for some future usage. The arrival in New York of the teenage Steve Gilmore required all of Marlon's attention and devotion. The two young men had a very special bond between them, in spite of the fact that Steve was three years younger than Marlon and was just a junior in high school.

The love affair of the two teenage boys had begun in 1942 when Marlon Sr. sent his son to his own alma mater, the Shattuck Military Academy in the sleepy little agricultural town of Faribault, Minnesota, where the "winters are as cold as a witch's tit," in his father's words.

Hating the idea of the regimentation of a military school, young Marlon wandered alone among the ivy-covered limestone buildings, "feeling abandoned and deserted." He was imbued with none of the patriotic fervor that blanketed America in the wake of the Japanese attack on Pearl Harbor in December of 1941. Even fifteen-year-old cadets couldn't wait "to go fight the Japs."

In Whipple Residential Hall, he was assigned to a room with fellow cadet John Adams, to whom he took an instant dislike. However, he did bond with a cadet, Barry Dillman, who lived in the same dorm.

After only two weeks at the Academy, he began to date an attractive and very proper girl, Betty Ferson, a student at nearby Saint Mary's School. Reportedly, her mother was a close friend of Dodie's, Marlon's mother. Their romance was relatively harmless, one of those adolescent boy-girl kind of things that many other cadets pursued. Marlon took her to tea dances and to military proms, and for long walks by the river.

Dillman recalled that Marlon had great athletic ability, although not much discipline. He was a superb long-distance runner, a crack swimmer, and the best football player at the academy. "He was in better shape than any of us," Dillman later said.

Marlon also excelled as a member of the Crack Squad, a precision drill team that required rigorous discipline. The squad won the national precision drill competition

At Shattuck Military Academy

that year and was invited to Washington to perform in front of President Franklin D. Roosevelt. To attract attention to himself, Marlon went to a drug-store hours before the performance and purchased a bottle of henna dye like Lucille Ball in Hollywood was using. With an outlandish head of hideous orange hair—a "grotesque carrot top"—he performed in front of Roosevelt, attracting the president's amused attention but also earning the scorn of his squadron leader.

Marlon, or "Bud" as his classmates called him, told Dillman one day that he'd decided to become an actor like his mother. To accomplish that goal, he began to read every play written by William Shakespeare. He also joined the Shattuck Players.

The head of the English department, Earle Wagner (known as "Duke") was in charge of the school theatrical troupe. This confirmed bachelor, known as "the gay blade" of campus, lived at Whipple Hall in a two-room studio, filled with antiques, leather-bound copies of the classics, Oriental carpets, and overstuffed leather chairs. He walked around campus in long, flowing black capes lined in silk in such flamboyant colors as chartreuse and magenta. He was often seen driving around in his highly polished black Packard with a 100-pound English bulldog—"the world's ugliest animal." He'd named the dog "Lord Byron" after his favorite poet.

The handsome, athletic Marlon and the rather effete acting teacher and aesthete quickly bonded. In between his sports, studies, and meals in the din-ing hall, Marlon was often locked up with Duke in his private studio.

Before Marlon, young cadets, each wanting to be an actor, often visited Duke for long hours in his studio. But after Marlon, invitations to the other cadets were no longer extended. Only Marlon was invited at night to visit Duke.

Britt Philip, a classmate, said he went by the studio one night to pick up a play. "Marlon was clad only in his underwear, lying on an Oriental carpet at the foot of Duke, who was reading to him. I got the play and left hurriedly."

Another classmate later claimed that it was in Duke's studio that Marlon "learned to use his sexuality like a weapon." It was later to be employed with greater career advancement when he met such vulnerable homosexual play-wrights as Tennessee Williams and John Van Druten.

"I'm not saying Marlon was testing out the casting couch, but it was obvi-ous to me that to get the best grades and the star parts in our school shows, you had to hang out with the master," the classmate claimed.

"I think Marlon while still a teenager came to realize that many men in the theater—playwrights, fellow actors, and drama teachers—were homosexual and that they were attracted to him," the classmate said. "He was extraordi-narily handsome in those days and had a perfect body. I used to stare at him in the communal shower. Marlon liked to show off his body in front of the other cadets, some of whom were homosexual. He never seemed embarrassed or even conscious of his nudity, yet he was incredibly conscious of it. I know that sounds like a contradiction. He liked to show off his assets. All the other cadets went to the showers with a towel wrapped around their midriffs. Marlon strode down the corridors buck-ass naked. He could often be seen walking around the corridors nude, and he always left the door to his room open, lying in bed completely naked. All of us got to see a lot of Marlon's 'wacky' that year whether we wanted to or not. I later followed, more or less, a homosexual lifestyle myself, and I think it was looking at Marlon's nude body that made me realize my own desires. Since I'm now married, more or less unhappily, I don't want my name used."

Duke became so enchanted with his new pupil that he even wrote Marlon Sr., claiming that his son might succeed best by pursuing a career in the theater. The old man exploded. "I've got a wife who's been in the fucking theater for no good reason that I can see. I'm not going to have this professor make a fairy out of my son, not when I'm having to shell out $1,500 in tuition money to make a real man out of him. Not someone who sits in front of the mirror applying woman's makeup. Not some faggot who shakes his ass in front of an audience every night." Although he threatened to have Marlon removed from drama classes, his father never carried through with that.

After his appearance in one of Duke's school productions, *A Message from Khufu*, a melodrama centering on Egyptology, the school newspaper hailed Marlon as "a new boy who shows great talent." That review would be the first of thousands—both good and bad—in every corner of the globe.

Unlike her husband, Dodie was thrilled with Marlon's initial success on the boards, telling her daughters that her son had found his true calling. "It's the stage for him. I know he'll succeed where I failed."

* * *

One afternoon after class Marlon strolled into Boosali's Olympia Cafe for a sandwich and a cup of coffee. An hour later, he emerged from the cafe with Steve Gilmore on his arm.

Steve, only fourteen at the time, was a boy of almost luminous beauty. He was about five feet ten, weighed less than one-hundred and fifty pounds, and had ash-blond hair and piercing blue eyes shaded by long velvety lashes. His features were almost perfect, especially his Cupid's bow, red-lipped mouth and his peaches-and-cream complexion.

21

Marlon's roommate, John Adams, reported that after "lights out," Marlon was tying two sheets together to form a rope and climbing down to the ground from the second-floor window. Sometimes he wouldn't return in time for the 5:45 wake-up call.

Marlon's fellow cadets thought he was slipping out at night to "screw the maids," mostly virginal country girls hired by the school as closely chaperoned workers.

Marlon was really visiting Steve off campus where he lived with his parents. Apparently, Steve and Marlon had conceived a plan whereby he could slip in and out at night without alerting the boy's parents.

During this time, Marlon made another friend on campus, fellow cadet William Langford, to whom he confided that he was secretly seeing Steve at night, although revealing none of the intimate details.

One day in town Langford met Steve as he was walking along with Marlon. Langford found the boy "rather soft like a woman. He was sweet and seemed to have a childlike trust in Marlon, whom he clearly worshipped. He gazed at Marlon with almost total rapture and hung on to his every word like those uttered by Jesus Christ himself. Steve was kind of moony, and it was obvious he was giving in to his hero's every wish. No doubt in my mind as to who was the top, who was the bottom."

One classmate called Steve and Marlon "the beauty and the brawn." There was a certain truth to that. All his life, Steve had been told, "You're so pretty you should have been a girl." The boy was not very masculine and had certain effeminate gestures, which led to lifelong ridicule and accusations of his being a "sissy."

To Langford's shocked surprise, Marlon and Steve made no attempt to conceal their intimacy in public. "If they felt like holding each other's hands, they did." One afternoon when Langford visited Marlon in his room at Whimple Hall, he found him in bed with Steve. "It was obvious they were nude under the sheets. Marlon didn't seem to give a rooster's fuck that someone would come in and catch the two of them in bed together. In fact, he seemed to be flaunting his relationship with Steve in a very defiant way."

Steve demanded sexual fidelity from Marlon but didn't get it. Marlon became notorious at the academy for his seduction of young girls. At one time, and by his own estimate, Marlon seduced twenty-eight girls that year, ranging from older waitresses at the town's cafes to virginal young farm girls in the agricultural community, many of whom were hired as maids by Shattuck. Cadet James Stewart later claimed that Marlon "was an equal opportunity fucker—the girls didn't have to be pretty, they could even be fat. They just had to be fuckable."

For a time Marlon was able to maintain two secret relationships—one

"I burned insects"

with Steve, another with Duke. It was obvious to fellow classmates, however, that Duke was becoming too possessive of Marlon. The teacher constantly referred to Marlon as "my protégé—my showpiece."

"Showpiece, hell!" said one classmate. "Codpiece would be more like it."

Then one fine day Duke allegedly went into what a drama student called "a queen's tizzy fit." Apparently, Duke caught Marlon sodomizing Steve in a secret little hideaway he'd discovered. It was in a stone-built *campanile* (bell tower) with a planked floor over the Dramatic Association's storage room where sets were stored, along with discarded costumes and various stage props.

"Marlon clearly broke Duke's heart," Stewart claimed. "From what I gathered, it would be the first of a number of hearts—both male and female—that Marlon would break."

After that day, the supportive relationship between Marlon and Duke collapsed. In defiance, Marlon began to miss rehearsals or flup his lines when he did show up. He clowned around on stage, even rewriting some of Shakespeare's lines and putting them into a more modern idiom. At one point during one of Duke's pretentious lectures, Marlon let a big, smelly fart.

At rehearsals, Marlon challenged Duke's interpretation of a role, whereas in the past he'd religiously followed his mentor's teachings. One afternoon, in front of the other actors, Marlon called Duke "an armadillo's asshole," a favorite expression of Marlon's at the time. Because Marlon possessed blackmail evidence on Duke, and could have destroyed his career, the teacher was forced to take the insult. "Marlon had a big pair of balls and didn't mind clanking them," Stewart said.

Marlon not only called Duke an asshole, but informed his former mentor that he could no longer "take your shitty directions—I don't interpret characters like you do. I can't play them your way. You're too superficial. I've got to get to the depth of a character."

Langford, an aspirant actor, said that he too got caught up in the ongoing conflict between Marlon and Duke. "Marlon became uncommonly sadistic. I had thought that he had a gentle soul. I remember one morning he'd broken from a precision drill to rescue a caterpillar about to get stomped on by the marching cadets. He removed the caterpillar to a grassy knoll before resuming the military march. But there was another side of him that came out on the opening night of a school play. In the play, he was supposed to beat up on me. Duke had provided a light piece of wood for the scene. But to fuck with him, Marlon on opening night substituted a hard oak broom. As I ran around the stage, he beat me black and blue. I was screaming, but the audience thought it was naturalistic acting. I had to be treated at the local hospital, and I was bruised for weeks. I never really forgave Marlon for that violent beating."

That opening night was the final straw for Duke. He could no longer tolerate Marlon in one of his acting classes and asked him to drop out. By that time, Duke had discovered another protégé, even handsomer than Marlon but not as talented an actor.

After Marlon's departure, Duke stayed on at the academy, but was eventually dismissed when another faculty member caught him having sex with a young male cadet.

Marlon's relationship with Duke wasn't all that was going bad that year. His grades began to plummet, and he was in danger of flunking out of school.

Instead of studying, Marlon began to dream up pranks, as the demerits on his school dossier rose dramatically. One morning he stole all the silverware in the dining room and hid it so the cadets couldn't have breakfast. On another occasion, he looted slabs of Limburger cheese from the school larder and placed the smelly stuff in air ducts, forcing the evacuation of a classroom. He frequently skipped classes, running away on one occasion with a fellow cadet to Chicago. In the big city, he patronized black jazz clubs, listening for hours to musicians from New Orleans. Late at night, he picked up hookers and bragged to fellow classmates that in a three-day weekend, he'd bedded "seven of Chicago's finest pieces of ass." He also claimed that two of the hookers let him go for free "just to get some fresh, young meat for a change."

One morning Marlon climbed the Shumway Hall Tower on campus, cutting the ropes and sending the chimes crashing to the pavement below, nearly killing a cadet. On another inglorious occasion, he emptied a chamberpot out of a dorm window onto the heads of three cadets in their stiffly starched uniforms. In yet another prank, he stole bottles of flammable hair tonic from the rooms of various cadets and started a fire in one of the dormitory buildings.

The administration at Shattuck could barely tolerate Marlon's pranks. But their tolerance for him was rapidly fading. As if wanting to get expelled, he managed to convince eight other cadets—all freshmen—to show up in the dining hall with dyed green hair. "It wasn't just spring green," Burford said. "It was fucking chartreuse."

Later that night, or so it is still rumored, Marlon invited his green-haired brigade back to his private room where they were caught by a faculty member engaged in an all-male orgy.

All that became too much for the administration. Marlon was expelled, his failing grades cited as the reason along with his frequent violations of various "probations." The president at Shattuck wanted to suppress evidence of the male orgy, fearing it would adversely affect future enrollment. The scandal was hushed up.

Sent packing, Marlon headed for the rail station, but not until he'd sodomized Steve for what he feared might be the final time. He had no idea he'd ever see his lover again.

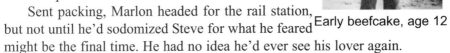

Early beefcake, age 12

That's why Marlon was doubly delighted when Steve showed up in New York. His rather wealthy father had been sent by his company to set up a junior branch in Newark.

Marlon would have weeks to be with Steve as the boy's parents apparently trusted the older man with their son. The exact details are lacking. But faced with seeing Steve every day, Marlon soon tired of him sexually, although the intimacy of their friendship would have decades to run before playing out.

It is believed that Steve pressed Marlon to run away with him, heading West. Steve was the first to suggest the possibility of future movie stardom for Marlon. The pretty young boy was flatly rejected. Marlon, or so it is believed, told Steve some very bad news. "I can't be faithful to any one person." Steve learned that Marlon, in addition to his love affair with the boy, was also engaged in a number of other intimate relationships. In addition to that, Marlon told Steve that he was also preferred anonymous sex with both men and women in a series of one-night stands.

Years later, when Steve consented to be interviewed about Marlon's life, he still couldn't bring himself to talk about the "destruction of all my hopes and dreams" with Marlon. He was more at liberty to reveal other secrets about Marlon but said that he never got over "my first heartbreak." At one point, Steve claimed that he'd contemplated suicide. "I spent the rest of my life loving Marlon," Steve said. "Throughout his stage career, I attended every opening. I went to every premiere of every film. When there was no premiere, I attended the first public showing of one of his movies. I became his most devoted fan."

"My second heartbreak came in the late 80s, when for no apparent reason, Marlon refused to take my calls," Steve said. "To get back at him, I began to reveal some of his darkest secrets. I wasn't going to let him cut me off in the way he did without seeking some sort of revenge!"

Chapter Two

By early January in 1944, Marlon was writing letters to friends and acquaintances in the Middle West, claiming that he was on the streets of New York "raising seventeen different kinds of hell." He never specified exactly what those different stages of hell were.

He continued to specialize in one-night stands, picking up both young men and women from the street. A fellow classmate at the New School, Jennifer Seder, claimed that Marlon dated "pure white trash, dirty-looking girls with stringy hair. I remember one horrible, ugly, and very fat girl with buck teeth he was dating. At the New School we called her Fang. Dating, Hell! That was the wrong word. Fucking was more like it. He was probably too ashamed of Fang to take her to a restaurant, even one of those late-night dollar-a-plate spaghetti joints on Bleeker Street."

Marlon wrote Don Henning, his confidant and headmaster back at Shattuck, that he was "having three serious relationships with at least three different women a week. Other than getting my rocks off, I have a more serious purpose. Clean underwear."

Brando at eight.

He wore his clothes until they started to smell, then he'd discard them for new ones. He was always in need of fresh underwear. At the apartment of one of his girlfriends, he would borrow her clean panties after a night of sex, leaving his soiled ones.

When he was spotted in the changing room at the drama workshop in women's panties, speculation arose that he was a transvestite. Actually, he wasn't. Although he'd occasionally dress in drag throughout his life, he was not into wearing women's apparel for a sexual thrill. The women's panties he wore were merely a "convenience of laundry."

During these vagabond days, he drifted from

one poorly furnished apartment to another, these temporary digs often borrowed from friends.

Marlon and his new "sidekick," Darren Dublin, became a familiar sight on the streets of Greenwich Village, hauling Marlon's possessions into a new home virtually every month. At the time, in addition to his wardrobe of T-shirts and blue jeans, plus one dark suit, Marlon owned a recorder, a small, easily portable red piano, and a tom-tom—and that was it.

Darren, a Bronx-born Jewish boy, was enrolled in classes at the New School with some vague hope of becoming an actor. The day Marlon met him, they became fast friends and didn't separate for forty-eight hours, talking until dawn. They fell asleep on costumes they piled onto a heap in the prop room at the New School.

One student described Darren's style as "early Woody Allen," but with protruding front teeth. He was small and unattractive, with a bad case of acne. Darren, or so it was said, was usually content with Marlon's "sloppy seconds," which often consisted of a string of black, Spanish, or Chinese girls. Whenever a Nordic-style blonde made herself available, her presence was a rare special occasion, like serving Beluga caviar at a family supper.

Often he'd take his dates, most often Darren, to a joint called The Cockatoo Club, where he'd beat the drums to entertain them.

Early in their relationship, Darren saw the Jekyll and Hyde side of his new friend, whom he referred to as "the poet, the sensitive side battling a raw animal nature."

In spite of his intensive dating, Marlon still found time for Stella Adler. She continued to call him "my puppy." He had taken to calling her "Mother Earth."

Stella Adler
"Pie in the face"

Through Stella, he was introduced to the (mostly male) artistic elite of New York. She called these men her *mishpocheh* or family. Marlon was soon hanging out with musician Oscar Levant, actor Lee J. Cobb, writer Irwin Shaw, composer Aaron Copland, critic Irving Howe, and even Stella's famous brother, Luther Adler, when he didn't have a stage or screen role.

When not hanging out with Stella's friends, "chewing the cud," as he put it, Marlon continued to take acting lessons from both Piscator and Stella. He even appeared in some school-sponsored productions.

At the New School, Piscator cast his unruly

pupil in George Bernard Shaw's play, *Saint Joan*. He did this in spite of having chased Marlon out of the auditorium the previous day when he caught him doing a wicked impersonation of himself. A future student of Piscator's, comedian Mel Brooks, would also do a devastating impersonation of the stern teacher. Brooks used Piscator as a role model when he inserted the character of the crazed German playwright of *Springtime for Hitler* into his hit show, *The Producers*.

Opening night on October 29, 1943 had marked Marlon's first appearance on a New York stage.

The Shaw play was followed about a week later, on November 5, with Marlon's appearance as Bartley, the son of an old woman in John M. Synge's *Riders to the Sea*. Before Christmas, he'd appeared in two more Piscator productions, both of them based on works by Tolstoy. Ambitiously, the teacher had condensed *War and Peace* into a three-hour stage drama. Shortly thereafter, Piscator adapted Tolstoy's *The Power of Darkness,* and cast Marlon in that adaptation too.

A male friend of Marlon's, Philip Rhodes, who eventually functioned as his makeup artist for four decades, saw both productions. Rhodes was especially impressed with Marlon's performance as Prince Anatole in *War and Peace*.

"Marlon was brilliant on stage," Rhodes claimed, "his presence mesmerizing. Though the other students were struggling through the heavy Russian drama, Marlon made his acting seem effortless—of course, that seeming non-effort may have been the greatest effort of all."

He also appeared in an English-speaking version of *Doctor Sganarelle,* a play by Molière, in which one critic claimed "Marlon Brando is an actor worth watching."

Showing that he was versatile, Marlon played Sebastian in Shakespeare's *Twelfth Night*, and later a giraffe in *Bobino*, written by Stanley Kauffman, who eventually became better known as a theater critic. The playwright Kauffman proclaimed that Marlon's role "consisted of being hit on the head and falling down, but he managed a way of falling that, without being obtrusive, was individual."

When Marlon was in costume for *Twelfth Night*, a fellow actor approached him backstage. The male student offered to help Marlon with his body posture, suggesting that he "lower your shoulders and put your chest out." The actor patted Marlon's crotch—not once, but twice—suggesting that he "pull this in a little."

At first Marlon stood motionless, taken by surprise. When the actor asked if Marlon were into "women, children, or men," Marlon punched him out. The errant actor ended up in the hospital with a broken nose.

Elaine Stritch

Piscator admonished Marlon for this violence, stressing that breaking someone's nose was not how professional actors showing basket in green tights handled propositions from fellow actors in the theater.

The actress (and later, comedienne) Elaine Stritch found Marlon's double role in Gerhart Hauptmann's *Hannele's Way to Heaven* "absolutely breathtaking." In the play, Marlon played both a prophet and a feeble old schoolteacher.

Although Marlon was pursued, he also pursued, being especially taken with Elaine, who was quite beautiful at the tender age of seventeen. Fresh from a twelve-year stint in a convent, she was virginal and relatively innocent at the time, thanks partly to her enrollment on 91st Street in a Roman Catholic finishing school which was strictly supervised by nuns.

At the time, Elaine was pretending to a sophistication she didn't possess, wearing outfits, usually with elaborate hats, which were inspired by the personal style of Stella Adler. Like Bette Davis in the movies, Elaine smoked cigarettes and tried to give "dramatic emphasis" to whatever she said.

In later years, Elaine claimed she fell big for Marlon "almost on first sight." He was extraordinary looking—very sensitive, artistic, and as wonderful as a character in a romantic novel."

Elaine's appearance may have misled Marlon. At any rate, he invited this daughter of a Catholic businessman from Michigan out on a date. Rather bizarrely, and in the spirit of a rather campy joke, he took her on a tour of some of the city's churches and synagogues, including stopovers at Greek Orthodox and Russian Orthodox churches. They ended up at a branch of the New York City Public Library, where he read passages to her from some of his favorite works, including Emily Brontë's *Wuthering Heights*.

Elaine had been expecting not this, but a night of sophisticated banter like those witty exchanges between Katharine Hepburn and Cary Grant in RKO movies of the late 1930s.

Finally, he bought her a plate of spaghetti, where she drank too much wine and consequently, could hardly walk. This cheap dinner was followed by a "dirty" burlesque show filled with bumps and grinds. This convent-schooled girl, who'd dressed like a Stella Adler clone for the evening, burst into tears at the nudity. Nonetheless, she accepted an invitation from Marlon to go back to his apartment to look at his cat.

Through the wind and flurries of a midwinter snowstorm, he guided her black-booted feet to a dingy apartment on West 12th Street. Giddy from drink, she rested on a battered sofa with the springs broken, as she tried to pet a female cat in obvious heat.

From the back of the apartment, Marlon emerged in red silk pajamas, the top unbuttoned to reveal his manly torso. Making hurried excuses, Elaine fled into the night, pounding on the convent door at three o'clock in the morning, long past the midnight curfew. Rising from her bed, the stern Reverend Mother opened the door, allowing Elaine inside and chastising her.

Marlon's reaction? He didn't speak to Elaine for an entire year, except on stage when he was forced to deliver lines to her, as he did in *The Petrified Forest*, the play that Bette Davis and Humphrey Bogart had adapted so successfully on the screen.

One of the few black men enrolled in classes at the New School was Harry Belafonte. As he had with James Baldwin, "color blind" Marlon formed a friendship with this Jamaican folk singer and actor. Piscator told Stella Adler that he suspected their student was having an affair with Belafonte.

Apparently not. Belafonte was strictly heterosexual. He did go out on several occasions with Marlon, however, but only to see a Broadway play. Belafonte most often saw the first act, Marlon taking over the ticket at intermission.

Later at a café over a glass of wine or else over a cup of black coffee, costing one nickel, they would discuss individual plays in depth, each telling the other how they would have interpreted one of the roles.

"Belafonte was definitely not one of Marlon's fuck buddies," Darren Dublin later said. "I'm sure Marlon would have loved for that to be, but, alas, there were some men and women in those days who eluded him—not many, though."

* * *

Stella Adler had formed a strong friendship with Clifford Odets during their shared experiences at the left-leaning Group Theater during the 1930s. She frequently and loudly proclaimed that his 1935 play, *Awake and Sing!*, dramatizing the struggles of an impoverished Jewish family, was one of the more brilliant works to come out of the Depression-era American theater.

For a few brief months, she entertained the idea that Clifford should write a play to introduce Marlon to Broadway audiences. When Clifford's 1937 play, *Golden Boy*, was made into a Hollywood film two years later, the role made a star out of William Holden, who was cast as the young boxer who wants to be a professional musician. She was convinced that Marlon in a play written by Clifford could become an even bigger star than Holden.

There was a problem: Arguably, Clifford was America's greatest living playwright at the time, and he didn't write dramas to order as a means of showcasing aspirant young actors. Aware of this, Stella developed another battle plan.

Knowing of Clifford's homosexual tendencies, and privy to the most intimate details of his long-running affair with Cary Grant, "she dangled Marlon in front of Clifford like a piece of meat," Bobby Lewis (who would later be a co-founder of the Actors' Studio) claimed. "As I was to find out from Clifford himself, he took the bait."

But not at first. Originally, when he'd seen Marlon in rehearsals at the New School, Clifford was not impressed. "That acting genius that Stella was ranting about was not apparent to the naked eye," Clifford told Bobby Lewis. "He looked to me like a kid who delivers your groceries. I tried to talk to him, and he was completely inarticulate. Yet I could tell he was bursting to talk. At the time of our first meeting, the words wouldn't come out. Later, when I got to know him, I couldn't shut him up."

Clifford was short and stocky, and he had a look of such intensity that his eyes seemed capable of melting ice. Under a wisp of unruly hair, he stared at you with probing eyes, as if he were about to ask you an earth-shaking question and that your answer would change life on this planet as we knew it.

Overheard by actor Lee J. Cobb, Clifford's first words to Marlon were, "Stella tells me you're a genius. Of course, everybody in America is supposed to be a genius. But rest assured that even if you're not a genius, there is something to be said for mediocrity in the arts."

Marlon turned his back on drama's greatest crusader for social justice.

Later, Marlon confided to Stella, "I saw fire in his eyes. But I had to turn my back on him or else I'd go up in the flames." During his first year in New York, Marlon often spoke in such melodramatic terms.

Clifford next encountered Marlon at a party at the Adler apartment about a year before the end of World War II. Marlon showed up in an ill-fitting suit obviously borrowed from a much smaller friend. "I tried to speak to him again,

Clifford Odets

but got absolutely no response," Clifford told Bobby, also a guest at the party. "Marlon just stood in a corner and didn't say a word. He seemed to be saying, 'I'll stand in a corner because the wall is solid. It protects me in the rear and on two sides. Therefore, I have to protect myself only from the front.'"

Marlon was in a much better form for his next meeting with Clifford, who had been the first to throw down the gauntlet. The breakthrough between Marlon and Clifford occurred at Child's Restaurant at Columbus Circle, a "summit" meeting attended by Stella herself, Bobby Lewis, Lee J. Cobb, and Stella's brother, Luther Adler.

As if he'd been rehearsed, Marlon tore into Clifford, claiming that although he had symbolized the essence of the American theater during the 1930s, Clifford no longer represented the Great White Hope of Broadway, but that instead he was in a meteoric decline, having sold out to Hollywood. "I understand that after showing early promise you are, in fact, being forced to have movie hack writers rescue your scripts."

To everyone present, it seemed doubtful that any lasting bond would ever take root between Marlon and Clifford. Bobby later confided to Cobb that he was surprised that Clifford didn't punch Marlon out.

To the surprise of everyone at the table, especially Stella, Clifford reacted by inviting Marlon for a nighttime walk in Central Park. No one knows exactly what happened during the course of that promenade, but apparently Marlon opened up to Clifford, and the two artists started to really communicate for the first time.

The next morning over Child's Restaurant's famously bitter coffee and buttermilk pancakes, Clifford told Bobby that it was the subject of Marlon's mother, Dodie, that unleashed the actor's floodgate of emotion. Clifford quoted Marlon directly, the exact wording as funneled through Bobby's memory. "When I was a boy, she was beautiful and tender, and I loved her above all others. But when I needed her and reached out for her, she wasn't there for me. My mother's an alcoholic. I thought I could solve her drinking problem through my love for her and hers for me. That didn't work. The more I loved, the more she drank. With her love of the bottle, there was no love left for me."

In this relatively unromantic setting, beneath the harsh lights and workaday setting of Child's Restaurant, Marlon's friendship with Clifford was launched, only to be deepened and strengthened within the shadows of Central Park after dark. It was a friendship that with a few ups and downs would last a lifetime.

A week later, Marlon confided in actor Joseph Schildkraut, one of Stella's best friends and a member of her extended *mishpocheh*. The thin, pale-faced movie villain listened in silent astonishment as Marlon confessed to him the depth of his relationship with Clifford. "Because I admired his mind, I gave

Clifford my body."

Clifford and Marlon were seen all over town together, going to dinner parties, the theater, art museums, actors' workshops, whatever. Clifford had the money to afford tickets to Broadway dramas. Marlon no longer had to share one ticket with an equally impoverished Harry Belafonte.

History does not record the long, intense dialogues between what some critics called America's greatest living playwright and America's greatest actor. Within days, Marlon had penetrated Clifford's shell, only to discover a deeply conflicted and self-destructive artist.

Harry Belafonte

"Clifford was not only struggling with his latent homosexuality, which wasn't so latent at this point, but he was fighting all sorts of inner demons," Bobby said. He once witnessed an hour-long discussion between Marlon and Clifford. "So intense was their dialogue that I don't think they were even aware of my presence at their table. They were talking about the relation between art and life, and it was fascinating to hear them. I already knew how brilliant Clifford was from having worked with him at The Group Theatre. But after that night in a café in Greenwich Village, I came to realize that Marlon, in spite of his age, had his own brilliant insights into the creative process. Of course, Marlon wasn't as articulate as Lee Strasberg, whom I adored and Marlon hated."

John Garfield

Clifford was a close friend of John Garfield's. It was a relationship that had begun in The Group Theatre and was solidified when Garfield had appeared in his play, *Golden Boy*. At the time of his first meeting with Clifford, Marlon, in lieu of anybody else, was using John Garfield as a role model for his own career as an actor. In a pattern that paralleled Stella's pressure of Clifford to write a play around Marlon, John wanted Clifford to write a play for him as a vehicle for a triumphant return to Broadway.

"For a man who liked other men, in spite of his marriages, Clifford must have been in hog heaven," Bobby said. "He was no beauty, but he had a lineup of handsome men who included Marlon Brando, John Garfield, and even Cary Grant vying for his attention. He must have felt like a king. Not only that, but women pursued him. After all, he'd been married, disastrously, to two-time Oscar winner, Luise Rainer. His friendships were legendary, even Albert Einstein. Clifford had spent weeks with that genius at his cottage on Long Island Sound. Clifford was even a friend of Charlie Chaplin, and later, Marilyn Monroe."

While married to Luise Rainer, Clifford had had numerous affairs with such actresses as the mentally troubled Frances Farmer, whom he'd met when she was in The Group Theatre. "He even stole Fay Wray from the arms of both Howard Hughes and King Kong for a brief interlude," Bobby claimed.

In the wake of his divorce from Luise Rainer, Clifford had met and married actress Bette Grayson on May 14, 1943. "Bette was his rosebud with great juicy melons instead of breasts, or so Clifford claimed at the time," according to Bobby.

But despite his recent marriage to such a sexy woman, Clifford and Marlon launched a sexual relationship, claimed Bobby, who was seeing both men almost daily during this white heat period of their lives. "The change between them was subtle and highly nuanced, but it was there. I have an instinctual ability to look deep into a man's soul, and I could tell they were in love, even though they tried to conceal it. For one brief interlude, I felt that Clifford fell for Marlon in a big way, even more than he had for Cary Grant."

"Marlon cured Clifford of one grand misconception," Bobby claimed. "Clifford felt that having a sexual climax would cut off the flow of his creative juices. He wanted to retain those juices—semen in this case—because he felt that by retaining them, it would lead to his writing great plays with memorable characters. Apparently, Marlon persuaded him that the flow of creativity had to parallel the release of semen. Marlon's point was that semen soured in your balls unless frequently released and replenished with a fresh supply. Both Marlon and Clifford, at least from what I gathered, were letting the semen flow between them, keeping their creativity juicy as well. The spigot between them was turned on full blast."

"And then one fine day, it was all over between them," Bobby said. "Clifford broke down and confessed everything to me about the affair. He'd fallen for Marlon, and he thought Marlon loved him back. But he'd failed to understand Marlon's mercurial personality.

Bobby Lewis
as Herbert Hoover

35

Marlon could be there for you one day, giving you the greatest time of your life, and then he'd be gone the next day. It didn't mean he was mad at you or even that he found you unfulfilling. In those days, and perhaps for the rest of his life, he was always moving on to some new world to conquer. Perhaps he'd decided that Clifford was never going to write that Broadway play for him."

Marlon used to be incredibly jealous of John Garfield who would eventually be offered the role of Stanley in *A Streetcar Named Desire*. During Marlon's early career, some critics had compared Marlon unfavorably to the better-established movie star.

The year before meeting Marlon, Clifford, in Hollywood, had been working on a screenplay for Warner Brothers based on the life of George Gershwin. In the scenario, Clifford had tailored the role of Gershwin for John, as improbable as that casting was. The film was shelved but would later be revived, retitled *Humoresque,* and even more closely tailored by other screenwriters for John, who was cast in the role of a temperamental violinist starring opposite Joan Crawford. Even though this script had been written by Clifford before he even met Marlon, it aroused a jealous fury in the actor when he discovered it one day in Clifford's apartment.

Almost overnight Marlon was no longer hanging out in cafés with Clifford but was seen walking arm in arm down the streets of New York with other loves of either sex.

It was to Marlon's credit that he later called Clifford in Hollywood and renewed their friendship, but not their love affair. With the passage of time, the sexual passion between them had dissipated.

Years later, in the early 60s, as Clifford lay dying on a hot Dog Day afternoon in a Hollywood hospital bed, fighting against the cancer eating his bowels, he didn't want most well-wishers to be allowed in to see him. His abdomen was swollen, and a tube was inserted in his nose. Another tube delivered wastes from his body into a glass jar at the foot of his bed. He was trying to decide who his true friends were.

Cary Grant, he'd decided, was no longer his bosom buddy. When the actor sent him a beautiful get-well card, Clifford called his former friend a "phony." He also rejected a massive bouquet of white carnations from "Mr. Hollywood," informing his male nurse to have the flowers delivered to another hospital room. When Cary showed up to visit him in the hospital, Clifford ordered his male nurse to turn him away. "I don't want him to see me dying."

Only a few select and local friends would be admitted, including Kim Stanley, Lee Strasberg, Harold Clurman, Elia Kazan, and, rather improbably, Danny Kaye, with whom Clifford had had a brief affair. Clifford also looked forward to a visit from Charlie Chaplin, "the only other actor I know with Marlon's genius."

For some odd reason, Clifford anticipated a visit from Frank Sinatra, until Elia Kazan reminded him that he was suing the singer for an alleged breach of contract.

At the top of Clifford's list of "the chosen few" was the name of Marlon Brando. "In this Lotusland of phonies, Marlon is all that's left of what is true, real, and sincere," Clifford told Kazan.

On his dying day on August 18, 1963, Clifford ordered the nurse to "send for Brando. Only he—not any doctor—can save me now."

Even near death, Clifford still dreamed about writing that long-overdue film script for Marlon. In the movie he envisioned, Marlon would be cast as Beethoven.

Rushing to the hospital, Marlon arrived just in time to hear the playwright's last words. Marlon remembered his lover from the darkest days of World War II as "leaking with the fluids of death from all parts of his dying body. He was a dripping, emaciated figure."

Marlon took Clifford's hand and held it up to his cheek before kissing the inner palm in a final farewell.

Clifford managed only a weak smile, looking intently into Marlon's eyes one final time before oblivion. In a very weak voice, he managed to say, "Life is about shitting in a towel."

* * *

Marlon's older sister, Jocelyn Brando, born November 18, 1919, had already preceded her brother to New York.

Weighing only three pounds at birth, "Tiddy," as she was nicknamed, was put in a cigar box instead of a crib and dressed in clothing intended for dolls.

Jocelyn Brando and "Stanley Kowalski" at rehearsal

By the time she'd reached the age of thirteen, Jocelyn often had to be a substitute mother for her beloved "Bud" (before he became Marlon) and his sister, Fran. As Jocelyn fried pork chops for the brood, Dodie was hanging out drunk in some sleazy Omaha bar, indiscriminately taking on lovers, often married men much younger than herself.

Like Dodie, Jocelyn decided early in life to become an actress. That ambition came to a head when the Brando family moved to Santa Ana, California, in 1936. Dodie found herself only fifty miles from the sound stages where her former lover, Henry Fonda, had become a famous movie star. Dodie and "Hank," as she called him, had begun their affair when he appeared on the stage with her in productions for the Omaha Community Playhouse.

Now Hank was a big star, having scored a hit with the 1936 release of *The Trail of the Lonesome Pine*, a drama about feuding Kentuckians and the first three-strip Technicolor production released by Paramount.

Dodie often drove both Bud and Jocelyn—but not Fran for some reason—to visit Hank on the Paramount set. It was not clear to the children at the time if their mother's affair with the handsome young actor was still ongoing.

Thrilled at getting to know such a famous movie star, Jocelyn "then and there" decided to become a big-time actress herself. Back at Santa Ana High School, she enrolled in the Department of Drama. A classmate recalled, "Almost from the beginning Jocelyn Brando was the star of all our plays. She was just better at it than the other kids and had perfect elocution." Later she enrolled in Santa Ana Junior College as a theater arts major.

Leaving Santa Ana, the Brandos in time moved to Illinois, returning to their roots in the Middle West.

In various interviews over the years, a portrait of early Marlon has appeared in Jocelyn's recollections. She remembered that her family had a big cow named Bessie. "She fell in love with Bud and would only allow his gentle hands on her teats."

While performing in plays for summer stock at the Lake Zurich Playhouse in the northern suburbs of Chicago, Jocelyn met and fell in love with a charming young actor, Don Hanmer. In time, she'd marry him.

"Jocelyn was prettier and sexier than Frances Farmer, to whom she had a remarkable resemblance," Don recalled. The young actress and the young actor became lovers that summer.

Sometimes Bud would show up at the playhouse, wandering backstage to check out the props and fondle the costumes. Perhaps he was already dreaming of becoming an actor himself.

When Dodie herself showed up at the playhouse, she quickly learned about her daughter's affair with Don. "It's your life," she told Jocelyn. "You have a responsibility to live it to the fullest."

Marlon Sr., despite his estrangement from other members of his family, also learned about Jocelyn's pre-marital liaison. As Jocelyn's relationship with Don deepened, he traveled to Libertyville, Illinois, to confront Marlon Sr. and to ask for his daughter's hand in marriage. Her father was skeptical, telling Don, "Fuck her all you want. But I don't want my daughter marrying a fucking actor without a fucking pot to piss in!"

Don didn't take Marlon Sr.'s advice. When Jocelyn was graduated from

Lake Forest College, about 30 miles from downtown Chicago, she and Don, although penniless, journeyed to New York on a Greyhound bus to search for work in the theater. Months later she made her Broadway debut in the 1942 production of *First Crocus*, a play which closed after only twenty-one performances.

Marriage to Don would follow, although Bud showed up and tried to prevent the wedding by telling Don—erroneously—that Jocelyn had the clap.

When she got a job as an understudy in a touring theatrical production, Don returned to Illinois and lived with the Brando family at Libertyville, a bustling little town some forty miles northwest of Chicago. Jocelyn was understudying in the play, *Claudia*, for Dorothy McGuire, who along with Hank Fonda, had become one of the most famous actors to come out of Nebraska. Delicate, pretty, and a heartfelt performer, Dorothy had appeared at the Omaha Community Playhouse opposite Hank in the play, *A Kiss for Cinderella*.

Claudia was a 1941 stage hit. By 1943 it would also become a successful movie starring Dorothy opposite Robert Young.

Delicate, Dorothy might have been, but relentlessly, she showed up every night to play the childlike newlywed coping with her mother's illness. Jocelyn, as understudy, was never allowed to go on in her place.

Back in Libertyville, Marlon often ridiculed his new brother-in-law, Don Hanmer, doing cruel impersonations of him.

With Don, Jocelyn returned to New York after her tour, paving the way for Marlon's eventual descent upon that city. She enrolled in the American Academy of Dramatic Arts and "appeared in a play or two."

When Marlon finally arrived in New York, he went to live with Fran, but saw a great deal of Jocelyn as well. She soon discovered that her baby brother "was screwing any and everything. He was just a boy who couldn't say no."

Although Marlon flaunted his affairs with women in front of Jocelyn, it appeared that he kept his liaisons with men a secret. At that point, Don was overseas serving in the Army in the middle of World War II. Jocelyn gave birth to a baby, David, and Marlon found himself an uncle for the first time.

When Dodie arrived in New York in 1944 to escape her husband and to reunite with her estranged family, she was often accompanied by Jocelyn when attending

Dorothy McGuire

AA meetings at a little church on 23rd Street.

If there were any professional sibling rivalry between Jocelyn and her more famous younger brother, she never showed it. Of course, Jocelyn's career would never come anywhere near to equaling that of Marlon's. She followed the usual pattern of a Grade B actress of the time, although she did appear on the Broadway stage again in 1948 in the cast of *Mister Roberts*, the only woman in the play. Her character of Navy nurse Lieutenant Ann Girard was known for "the strawberry birthmark on her ass."

Despite her promising start, a big movie career for her never materialized. She did, however, land an important role in Fritz Lang's *The Big Heat*, released in 1953. Glen Ford, the star of the film, remembered that "she looked like Marlon Brando in drag."

Her film career was hampered because she was blacklisted by the House on Un-American Activities. Years before, she'd innocently lent her support to a Communist front group.

Marlon brought her back to the screen in 1962 to appear with him in *The Ugly American*, but the movie was a box office bust and did nothing for either of their careers.

Marlon brought Jocelyn back to the screen once again to appear with him in another unsuccessful film, *The Chase*, in 1966, which also starred Jane Fonda and Robert Redford.

By then, it was too little too late. In 1981, when Jocelyn appeared in a minor role in that libelous portrait of Joan Crawford, *Mommie Dearest*, as Barbara Bennet, her screen career was flickering to dim. She lacked the superstar charisma of her brother.

She was more successful in television dramas, appearing in the 1960s in *Alfred Hitchcock Presents* and also on *Dr. Kildare* in the 60s. She would also appear on TV in a recurring role on *Dallas* in the 70s.

In spite of an alcoholic mother and a philandering father, Jocelyn always retained fond memories of her baby brother, calling him "a blond, fat-bellied little boy—quite serious and very determined. As a boy, he was always miming movie death scenes and doing so very realistically. He would die but rise from death to be born again, only to die again. The story of Bud's life, I guess."

* * *

Throughout their lives, Wally Cox and Marlon Brando were referred to as the odd couple. Whatever labels were associated with their friendship, the two men became "best friends for life."

The same age as Marlon, Wally Cox was also destined for fame in show

40

Wide-eyed Marlon and his mother, Dodie

business. One friend was well muscled and masculine, the other frail, jug-eared, chicken necked, and a bit effeminate, speaking in a reedy voice. Today Wally is still remembered for his voice characterization for the animated superhero, "Underdog." His famous quote was, "No need to fear. Underdog is here!" But it was the hit TV series, *Mr. Peepers* in 1952, that made Wally Cox a household word throughout America.

Wally wasn't at all like the character he presented on television. In 1976, three years after Wally's death, Marlon told a reporter: "Wally didn't even remotely resemble that Mr. Peepers character. Instead, he had the mentality of an ax murderer. I can't tell you how much I miss and love that man."

Marlon was nearly ten years old when they met. Because of his father's work, the Brando family had moved to Evanston, outside Chicago, where the children were enrolled at Lincoln, one of the best public schools in America.

With his horn-rimmed glasses and with his frail body, Wally was the type of little guy bigger boys "liked to beat the shit out of," in the words of classmate Ernest Hopkins.

Although born in Detroit, Wally's parents had also moved to Evanston. "God knows where Wally's father was," Dodie recalled after meeting the boy's stepfather, Ben Pratt, a radio writer, and his mother, Eleanor Cox, who had penned several mystery tales, even a boring novel, *Seedtime and Harvest*, about Swedish farm workers.

Dodie later remembered that Wally's mother, an alcoholic like Dodie herself, fell in love with a "tough, butch woman and disappeared into nowhere" for a long time, although when she grew ill she later came back for a reunion with her abandoned son. Dodie and Eleanor may have met at an AA meeting in Evanston.

Marlon's first encounter with Wally was on the school play yard at Lincoln. On the ground, Wally was using his thin arms to shield his face from the kicks and blows raining down on him. He was being beaten up by three of the school tough guys who were calling him "sissy" and "fairy."

To his rescue, Marlon rushed the thugs and slammed punches into their noses and guts. Faced with a tornado of violence themselves, the tough boys didn't seem so tough any more and fled from the massacre.

Picking Wally up off the dusty ground, Marlon brushed the young boy off and introduced himself. According to Wally later in life, his rescuer's first words to him were, "Hi. I'm Marlon Brando. I've just become your new best friend."

From that very day, the two boys became inseparable, recalled classmate Eric Panken. "They went for long hikes in the woods. Wally was a budding botanist, if I recall. He pointed out the wonders of nature to Marlon and taught him the names of wildflowers. They argued, they fought, they broke up, and then they came back together again and all was forgiven. One time when Marlon got mad at Wally, he took a rope and tied him to a tree in the forest where Wally remained all night, waiting patiently for Marlon to come in the morning and untie him. Apparently, this did not seriously piss off Wally, because later that afternoon the two boys were seen walking arm in arm. Sometimes Marlon would protectively put his arm around Wally on the school grounds as if to signal to the bullies that he'd beat the shit out of them if they so much as laid a hand on Wally. They were very physical with each other, but I don't know how far that went. Are ten-year-old boys capable of having sex with each other? I know that one time when they went on a camping trip, they slept cuddled up naked with each other in their own tent. We could hear them laughing and giggling late into the night."

Eric recalled that once he was with some of the boys from the Lincoln School, and they were talking about girls, "a subject we knew nothing about. Marlon was with us but saying nothing. He had a pained expression on his face. 'What do I need a girl for?' he asked us before walking away. We didn't know a lot about homosexuality in those days, so none of the boys drew any ugly conclusions. It was okay for boys to bond real close back then. Many young men in the U.S. Army, or so I learned later, were doing the same thing. It was the thing to do. It was just assumed that as you grew older, you'd give up your boyfriends and bond with a girl."

Eric claimed that after Wally moved away from Evanston, Marlon did just that. "Suddenly, he was talking about girls all the time. He was always telling us about his sexual conquests, especially when he reached the age of fourteen and puberty. He said that he'd lost his virginity to the family maid back in Omaha. His libido seemed to be out of control."

Later, when he'd reunited with Wally again, he told him and other friends that he also "fucked the family's black maid" when the Brandos moved to Libertyville. Marlon would contradict himself, telling other friends that his first sexual experience with a black woman would be in New York.

He bragged to another classmate, George Robin, "I can have any gal I want. All I have to do is ask. Sometimes I don't even have to ask. The bitches come to me to get fucked."

One of his early girlfriends, who did not want her name used, would always remember her first date with Marlon, which led to her seduction. "I was a virgin and didn't know what was happening. He seduced me. There was no foreplay. Not even a kiss. He pulled up my skirt, pulled down my panties, and plowed me like a bull. I bled. It was very painful. I begged him to stop. He didn't until he'd finished with me. He really hurt me. Of course, I never went out with him again."

Wally Cox

Richard Loving, the artist who married Marlon's sister, Fran, once recalled that "Young Marlon was the most highly sexed individual I'd ever met. Primal, really, or maybe primitive is a better word."

At some point, Eleanor Cox broke up with her butch girlfriend and came back for Wally, taking him to New York in 1942. She enrolled her son at City College where he studied botany. He still corresponded with his friend Marlon, who at the time was enrolled at the Shattuck Military Academy.

In New York, Eleanor was stricken with partial paralysis and could no longer be the breadwinner for her son. Both men and women lovers seemed to have faded from her life, and she was totally dependent on Wally.

Her son immediately got a job working for an old-fashioned Polish cobbler in Brooklyn.

The reunion of Marlon and Wally in New York became part of the enduring legends of both men. Fran and Marlon were on Seventh Avenue, having gone shopping at a New York grocery store. Still a prankster, Marlon was trying to coerce Fran to get into a pushcart so he could race her up the avenue through traffic. The more mature Fran asked him, "Why don't you grow up? You're not in military school any more."

Wally Cox

As if by magic, Wally accidentally came upon them. Although both men had changed enormously since their school days, Marlon recognized "the little shrimp right away."

"He was so casual about running into Wally again after all these years," Fran recalled. "He didn't make a fuss about it at all."

"Hi, Wally," was all Marlon said. Instead of inquiring about how Wally had been after all these years, Marlon complained that Fran wouldn't get into the pushcart. He accused her of trying to spoil his fun.

Wally, still looking "half-baked," in Fran's words, immediately climbed into the grocery cart without a protest. Thrilled at this, Marlon pushed the cart into traffic and rolled Wally up Seventh Avenue "for the ride of a lifetime," both young men narrowly escaping the jaws of death from the wartime traffic in the streets of New York.

Fran remembered that her brother was gone for three days and nights. Later Marlon claimed that he and Wally had a "lot of catching up to do. On matters like life and death, sex, our hopes and dreams, funny things that had happened to us while we were apart. And, yes, tragic ones. Those too."

By the time Marlon returned to Fran's apartment, he'd become "bonded at the hip for life" with his long-lost boyhood friend.

After that pushcart incident, Fran would later tell a reporter for *Coronet* magazine: "Wally and Marlon have been in complete rapport ever since."

Wally had another close friend at the time, a writer, Everett Greenbaum, who would create the shy, mild-mannered school teacher, Robinson Peepers, for Wally's hit TV series, a role, incidentally, that Wally detested.

"Wally and I were close back in those days," Everett later recalled. "But when Brando came back into his life, I played second fiddle. It was obvious that Wally's heart belonged elsewhere, although our friendship continued on a more subdued basis. He always called his friend, 'Marlon Brando, the actor,' and Brando always called Wally 'Walrus.'"

Soon Marlon was insisting that Wally wear his own characteristic jeans and T-shirt, and Wally complied with this dress code. "Marlon had the muscles to fill out both his T-shirt and jeans," Everett said. "Wally did not. He always looked like the skinny kid in the Charles Atlas ad, the one who gets sand kicked in his face."

"I never really knew what Wally and Brando talked about," Everett said. "Sometimes they'd sit for hours talking. It was hard to shut Wally up. Brando must have been a good listener. Both young men had a passionate interest in almost everything and would even read every page of *Scientific American*. I don't think they could afford to buy a copy of that magazine so they must have stolen it from some newsstand."

Marlon urged Wally to enroll in the New School, which he did, studying acting under Stella Adler. "To say that Wally Cox was not what he appeared to be would be the understatement of the ages," Stella later said. "Behind that mild-mannered, even meek façade, was a sarcastic little bastard with a rapier-like wit. He was the only person in the world who could cut Marlon down to size. And he did. Frequently. And Marlon shut his mouth and took it from this tough little mutton chop."

"Wally was always getting arrested back in those days," a friend, David

44

Geller, recalled. "Not that he did anything illegal. But any time one of New York's finest took a good look at poor Wally, they imagined him a rapist or at least one of those guys on a most wanted poster in the post office. Perhaps an escapee from a mental ward. Wally was routinely hauled in for questioning. Marlon would always show up later to help his pal get released. Marlon used to tell Wally that if he ever became famous and wrote memoirs, they should be entitled *Tell It to the Judge*."

Marlon helped Wally care for his invalid mother, Eleanor. Sometimes Marlon would buy a cup of hot soup from the deli and come to Wally's apartment where he would spoon-feed it to Eleanor. When she died, Marlon and Wally had a picnic on her grave but not as a sign of disrespect. "We loved her," Marlon later said, "and just wanted to be with her."

In the middle of World War II, Wally was drafted into the U.S. Army. Frail though he might have been, he passed the physical and began a rigorous military training program. After only two weeks at a South Carolina camp, he collapsed from heatstroke and hovered between life and death for three days. Apparently, the Army decided he wasn't soldier material and sent him packing back to New York with an honorable 4F discharge.

Reunited with Marlon once again, Wally managed to eke out a poverty-level existence by becoming a puppeteer—his first show-biz gig. He also enrolled in New York University's School of Industrial Design.

At a party in Greenwich Village, Wally met "a fellow stringbean," Richard Loving, and the two frail young men decided to launch a jewelry business together. A skilled craftsman, Wally taught Dick how to fashion jewelry out of sterling silver. Soon the two young men could be seen hawking their jewelry on the streets of the Village.

Portrait of an artist
as a young man

Wally introduced Dick to Fran, and it was love at first sight. They began "intense dating," which eventually led to marriage.

Fran and Dick took an apartment together—called "a railroad flat" back in those wartime days. Wally, in an even more dilapidated apartment, lived across from Fran and Dick.

Bobby Lewis recalled seeing a lot of Marlon and Wally in those days. "Those two attended parties together, and everybody just assumed they were a couple. Marlon told everybody he met that Wally was 'a genius at comedy.' At private parties,

Wally performed milquetoastish, ad-libbed, and hilarious monologues. Once those guys borrowed *Lederhosen* from the prop room of the New School and showed up at a Village party dressed like Hitler Youth with Nazi armbands. Believe me, wearing Nazi armbands on the streets of New York in the mid-Forties wasn't a smart thing to do. In spite of that, they were the hit of the party, performing a whistling act followed by a Swiss yodel that had all of us in stitches."

As his friendship with Wally and Marlon grew, Bobby showed up frequently at Wally's cold-water flat in Hell's Kitchen along Tenth Avenue. "It was a hell hole. I felt that a big rat would devour me at any minute. Wally had furnished the place with junk picked up from the street. There was a nasty little bedroom to the side, a kitchen where no dish was ever washed, and a living room with a battered sofa with the springs broken, and the most disgusting urine-stained mattress I'd ever seen in my life with nothing to cover it."

"I have to sleep on this mattress when Marlon takes over the bedroom to bang some fresh pussy," Wally told Bobby.

"It was obvious to me that Wally had fallen, and fallen big, for Marlon," Bobby claimed. "I may be completely wrong, but I think back then that Wally stood on the border between being gay or straight. Marlon could have tipped the preference either way. I felt that Wally was ready to commit to Marlon, and I'm sure they were making love. Wally was obviously playing the role of the dutiful wife. But Marlon could never commit to anyone, much less a man. He loved his women too much. I could see the love in Wally's eyes as Marlon, with his well-muscled body, paraded around in the nude in front of Wally and

me. Poor Wally looked at Marlon with such desire that it was almost pathetic. As if to humiliate his friend, Marlon often brought his girlfriends over to Wally's apartment to screw them. He'd take over the bedroom and make Wally sleep on that filthy mattress in the living room. Wally had to listen to the sounds of Marlon's love-making all night. It was sadistic, really."

In spite of his relationship with Wally, and in spite of the random pick-ups, Marlon was still dating Celia Webb. In addition, he'd occasionally show up at parties with a young woman he introduced as Faith Dane. He frequently took Ellen Adler, Stella's daughter, to the the-

The intensely shy, private Marlon

ater.

One friend at the time, who didn't want to be named, said he was a closeted homosexual during the days he knew Wally and Marlon as two struggling actors. "Wally had girlfriends on the side—not as many as Marlon, of course. But I don't think he had sex with any other man but Marlon. Marlon, on the other hand, would show up at Wally's apartment with both men and women. The gals came in all sizes—some ugly, some pretty. But some of the guys he picked up in Central Park looked like creeps. Druggies, whatever. Nearly all of them needed a bath and a haircut. Maybe a de-licing."

"The way I saw it, Marlon fucked Wally when he didn't have anyone else to fuck," Bobby Lewis claimed. "That's it: plain and simple. Wally was so anxious to have a piece of Marlon that he put up with any humiliation. Remarkably, and after a passage of many, many months, Marlon gradually fell in love with Wally, but not to the exclusion of his others. Never that! Wally came to understand that Marlon would never be his, and his alone. That was the best thing for Wally because he got on with his own life after a few, brutal, painful months of being a lovesick fool. Instead of going away, he reacted to Marlon's new set of rules by becoming a bit of a womanizer himself. Other than Marlon, there is no evidence he ever indulged in any other homosexual relationships—in fact, he married two women, Patricia Tiernan and Marilyn Gennaro. But if Marlon called, Wally dropped whatever he was doing and came running like a faithful puppy dog to his master. I think that Wally continued to love Marlon until he drew his last breath on that windy day in February, 1973, in Los Angeles."

"Without really explaining himself, Marlon once told me, 'I get something from Wally I don't get from anybody else,'" Bobby said. "'It's very real, very important to me.' From what I gathered, although Marlon and I grew apart, I think that Wally Cox remained the only enduring love of Marlon's life. Other friendships, other loves, would come and go. But his bond with Wally lasted beyond the grave."

* * *

Marlon Brando might never have become a screen legend were it not for a tall, willowy, ash-blonde beauty whose eyes changed colors to match light reflections. Born of proud American prairie stock in Grand Island, Nebraska, in 1897, Dorothy Pennebaker Myers, nicknamed "Dodie," was the daughter of a bookkeeper by day, and an adventurous gold prospector on the weekends, who hoped to get rich quick in the Colorado Rockies.

In her own drunken words, she was "the best God damn actress ever to come out of Nebraska, and to hell with that other Dorothy." Her reference was to filmdom's Dorothy McGuire, a fellow actress at the semi-professional Omaha Community Playhouse. McGuire was twenty-one years younger than Dodie. Beginning with a squabble over the affections of Henry Fonda, also Nebraska born, the two Dorothys became life-long rivals.

Henry Fonda

"I brought realism and drama to the stage," Dodie once said. "That bitch, McGuire, had one emotional beat—that of home-fired warmth and mother love. If there's one thing I find disgusting, it's motherly love on the screen. It's worse enough in real life." Dodie didn't always believe her statements. She liked to utter strong opinions to shock what she called "tea-drinking Republican women who take their brew in delicate china cups painted with Pompadour pink roses. Instead of tea, give me a little Prohibition home-brew any day."

Her father died when Dodie was only two, and she experienced a chaotic childhood before entering into an even more chaotic marriage to Marlon Brando Sr., who had been born into Alsatian stock with an original name of "Brandeau." When he grew up, he made his living by selling chemical feeds and insecticides.

From the beginning of her marriage and even after the birth of her three children, Dodie had a total disdain for child-rearing and housekeeping. She did not believe in heavy discipline for her kids but preferred that they "discover their own true natures."

For young Marlon, that often "meant running wild through the town, raising hell, and causing trouble," in the words of former Omaha neighbor, Mrs. Casey Culler. "The kid was a total menace. The father was always on the road with one of his whores, the mother out drunk in some cheap motor court with someone's husband. That little brat, Brando—they called him Bud—once dropped my cocker spaniel into my well. I was glad when Omaha saw the last of that brood. I never went to see one of his films when he became a big movie star, and I'm sure I didn't miss out on anything."

When Marlon Sr. did return home from his womanizing and selling "all that poison to people," as young Bud put it, he went to sleep listening to his parents argue and shout at each other, hurling denunciations. Both of his parents accurately accused the other of committing adultery.

Their tempers were fueled by their "Prohibition brew." Once to shame his parents about their excessive beer-drinking, Marlon rounded up all the empty bottles, placing them prominently in front of their Omaha home to shock the

Prohibition-supporting, church-going neighbors who listened to long Sunday sermons on the evil of drink.

In spite of that act of rebellion in trying to humiliate his mother, Marlon was very supportive of her throughout her alcoholic binges. In 1932, she'd broken her leg while driving drunk to a secret rendezvous with a married Army officer, with whom she'd been having a months-long affair. When she was brought home from the hospital, he took her meals to her and even helped her with her bath. He told his sister, "Dad drives her to drink."

When Dodie sobered up, and she would for long periods of time, she was usually involved in a production at the Omaha Community Playhouse, where she was both a producer and, very often, the lead actress.

Eyewitnesses and newspaper reviewers of that era acclaimed her ability as an actress. "She was one of our best," said theater critic Nathan Palley. "It's too bad she had to leave Omaha and go to Illinois. It broke her heart to give up the theater. She could have been a big star. She was starting to attract a lot of attention when her husband took his family to Illinois because of his work."

In 1925, only a year after Marlon was born, Dodie starred in the play, *The Enchanted Cottage*, by Arthur Wing Pinero. Ironically, it was this same play that Dodie's nemesis, Dorothy McGuire, would turn into a highly successful movie in 1945.

When he became one of the big stars of Hollywood's Golden Age, Henry Fonda always thanked Dodie for launching him into acting. He remembered lying around his home one summer in Omaha, having dropped out of the University of Minnesota where he'd gone to study journalism. A call came in from the Omaha Community Playhouse. It was from Dodie, who was a friend of Hank's mother, Herberta. The juvenile lead had dropped out of a production, *You and I*, written by Philip Barry, who achieved far greater fame by writing *The Philadelphia Story* for Katharine Hepburn.

Although the play didn't run long, Hank fell in love with the theater and stayed around that summer to help paint the sets and sweep the floors. At some point during that summer, one of the longest and hottest in the state of Nebraska, Dodie fell in love with the handsome, lean young actor in spite of his shyness, or maybe because of it.

He was eight years her junior. Actually, Dodie seduced Hank. The young actor had lost his virginity earlier that summer in a seedy whorehouse in Omaha. He later said, "the experience was so horrible—just a wham-bam— that I was repulsed and very turned off women." Dodie may also have sensed that young Hank had homosexual tendencies, which would reach fruition when he met and fell in love with another aspirant, struggling young actor, the equally handsome James Stewart.

From all reports, Dodie was very patient with Hank, and somehow man-

Marlon Sr. & Jr.

aged to find satisfaction with him sexually in spite of his lifetime reputation as a premature ejaculator.

Long after leaving Dodie's bed, Hank would become known as a milquetoast husband, especially during his marriage to the nymphomaniacal Margaret Sullavan. Playwright Edward Albee originally wrote *Who's Afraid of Virginia Woolf* for Hank to star in.

Hank's hanging around backstage at the Playhouse eventually paid off. He was cast opposite Dodie in 1927 in Eugene O'Neill's *Beyond the Horizon*, opening to good reviews for both of the lovers. It was at this point that Dodie was trying to persuade Hank to marry her. She promised to divorce Marlon Sr. and wed him right away. He turned her down, although surprisingly, they maintained their sexual liaison for years to come.

Dodie faced plenty of competition from other women. When he was cast in *A Kiss for Cinderella*, opposite that "steel magnolia," Virginia-born Margaret Sullavan, he fell in love with her and would eventually marry her. Dodie felt she could hardly compete against such a formidable challenger.

What infuriated her was when Hank repeated the same role in Omaha a few years later. He chose as his Cinderella a beautiful thirteen-year-old girl, Dorothy McGuire, as his co-star. When reports reached Dodie that the much older Hank was having an affair with this teenager, Dodie was enraged. She threatened never to speak to Hank again, claiming "I detest child molesters."

Hank could be very persuasive when he wanted to, and eventually he got Dodie to forgive him. However, she never forgave "that little Lolita tramp, Miss McGuire."

Once when Dodie encountered Hank in Hollywood, following his disastrous marriage to Margaret Sullavan, he reportedly told his Omaha love, "I need a loving woman like you to restore my male confidence. Maggie told me I was a 'fast starter and a lousy finisher'—and she also made me feel like I had two cents in my pants along with two inches."

Dodie, inviting Hank back to her room, assured him that she would restore his manhood. In that, she must have succeeded. He went on to marry three socialites, including Frances Seymour Brokaw (mother of Jane Fonda), Susan Blanchard, Afdera Franchetti, and, finally, an airline stewardess, as they were called back then.

In 1944, after discovering "too many lipstick collars" on her husband's white shirts, Dodie had had enough. Forgetting that she too frequently engaged in adultery, she informed Marlon Sr. that she could no longer tolerate his philandering. She packed her bags and headed for New York to join her three artistic children.

Left with his chemical feeds and insecticides, Marlon Sr. remained in Chicago, but agreed to pay the rent. His final message to Dodie was "to give up drinking once you hit the streets of New York."

Arriving in New York in April, Dodie had a reunion with each of her offspring, including Marlon. She was astonished at how his body

Margaret Sullavan

had developed and was impressed with Stella Adler's report of his acting talent. Dodie rented a ten-room apartment on West End Avenue in the Seventies, and invited all of her children to move in with her, since she had found them living "in God awful apartments under unsanitary conditions."

Bobby Lewis was one of the first visitors to the new apartment, which quickly became an "open house" to many struggling actors of that day. "It didn't have much furniture," Bobby said. "A piece here, a piece there. . .very minimal. It was furnished with items from the junkyard."

He learned from Marlon that Dodie had resumed her heavy drinking. "Even drunk, she put on a good show for the young actors who flocked around her. Sometimes she gave dramatic readings, and she was very good. She always said she was better than the great Katharine Cornell, with whom her son was about to get involved, and I believed her."

"People dropped in at all times of the day and night to the Brandos," Bobby said. "Often they slept on her living room floor. And yes, fornicated there as well. I met all sorts of people, including a woman who I think later became the wife of J.D. Salinger. Back in those days they called us bohemians, and the word stuck around for a long time until Gore Vidal told us it was no longer fashionable to use it."

"Sometimes I'd join Marlon in a search of the neighborhood bars for a drunken Dodie," Bobby said. "At other times Wally Cox would go on the hunt. Wally told me that one time they found her drunk on the street and had to carry her home and up the steps like a slab of beef."

He also claimed that a story was making the rounds at the time, and he didn't know if it were true or not. But it was believed that a drunken Dodie was picked up one night by two sailors and taken to a flophouse in the West

Sixties. It was rumored that she was repeatedly gang-banged by an untold number of sailors until Marlon somehow found out about her whereabouts and went to rescue her. Marlon himself told Bobby that one morning he discovered his mother in bed with a discharged Army man who'd lost one leg and one arm on the battlefields of Europe.

"Through all the crap she put him through," a close friend, Ann Hastings said, "Marlon continued to worship his mother. He forgave her for everything she did, all the bad stuff. She worshipped him as well. She frequently called him 'that acting genius that popped out of my womb.' She claimed that he'd one day set the theater world on fire with his acting talent. She also boasted that if her husband hadn't sabotaged her own career, that she too would have been a big star."

Ann also reported that one afternoon when she dropped in on the Brandos, she'd brought a large macaroni and tuna casserole since the family always seemed short of food. "Once inside the apartment, I saw the strangest sight. Marlon was sitting in the sparsely furnished living room. He had on one of Dodie's street dresses and a pair of those Joan Crawford fuck-me shoes, as ankle-strap high heels were called in those days. He was fully made up, lipstick and all. He didn't seem at all embarrassed for me to see him dressed like that. He asked me to put the casserole on the kitchen table and thanked me. He told me that Dodie didn't feel well and was resting. I just knew she was trying to sober up from a drunk. After leaving the kitchen, I hurried out of the apartment. It was all too weird for me."

Two weeks later, Ann had a falling out with Dodie, claiming that, while drunk, Dodie had made a pass at her husband. The two former friends never spoke to or saw each other again.

Perhaps Ann was merely trying to get even, or else telling the truth, but after their initial estrangement, she went on to claim that Dodie was indulging in sexual intercourse with her own son. The charge could be dismissed as completely untrue were it not for some supporting testimony from Bobby Lewis.

Bobby claimed that he knew for a fact that Dodie often slept in the same bed with Marlon. "This was a very suggestive thing to do—after all, Marlon was a grown man. I have no evidence that his relationship with his mother was sexual. At the very least, I'd call it extremely intimate. One night while I was alone with Marlon and Dodie in their living room, listening to classical music, they seemed to have forgotten that I was there. Although she was wear-

The slicked back look

ing a housecoat, fully dressed, he snuggled into her breasts as part of a nursing ritual learned long ago. In spite of her heavy drinking, Dodie always kept that special bond with her son. It was very Oedipal. A little too Oedipal for my tastes. At some point, I stopped visiting their apartment, preferring to see Marlon and Wally on the outside. In the theater, I was always uncomfortable with the theme of incest. I guess I should have put my own personal feelings aside and been more of a tough-assed artist."

* * *

Piscator was just too autocratic and Marlon too rebellious for their teacher/pupil relationship to last. Nonetheless, his teacher invited Marlon to join a summer stock troupe at a theater he operated with his wife, Maria Ley, at Sayville on Long Island across from the promiscuous gay enclave of Cherry Grove on Fire Island. It was a beautiful white colonial style theater that opened onto a country lane bordered with wildflowers. The setting was on a white sandy beach fronting an azure bay, a cliché of Long Island charm, the kind of place where Katharine Hepburn might build a house.

The actors were told to take whatever bed they could find and make it their own little nest. For his roommate, Marlon made an odd choice in Carlo Fiore, who would soon become his best friend. A Sicilian, he spoke Brooklynese and dressed in a zoot suit and wore blue suede shoes long before they were popularized by Elvis. He wore his jet-black hair in a greasy pompadour forming a ducktail at the neck line. Instead of Sayville, Carlo would have been more at home cast as an extra in that 1955 movie, *Guys and Dolls*, that lay in Marlon's future. On being introduced to him, Elaine Stritch mistook him for a gangster.

"I'm just a nomad," Marlon told Carlo. "I lived in three states and five different houses before I was six years old. If I go into the theater at all, it will be for one reason. I love to put on makeup and wear wigs."

"Are you a faggot?" Carlo asked.

"On nights the full moon rises," he said enigmatically before walking away.

Piscator warned his horny young actors, especially Marlon and Carlo, that all the female members of the troupe were virgins and he wanted to keep their chastity intact—"no unwanted pregnancies," he cautioned. If a male member of the cast were caught having sex with one of the young

Brando and Carlo Fiore

actresses, the offender would immediately be sent packing back to New York. What was unknown to Marlon and Carlo at the time was that Piscator himself planned to deflower each of the virgins himself, one by one, before the first autumn wind blew.

"Yes, *der Meister*," Marlon said provocatively to Piscator. "*Der Shtudents* will obey. 'Ja. 'Ja. 'Ja!"

Piscator did not condemn homosexual contacts among the young actors, and even slyly suggested that in lieu of not having women, the male members of the troupe might turn to each other for sexual relief—"the way it's done in prison," he said. Maria once asked her husband if he were condoning homosexuality. "Not at all!" he replied. "But it's a harmless pursuit and keeps the boys in line. The main thing is that it doesn't lead to unwanted pregnancy. In my young days in Germany, I often indulged in male/male sex. It can be very satisfying, different from a woman."

Marlon invited Carlo to be his bunkmate in a weather-beaten, unpainted old New England barn loft reached by a rickety ladder that led to a trap door upstairs. They lugged a mattress up the ladder, and it was there they spent their first night together talking until dawn came and Marlon fell asleep. Carlo made the unpleasant discovery that Marlon snored "like the thunder and lightning that sparks the sky before a summer storm."

Marlon would often take the ferry boat by himself over to the beaches of Fire Island where he was seen walking nude up and down the beach at Cherry Grove.

A longtime resident, Jay Garon, who was later to become a famous literary agent, claimed, "By the late 1960s nudity was commonplace on the beaches of Fire Island. But to my knowledge, Marlon was the first to drop his swimsuit. All of us had Marlon that summer. All you had to do was to invite him to come with you into the bushes. He only let himself be serviced. Strictly rough trade. But at least he didn't charge."

"Bare-assed swims" in the blue bay with Carlo were followed by dinners of French fries—"second helpings with lots of catsup"—and thick chocolate malts. Marlon always complained that the malts weren't thick enough like those he'd enjoyed as a child in Omaha.

Dinners were followed by the "deflowering of young virgins," especially those that Piscator had warned them not to seduce. In his memoirs, Marlon admitted that there was a "lot of unbridled fornication" that summer and that "I was in the thick of it."

Marlon and Carlo found a young woman from Sayville who worked as a maid in a nearby hotel. She spoke with a heavy German accent, had a bad case of acne, and wore her hair in pigtails. Nonetheless, Marlon was attracted to her. Carlo wasn't particularly enthralled but was "horny as hell" and agreed to go along. Marlon and Carlo took her back to the barn and climbed the ladder before hoisting it up inside the trap door which they bolted. Once in bed, the Fräulein wanted to have sex only with Marlon, not with Carlo. He lay only two feet from his friend, "who pounded the hell out of the Nazi bitch."

In mid-intercourse, Marlon took his hand and ran his fingers across Carlo's face, lingering under his eyes. In the middle of his fuck, Marlon said in a soft whisper, "I just wanted to see if you were crying."

As Marlon got to know his new friend, Carlo, he learned more about him—and not just that he'd been a factory worker in Age 16: Bad Boy of Libertyville Brooklyn, steam-pressing men's trousers. Carlo had "an affinity for drugs," especially heroin. Marlon was against drugs, but sympathetic to his new friend's addiction. In the years ahead, drug consumption would increasingly become a problem for Carlo.

At Sayville, to an audience consisting mainly of vacationing New Yorkers, Marlon repeated a role he'd performed in a New School production of Gerhart Hauptmann's *Hannele's Way to Heaven.*

In front of the eponymous heroine, Hannele, Marlon flung off his black teacher's robe and stood in the spotlight in a suit of gold satin. "You could hear the gasps all over the audience," Elaine Stritch said.

"He was a young blond god, totally beautiful," exclaimed Glenda Johann, who was in the audience that night. "A nineteen-year-old playing Jesus Christ. It was fantastic. He was luminescent. I just knew he'd go on to greatness."

Elaine found his performance "absolutely breathtaking—you knew you were watching an acting genius on stage that night."

When Carlo told Marlon of Elaine's praise, he said, "I'm tired of being called an acting genius. Frankly, I haven't made up my mind if I want to be an actor at all."

In the theater, hearing the audience gasp, sat Maynard Morris, a powerful theatrical agent for MCA, the world's largest talent agency. After the show, Maynard came backstage to congratulate Marlon and ask him if he could represent him and send him out on auditions for Broadway shows.

Marlon startled him by his indifference and his comments. "Actually, my top priority this summer is to get laid. . .and frequently. I have a friend, Carlo Fiore, who says I'm an actor in a state of perpetual erection. My father wants me to join him in the chemical feed business in Chicago, and that sounds like a nobler profession than acting." In spite of Marlon's indifference, Maynard pressed his case until Marlon agreed to sign with MCA.

The next opening night didn't go as well. Dodie took the train from New York to see her son play Sebastian in *Twelfth Night*, a play she'd also appeared in in Omaha.

Piscator had been away in New York preparing a play for Broadway, and had turned the direction over to his mild-mannered and rather weak-willed wife who could not control the unruly and often rebellious actors. As opening night came, many of the players, including Marlon, had not learned the Bard's difficult lines.

After having heard raves about her son's acting, Dodie sat in the audience in stunned disbelief as Marlon gave one of the worst performances of his life. When he didn't know a line, as was often the case, he mumbled.

Later that night she told him either "take the theater seriously or get out of it."

Marlon informed Carlo that he'd never again appear in a play by Shakespeare, obviously changing his mind in 1953 for his performance in the movie, *Julius Caesar*.

With a Roman haircut

After the performance, Marlon invited Carlo and Dodie to the late-night Blue Moon Cafe. At table, Carlo ordered a gin martini and asked Dodie to join him. In front of Marlon, she confessed to being a recovering alcoholic and turned down the offer. "I can't even have one drink because it will lead to another and another," she said. "Even a thousand drinks will not be enough for me."

When a trio of musicians—a black sax player, a piano player with a bald head, and a fat bass player— played the cafe's theme song, "Blue Moon," Dodie asked Carlo to dance. He later admitted that when she lodged her still-attractive figure against his body, he got an immediate erection and wanted to take her right there on the dance floor, even though Marlon was hawkeyeing their every move.

Erwin Piscator (left) directs Carlo Fiore rescuing Dorothy Spaulding in *Twelfth Night*

On the way back to their barnloft that night, Marlon bluntly asked Carlo, "You want to fuck my mother, don't you? Don't deny it."

Fearing that Marlon would see through a lie—"I was always a bad liar"—Carlo confessed that he did from time to time have "an itch for older, attractive women." But he promised never to touch Dodie, even if she came on to him. "There's no way I could do that to my best friend."

Marlon seemed to accept that.

Later, Dodie did come on to Carlo. Even though he wanted to seduce her, he turned her down, claiming that he couldn't go to bed with the mother of his best friend. "It just wouldn't be right."

"I find you very attractive," she told him before walking toward her motel room alone.

The next morning, after Marlon had put Dodie on the train back to New York, he told Carlo, "I'm in love."

"What?" Carlo asked jokingly. "With the sound of your own voice."

"Cut the shit!" Marlon flashed anger. He wanted to be taken seriously. "No, I'm really in love for the first time. It's Blossom."

* * *

Her name was unusual. Blossom Plumb was often ridiculed as "Plump Bosom." Reared in Connecticut, she came from a prosperous WASP background, even though Marlon preferred "women with skins of color," in his own words.

A fellow workshop student at the New School, she bore a resemblance to a budding young actress, Eva Gabor. Maureen Stapleton remembered seeing her in the cafeteria of the New School with Marlon. "It was Mr. Gorgeous dating Miss Gorgeous," she said. "Until Blossom came along, I thought Marlon liked only ugly girls—often fat."

Blossom Plumb and Brando rehearsing *The Twelfth Night*

Marlon really got to know Blossom when he worked backstage with her on the set of *Charley's Aunt*. "Blossom was tall, pretty, and well stacked," Carlo remembered. "A regular Betty Grable who was all the rage at the time. But definitely not Marlon's type. She reminded him of Dodie."

A technician at Sayville had also tried to date Blossom but had been turned down. He recalled her as having "eyes as blue as an alpine lake, hair as the color of a Kansas wheat field, and skin that evoked a bowl of peaches and cream." Instead of installing wiring, perhaps he should have been a poet.

There have been many conflicting versions about what happened to end Marlon's stay at Sayville. The most believable is that Piscator caught Blossom in the hayloft naked with Marlon. Carlo maintained that "it was all innocent. They'd been rehearsing lines together in the loft and had fallen asleep on our bed." Protective of his friend, Carlo delivered a version that was a little too innocent to be believed.

The next morning, after catching them in bed together, Piscator dismissed both of them. Blossom cried and begged to stay on. Marlon, it was reported, was rather indifferent—in fact, according to some, eager to "get back to the fleshpots of New York where there will be no restrictions on my libido."

Before departing on the train back to New York, Marlon confided in Carlo that, "I want to go back to the city where all the girls like you to screw them doggie style."

Having gotten kicked out of military academy, Marlon faced his second banishment, again for so-called "immoral" behavior.

Before leaving Sayville, Marlon told members of the cast. "It's a shame, really. Mother Nature made man to want to get his rocks off. In answering the call of nature, we are often condemned for doing the very thing we were put on this earth to do. When will they ever learn?"

It's not known what Marlon thought about on that train ride back to New York. Even in his wildest imagination, he might not have known that he was about to plunge into a series of events that would make him a household name around the world.

Chapter Three

Marlon's new agent, Maynard Morris, was eager to launch his discovery. He suggested that Marlon, 20 years old at the time, might be "ripe" to play the part of the fifteen-year-old, Nels, in an upcoming play, *I Remember Mama*. It was being produced by Richard Rodgers and Oscar Hammerstein II as their first nonmusical after the historic success of their *Oklahoma!* "We were going to the bank every day with a wheelbarrow of money from that one," Rodgers claimed.

I Remember Mama had been written by John van Druten, the English playwright, who was fresh from his success of the previous year, *The Voice of the Turtle*. In 1947 that play would be made into a film, starring—of all people—Ronald Reagan.

Van Druten had based his play on Kathryn Forbes's *Mama's Bank Account*, a series of recollections about a struggling Norwegian family growing up on Steiner Street in San Francisco at the turn of the century.

Marlon accepted a copy of the script and took it to Dodie's West Side apartment where she read it aloud, not only to him, but to her two daughters as well. Marlon remembered falling asleep before the first act had ended. "This is the dullest play I've ever read," Dodie claimed. "It's not for you, Bud. Besides, you're too old to play an early teenager."

Dodie dismissed the play as a rip-off of the long-running hit, *Life with Father*—"pure schlock to take a New Yorker's mind off the war."

When Marlon presented the play to Stella Adler, she disagreed with Dodie, predicting *I Remember Mama* would become one of the biggest hits of the Broadway season. She urged Marlon "to go for it."

In spite of his respect for Stella's theatrical taste, Marlon felt little affinity for the role of the timid, rather shy Norwegian-American boy who entertained dreams of becoming a doctor. "It's not something I can sink my teeth into," he told Stella. "Besides, I hate reading before producers."

"How can you hate what you've never done before?" she asked.

"I'll feel like I'm standing there in front of them with my dick hanging

John van Druten

out," he predicted. "To me, a reading is like coming out on stage naked and having some shithead appraise your equipment. I've auditioned before. Back in Libertyville, I tried to get a job as a drummer in this swing band. The guys not only turned me down, they laughed at me, claiming I had no talent as a musician. After going through all that crap, I need some assholes to tell me I don't know how to act?"

"I'm sure it won't be a waste of your time," Stella said. "Who knows?" A smirk came across her face. "If you don't get cast as Nels, maybe Rodgers and Hammerstein will cast you as a cowboy in *Oklahoma!*"

Stella overcame his objections, and Marlon reported to the office of Richard Rodgers for the dreaded audition "against better judgment. Like, I could use the money. But not through some shitty Broadway show."

Rodgers was present, as was Oscar Hammerstein. Also in the office was John van Druten himself. He was amusing the producers with a story of how David O. Selznick had paid him $7,000 to write a draft of the screenplay for *Gone With the Wind*, which the producer had then rejected.

In front of the three show business veterans, Marlon gave "the second worst reading of my life." (The very worst reading, he'd soon learn, lay ahead in his immediate future.) "He stumbled, mumbled, and fumbled," as van Druten remembered it. Before he'd finished, Hammerstein told Rodgers, "Get this fucking kid out of here. What a waste of time!" Turning to Marlon with contempt, he said, "Jump back on the turnip truck, kid."

Van Druten moved toward Marlon, looking over his body very carefully. He was dressed in a very tight-fitting T-shirt that showed off his manly chest and muscles and a tight-fitting pair of jeans that emphasized his endowment. The playwright turned to his producers. "Let him stay. I think I can work with this one. Trust me, I see hidden talent here."

Aware of van Druten's homosexuality, Hammerstein said, "I know what you see hidden." He invited Rodgers out for a Broadway lunch, leaving the playwright and the actor alone in the office.

"Don't worry," van Druten called to their backs. "There's a spark here. As director, I can ignite it."

When the producers had gone, van Druten faced Marlon. "That was the single worst reading I've heard in the theater on either side of the Atlantic."

"*Adios!*" Marlon said with contempt, moving toward the door.

Van Druten raced after him, taking hold of his muscled arm. "Don't be so hasty. You've got the part. I can convince Rodgers and Hammerstein."

60

Born near the turn-of-the-century, in the last year of Queen Victoria's reign, van Druten was twenty-three years' Marlon's senior. As Marlon was later to report to Maynard, "The old letch really came onto me, telling me what a sexy young man I was. He said that one day he'd write a really hot part for me where I'd literally exude sex appeal on the stage. He told me that in the meantime I had to get my start on Broadway somewhere, and *I Remember Mama* might be the right launch pad for me. I went along with this homosexual who was practically salivating for me. By eight o'clock that night, after a few drinks, I was in the fucker's hotel room where he was devouring my cock."

The next day, Marlon signed for the role, getting seventy-five dollars a week. He told Morris, "I should get two-hundred a week for letting van Druten taste my noble tool."

Beginning with rehearsals for *I Remember Mama*, Marlon began to refer to his penis as "my noble tool."

He would do so for the rest of his life, at one point making the pronouncement, "I've never been circumcised, and my noble tool has performed its duties through thick and thin without fail."

* * *

Dodie was wrong and Stella was right. *I Remember Mama* opened at the Music Box Theater on October 19, 1944. It was an instant hit, with lines forming at the box office. The review in *The New York Times* didn't even mention Marlon by name. That was the last time that that prestigious newspaper would overlook him. However, Robert Garland, writing in *The Journal-American*, said, "The Nels of Marlon Brando is, if he doesn't mind me saying so, charming."

No longer claiming Rangoon as the place of his birth, Marlon insisted to the play's publicist that he'd been born in Calcutta where his father was engaged in geological research. He also falsely claimed that he'd come to the United States when he was only six months old. The publicist didn't quite believe him. "Are you sure you weren't born in Mukden, China?" he asked sarcastically.

"Hey, I never thought of that," Marlon said. "I'll use that as my birthplace in the next playbill." When the publicist suggested that it might be better to say he was born in Nebraska like

Mady Christians and Brando in *I Remember Mama*

movie stars Henry Fonda and Robert Taylor, Marlon dismissed the idea. "After all, what is theater but illusion?"

His sisters, Fran and Jocelyn, turned up for opening night, as did girl-friends Ellen Adler, Blossom Plumb, and Celia Webb, and best buddies Wally Cox and Darren Dublin. Only Dodie was noticeably absent. She was home drunk.

Bobby Lewis showed up too. "Marlon was fantastic," he later recalled. "When he came wandering downstage munching an apple, he was so natural I really believed that he lived upstairs. He was completely relaxed."

When Marlon was told of these comments, he dismissed them. "Like hell! I was so fucking scared I was developing a blood clot."

Veteran character actors and popular stars at the time, Mady Christians and Oscar Homolka, both from Vienna, and both cast within the same play, were stunned when Marlon's exit line met with thunderous applause. All he said was, "Good night, Mama. Good night, Papa." Stella Adler claimed that it was Marlon's "unprecedented naturalism" that inspired the audience to such a fever pitch. "He stood in perfect contrast to the overacting of Homolka and Christians, who were practically eating up the scenery. Marlon showed what subtlety on stage can accomplish."

Marlon remained contemptuous of the play, in spite of its success. He called it "sentimental slosh—bourgeois theater of the most blatant sort, strictly women's club matinee stuff."

The play would run for 731 performances, although Marlon would stay with the troupe for only a year. He easily became bored, repeating the same lines night after night. Growing impatient and restless, except during his eloquent coming-of-age speech in the third act, he began to improvise. At first he infuriated van Druten by inserting new words, or even a different line here and there, into the script. However, when presented with Marlon's noble tool in his dressing room, the author usually forgave the errant actor.

Noël Coward

"A rebellious lad," van Druten told his close friend and fellow playwright, Noël Coward. "But so sexy you'll forgive him of any transgression."

"I can't wait to meet the dear boy," Coward said. "He sounds delightful. I always like to audition fresh meat on both the American and British stage."

"Tell me something I don't already know," van Druten responded archly.

Van Druten obviously wasn't all that upset with Marlon's improvisations. When the final script of *I Remember Mama* was published, it con-

62

tained many of Marlon's "little things."

During the run of the play, actress Frances Heflin complained to van Druten that Marlon wasn't bathing regularly. Van Druten seemed dismissive of her comments. "There is nothing wrong with a man smelling like a man. I, for one, like the natural smell of a man."

By the third week, a bored Marlon was conflicting with both of the stars, Mady Christians and Oscar Homolka, each a classically trained actor.

At one point in the play, Mady was to drink a cup of coffee and proclaim that it was so good she

Oscar Homolka

wanted a second cup. Before curtain time, Marlon poured lots of salt and several generous sprinklings of Tabasco into the pot. Mady not only drank from this "cauldron of horror," but managed a second cup without letting the audience know anything was wrong.

Marlon admired her "professionalism under duress." When the final curtain went down, she seemed to know who the culprit was. Backstage she pounded into his chest and slapped his face repeatedly.

Almost from the beginning, Marlon conflicted with Oscar. Marlon found the Austrian "brusque, unpleasant, pompous" and very Nazi-like. He enjoyed irritating this scene stealer with some scene stealing of his own, like picking his nose during the actor's big scene, or, even worse, unbuttoning and rebuttoning his fly.

When he deliberately pretended he'd never heard of the actor, Oscar began reciting his impressive list of credentials, including performances in *King Lear* and *The Emperor Jones* on the stages of Europe where his name was a household word. Marlon pretended that he wasn't impressed.

Oscar was contemptuous of American actors, viewing them as "just removed from the barbaric stage. They only recently started wearing clothes instead of cowskins," he was fond of saying.

One night Mady went to Marlon's dressing room to complain about his tendency to change lines and stage movements every night. When she knocked, he yelled for her to come in. She was startled to find him naked on the floor having intercourse with a half-clothed Stella Adler. "He seemed completely oblivious of my presence and kept going at it like it was Christmas," she told Oscar.

When he heard of this, he wryly replied, "Thanks for the warning. If I want to keep my virtue intact, I'll have to stay out of Brando's dressing room."

Mady noted her surprise that Marlon was seeing both Stella and her daughter Ellen. "The fifteen-year-old girl was very different from her mother. Unlike blonde Stella, Ellen had jet-black hair like a gypsy flamenco dancer from Seville. She was very advanced for her age. Fifteen going on thirty."

A minor actor, Herbert Kenwith, said he had to move out of the dressing room he shared with Marlon because of the constant stream of visitors, both male and female, that Marlon received most evenings after curtain call. Usually the women were dark skinned or even quite black—"yes, even blue black, but more often Eurasian."

Oscar was scornful of the "flighty young men flocking backstage" to greet Marlon, who was just beginning to bask in the power he had over young homosexuals. "He relished their attention," Oscar later said. "I think the word got out in New York fairy circles that if you wanted to get fucked and had a tight ass, you could go backstage and get it from Brando every night."

A friend of the Brando family from Evanston, John Bingham, showed up one night to see the play and go backstage. "Marlon's dressing room was filthy. There were even sanitary napkins lying about, and bloody ones at that. When Marlon talked to me about Evanston, he left the bathroom door open when he went to take a crap. He got up off the stool and didn't even wipe. I was a bit taken back when I saw that he wore a lacy pair of women's underwear. But I'd heard rumors that he'd turned homosexual when he got to New York."

One night a young mulatto woman showed up and slipped backstage when the guard had gone to the toilet. She threatened to disrupt the evening's performance if Marlon didn't give her two-hundred dollars for the abortion she wanted. Not having the money, Marlon went to every actor and member of the crew, requesting donations. Finally, he raised the money.

Mady gave twenty dollars. "Why not send her over to Hoboken?" the star asked. "I understand that Frank Sinatra's mother will arrange an abortion for anyone who asks."

The most serious complaint lodged against Marlon from his fellow cast members was that he stood in the wings every night, waiting for his time to go on. While doing so, he'd fondle himself into a full erection, which was clearly visible through the tight knickerbockers he wore on stage. Not believing that the tale was true, van Druten sat out front one night to watch the performance. Marlon's erection was clearly visible, and some female members of the audience let out audible gasps.

Backstage, van Druten confronted Marlon, charging that "your protuberance is very distracting."

"In that case, if you don't want me to go out with a hard-on, you'll have to suck me soft every night."

"Marlon continued to show it hard when he walked out on stage," Carlo

Fiore later said. "You could hear the women in the audience swoon. I guess that's one way to become a star."

* * *

Clad only in his boxer shorts, Marlon answered the door to his dressing room in response to an urgent yet delicate knock. He was feeling good that night, thinking he'd delivered his best performance in *I Remember Mama*.

Mady Christians had told him that there were a lot of movie stars out front. She was going to name them, but he dismissed her, telling her that, "I'm not interested in movie stars. Maybe if Rin Tin Tin shows up. Otherwise, no!"

The female star who stood at his door was one of such sexual ambiguity and allure that he could hardly ignore her. He gently took her hand and eased her inside.

He still hadn't spoken to her. For a stage actor dismissive of movie stars, he was in awe of this icon of beauty and glamour. She was the century's embodiment of erotic sophistication, the mysterious Shanghai Lily of his childhood, taking the *Shanghai Express*. She was the brazen Frenchy getting doused with a bucket of water in *Destry Rides Again*. Although her legs were hailed as among the world's most beautiful, they were covered in trousers tonight.

To his further astonishment, she gently glided to the floor on her knees. Reaching inside the flap of his boxer shorts, she removed his uncut penis, skinned it back, and proceeded to give him what he would later claim was "the world's most perfect blow-job—before or since."

It was only when she'd swallowed his offering and had risen to her feet, did the actress introduce herself. "Forgive me," she said, "I should really tell you who I am. I am Marlene Dietrich. I admired your performance tonight very much. I think you'll go far on the Broadway stage."

Marlene Dietrich

"Since you know who I am," he said, "and since you're already very well acquainted with my noble tool, I won't bother to waste time introducing myself."

The exchange between Dietrich and Marlon would have been lost to history had not Marlon bragged about it to John van Druten the next day. The gossipy English playwright told not only Noël Coward, Dietrich's friend, "but virtually everyone else," or at least that's what Oscar Homolka claimed.

Unknown to Marlon at the time, Dietrich's

"tribute" to his acting talent was not unique. In her heyday, she had a custom of performing the same act of fellatio on artists and writers she admired. When she first met George Bernard Shaw, at least according to her husband, Rudolf Sieber, she knelt at his feet, unbuttoned his fly, removed his penis, and then "worshipped it." Only after the playwright had climaxed, "could we talk seriously," Dietrich later claimed.

Surveying the disaster that he called his dressing room, Dietrich said, "My, oh my, we'll have to clean up this place. My husband is a chicken farmer, but even his hens wouldn't call this place home." An alluring smirk moved across her face. "We'll have to invite Joan Crawford over. Even when she's visiting friends, she drops down on her knees, not to do what I did to you, but to scrub toilets. In some ways, I'm like Joan. They call me a *femme fatale*. But I'm just a *Hausfräu* struggling to get out."

In a long black limousine, en route to her hotel suite, Dietrich told Marlon that, "You are the most natural actor I've ever seen on the Broadway stage. I adored how you vaguely hinted at a Norwegian accent but didn't ghoulishly overdo it." She rubbed his cheek with a pink-gloved hand. "Just the right touch of blush, and I noticed it was natural—not makeup. You have that scrubbed open-faced look that a young teenage boy of Norway would have. However, I don't know how anything wholesome looking could emerge from that pig sty of a dressing room. And you look. . . what's the word? A bit chunky. Perfect for the part. I know you're not Norwegian. What is your ancestry?"

"Part Dutch, part Alsatian. . ."

She interrupted him. "German! I just knew it. You're a fellow *Kraut* like me."

Back in her hotel suite, he felt awkward with her before she retreated to the bedroom "to slip into something more comfortable." He'd bluntly told her he was hungry, thinking she would send down for room service. Instead she preferred to cook him "a special omelette" in the small kitchen attached to her suite.

In a few minutes she came back into the living room in a sheer, see-through night gown. His next move surprised her. Instead of moving toward her to seduce her, he went over and raised the living room's window. Crawling out through the open window, he disappeared into the dense fog that had blanketed New York that night, in the open air, ten floors above street level. "*Auf Wiedersehen!*" he called to her.

Obviously figuring that he was just playing a game as a means of frightening her, Dietrich, pretending nonchalance, went to the kitchen to prepare his omelette.

In fewer than ten minutes, Marlon appeared outside the suite's open kitchen window, then swung himself inside, eventually standing beside her, next to her little stove. He'd emerged from the fog like a ghost. "There's no ledge outside to grab onto," he said. "But there's a gutter and a drain pipe that I used to haul me across instead."

"This is a very old hotel," she said matter-of-factly. "With a war going on, probably no one's inspected those drain pipes since the 30s. Drain pipes rust and rot away, like people you know."

"Maybe I could have fallen to my death," he said as if the idea had never occurred to him.

"Potentially at least, America could have lost one of its greatest young actors. Such a shame." She placed a potato omelette in front of him and invited him to sit down at the little table. "Enjoy, and finish every bite. You'll need all your strength for the fun and games I have in mind for us tonight."

* * *

His one-night stand with Dietrich forgotten, Marlon received another female visitor backstage after a performance of *I Remember Mama*. Tall and statuesque, she was a champagne blonde tastefully dressed in a black suit. As an associate of Maynard Morris at MCA, the forty-five-year-old woman came not to seduce Marlon, but to advance his career.

"Until I met Marlon," Edith Van Cleve recalled, "I had nothing but clients with more ambition than talent." The brilliant exception to her stable was Montgomery Clift, who was as talented as Marlon himself. "All of my clients wanted to become as big as Barbara Stanwyck, who at the time was the highest paid woman in America. In spite of his prodigious talent, Marlon just didn't seem to care if he made it or not. On our first meeting, I wanted to sign him to a contract. He was already represented by my colleague, Maynard Morris, but he hadn't signed a personal contract. Maynard had had great success, helping launch Gregory Peck and Tyrone Power. But I wanted to move in and take over Marlon for myself."

At first Edith tried to impress Marlon by promising to use her connections to get him various screen tests. "Every young actor in the 1940s wanted to be a screen star, so I just assumed Marlon did too."

"Keep those movie people away from me," he cautioned, taking her by surprise. "Do you really think I could become the next Betty Grable? I've got great legs myself, but hers are better."

"He had the body of an Olympic athlete," Edith said. "The beauty of a matinee idol. The talent of a young John Barrymore. But he just didn't seem to care if he capitalized off the package or not."

"Do you want to fuck?" he bluntly asked Edith.

Brando and Carlo Fiore

She assured him that she never mixed business with pleasure.

"Your loss," he said with seeming nonchalance.

Marlon was nothing if not a bundle of contradictions. In spite of his ranting against the movies, he agreed the following week for a screen test with 20th Century Fox. "I heard they're looking for a replacement for Shirley Temple," he jokingly said to Carlo Fiore. "The tough little slut is getting a bit long in the tooth." The expression, "tough little slut," as it applied to Shirley Temple, had been borrowed from silent screen star Louise Brooks.

Richard Gregor, who directed Marlon's first screen test, recalled the event decades later in his modest home in West Hollywood. He was very "out." "I thought Marlon was one humpy number when he showed up for the screen test in a form-fitting white T-shirt and jeans so tight that they showed the outline of his dick. I suggested that he remove his T-shirt for the test. Actually, that wasn't often done, but I wanted to get a look at those muscles. He refused to take off the shirt. 'I will do one thing for you, though,' he said. 'I'll take my dick out and piss for you if that is what's called for.' It didn't take me long to learn how rebellious he was."

"At one point, he pulled a big bugger of dried snot from his nose-right on camera," Gregor claimed. "He was supposed to have memorized a few lines from an old Tyrone Power script. But all that came out of Marlon's mouth was a few noncommittal grunts and a mumble here and there. Naturally, the test bombed."

Edith sent Marlon to test for Metro-Goldwyn-Mayer. After viewing the results, an MGM talent scout claimed that snot from Marlon's nose "dribbled down his face like soft ice cream." For his test at Paramount, he carried a Yo-Yo with which he proceeded to play with on camera. For Warner Brothers, he demonstrated on camera how to eat a raw egg.

At night he amused himself by going to the rooftops over jazz joints and dropping brown paper bags filled with water onto the heads of drunken patrons who staggered out at four or five o'clock in predawn New York.

Before his death in 1964, Maynard recalled that, near the end of the war, all the big studios were looking for new faces to fill the gap caused by some of the biggest stars, such as Clark Gable, being involved in the war effort. "Until the real stars came marching home, I felt there was a great opportunity in Hollywood for Marlon. Obviously he didn't agree. How else to explain why he sabotaged every screen test Edith ever sent him on? Of course, he would eventually conquer Hollywood, but that would have to wait until later."

Abandoning hopes of a screen career for her new client, Edith sent him to try out for stage roles, since his year-long contract with *I Remember Mama* was running out, and he didn't want to renew, finding the same role boring.

Although she was relatively new as an actors' agent, Edith, a former actress herself, was a powerhouse. She knew some of the most legendary figures in the American theater.

Despairing of her new client succeeding on the screen—"his heart just wasn't into it"—Edith sent him out for an audition with two of the "living legends" of the American theater: Alfred Lunt and Lynn Fontanne.

* * *

Marlon was sent by Edith Van Cleve to audition for *O Mistress Mine*, a drawing room comedy with a role for a sixteen-year-old boy. The author was Terrence Rattigan, a homosexual London-born playwright. Rattigan would be at the audition, along with the stars of the play, Lynn Fontanne, also English born, and her equally famous husband, Alfred Lunt. Like Marlon himself, Lunt was from the Middle West—Wisconsin in this case. Lunt and Fontanne had enjoyed a hit run with their play in London. Known to British audiences as *Love in Idleness*, it was renamed *O Mistress Mine* for Broadway.

Along with Rattigan, Lunt and Fontanne were sitting in the front row, immaculately attired as always. "Marlon looked like a bum who'd been picked up in the Bowery," Rattigan later recalled from his home in Bermuda. "I don't think he'd shaved for days. His T-shirt was dirty, and his jeans looked like he'd last washed them at the time of the Spanish-American War. Worse than that, he seemed to have a perpetual scowl. Actually, it was a kind of glower, as if he didn't belong on stage auditioning for us. Even though the Lunts were theatrical royalty, he greeted them with obvi-ous defiance and arrogant hostili-ty. The well-mannered Lunts were taken aback. As for me, I was more or less attracted to the beast.

Alfred Lunt

Lynn Fontanne

Beneath his sloppy appearance was a very handsome and very sexy young man with a certain amount of raw animal magnetism."

"I'm Marlon Brando," he said, even mumbling his name. Lunt heard the name as "Brindel," and addressed Marlon as such. Marlon didn't bother to correct the actor, who was known for his perfect elocution.

"Are you ready to begin?" Lunt asked rather impatiently. The availability of the role had been widely advertised, and backstage, Marlon had found himself part of a cattle call. At least fifty young men—maybe more—had shown up for the audition, their various ages, according to the stage manager, ranging from twelve years old to "at least one who wasn't a day younger than thirty-five."

Marlon frowned as he studied Rattigan's script. Although near-sighted, he vainly chose not to wear glasses. Finally, he tossed the script into an empty seat in the front row. "I can't say these words." Perhaps he couldn't even read them. "I just can't do this." Before the astonished theatrical trio, he walked off the stage.

Lunt called after him. "Don't make such a hasty retreat, young man," Lunt said. "Anyone as rude and as insolent as you must be hiding a great deal of talent. If you don't want to read the script, recite anything. At this point, Lynn and I—Terrence, too—mainly want to hear the sound of your voice."

"Recite your favorite verse to us," Fontanne chimed in. "Perhaps from Shakespeare."

Marlon stood stiffly and recited a nursery rhyme Dodie had taught him:

Hickory, dickory dock,
The mouse ran up the clock.
The clock struck one, the mouse ran down,
Hickory, dickory, DUMB.

He placed a heavy emphasis on the word *dumb.*

The recitation elicited utter disdain from the Lunts, but brought a smirk to Rattigan's face. Marlon stormed off the stage. "You're much too old for the role," Fontanne called after him. "Sorry. We won't be calling you."

"Be sure *not* to leave your name with the stage manager," Lunt said to Marlon's departing back.

The confrontation became part of the legend and lore of Marlon Brando. But there was more to the story than has ever before been told. It didn't just end with the recitation of the nursery rhyme.

Sitting in the back seat of the darkened theater was a handsome, debonair man. He was Jack Wilson, the lover of Noël Coward. He was also that playwright and entertainer's business manager, producer, and director. Like his

Jack Wilson

homosexual friend, Rattigan, Wilson was very intrigued with the young Brando, despite the actor's insolence.

"I don't think I'd ever seen an actor on stage in such tight jeans," Wilson later recalled to his friend, the Austrian chanteuse, Greta Keller, who was also a close friend of Noël Coward's. "There was something special about Brando. I thought he had enormous sex appeal. I think if cast in the right role, he could inspire rape fantasies in the female members of the audience. Perhaps some male ones too, if they're so inclined."

Wilson admitted to racing backstage. There, he introduced himself to Marlon, explaining who he was. "He barely noticed me, although I convinced him to give me his address," Wilson later recalled to Greta. "I told him that I had the perfect play in mind for him, one by Sir Noël himself." Brando seemed utterly indifferent to the idea, but agreed to show up when I called him for an audition."

Later, Wilson confided in Rattigan, "That's the most natural appearing actor I've ever seen on the stage."

"Cut the shit, you old sod!" Rattigan chided Wilson. "You just want to sample the package in those jeans that he must have had sewed onto his body."

"That, too," Wilson admitted, "except Noël will want him too."

* * *

Admitting that she was "crazy about the bastard," Dodie announced her departure from the apartment on West End Avenue. She was returning to Illinois and the arms of Marlon Sr.

Marlon Jr. did "everything in my power" to get her to stay. He even held out the prospect of sex with Carlo Fiore, whom he still called by the nickname of "Freddie," even though his friend didn't like that.

Marlon's second wife, Anna Kashfi, once claimed that Marlon's "submerged sexual longings for his mother had to be vented" in some way. Since, in her words, he had an "ingrained incest taboo, oedipal intercourse could be realized only vicariously."

Marlon was well aware that from the beginning Dodie had been attracted to Carlo, and he to her. Marlon hoped that if his mother fell in love with Carlo, he might be able to keep her in New York. He urged his friend to seduce his mother. Carlo wisely turned down the invitation. Years later in discussing this with Anna, Marlon dismissed Freddie as a "left-handed homosexual."

Despite Marlon's resistance, Dodie took the train back to Chicago. In his own words, Marlon later admitted that he experienced "a kind of nervous breakdown." He was left alone and felt abandoned in the big West End Avenue apartment.

Marlon viewed his mother's departure as his own personal failure. "I had another chance to offer her my love, which I did, but it wasn't enough for her."

Unable to afford it, he soon got rid of Dodie's large apartment and moved to a one-room studio at Sixth Avenue and 58th Street. He kept it in the same "pig-sty" style that Marlene Dietrich had found in his dressing room.

"I stopped eating," Marlon said, "lost ten pounds, and felt depressed and vulnerable, but didn't know why. I still acted every night, but I was in emotional disarray."

He credited Stella Adler with "saving my sanity." He spent night after night at her apartment, even going into her bedroom to "see that she dresses properly." Often her husband, Harold Clurman, or her daughter, Ellen, whom Marlon often dated, would be sitting right outside in the living room.

In his autobiography, Marlon denied ever having an affair with Stella. "He merely wanted to protect Stella's reputation—after all, she was a married woman," Bobby Lewis claimed. "Actually, he was banging the hell out of his mentor night after night."

Bobby said that on several occasions Clurman admitted to him that he was well aware that his wife was having an affair with Marlon. "I know I should feel a jealous rage, but I don't," Clurman told Bobby. "I have to ask myself several times why I'm not furious, why I don't kick Marlon out of the apartment. But in my own mixed-up way, I love the guy. I feel Stella's entitled to a little affair on the side. She works hard and is very dedicated to the theater . . . and to Marlon, perhaps even to me on occasion."

When not with Stella, Marlon engaged in anonymous sex. He'd go to toilets frequented by cruising homosexuals, where he'd allow anonymous fellatio to be performed on himself. Or else he'd pick up women randomly on the streets and bring them back to his small apartment. Darren Dublin remembered that on one occasion he saw Marlon disappear into his bedroom with three young women. "All ages, sizes, and hair styles appealed to Marlon," Darren claimed.

In the meantime, Jack Wilson, when not in bed with Noël Coward, continued his pursuit of Marlon, holding out the prospect of various theatrical offers to the struggling young actor. Marlon found no work after turning down the road tour of *I Remember Mama*. "He was accessible to many offers at the time," Bobby Lewis said. "He also considered himself ambrosia to various homosexual playwrights, and took delight in offering himself on a platter to them. John van Druten—or perhaps Clifford Odets—was just the beginning of Marlon presenting himself like a slab of meat to artists. He liked the way he could make them salivate and often bragged about his power over them. In his future lay Tennessee Williams."

* * *

A former American stockbroker, Jack Wilson was known for his matinee idol good looks. He exerted almost as much personal charm as did Noël Coward himself. Jack had a sharp wit and could make Marlon laugh, especially when he told the most indiscreet stories about "the gods and goddesses" of the theater, both British and American. Marlon quickly learned that Jack had been nicknamed "Dab" by Coward and that the playwright himself was called "Poppa."

Wilson managed to keep his affair with Marlon a secret until Coward heard about it via the Cole Porter grapevine and wanted to meet "this darling boy." To cover up for himself, Wilson said that he'd been seeing Marlon with an eye toward casting him in his mentor's drawing room comedy, *Present Laughter*. Of course, Marlon was all wrong for the role, and the savvy Wilson knew that. Still, he persisted.

Instead of having the audition in a theater, it was conducted in Coward's hotel suite which he shared with Wilson. That evening Coward had been entertaining his friend, the composer Cole Porter, in his suite. Wilson, Coward, and Porter sometimes traveled together as when they showed up on Venice's Lido, looking suitably bronzed for the photographers. All three men were bonded with their mutual interests in the theater and homosexuality.

Both Stella Adler, who'd read *Present Laughter*, and Marlon dismissed the play as "mere Coward fluff." Stella went so far as to say, "It's not worthy of him. Second rank Coward, or maybe not even that."

For bizarre reasons of his own, Marlon agreed to the audition. Apparently, it was not his intention to read the play's dialogue. Instead he showed up at Coward's suite with two black Jamaican drummers.

In front of the astonished, but delighted trio, Marlon danced in a jewel-studded G-string to the accompaniment of the black drummers. He'd been studying at Katherine Dunham's School of Dance and moved with perfect rhythm to the West Indian

Greta Keller

73

drum beat, his G-string held on by two snaps. At the end of the number, he snapped off the brief and stood nude before his appraisers.

"After I gave each of the drummers a hundred dollar bill," Wilson later told Greta Keller, "just to get rid of them, Cole, Poppa, and I had Marlon like we were at a smörgåsbord table."

After the fun, Marlon decided to tell the suave Noël Coward what he thought of *Present Laughter*. In nearly all biographies of Brando, Marlon stands before Coward and says "Don't you know there are people starving in Europe?" He is then alleged to have walked out on the playwright, after having dismissed his latest efforts as trivial.

According to Wilson, however, that incident never happened. "Marlon spoke bluntly to my darling Noël."

"There is no laughter in your play, present or past," Marlon said to Coward, if Wilson is to be believed. "It's like having a diarrhea attack with no toilet in sight." Marlon then left the apartment, having dressed in his jeans and T-shirt.

Apparently, Coward never forgave his rudeness. Still panting after Marlon, Wilson, however, was most forgiving.

The following day, using a sibilant *s*, Marlon swished in front of Carlo, singing Coward's "Mad About the Boy."

Marlon was still casting about for work. Even though Wilson never pressed Marlon to appear in *Present Laughter*, he suggested another job opportunity for him when the actor told him he'd run out of money and was not getting any more from back home.

Back in his stockbroker days, Wilson, hoping to win an account, often acquainted potential homosexual clients with the services of Kenneth London. The British-born "madam" ran an escort service, euphemistically called "Gentlemen for Rent."

* * *

Originally, London set up his service as an agency where handsome young men could be rented out for the night to women seeking escorts. The fee was one-hundred dollars a night, a rather large sum of money in those days. If a tuxedo were required, the bill would be twenty-five dollars extra. If sex were involved at the end of the evening, that would be a private negotiation between the young man and the client.

London himself didn't engage in the male prostitution aspect of the service. He always said, "Any sex was strictly between the boy and the woman." Of the hundred-dollar escort fee, London took fifty of it.

He claimed that during the first few weeks in the life of his company, all

Ruth Warrick

of the incoming calls were from womer
well-known actresses from Hollywood vis.
York and having need of an escort. As time we.
London began to receive calls from "respectable ge.
tlemen," as he put it, requesting the escort services of
a member of his handsome all-male staff. After checking with "my boys," London learned that at least half
of the boys would agree to go out with a male.
However, for that extra service, they wanted twice as
much money. Soon London was offering escorts to
both men and women.

"One of my boys even fell for a client, a rich busi-
nessman from San Francisco," London said, "and that's the last I ever heard
of either of them."

Wilson introduced Marlon to London, who signed him as an escort.
"Brando worked for me for about five to eight weeks, I don't remember
which. He earned about three-thousand dollars for his time. He also agreed to
escort both men and women. I don't know if sex was part of any of his deals.
Frankly, I didn't want to know. Such knowledge could have led to my arrest
for prostitution. Personally, I think Marlon did it for the thrill of it instead of
the money. I could be wrong."

Rumors about Marlon being a "callboy" in the mid-Forties clung to him
all his life, seeing print for the first time in *Brando: The Unauthorized
Biography* by Joe Morella and Edward Z. Epstein. The two authors dismissed
the rumors as "ridiculous" denying that Marlon had posed for a picture for a
special "catalog" sent to London's rich clients.

Yet some highly placed sources, although not unimpeachable, claimed
that Marlon did work for the agency, and, as mentioned, London himself confirmed it. Greta Keller claimed that Jack Wilson told her that Marlon worked
briefly as a $100-a-night callboy.

Actress Ruth Warrick played Charles Foster Kane's very proper first wife
in Orson Welles's *Citizen Kane* and became a legend in daytime TV drama
with her appearances as Phoebe Tyler in *All My Children*. She also claimed
that she first met Marlon when she called London, requesting an escort to take
her to the opening of a Broadway show.

When pressed if sex were part of the deal, Warrick said, "Darling, I was a
Forties movie star. In those days, we drew the shades when such activity happened after 'The End,' flashed across the screen. Let's keep it that way!"

* * *

Katherine Dunham

Impulsively, Marlon had decided to become a dancer instead of an actor—and "not just a white boy dancer." He wanted to become a black dancer, as irrational as that goal was. "I want to dance to the rhythms of divine drumbeats," he told best friends Carlo Fiore and Darren Dublin. "That is, when I'm not playing the conga drums myself."

His dream, which was shortly to be realized, involved meeting Katherine Dunham, doyenne of black dancers who had been hailed as "the hottest thing to hit Chicago since Mrs. O'Leary's cow kicked the bucket." Moving from Chicago, she had opened a dance studio in New York, composed mostly of black, especially Haitian, and Puerto Rican dancers, with a "scattering of Cubans."

Her school was on 43rd Street near Seventh Avenue. By a coincidence, Lee Strasberg had opened what became an early branch of the Actors Studio in one part of the loft he shared with Dunham. Although he still detested Strasberg, Marlon, for reasons known only to himself, attended a few of Strasberg's classes over Stella Adler's objections. His excuse to her was, "I want to see what the enemy is teaching." He attended only a few classes. "Once he heard the sound of those bongo drums, he wandered next door and never came back to class," Strasberg later said.

Marlon was captivated by Katherine Dunham and went up to introduce himself and to get permission to join her school. The performer was already deep into her legend, having made her debut as a dancer on Broadway in the 1930s, sporting a birdcage on her head and a cigar in her mouth.

He told her that he'd seen the 1943 film, *Stormy Weather*, six times. In the movie, Dunham appeared as herself. He also told her that he'd seen her 1942 *Star Spangled Rhythm* the same number of times. Dunham had appeared again as herself in a "Smart as a Tack" number.

She might have been flattered by the attention of the handsome young Brando. A bit reluctant, she signed him up the same afternoon she met him.

Her suspicion at the time was that Marlon might want to join her school because he was a devotee of black women and wanted to use membership in the troupe "to get close to a lot of hot mammas." To some extent, Dunham's suspicion was true. But he also sincerely wanted to learn to dance.

Evocative of how enraptured he'd been by another mentor, Stella Adler, Marlon became "addicted" (his words) to Katherine Dunham in the days ahead. It was obvious to the rest of the troupe that he'd developed a crush on her. Seduction, however, appeared out of the question, as she was still in love with her husband, John Thomas Pratt, whom she'd married in 1941.

Marlon wanted to learn all he could not only about black dance but about Dunham herself. She willingly shared stories of her life with him. Born in Chicago in poverty, she had a French-Canadian mother and an American father who traced his ancestry back to a slave ship arriving from Madagascar. When not directing the dancers, Dunham was often seen sitting with Marlon in a corner of the studio, reading Tarot cards to him.

He watched rehearsals every day, but didn't join in. As best as he could figure it, the Dunham technique of dance combined West Indian movements with traditional ballet, sprinkled with "Darkest African rituals," a strong dose of black American rhythms.

In just three weeks, Marlon had learned enough to join the regular class in rehearsals. "It's hard to believe that Marlon wasn't a nigger like us," said Jean Desirée, one of the Haitian dancers who had moved to New York from her native Port-au-Prince. "He was totally into the black experience. Over a period of time, he fucked nearly all the gals in our troupe and a lot of the beautifully muscled black skin boys too. He went black all the way. We had a brief affair but he quickly dumped me for some other meat."

After a short time, Marlon pronounced himself an expert at the cakewalk and the bebop, two dances that Dunham believed had "roots in darkest Africa." Even if he weren't the school's leading male dancer, Marlon became an exotic member of the troupe with his white-skinned body contrasting with dark-skinned men with their perfect physiques and well-developed muscles. He told friends that he loved to dance with the "budding Lena Hornes," referring to the brown-skinned female dancers with their sexy mesh stockings, their spike heels, and skimpy outfits whose fabric barely concealed their breasts.

"Dance, Marlon, dance," Dunham would call to him. "Dance with the same pounding beat I understand you use in making love. That way, you'll become a big star. In my dances, think of the rhythms as wild, pounding love acted out to the beat of a conga drum. No pirouettes from *Swan Lake!*"

Marlon danced nude except for a tattered old leopard skin apron (a handkerchief, actually, with long strings that tied behind his waist) that barely concealed his genitals, but completely exposed his buttocks. He never wore a jockstrap or pouch, claiming that no true African dancer would ever do that. When he danced, that flap went up in a twirling motion, revealing his cock and balls. No one objected, not even Dunham who found the costume "authentic to the African experience."

"As a dancer, Marlon was okay, I guess, but not great," Desirée claimed. "Actually, he was the worst dancer in the group and was far better on drums."

Marlon met a beautiful mulatto member of the troupe, a dancer from St. Louis, who was working on a number called "Incest." It dealt with her being raped nightly by her father, while her abused mother sat in the other room crying over what her daughter was subjected to. Marlon could never remember what her name was, but he had a brief affair with her before going on to other women. He told Carlo that, "I could become addicted to brown belles. They are much hotter in bed than white women."

When he tried this line out on his friend, James Baldwin, the author angrily rejected such a notion as a "typical black stereotype, perpetuating the myth that all of us 'colored boys,' gals too—are oversexed." In spite of his friend's protest, however, Marlon throughout his life still held to his original impression.

Marlon could not remember the dancer who wanted him to play the lead in her "Incest" number. Both the dancer and Marlon were hoping that Dunham would agree to stage it. When he ran through the number with the young dancer in front of Dunham, she completely rejected it, perhaps on personal grounds. It may have set off a bad memory for her. In her autobiography, *A Touch of Innocence*, Dunham wrote candidly that her father took an unhealthy interest in his growing daughter. She recalled his wanting her "to sit close to him in the truck or kiss him goodbye, or the touch and fondling that made everything about my life seem smudgy and unclean."

With his star role in modern dance fading quickly, Marlon became "just one of the dancers," definitely in the background. The star parts were taken over by Dunham's more skilled pupils. Even so, he seemed delighted just to be a member of the troupe.

Marlon became "besotted with Miss Dunham," in the words of Ralph Feernan, who was one of the major fans of black dance and planned to write a book on the movement that never materialized. "I talked to Marlon several times in those days, and I honestly believe he wanted to become black himself. At one point, he suggested that he might appear on stage in black face to blend in better with the other dancers. Miss Dunham completely rejected that idea as 'vulgar, even obscene.' But Marlon definitely wanted to go native."

In addition to dance, he studied drums under Henri Augustine, the troupe's *hungan*, a name that was used back in his native Haiti for a voodoo priest.

Marlon called him "Papa." The drummer gave Marlon a phallic symbol, which he wore at all times around his neck, telling friends that it not only warded off the evil eye but made him more virile in bed.

Desirée recalled that Marlon was transfixed when Papa played the drums. Trying to imitate Papa, he would play the drums for hours on end. "I think one of the boys in the troupe was giving him something too," she said. "Marlon was high all the time."

He told friends at the New School, where he still studied acting, that "he'd become a high priest of voodoo" after a special initiation one night in Harlem. He never fully explained exactly what went on that night in Harlem except to say that part of the initiation involved biting off the head of a live rooster and drinking the blood of a thirteen-year-old virgin after her hymen had been pierced by a large black dick.

"One night he played drums—congas, bongos, I don't remember—for eight hours straight," Desirée said. "He wouldn't stop, even when he had to ask one of the boys to bring him a quart jar to piss in. The dancer reached for Marlon's pouch, pulled it back, and held his dick while he pissed in the jar. I'm sure the boy was one of Marlon's fuck buddies to be that intimate."

Marlon became a good enough dancer to make his first appearance at one of the *boules blanches* that Dunham staged monthly as a fund-raiser for her perpetually underfinanced dance school. These benefits drew a monied and cultural elite, often white. "The audience, and I'm guessing, was about thirty-five percent gay, the rest straight . . . sorta straight," Desirée recalled.

In the audience you were likely to find Betty Furness, Langston Hughes, James Baldwin, even Noël Coward, Cole Porter, and Monty Woolley. Throughout their lives, Porter, Coward, and Woolley had a fondness for black men.

As Marlon was dancing in a sarong, he noticed a tall yet graceful white woman ogling him. She never looked at the other dancers, only at him. Hoping to impress her, he put more energy into his dance than he usually did.

Dripping with sweat at the end of the number, he came over to her. Her face looked vaguely familiar. Perhaps she was some actress he'd seen on the silver screen.

"Hi," he said. "I'm Marlon Brando."

"Miss Dunham has told me who you are," she said in a well-modulated, educated, East Coast charm school voice. She extended her hand.

"I'm Doris Duke."

* * *

The tobacco heiress, Doris Duke, was the wealthiest woman in the world. Her father, James B. Duke, had taught the world how to smoke readymade cigarettes, and made a $100 million fortune in the process, much of it passed on to his daughter when he died.

In the dance hall, Marlon was immediately attracted to the "Million Dollar Baby." The eccen-

Doris Duke

79

tric heiress was only in her mid-thirties at the time. He'd heard that Duke thumbed her nose at society. "I have a weakness for pleasure," she told him, "and a big appetite for adventure."

On his first night with her in her penthouse in New York, she revealed to him that her former lover, Errol Flynn, had been a Nazi spy during the early years of the war. She claimed that she'd dropped him for that reason, since she was a very patriotic American.

But something good, she claimed, had come out of her love affair with the swashbuckling actor. Flynn was a great believer in reincarnation, and he'd interested her in his passion. She'd consulted various reincarnation experts around the world, as the subject held great fascination for her.

"When I saw you dancing, I knew that we'd been lovers in a previous life," she told Marlon.

"Let's pick up where we left off," he said.

The details of the burgeoning Brando/Duke affair would never have been known were it not for one man. For several years in the Forties, Duke took as her confidant, Jimmy Donahue, the grandson of the millionaire Frank W. Woolworth. Jimmy was widely hailed at the time as the "playboy of the Western world." This was in the years before Jimmy launched his affair with both the Duke and Duchess of Windsor. "That insane camp," as Noël Coward called Jimmy, was also the cousin of the Woolworth heiress Barbara Hutton. In spite of that, and in spite of Duke being the chief rival of Hutton, the tobacco heiress still took Jimmy into her confidence. That turned out to be a mistake.

Jimmy amused gay friends with hilarious stories about both Duke and Hutton, especially their romantic imbroglios. Much of what is known about Marlon and Duke is preserved through Jimmy's "oral history." He may have exaggerated certain details, as was his way, but the essentials of the affair appear to be basically what really happened.

Of course, Marlon himself contributed to the details of the affair in stories he told friends at the time. After his conquest of Duke, he openly bragged about his exploits at the New School. "For a young man born into modest circumstances in Nebraska, Doris Duke was the biggest feather in Marlon's cap," claimed Stella Adler, who seemed a bit peeved, even jealous, of Marlon's new, rich friend. Stella, however, immediately accepted Marlon's new friend because she saw Duke and her tobacco millions as a possible "angel" to fund various theatrical projects she might want to present in the future.

Jimmy Donahue

80

"The sex was glorious," Marlon told Carlo. "She went around the world on me, not missing a spot. She has an amazing curiosity and fascination with the male body, wanting to taste every inch of it. She likes to pet, fondle, and then lick voraciously. I had three orgasms before the butler arrived at ten o'clock the following morning with our eggs Benedict."

Marlon had more to say. "Doris is the first woman I've ever met who asked me what gives me pleasure in bed. With most women, I have to pleasure them. With Doris, she pleasures me. Listen, she's got great legs. Better than Betty Grable's. And great skin, too. Real smooth, like a baby girl's."

Not even asking Marlon if he smoked, Duke presented him with a sapphire-studded gold cigarette case before he'd left her suite on the morning following a night of seduction. "In Doris's world," claimed her first husband, James Cromwell, "she just assumed that all real men smoked."

On the first weekend of their meeting, Duke personally drove Marlon to Rough Point, her sprawling, drafty estate in Newport, Rhode Island. Jimmy Donahue was there, already drunk on champagne at two o'clock in the afternoon.

Marlon was fascinated by Duke's "cottage," the former summer home of the Vanderbilts. He went exploring from room to room, even though Duke told him that in all the years she'd lived at Rough Point, she'd never actually visited every room.

After lunch, Duke took both Jimmy and Marlon on a tour of her vast flowerbeds. "Doris insisted that flowers be blooming at all times during the growing season," Jimmy maintained. "She could not tolerate one dead flower in her beds. She constantly had the flowers rotated once they started to die down. She had all sorts of flowers, mainly gardenias and orchids, shipped in from Boston. She detested seeing a flower in its dormant period and demanded that it be dug up and a new one substituted."

"I was bored out of my mind," Jimmy said, "but Marlon seemed fascinated by her flowers. He told her that he had a friend, Wally Cox, who was a botanist. He said that Cox had given him an interest in all growing things."

"At one point on the tour, Doris went berserk," Jimmy said. "She discovered a dead petunia and immediately threatened to fire all her gardeners. To see Doris explode made the tour worthwhile for me. What's the use of having servants if you can't fire them in anger?"

Over dinner, while Jimmy drank, Duke hand fed Marlon almost an entire apple pie freshly baked from her kitchen. She told him that she'd grown impatient with New England and wanted to return to Hawaii to survey her estate, Shangri-La, there. "She invited both of us to go with her," Jimmy said. "Marlon accepted, I didn't, although I eventually ended up going anyway."

Over a late breakfast the following morning, Marlon told Jimmy of a strange experience he'd had the night before. In the middle of the night, Marlon had gone downstairs for a glass of cold milk. He claimed that he'd encountered a "robber baron ghost" on the stairwell. "The ghost threatened to kill me. I ran all the way back up the steps and into the protective arms of Doris."

"Doris really seemed fascinated by Marlon," Jimmy claimed. "At one point she told me she was considering urging him to give up his career in the theater and come and live with her. I advised against that, although Marlon didn't have much career to give up at that point."

Apparently, at some point Duke made her offer to Marlon. He turned her down, later telling Stella Adler that he didn't want to be "the kept boy of the richest woman in the world."

Duke continued to keep Jimmy informed of her trysts with Marlon. She called him "a real man—and not one of those homosexuals I'm used to sleeping with."

Allegedly, she told Marlon that "life doesn't last forever and we owe it to ourselves to seek fulfillment and pleasure, even at the price of pain to others."

One night, according to Jimmy, Duke took Marlon to the Stork Club in New York. At one point, after a dialogue with columnist Walter Winchell, she went into a screaming rage. A drunken Winchell had asked Duke if he could be introduced to her "new boy." Duke summoned the *maître d'* and ordered Winchell "expelled" from her presence.

Jimmy found her story amusing. For many years, Duke had resented what Winchell wrote about her in his column. He always referred to her as either "the richest girl in the world," or "the girl who has everything."

"How can he possibly say I have everything?" she asked Marlon as her anger faded. "I don't have everything. At times I feel I have almost nothing. Life has not been fulfilling to me. In the decade coming up, I'm going to devote my life to fulfillment, both pleasure for my body and solace for my soul." Duke had frequently expressed such sentiments to Jimmy as well.

Marlon apparently agreed that "your way is the way to go. Full steam ahead. I'll be following right along in your footsteps." In the years ahead, Marlon, more or less, would follow Duke's battle plan.

Jimmy said that, at one point, Duke confided to him that she'd once picked up a muscled Hawaiian boy on the beach. "I just wanted to feel what it's like to have a fourteen-year-old make love to me." In his later years, Marlon too would be attracted to early teenagers, both boys and girls.

It seemed that neither Duke nor Marlon worried about legal consequences of child molestation. "I'm above the law," Duke once said to Jimmy. "If I get into trouble, I'll merely buy my way out. When you have unlimited money, you have unlimited power."

82

Jimmy believed that as the days and weeks went by, Duke was falling in love with Marlon. "He's not boring," she told Jimmy. "Always full of surprises, always holding out some new adventure for me. One night he took me along the dangerous part of the New York waterfront, and we checked into a two-dollar-a-night hotel. He seduced me in this rat hole. It was one of the most thrilling nights of my life. All men I've met before have wanted my money. Not Marlon. He seems completely unconcerned about my fortune. If he's got twenty dollars in his pocket, he'll spend it on me and to hell with tomorrow. For once in my life, I want to experience what it's like to be a vagabond. Marlon has even suggested to me that I hitchhike with him across the country to California. That we leave New York with absolutely no money and test our wits by living off the fat of the land."

Jimmy advised against that. "Oh, shit, Doris, that would kill you," he said. "You can't live without your gold bars, including some stored in Zurich with Hitler's Swastika on them."

Marlon soon discovered that Duke tired quickly of sex in the missionary position. She constantly referred to her posterior as "my pleasure spot," and admitted her fondness for sodomy to Jimmy. "She demanded that Marlon sodomize her repeatedly, and he seemed willing to indulge her passion," Jimmy claimed. "Doris was long known for taking it up the ass. From what I heard, she turned Marlon on to heterosexual ass-fucking. I could have done some ass-fucking with Marlon myself, if he had been willing. In his post-Doris era, I understand that Marlon liked to sodomize both young boys and girls, but he can thank Doris for teaching him one of life's greatest pleasures."

Duke had a sexual fetish, known to all her lovers and eventually to Marlon. Before intercourse, she demanded "one hour of foot worshipping" as sexual foreplay. "I've never eaten so many toes in all my life," he confided in Jimmy. "Until I met Doris, I think my record for eating toe jam was about five minutes. But she expects me to play with her feet for hours."

On what became Marlon's last weekend at Rough Point, where Jimmy was also "in residence," Duke confided to the two men that all her life she'd been frightened of being kidnapped. When she was only a young girl, her father had received endless kidnapping threats. "I always felt I was going to be abducted and held for ransom. My worst fear was that my daddy wouldn't pay the kidnappers one dollar of ransom and that they would kill me."

She claimed that a psychiatrist in Hawaii advised her to act on her worst fear. "I decided to face my fear of kidnapping but to tie it in with a sexual fantasy. Not only did I want to be kidnapped, but I wanted to be held in bondage and gang-raped. I think all women dream of being gang-raped."

"I know I do," Jimmy chimed in.

"Eventually, one of her lovers," Jimmy said, "actually staged a 'kidnap-

Rudolph Nureyev

ping' of Doris in Honolulu. He'd rounded up several handsome, virile boys on the beach and some muscled sailors along the waterfront. Each man was given a hundred dollars. Stripped nude and held in a beach house, Doris was repeatedly raped and frequently sodomized during her three-day ordeal."

"It was one of the most thrilling experiences of my life," she later told Marlon and Jimmy. "All my life I've exerted great power over others. For the first time, I was the victim, forced to do the bidding of my attackers. Frankly, I would never want to go through that experience again. But I got it out of my system, and I'm glad I did. I'm a better person because of what I've experienced. My body, bloody and bruised, was delivered back to Shangri-La with memories to last a lifetime. I immediately checked into a hospital."

On Marlon's "dates" with Duke in New York, they indulged their mutual passion for jazz piano, and were often seen at various Harlem night clubs. In some of these dives, Marlon would play the conga drums. On a few occasions, she took him on Sundays to a black church "somewhere in New Jersey" where she startled him by singing in the choir.

Faced with the possibility of other conquests, a seemingly endless parade, Marlon drifted away from Duke. Even so, they remained friends for life. He made several trips to visit her mansion at Shangri-La in Hawaii.

In later life, when Marlon became passionately involved in the plight of the American Indian, he interested Duke in his cause. He got her to contribute financially. At one point she donated 250 head of prime cattle to the Rosebud Indian Tribe.

Peter Brooke, a freelance journalist who was occasionally hired to do "undercover work" for Duke, took a cynical view of the Brando/Duke friendship. Brooke recalled a dinner attended by Marlon at Duke's New York penthouse. "Brando was just using her," Brooke claimed. "He was such a pompous ass."

Nonetheless, the friendship endured. A gardener at the Duke estate in Somerville, New Jersey, recalled being surprised one morning to see Marlon, clad only in a pair of jockey shorts, jogging across the front yard.

It was later learned that Marlon had come to visit Duke on her estate because he needed

Rudolph Nureyev

financing for a film script that interested him. It dealt with the plight of the American Indian. In the movie, Marlon would be cast as a hard-nosed government agent who comes onto an Indian reservation. There he meets and falls in love with a beautiful Indian maiden who wins his support for the plight of her people. According to the script, he resigns his government post and goes to live among the Indians, exposing the atrocities of the government. After showing some early enthusiasm for the project, Duke lost interest and never financed the film.

Surprisingly, according to Duke's servant, Leo Moffatt, the dancer, Rudolph Nureyev, was also visiting Duke at Somerville that weekend. He, too, had a film he wanted financed. The Russian's project was more fully developed than Marlon's vague idea.

Over dinner that night, Marlon patiently listened to Nureyev. He wanted to make a film based on the life of the legendary dancer, Nijinsky. Costing an estimated three million dollars, his film would be written by none other than Edward Albee and would be directed by Franco Zeffirelli.

On this film, Duke put up an initial $100,000, but soon learned of trouble once shooting began. Instead of the great Nijinsky as the film's centerpiece, Nureyev wanted to adapt the picture so that its story line became an autobiographical rehash of his own life.

"Duke pulled the plug," attorney Wes Fach of Somerville said.

Moffatt recalled a strange sight he'd seen when he went to round up Duke and her two male guests for lunch. "I was astonished to see Nureyev completely nude teaching Miss Duke and Brando how to belly dance. Miss Duke was without her top but had on some panties. Brando was in jockey shorts. But Nureyev, who looked amply endowed, was letting it flop around, as he taught them the movements. All my life I've regretted I didn't have a film clip of this unholy trio. Surely my clip would have become as famous as that of Marilyn Monroe singing 'Happy Birthday, Mr. President' to JFK."

Who you lookin' at?

Chapter Four

In his highly unreliable memoirs, Marlon remembered meeting Monty when he, Marlon, was appearing in *Truckline Cafe*. Marlon claimed that he went to see Monty's performance in *The Searching Wind*, the Lillian Hellman play in which Monty was cast opposite Cornelia Otis Skinner. Marlon, according to his memory, introduced himself to Monty and invited him out to dinner. That was simply not the case.

Instead, it was Edith Van Cleve who brought young Montgomery Clift— "the rage of Broadway"—backstage to meet Marlon near the close of his run in *I Remember Mama*. Provocatively, Marlon asked his potential rival a question even before introductions were made by the agent. "So, what's the verdict?" Marlon asked Monty, who was four years older. "Who's better looking? You or me?"

"Every day I get up in the morning, look at my puss in the mirror and ask myself the same question," Monty said, half-mockingly. "Mirror, mirror on the wall, who is the fairest lad of them all? Montgomery Clift or Marlon Brando?"

"If you want my opinion," Edith chimed in to break the tension, "you're both the two hottest pieces of male tail ever to arrive in New York."

Because of his baby face and his almost poetic beauty and sensitivity, Monty looked even younger than the more masculine and well-built Marlon.

The following night, after composer David Diamond, while on the arm of Stella Adler, heard of this exchange between Monty and Marlon, he came up to Marlon at a party. "If it's some competition between Monty and you, I can tell you who's better looking, if you must know. Monty is actually better looking because your nose is all wrong. But you've got big balls, baby, and on stage it's the *cojones* that counts in an actor, not matinee pretty boy looks."

"I'll take your word for that, you Diamond in the Rough bastard," Marlon said, smiling.

Back at Marlon's dressing room for *I Remember Mama*, the actor suggested that Edith find herself some other male escort for the evening. Marlon put his arm around Monty and squeezed so hard that Monty winced in pain. "I hear you were born in Omaha," Marlon said. "That's my hometown. Omaha's not big enough for two talents such as ours, so I guess it's just as well that we came to New York."

"The question is, is New York big enough to contain the two of us?" Monty said. "Or, are we going to clash? Be up for the same roles."

As Edith recalled, Marlon wanted to immediately assume some dominance over the less developed and more fragile Monty. Right in front of his agent, he gave Monty a kiss with tongue. "Before the rooster crows, you'll know who's the better man."

"How do you know *I'm* not the better man?" Monty asked, somewhat taken aback by Marlon's male aggression.

"Before dawn breaks, sweetcakes, I'll be on top. You, the bottom."

"Maybe the other way around," Monty said.

"The next few hours will tell."

Edith watched as the dazzling pair headed out of Marlon's dressing room and into the night.

What happened next was pieced together by Monty's brother, Brooks Clift, and their mutual friend, Bobby Lewis. Other friends over the years have also added their opinions.

"Their friendship—dare I call it an affair?—was brief and intense," said Stella Adler. "So intense that it was destined to burn out quickly. It was rivalry that tore them apart. They were both the two young geniuses of 1940s Broadway and later the two young geniuses of Hollywood."

"Many critics compared their acting style, but they were quite different," said director Elia Kazan. "Both, of course, were often cast as deeply troubled young men, their characters the victim of an uncaring society. Monty was more intellectual in his approach to a role. Marlon acted more out of instinct. Monty was soft, even fragile in his characterization. Marlon was more brutish, as best exemplified by his role as Stanley. Monty was so uptight that Marlon once told me that he felt Monty walked like he had a Mixmaster up his ass!"

Actor Kevin McCarthy and his wife, Augusta Dabney, whom he'd married in 1941, were Monty's best friends. McCarthy was the younger brother of famed writer and novelist, Mary McCarthy, and the cousin of former U.S. senator and presidential candidate, Eugene McCarthy. Over the years, Kevin made many comments about his doomed friend, Monty.

Kevin McCarthy

"A former child actor, Monty was a marvelous technician on stage," Kevin said. "Marlon, on the other hand, was the more sensual animal. Monty took it all very seriously, and Marlon more or less viewed acting as a joke, not a respectable way for a real man to make a buck."

On their first date, according to Brooks Clift, both men had to explain to each other why they were 4-F. Monty said he was turned down because of chronic diarrhea caused by "some bug I picked up in Mexico." Marlon explained why he didn't make the grade, but assured Monty that "I'm a perfect specimen in every sense."

Monty Clift

Brooks said that the two young actors headed for the Battery on their first night together and raced each other for most of the way. "From what Monty later told me, they collapsed panting and out of breath. Monty always liked a bit of rough house, and he played with great intensity to release pent-up energy. He said that when he fell on the street, Marlon wrestled him to show him that he had more muscle and strength."

Brooks didn't know which man was the first to suggest it. But at one point in the evening Marlon and Monty decided to pull off their clothes and run through the almost deserted canyons of Wall Street. A military policeman spotted them and gave chase, but somehow they eluded him. "Both of them could have been shot," Brooks later said. "Those were tense times back then." Since they'd left their clothing on some dark street corner, Marlon and Monty were wearing "newspaper dresses" when they finally arrived at Marlon's apartment.

"They must have had a great roll in the hay," Bobby Lewis later said. "Because in the days and weeks ahead, they were seen everywhere together. When I went for a walk with them in Central Park, they even held hands, much to my embarrassment. Those were not tolerant times we lived in back then, but those two wildcats didn't seem to give a fuck."

Bobby claimed that their affair didn't last long. "Monty fell big for Marlon. They were both crazy. Two real lunatics. They'd do any stupid thing, like run out in front of traffic and see if cars could brake fast enough. They'd go to an expensive restaurant, then run out without paying the bill, flying down the street as a waiter gave chase. One night they pulled off their clothes and jumped nude in front of the fountain at the Plaza Hotel, splashing about. A cop arrested them, but somehow they got off with a small fine. Their agent may have come to the rescue, I'm not sure."

"Monty and Marlon could be two crazies on a Saturday night," Brooks said. "But there was a big difference. Marlon could pull himself together by Monday morning. Monty, on the other hand, couldn't come back from the brink so easily. Even in those early years, he could move into a whirlwind of despair, and no one could pull him back. Amazingly, he'd recover from his bouts of depression. But as the years went by, those bouts of depression grew longer and longer until he couldn't escape his demons, regardless of how hard he fought to do so."

Kevin found that Monty was one of the most ambitious actors he'd ever known. Marlon seemed indifferent to future stardom. As proof of Monty's ambition, he told his new friend, Marlon, that, "I want to be the greatest actor in the world. And I know that means going to Hollywood. So far, I've resisted all offers. But it's almost a foregone conclusion that I'll be a big star sooner than later in Hollywood. I hate the idea of those fucking seven-year contracts. I don't want to become Louis B. Mayer's prize bull. If I do go to Hollywood, I'm going to demand the greatest of roles, the best of scripts, and directors like Howard Hawks."

"You talk big," Marlon told Monty, their exchange later reported to Brooks. "I think all of this shit talk shows a lack of self-esteem. It's very sad. I'll have to fuck these conceits out of you tonight."

Marlon later told Stella Adler that he thought Monty was a lost soul. "I know how to pace myself," Marlon assured his mentor. "Monty doesn't. He'll be a big, bright star but he'll soon flicker out." In that remark, Marlon turned out to be a prophet. "As for me, I'm in for the duration like a prizefighter who knows how to pace himself. The decades will go by, and I'll be out there emoting—not Monty."

Monty surprised acquaintances such as actor Tom Ewell, who said, "I often saw him at parties. On one occasion, at a party in Greenwich Village, Monty sat in Marlon's lap, fondling him and kissing him throughout the entire party. Admittedly, it was a mostly gay party. The straights there were very tolerant. But, even so, things like that were frowned upon. I once saw Kevin McCarthy and his wife, Gussie, with Monty. He was definitely a hugger and kisser, especially with the McCarthys. Monty was practically making love to his best friends."

Tennessee Williams always claimed that Monty had intense feelings for the handsome actor. "I think Monty was in love with him," the playwright maintained. "Kevin was the love of Monty's life." Kevin, however, was a heterosexual. Though he loved Monty as a friend, he did not want the relationship to become sexual.

"What Monty wasn't getting from Kevin, he got from Marlon," Bobby Lewis claimed.

The first rift in Marlon's relationship with Monty came because of a girl. Ann Lincoln, whom writer Robert La Guardia called "a cross between Judy Holliday and Margaret Sullavan." A rising young actress at the time, she met Monty when she appeared opposite him in *Foxhole in the Parlor*. Marlon remembered her as hard drinking and aggressive, with a strong sex drive.

In his memoirs, Marlon wrote that Ann told him that Monty might be homosexual. "I found it hard to believe," Marlon said in those memoirs. "I imagine he was torn asunder by it." In so reporting, Marlon was completely misrepresenting himself. "How could he have found it hard to believe Monty's homosexuality when he was pounding his ass every night?" Bobby Lewis asked.

Marlon did have a point about Monty being torn apart by his gay streak. Monty went through his entire life struggling against his homosexual impulses.

"As for Marlon, he didn't seem to give a damn what anybody thought," Bobby said. "He moved from the bed of a woman to the bed of a man with no soul-searching at all. Marlon seemed to say, 'I am what I am,' and if you don't like it, go stick a feather up your crusty ass."

When Monty began to stray in his relationship with Ann Lincoln, she turned to his brother, Brooks, with whom she had an affair. When Monty found this out, he was enraged.

More pain was on the way. Soon after, perhaps as a means of making Monty jealous, Ann launched an affair with Marlon as well, all the while insisting that she still wanted to marry Monty. Whether it was true or not, word reached Monty that Ann was telling their friends in the theater that Marlon was far more preferable as a bed partner than Monty.

As the years went by, Monty and Marlon would grow apart, each of them rivals for the same dramatic roles. It was Monty, not Marlon, who was origi-

Tennessee Williams
hanging out

nally offered the lead in *On the Waterfront*. He turned it down. In 1958 Monty would be cast opposite Marlon in *The Young Lions*, and in 1967, it was Marlon who took over Monty's role in *Reflections in a Golden Eye* opposite Elizabeth Taylor. Originally Monty, at Taylor's urging, had been cast as the gay Army major in love with a handsome young soldier. Regrettably, Monty died of a heart attack before filming began.

Later, during the actual shooting of the film, Marlon told Taylor, "Your friend Monty and I were alike in only one regard. Both of us had desperate hopes and nursed unspeakable desires."

When Taylor asked him to explain himself, Marlon said, "Both Monty and I have human hearts. But they beat in the wrong places."

Brooks once asked his brother to define his brief but intense relationship with Marlon. Monty's response was enigmatic. "A mother substitute—that's all!"

* * *

"Except for Wally Cox, Marlon's affairs with men were launched with great intensity, but flickered out like a firecracker," Bobby Lewis claimed. "At one moment, insiders on Broadway would be talking about Marlon and Monty; and a moment later, the gossip was about Marlon and somebody else. Despite his many dalliances with men, especially in the Forties and Fifties, I think Marlon was basically straight. From all reports, he was particularly active as a homosexual in the 40s, less so in the 50s. After that, as he grew older, it appears that he led more or less a straight life—or so I heard. But with Marlon, you could never be sure."

Best pals Bobby Lewis, Wally Cox, Carlo Fiore, and Darren Dublin were always amazed at the clever balancing act Marlon maintained with his women. "I don't know how he did it, but he kept all of them dangling in the wind even though all his gals were aware of the existence of the others," Bobby said. "Not only that, but Marlon managed to pick up strays every week. He was so sexually magnetic that his women kept returning to his arms, even though by the time one of them woke up in the morning, Marlon might be gone from their warm bed and into an even warmer bed somewhere else. Marlon was definitely going through the most sexually charged period of his life. Maybe it was his Wheaties."

While enjoying intimacies with Celia Webb, Ellen Adler, and Blossom Plumb, Marlon also managed to launch an affair with Julie Robinson, an exotic-looking dancer from Katherine Dunham's troupe. Because of her relatively dark skin, and because she was a member of the Dunham dance troupe, many people thought Julie was a mulatto from the West Indies. Actually, she was Jewish, born of liberal New Yorkers who were described as comfortably well off.

Julie's best friend, Joyce Crosbie, another Dunham dancer, said, "Julie had charge accounts all over town when the rest of us had to sell pencils to pay for a cup of espresso at a Greenwich Village cafe."

From all reports, Julie fell in love with Marlon "and he with her," Crosbie maintained. "That is, Marlon fell in love with Julie in his fashion. However, I suspect that Marlon's true passion was the image that greeted him in the mirror each morning."

Even during the white heat of his affair with Julie, Marlon still hung onto

92

his other beauties. Julie was well aware of this. She constantly pressed Marlon for a commitment, because she believed she was his own true love. At least he told her that she was. "God only knows what he was telling his other women," Crosbie said.

Katherine Dunham also believed that "Marlon—at least for the moment—was in love with Julie. She urged marriage but he stalled her. Her affair with Marlon lasted, I guess, until his friend, Harry Belafonte, sang 'Yellow Bird' in Julie's ear."

After many a year—in 1957, to be exact—Julie and Belafonte got married. "Even when Julie more or less became Belafonte's woman, Marlon still pursued her," Dunham claimed. "She was one of my leading dancers, and I remember Marlon showing up in Cannes one afternoon hoping to win Julie back. He did handstands on the beach for her. But that didn't do the trick."

Both Belafonte and Julie were enrolled in drama classes at the New School with Marlon. As a West Indian with a father from Jamaica and a mother from Martinique, Belafonte found that his career as an actor was going nowhere. "Only Uncle Tom parts were offered to me," he told Marlon.

Eventually Marlon's interest in Julie subsided. As Marlon's own career soared with *A Streetcar Named Desire*, Belafonte by 1950 was found at Martha Raye's Five O'Clock Club in Miami Beach, singing such "white women's songs" as Patti Page's "The Tennessee Waltz" or Rosemary Clooney's "Come On-a My House."

One day in the early Fifties, Marlon unexpectedly encountered Belafonte on the sidewalks of New York. Embittered and depressed, Belafonte had returned from his experience as an obscure entertainer in Florida. He told Marlon that on Miami Beach "there are curfews for people of my skin. A Negro can stay only in special hotels or drink from a special fountain for coloreds. He must use special but hardly equal facilities. It's special everything. I even had to have a goddamn pass to cross over from the colored section of town into the white."

Marlon listened with great intensity to tales of these atrocities, and promised that when he became "an even bigger star than I am now, I'm going to do something to right these injustices."

"Good," Belafonte said. "You can make a difference. Each and every one of us can make a difference. We have the power."

"One day we'll be marching arm in arm like brothers onto Washington," Marlon predicted.

Even though that day didn't come as Marlon envisioned it, he did in his way honor his long-ago commitment to Belafonte and to the civil rights movement.

Known in the 1880s as a tranquil, sleepy fishing village with a high percentage of Portuguese immigrants, Provincetown, at the tip of Cape Cod, had long been a retreat for artists, writers, and various "queer folk." Around the end of World War II, Marlon and Darren Dublin arrived there too.

Preceding them had been a long list of literari, including novelist Edna Ferber, whom Noël Coward always insisted was a man in disguise. "The other Edna," Edna St. Vincent Millay, had also been a visitor. Even Gertrude Stein was once seen wandering alone on the sand dunes. The diarist, Anaïs Nin, had also been a visitor during "one of her frequent lesbian periods," according to author Henry Miller, her lover, confidant, and muse.

Checking in for the first time during the summer of 1940, Tennessee Williams himself had called Provincetown "the frolicsome tip of the Cape." He'd been a regular visitor ever since.

"The playwright and the actor were destined to meet," said Peggy Guggenheim, also a frequent visitor to P-town. "Tennessee was born in St. Louis in 1911, and Marlon in Omaha in 1924. What an odd couple. But each artist needed the other. Tennessee supplied Marlon with the words; Marlon supplied the emotional intensity needed to bring those words into a memorable reality in the theater. Forget all those memoirs about them meeting much later. They knew each other—rather intimately, I suspect—long before Marlon ever took a ride on *A Streetcar Named Desire*."

Not as sophisticated in the early Forties as he later became, Tennessee—still imbued with some Midwestern mores—at first found the "behavior of the beach crowd shocking." The author, who would later write boldly about such subjects as cannibalism, compared himself to "an old auntie" at the time, suggesting that "I leave my glasses in my bedroom if I plan to go to the beach."

As the summers quickly passed, Tennessee more readily adapted to this new environment. "P-town was a place back then—perhaps even today—where one took one's pleasure as one found it," he told the author. "What I liked about the place was that it was unnecessary to disguise one's eccentricities. P-town offered liberation to those of us who harbored souls that had suffered repression somewhere else in America, as I did in the Middle West. Considering some of the secret passions that resided in the hearts of many of the summer residents, homosexuality was viewed as one of the lesser evils."

"The gay colony—I don't think we called it gay back then—was tolerated by the supposedly straight Portuguese fishermen and sailors in town," Tennessee said. "We queer ones provided a quick and easy way for them to supplement their meager incomes. Not bad. Two dollars in exchange for a fast blow job. Two dollars was the going rate until some vicious queen arrived

94

from Brooklyn Heights one summer. He started giving these men three dollars. We practically lynched this flamboyant dandy for causing immediate inflation after dark."

Sidney Shaw, a homosexual lyricist linked to the Dunham dance troupe, had turned Marlon on to the glories of summertime P-town. Planning to spend the summer at the Cape, Marlon arrived with only eighty dollars. "Bronzed, blond, and muscled, he was addicted to wearing jeans so tight you could tell that he was uncut," claimed summer resident Jesse Steele, one of the first to make the actor's acquaintance.

Yours truly

Completely lacking in talent, according to Peggy Guggenheim, Steele called himself a landscape painter. He was the scion of a wealthy auto-manufacturing family from Detroit, who sent him monthly payments to stay out of Michigan.

In those days, Steele was known as a "mincer." He dressed in flamboyant attire—"colors to challenge the rainbow," according to Tennessee—preferring pink and lavender. In spite of his effeminate manner and slight lisp, Steele was a favorite of the fishermen at the port, a scattering of beach boys, New England boat builders, and itinerant sailors.

His parties were "all the rage" that summer, attended not only by Tennessee, but by Peggy Guggenheim herself, along with her "lover of the moment," perhaps Max Ernst or Jackson Pollock.

The town's foremost sexual predators—Tennessee, Steele, and Guggenheim—bonded. All three shared a mutual belief. "A small stipend discreetly slipped to your man of choice for the night will guarantee a much more reliable erection," Steele claimed with a great degree of accuracy.

Tennessee and Steele would have frequent arguments and not speak for a few days. But the following day, all the wounds would heal, and the two of them would be seen biking along the main street of the town.

"Tennessee, with a few drinks in him, would often criticize what he called my profligate ways," Steele said. "Actually, he indulged in far more daring and dangerous sex than I did. At one point, his behavior became so outrageous that the couple with whom he was staying kicked him out. He was bringing back some of the more well-developed teenage sons of the local families. He was bragging about a steady diet of fifteen-or sixteen-year-old semen, which he told me was good for the skin. He was kind in his assessment of the age of these boys. I saw many of them. Fourteen if they were a day. His only requirement was that a young boy should have reached puberty. As for myself, I preferred more mature and manly men, those with a lot of experience. A man like Marlon Brando."

"I must have met Marlon his very first day in town," Steele claimed. "I'm not exactly saying that he was in town hustling. Well, not exactly. But if you wanted to give him a free dinner—and a big one at that—free lodgings in your home, and free drinks, he wasn't opposed to accepting such gratuities. All of us had Marlon that summer. He was passed around from one queen's mouth to another like Southern fried chicken at the communal table of a boarding house."

According to Steele, the big debate in bars that summer was over the size of Marlon's dick. Was it six inches or ten inches? "The actual measurement, depending on the queen telling the story, varied at least four inches. I was often asked to appraise Marlon's equipment, since everybody in P-town knew

I'd had him. I always said, 'I've had bigger but never tastier.' Marlon called it his noble tool, and I think that's the best description. We don't need to be vulgar size queens running along with a ruler."

If Steele is to be believed, and he often exaggerated, Marlon for a week or so was seen around P-town with Dame May Whitty on his arm. A dame by Order of the British Empire, the dowager of the British and American stage had been born in Liverpool, England, in the closing year of the American Civil War.

In 1945, she was appearing at the Provincetown Playhouse, repeating her role in *Night Must Fall*, in which she'd scored a hit on both the London and Broadway stages. She'd even repeated the role in 1937 in a film version opposite Robert Montgomery, for which she won an Oscar nomination.

Dame Whitty had seen Marlon's performance in *I Remember Mama* and had made his acquaintance backstage. "It's ludicrous to speculate anything sexual between those two," Steele said. "Her Majesty just enjoyed Marlon's company. She was to die in 1948, and I'm sure that she was no longer susceptible to the pleasures of the flesh by the time she began hanging out with Marlon. She did pick up his tabs, however, and so word got out that Marlon was her kept boy."

It was Dame Whitty who introduced Marlon to his benefactor that summer, Clayton Snow, hailed at the time as "The Queen of P-town," a title that Steele also claimed for himself. With a shrug, Steele maintained that "Claytina," as everyone called Snow, "looked like First Lady Eleanor Roosevelt in 1934."

Clayton worked as the chief bartender at the Central House, a dive opening onto the water, next door to the Provincetown Playhouse. "Like the wartime queen of England, Dame Whitty liked a nip of gin every night," Steele said. "Sometimes more than one. Marlon was always at her side."

Dame Whitty suggested to Claytina that her actor friend needed a place to stay for the summer. By the very next day Marlon was living in Claytina's two-room cottage on a lane called Pumpkin Hollow, named after the large pumpkins an old grandmother once grew there for Halloween.

Dame May Whitty

"If there was a streak of cruelty in Marlon's character, it involved the devastating impressions he'd perform of Dame Whitty after she'd retired for the evening," Steele said. "His impressions weren't vicious, but deadly accurate. He had the bar in stitches. I also heard that when I wasn't around, he did swishy impressions of me too."

In the days ahead, Claytina was announcing to half of P-town that, "I've had Marlon. We've made a deal. In exchange for one rough-trade blow job a day, I'm giving him room and board. Claytina said that he'd told Marlon that he'd have to hustle his own drinks and spending money from the other P-town queens.

"Darren Dublin seemed to fade in and out of the picture," Steele said. "He wasn't always with Marlon. I have no idea what he was up to."

"Later reports claimed that Marlon rarely drank," Steele said. "But believe me, he was often drunk that summer in P-town. I don't want to leave the impression that he made out only with men. I knew more about his male conquests than his female ones. But I heard that he made out like a bandit with a lot of young women that summer, mostly actresses or dancers at the Playhouse. From what I observed, he liked women with dark skin. I don't think he was with these women for more than two or three nights, before moving on to some other belle. Marlon looked upon sex as a giant smörgåsbord, and he wanted a taste from every platter. One drunken night at Central House he told me that he'd acquired an appreciation for cunnilingus. 'Before this summer, I wasn't too much into going down on a woman,' he told me. 'Now I like it, not necessarily for the taste, but for the power I have over a woman while I'm performing the act.'"

Sometimes Marlon tried to pick up the wrong woman. One night at Central House, he ended up in the hospital. Approaching an attractive young Portuguese woman at the bar, he asked her to go to bed with him. Suddenly, at his back, Renaldo Salgado appeared. In the words of Steele, "this burly fisherman pulverized Marlon's pretty face, and I had to take him to the hospital for treatment. Later I told Marlon that in P-town we hit on the fishermen, not their wives. God, he could be dumb and daring at times."

Established in 1933, The Flagship was the oldest restaurant in P-town. Gertrude Stein and Anaïs Nin were long gone, but Tennessee was a regular patron. He appeared almost nightly with his lover, Pancho Rodriguez y Gonzalez, the strikingly handsome young desk clerk he'd met at La Fonda de Taos in New Mexico.

Arriving without Darren that night, Marlon was invited to join Tennessee's table by James Bidwell, an acquaintance of his. Tennessee had no objection. The playwright's *The Glass Menagerie* had opened at The Playhouse on 48th Street in New York on Easter Eve, 1945. Marlon had gone to see the play and its star, the incredible Laurette Taylor, whom he'd praised as "the world's greatest actress."

Admiring his work in the theater, Marlon was eager to meet Tennessee. Whether Marlon secretly hoped that the writer would be charmed by him and cast him in his next play is not known.

98

At the time of their historic meeting, Tennessee was struggling with a play called *The Poker Night*, whose title he later changed to *A Streetcar Named Desire*.

To the astonishment of the table, Marlon presented a drunken, cackling Tennessee with a piece of silver jewelry handmade by Wally Cox. Graciously accepting it in the style of Tallulah Bankhead, Tennessee slipped on the silver bracelet and dangled it in front of the other guests for an inspection.

"Then his eyes moved in on Marlon with that inner radar he seemed to possess," said Bidwell. "It was love at first sight, at least on Tennessee's part."

"Does that mean we're engaged?" he asked Marlon, laughing at his own remark.

Sitting beside Tennessee, Pancho stared at the new boy in town with a barely controlled fury. He refused to speak to Marlon when introduced by Bidwell.

"Oh, that blond hair," Tennessee proclaimed not only to Marlon but to the table at large, as he took in the actor's sensitive, poetic face, devoting equal time to the muscles encased like sausage in a white T-shirt and the tight jeans. Tennessee looked over at Pancho, who, in spite of his stunning looks, was a brunette. "All summer long, I've been famished for blonds." He would later insert that same sentiment into his play, *Suddenly, Last Summer*. "Now the gods have rewarded me for writing *The Glass Menagerie*. They've sent a Viking god directly from the shores of Valhalla."

He extended his hand to Marlon, the Wally Cox bracelet dangling from his arm. "I am Tennessee Williams. Soon all the world will know of me. I already know who you are. Marlon Brando. Soon all the world will know of you too. As I told John van Druten after sitting through his *I Remember Mama*, I didn't remember Mama at all. But who could forget Marlon Brando and that fabulous erection you were showing on stage?"

* * *

Much to Pancho's regret, Marlon continued to show up at the Flagship where he would "bum a meal off Tennessee." Increasingly isolated, Pancho sat beside his lover nightly, being virtually ignored as Tennessee amused Marlon with stories.

Occasionally, Tennessee would look over at Pancho and make some comment as if he weren't there. "Pancho fears he will lose me to the seductions that fame will bring. When one becomes famous, one must share oneself with the world, like it or not. When you become famous, Marlon, and I'm sure you will, you will understand the great burden that fame imposes on a life. Your own life will never be yours again."

The playwright also told Marlon that Pancho preferred a "one-to-one relationship, but at night my heart is a lonely hunter. I have never endorsed the idea of sexual exclusivity. One must venture forth each night onto the lonely beaches to encounter another like-minded but lost soul. In him, we can sometimes find greater tenderness and a rawer and immediate emotion than one can encounter in more stable relationships." At that point of Tennessee's monologue, according to Steele, Pancho stormed out of the cafe. "When Tennessee suggested that I, too, should leave him alone to talk theater with Marlon, I made my exit like Lynn Fontanne on her final curtain call," Steele said.

On other nights, in front of Marlon, Steele, and other members of the gay colony, Tennessee amused his listeners, who rarely contributed. "It was important to Tennessee that everybody be an audience," Steele said. "Most of us had already heard his stories, everyone except Marlon. He took in every word that Tennessee said, viewing it as Holy Writ."

Tennessee amused the table with stories that he'd received a letter from Joan Crawford, stating her desire to appear on Broadway in his play, *Battle of Angels*. "With a lot of rewriting, I think you might tailor this role for my particular talents," Crawford wrote. "I see that it might become a vehicle for myself." Cackling, Tennessee dismissed the idea of Crawford. In the pre-*Mildred Pierce* months in which she'd written the letter, her career had virtually collapsed, and she was hoping to rekindle it by appearing on Broadway.

Tennessee said he'd taken the play to Tallulah Bankhead and had come back in five days to get her reaction. "Darling," she told him, "let's have some bourbon and branch water while I tell you what a dreadful play you've written. It's indecent."

He finally persuaded Miriam Hopkins to take the role. After bombing with it, according to Tennessee, she shouted at him, "Damn you, Tennessee Williams. First, I lost the role of Scarlett O'Hara. Now this atrocity you inflicted on me."

On yet another night Tennessee entertained Marlon with stories of his short term at Metro-Goldwyn-Mayer. He'd been instructed to write what he called a "celluloid brassière" for Lana Turner, entitled *Marriage Is a Private Affair*. The playwright confessed that he spent most of the day working on his script, *The Gentleman Caller,* which was later entitled *The Glass Menagerie*.

"My writing wasn't going well," he said. "One very hot, muggy afternoon I was smoking far too many cigarettes and drinking much too much bourbon. Suddenly, there was such a rap on my door that I thought the Devil himself had been sent to reclaim me. Hiding the bourbon in my desk, I answered this urgent summons. To my surprise, little Margaret O'Brien was on the other side of the door. She was actually scheduled for an appointment in some other office and had gotten lost. The little tramp took one look at me and informed me that I was drunk, information I already possessed. I didn't need this smaller and more loathsome version of Shirley Temple to tell me that."

Neither Steele nor anyone else knew on what night Tennessee invited Marlon for a walk on the beach. It probably occurred the weekend that Pancho traveled alone to Boston, Tennessee refusing to go with him. The playwright took the actor for a moonlit walk to one of the Peaked Hill "dune shacks," informing him that Eugene O'Neill had once occupied one of these shanties. Marlon asked Tennessee what he thought of the plays by O'Neill. "Isn't money beautiful?" was Tennessee's enigmatic reply.

Over "pillow talk" with a future lover, Frank Merlo, Tennessee reported what took place that night between Marlon and himself.

"I think you and I might find a bit of comfort with each other," Tennessee said to Marlon. "Perhaps you can find solace for your pain by suckling on my not altogether fallen breasts."

Marlon erroneously told Tennessee that he was straight.

"Yes," Tennessee said, "don't you find that the land here, especially the weather at night, all gray and foggy with strange lights, evokes a stage setting? As for being heterosexual, that is a lofty ambition not achieved by all of us. On many a dark night, when the heart feels desolate, you might need my nurturing. All you have to do is lie back on the warm sands, perhaps with the ocean water cleansing your feet. I'll transport you to a sublime shore in a far and distant land. Your heterosexuality will not be compromised in any way. I'll even pay. I know you're short of money, and I'll give you five dollars, and that's my highest price ever."

"I don't do it for money," Marlon said, conveniently forgetting his recent job in New York with the London agency.

Marlon turned him down that night. But, according to Frank Merlo, "Tenn got his man about two weeks later." To Frank, Tennessee remembered seducing a slightly drunken Marlon as the "tide lapped under the wharf and the hungry seagulls screeched overhead."

"I managed to extract two offerings from that magnificent tool before I would remove that treasure from my mouth," Tennessee said. "By the time Marlon's cannon shot for the last time, the early streaks of dawn were in the sky. I had found my new Kip in spite of my other romantic entanglements at the moment."

Tennessee was referring to Kip Kiernan, a handsome blond youth and former lover of his who had died of a brain tumor at the age of twenty-six.

"For a brief time," Tennessee told the author but not for publication, "I had a vision of myself becoming Mrs. Marlon Brando, living in some rose-covered cottage on the Cape. There in our cozy nest by the sea, we'd settle in and enjoy everlasting happiness until the end of time. Although Marlon that summer temporarily turned his splendid body over to me, it was a vessel I was to possess only briefly. He was destined to share his magnificence with others. *So many others.*"

* * *

Having given up a steady acting job with *I Remember Mama*, Marlon faced an uncertain future on Broadway when cast in the Maxwell Anderson play, *Truckline Cafe*. It was the first presentation of Playwrights' Company, a theatrical partnership formed by Harold Clurman and fast-rising Elia Kazan. The new company had grown out of their shared Group Theatre experiences in the 1930s.

Kazan was already a name when he agreed to produce *Truckline Cafe*, with Clurman directing. Monty Clift had already sold Kazan to Marlon by raving about his staging of Thornton Wilder's *The Skin of Our Teeth* in 1942, in which the young actor had appeared opposite such veterans as Tallulah Bankhead, Fredric March, and Florence Eldridge. Kazan was also fresh from his film success, *A Tree Grows in Brooklyn*, based on the best-selling book by Betty Smith.

Stella Adler had threatened Clurman that if her husband didn't cast Marlon in the small but meaty role of Sage MacRae, he would no longer get laid.

Marlon's part-to-be was that of a psychologically troubled returning veteran from World War II, who drowns his unfaithful wife in the Pacific Ocean before turning himself in. Kazan's motives for agreeing to produce the play still remain unclear, because from the first reading of Anderson's script, he'd pronounced it "God damn dull." Clurman, however, saw possibilities not only in the play but in Marlon himself.

The setting for the seedy cafe is somewhere along the coastal road between San Francisco and Los Angeles. Most of the action, such as it is, takes place offstage and is described by the actors.

Marlon's first reading in front of both Clurman and Kazan was a disaster. He mumbled all his lines and couldn't even be heard in the second row, according to Clurman. Infuriated, Kazan stormed out of the theater. "This might be your wife's fuck buddy," he

Wet entrance on
stage in *Truckline Cafe*

called out to Clurman in front of Marlon, "but he's no actor."

Eventually the director convinced Kazan that he could "force" a perform-ance out of Marlon. But Kazan remained doubtful. When Edith Van Cleve, in her role as Marlon's agent, presented his salary demands of five hundred dol-lars a week, "Gadge"—his nickname—"practically threw me out of his office," she recalled. After fierce negotiations, often riddled with denuncia-tions, Edith got Marlon a salary of two-hundred and seventy-five dollars a week.

Marlon was the most inexperienced actor in the troupe which Kazan and Clurman had assembled. Also appearing in the play were Kevin McCarthy, Lou Gilbert, Karl Malden, Richard Waring, and Ann Shepherd cast as Marlon's soon-to-be-murdered wife.

Marlon was already a friend of Kevin McCarthy. And from the beginning, Marlon liked Karl Malden and admired his work. It was to become a mutual admiration society. Neither Karl nor Marlon knew that at that moment of their coming together, Tennessee Williams was laboring over a play that would bring fame to both actors.

Kazan was not alone in his disappointment with Marlon's acting. Maxwell Anderson, who had scored major successes with such plays as *Winterset* and *Abe Lincoln in Illinois*, thought Marlon was the worst actor ever to set foot on a Broadway stage. He referred to him as "that idiot."

It was Clurman who had introduced Marlon to Anderson, a playwright who had been described by the drama critic John Mason Brown as a "great, shy bear of a man." It was hardly a historic moment in the theater. The play-wright and the actor traded insults.

"Why don't you appear in a play by Lillian Hellman instead of ruining mine?" Anderson provocatively asked. "Maybe something by Eugene O'Neill. Let *that one* suffer a bit."

"I understand you're a playwright of ideas," Marlon countered. "That you are taken most seriously, mostly by yourself." After delivering that line, Marlon stalked away.

At dress rehearsal Marlon showed up "in the tightest pair of green fatigues ever worn on a Broadway stage," said Richard Waring. "It showcased his gen-itals."

On seeing his wardrobe, Kazan shouted at Marlon. "We're not putting on a male burlesque show, Brando. Make those fatigues two sizes larger—and that's an order!"

Kazan was so disappointed at dress rehearsal that he urged Clurman to fire Marlon before opening night and find an immediate replacement. Originally, Kazan had wanted veteran actor Burgess Meredith for the role.

In a last-ditch effort to rescue Marlon in the part, Clurman came up with a scheme. Only the night before, he had told Stella, "Marlon is withdrawn, completely inarticulate. He throws away his lines upstage. He talks like he's got marbles in his mouth. He is, in essence, catatonic."

He felt that "Marlon can't connect with the deepest part of himself. His pain is too great. That's why he mumbles. He's trying to cover up his real emotions."

While the rest of the troupe broke for lunch, Clurman asked Marlon to stay behind. Once the theater was emptied, he ordered the actor to climb a rope hanging from a gridiron above the stage. As he climbed the rope, Clurman yelled for Marlon to shout your lines "until your lungs burst." When Karl Malden returned from lunch, he was shocked to discover Clurman kicking Marlon, who lay screaming hysterically on the stage floor.

"Like a wild horse, Clurman had tamed Marlon," Malden said. "From then on, he could get the lines out of this throat. Before that brutal ordeal he went through, his lines seemed permanently lodged in his throat."

Even though Kazan at first "detested" Marlon, he very gradually won over the director's begrudging respect. "The Devil himself keeps the heart beating of this son of a Turkish rug salesman," Marlon told Clurman.

With his stocky build and dark complexion, Kazan was thirty-six years old when he met the young actor with whom he'd be forever associated in the public's memory, both in the theater and on film.

Truckline Cafe opened at New York's Belasco Theatre on February 27, 1946. For the purposes of what appeared about him in the program, Marlon switched the place of his birth once again, claiming to have been born in Bangkok, Siam.

Carlo Fiore watched the performance from backstage, claiming that Marlon had traversed the full circle, "a metamorphosis from dilettante to dedicated actor."

In preparation for his final scene, Carlo had watched Marlon race up and down an iron spiral staircase so that he'd arrive on stage breathless. A few seconds before his appearance, two stagehands doused him with buckets of ice-cold water, so that it would appear that he'd just emerged from the chilly Pacific.

At the close of the play, Marlon's confession of the murder, a five-minute monologue, stopped the show and brought on a thunderous ovation. In his performance, he perfectly captured the war vet's sensitivity with an underlying hidden violence that could erupt at any moment. The conclusion of the play involves a posse that bursts

Brando and Carlo Fiore

104

into the cafe to seize and haul him away, perhaps for a lynching. "Marlon pranced off the stage as if performing a dance of death, eager for his annihilation which he'd lacked the courage to do himself—either by a bullet to his head or drowning in the ocean," according to Carlo Fiore.

Writing for *The New York Times*, critic Lewis Nichols suggested that Anderson must have penned his play "with his left hand in the dark of the moon." John Chapman of the *New York Daily News* lambasted *Truckline Cafe* as "the worst play I've ever seen in my history of reviewing plays."

Yet Marlon's personal notices were raves. One critic, whose name seems to have been lost in the controversy surrounding the play, wrote, "Montgomery Clift, sit up and take notice! A Broadway star has come along to challenge even your brilliance." That remark was the beginning of a professional battle between the two handsome young actors that would last for years.

Backstage at the play, Marlon met veteran actress Jessica Tandy, who'd come to his dressing room not for seduction, as was so often the case with Marlon, but to compliment him on a "performance that is truly brilliant." Jessica was just months away from playing Blanche to Marlon's Stanley in *A Streetcar Named Desire*.

Director Jules Dassin was more to the point. "Oh, shit, this kid is great!"

To counter the bad reviews, the Playwrights' group took out ads attacking the critics, hoping to turn *Truckline Cafe* into a *cause célèbre* on Broadway. The ploy didn't work, even though Anderson lambasted his attackers as "the hound dogs of the press." The show would run for only eight performances, with Marlon finding himself out of work.

Even so, his short performance had made him the toast of Broadway. He was suddenly famous, vowing to punch anybody in the nose who called him "the new Montgomery Clift."

Marlon himself claimed that "Nothing, I learned, attracts women more than fame, money, and success."

Once again, Hollywood agents were pounding on his door. In bed, Marlon instructed his lover *du jour*—male or female—"to tell the fuckers I've gone home to Nebraska."

He did agree to meet with Margaret Webster, the British director and actress, at her apartment. She offered him the role of *Hamlet* in her repertory company production. He told her he'd get back to her. In a few days, he showed up at her door with a tinned can of imported French pâté as a gift. Attached to it was a note. He'd scribbled, "To be or not to be, alas, but for poor Marlon it's not to be."

* * *

On most lists of Marlon's lovers appears the name of Leonard Bernstein, the flamboyant composer and pianist who would captivate Broadway with such smash hits as *On the Town* or *West Side Story*.

It was generally assumed that Marlon met Bernstein through their mutual friend, Stella Adler. Apparently not. His first encounter with this musical giant, known for his versatility and boundless energy, was far more casual than that.

Before he started earning a decent living as an actor, Marlon often "crash-landed" at the seedy Park Savoy Hotel. His sometimes girlfriend Celia Webb lived in a room with him at this hotel with her young son.

Leonard Bernstein

The hotel stood on 56th Street, off Seventh Avenue. Since it was only two blocks from Stella's apartment, it was easy for Marlon to continue his visits—and presumably his affair—with his mentor.

The Park Savoy attracted struggling young actors from the Broadway stage, all of whom seemed to be perpetually out of work. At various times, actor Tom Ewell was in residence, and could be seen bringing home sailors—his favorite seafood—that he'd picked up in waterfront bars. During her so-called "lesbian period," Judy Holliday also lived here, as did Adolph Green and Betty Comden.

"On the same floor, where we shared a communal kitchen, one room would be filled by an out-of-work hoofer, the next room by an old-age pensioner, and yet a third room by a very busy Times Square hooker," Tom Ewell revealed in Key West during the filming of *The Last Resort*. "I met and became very friendly with Marlon at that time. He'd change lovers, both male and female, several times in the course of a week. He was never faithful to that poor Celia Webb."

Marlon's friend, Darren Dublin, lived at the hotel for a while, as did actress Maureen Stapleton. The landlady, Estelle Rose, weighed in at 225 pounds and spoke in a thick Brooklyn Jewish accent. She had a love/hate relationship with Marlon. She loved him when he paid his $18-a-week rent and hated him when he didn't. Ewell said that on several occasions Rose padlocked Marlon's door and wouldn't grant him access to his possessions until he came up with the money.

"Rose had been an old hoofer herself back in the Twenties," Ewell said. "She was a sort of a clone of Sophie Tucker and reputedly had the most vulgar act in show business. Marlon always seemed enchanted by her and would listen respectfully for hours to her stories of the old days on Broadway. One night he told me he fucked her. He might have lied, but I believed him. You could not believe the types he hauled into his hotel room. Types that could never get picked up by anybody but Marlon."

Locked out one night, Marlon crashed at the pad of two transvestites who did a revue every Saturday night on Bleeker Street in The Village. "His friends at the hotel just assumed he was fucking them too," Ewell claimed. "On some nights when he found his door bolted, Marlon crashed in Darren's room, sleeping on the floor."

One night, at least according to Ewell, Marlon came home at two o'clock in the morning to find his room padlocked once again. He'd forgotten to pay the rent and had spent all his cash. Just as he was pounding on the door to Rose's room, Leonard Bernstein entered the building. Learning of Marlon's plight, the brilliant young composer invited the young actor to share his room for a sleep-in.

Bernstein had been appointed music director of the New York City Symphony Orchestra, so why he still kept a room at the low-rent Park Savoy when necessity no longer dictated it is a matter of conjecture. Ewell speculated that the room "came in handy for Lenny's off-the-record assignations."

Although he could never be sure, Ewell was convinced that Marlon didn't sleep on the floor that night but was invited into Bernstein's bed. "All of us knew in those days that Lenny was far more gay than he was straight. Marlon was very handsome back then. I propositioned him once or twice but he turned me down. Frankly, I think I looked better than some of the riffraff he dragged in."

In an affair that evoked the one Marlon had had with Clifford Odets, "he and Lenny became an item," Ewell claimed. "They were probably lovers for a month at least. After the semen stopped flowing, they remained friends for years to come. Marlon always had this thing for accomplished Jewish artists, be they female or male, and Lenny was just his cuppa . . . at least for a while."

Years later, in 1954, it would be Marlon who would convince Bernstein to craft the musical score for *On the Waterfront*. Until then, the composer had resisted writing music for the film industry, but Marlon was very persuasive. Bernstein told Marlon that, "I find it very unsatisfactory to write a score whose chief goal is to be unobtrusive."

Tom Ewell

On the set of *On the Waterfront*, Director Elia Kazan remembered that "Lenny always gave Marlon a tongue to taste when greeting him, usually right in front of the whole cast. I always turned away at such displays of male bonding." Monty Clift maintained that Kazan was a homophobe.

Bernstein later confessed to fellow gay composer Benjamin Britten and others that, "Marlon was my one true love. Now I know what Judy [Garland] meant when she sings so beautifully about the man who got away. Marlon broke my heart. While it lasted, it was wonderful. Reason enough to be born." High praise indeed. Even assuming that Bernstein exaggerated the affair, he did harbor "a passionate affection for Marlon," as he confided to Stella.

"As for Marlon," Ewell said, "I don't think he gave sex with Lenny his primary attention."

Marlon did agree to disappear with Bernstein from the New York scene for about ten days. None of their friends knew what had happened to them.

Dorothy Raymer, a longtime columnist for *The Key West Citizen*, said that Marlon and Bernstein landed in Key West, where she encountered them on several occasions in the bars along Duval Street. Bernstein had discovered the glories of Key West in 1943, and wanted to share the town with Marlon. Marlon told Dorothy that he liked the old ramshackle seaport more than he did Provincetown, and he thought the redneck locals—called "conchs"—were, in his words, "fun as a fart and a half."

"They acted here like two men very much in love," Dorothy claimed. "But in Key West we've always been accustomed to that. In those days, I wore hibiscus in my hair. I remember that Marlon and Lenny took the flowers from my hair and wore them in their own hair at one of the local clubs. It was all very gay. Actually, back then we called it queer."

"Once," Dorothy said, "at a club on Duval called Sloppy Joe's, Marlon, accompanied by Bernstein on the piano, came out dressed like Dorothy Lamour in a sarong. He had a pet chimp with him. Borrowed from God knows who. He called it Bogo like the chimp who appeared with Lamour in that film, *The Jungle Princess*. Pretending, like Lamour, to be the tropical babe Ulah, Marlon gave a brilliant impersonation of Lamour singing *Moonlight and Shadows* as he cavorted with Bogo."

"The only trouble I ever had with Lenny," Dorothy claimed, "was that he liked to stick his tongue down my throat every time he greeted me. Marlon might have liked that but not me. I feared where Lenny's tongue had only recently been."

* * *

Veteran character actress Estelle Winwood, performing in James Leo Herlihy's play *Crazy October*, reflected on her marriage to Guthrie McClintic, the eminent producer and director. "I did have one homosexual husband. At least. Guthrie McClintic. He was an extremely famous Broadway producer

108

Estelle Winwood

who loved his fellow man—often. I wasn't the only actress he married. He married Katharine Cornell. But it was different for her than me. Like her husband, she was attracted to her own kind. You know: Birds of a Feather fornicate together."

One night, near the closing of *Truckline Cafe*, Guthrie was sitting in the audience, mesmerized by Marlon's performance. Talking with Marlon backstage after the performance, Guthrie proposed that Marlon should consider auditioning for the role of the fey poet, Eugene Marchbanks, in George Bernard Shaw's *Candida*, opposite his wife, Cornell. "It'll give you a chance to star opposite America's Duse," Guthrie said.

"I will only audition if you audition for me as a director," Marlon told the startled Guthrie. Instead of being insulted, Guthrie seemed wryly amused at Marlon's insolence, and, as was obvious to the rest of the cast of *Truckline Cafe*, the producer/director was powerfully turned on by Marlon.

There has been much speculation about why Marlon accepted a role so unsuited to his talents. At the time he was well aware that his friend and rival, Monty Clift, had appeared with Alfred Lunt and Lynn Fontanne in Robert E. Sherwood's *There Shall Be No Night* at the Alvin Theatre in New York in 1940. Depending on which critic you talked to, Lynn and Fontanne were the first couple of the American theater. Others considered Cornell and Guthrie the first couple of the American theater. Ironically, both the Lynn/Fontanne and the Cornell/McClintic marriages were called "lavender," meaning in name only, with Lunt and McClintic preferring men as lovers, and Fontanne and Cornell pursuing women, often young actresses.

During the run of *There Shall Be No Night*, Lunt fell madly in love with Monty, then only nineteen.

Bobby Lewis speculated that Marlon planned to duplicate the experience Monty had with Alfred Lunt but with Guthrie McClintic instead. "It was an amazing symmetry," Bobby said, "and I don't believe it was without design. When it came to experiences, Marlon didn't want Monty to have one up on him. Marlon also knew that Monty wanted the role of Marchbanks for himself. Actually, Monty would have been far more convincing as the effete poet than Marlon."

Cornell had first appeared in *Candida* in 1924. She had revived the play several times

Katharine Cornell

since, scoring great hits with Orson Welles in 1937 and Burgess Meredith in 1942 playing Marchbanks. McClintic planned to rotate performances of *Candida* with a modern dress adaptation of Jean Anouilh's *Antigone*. In that play, Marlon would be cast in a minor role as "The Messenger."

Marlon's involvement with the plays almost fell apart during his first meeting with Cornell, the *grande dame* of the American theater. A few minutes after their initial greetings, Marlon said, "I read Shaw's play. The part calls for you to be thirty-three years old. I hear you *admit* to being fifty." Actually, Cornell was forty-eight years old at the time. But her Guthrie was a ripe fifty-three years old when he fell for Marlon, whom he offered a salary of three-hundred dollars a week, a very respectable fee for Broadway actors in the mid-Forties.

Having successfully coped with the insults of another young *wünderkind* in the theater, Orson Welles, Cornell forgave Marlon for his impertinent remark. Rehearsals began at their townhouse at 23 Beekman Place, a brownstone the couple had purchased in 1923 for twenty thousand dollars.

The joke around Broadway at the time was that Guthrie was successful at directing his wife because he secretly wanted to play all her roles himself, everything from Juliet to Elizabeth Barrett Browning.

Almost from the beginning, Guthrie realized that he might have cast Marlon in the wrong play. The macho-looking young actor had been cast as an effeminate, eighteen-year-old poet with a delicate, childish voice. Shaw's stage instructions had called for the character of Marchbanks to appear with a "haunted, tormented expression and a shrinking, shy manner."

"At least Marlon got *that* part of his character right," Guthrie would later say.

Cornell represented the old-fashioned school of acting, as opposed to Marlon, who was a Method-trained exponent of psychological naturalism. In her exalted romantic style, Cornell delivered her lines in a striking vibrato, using gestures so extravagant that they'd have been better suited to the character of Norma Desmond as portrayed by Gloria Swanson in the upcoming film, *Sunset Blvd.* "Acting with Cornell is like trying to bite down on a tomato seed," Marlon wrote sister Fran.

Attending rehearsals was veteran character actress Mildred Natwick who had appeared in *Candida* in 1937 and again in its revival in 1942, playing the role of Prossie. "As long as there are spinster and biddy parts," Mildred told Marlon, "I'll have a job." That drew a laugh from him. He adored Mildred, and the two actors became fast friends. Unlike Cornell, Mildred did not take herself too seriously.

"By the second week, it became apparent to me that Guthrie was seducing young Marlon," Mildred recalled years later. "Cornell was well aware of what was going on. In my opinion, she encouraged the affair. It kept Guthrie happy and off the streets. Some of his rough trade pickups in the past had led to trouble. Kate feared scandal. At least with Marlon, there would be no scandal."

"If there was trouble, and there was, it came when Guthrie fell madly in love with Marlon," Mildred later said. "The love affair was doomed from the start. I'm sure Marlon did not feel the same way about Guthrie that this middle-aged man felt for him. He did find Guthrie amusing, however. No one was filled with more theater lore than Guthrie, and no one could be more entertaining when he wanted to. He was a regular *bon vivant*. It was sad to watch, however. Guthrie was following Marlon around like a little puppy. Marlon seemed indifferent to the whole matter. He did share Guthrie's bedroom. At the townhouse, Kate and Guthrie occupied separate master bedrooms."

Sir Cedric Hardwicke was appearing in the play as Cornell's pastor husband. "Marlon was contemptuous of this gifted but old-style performer," Mildred said. "Marlon told me, 'When I'm around that guy, I always try not to stand in a downwind.'"

Hearing the remark, Hardwicke got even with Marlon in his memoirs, *A Victorian in Orbit*. He declared Marlon "useless as Marchbanks." Marlon countered that Hardwicke was a "Johnny One- Note actor."

When Marlon wasn't at the Beekman Place address, he was sharing the apartment of Wally Cox on 57th Street. "It was like Grand Central station," Maureen Stapleton later remembered. "People came and went at all hours of the day and night. I don't think Marlon and Wally ever locked their doors—not that there was anything to take if some bandit dropped in."

"Marlon might have been involved with a number of famous men in the theater," Mildred said, "and was in fact a serial seducer of such gentlemen. But he was seducing far more girls at the time, at least from what I could see. I visited Wally and Marlon several times at their wretched flat. At the time, I heard that Wally and Marlon were having an affair, and I believed that. But he was also dating every dark-skinned, exotic young woman in New York. I remember seeing him at one time with an incredibly short girl from Nicaragua, another time with this beauty from Thailand. Girls he dated were definitely the type who couldn't get an escort for Saturday night. I recall one particularly overweight beast of burden. When Marlon caught me appraising her, he whispered in my ear, 'Fat girls need a good fucking from time to time—not just the skinny ones.' I truly am convinced that even though Marlon pursued sex daily, it didn't really mean that much to him. He rather bluntly shared

Maureen Stapleton

his feelings with me one night. 'I need to take one good crap a day or I feel rotten,' he said. 'I also need at least one good lay a day. I can live without the fuck but I'm miserable without the shit."

"Almost from the beginning of their relationship, Marlon made it clear to Guthrie that if he wanted him, he'd have to put up with his many affairs with women," Mildred said. "There was a young girl I remember that Marlon brought backstage. I think her name was Donna Bedford. A struggling actress at the time, she seemed very much in love with Marlon. He paraded this unfortunate creature in front of Guthrie who became very jealous and ordered her out of the theater. It was like Marlon was sending a signal to Guthrie. In essence, Marlon was saying, 'Listen, you old pervert, this is what I'm really into. Not you.' He could be cruel to his lovers. And never faithful. No, not that."

Once at Wally's apartment, Bobby Lewis challenged Marlon about his growing reputation on Broadway for sleeping with influential men in the theater. "I know you've got talent but some of your enemies are saying you only win parts because of the casting couch. I thought I'd really piss Marlon off by telling him that. Maybe it was the wine speaking for me. But he didn't seem to take offense at all."

Bobby struggled to recall Marlon's words at the time. "'To be an actor,' he said, 'I have to taste and sample much that life offers. That taste, like the lemon, is bitter. Yet under the right conditions, the lemon yields one of the great flavors on earth. Often I don't stand around to see what life offers, but I go out and discover what it can offer. That means the good, the bad, and the ugly. I need to experience it all, even if it means dealing with Cornell and Guthrie and their endless demands. I'm storing away experiences in my subconscious. I can summon these experiences when I need them on the stage. It's like removing a box from storage in my own personal warehouse. It's my duty to have as many experiences as I possibly can so that I can interpret the various stages of life's realities.'"

In a more refined version that he'd polish over the years, Marlon gave very similar views in a statement on acting he made in 1960, repeating the same sentiments again in 1962 before going silent on the subject.

On opening night, with some exceptions, the critics were unkind to Marlon. Stanley Kauffmann found that he "talked like a cab driver and moved like a third baseman." Writing in *The New York Times*, Lewis Nichols found Marlon's interpretation of Marchbanks "more sniveling than spirited."

Hollywood columnist James Henaghan later said, "I couldn't believe how effeminate Brando was in the role. Later when I went to see his macho performance in *A Streetcar Named Desire*, I couldn't believe it was the same actor."

Mildred Natwick

Marlon Sr. showed up in New York to catch Marlon's performance opposite Cornell. Backstage he was introduced to the star and to Guthrie. "Marlon's father detested Guthrie," Mildred said. "After Guthrie walked away, he told me that he was nothing 'but an old fag.'"

Marlon Sr. had come to New York for reasons more compelling than to see a stage play. Once again, Dodie had fled back to New York to escape her marriage. She had resumed her heavy drinking and often disappeared for days at a time. Marlon Sr. wanted to track her down and win her back.

In spite of the bad notices of *Candida*, Louis B. Mayer sent one of his agents to the theater to deliver a handwritten note to Marlon. He offered him a seven-year contract at Metro-Goldwyn-Mayer with a guaranteed salary of three thousand dollars a week for the run of the contract. Marlon had never been offered such a high salary before.

"Would you believe it?" Mildred asked. "The young fool turned it down. Backstage all of us were practically drooling at the offer."

An offer also came in from Elia Kazan, who wanted Marlon to play the juicy third role of a Jew in *Gentleman's Agreement*. Marlon turned that down too, the part going to his rival, John Garfield.

On reflection years later, Marlon found Cornell "empty-headed," an actress who depended on stage presence more than talent to attract attention. "It was like two people dancing to a different beat," he recalled of their time on the stage together.

In 1972 she was far kinder to him in her appraisal, claiming that he was "the finest Marchbanks I ever appeared opposite in spite of his often erratic performances."

In recalling Guthrie years later, Marlon provided no clue as to any sexual interlude that might have existed between them. He remembered only Guthrie's bizarre sense of humor and "a hernia that kept popping out when he laughed. When that happened, he punched himself in the groin and pushed it back into his gut."

It was at the final performance of *Antigone*, not *Candida*, that a friend of both Cornell and Guthrie appeared backstage. Newly arrived from London, he was handsome, dashing, and debonair, "with a speaking voice better than God himself," as Mildred put it.

"The Englishman had arrived to congratulate Marlon on his performance," Mildred said, "even though it was just a walk-on. He hurried past his dear friends, Kate and Guthrie, and headed straight for Marlon. I don't know if Kate ever forgave him for that. I was standing nearby when God's anointed came up to Marlon. Instead of shaking his hand, he kissed both of Marlon's rosy cheeks. Finally, he broke away and extended his hand to Marlon. 'Great performance! I'm the man who married Scarlett O'Hara.' "

* * *

Backstage at *Antigone*, Laurence Olivier was utterly captivated by young Marlon. He told reporter Sheila Beckstein that, "Brando has only a very small role—no more than one speech really. But his performance was electrifying. Truly exciting theater. It's obvious to me that Marlon Brando is a star on the rise."

Mildred Natwick was invited to join Olivier and Marlon for a late-night supper at the home of Katharine Cornell and Guthrie McClintic. Years later, she would claim that she saw the affair between Marlon and Olivier developing "right before my eyes." She also noted that it was taking place right under the jealous eyes of Guthrie and in his own home, where Olivier was a house guest as he'd been several times before. It is not known if Olivier was aware of Guthrie's romantic interest in Marlon.

"I really believe that if he did know, it would not have made the slightest difference to Larry," Mildred would later claim. "He was of the school, 'All's fair in love and war.' John Gielgud slept with Larry on several occasions, or so he said. He once told me that whenever Larry spotted a handsome actor, especially one in green tights, he went after him with an unusual determination—and most often got his man. I mean, back in those days what aspirant actor would turn down *Macbeth*, much less *Hamlet*?"

Producer David Lewis once said of his friend Olivier, "He would sleep with anyone."

During the run of a rather silly play, *No Time for Comedy*, opposite Katharine Cornell, Olivier had launched an affair with Guthrie. In the play, Olivier had been cast as "Gaylord Esterbrook" at the time his lover, Vivien Leigh, was in Hollywood shooting *Gone With the Wind*.

Guthrie was hardly Olivier's first homosexual liaison. His first wife, actress Jill Esmond, was a lesbian, and during his marriage to her, he'd been free to carry on whatever relationships he

Laurence Olivier

114

wanted, usually with men of the theater. According to Jack Wilson, "Noël and Larry had an affair that lasted for years—or at least until I came along."

Olivier also had affairs with actors who ranged from dashing Richard Burton to dashing Errol Flynn, even the Frankenstein director, James Whale. References to these affairs were edited out of Olivier's autobiography at the request of family members and his third and final wife, actress Joan Plowright.

Under pressure, Olivier agreed not to publish these controversial revelations, including his description of his longtime affair with comedian Danny Kaye, but copies of the original chapters were made and widely distributed in publishing circles in New York. Olivier did go on record as saying, "I am prepared to believe that the sense of romance in those of our brothers and sisters who incline toward love of their own sex is heightened to a more glazing pitch than in those who think of themselves as normal."

Mildred believed that Olivier's seduction of Marlon occurred the very first night of the Cornell/McClintic late-night dinner. It continued, according to her suspicions, at the couple's retreat in the village of Sneden's Landing on the Hudson River. In previous years, Cornell and Guthrie had invited Vivien Leigh, Olivier's wife at the time, to spend time there when Vivien and Olivier were hoping to star together in the film, *Rebecca*.

"I remember bits and pieces of the dialogue between Larry and Marlon at the Cornell home," Mildred said. "Larry was complaining that he and Vivien were regarded as 'mere *arrivistes*' by the American press. 'Sometimes autograph hunters over here mistake me for Maurice Evans. In most whistle stops, I'm considered a movie star. I don't think most Americans are aware of my career on the stage.'"

Olivier suggested to Marlon that in "just a few short months, and I predict this, you'll be followed everywhere by autograph hounddogs. Once I was standing at a latrine at the Plaza Hotel. The man next to me used that inopportune moment to request an autograph. I rather testily told him that his dick wasn't long enough for me to write Laurence Olivier. I buttoned up and walked out as grandly as I could." He also told Cornell, Guthrie, and Marlon that Vivien knew how to handle autograph seekers at her stage door. "She routinely shouts at them, 'Fuck off—now *fuck off*!'"

According to Mildred, Marlon laughed at this. He told Oliver, "If one of those hounddogs comes up to me, I'll tell him he'll get his autograph if he'll show me his ass. I'll write 'Marlon' on one buttock, 'Brando' on the other."

Mildred remembered Marlon asking Olivier why he wore so much perfume. "I know it's gilding the lily," Olivier said, "but I sweat a lot in crowds and under lights. I like to smell kissable at all times. You wear no cologne at all?"

"Just my natural smell," Marlon said. "Sometimes I don't even take a shower, much less a bath. I just throw a glob of spit into the air and run under it."

"Olivier laughed and it was obvious to me that he was both attracted and repulsed by Marlon's vulgarity," Mildred claimed. "Marlon's crude sexual animalism mesmerized Larry. I don't want to say that Larry had his tongue out panting for Marlon that night, but seduction was obviously on Larry's brain."

Before the night ended, at least according to Mildred, "Marlon and Larry were exploding off each other. There was a great chemistry between them, even though they were from entirely different sides of the pond. Different worlds, really. Before midnight, when I went home, Kate, Guthrie, and I could have been invisible ghosts. Larry had eyes only for Marlon—and Marlon only for him. Romeo had met his Juliet in an unlikely form."

Three days later when Mildred once again encountered Olivier, he told her, "I am the happiest man alive."

"Strong comments coming from a man who in the past had been so unhappy that he'd contemplated suicide," Mildred said.

"Our love is triumphant," Olivier told her. "In Marlon, I have found what I've been seeking but never came across in all my life. Vivien will have to understand. Her Ladyship is very understanding. I'm moving Marlon in with us."

Those plans, alas, did not materialize, at least not immediately. After less than a month, Marlon abandoned Olivier, giving him the same treatment he'd given such luminaries as Clifford Odets and Leonard Bernstein.

"One morning, he was lying nude under the sheets with Larry," Mildred said, "and the next day he was gone from the bed. Marlon dumped Larry to resume his one-night stands. Hamlet got jilted for late-night pickups."

The full story of Marlon and Olivier, catalyzed by the ongoing presence of Vivien Leigh and a film version of *A Streetcar Named Desire,* hadn't yet evolved. "Marlon merely put Larry on hold until some future date," Mildred said.

Marlon later confided to Stella Adler and Bobby Lewis, as well as others, that he'd been with Olivier "merely to listen to the sound of his voice." He told his friends that Olivier himself had admitted to "imitating absolutely and unashamedly" such stars as Ronald Colman, Alfred Lunt, and John Barrymore. He did caution Marlon, however, that "imitation is good provided you don't mold yourself around that one actor you admire—that you don't merely imitate. In your case, I just know you'll allow your own conception of a character to develop. Make it your own!"

Stella Adler once said that she was amazed at the future comparisons others would make between Marlon and Olivier. The debate would rage for decades, and it's still going on: "Who was the greatest English-speaking actor of the 20th Century?"

John Gielgud found comparisons between Marlon and his friend, Olivier, "odious. How can you compare a young man who appeared on the stage for the last time in 1947 at the age of twenty-three with a gifted performer who first walked on the stage at the age of ten, and who would later define theater as we know it today?"

Gielgud was practically alone in deriding comparisons. William Redfield, in his *Letters From an Actor*, wrote: "Ironically enough, Laurence Olivier is less gifted than Marlon Brando. But Olivier is the definitive actor of the 20th Century. Why? Because he wanted to be."

Tennessee Williams himself pronounced Marlon "the greatest living actor ever . . . greater than Olivier."

As amazing as it seems, considering what different characters and actors they were, Olivier and Marlon were sometimes up for the same role. In one of the ironies of Hollywood, it was Olivier, not Marlon, who was the first choice to play Don Corleone in *The Godfather*. In yet another irony, on the night of March 27, 1973, in Los Angeles, Marlon would find himself competing with Olivier for an Oscar for the best actor of the year, Marlon for his role in *The Godfather*, Olivier for his star turn in *Sleuth*.

The Olivier/Brando coupling was too good a story not to make it to London. At a party attended by Vivien Leigh, the British theater critic, Kenneth Tynan, confronted the emotionally unstable actress. He too had had an affair with her husband and would later have an affair with her future costar in *A Streetcar Named Desire*. Although not wanting to cause her even more pain than she was experiencing because of her personal demons, he became a little bitchy after a few drinks. He told her all that he knew of her husband's affair. Vivien listened politely, then said, "Oh, my. What fiddle-faddle! If that's true, I only hope that poor Larry knew what to do. Marlon Brando. I must try him myself one day!"

With that pronouncement, she turned on her heels and walked away. All Tynan saw was the curve of her back as she graciously made her way across a crowded London living room to greet the just-arriving Noël Coward and his partner, Jack Wilson. Both of these men already knew what Vivien didn't know.

What Marlon Brando was like in bed.

* * *

In the autumn of 1946, Marlon left the Cornell/McClintic townhouse never to return. That very same week he was given an inch-and-a-half thick script by his agent, Edith Van Cleve. He was asked to read it that very night for an audition she'd arranged in the morning in front of Broadway producers Edward Dowling and Margaret Webster.

After devouring a heavy pasta dinner cooked by Wally Cox, Marlon started to read the script of Eugene O'Neill's latest play. In spite of the playwright's reputation, Marlon had never been impressed with O'Neill's works, finding his plays "dour, negative, and too dark." After only fifteen minutes, he fell asleep on the sofa.

The following morning at the audition that never came to be, Marlon attacked O'Neill's play in front of an astonished Dowling and Webster. "It's a piece of shit," Marlon claimed. Even though he hadn't read the script, he said it was "full of long, boring speeches. O'Neill sounds like an asshole on a soap box. The play is meaningless. The audience will fall asleep only ten minutes into the first act. I saved many plays before but even I can't rescue this turkey. I wouldn't even be caught dead performing in it." He walked off the stage before the producers could even respond.

On the opening night of *The Iceman Cometh*, O'Neill received perhaps his greatest critical acclaim. One critic called the play "the best of the decade." Marlon told Edith that, "I read the reviews and wept at what might have been. With me in it, it could have become O'Neill's masterpiece and my greatest hour upon the stage."

That same week Marlon was rescued by another offer, not from Edith but from Luther Adler, Stella's more famous actor brother who was making his Broadway debut as a director with a play called *A Flag Is Born*. "You'll be the only goy in the cast," Adler told him. He'd had doubts about offering Marlon the role but had done so at Stella's urging.

With music by Kurt Weill, the play was written by Ben Hecht, arguably the screen's most gifted writer and winner of three Academy Awards. His big hits had included *The Front Page* and *Twentieth Century*.

In *A Flag Is Born*, Hecht had lost his usual screen-writing brilliance. The play—actually a pageant masquerading as a play—was a cornball propaganda piece showing Hecht's zealous commitment to Zionism. *A Flag Is Born* was a virtual petition calling for the creation of the new State of Israel. It was also bitterly anti-British. The Royal Navy was preventing Jewish refugees from Europe, often survivors of Nazi concentration camps, from traveling to colonize the Holy Land. Long an admirer of the Jewish people, Marlon shared their dream of establishing a new homeland in Israel. He told his director, "the Adlers are my kind of people, not that ritzy Cornell crowd."

Marlon was cast as a young Jewish firebrand named David. He would be working opposite Celia Adler, who was Stella's sister, and Paul Muni. Muni was one of the few actors who appeared in pictures that Marlon admired. He'd seen all of his pictures and was especially impressed with his role as a gangster in *Scarface* and a Chinese coolie in *The Good Earth*. Marlon found the veteran actor's accents, disguises, and versatility amazing.

Ben Hecht

Muni did not return the compliment. He chastised Marlon's acting in front of Adler, telling his director that he should fire Marlon and find some Jewish actor to take over the $48-a-week role as David. Muni claimed that Marlon was "completely miscast and completely unconvincing in the role." Unaware of what Muni was saying behind his back, Marlon stood in the wings watching Muni emote, telling Adler that "he gives me goosebumps."

A Flag Is Born opened on September 5, 1946 at the Alvin Theatre, playing mainly to Jewish audiences. On opening night, Muni's character was to die on stage at the end of the play. Marlon had to drape the flag of Israel over Muni's body and then launch into his moving, eloquent speech of the evening.

It was the highlight of his performance. Before they went on stage. Muni had instructed Marlon not to cover his face with the flag, but to leave it exposed as part of his death scene. In the nervousness of opening night, Marlon forgot and completely covered the older actor's face.

Although he'd mumbled through most of the rehearsals, Marlon was at his most ferociously intense during the play's final speech. Many members of the audience were awed by the clarity of his voice and the brilliance of his performance. He would, in fact, draw more applause than Muni at the end of the show. This enraged Muni.

Marlon's back faced Muni's coffin as he delivered his moving speech. Bit by bit, the "dead" Muni, with his hand concealed, tugged at the flag inch by inch until his previously covered face was exposed to the audience. Titters could be heard throughout the audience.

It was only when the curtain went down that Marlon learned what Muni had done. In his dressing room, Marlon told Adler, "The son of a bitch wanted to keep acting even while he was supposed to be dead. Maybe he wanted

Paul Muni

to act his way through rigor mortis. Maybe act his way to show the flesh rotting from the bone. What a fucking ham!" The next day Marlon forgave Muni but never again covered the actor's face with the flag for the duration of the run.

A Flag Is Born was Marlon's first experience with a political commitment that in time would lead to his fight for the rights of the American Indian. At the time, American Jews were divided over how a Jewish homeland should be established in Palestine. Marlon backed the more militant wing, the Irgun, a group led by Menachem Begin, that advocated violence and was anti-British. Most American Zionists, however, leaned more to the Haganah movement advocating a less violent approach, as proclaimed by the more moderate David Ben-Gurion.

After the play had run its course, Marlon actually traveled across the United States, raising money for the Irgun. "I was a hot-headed terrorist back then, advocating violence," he recalled later in life. "As I matured, I came to understand all sides, even the Arab point of view. I was a bit over the top when I proclaimed in speeches that British troops blocking Jewish immigration to Palestine were committing far greater atrocities than the Nazis. Blame it on my youth!"

Ben Hecht lost his sense of fairness and balance when he zealously took out a newspaper advertisement in the *New York Herald Tribune*. In that ad, he proclaimed that every time a British soldier dies, "I have a little holiday in my heart."

This support of Irgun terrorists would eventually cost Hecht his movie career. It certainly led to a boycott of all his work in Britain. Even such leading Jewish figures as Edward G. Robinson dropped his support after Hecht's blatant advertisements.

But Marlon remained loyal to Hecht, and basically agreed with the screenwriter. In his memoirs, Hecht claimed that *A Flag Is Born* raised one million dollars for the Irgun "Freedom Fighters." Actually, it raised $400,000. That money went to purchase a large ocean liner, named the *S.S. Ben Hecht*, which ferried nine hundred refugees to Palestine in March, 1947. The British Navy captured the ship and sent six hundred of its passengers to detention camps in Cyprus. The rest of the passengers escaped to Palestine where they joined the ranks of the militant Irgun. Later the *S.S. Ben Hecht* became the flagship of the Israel Navy.

Although Marlon was appearing in a political role, his presence as a sexual animal on stage did not go unnoticed. "Scads of young Jewish girls flocked every night not to listen to the message of our play but to see Marlon perform," Luther Adler said. Marlon wore a black turtleneck sweater that showed off his powerful physique and a pair of black trousers tied with a rope belt. One male writer proclaimed that he was "breathtakingly handsome, a figure of charismatic, mythic beauty."

"I think during the run of the play, Marlon must have fucked half the Jewish gals in New York," Adler said. "They flocked backstage to meet him, and he took his pick every night."

In the words of his second wife, Anna Kashfi, "Marlon seduced an ardent harem of voluptuaries. He told me, 'I wanted a house filled with women. One for every occasion—a picnic in the woods, a day at the beach. One to screw in bed. One to screw standing up.'"

Not all visitors arriving backstage were female. One night Frank Sinatra showed up in Marlon's dressing room to congratulate him on his performance. Marlon later told Stella Adler, "All flash, an overbaked Guinea Pie. As for his singing voice, I'd prefer a castrated rooster at dawn." When the two stars made *Guys and Dolls* together, Marlon would have even harsher comments to make against Sinatra.

In Paul Muni, Marlon survived one legend on the stage. During his next venture, he would not survive the second stage legend.

The incomparable Tallulah Bankhead was about to barge into his life, the same way she'd aggressively barged down the Nile in her performance of *Cleopatra* in 1937.

She called Jack Wilson, the producer of her new play. In her throaty, bourbon-and-branch water voice, she instructed him, "Get me Marlon Brando! I can't stand Method actors, but get him anyway. From all reports, even if he can't act, I'll get royally fucked every night of the performance!"

Of Poetic Sensitivity

Chapter Five

Edith Von Cleve was not only the agent for Monty Clift and Marlon, but she was one of Tallulah Bankhead's closest friends. Tallulah told her that she was looking for a leading man to appear opposite her in the Jean Cocteau play, *The Eagle Has Two Heads*, originally called *Eagle Rampant* and a previous hit in London and Paris. Edith had reservations about the possible "chemistry" between Tallulah and Marlon, but recommended him anyway for the co-starring role.

Tallulah agreed to interview Marlon at her country home, "Windows," in Westchester County's Bedford Village, north of New York City. Her friend, Bobby Lewis, lived a mile away at Pound Ridge. He claimed that, "I could clearly hear her if the wind was right."

In Cocteau's romantic Graustarkian fable, the lead role of Stanislas is based on an impassioned young revolutionary poet who comes to assassinate the queen of an Eastern European country, but stays to love her, an improbable plot if there ever was one. In Cocteau's play, the queen is actually thirty-one years old. In real life, Tallulah was forty-three years old, Marlon a mere lad of twenty-two. Before meeting Tallulah, Stella Adler had warned him that Tallulah was a lesbian, but Marlon was soon to find out that that wasn't completely true.

In France, Cocteau had written the play for his lover, the actor Jean Marais, known at the time as "the handsomest man in France." Marais had instructed his playwright-lover to "Write a play in which I say nothing in the first act, talk all through the second act, and die dramatically in the third." In the play, as conceived by Cocteau, Stanislas shoots the queen before draining a fatal quaff of poison.

Before actually meeting Tallulah, Marlon arranged a luncheon with Bobby Lewis at his country retreat. Marlon was seeking advice from Bobby about how to handle "this bitch, this termagant, this vixen."

After getting lost and arriving by train in the wrong town, Marlon was eventually picked up by Bobby in his car and driven to his home. With Marlon was his on-again, off-again girlfriend, Blossom Plumb. She struck Bobby as "related to that Charles Addams character with the dead white face, dank hair, and with her dress ending in a pool of blood on the floor."

After a lunch that had already been ruined by Marlon's late arrival, he went upstairs and stripped down to very revealing briefs on the terrace to take advantage of the late autumn sun. Blossom also stripped down, removing her bra but retaining her panties. Almost immediately, Blossom and Marlon got into a terrible row over Marlon's dating of a young woman who'd just arrived from Antigua, wanting to become an actress. In tears, Blossom ran from Bobby's house never to return. Marlon seemed indifferent and had no plans to go after her.

"After she'd disappeared, we settled down for a talk about Tallulah," Bobby recalled. "Marlon was smoking a lot. I surrounded him with ashtrays, warning him that we'd had a dry spell and asking him not to flip his lit cigarette over my balcony into the yard where the autumn leaves lay in dried-out piles. Ignoring me, Marlon did just that. His lit cigarette started a fire in my garden. I rushed down to put it out. When I returned, Marlon had stripped naked, claiming he wanted 'to be brown all over.'"

Back on his roof terrace, Bobby warned Marlon that "seduction will be part of the deal if you agree to play opposite Tallulah. She always insists on fucking her leading man—it's practically written into her contracts. When she comes on to you, and she will, just grin and bear it. Think of God and country as you do the dirty deed."

"I get it," Marlon told Bobby. "Aging actress and former beauty hopes to reclaim lost youth through the semen of handsome young men." He told Bobby that he didn't think Tallulah was bad looking, recalling having seen her in a movie she'd made in 1932 called *The Devil and the Deep* in which she'd costarred with Gary Cooper.

Bobby warned that Tallulah no longer looked as she did when she was made up like Garbo in that film. "All of her hard drinking has caught up with her," he told Marlon. Bobby also predicted that Marlon and Tallulah would not be compatible as actors.

Tallulah Bankhead

Marlon assured him, "I think I can handle Miss Bankhead. She wouldn't be the first aging actress who has come on to me."

Bobby later expressed his apprehension about the pairing. "Since Marlon and Tallulah employed widely different work methods, and since they both had an unshakable independence of spirit, a clash of personalities was a distinct possibility. With this in mind, I suggested that he ask for a contract with a two-week notice cause in it. If things got impossible on the road tryout, he could leave the play. I then deposited him at Tallulah's."

Tallulah, "in a new frock bought for the occasion," greeted Marlon in the foyer of her home. "I even wore my most stunning jewelry, a gift from that tiny little prick, the Prince of Wales."

She was disappointed that he hadn't shown proper respect for her by showing up in a suit, white shirt, and tie. Instead he wore a dirty white T-shirt, tight jeans, and sneakers. "Dah-ling," she later told Edith. "He looked like he'd just finished eighteen rounds of baseball. Not only that, but right in front of me, he scratched his private parts."

In spite of his clothing, she found the body underneath his sloppy dress immensely appealing and invited him into her living room. A maid appeared to take their drink orders, Marlon requesting lemonade and Tallulah demanding her usual bourbon and branch water. Noting that she was already tipsy, Marlon asked, "Are you an alcoholic?" "No dah-ling," she replied, "just a heavy drinker."

Marlon continued with his insults. "You are roughly my mother's age," he told her, an actress who had practically gone into hysterics when turning forty. "My mother's name is Dodie. She is an actress too. And an alcoholic."

"I'm sure your mother is delightful," Tallulah responded. "We must invite the dear heart to rehearsals."

"Dodie was the lover of Henry Fonda," Marlon boasted.

"Oh, please, dah-ling, don't mention Hank to me," she said. "I went to bed with him only one time. He failed to produce an erection. Now I know why that magnolia Southern bitch, Margaret Sullavan, dropped him."

A bit stunned by her response, Marlon said, "I'm here to talk about the play. I have to be blunt. I think it's a turkey. It may, in fact, be the worst play in the history of the theater."

His words were dismissed by Tallulah. "Dah-ling, what does the fucking play matter? The audience will flock to see your Aunt Tallulah in it, not Cocteau's fantasy. *Me*, dahling. *The star!* Dah-ling," Tallulah continued, "I first met Cocteau in Paris in the late Twenties. I was appearing every night in lingerie on the London stage and I'd gone on a vacation to France. He forced opium onto me. At the time I had promised my daddy that when I went to Europe I wouldn't drink or go out with men. To get around that restrictive little promise, I took drugs and dated women. But *opium*, my dah-ling! Hardly my drug of choice. I felt like the bride of Fu Manchu and threw up *constantly* for a week."

As they sat discussing the play, Tallulah's withered hand began to wander up the leg of his blue jeans.

Later when Marlon stopped off again at the home of Bobby to report on his "audition," Bobby asked the pertinent question. "What did you do?"

"I didn't stop her," he said. "Actually, I was interested from an engineering standpoint if it were possible for her to obtain her objective. I mean, my jeans were pretty tight. Amazingly, Tallulah scored. She not only got to feel my noble tool, but my balls as well. All the time we were carrying on with this silly blah-blah about this stinker of a play."

"Okay," Bobby said. "Now for the big question. Did you fuck Miss Bankhead?"

"I did the deed," Marlon claimed. "She's voracious. She drains a man so completely there's nothing left for tomorrow. It wasn't the greatest fuck I've ever had. I felt she expected me to, so I fucked her. My task was made more difficult because of the foulness of her breath. Her breath came out of her mouth and hung in the air like a poisonous mist. I guess I passed my casting couch audition. I got the part, although I'll probably regret it."

He told Bobby that Tallulah would be perfectly cast as the Wicked Witch of the West in *The Wizard of Oz*. Her body "smelled of Russian Leather perfume, her breath of rotgut bourbon. She smoked British cigarettes from a scarlet red box. She pressed these cigarettes into a long silver holder, a gift from Cecil Beaton, she claimed." Marlon told Bobby that even though Tallulah offered him the role of Stanislas, "I think she is more interested in me for sex."

Unknown to Marlon at the time, Tallulah had already been on the phone to the show's producer, Jack Wilson. "Picture me as Salome, dah-ling," she told him. "I want Brando's head delivered to me on a silver platter. I will have no one assassinate me but Brando. He throws a mean fuck. But, dah-ling, I'm sure you and Noël auditioned him long before your Aunt Tallulah."

Jack Wilson still had a powerful crush on Marlon and planned to seduce him during the tryouts of the play, as he had on several occasions before. "I found myself iced out, once the contract was signed," Wilson told chanteuse Greta Keller. "On our second time around, Marlon wouldn't even give me a tumble, even though everybody raves about how dazzlingly handsome I am."

Back in New York, on at least ten different occasions, Tallulah invited Marlon to her suite at the Elysée Hotel. The ostensible reason was to rehearse scenes from the play. She always showed up at the door to her suite in revealing Parisian lingerie designed to show off her not altogether fallen breasts and her vagina.

After repeated seductions, Marlon wrote to his sister Fran that, "My mind feels like ten octopi in a space the size of a matchbox, each trying to manicure just its own toenails."

One night Marlon abruptly cut off the sex, refusing to meet with Tallulah at the Elysée. She did not take rejection very well.

As they went on the road for tryouts in Wilmington, Delaware, and

126

Washington, D.C., she attempted to rekindle Marlon's passion for her. Often these crude attempts were played out in front of preview audiences.

"She was supposed to kiss me in the play," Marlon told Bobby Lewis. "I came to dread those nightly kisses. Her tongue was especially cold. It was like an eel trying to slide backward into a hole. Her tongue would explore every cranny of my mouth before forcing itself down my throat." To counterattack, Marlon ate a bulb of raw garlic backstage before going on with the kissing scene. Learning that she detested the smell of peanuts, he ate a bag before going on.

The tryouts on the road were a disaster as the aging star and the future star clashed. "Tallulah, for all her fiery talent, clung to the old tradition of certain stage stars, namely that when they are holding forth in a scene, everyone for miles around should be immobilized," Bobby said. "They interpret any move or reaction from the other actors as distractions. Marlon, on stage, is the kind of actor who has a continuous life going for him, a life which results in scenes rather than star arias surrounded by accompanying robots. Tallulah even placed spies out in the audience to report to her if Marlon was acting behind her back in sections where she couldn't keep an eye on him."

In the play, Tallulah had to deliver a thirty-minute monologue, perhaps the longest soliloquy in theatrical history. She had instructed Marlon to remain motionless behind her back while she delivered this long, drawn-out speech.

"Marlon did everything he could to upstage Tallulah," Bobby said. He came down to Washington see the tryouts. "One night, or so I heard, he let out a loud fart during her monologue. He scratched his balls. Later backstage that night, Tallulah told me that she would like to give Marlon a good kick in those balls."

"During Tallulah's speech, Marlon would unbutton, then rebutton his fly," Jack Wilson said. "He would squirm during her speech and was especially adept at picking his nose. He would leer at the audience, wink at a stagehand standing in the wings. One night he scratched his ass, and I mean really scratched, going for those dingleberries. Not just onstage but backstage, Marlon was 'driving me nuts,' in Tallulah's words, with his constant sit-ups and push-ups. She called them nipups."

By the time of opening night in Boston, Tallulah herself was calling Eagle *The Turkey with Two Heads*. Marlon was at his most outrageous on opening night. During Tallulah's long speech, he turned his back to the audience, spread his legs, unbuttoned his fly, pulled out his cock, and urinat-

Tallulah Bankhead

127

ed against the stage scenery. The audience could clearly see his yellow urine raining down. With her back to him, Tallulah didn't know why the audience was laughing at her dramatic monologue.

It was all too much for her. After the curtain went down, and she learned what he'd done, she demanded, successfully, that Jack Wilson fire him as soon as possible. "Get me Monty Clift," she demanded, "if he's free. He and I did all right together in *The Skin of Our Teeth*. Like Brando, Monty is from Omaha too. It must be something they put in the water out there that makes their men so drop-dead gorgeous. Marlon is a beautiful but dangerous animal—like Monty Clift, but without the neuroses." She obviously didn't know Marlon very well.

Knowing that he'd been fired, Marlon planned a farewell performance, something that would even top his pissing scene. A perilous *coup de theater* scene came at the end of the play.

Standing at the top of a staircase, and looking as regal as possible, Tallulah is supposed to be shot by Marlon, playing Stanislas, before plunging head first down the stairs in one unbroken line. "This would be hazardous duty even for a trained stuntwoman, and certainly a daring challenge for a middle-aged drunk like Tallulah," Wilson said.

For his farewell performance, Marlon removed the blanks from his stage pistol. When he "shot" Tallulah, no sound came out. "Bang, bang!" he said as the audience laughed. Ever the trouper, she plunged down the stairs.

"Marlon then drank his poison as Tallulah lay dead at the foot of the stairs," Wilson said. "But Marlon wasn't ready for the coffin. Like Paul Muni in *A Flag is Born*, he prolonged the death scene. After swallowing the lethal potion, he staggered dramatically around the stage, gasping for breath. He clutched his throat in a virtual dancing jig of death. It was the longest death scene ever presented to a stage audience. Mercifully, I ordered the curtain. Otherwise, it would be midnight and Marlon would still be dying. By the time the curtain fell, none of the audience remembered Tallulah's daring staircase death scene. Marlon had completely taken her fire. Infuriated as the curtain fell, Tallulah rose from the dead. Backstage, she refused to take even one curtain call. 'I want Brando's blood,' she told me. 'I'll personally see to it that he never works another day in the American theater. The British theater as well.'"

A Boston theater critic had fun ridiculing both

Faking it

128

Marlon and the play. He claimed that "Bankhead's Southern contralto hammered away at Cocteau's delicate conceits and left them a rubbish heap of mystifying words." Regarding Marlon's prolonged death scene, he wrote, "Brando looked like a car in midtown Manhattan searching for a parking space."

In the type of grand theatrical gesture for which she was known, Tallulah surprised the cast when she rushed to kiss Marlon good-bye as he was making his final exit from the theater. "In spite of our differences," she proclaimed loudly in front of the cast, "I think you're going to become a famous American actor. Note that I said famous. Not good! And, dah-ling, that prediction comes from a woman who has fucked all the big names in the theater. John Barrymore. You name them. Remember, yesterday and today make for tomorrow." She turned and walked away from him, heading for her dressing room.

Once seated at her vanity table, she began to remove her makeup after calling for her secretary to draft a note to Tennessee Williams. Only the night before, she'd read his play, *The Poker Night*. It was set in New Orleans, and the star of the play was the character known as Blanche DuBois, who was to appear opposite her brutish brother-in-law, a character named Stanley Kowalski.

Even though she'd brutally rejected *Band of Angels*, the first play he'd sent her, Tennessee bravely sent her this other drama of his. "While I was writing this play, all of the speeches seemed to be issuing from your mouth, Miss Bankhead."

The note she drafted that night presumably no longer exists. Later, Tallulah denied ever having written it. But Tennessee for years maintained that he received it. As he recalled it, the note went something like this:

My Dear Mr. Williams:

Thank you for showing me your latest little play, even though I turned down the first one offered. Poor Miriam Hopkins was foolish enough to appear in that play that I knew would be a disaster. Regrettably, I must turn down the role of Blanche DuBois in The Poker Night. You and I are both Southerners. But I fear that you were born on the wrong side of the tracks in the South. You simply do not understand genteel and aristocratic Southern women. How we talk. How we behave. Therefore, I cannot be your Blanche DuBois because I find the character completely unreal. Instead of a faded Southern lady, you have depicted a strumpet.

When she presented the draft of your play to me, Edith also gave me a black Mark Cross purse, which I know you must have purchased with your earnings from The Glass Menagerie. Thank you for the lovely gift which I am forced to return. How dare you send me a black purse! A lady always travel in brown. But I suppose that it's impossible for you to understand what a lady does.

I do have one suggestion for casting. I know of an actor who can appear as this brutish Stanley Kowalski character. I mean, a total pig of a man without sensitivity or grace of any kind. Marlon Brando would be perfect as Stanley. I have just fired the cad from my play, The Eagle Has Two Heads, and I know for a fact that he is looking for work.

Also, my darling man, I will never appear in a play where the word 'nigger' is used.

Good luck with your play. Perhaps Miriam Hopkins will give you another chance, although I doubt if even Miriam will go for this turkey.

With sincere best wishes,
Miss Tallulah Bankhead.

* * *

In his autobiography, Marlon erroneously wrote that "my virtue was still intact" after his ordeal with the two-headed *Eagle* and with Tallulah. "I would

Launching the t-shirt industry

rather have been dragged over broken pottery than make love to Tallulah," he wrote. But that's not the story he related to Stella Adler, Bobby Lewis, and Edith Van Cleve. And that's not what he would later tell Tennessee Williams.

Tallulah herself, years later at her New York townhouse and in front of James Leo Herlihy, James Kirkwood, and the author, discussed in detail her seduction of Marlon, portraying herself in a far more glamorous light than the portrait that he painted of her.

On the train going from

130

Boston back to New York, Marlon wrote a letter to his family, revealing to them that he'd been fired from the play. "The next time T. Bankhead goes swimming, I hope that whales shit on her."

As he was writing the letter, word of his dismissal was just reaching the small, gossipy world of Broadway. "The verdict was in," Bobby Lewis said. "Marlon was viewed as difficult, temperamental, and not dependable. You might say that for a short time at least, he could have been labeled Broadway poison. At the time, I didn't know any producer who wanted to take a chance on him. Even Hollywood was cold shouldering him."

All offers for Marlon to work on Broadway or in Hollywood dried up. Marlon hinted that he "just might be available for at least one movie." But Lew Wasserman, president of MCA, informed Edith that "Hollywood is finally wise to the ways of Brando. No studio wants him any more. I predict he'll never find work in this town. He was a young upstart on Broadway that got some attention. His day has come and gone. Call him the star that never was. Besides, we now have Burt Lancaster. With Burt about to become the King of Hollywood, no one out here is talking about Brando any more. I suggest he buy a one-way ticket back to Omaha."

After writing the letter on the train, Marlon fell asleep. When he woke up, his wallet containing eight hundred dollars was missing. That represented all his earnings from *The Eagle Has Two Heads*. He was left penniless and he didn't know what to do. A panic set in.

In an amazing coincidence, from the far side of the rail car, he saw a young man emerging. As that man moved closer to him, Marlon was astonished to meet up with Monty Clift once again. What Monty chose not to reveal was that he, too, had been up in Boston. Tallulah had called him and requested that he come to Boston to replace Marlon in *The Eagle Has Two Heads*. Curious about the role, Monty arrived in Boston. But he turned down the role and immediately took the next train back to New York.

"Instead of talking about the play and my role in it," Monty later confided to his brother, Brooks, "all Tallulah wanted to talk about was Brando. She claimed he left her with 'history's worst case of crabs.'"

Back in New York, Monty told Edith that Tallulah didn't actually audition him for the play. When not talking about Brando, she attacked the Stanislavsky technique of acting, which she claimed was "fake and impractical—any actor who loses himself in a part is a stupid ass." When Monty queried her about her own acting technique on stage, she said, "If the scene gets very emotional, I don't get carried away with it. Instead of thinking—say, of murdering my husband on stage, whatever the script calls for, I often say my lines thinking about the big, juicy steak I'm going to order—blood red—right after the curtain falls."

Marlon was replaced with Helmut Dantine, who was thirty years old at the time. Before 1938 he'd been the leader of the anti-Nazi youth movement in Vienna. Placed in a concentration camp when the Nazis annexed Austria, he remained incarcerated there for three months before escaping to the United States. He is still remembered today for his attention-grabbing role as the downed German flyer who confronts Greer Garson in the classic, *Mrs. Miniver*, in 1942. That same year, he also had a small role in Bogie's *Casablanca*, playing a careless newlywed who gambles away his visa money.

For some perverse reason, and knowing that they were, at least in theory, competing for the same role, producer Jack Wilson booked both Monty and Helmut into a shared double bedroom at a Boston hotel. He was well aware that both young actors were viewed as "switch hitters."

Monty later confided to Brooks that he and Helmut had had a "one-night stand," even though they were technically rival actors vying for the same part.

Both Marlon and Monty had rejected Tallulah, but Helmut was only too happy to oblige as both her leading man and bed partner.

The young Irish playwright, Kieran Tunney, Tallulah's longtime friend, described Helmut as "handsome, butch, bronzed, muscles rippling, hair on chest showing." But when Tunney wrote that Helmut "unfortunately didn't have the inner equipment needed," Tallulah corrected him. "Believe you me, my dah-ling," she said. "He has the right equipment. And that comes from a woman once married to John Emery, who has the biggest cock in Hollywood."

She later told Jack Wilson what he already knew. "Helmut is the answer to a maiden's prayer." Wilson had already auditioned Helmut on the casting couch.

Upon his return to Manhattan, Marlon revealed his cruel streak as he spread vicious anti-Tallulah stories. At one point, he told his friend Tom Ewell at the Actors Studio that "Miss Bankhead lets her God damn dog fuck her. She also masturbates and lets the mutt lick up the pussy juice."

With columnist Earl Wilson, he was more subdued. "Tallulah considered me a weirdo. I got bounced from the show. The play was no good. Every day they had the janitor in to help rewrite the script. Tallulah didn't like me very much. She always wanted to go out and order champagne. Then she'd say, 'Oh, do let's paint the walls with fish.' I just about lost my mind."

In New York, *The Eagle Has Two Heads* opened on March 19, 1947, at the Plymouth Theatre. Trounced by the critics, it closed after twenty-nine performances. Cocteau denounced the production as a "vulgarization of my work." Dressed in dirty jeans, mud-caked sneakers, and a tattered shirt, Marlon sat in the first row on opening night. He got up and walked out before the curtain was drawn on the first act.

Marlon's experience with temperamental Tallulah drove him to a psychoanalyst, Dr. Bela Mittelman. His therapy would continue throughout his twenties. He later recalled, "I was blessed with enough sense to realize that if I wanted well-being, psychoanalytic help was just about the only, and last, way I could get it."

Out of work, Marlon continued to live with the also penniless Wally Cox. They survived on peanut butter sandwiches. For amusement, they would gather horse droppings in Central Park from the stallions ridden by policemen. At night from their tenement floor on West 52nd Street and 10th Avenue, Wally and Marlon dropped bags of these horse turds on unsuspecting passers-by down below.

With stage money he'd earned, Marlon had purchased a motorcycle. He could be seen speeding through the canyons of New York with Wally "holding onto him for dear life." Often they'd zoom through the deserted streets of New York at three o'clock in the morning. Sometimes policemen would chase them, but Marlon always claimed that he managed to elude them.

When he wasn't "acting crazy and cutting up" [his words], he drifted into long, dark, and moody depressions that would last for days or even weeks.

Monty later recalled that, "Marlon seemed to occupy some secret place where he'd retreat in bad times. Perhaps it was on the other side of Oz. There he would contemplate his navel and his life. I remember visiting Wally and Marlon one night at their apartment. Marlon had taken a crude piece of cardboard. With a red crayon, he'd scribbled on it, 'You ain't living if you don't know it.'"

* * *

At a bleak point in Marlon's life, along came Shelley Winters. A whole generation has grown up identifying her as an earthy, outspoken, and overweight lady. But oldtime movie fans remember her as sexy, vampish, and svelte, a "hot blonde," in the words of Luther Adler, Stella's brother, who would later costar with her in *South Sea Sinner* in 1950. "She was the kind of gal your Jewish father wanted you to lose your virginity to but not to marry."

"Shelley was destined to play vulgar women, brassy, exciting, the kind you meet in a strange town on a bar stool," said George Cukor, who directed her in *A Double Life* with Ronald Colman.

Marlon himself later said that "Shelley was perfect for playing a loose woman. She was the woman you knocked up in a cheap motel room before moving on to classy Elizabeth Taylor."

He uttered these remarks after seeing Shelley appear with his former love, Monty Clift, and Elizabeth Taylor, in *A Place in the Sun,* released in 1951. In that film, Shelley, the sad, whining factory girl, gets knocked up and bumped off, which earned her an Oscar nomination.

The meeting of Marlon and Shelley at Actors Studio was inevitable. Along with his sister, Jocelyn, Marlon frequently showed up for Elia Kazan's acting classes, joining an all-star student body that included Kevin McCarthy, Tom Ewell, Maureen Stapleton, on occasion Monty Clift, Arthur Kennedy, and Miss Shelley Winters herself.

As a blonde bombshell, Shelley—actually Shirley Schrift of Brooklyn—was seen at such clubs as El Morocco dressed in cheap finery on the arms of such playboys as actor Franchot Tone, who'd long ago been dumped by Joan Crawford.

The Beau with the Pink Carnation

Over the years, Shelley was an A-list seducer, her conquests including the likes of Ronald Colman, Sean Connery, Robert De Niro, Albert Finney, Howard Hughes, John Garfield, Sterling Hayden, Burt Lancaster, John Ireland (her biggest thrill), and legends such as Clark Gable, Errol Flynn, and even pretty boy Farley Granger, an astonishment to much of Hollywood who didn't realize he swung in that direction.

At the top of any list of Shelley's seductions appears the name of Marlon Brando. From the day he'd first met her in class, Marlon was drawn to what Frank Sinatra called "this bowlegged bitch of a Brooklyn blonde." Marlon liked her outspoken quality. "She called them like she saw them," he once said, "and if the emperor didn't wear any clothes, she was likely to tell His Majesty that he was jaybird naked with a pecker he should be ashamed of."

Once, when a director on one of her pictures asked her why she'd shown up late Monday morning for work, she informed him that, "I had to fly cross-country for the weekend because I desperately needed to get fucked."

In some respects, she was just as outrageous as Marlon himself. Seated next to Dylan Thomas at a dinner party in Los Angeles, she was told by the Welsh poet that he'd come to Hollywood "to touch the titties of a beautiful blonde starlet and to meet Charlie Chaplin." To fulfill part of his fantasy, Shelley surrendered her breasts to him.

When Marlon started to date Shelley, he couldn't afford to take her to "21" or the clubs to which she was accustomed when hanging out with the likes of Cholly Knickerbocker.

Nonetheless, she found him "sexual lightning," and there was a powerful chemistry between them. She ignored his reputation "for seducing anything on the hoof," feeling he couldn't possibly have the time for such wholesale conquests. She would later learn otherwise.

One night Marlon invited her to dinner at his apartment after her performance in *Oklahoma!* at the St. James Theatre. Shelley had recently replaced Vivian Allen as "Ado Annie" in the hit show. Even though New York that night was hit with one of the worst blizzards of the Forties, she braved the chill in her beaver coat to climb five flights of stairs leading up to the rundown apartment Marlon shared with Wally Cox, who was often more than a roommate.

Arriving at Marlon's doorstep "in so many layers of clothes I looked like Marie Dressler on a bad night," Shelley was ushered into the coldwater flat. She nearly stumbled over an open can of midnight blue paint.

Marlon explained that he and Wally were redecorating. "They had dabbed a few feet of paint on one wall," Shelley said. "For one solid year, the canvas, the buckets of paint, and the brushes lay in the middle of that floor. No one had touched anything since my first visit. Every visitor just stepped over the paint which had long ago dried up."

Shown into the ramshackle apartment, she refused to remove her coat because she was freezing. "No Eskimo igloo was ever as cold as that damn apartment," she would later recall.

Marlon introduced her to his pet raccoon. "The beast smelled like it had just let eighteen farts," Shelley said. "The sole electric heater in the apartment was turned on that little beast. He looked so warm I wished I could have traded my beaver coat for his raccoon fur."

"When I innocently asked why Wally and Marlon didn't furnish the place better, he turned on me in anger. 'Listen, Miss Rich Bitch,' he told me. 'You're working in a hit Broadway show. I haven't worked in six months. Wally hasn't had a gig in a year.'"

As if on cue, Wally emerged from the bedroom of the two-room apartment. He appeared to be with a girl, although Shelley wasn't sure. Both of them were heavily bundled against the cold. Later, when the woman revealed more of herself, Shelley remembered her "as a very pretty girl with big glasses." She believed, but wasn't sure, that this was the woman who Wally would eventually marry.

In gray sweatpants, Marlon performed gymnastic exercises, as Wally prepared dinner. He removed all the food from the bitterly cold windowsill. "It was my first frozen food meal," Shelley later recalled. In her subsequent memoirs, she immortalized the meal of canned tomato soup served in broken mugs, cold cauliflower dipped in sour cream, and heavy brown rice cooked with nuts and kasha studded with raisins and green peppers. Cheap wine

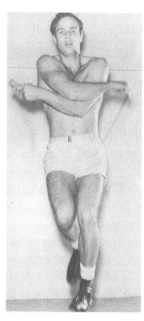

1, 997...1,998...1,999...

spiked with gin made the whole table warmer, although Shelley still refused to remove her heavy garments. For dessert, Wally fried grapefruit in an iron skillet on the gas stove, later glazing it with brown sugar.

In front of Wally and his girlfriend, Marlon told Shelley that his roommate "is an old, fragile, beautifully embroidered Chinese ceremonial robe with a few Three-in-One Oil spots on it."

Wally flattered Marlon by claiming that "my friend is a philosopher but only on the deepest level. A deep thinker like the Rodin sculpture. But mainly he liberates everybody he comes into contact with."

"Honey child," Shelley said. "Your mother here doesn't need any liberating, baby!"

As dawn was breaking over the New York skyline, Wally and "his bohemian girl" disappeared into the bedroom. Still shivering, Shelley was left alone with Marlon and the raccoon in the kitchen, where a double bed had been placed. He invited her to join him in bed, promising that "My body generates a great deal of heat." In the early hours of the morning, as most New Yorkers were heading for work, she found that to be true.

Marlon and Shelley remained in the kitchen bed until about one o'clock in the afternoon of the following day, when she woke up in his arms. He made her coffee in an electric percolator. The flat had no electrical outlets, so he removed the bulb from over the kitchen table, screwed in an electrical adapter, and plugged the coffeepot in there. He then lit a candle "to take the curse off the darkness." The light was desperately needed since the kitchen had no window to let in the noonday sun.

Back in her beaver coat and her felt-lined galoshes, Shelley expressed her concern that he was out of work for so long. She casually mentioned that Mary Martin, then the reigning Broadway musical star, had visited with the cast backstage when she'd come to see *Oklahoma!* "She told me she's come across this most divine play by Tennessee Williams. He's calling it *A Streetcar Named Desire*, and Mary thinks it'll be even bigger than *The*

Shelley Winters

136

Glass Menagerie. She wants to star in it. She also told me there's a great role for a young man. A brute of a character called Stanley Kowalski."

"I don't do musicals," he bluntly told her.

"It's heavy drama, baby," she said. "Bette Davis has even threatened to star in it to put some life back into a stalled career. I know Pauline Lord and Fay Bainter want it. But for my money I'm voting for that steel magnolia herself, Margaret Sullavan."

"Who's up for the Kowalski part?" he asked.

"Kazan is directing it," she said, "and I hear he wants a real big name. 'Only John Garfield will do,' he told me yesterday. He said the role calls for—and get this—'a quintessential semi-Simian actor of undiluted virility.' Quote, unquote."

"Fancy words for a brute."

"At the same time he said only John Garfield would do, he mentioned Burt Lancaster in the same breath," she said. "All that means is that he's undecided. Don't tell a soul about this, but I heard it for a fact that Irene Mayer Selznick, who's producing the show, doesn't want Garfield or Lancaster. She's after Monty Clift." The remark about Monty was not true, and Shelley knew it wasn't. Apparently, she was throwing in the name of Monty Clift to goad Marlon into action and get the role for himself.

"#*#!!#**!#&!!!" was his response.

From the stairwell, she called to him. "You passed the kitchen bed audition last night. I'm ready for a repeat. Meet me backstage at *Oklahoma!* tonight. I think this is going to be the beginning of a big love affair. But you've got to get rid of that goddamn, stinking raccoon first!"

* * *

At the New School, it was her thick accent, which sounded Texan to him, that drew Marlon to a beautiful blonde from Tularosa, New Mexico. Normally, he did not pursue blondes. But, as he told Wally Cox, "after a steady diet of chocolate, a vanilla cone tastes good, all sweet, virginal, and pure like the nourishing liquid I used to drain from our family cow."

The blonde introduced herself as Kim Stanley. Although normally a bit reserved, she was quite talkative around Marlon. "I just hit town and I've got only twenty-one dollars to my name—and it's going fast. To economize, I steal two oranges a day, but only from the most prosperous looking street vendors, and just one banana."

"I also go by Horn and Hardart on 57th Street just at closing time," she said. "A kindly man I know there—I think he has a crush on me—sells me the stale unsold sandwiches at ten cents apiece. He would throw them in the garbage anyway if he didn't sell them to me."

"After I pay my rent this week, I won't have any money left at all," she said.

"Your problems are solved," he told her. "I'll get you a room at a real ritzy place, called the Park Savoy. Doesn't that sound impressive? I'll pick up the rent bill for you."

"You mean, I'm about to become a kept woman?"

"Welcome to the club. Half the women living in New York are kept."

"You're full of surprises," she said. "Some of the kids at school told me you have homosexual proclivities. I didn't feel you'd want a broad from the Southwest like me."

"That homosexual thing—don't pay any attention to that talk," he assured her. "What those kids actually meant to say is that I'm a lesbian in a male body."

She looked confused for a moment. "Well . . . since you're a man, I guess that lesbianism is okay. When I left New Mexico, my family warned me not to get involved with lesbians. But since you're a man . . . well, as I said, I guess it's okay. But the way I figure it, if I don't hook up with you, it's a bench in Central Park for me."

Kim's opening dialogue is known today only because of Brooks Clift, Monty's brother. He was soon to meet and have an affair with the actress, and she related her experiences with Marlon presumably over pillow talk with Brooks. These recollections were included in his unpublished memoir. The bulk of that memoir was devoted to theatrical personalities he'd known, with many pages that described his troubled brother.

Marlon, as promised, got Kim a room at the rundown Park Savoy, that rat-infested hell hole for out-of-work actors. It was far from being the ritzy palace he'd promised. Although living with Wally, Marlon was a frequent visitor to Kim's ragtag room with its beat-up furniture. Casey Sullivan, a homosexual actor who lived next door "with whatever rough trade I could find," often knocked on Kim's wall urging her to quiet down. "When Brando came to visit, the springs in that bed creaked all night."

Kim Stanley

"I was a virgin until Marlon deflowered me," Kim once told Brooks.

Gradually Marlon helped Kim get rid of a lot of her thick southwestern drawl. When not fornicating, he gave her elocution lessons. She told him that when she'd first enrolled at the New School, one of the teachers had advised her to "take the first Greyhound bus heading back to

138

Texas."

Through some unknown connection, Marlon found work for Kim. She was hired as a cocktail waitress at the Astor Hotel Bar near Times Square. Between pushing cocktails on the primarily homosexual clientele, she was a dress model at Macy's.

Marlon introduced her to both Lee Strasberg and Elia Kazan, and soon, she was enrolled in the Actors Studio. After about five weeks, her accent began to disappear, enough so that she was cast in a small part in a bad play by Gertrude Stein. Called *Yes Is for a Very Young Man*, Kim appeared opposite Anthony (Tony) Franciosa, a future husband of Marlon's other girlfriend, Shelley Winters. Although he disliked the play itself, Brooks Atkinson, drama critic for *The New York Times*, singled out Kim for special praise.

One day on a hand-holding walk through Central Park, Kim told Marlon, "All I ever wanted to do was to be the May Queen back in Santa Fe. Here I am trying to get an acting job in New York City. *New York City of all places!*"

After seeking Katharine Hepburn in a road show tour of *The Philadelphia Story*, Kim decided "it was the theater for me, although I have a degree in psychology. I can psychoanalyze you if you want me to."

He took her up on that offer. As Kim later revealed to Brooks, "Marlon told me some of his deepest, darkest secrets, including his fear of being forever a mama's boy."

He also claimed that after a particularly intense affair with a man, such as Monty Clift or Leonard Bernstein, that he indulged in promiscuous sex, "screwing every girl who will go to bed with me—and very few of them say no."

"I have guilt about sleeping with men, and, almost to atone for it, I go in the opposite direction," he said. "The more the merrier. That way, I manage to convince myself I'm a bona fide heterosexual until the queer side of me comes out again."

Kim advised him that he'd make an excellent case study for Dr. Alfred Kinsey, a sex researcher who was getting better known every day. She claimed that she was very impressed with Dr. Kinsey when she heard him lecture on sex. "For the first time," she said, "I understood what sex was about and how it should be approached." At first Marlon volunteered to be interviewed by Dr. Kinsey, but he later bowed out, giving no reason.

Even though he may have kept it a secret from such close friends as Wally Cox and Stella Adler, Marlon, in the weeks leading up to his being cast in *A Streetcar Named Desire*, developed a fondness for group sex. During his "analytic" sessions with Kim, he confessed that at least once a week he attended an orgy in the Village. Group sex became especially popular in the Village in the months after World War II. "The war liberated both men and women,"

A pensive moment in
sister Fran's apartment.

Tom Ewell later said. "It was a great time to be alive and to be in New York."

Sometimes groups, often all male, and with Marlon in their midst, would meet in a private apartment for an orgy. Other groups preferred a combination of men and women. Marlon confessed to Kim that he had "an insatiable appetite" at these orgies. He boasted that during one session in particular, at least a dozen young men and women got to enjoy "the pleasures of my noble tool." He even invited Kim to join him at one of these orgies. That wasn't her lifestyle, and she politely turned him down.

In an amazing turn-around, Marlon the patient began to analyze Kim the psychologist. He predicted that her luminous presence would one day light up the Broadway stage, and with that pronouncement, he demonstrated a gift for prophecy. But he also found that she had a very dark side, and he identified with her frequent bouts of depression and self-doubt. She shrank from the perceived pressures of future stardom, telling him that she could never be "comfortable in my skin" as a star. He shared the same feeling. She noted that he had attempted to deliberately sabotage his future stardom by "fucking up so badly in that *Eagle* play opposite Bankhead."

Kim's romance with Marlon lasted for about six weeks. "It was just too intense," she said. "Like a short candle, it burned out."

"I thought they were truly in love," Bobby Lewis said. "I was with them on several occasions. Their talk wasn't just about sex. They could go on for hours about Method acting. I often joined in on these sessions. Kim always claimed to anyone interested that Method acting had helped her become as 'free as possible.' She adored Lee Strasberg as much as Marlon continued to detest him. Although we didn't call it such in those days, Lee was actually Kim's guru."

Bobby would later work with Kim professionally, notably on Colette's *Chéri*. When interviewed years later by *Newsweek*, he called Kim "our greatest actress," and the magazine ran that accolade without attribution.

Although Marlon unceremoniously dumped Kim, he remained her friend like he had with so many of his other loves. That friendship continued as she went through hasty marriages to actors Bruce Hall and Curt Conway.

Marlon avidly followed her career in the years ahead and was "thrilled," he later said, when he saw her perform in the 1955 William Inge play, *Bus Stop*. In her most memorable stage role, Kim played Cherie, the worn-at-the-edges nightclub singer. Refusing the screen role, she saw it go to Marilyn Monroe, who delivered one of her most memorable performances.

By coincidence, Marlon briefly considered appearing opposite his friend, Marilyn, in the role of the feisty cowboy who wins Cherie's heart.

When Marlon bowed out, the role was offered to Elvis Presley. It could have been a career-making move in Hollywood for Elvis. Many producers in Hollywood salivated at the prospect of Elvis and Marilyn in the same movie. But his manager, Colonel Tom Parker, turned down the juicy role, preferring Elvis to remain in the exploitation films he selected for him.

In one of her infrequent forays into film, Kim played the lead in a 1958 movie, *The Goddess*, loosely based on Marilyn herself. Sitting through the film twice, Marlon pronounced it "the greatest movie ever made—you can forget *Citizen Kane*."

By 1964 Kim had persuaded Lee Strasberg to have the Actors Studio present a production of Chekhov's *Three Sisters*. Her old mentor, Lee himself, would direct. Cast as the other two sisters were Geraldine Page and Shirley Knight.

"In their day, both Geraldine Page and Kim Stanley were hailed as the two greatest actresses on Broadway," Bobby Lewis said. "But long before each of them became famous, Marlon got in there first. Kim had met and befriended Geraldine many years before they worked together. If Kim wanted to hang on to Marlon between his group sex sessions, she made a big mistake. One night at a coffeehouse on Bleeker Street in the Village, Kim introduced the handsome young Marlon to the vibrantly engaging, if not beautiful, Geraldine Page. The chemistry was so hot between them I think he fucked Gerry on the first night of their meeting. Poor Kim went home alone."

After her self-imposed exile in New Mexico in later years, where Kim suffered a nervous breakdown, Marlon corresponded with her only rarely. She wrote letters on occasion to Brooks Clift, Marlon, Lee Strasberg, and Geraldine Page, whom she'd forgiven for stealing Marlon from her. In these letters, she expressed a frequent sentiment, also shared with pupils in classes where she taught acting. "You can't be good in the theater until you've immersed yourself in the marvelous detective story of the human spirit. But it's difficult, so terribly difficult."

Her last known contact with Marlon was in 1979 when she returned briefly to New York, launching an acting troupe in SoHo. She wrote him asking him to "use your star power to help me get financing to make a film about Virginia Woolf."

After mulling it over and placing a call to a producer or two, he found no enthusiasm. He never answered her urgent request.

But he did watch her 1984 TV version of Tennessee Williams's *Cat on a Hot Tin Roof* in which she played Big Mama. Kim had made her London debut in the play in 1958, but in that production she'd played not Big Mama, but "Maggie the Cat" herself. In 1984, cast as Big Mama, she appeared opposite Jessica Lange as Maggie.

"Perhaps the most brilliant interpretation of one of Tennessee's characters since Vivien Leigh took *A Streetcar Named Desire*," Marlon told his friends in Hollywood. "Watching Kim emote last night made me realize that she was the love of my life." He no doubt believed his assessment of her performance. But surely the second sentiment was said only for dramatic effect.

* * *

Among New York studs, Marlon became one of the first—and perhaps the only actor—to "audition" both Kim Stanley and Geraldine Page. Long before any theatrical agent fully understood the depth of their enormous talents, he was loudly and accurately proclaiming that each of them in her own way would become the greatest of all Broadway actresses, far better than either Lynn Fontanne or Katharine Cornell. The Stanley/Page debate still rages today as theatrical memory fades.

There is no doubt that Missouri-born Geraldine Page, called Gerry by her friends and the same age as Marlon, received the most acclaim. When friends told Marlon that Gerry was primarily a stage actress, not really suited to film, he'd say, "What the fuck? How many stage actresses do you know who can count eight Oscar nominations for their screen work? Gerry was nominated for Academy Awards even when she shouldn't have been." He was no doubt referring to her cartoonish performance in the anything-goes comedy, *You're a Big Boy Now*, in 1966.

One night in Key West, on the back porch of a local conch, Danny Stirrup, Gerry related her involvement with Marlon to an amused Tennessee Williams, his lover, Frankie Merlo, novelist James Leo Herlihy, art director Stanley Haggart, and the author.

"Yes, that dear Marlon took me to bed on the first night we met," Gerry said. "Such sensitive hands. We just deserted poor Kim Stanley. Marlon told me that he and Kim were merely friends. I believed the devil. Later, I found out that Kim was madly in love with him. I would never have walked off with the trophy of the night had I known that. Deliberate cruelty is not part of my

142

character."

She laughingly recalled, "I was no virgin when I met Marlon. I grew up in the Middle West where the corn-fed boys could outrun me, so I approached Marlon's bed already properly deflowered. From the first night, I realized that Marlon had nothing in common with other boys I had known. No man ever fascinated me as much until another actor with the unlikely name of Rip Torn came along. And, as you know, I married him."

"Bobby Lewis told me I'd have a two-month run with Marlon, if that," she said. "It became 'if that.' If I remember properly, our love affair didn't last an entire month. But our friendship has endured forever." She reached over and patted Tennessee's hand. "It was because of your characters that we achieved whatever notoriety the both of us enjoy. Without those plays of yours, what would Marlon and I have become? Marlon and I rarely see each other today. We have a phone relationship. I share my latest humiliations with him, and he shares his even more horrible humiliations with me."

At that point, her host, Danny Stirrup, arrived with a slice of Key Lime pie for her. "Carrot cake is my favorite," she told him, "but I'll go for this too. At our home in Chelsea—we call it Torn Page—Rip does the cooking and I do the eating. Anytime anyone invites me for dinner, I tell them I love everything but eggplant. It was food that brought Rip and me together. I was licking a strawberry ice cream cone. It was at the Actors Studio in 1955. This handsome but strange man comes up to me and asks me for a lick. I give him a dirty look. Then I look into his face again and let him have a lick. Rip has been taking licks ever since."

"If not for Rip, I would have married Marlon years before," she claimed, "but he never asked me. The closest we ever came was on a street in the Village. He bought me a two-dollar beaded necklace from this street vendor. The gems were red beans. He put the necklace around me and kissed me.

'That means we're officially engaged,' he said. I told him it was more customary to present a young woman with an engagement ring. 'No, that's old-fashioned,' he said. He'd read somewhere that some tribe on the planet used beads instead of an engagement ring. After that sort of proposal, there was never any talk of marriage again."

During their courtship, Gerry quickly learned that she wasn't the only girl in Marlon's chaotic life. "Sometimes when out on a date with me, he would walk off with another young woman he'd casually introduced himself to. One time we went into this drugstore. He walked up to the girl behind the

Geraldine Page

"I've got rhythm, I've got music..."

counter and asked her to go away with him. He had this seductive way around women. The girl literally walked off her job to go with him. As for me, I sat on the drugstore stool alone ordering a double chocolate malt. Some abandoned women would never have spoken to Marlon again. But I forgave my errant lover. In a way, dealing with him prepared me for my future husband. I learned to ignore all the young women Rip was secretly dating behind my back."

Geraldine continued with her memories: "One night Marlon boasted that he had 'at least six women pregnant' that month. He told me that somehow he was going to raise enough money so that these women could have illegal abortions. 'I'm very careless when I have sex,' he told me, as if I didn't already know that. 'I don't like to use protection,' he said. 'It desensitizes my noble tool.'"

"In those days, according to Marlon," Gerry said, "an abortion performed by a legitimate doctor cost five hundred dollars. A doctor in Brooklyn, Sam Segal, often performed these abortions. Marlon said that he always accompanied his pregnant girlfriend—by then, often his ex-girlfriend—to these abortions, paying for them with God knows what money," Gerry claimed. "He told me that in most cases he never saw the girl again after she had recovered from the procedure."

On one occasion," Gerry claimed, "Marlon actually invited her to an abortion party on Sullivan Street in the Village. "There must have been fifty people there. Wally Cox was at the entrance door collecting five dollars per head. Once I got inside the crowded little flat, I learned that an abortion had already been performed on a stringy-haired ballet dancer in a black leotard."

When another money taker took over at the door, Wally went to get Gerry some cheap wine in a broken glass, and she talked briefly with him. "Marlon and I are rooming together," he told her. "Marlon is the right shoe and I'm the left. People don't understand our strange friendship because the two of us are so different. But I'll let you in on a secret. I'm not beefy like Marlon as you can see. He gets all the women. I get very few. But hanging out with him I get his rejects. With the exception of your lovely self, his rejects aren't all that special. Marlon is known for dating pigs. Even though we're very different, we share one common trait. Marlon and I will go to bed with just about anybody who walks."

When the party was in full swing, and all the guests had arrived, "the fetus—or at least I thought it was a fetus—was passed around for everybody to examine," she said. "It had been placed in a clear Mason jar with a tin lid on top. When the jar was passed to me, I nearly dropped it. One look and I wanted to throw up. It was the most disgusting looking thing that ever came out of a human body. Maybe it was just a piece of chopped liver from the deli. But I just knew it was a fetus. I was so shocked I begged Marlon to take me home. He refused to go with me. He said he was going to play the bongo drums to entertain the guests. I went home vowing never to see Marlon again. The next night, I'd forgiven him and our romance resumed."

In the days ahead," she said, "Wally often joined us on our dates. Sometimes we'd do nothing more exciting than stop at Marlon's favorite place, Bernie's Juice Bar. I'd never had beet juice before, much less carrot, much less beet and carrot juice combined. I drank this horrible concoction to please him. Frankly I preferred orange juice."

"All of Marlon's friends, especially Wally, did whatever they thought Marlon wanted to do," she said. "He was definitely the ringleader and plotted all the amusements for his gang. Sometimes he took me motorcycle riding, no doubt in rehearsal for a future film of his. Once he took me to Chow-Chow, his favorite restaurant in Chinatown. There he taught me to eat with chopsticks. I think we ordered chop suey. In those days, eating Chinese meant ordering chop suey."

"One night—it was very late—he took me to this little dive in the Village," she said. "You know, candles dripping from cheap Chianti bottles. I had a glass of wine and suggested he might like one too. I knew he wasn't a big drinker. To my surprise, he ordered a large tumbler of straight Scotch— 'the more rotgut the better,' he told the bartender. In one gulp he downed all that Scotch. I was stunned."

"To my horror," she recalled, "he took the glass and broke it over the wooden table. Before I knew what was happening, he took the most jagged edge of the glass and slit both his wrists. The blood was gushing out of both arms. The next hour passed like a blur for me. The bartender must have summoned an ambulance. We got him to the hospital. His life was saved."

"The next day I showed up at the hospital with flowers," she recalled. Marlon, with his wrists bandaged, was resting peacefully. I remember saying to him, 'How could you? What on earth drove you to try to commit suicide? You've got everything to live for.' He looked up at me. With the most sincere eyes I've ever seen on a human being, he answered me—and I felt his reply was genuine. 'To tell you the truth, I don't know why I did that. I truly don't. I hardly remember last night.'"

After that hospital visit, Geraldine's relationship with him tapered off.

"His intensity, the depth of his feeling about everything, frightened me. I wasn't all that emotionally stable myself in those days, and I feared Marlon would take me to the brink. He was more than I could handle."

She remembered that she hadn't seen him in a week, but that she had agreed to meet him at her apartment for a six o'clock rendezvous. Because of a rehearsal, she didn't get home until after eight that night. "I couldn't get in touch with him to tell him I was held up," she said. "I turned the key and went inside my dark apartment. In the kitchen when I turned on the overhead light, I noticed that my kitchen window had been broken into and someone had come in through the fire escape. I heard someone call out my name from the bedroom. I recognized Marlon's voice. I went into the bedroom where he'd taken a candle from the living room. In the glow, I could see he was lying on the bed nude in my silk lingerie, the only silk I owned at the time. 'I love soft fabric on my skin,' he told me. 'Now come and get in bed with me. I want to fuck you silly.'"

Gerry claimed that during her relationship with Marlon she was well aware of the other women he was dating. "I overlooked a lot, but what I could not forgive in some cases was the age of the girls he dated. Pure jailbait. Fifteen years old if that. More likely thirteen or fourteen years old. He claimed he was the champion hymen-buster of young girls in New York City."

"At one point," she said, "he even bragged of taking the virginity of a twelve-year-old girl still in the convent. Her parents were circus performers and had dumped her with some nuns. I have never interfered in the sexual pastimes of others and always try to withhold judgment. But I do not endorse child molestation. You remember all the trouble Errol Flynn had in the early Forties with statutory rape, and, of course, Charlie Chaplin is famous for his Lolita types. So was Howard Hughes. Becoming moralistic, I warned Marlon that he might be ruining the lives of these young girls. He merely shrugged his shoulders. In some ways, he could be the most sensitive man I've ever met. But he appeared completely indifferent to any harm he might be causing. About virgins, he had a completely Dr. Jekyll and Mr. Hyde personality. He once told me that if he caused any harm at all, it was that he ruined these girls for all other men after only one night with him."

"After I drifted away from Marlon, I started dating this handsome young actor who had dreams of becoming a movie star," she said. "He later went to Hollywood and became one of its biggest stars, even though he was a closeted homosexual. So as not to cater to your voyeuristic pleasure, I won't name him. I'm sure everybody here knows who I have in mind." She waved her arm expansively in a gesture that included everyone on Danny Stirrup's back porch.

"Unannounced, Marlon came over to my apartment one night," she said.

"I was in bed with what's-his-name. Marlon barged in on us. That night, the window opening from my kitchen onto the fire escape had been left open so that we could get some air. Even though Marlon was the most promiscuous actor in New York, he called *me* the whore. He said his own mother, Dodie, was also a whore and that she'd betrayed him with other men. It sounded most incestuous. 'What is it with you women?' he asked me. 'Do you have to sleep with any man in pants?' He stormed out of my apartment, never to return. Later, at the Actors Studio, as a means of getting even with me, Marlon told me that he too had slept with what's-his-face, and my errant lover went on, according to Marlon, to claim that Marlon was better in bed than I was. I was hurt and Marlon retreated into a defensive withdrawal. Our relationship was over. I didn't see him after that unless he showed up at one of my plays."

Geraldine went on to state that despite their conflicts, she continued to call Marlon for advice about which roles to accept. And sometimes he'd call her to discuss if he should accept a particular script or not. "What was amusing," she said, "is that we always called each other but never took any of the advice. He told me to take the part of the mother in *The Exorcist*. But I'd read the book and wanted to throw up. I was offered the role of Nurse Ratched in *One Flew Over the Cuckoo's Nest*, and Marlon told me to go for it. Once again, I didn't listen to him. My biggest mistake was in turning down Edward Albee's *Who's Afraid of Virginia Woolf*. The Tony that year went to my acting teacher, Uta Hagen, who immortalized herself with that juicy part. When I first read the play, I thought it was all just dirty talk. I almost turned down John Wayne in *Hondo* because I considered him a notorious right-wing bigot reactionary. When Marlon too advised me against *Hondo*, I decided to accept the part."

As long as there is an eccentric and kooky lady to play," Gerry told Tennessee, "there will be a role for me. A drunken, fading actress. A neurotic schoolteacher. An aging spinster. A vulnerable lady hanging on to life by an emotional thread. I work in spite of what critics call my 'habit of pouring on the weird tics a bit.'"

In the years that lay ahead, Marlon would see all her films, even the bad ones. He was mesmerized by her trademark fluttery gestures and seesaw voice. Rivaled only by Vivien Leigh, whose performance in many ways defined *A Streetcar Named Desire*, she was the ultimate Tennessee Williams troubled heroine, as exemplified by her stage portraits of the love-starved Alma in Williams's *Summer and Smoke* in 1952 and in her role as the fading movie star Princess Kosmonopolis (also known as Alexandra Del Lago) in the playwright's 1950 *Sweet Bird of Youth*. She would later earn Oscar nominations for these two roles on the screen.

For the part of the doomed hustler, Chance Wayne, in *Sweet Bird of Youth*, Marlon himself flew to Key West to discuss his possible appearance in the film with its author, Tennessee. Marlon dropped out when he learned the producers really wanted pretty boy Paul Newman.

Marlon later regretted that he didn't pursue the role of Chance more aggressively. "I know more about hustling than Newman," he said. He also regretted not appearing in *Cat on a Hot Tin Roof* opposite Elizabeth Taylor. "I know more about being a homosexual than Newman," he said. "It's very clear to me that Tennessee modeled Alexandra Del Lago after Tallulah. I surely know how to appear opposite a Tallalah character better than Newman. Besides, I hear my prick is bigger than his."

* * *

Even before *A Streetcar Named Desire* went into rehearsal, rumor was rampant on Broadway that it would become the hit of the 1947 season. Its author was none other than Tennessee Williams, who had already scored a Broadway success with *The Glass Menagerie*.

Originally called *The Poker Night*, *A Streetcar Named Desire*, in its simplest form, was the story of a neurotic aristocratic southern belle, Blanche DuBois. She'd lost Belle Reve, her family estate, and with her illusions still intact arrives in New Orleans, after having been run out of her hometown because of her profligate ways. She seeks refuge with her sister, called Stella in the play, and her brutal brother-in-law, Stanley Kowalski.

From her sixteen million dollar fortune, the producer, Irene Mayer Selznick, invested only $25,000 of her own money to get *Streetcar* launched. To make up the rest of the projected $100,000 budget, she called on old friends, Cary Grant and John Jay Whitney, for cash.

Pointedly, she did not ask her father, Louis B. Mayer, to invest, "because Dad liked only happy endings." Also ignored as a potential "angel" was her estranged husband, David O. Seznick, who was carrying on a torrid affair at the time with the beautiful young actress, Jennifer Jones.

Originally, Irene had wanted Josh Logan, the hottest director on Broadway, to handle *Streetcar*. But Tennessee had insisted on Elia Kazan after seeing him direct rival playwright Arthur Miller's *All*

Watch out for my spear

148

My Sons. Irene found Kazan a tough bargainer. He outrageously demanded and eventually forced her to agree to turn over 20 percent of *Streetcar* profits to him. He also wanted a guarantee of "complete control" over the production. Not only that, but he held out for the billing to read: IRENE SELZNICK PRESENTS AN ELIA KAZAN PRODUCTION.

As Irene and Kazan set about to cast the play, the relationship between the producer and director was tense. From the beginning, Irene interfered so much that Kazan warned her that, "I'll walk if you don't get out of my face. If your suggestions are so great, call your Dad. I hear he's in danger of getting kicked out of MGM." Although he could be cruel to her, she would always forgive him.

Irene insisted on casting stars "so I'll get back my investment." With that in mind, she invited Tennessee and Kazan to visit her at her lavish Hollywood home, where she was entertaining her best friend and rumored lover, Katharine Hepburn. At some point, Irene had tried to interest Miss Hepburn in going onto the stage as Blanche. Hepburn read the play but ultimately turned it down. "Why didn't your fucking husband cast me as Scarlett? Now, that's one Southern belle I could have played the hell out of." Unknown to all but her closest friends, Hepburn "cursed like a sailor," in the words of director George Cukor, "whenever the cameras weren't rolling."

While Kazan, Tennessee, and Irene were sitting in the garden of her mansion, "getting plastered," as Tennessee later recalled—"or at least I was having one wee dram too many"—a call came in from Hume Cronyn. "A call and an invitation."

Cronyn, a Canadian actor, had left behind a career in law to become an actor and the partner, both on the screen and in real life, to British actress Jessica Tandy. Tandy, whom he married in 1942, would, of course, become one of the great actresses of the English-speaking world, a position she'd eventually maintain for five decades. But that lay in her future.

Knowing that his wife's career in Hollywood was going nowhere, Cronyn staged an early one-act play of Tennessee's, *Portrait of a Madonna*, at the Actors' Lab in Los Angeles. The protagonist in this play was an early version of Blanche DuBois, whose characterization was to be fully realized in *A Streetcar Named Desire*. Cronyn directed Tandy in the part, and invited Tennessee, along with Kazan and Irene, to see the production.

Both Kazan and Tennessee were enthusiastic about Tandy's performance. "Since you won't allow me to play the role of Blanche myself," Tennessee said,

Hume Cronyn

campily, "I guess we've found our star."

Kazan agreed. "Let's go backstage and offer her the part."

As producer, Irene was not so sure. She'd grown up in the world of the star system and wanted big names. Before going backstage, Irene expressed her fears about Tandy to both Tennessee and Kazan. She warned that Tandy was far too strong an actress to play the frail, aging Southern belle who dressed in gossamer. "We need a Vivien Leigh type. We probably can't get her, but I bet Margaret Sullavan can do it. Vivien would be better, however. I could just see her emoting like a moth attracted to the flame that will kill her."

Ultimately Tandy won the role. Before she was signed, Irene, daughter of the studio system and a strong advocate of star power, had pushed Mary Martin as Blanche and Gregory Peck onto the somewhat astonished Kazan and his playwright. "When they were shocked, I told them that my choice for the roles was no stranger than David actually casting Humphrey Bogart in the role of Rhett Butler in *Gone With the Wind*. At least David entertained the idea of Bogie for a week before sanity took over."

Even though Tandy would go on to win a Tony award for the best stage performance of the year by a female, Irene had been right. Tandy was wrong for Blanche.

With the female role cast, Irene suggested actors for the role of Stanley Kowalski. "Earnest and dependable" Van Heflin appealed to her. But Tennessee and Kazan refused. She then put forth the name of Edmond O'Brien. "A face permanently fixed in a troubled squint and with a voice that sounds as if it brings only bad news," was Kazan's assessment.

Finally, Irene stunned Kazan and Tennessee by suggesting John Lund. "The boy from Rochester," Kazan said, dismissing the idea. "Decidedly square and stoic. Not our Stanley."

The name of Marlon Brando was put forth by Kazan. Irene, Tennessee, and Kazan himself had seen all of Marlon's performances on stage. He was, in fact, Kazan's pupil at the Actors Studio. "Too young," Tennessee claimed. "He looks like a boy. I see Stanley as a thirty-year-old Polock."

Kazan had just finished making *Gentleman's Agreement,* in which John Garfield had appeared opposite Gregory Peck. The two men had worked together in the Group Theatre in the 1930s. "Julie would be perfect for this blue collar role."

Tennessee wasn't so sure, but Irene applauded the idea. "Let's go for Garfield!" she said.

Tough, cynical, and edgy, both on and off the screen, New York bad boy John Garfield had burst into stardom. Half the world, or so it seemed, saw him emote with Lana Turner in *The Postman Always Rings Twice* and opposite man-eating Joan Crawford in *Humoresque*.

Arriving in New York fresh from his hit in the film, *Body and Soul*, in which he played a dim-witted boxer, Garfield was cocky and demanding.

On a deserted stage, Garfield did a fresh read-through of *A Streetcar Named Desire*, with Kazan playing both Blanche and Stella. In Garfield's judgment, "The male role is very secondary," he told Kazan. "This Stanley character is a mere prop for Blanche's histrionics."

He did not turn down the part but instead issued a series of demands. Before he'd sign for the role, he wanted Tennessee to rewrite the play, making Stanley's part the focus of the drama and expanding his role. He also wanted a guarantee that he could leave the play after only four months and that he would be offered the movie role. Tennessee turned down the request for a rewrite, and Irene refused to meet Garfield's other demands.

At the Actors Studio, Marlon confronted his teacher, Kazan. He'd heard that Garfield "all but had the part of Stanley." Marlon told Kazan, "I think Garfield would be perfect as Stanley. My only problem with him is that his old buddies from the Thirties, guys like yourself, call him 'Julie.' Is there some secret life about Mr. Macho that you're hiding from me?"

"I can assure you that John Garfield is the most heterosexual actor you'll ever meet," Kazan said. "I'm not known for hanging out with fags."

"Not that I'm saying Tennessee is a fag—far from it—but you hang out with him," Marlon countered.

"There is always the exception to the rule," Kazan said, "even a rule of my own making." He turned and walked away.

Although out of the running himself, Marlon was eager to learn any news he could about how casting for *Streetcar* was going. Karl Malden himself told Marlon that he'd been assigned the role of Mitch, Stanley's sidekick.

Marlon also learned from Kazan that the relatively unknown actress, Kim Hunter, had been cast as Stanley's brutalized wife, Stella.

At the Actors Studio, Kazan remembered that Marlon was "stunned" when he told him that Garfield was out and Burt Lancaster was flying into New York to read for the part.

"A circus acrobat," Marlon said. "I'm sure that's the kind of background Tennessee had in mind when writing the character of Stanley."

"Are you being sarcastic?" Kazan asked him.

"No, sincere."

Defensively, Kazan read to Marlon a newspaper clipping he was carrying with him. It was by Shelia Graham, the popular Hollywood columnist and former mistress of the novelist, F. Scott Fitzgerald.

Gushing with praise after seeing Burt emote in *The Killers,* a short story by Ernest Hemingway, Graham wrote: "Masculinity was oozing from every pore. He was thirty-two but looked twenty-two, and what a physique! I could see the muscles rippling up and down beneath his open shirt. It was a pleasure being with a future star at the beginning. He is always so friendly, so eager to please."

"Sounds to me like you want to turn *Streetcar* into a male burlesque show," Marlon said.

"Eat your heart out, Marlon!" Kazan told him.

"I was told that Burt, while in the circus, posed for the meat magazines," Marlon said. "You know, in those homoerotic Greco-Roman stances. And there are a lot of candid frontal nude shots of him in circulation. Maybe you could acquire one of them and run a nude billboard of Burt outside the theater. That surely would guarantee you business for *Streetcar*."

Kazan remembered losing his patience with Marlon and actually slapping him. "Fortunately, he didn't hit me back. 'Don't let your jealousy overwhelm you,' I told him."

"I've got a great body too!" Marlon protested. "I work out all the time."

"Your body's fine for Stanley," Kazan said. "I've told you before, you're just too young. What I didn't tell you, and I'll tell you now that I'm mad at you, you don't have the role in you. The part of Stanley Kowalski is just too big for your limitations as an actor."

"You're a rude, stupid man," Marlon said. "I'm dropping out of your class—you're a rotten teacher anyway—and out of the picture entirely. Someday I'll be the biggest star on Broadway. You'll come begging to me. Just you wait and see."

* * *

What happened next has become part of Broadway legend and lore. Even today, the scenario is a bit hazy, and all the eyewitnesses are dead, leaving only sketchy reports. "No one," Kazan recalled years later, "was exactly in the loop about that strange and long-ago week that Marlon and Burt Lancaster spent together in New York."

Burt arrived in New York with his agent, Harold Hecht, a former dancer for the Martha Graham company and the son of a Brooklyn iron contractor. Burt, whose career was soaring, was clearly Hecht's new meal ticket, and he was ferocious in his attempt to make a big star out of his newly acquired client. The role of Stanley Kowalski in *Streetcar* was only one of several offers Burt was considering. Most of the excitement over him was generated for movie roles, not coming from the Broadway stage, except in the case of Kazan and Irene Selznick. Hollywood producers, not just Shelia Graham, saw his star potential.

Along with Hecht, "guarding him like a box of gold from Fort Knox" in

Burt Lancaster

Irene's words, Burt arrived at her grandly furnished Fifth Avenue apartment. She was impressed with the actor's good looks, physique, and male charm. But she later told Tennessee and Kazan that she felt Burt was more interested in securing the movie contract to play Stanley than he was in appearing on Broadway.

On her first meeting with Burt and Hecht, she told them of her triumph earlier in the day. She claimed that "I fished out Tennessee's best line from his wastepaper basket. 'I have always depended on the kindness of strangers.'"

"I just wish that Williams had put a line or two that good in the mouth of Kowalski," Burt told her.

Over drinks, he agreed to appear at the New Amsterdam Roof Theatre on 42nd Street and Broadway the following morning for a read-through of the play. Once again, as he had with Garfield, Kazan assumed the roles of both Blanche and Stella. At the rehearsal hall, perhaps to show off his manly physique, Burt insisted on removing his shirt.

It is not known how Marlon managed to slip in undetected to see Burt's read-through. Kazan later speculated that Marlon had disguised himself as a janitor. However he managed to conceal himself, Marlon saw Burt go through his first "blind read" of the play. It was the only time that Burt would "appear" as Stanley in front of anyone. Marlon was impressed with Burt's reading, Bobby Lewis later claimed, "although Marlon still felt that Garfield was the ideal choice for Stanley."

After performing as Stanley, Burt said he liked the role and "saw possibilities here." Hecht didn't comment, claiming, "I'll have to talk it over later with Burt."

Kazan left the studio for a meeting with Jessica Tandy, and Hecht had to see some old friends from his Brooklyn days. It was at this point that Marlon appeared, or so it is believed, and made the acquaintance of Burt, who had been left alone in the rehearsal hall.

"Marlon never told me the complete story," Edith said. "I was his agent, but I didn't even know how to get in touch with him most of the time. Technically, he was rooming with Wally Cox and that smelly raccoon. But whenever you needed him, he was never there but stashed away in some bed somewhere in God knows whose apartment. He never had a phone. You literally had to go over to that rattrap where he lived with Wally and leave him a hand-delivered message. The door was always open to their apartment, and

153

complete strangers wandered in and out at random. In those days it was the house party that never ended."

Within forty-eight hours, Hecht called Kazan to tell him that Burt would not be appearing on Broadway but was returning to Hollywood to make a film for producer Hal Wallis. Hecht also told Kazan that he wanted "Burt to be your first choice for Stanley when the film version is made."

Despondent over not being able to cast the right actor in the role of Stanley, Kazan met with Irene once more to reconsider Marlon. In spite of their temporary split, the director finally concluded that Marlon "would be a more dimensional Stanley than either Garfield or Lancaster once he finds himself in the role, which will take weeks, of course."

Irene and Kazan finally decided to send Marlon on a trip to Provincetown where Tennessee was applying his final polishing to *Streetcar*. "If Tennessee approves of Marlon in the role, he'll be our Stanley," Kazan said, "but only if our favorite homosexual says yes. One look at Marlon, and I bet Tennessee will get a hard-on." At the time, Kazan was not aware that his playwright not only knew Marlon but had already seduced him.

The only problem was, no one, especially Edith, knew where Marlon was. "Wally Cox was no help whatsoever," she said. "Wherever Marlon was, he wasn't rooming with Wally. He also hadn't informed Wally where he might be hanging out."

Marlon's former girlfriend, Geraldine Page, once said that he reminded her of a dog you take for a walk in the park. "He pisses on the elm tree. He pisses on the birch. Then, for a change of pace, he pisses on a fire hydrant or a patch of grass. His actual address shifted from day to day, depending on who—in his case, *what*—he was seducing. His ass *du jour*, so to speak. He once told me that he had to shift his address constantly, because so many of

Burt Lancaster

the young women he dated ended up stalking him after he dumped them, which he invariably did, including *moi*."

Where Marlon was hiding out, it was later learned by Edith, was in the "bed of that gorgeous Burt Lancaster. Surely there were no two more beautiful men that God created than Burt Lancaster and Marlon Brando. What great porn stars they would have made as a screen duo. I don't know how Marlon persuaded Burt to disappear with him from that rehearsal hall, but away they went. I think on their first date that day after the *Streetcar* read-through, Marlon invited Burt to go with him to a gym. There, they worked out together and presumably showered together. Somehow in the shower a torrid but very brief affair was launched."

"Obviously Burt was competition for Marlon, and the two actors would not only be compared frequently in Hollywood, but would often be up for the same parts," Edith said. "Even though I was Marlon's agent and close to him, a confidante about his affairs with both men and women, I never fully understood him. Instead of being hostile to actors with whom he was competing, Marlon tried to seduce them. It was as if the act of seduction gave him the edge. I assume that meant topping the victim in bed. Take poor Monty Clift, for instance. Instead of being leery of Monty, Marlon overpowered him sexually. At any rate, when I combed all of New York for Marlon to tell him he was on again for the part of Stanley, he was screwing Burt Lancaster. If I had been a man, I too would have wanted to screw Burt Lancaster."

"The two men partied, they drank together, and they may have even shared a woman or two in Burt's bed," Bobby Lewis said. "I heard they liked to roughhouse with each other, wrestle each other on the carpet, shit like that. These childish escapades, from what Marlon later told me, went atomic."

Encountering Kazan in Hollywood long after the film success of *Streetcar*, Burt told the director that, "I would not have been the great Stanley Kowalski that Brando was. He's a genius. But genius is too erratic. A pretty dangerous thing. It's better just to be talented. I am different from Brando—not better, just different. Where I've got one up on the fucker is that I have discipline. He doesn't."

In the years to come, Marlon followed not only Burt's career, but was always eager for gossip about his personal life. Marlon, Kazan, and Burt would each be cited in *Counterattack* magazine on August 4, 1950. The article claimed that all three men had a "Communist front record."

On many occasions Burt learned that directors wanted Marlon for a particular role, but that they had eventually settled for him instead. Marlon was Luchino Visconti's first choice for the role in *The Leopard*, which eventually went to Burt. Marlon had also been Tennessee's first choice for the role of Alvaro Mangiacavallo, the buffoonish truck driver opposite Anna Magnani's Serafina in *The Rose Tattoo*. Marlon turned it down, the role going to Burt.

Burt's biggest disappointment came when he lost the chance to play Don Vito Corleone in *The Godfather*, based on Mario Puzo's kitschy best-selling novel. Paramount had been pushing for Burt in the role until Francis Ford Coppola awarded it to Marlon. For the rest of his life, Burt hated Marlon for "stealing my part."

Even more painful for Burt was when Marlon replaced him as the love interest in the life of Shelley Winters. The blond, brassy beauty had originally broken off with Marlon when *Streetcar* played on Broadway, but had resumed their relationship in Hollywood.

Burt fell for Shelley in a big way, although he was married. She called their affair in the winter of 1951 "a lovely and sad backstreet romance." Her romance with Burt came to a crashing end when she encountered Marlon once again.

Burt was heartbroken when Shelley teamed up with Marlon once again. Reportedly, on some evenings, Burt sat in a parked car for hours at a time, watching Marlon come and go from Shelley's apartment.

"First the juicy roles," Burt told James Hill, who was his partner and the husband of Rita Hayworth. "Roles intended for me. Now he steals Shelley." He astonished Hill by telling him that he had fantasies of killing Brando. "No, not killing him myself," Burt said. "Hiring killers to do the job for me. I really mean that!"

* * *

On a windy, blustery New York day, Kazan encountered Marlon at the Actors Studio where he'd returned in spite of his threat to resign. "I've called Tennessee," Kazan told him. "He's waiting for you on the Cape. He wants to hear you read for the part of Stanley. If he goes for you, you've got the part. Of course, we can always have your blond hair dyed brown."

"How am I going to get up there?" Marlon asked. "I'm broke."

"I'll lend you twenty," Kazan said, reaching into his pocket.

Years later, Kazan recalled that moment in the history of the theater in a rather melodramatic way. "Marlon headed for the Cape to meet Tennessee. It was to be a date with destiny!"

Chapter Six

With the twenty dollars in his pocket that Kazan had given him, Marlon devoured all the food he could eat. "I was starving," he recalled. "Hadn't eaten a square meal in two days. Just peanut butter without any bread."

With the money he had left over, he bought groceries for Celia Webb and her son. Stashing the young boy with a friend, Celia joined Marlon on the trip to Provincetown to read for Tennessee. Since neither of them at this point had any money, Marlon stuck out his thumb, hitchhiking along the way and bumming food where they could find it. Celia and Marlon arrived in P-Town three days late. "In a tizzy," Tennessee had given up all hope of Marlon ever showing up. Kazan had warned him how undependable the actor was.

It turned out that Marlon and Celia had to hitch rides with at least eight different drivers before finally reaching the tip of Cape Cod.

In Tennessee's battered cottage, Marlon recalled that, "The toilet was overflowing with shit. That shit was swimming onto the tile floor—no one had mopped it up. I dug my bare hand into the toilet and pulled out what looked like a human feces before delivery. Before I got there, Tennessee's motley crew had been using the bushes. Even the lights were out. Tennessee said they had been 'plunged into everlasting darkness.' I even fixed the God damn electricity using copper pennies."

Sharing the house with Tennessee were two strong-willed dames from Texas, producer Margo Jones and her estranged companion, Joanna Albus. The two women had come to the Cape to meet with Tennessee about mounting a production in Texas of *Summer and Smoke*.

Nicknamed "The Texas Tornado" by Tennessee, Jones had directed plays on Broadway before heading to the Southwest, landing in Dallas where she'd launched a repertory group, Theatre '47. Tennessee referred to Joanna as "the Tornado's sidekick."

Later, Joanna would become assistant stage manager when *Streetcar* opened on Broadway. Early gossip in P-Town linked Tennessee romantically with Margo until Joanna arrived on the scene to "set these gay boys straight." In Key West, Tennessee once said, "I have never been especially attracted to lesbians, although there has been a notable exception here and there."

Also sharing the cottage was Pancho Rodriguez, Tennessee's Mexican lover. At first Pancho threatened to leave P-Town and return to New Orleans

157

if Marlon spent the night. He was just as jealous of Marlon as he'd been on the first night they'd met years before. Tennessee prevailed upon Pancho to stay, and he did, although he refused to stick around for Marlon's reading.

As he had before that summer in Provincetown, Marlon bonded with Tennessee, finding him "a pristine soul who suffered from a deep-seated neurosis, a sensitive, gentle man destined to destroy himself."

In his autobiography, Marlon noted, but only casually, that the playwright was a homosexual, "but not effeminate or outwardly aggressive about it, and he never made a pass at the actors in his play. There was something eating at his insides that ultimately propelled him to his death."

Tennessee later recalled that "all of us were drunk when Marlon read for the part of Stanley." Taking the role he secretly coveted for himself, Tennessee played Blanche. He didn't need a script.

"The reading lasted less than two minutes," Margo recalled. "We just knew that Marlon was destined to be Stanley. I let out a Texas whoop like I do at the rodeo."

At first Tennessee didn't say anything after hearing Marlon read. His face looked as if he had disappointed Tennessee, who just sat there in a wicker peacock chair intently studying Marlon as he sucked smoke through a hygienic cigarette holder full of absorbent crystals. "The part is yours!" Tennessee finally said.

Leaving the women to prepare the beds for the night, Tennessee invited Marlon for a midnight stroll on the same beach where he'd seduced him some time before. Pancho had gone to the bars in P-Town, and the playwright didn't expect him to return to the cottage any time soon.

Tennessee later recalled that neither Marlon nor he said a word. "No mention was made of *Streetcar*. In the moonlight, I had never seen a man of such extraordinary beauty."

The myth about Tennessee never making a pass at his actors has been perpetuated, often in biographies, for decades. The playwright's longtime lover,

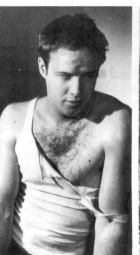

Stanley Kowalski (*Streetcar*) and
Val Xavier (*The Fugitive Kind*)

Frank Merlo, Pancho's eventual replacement, claimed the statement was true in a technical sense. "But we're splitting hairs here. Tenn never made a pass at actors. They made passes at him. Or, rather, they made themselves available to him. On the beach that night, and Tenn told me this himself, he didn't have to grope Marlon. Marlon whipped it out for Tenn. What gay man worth his salt wouldn't have taken advantage of that? Tenn was only human. And Marlon was his sexual fantasy. In Tenn's mixed-up head, Marlon and Stanley Kowalski had meshed into the same erotic image. Theirs was hardly a love affair, like Tenn and me. Marlon was rough trade to Tenn. He didn't mind servicing the stud, swinging on what Marlon always called his noble tool."

Tennessee was less than candid in his memoirs, claiming that he kept the relationship businesslike between Marlon and himself. "I have never played around with actors," Tennessee falsely claimed. "It is a point of morality with me. And anyhow Brando was not the type to get a part that way."

Perhaps that was true, but it didn't take into account that Marlon had seduced playwrights before, often very famous ones.

Back in his cottage at one o'clock in the morning, Tennessee noted that Pancho still hadn't returned from the bars. Marlon claimed he was starving. No great chef, Tennessee went into the kitchen and made him a ham sandwich. The ham was dry, the bread stale. He also poured Marlon a glass of milk. In one gulp, Marlon finished the milk and then requested the whole quart, which he proceeded to finish off. "Pure Stanley," Tennessee said.

He kissed Marlon on the lips and headed for his own bunk bed. He noted that Celia was asleep under a quilt in a corner of the living room, where Marlon went to join her for the night.

The next morning, Tennessee said that Pancho had not returned all night, but Marlon didn't seem unduly concerned. Tennessee lent Marlon twenty dollars so he could buy bus tickets back to New York. Leaving the cottage, Marlon told Celia that "Tennessee is a very easy touch."

On the Greyhound bus going back to New York, Marlon never spoke to Celia. He was lost in a world of his own. "I didn't have anything to say to her because my mind was completely occupied with how to play Stanley. I feared the part was too big for me. A sense of terror, unlike any I'd known before, came over me. I was shaking and sweating a lot. Celia tried to comfort me, but no one could. A demon was taking over inside me and squeezing my guts."

With Marlon out the door, Tennessee called Kazan in New York. "I want Marlon to be Stanley Kowalski. He's far better than Garfield could ever be."

When Kazan put down the phone, he called Irene Selznick. "That son of a bitch of a faggot up there on the Cape is riding a crush on Marlon."

Back in his cottage, Tennessee was writing a letter to his agent, Audrey Wood, calling Marlon a "God-sent Stanley." He seemed delighted to cast the role eight years younger than he had written it. In the letter, he praised Marlon for delivering "the best reading I have ever heard," and that coming from an actor already notorious for his bad readings in which he mumbled. In his letter, Tennessee noted "the physical appeal and sensuality of Marlon, at least as much as Burt Lancaster."

Back in New York for the rehearsals of *Streetcar*, Marlon is credited with causing the final break between Tennessee and Pancho. During one particularly violent and jealous argument over Marlon, Pancho grabbed Tennessee's typewriter and tossed it out of the hotel window, seriously injuring a pedestrian below—in fact, almost killing him.

That was all too much for Tennessee. He bought Pancho a one-way ticket to New Orleans and gave him a thousand dollars "to jump-start another life for yourself." Pancho had calmed down after the typewriter incident. Pleading and even crying before Tennessee, he begged him to let him stay. "It's over," a somewhat callous Tennessee said. "Time to end what should never have begun in the first place."

On the way out the door, Pancho said, "I hope you and Brando will be very happy together. He's your fantasy both on stage and off."

According to Frank Merlo, Tennessee, post-Poncho, "made himself available" to Marlon on several occasions during rehearsals and during the long run of *Streetcar*. As reported by Frank, Tennessee told him, "The last time I enjoyed Marlon was that night on the beach at the Cape. It is a memory I'll always treasure. If he had wanted to come and live with me, I would have asked Pancho to leave much sooner. The relationship with Marlon never got beyond a blow-job. In my already broken heart, I knew even then that it is a hopeless pursuit every time we go after the unobtainable."

* * *

Marlon began rehearsals on October 5, 1947 in the hall on top of the New Amsterdam Theatre where Burt Lancaster had gone through his reading. By the third day, Marlon stormed out of the hall. Kazan chased him down the corridor. "I can't play this character," Marlon told Kazan, who remembered Marlon "all sweating and trembling with grief and anxiety."

"I hate Stanley Kowalski," Marlon shouted at his director. "He never doubts himself. His ego is so strong. He's always right—or at least thinks he's right—and he's never afraid. He's the complete opposite of all the things I am."

Slowly Kazan lured him back into the rehearsal hall, putting his arm around Marlon to offer him comfort. "Just think of Stanley as a complete hedonist," Kazan said. "The type of guy who sucks on a cigar all day because

160

he can't suck on a teat. He conquers with his penis like you conquer dame after dame with what you call your noble tool."

During the first week of rehearsals, Tennessee showed up on the roof of the New Amsterdam where Florenz Ziegfeld in the 1920s had staged midnight musical revues. He went around speaking to each cast member individually. "I'm dying of pancreatic cancer," Tennessee claimed. Marlon and Jessica Tandy, along with Karl Malden and Kim Hunter, were stunned at the news and didn't know what to say, other than muttering their condolences.

Kazan was already aware that Tennessee "was the world's most hysterical hypochondriac." He went over and embraced Tennessee. "Don't worry," he told the playwright. "You're a tough old bird and will live to be one hundred years old—maybe more. Now, let's get on with the rehearsals of this poetic tragedy."

Tennessee had originally intended that sympathy generated by the play be directed toward Blanche. Sitting with Kazan during the weeks of rehearsals, he clearly saw that Marlon was altering his intention. Instead of telling Kazan to restrain Marlon, Tennessee proclaimed, "The boy is a genius! Let's see what he can do. He's a Lawrencian fantasy of the earthy proletarian male." He paused. "A regular midnight cowboy." Years later in Key West, Tennessee would share his early reaction to Marlon with his neighbor, novelist James Leo Herlihy. The writer so liked the expression, *Midnight Cowboy*, that he wrote a novel about it, which was made into the Oscar-winning film of 1969.

Bobby Lewis visited *Streetcar* rehearsals to watch Marlon emote with Jessica Tandy. "Marlon was playing against Dodie, not Tandy as Blanche," he later said. "In Tennessee's character, Marlon found the same heavy drinking, the coquettish sexual flirtations, the lost hopes and dreams that he'd experienced with his own mother. He was seeing Dodie up there on that stage—not Tandy. In the rape scene, he finally fulfilled his incestuous wish to deflower his own mother."

Bobby dismissed talk of how Marlon was slowly "discovering Stanley" as he got deeper and deeper into the role. "Marlon used his portrayal of Stanley as an excuse to pick up a lot of blue-collar New Jersey truck drivers and give them blow-jobs. That's how he imbued himself with the semen of Stanley."

Kazan was not completely aware of all of Marlon's nocturnal adventures during rehearsals for *Streetcar*. Often his star actor showed up late. "On some occasions Marlon looked like the shit had been beaten out of him," Kazan recalled. "Which it probably had. All of the cast knew that Marlon was fucking every woman in sight and, for a change of pace, picking up rough trade along the waterfront. I hoped he wouldn't get knifed before opening night."

Along with Shelley Winters, Carlo Fiore—at Marlon's invitation—attended a rehearsal of *Streetcar*. "I was shocked at Marlon's transformation into

Karl Malden and Kim Hunter preventing backstage brawls between Brando and Tandy

Stanley," Fiore said. "He had put that pelvis-thrust-forward slouch of his to good use and turned his petulant pout into a snarl. His T-shirt disclosed the heavily muscled torso of a truck driver. He mumbled like a moron. He scratched his asshole, digging in deep to get at the itching. To show that he had a perpetual hard-on, he wore tight jeans to outline the bulge of his genitals."

For his appearance in *Streetcar* in a dirty, tight-fitting T-shirt and equally tight-fitting blue jeans, Marlon made a fashion statement that would be adopted by young men across America in the Fifties.

Lucinda Ballard, the costume designer, didn't just put a pair of jeans onto Brando. "The skin-tight jeans were tapered to show the muscles in his thighs and to showcase his genitals," she recalled. "During fittings, Marlon insisted on wearing no underwear. 'I want them to fit like a second skin,' he told me. After our first fitting, I went with him to get his blond hair dyed brown. He was becoming more and more like Stanley Kowalski each day."

The next day Lucinda came up with an inspiration. She went up to Marlon and tore the right shoulder of his red T-shirt, leaving it ripped. "I wanted to suggest that Stella might have attacked Stanley in an angry fit."

Lucinda was well aware that Marlon liked to show off his genitals. She'd designed his costume for *I Remember Mama*. He'd also been impressed with her work on the costumes for Tennessee's *The Glass Menagerie*.

From the very first, Kazan realized that Irene Selznick had initially been right: Tandy was too strong an actress to play a weak, vulnerable soul such as Blanche DuBois. At one point, he amazingly ordered a stagehand to tie Tandy in ropes. The other actors in the cast, including Kim Hunter and Karl Malden, were ordered to attack her and make fun of her in the most demeaning way. That meant attacking her "small tits," her "pus-laden vagina," her "lack of talent," even her "cunty smell."

She was reduced to tears when Marlon stepped up to her. As she lay helplessly on the stage floor,

Marlon and Jessica Tandy in *Streetcar*

still tied in ropes, he unbuttoned his blue jeans and whipped out his penis to urinate on her. At that point, Kazan intervened. He rushed up to Marlon. "Button up, boy! Can't you see Jessica is hysterical? We've already pushed her over the deep edge."

* * *

Two weeks into rehearsal, Marlon called Irene and asked if he could come over and visit her in her plush apartment. She agreed to see him, and later said that she felt that he might want to talk over the trouble he was having with his role. "He arrived in dirty blue jeans and a T-shirt," she said, "with some old Air Force leather jacket. For one hour we talked absolute nonsense—mostly about motorcycle riding and bongo drums. Then he got to the point of our rendezvous."

"I hear your old man is shacked up with Jennifer Jones," he told her, referring to her estranged husband, David O. Selznick. "I also hear you're divorcing the cad. After you divorce him, I might marry you. I've been thinking about proposing. Consider yourself flattered because I'm not the marrying kind. But I'm thinking it might be cool married to a classy dame like you. L.B. Mayer's daughter and all that. *Tout* Hollywood."

"But you don't know me," she protested, still not believing his words.

"After we're married there will be plenty of time to get to know each other. I must warn you one thing about me, though."

"No doubt one of your bad habits?"

"Not that. You should know in advance—it's only fair to tell you. Since your husband is Jewish, I have to assume he's cut. I must warn you that I'm not. But I'm good in bed. The foreskin of the male penis actually gives you a more sensitive tool to work with."

She told him that she'd take his marriage proposal under consideration. In all of their subsequent meetings, the subject of marriage never came up again.

* * *

Marlon detested Jessica Tandy, but became friends with his "wife" in the play, Kim Hunter who played Stella. Born Janet Cole in Detroit, she was two years older than Marlon. From the first meeting, these two actors bonded. He soon discovered that her liberal positions on Civil Rights matched his.

Kazan often found them huddled backstage somewhere "with their heads together like they were plotting an overthrow of the government. I just assumed Marlon was fucking her. He fucked everybody—maybe not Karl Malden or Jessica Tandy. But for all I know, he had them too." He smiled to indicate he was absurdly joking. "Some little gossip even told me he fucked Tennessee Williams. Now, *that* I can believe. Throughout the entire run of the play, Tennessee was absolutely mesmerized by Marlon, even when he acted like a silly ass and sabotaged the play on more than one occasion."

In Marlon, Kazan later reflected, he found a "soft, yearning, and even girlish side. But I warned him to save that for some other role, perhaps when he would play a homosexual in some future part. 'For God's sake, don't play Stanley Kowalski as a fag,' I warned him. 'You're Tennessee's ultimate wet dream fantasy!'"

Marlon wasn't Kazan's only problem in casting. His initial attempt to direct Kim Hunter in her role as Stella failed utterly.

At one point Kazan claimed he was so disappointed in Kim's role as Stella that he was considering replacing her with another actress. Then an amazing change came over him, as Jessica Tandy noted. "Far from condemning Kim, Gadge had only the highest of praise for her performance. He was spending all his time directing her instead of concentrating on my performance as Blanche. After all, the burden of carrying *Streetcar* fell on my shoulders."

Marlon had a different take. "Kazan fell head, heels, and prick in love with Kim herself. In love in this case meant five weeks. Our director believed in seducing and moving on to the next victim."

Carlo Fiore, in his so-called "tell-all" memoir about Marlon, was less than candid about what he knew about Marlon's own involvement with Kim. Yet

Marlon and Kim Hunter embracing in *Streetcar*

he remains the only source for information about Marlon's seduction of his stage wife.

"The way Marlon told it, he came to Kim one night and said that for the purposes of artistic integrity, he had to fuck her," Fiore said. He quoted Marlon as saying, "In the play our entire relationship is based on you hanging with me because of the carnal pleasure I provide for you nightly. Why else would a fine aristocratic Southern dame like Stella end up with Stanley? It just doesn't make sense. Tennessee himself told me that the only reason Stella stays with Stanley is because of the way he fucks her. You and I can't actually play our parts with any truth unless we go at it like animals, the way that Stanley plows it to Stella."

Amazingly, and again Fiore is the only source for this, Kim agreed to go to bed with Marlon. Apparently, the seduction occurred only one time. Marlon took her back to the apartment he had rented, along with Wally Cox, on West 52nd Street. It had been sublet from songwriter Vernon Duke. Once there—fortunately Wally wasn't home that night—he introduced her to his smelly friend, Russell the Raccoon.

Without admitting to a seduction, Kim later recalled a visit to Marlon's apartment. "There was a restaurant downstairs. Also nearby was a night club where, as I understood from Marlon, white senators from Alabama went to indulge their tastes in brown belles. It was a very garish and noisy part of town—not only night clubs, but jazz joints, sloppy joe eateries, and tourist traps hawking cheap souvenirs. Marlon told me he wasn't bothered by the loud sounds of the night. 'That's why I keep my windows open,' he told me. 'The noise lulls me to sleep like a baby.'"

She recalled that there were four urine-stained mattresses spread helter skelter across the living room floor. "Marlon told me he liked to keep his hi-fi blaring late into the night. He also said he liked the apartment because he could play his bongo drums all night, and no one complained about the noise. In one part of his living room, I noticed a set of barbells, some boxing gloves, and a punching bag. I guess that's how he kept himself in such splendid shape."

Later, after the deed was done, he took her downstairs for a pasta dinner at Leon & Eddie's. To cap the night, Kim recalled, he invited her for a midnight ride through the streets of New York on "this powerful Indian motorcycle he'd purchased with his first paycheck from *Streetcar*. I later learned that some of the most famous actresses in the world were invited to weave dangerously through New York traffic on that motorcycle, wildly holding onto Marlon for support. That also gave these women a chance to feel those muscles. To ride on Marlon's motorcycle from the Ethel Barrymore to his messy apartment for the purposes of getting royally screwed became a status symbol for women flying in from Hollywood. Some deliberately flew in just to see Marlon emote in *Streetcar*. Poor Jessica. Poor Karl. Poor me."

Apparently one night with Marlon was enough for Kim, who never revealed if Marlon in real life lived up to her on-stage husband of Stanley.

At least a friendship emerged from this one night of passion. In speaking to the press, Kim had only raves for Marlon the actor, saying nothing about Marlon the man.

She claimed that he had "an uncanny sense of truth as an actor. It seems absolutely impossible for him to be false. It makes him easier to act with than anybody else ever. Anything you do that may not be true shows up immediately as false with him."

Fiore claimed that the only comment Marlon ever made to him was, "I'm afraid that as bed partners Kim and I aren't really Mr. and Mrs. Stanley

Kowalski. Only on stage. But she's a fine actress in every way. She's going back to Hollywood, but she's too liberal and sophisticated for those constipated assholes out there."

His words were prophetic. In Hollywood, after appearing in such films as Bogart's wife in *Deadline, U.S.A.*, she was eventually blacklisted because of her strong pro-Civil Rights stances.

However, she returned and became familiar to a whole new generation because of her simian face in those *Planet of the Apes* films.

In 1968 she called Marlon in Hollywood, telling him that, "I'm trying to keep my dignity intact while buried under all this fucking monkey makeup."

Men wanted to be him. Women (and others) wanted him.

"I've made a monkey out of myself on the screen before," he told her. "Stella, we really wooed them a long time ago, didn't we? You and I will live forever as Mr. and Mrs. Stanley Kowalski."

* * *

In the out-of-town tryouts, Tandy complained to Kazan that, "If Brando feels bored or tired, he acts bored or tired. If he feels gay, he acts gay." Her remarks were later misinterpreted. It has been written that Tandy was charging Marlon with homosexuality. The word "gay" meaning homosexual was not quite in vogue then, and Tandy could have used the word in its old-fashioned sense.

"Knowing Jessica, she could have meant homosexual," Kazan said. "One night in New Haven, Marlon got so bored he played Stanley as a swish. The next day both Irene and Tennessee showed up to chastise him for this outrageous performance. Tandy was furious at him, denouncing him as 'the most unprofessional actor I've ever worked with.'"

But sometimes it was Marlon who lost his patience with Jessica. At one point, he stormed off the stage in complete disgust at her interpretation of Blanche. "My God, how can I play opposite Ophelia? She thinks she's appearing in Gielgud's *Hamlet*."

As Stanley, Marlon threw himself into the character, becoming an animal on stage. "He eats like one," Tandy said. "Moves like one. Talks like one!"

166

She complained to both Kazan and Tennessee that out of sheer boredom Marlon was shifting the emphasis of the play almost nightly. She never knew what to expect from him. She had good reasons to complain. In New Haven, she was delivering one of her most poignant speeches as Blanche. The audience snickered at her. She turned around and, to her horror, caught Marlon puffing a cigarette through his nostrils.

When she complained to Tennessee that Marlon was "destroying the integrity" of *Streetcar*, he attended a performance. After watching some of Marlon's alterations, Tennessee proclaimed to Tandy that "Marlon is adding a new dimension to *Streetcar*."

With a sense of despair, she endured night after night, living in dread of what Marlon might do at that evening's performance. Broadway loomed in her future, making her wonder if she'd survive opening night playing opposite an actor she called "Broadway's bad boy."

Unlike Tandy, Karl Malden liked Marlon but admitted that he got so frustrated with being constantly upstaged that he once smashed his fist into a brick wall. "At times I enjoyed acting with Marlon," Malden said. "He was a constant challenge. At other times I could have wrung his little neck."

Marlon's experience working with his costar, Tandy, in *Streetcar* wasn't as disastrous as his appearance with Tallulah Bankhead. But Marlon and Tandy, two very different stars, were completely incompatible. Marlon later summed it up this way: "We don't see eye-to-eye on some things. She believes you should shave and get dressed for a day in the country. Besides, she doesn't like peanut butter sandwiches."

Tandy's view of Marlon? "A selfish, psychopathic bastard."

There was obviously no sexual magnetism between the two players. That would have to wait for Marlon to be cast opposite another actress in the film version.

Tandy, with her Royal Academy training, was opposed to Method acting and the Stanislavsky system. Even in rehearsals, she wanted to "freeze" the play, its movements and its action.

Tryouts in New Haven preceded the play's shift to Boston where Kazan feared "the blue bloods would object to the raw, animal sex of the play." But *Streetcar* was well received. The cast continued with its optimistic streak as *Streetcar* opened to rave reviews in Philadelphia.

Kazan felt that the early success of the show would "have New York critics sharpening their knives for us. New York critics didn't always follow the praise that came 'from hicks in the boondocks.' I told the cast in Philadelphia that *Streetcar* could be compared to oysters. 'Remember,' I cautioned them, 'not everybody likes oysters.'"

A handsome young actor, Sandy Campbell, had asked Tennessee if he could play the role of the Young Collector in *A Streetcar Named Desire*. Sandy was the lover of Donald Windham, one of Tennessee's best friends. Tennessee and Donald had co-authored a play, *You Touched Me!* which had starred Monty Clift on Broadway.

In a letter dated September, 1947, Tennessee wrote Sandy, telling him that, "I would love to have you in the part if it were at all suited to you, but if you remember the scene, the boy's name is Shapiro and Blanche says 'he looks like a young prince out of Arabian Nights!' He *has* to be dark."

In spite of the rejection, Sandy, with his hair dyed black, ultimately prevailed. He replaced the original actor cast in the Broadway company, and even returned to the role in 1956 when Tallulah Bankhead, in one of the worst mistakes of her career, finally agreed to appear as Blanche DuBois and was practically laughed off the stage by gay audiences who interpreted her involvement in the play as an act of high camp.

If Tennessee believed in the casting couch, Sandy would have gotten the role much earlier. In a letter sent to Donald Windham in October of 1948, Tennessee admitted that at a party he'd attended with Sandy, that the young actor/writer had gotten "very drunk and was so cute I had a letch for him. That is, I felt like I wanted to kiss him and hold him in my arms, but of course I didn't."

"Like hell he didn't," Frank Merlo, Tennessee's later lover, once said.

Even though Sandy was embarked on a relationship with fellow writer, Donald Windham, a love affair that was to span forty-five years, he was, in the words of Tennessee, "a star fucker of the literati."

Donald Wyndham
& Sandy Campbell

His affairs included the likes of Truman Capote and lesser literary stars of the late Forties and early Fifties. He did not specialize in actors except for Monty Clift and Marlon Brando.

"Until Sandy came into Marlon's life," Kazan later recalled, "Marlon was always in the driver's seat with both men and women who fell for him. For the first time, he was smitten. The love bug bit hard. Personally I think Marlon fell head over heels for Sandy. I don't really understand these male/male love affairs. All I know is that my male star of the show was following Sandy around with his tongue wagging. I'd never seen Marlon act like this before. He was love sick. Perversely, I thought Sandy was Marlon's payback for all the ways he'd abused lovers in the past."

Kazan and other members of the cast watched the love affair unfold before their eyes. Tandy recalled seeing Marlon and Sandy standing in the wings holding hands before Marlon was called onto the stage. "If I admired anything about Marlon," Tandy later remembered, "it was how open he was in flaunting that homosexual streak in himself. At a time, when he was seducing every woman who came backstage, including some of the biggest stars in

Monty Clift

Hollywood, he was still openly carrying on with Sandy, who was a dear, darling boy. Anybody would have loved Sandy. He was very precious and very ingratiating. In some ways, I think Marlon pursued Sandy so aggressively because he knew that boy was unobtainable and committed to another relationship with Donald Windham."

She recalled that Monty Clift came several times to see Marlon perform in *Streetcar*. The young actor had by then become very jealous of Marlon's success. The backstage gossip of the time was that Monty had fallen for Sandy at one point in his life. "I don't know when Sandy first met Monty," Tandy said. "Maybe he was around at the time Monty and Donald did that play, *You Touched Me!* All I know is that Monty had had an affair with Sandy. Sandy had rejected him in favor of Donald. When Monty learned that Sandy and Marlon were an item, he seemed furious. He came to visit me on several occasions. He told me that he did not like Tennessee because the playwright did very little to conceal his homosexuality. 'He's too God damn open about it!' Monty told me. He also told me that he believed some secrets, especially homosexuality, should be kept confined to the bedroom with a lock on the door. He also predicted that Marlon carrying on so openly backstage with Sandy would destroy Marlon's chance for a career. 'He'll be confined to the stage,' Monty predicted. 'On Broadway, you might get away with all this hand holding. In Hollywood, it'll be the kiss of death for Marlon.'"

Kazan never condemned Marlon for his open display of affection for Sandy. Instead the director seemed to grow more and more curious. Although still viewed as a homophobe by the gay members of the *Streetcar* crew, Kazan was showing more and more interest in the subject. Tennessee once speculated that he felt that the womanizing Kazan was a closeted homosexual. "Just show me a womanizer," Tennessee said, "from Errol Flynn and Howard

Hughes on down, and I bet you'll find a lavender streak in there somewhere."

One night Kazan confronted Marlon backstage. The director asked to speak to him in private. Marlon later told Kim Hunter what had taken place. Kazan, according to Marlon, came to him and said, "I really want to know what takes place when two faggots sleep together. I mean I can picture it in my mind, but I don't quite get the logistics." Marlon suggested that Kazan watch an underground gay film, as many were in circulation on the black market at that time. Kazan told him that he was seeking a closer encounter than that.

On a dare, Marlon invited him to share a hotel room. "We'll have twin beds," Marlon said to reassure his director. "Sandy and I will be in one bed. You and your lady of the evening can be in the other bed. We'll watch you, and you can watch us."

To the surprise of Marlon and Sandy, Kazan showed up with Kim Hunter. Both actors had heard that Kazan had been "having an affair with Blanche's sister," but this was their first confirmation of the rumor. Sandy recalled that both Kazan and Kim were a little drunk.

Sandy later told Tennessee and his lover, Frank Merlo, "We put on a great show for them. I wanted to perform my best, throwing more gusto in the sex than I usually did. After all, if I wanted a future career in gay porn, here was my golden opportunity." He smiled to indicate that he was joking. "We really went to it. Earlier, Marlon had suggested that we go at it like two animals in heat, getting into every conceivable position that we could think of. I called it

Was it Truman or Sandy Campbell?

170

our gymnastic romp. As far as I could tell, Kazan seduced Kim in a rather boring, old-fashioned missionary position."

Sandy Campbell is the only source of this amazing story. At first his claim might be met with a degree of skepticism, but not after 1988 when Knopf published *A Life*, Kazan's memoirs. In this autobiography, Kazan admitted that he extended the same invitation to Tennessee for a double date. While he occupied a twin bed with "a young lady" (unknown), Kazan watched Tennessee and "a Mexican jungle cat" (a reference to Pancho Rodriguez) make love. Kazan's critique of Pancho's lovemaking? "In a word, rambunctious."

At no point in the memoirs did Kazan admit to watching Marlon and Sandy go at it.

After a year's run of *Streetcar* on Broadway Kazan could admit that homosexual love "was no longer a mystery to me."

Kazan later told Tandy, "I have seen two stately homos perform—Mr. Williams and Mr. Brando. In Marlon's case, I should say bisexual—let's at least give him credit for that."

* * *

Author Truman Capote, Marlon's future nemesis, was on his way backstage to search for his friend, Tennessee Williams, long overdue for an agreed-upon luncheon date. As he was to later recall, "I stopped in my tracks when I encountered a young man asleep."

"It was a winter afternoon," Capote said. "I found the place deserted backstage except for this brawny young man stretched out atop a table on the stage under the gloomy glare of stage lights. He was sleeping soundly. He wore a white T-shirt and denim trousers that did little to conceal the outline of his genitals. He had a squat gymnasium physique and weightlifter's arms. It was definitely a Charles Atlas chest but he had a copy of Freud resting on the chest of that perfect body. I took him for a stagehand, one who definitely moonlighted for pay with the queens of Broadway."

"I looked closely at his face hoping to wake him up gently and perhaps arrange a rendezvous with him later where I would personally audition him," Truman continued. "It was as if a stranger's head had been attached to the brawny body, as in certain counterfeit photographs. For this face was so very untough, superimposing, as it did, an almost angelic refinement and gentleness upon hard-jawed good looks: taut skin, a broad, high forehead, wide-apart eyes, an aquiline nose, full lips with a relaxed, sensual expression."

"Finally, I realized it was Marlon Brando," Truman said. "He didn't have the least suggestion of the unpoetic Stanley Kowalski. It was therefore rather an experience to observe, later that afternoon, with what chameleon ease

171

Tennessee Williams

Marlon acquired the character's cruel and gaudy colors. Superbly, like a guileful salamander, he slithered into the part. His own persona evaporated."

Truman remembered how Marlon, lying on that table, opened only one eye at first to see what stranger had invaded his lair. "He looked at me as if I were green and a four-headed monster who'd just gotten off the ship from Mars," Truman said. "It was obvious to me that from the first Marlon was fascinated by me. Perhaps he'd never met anyone like me. I am, after all, unique. Sometimes I have this peculiar effect on men. When I first met Errol Flynn, he thought I was the sexiest thing since he'd last fucked a Tasmanian Devil. Even Mr. Macho, Bogie himself, was captivated by my charms. He told his wife, Lauren Bacall, that, 'I want to put Capote in my pocket and bring him home.'"

The fact that Truman Capote met Marlon is true, and the details, as noted above, have been reported in numerous biographies. But the choreography of the meeting that's outlined above didn't involve Marlon and Truman, but, rather, Marlon and Sandy Campbell.

The young actor had told his friend, Truman, about how he'd first met Marlon. Truman put a spin on the incident, eliminated Sandy from its context altogether, and substituted himself instead, as he so often did in many other incidents.

In reality, after *Streetcar* had opened on Broadway, Truman was taken backstage by Tennessee and introduced to Marlon in a way that was a lot more conventional than in Truman's more elaborate and romanticized version, as noted above.

From the moment they first met, Truman set about to ingratiate himself with Marlon. On one drunken night in Key West, Truman later claimed that, "Tennessee got him first, but I wanted to be next in line. After getting to know Marlon a bit better, I realized to my regret that the line stretched around the block. I had to persevere. I couldn't let Tennessee have one up on me."

* * *

The opening of *A Streetcar Named Desire* made theatrical history as the curtain went up at the Ethel Barrymore Theatre on December 3, 1947. The word had been out there for months that this was going to be "the play" to see that winter. For days in advance, lines had formed around the block, as theater-goers eagerly sought to buy tickets. Scalpers were having a field day, hawking tickets for fifty dollars each.

"Sex sells," said theater doyenne Jean Dalrymple, who was one of the distinguished guests on opening night. She joined a wide array of VIPs that also included a well-dressed Marlon Sr. and a sober Dodie, as well as Tennessee's mother, Edwina Dakin Williams, and the playwright's rather jealous brother, Dakin.

Even David O. Selznick showed up, although Irene had specifically asked him not to. She had suggested that her husband "and your trollop," an unkind reference to his mistress, Jennifer Jones, go elsewhere that evening. Selznick had aggressively promoted Jones for the role of Blanche DuBois, casting that was simply unthinkable to Irene.

"We had been told that *Streetcar* was filled with more raw sexual passion than anything that had ever been presented on Broadway," Dalrymple claimed. "The word was also out on Brando. Gossip had it that after *Streetcar* he was going to be the hottest actor on Broadway."

"From the moment Brando walked out on the stage, all eyes were riveted on him," Dalrymple said. "In his sweaty, tight-fitting red T-shirt, and in those even tighter jeans that were very revealing, he was like an animal in heat. It was an exciting moment in the theater."

"You could almost hear the women in the audience swoon as if they had suddenly found the rapist of their dreams," Dalrymple said. "Brando was a savage but what a sexy one! He was violent, crude, and totally mesmerizing. I don't recall having seen such utter rapture in a drama, and, believe me, I've seen the greatest performances of anybody of my generation—all the greats, from John Barrymore to Katharine Cornell. When the curtain went down that night, it was more than a new star had been born. We were actually devastated as if a quart of our blood had been drained from us. I knew that after Brando's performance that night in *Streetcar*, that acting, and Broadway itself, had changed for all time."

Jessica Tandy as Blanche DuBois

Sitting in the front row, along with Irene and Tennessee, were such famous faces as Monty Clift, Edward G. Robinson, Paul Muni, and Cary Grant.

Bobby Lewis was also in the audience that

night. He would later reflect on that memorable evening in the theater. "Marlon paved the way that night for other actors to come. You just name them, beginning with Marlon's understudy, Ralph Meeker, who in time also played Stanley. The parade of Marlon clones continued: Rip Torn, Paul Newman, Steve McQueen, and most definitely James Dean."

When the final curtain fell that opening night, it was Dodie who was first on her feet to launch applause for Marlon that lasted thirty minutes. "Backstage, Jessica was furious," Kim Hunter recalled. "She knew that all that clapping was for Marlon and not for her star part."

One of the investors, Cary Grant, was the first to rush backstage to greet Marlon with a theatrical kiss on the lips. "I'm going to get back my money in the show," he proclaimed to a startled Marlon. "I see a future in Hollywood for you. Irene knows how to get in touch with me. When you get to Hollywood, I want to show you around. You'll find no better tour guide." Having had several drinks before show time, he was in a gay mood, as he retreated to make way for an onslaught of other well-wishers. As he departed, Marlon and Irene heard him yelling, "Hey, Stella. Hey, there, Stella, baby!"

Following Cary backstage was Geraldine Page, Marlon's estranged girl-friend. "You've become a star overnight!" she gushed.

"Cut the shit, Gerry!" he said, softening the harshness of his words with a seductive smile and a kiss on the lips.

Today it might be hard for modern theater audiences to understand what all the fuss about *Streetcar* was in 1947. Of course, the world people inhabited then was a far and different place. As one critic put it, "*A Streetcar Named Desire* was awful and sublime. Only once in a generation do you see such a thing in the theater."

Years later, another critic would proclaim that "Brando, the wild, sexy rebel, all mute and surly bad attitude, prefigured the great art form of the Sixties generation: rock and roll."

For appearing in *Streetcar*, Marlon was paid $550 a week (the equivalent of $7,500 a week in today's currency), $400 of which he sent every week to Marlon Sr. to invest. His father foolishly invested in such money-losing enterprises as oil fields in Indiana and his Penny Poke cattle ranch in Nebraska.

After the show, Tennessee invited his mother Edwina and his brother Dakin to join him for a party at "21." Director George Cukor was the official host, but behind the scenes, Irene was picking up the hefty tab. On the way there, Edwina told Tennessee that before the curtain she had met the Brandos, as he would later recall.

"They looked very respectable to me," she said. "I don't know how they could have produced a wild thing for a son. And, frankly, if you really want to know my opinion, I think Dakin is far handsomer than Brando."

174

"Speaking of wild things," Dakin chimed in, "at this fancy party, they just might be asking how a God-fearing woman like you could produce Tom here."

"Tom," she said, gently reaching for her son's hand, "for the life of me, I don't know why you insist on writing about Southern decadence when there are so many more spiritually uplifting subjects about the South that you could write about. You just give Yankees ammunition to use against us. I mean, even if Blanche and Stanley weren't blood-related, it's still *incest!*"

Uncharacteristically, Marlon showed up at "21" in a dark suit and tie, accompanying

Truman Capote

Dodie and Marlon Sr., who were beaming and smiling at their son's success. Throughout the evening Irene kept rushing over to the Brando table, quoting excerpts from reviews as they arrived by special delivery. "Just hear this," she told the Brandos. "It's right here in print: 'Our theater's most remarkable young actor at his most memorable!'"

Later that night, Dodie went off the wagon. She'd been "dry" for weeks leading up to opening night, but could not resist when Karl Malden came around offering champagne. Irene would remember Dodie tap-dancing for the amusement of her guests. Dodie had been taking lessons. "My Dad's not going to replace Ann Miller with Dodie," Irene told Kim Hunter, "but Marlon's mom wasn't bad."

* * *

After *Streetcar* opened and perhaps to impress Marlon, Truman Capote showed up backstage one night with the photographer, Cecil Beaton on one arm, Greta Garbo on the other. Kim Hunter and Jessica Tandy were part of the "audience" at this moment in theatrical history, although they remained out of the loop, except as eyewitnesses to later report what occurred.

After congratulating Marlon on his brilliant performance, Garbo told him that she was here tonight because she'd promised Tennessee that she'd go to see the play since he wanted her to star as Blanche DuBois in the eventual film version of the work. If Garbo were aware that she was speaking in the presence of Jessica Tandy, who wanted to appear in the film version herself, she didn't seem to have any sensitivity to that.

"I must turn Tennessee down," Garbo told the private audience standing in awe of her. "Blanche DuBois is a bad woman, and never again will I play a bad woman on the screen. The character is difficult, much too unsympathetic. I'm an honest and clear-cut woman. I see things with lucidity. I could never play such a complicated woman. I couldn't bear to tell lies and see things around the corner instead of straight-on. Besides, who would believe me as an aging Southern belle on the verge of madness? I couldn't play Scarlett O'Hara either."

"What sort of role would entice you to return to films?" Marlon asked. Truman later recalled that Marlon was obviously impressed with Garbo and a bit tongue-tied, but he was trying to keep his cool and not show it.

"I always wanted to appear as Dorian Gray," she said. "If some producer offers me that role, I will return to the screen." Three years later when Katharine Cornell talked to Garbo about a possible comeback, the Swedish actress still insisted that only the role of Dorian Gray would bring her back to the screen. Except she had now added one condition. Garbo had recently seen Bette Davis in *All About Eve*. It wasn't Davis that impressed Garbo but a young blonde actress named Marilyn Monroe. Garbo told Cornell she'd do the picture only if the director cast Marilyn Monroe as the young girl that Dorian deflowers, ruining her life. As an afterthought, Garbo added, "And, yes, I think Miss Monroe should be photographed nude at one point in the film."

Throughout her meeting with Marlon, Garbo remained standing, refusing a chair offered by Jessica Tandy. Garbo also failed to comment on Tandy's performance, or the role of Stella as portrayed by Kim.

Garbo went on to assert that although she'd most prefer to play Dorian Gray, it was likely that she'd return to the screen in *The Eagle With Two Heads*. "That brought a look of such astonishment to Marlon that I wish it had been captured on film," Truman said.

"You've seen that turkey?" Marlon asked.

"Not with you in it, darling," Garbo said. "I saw it on Broadway with that

awful woman from the South, Tallulah Bankhead. It's a play of great wretchedness. But even bad plays can be fixed for the screen. If I'm to wear décolletage in the film, there's a lot I've got to arrange. Much exercising for me. Much coaxing of my body to get back in shape. Of all the films being offered to me right now, and they are considerable, it's the role of a queen that I am going to select for my return to the screen. As you know, I've played queens before. But perhaps you're too young to remember my films. I was a star when you were born."

Greta Garbo

176

Marlon didn't comment.

"If I agree to do the play, and it's not final yet, I want you to be my leading man," Garbo said. "What actor could turn down a costarring part in Garbo's return to pictures? Incidentally, I hate the word 'comeback.'"

Months later, Billy Wilder heard of that remark, and put much the same sentiments into the mouth of Norma Desmond, as played by Gloria Swanson, in *Sunset Blvd.*

Cecil Beaton

At the door to his dressing room, Garbo impulsively kissed Marlon on both cheeks as a parting gesture. She reached for a rose held in the hand of Cecil Beaton and handed it to Marlon with a certain passion. She seductively kissed the rose before passing it to him. "That will put the dew on it," she said before adjusting her gray highwayman hat and departing into the night.

Cecil remained behind to make a request of Marlon, asking him if, over the weekend, he'd pose for a series of pictures for *Vanity Fair*. "Normally, Marlon would turn down such a request from what I'd heard about him," Truman recalled. "But I think he was charmed by Cecil. He must have known that Cecil was primarily homosexual. I'm sure Marlon had heard that Cecil regularly fucked Garbo. For some reason, that held enormous intrigue for Marlon as I was later to find out. I think Marlon wanted to learn what this mysterious Cecil was all about. In other words, what did a primarily gay photographer have that would make Garbo, who was primarily a lesbian, want to go to bed with him? I fear Marlon never found out the answer to that riddle. But he did agree to the photographic session. I invited myself to attend. This, I just knew, was going to be the best show in town."

The next day Marlon encountered Tennessee and reported on his exchange with Garbo, telling the playwright that the actress had turned down the role of Blanche DuBois.

"Just as well," Tennessee said. "I got carried away when I offered her the role of Blanche. Garbo is wrong for Blanche." He looked at Marlon as if he were a judge at the Spanish Inquisition. "Have you ever seen a drag queen impersonate Garbo?"

Marlon said that he had not.

"That's because she is unique," Tennessee said. "Almost impossible to capture in an impersonation. Actually, she's a hermaphrodite, with the cold quality of a mermaid. Definitely not Blanche." As an afterthought, Tennessee added, "I could play Blanche better than Garbo, as you already know from my reading with you that night back on the Cape."

Inviting Marlon for a drink, Tennessee told him that when he'd first gone to see Garbo about the role of Blanche, he'd gotten so nervous that he actually pitched another story idea to her. "I told her all about this film script I was working on. It's called *The Pink Bedroom* and it's about this actress and her agent lover. For an hour, I babbled on about the script with frequent interruptions of 'Wonderful!' from Garbo. Finally, when I finally shut up, Garbo rose to her big feet to dismiss me. 'Give it to Joan Crawford,' she told me."

Truman attended the photo shoot of Marlon the following week. He showed up in his dirty T-shirt and tight jeans from *Streetcar*. At some point, according to Truman, Cecil took at least a hundred pictures of Marlon. After Cecil was satisfied he'd had enough of those, he asked Marlon if he would remain behind and pose "for some figure studies," as Truman later quoted Cecil.

"Cecil was well aware that Marlon did not wear underwear under his jeans," Truman said. "Everybody along Broadway had heard that fascinating tidbit."

With absolutely no embarrassment, Marlon pulled off his shirt and unfastened his jeans. In a minute, he was stark naked for Cecil's camera. "I decided then and there that this handsome young man could be had," Truman said.

Years later in Key West, Truman became a bit coy, especially when talking about what happened after the photo shoot. "Both Cecil and I had Marlon that night in the same bed," he claimed. "He was strictly rough trade, but we managed to coax two loads from him—one for Cecil who got the first eruption, the next for Yours Truly."

After that, Truman claimed in front of Tennessee, Frank Merlo, and James Leo Herlihy, that he "serviced" Marlon frequently in the weeks to come. Truman not only lied on occasion about many of his involvements, but exaggerated those that really took place. He was also known for altering the facts to make a good story even better.

Frank Merlo and Tennessee Williams

But both Tennessee and later Elia Kazan felt that Truman told the truth in this case. "Even so, I think Truman highly exaggerated the extent of his romantic friendship with Marlon," Tennessee said when Truman left Key West. "Truman might have fallen down once or twice on bent nylon and given Marlon a blow-job, or even two or three. But I'm sure that the so-called love affair between

Marlon and Truman took place only in the wee one's churning brain."

There is no way at this point of determining if Truman told the truth. Marlon never commented, as far as it is known. Nor did Cecil.

The nude shots of Marlon became the talk of gossipy underground Broadway. They have never been published, at least for public consumption. Marlon later denied having posed for the nude shots.

Apparently, the pictures were not part of the vast repertoire of photographs and diary entries that Cecil left behind at his death.

There is speculation that Cecil in the 1950s sold the nude pictures to a very rich and very devoted fan of Marlon's, where they may reside to this day, waiting for some future heir to some estate to sell them to the highest bidder as a collector's item.

* * *

When *Streetcar* opened on Broadway, Tandy, in a spirit of reconciliation, brought columnist Sheila Graham to Marlon's dressing room. "Marlon, I have someone who's dying to meet you," Tandy said. She stood back and presented the columnist, who was especially vain about her looks.

"Who?" Marlon asked. "Your mother?" Perhaps he was paying Graham back for her effusive praise of Burt Lancaster's physical charms. At this point, Marlon had begun to regard Burt as a serious competitor.

Irene forced Marlon to grant some newspaper and magazine interviews, a task he loathed. Every one of "my inquisitors" wanted to know about his private life. He told them he swallowed one raw egg every morning for breakfast. "The rest of my diet consists of peanut butter and pomegranates. My hobbies are bongo drums, tom-toms, and riding motorcycles through the streets of New York. I like to box and swim in the nude. My reading matter consists entirely of Spinoza. My pet peeves are wearing shoes and giving interviews."

"What about your love life, Brando?" one impertinent interviewer asked. Marlon gave him a puzzled look as if he didn't understand the question. "I can't talk about something that doesn't exist."

* * *

Deep into the run of *Streetcar*, and only a few minutes before curtain time, Jessica Tandy received a call from Irene Selznick. The producer told her star that her father's favorite motion picture star, the crowned King of Hollywood, Clark Gable himself, was in town. Irene had presented him and "this little starlet" with two tickets for the best seats in the house.

For the past week, Jessica had not spoken to Marlon because twice in a run of only three days, he'd upstaged two of her most evocative scenes. But she decided to break her silence to report this epic news.

Knocking on Brando's door, she stood bravely to confront him. "Yeah," he said when he threw open the door and discovered his nemesis. "What do you want?" he mumbled. He hadn't put on his jeans yet, which meant he was naked from the waist down. He pulled down his dirty red T-shirt to cover his privates, which he often didn't bother to do with many of his dressing room visitors.

"Marlon' she said with a stage smile, keeping her eyes averted skyward. "I just had to share the news. Clark Gable is out there in the audience right this minute waiting for us to go on." In those days, such an announcement was like saying that President Harry Truman was in the audience.

Jessica later recalled that she'd been surprised at Marlon's stunned reaction. "I just assumed that Marlon would be contemptuous of Gable and everything he represented as an actor. Gable represented old, established Hollywood. Marlon represented the Hollywood of the future.

Even though Marlon hadn't made a film yet, Gable had heard through the grapevine that the hot new Broadway star was being besieged with film offers. Before going to the theater, Gable had told Irene that, "I thought while I'm in New York I'd better check out tomorrow's competition. I'm getting a little long in the tooth, and I want to see who my replacement is going to be."

Gable's intuition was working just fine. It was as if he'd sensed that the sex symbol of the 1930s, as represented by himself, was about to meet the future sex symbol of the 1950s, as evoked by Marlon.

Jessica feared the end of the night's performance when Gable would actually meet Marlon. "On one occasion when we were discussing acting—that is, on one of the days we were actually speaking—Marlon cited a list of the

phoniest 'non-actors' in Hollywood," Tandy said. "If I remember correctly, Gable led the list, followed by Lana Turner, Victor Mature, Betty Grable, and John Wayne. Singled out as the phoniest actress of all time was Joan Crawford, who he was yet to meet."

"His cool air of detachment almost collapsed when I told him about Gable being out front," Jessica recalled. "I think Marlon almost forgot to put on his blue jeans that night."

"When Marlon went on stage, he absolutely froze," she said. "He was totally wooden. I did something that night I had failed to do so far: I

Clark Gable

completely stole the show from him. I acted rings around this wooden Indian in a cigar store. I'm sure that Gable, seeing Marlon on the stage for the first time, must have been puzzled as to what the excitement was all about."

Later, Irene reported a story her father, Louis B. Mayer, told her. Upon his return to Hollywood, when Gable called on Mayer, he is quoted as saying to the studio mogul, "I think Brando was great! Just great!" Gable didn't disguise the sarcasm in his voice. "I think you should acquire the screen rights from your daughter. Peter Lawford would make a perfect Stanley. Van Johnson, an even better one. Of course, Roddy McDowell would show them both up. That Kowalski needs a dog for a pet. If Roddy is assigned the role, you could put Lassie in the picture. On the other hand, that Kowalski guy would go only for a poodle dyed pink. For Blanche, I'd suggest Lana Turner. You could paint wrinkles on her face. And for relief, get Judy Garland to sing two or three New Orleans jazz numbers. That will attract the homosexuals."

Mayer brushed aside Gable's ribbing. He'd seen the play in tryouts in New Haven. "I don't think it's a family picture. I urged Irene to get Williams to rewrite the ending. I told her it had to have a happy ending if the picture's going to be a success. Also, a lot of the subject matter—references to homosexuality, rape, shit like that—would have to be removed before it can ever be filmed."

Back in the theater on that fateful night, Marlon faced not only Gable but an audience of fourteen hundred patrons. He remembered the night later in his life. "I came to an absolute, complete void. I just stood there looking at the audience with a grin on my face. I looked up at the people in the balcony and all over the house, and it seemed terribly amusing. There were all these people waiting for me to say something, and I didn't have the slightest notion of what it was supposed to be. Kim Hunter was in the scene with me, and she is inclined to come apart in such situations. Her eyes got as big as saucers, and all she could do was ask me questions like 'What did you do then?' Or, 'What did she say?' Somehow we managed to get through it."

Throughout the night Marlon mumbled. Some irate members of the audience shouted "Louder!" at him. Kim Hunter later claimed that "Marlon in front of Clark Gable that night gave the single most disastrous performance of the entire *Streetcar* run."

To make matters worse, Marlon was also served the most stinking stage

Irene Mayer Selznick

dinner in the history of the theater. Each night he was supposed to eat a chicken dinner on stage. The food was supplied by the prop man. At each performance, according to Marlon, that chicken "got tougher and meaner." After curtain call one night, he told the prop man, "it was godawful—I'd rather eat dog shit."

On the night Gable showed up, the prop man served Marlon his stage dinner. When he lifted his napkin, he was in for a surprise. "It was the real thing," Marlon recalled. "All yellow, runny and smelly like a good dump by a dog should be. Not wanting to break character, I was for just a second tempted to take a bite just to show that shithead prop guy. But I quickly decided not to. The way I figured it, a paycheck of $550 a week just wasn't worth tasting a fork of shit."

Not telling Marlon what he thought of his performance, Gable graciously came backstage after curtain call and introduced himself to the actor and presented his starlet date for the evening. Someone had arranged a blind date for Gable, and later in the evening, he would seduce the attractive young woman, little knowing that one day her fame would eclipse his.

Gable told Marlon that if he looked like he did in the movies of the early Thirties that he could have played Stanley. "You didn't know that I once wanted to be a stage actor, did you?"

In front of Kim Hunter, Marlon confessed. "I'm sorry, Mr. Gable, but I'm not familiar with your career."

"Not even *Gone With the Wind*?" asked a startled Rhett Butler.

"Not even that," Marlon said, perhaps telling a lie.

He later told Kim, "I didn't want to inflate an already overinflated ego."

Gable invited Marlon to join him and his starlet for an after theater supper at Sardi's. Somewhat mesmerized by Gable in spite of his surface hostility, Marlon accepted.

"One day, kid, you're gonna draw more fan mail than I do," Gable predicted to Marlon in front of Kim. He paused as if to reflect for a moment. "Perhaps, I should say, more fan mail than I used to get. After I got back from the war, I found the gals don't write like they used to."

After dinner with Gable and his friend, Irene was the first to contact Marlon in the morning to find out what happened. He gave her few details, saying, "The King and I didn't have much in common."

Actually they had more in common than either man realized at the time. While making the original *Mutiny on the Bounty* in 1935, Gable had had a torrid affair with the Mexican actress, Movita, who was playing his Tahitian girlfriend in the movie, and who at the time was only a teenager. Gable, like Errol Flynn in later life, could have been charged with statutory rape. In the midst of the affair, Gable nicknamed Movita "Chili." He was amused by her hot

182

temper. Any time someone angered her, she said, "Go *feck* yourself." Unlike most other studs in Hollywood, Gable would often laugh at his own sexual inadequacies. He once told fellow *Mutiny* co-star, Franchot Tone, that when he did not satisfy Movita sexually, she'd scream at him: "Get off me, you son-of-a-beetch."

Marlon would take this same Movita for his second wife in 1960. In the autumn of the same year, Marlon would meet the underaged Tarita Tumi Teriipaia, who played his

Kim Hunter and Marlon in *Streetcar*

Tahitian girlfriend in his own version of *Mutiny on the Bounty*. Following in the footsteps of Gable with Movita, Marlon, too, launched an affair with this "jail bait" actress, who would become in time his third and final wife.

Gable and Marlon would surely have had more to say to each other if the King had known that "this new young upstart" would one day make his own version of *Mutiny on the Bounty*.

Gable had initially protested loudly against playing the role of Fletcher Christian "in knickers, pigtails, and a face as smooth as a baby's ass." Gable told Louis B. Mayer that he thought the character of Christian was actually a secret faggot. But Irving Thalberg insisted that he be cast in the role.

Gable played Christian Fletcher as unwaveringly masculine. But Marlon did the sissified version, beginning with his appearance with a red cape swirling around him, a true drawling fop. Gable surely would have been horrified at the remake of one of his most famous roles.

At some point during that evening at Sardi's, perhaps when Gable went to the men's room, Marlon turned his attention to the starlet, out on her first date with the King. Before Gable returned, Marlon must have worked fast, getting the brunette's phone number. When he arrived in Hollywood months later, he would take advantage of that number and call the actress.

Much later in life, he would confide to Edith Van Cleve. "Nancy was the First of the First Ladies I seduced."

He was referring to Gable's girlfriend, Nancy Davis, who eventually became better known as Nancy Reagan.

* * *

One night after a performance of *Streetcar*, Kim Hunter rapped on the door of Marlon's dressing room. She wanted to introduce him to Humphrey Bogart. Marlon at this point was getting used to visits by Hollywood royalty. In those days, movie stars haunted Broadway plays looking for hot new material.

At the time of his first meeting with Marlon, Bogie was in the process of raising money for a film adaptation of the new bestseller, *Knock on Any Door*, a novel by William Motley. It was the story of a juvenile delinquent portrayed as a victim of his own childhood.

Bogie arrived with two different missions, one concerning Marlon himself. The other focused on Kim. He was evaluating the actress as a future leading lady. Bogie told Kim, "This kid and I could become the hottest movie ticket since Fred Astaire danced off with Ginger Rogers."

Bogie tended to disguise his most serious intentions with facetious remarks. But, as Kim later remembered, "He definitely seemed interested in linking himself to Marlon. Old Hollywood teaming up with what potentially could be New Hollywood as represented by Marlon. Bogie also told me backstage that 'if you can't beat the competition, join them.'"

Marlon later recalled to Bobby Lewis details about his first encounter with Bogie. "The night he came backstage, I had nine pussies waiting in line to fuck me. That had become a regular occurrence every night. All I had to do was make my choice for the evening and apologize to the rest of the disappointed ladies. Then Bogie came backstage asking me to go with him to Sardi's. Now, how in hell could I turn down Bogie for a pussy? I had to put the hot twats in the deep freeze until the following night."

Marlon dined with Bogie at Sardi's, where they were frequently interrupted by rubber-necking autograph seekers. In his lisp, the veteran actor pitched to Marlon the role of Nick Romano in *Knock on Any Door* as his screen debut. "It's a great part!" Bogie assured him. "And with me in the lead, it'll be a box office smash. We can make beautiful music together."

Marlon later said that what intrigued him about the role was the credo as expressed by the character of Nick Romano. Nick's rule of life was, "Live fast, die young, and leave a good-looking corpse."

Marlon promised Bogie to read both the novel and an early version of the screen treatment. To solidify the deal, producer Mark Hellinger flew to New York for further talks with Marlon, telling the actor that "Bogie believes so much in this film that he's put up $25,000 of his own money, the exact amount that Irene posted for *Streetcar*."

Hellinger had Marlon more or less moving toward contract signing. But he died suddenly, and Marlon lost interest.

Humphrey Bogart

Before the role was recast, Bogie placed one final phone call to Marlon at the Ethel Barrymore. As always, but especially during the context of this call, Bogie was half serious, half tease. He said, "I understand that on every fourth night you like to fuck a guy in the ass instead of pumping every twat in the city. If you'll agree to play Nick, I'll turn over my own juicy rosebud to you for one night. But don't get your hopes up that this is going to be any permanent arrangement. One night—that's all, pal!"

The sound of Marlon's laughter traveled across the coast into Bogie's living room. "As tempting as that offer is," Marlon told Bogie, "I must still say no."

Before hanging up, Bogie said, "Too bad. I could have ordered the scriptwriters to put in a love scene or two between us." He made one final macho-chivalrous pitch, perhaps realizing at this point that Marlon would never change his mind. "I'll even let you fuck my wife as part of the deal," he blurted out.

"Not even that can tempt me, as lovely as she is," Marlon said. Flattering Bogie as a means of softening the rejection, he added, "After you, I would surely be a disappointment to Lauren Bacall."

When *Streetcar* was being filmed in Hollywood, Bogie slipped onto the set, hoping in vain to conceal his appearance. But he was discovered by the makeup artist, Phil Rhodes. "To what do we owe this honor?" Rhodes asked.

"I just wanted to get a peek at this hot-shot kid," Bogie said. "He was supposed to have made his screen debut with me in a serious drama—not all this decaying Southern magnolia slush conjured up in the faggoty mind of Tennessee Williams. One way or another, I got to see Brando act for the screen."

"What's the verdict?" Rhodes asked.

"This guy Brando—he'll be doing *Hamlet* when the rest of us are selling potatoes."

Later, in 1951, it was with a certain irony that Bogie found himself pitted against Brando for the best actor award on Oscar night. Marlon, of course, had been nominated for *A Streetcar Named Desire*, with Bogie weighing in for his performance in *The African Queen*. Up until the last minute, Bogie kept insisting to director Nicholas Ray and others, "Brando is going to win. I have a gut instinct for this thing."

But despite his premonitions, Bogie walked off with the Oscar. "That night Hollywood voted its heart and gave Bogie the Oscar he should have won in 1943 for *Casablanca*," costar Ingrid Bergman later said. "Just imagine giving Paul Lukas the Oscar for *Watch on the Rhine* when Bogie really deserved it for Rick. Hollywood!"

* * *

There was no more dramatic moment in *A Streetcar Named Desire* than when Marlon rushed onto the stage with blood gushing from his nose. Preceding that, he had a twenty-minute break before he was due to reappear on the stage. To keep his energy level high every night, he often boxed backstage with whatever man was available. On occasion, his sparring partner was his friend, Carlo Fiore. On another occasion, it might be Karl Malden.

"One night no one wanted to box with me," he told Fiore. "I saw this fireman standing around, doing nothing, so I asked him if he'd go a couple of rounds with me. He was a shy kid and somewhat reluctantly put on the gloves. We squared off, circling each other. All of a sudden, he winds up throwing a haymaker at me. I saw it coming, but it was too late. Next thing I know I was flying ass over heels into a pile of wooden crates. I saw stars and began bleeding from the nose like a stuck pig. In the dressing room I put some cold compresses on my beak but couldn't stop the bleeding."

Marlon later related that when he heard his cue, he appeared on stage. "I held my nose, but from the break in the bridge a regular geyser of blood shot about ten feet across the stage." He managed to get through his scene with a stunned Jessica Tandy. As the curtain went down, she came up to him. "You stupid ass!" she said. From the loss of blood, he fainted at her feet. She stepped over him and headed for her dressing room.

Stagehands rushed to Marlon's rescue. Even before the curtain went down, the stage manager had already summoned an ambulance to rush him to the hospital.

In a hospital bed, Marlon encountered a staff doctor whom he would later call "a sadist and a butcher." After putting Marlon through excruciating pain, the staff doctor set his nose badly. "That perfect face, those classic looks, would never be the same again," Tennessee would later lament.

Marlon recovered quickly and could have returned to the play if he had really wanted to. But he told Fiore, "It's become a fucking bore. I need a rest. Why not a hospital?"

A theatrically smart woman like Irene real-

Elia Kazan

186

Jack Palance

ized that audiences were flocking to see Marlon, not Jessica.

During his absence, she'd hired actor Jack Palance to replace Marlon. He'd flown in from Chicago where he was understudying Anthony Quinn, who at the time was playing Stanley Kowalski to packed crowds in the Windy City. Palance would soon become one of Hollywood's fiercest villains in films, menacing Joan Crawford, for example, in the 1952 film, *Sudden Fear*. Standing six feet, four inches, this former prize fighter and Air Force bomber pilot was, in the words of Kazan, "the most menacing, the most sinister, and the most frightening Stanley Kowalski ever to appear on the stage."

With box office receipts falling off, Irene made a visit to Marlon in the hospital. Hearing that she was on the way, he bribed a nurse to paint spots of iodine on his face to discolor it and to "wrap me up in other places like a mummy."

When Irene saw him, she screamed. Rushing to his side to comfort him, she said. "You poor, poor boy." Somewhat unconvincingly, she told him she'd allow him plenty of time to recover, even if it meant closing down the play.

When she'd gone, he was removing the bandages as Fiore arrived in his room for a visit. His friend helped him get rid of the unneeded gauze. That night, or so Marlon assured Fiore, he was going to "call one of my anonymous broads to come over. Right in this hospital bed, I'm going to fuck the shit out of her."

Once released from the hospital, Marlon seriously studied his new face. He told Fiore, "My face was too beautiful for theater-goers to take seriously. Now, my nose is no longer straight and narrow. It's slightly aquiline. I like my new nose. It gives my face character. From this point on, I can play character roles—not just be a pretty boy."

Anthony Quinn

Back at the theater, Irene was blunt. "You're just not as handsome as before. But all is not lost. I suggest that you have your nose rebroken, then set properly."

He refused such a suggestion.

"Then live with your Halloween face!" she angrily told him.

Only two weeks after his seven-day rest in

187

the hospital, Marlon took up boxing again. His sparing partner at Stillman's Gym was none other than Rocky Graziano, the former middleweight champion. Marlon told the champ that his nose had been recently broken, so Rocky was careful not to pound the actor's face.

The next afternoon as both men showered together, Rocky asked Marlon what he did for a living. "I'm appearing in this play on Broadway. It's called *A Streetcar Named Desire.*"

"What role do you play?" Rocky asked. "A conductor?"

"Something like that," Marlon said. He invited Rocky and his wife for the Saturday night performance. The next day Marlon arrived at the gym with two free passes for the best seats in the house.

That evening, when Marlon swaggered on stage as Stanley Kowalski, and Rocky realized for the first time that his sparring partner was a bigtime star, the boxer jumped to his feet. "That's him!" he shouted. Fellow members of the audience angrily told the champ to sit down and shut up.

The next morning when Rocky joined Marlon in the ring, he said, "I don't know if I want to box with you any more. I'll be holding back too much. After all, I don't want to fuck up the pretty face of a bigtime future movie star."

* * *

When she saw that ticket sales were gradually declining, Irene Selznick persuaded Marlon with his new nose to go on television to promote *Streetcar*. He only reluctantly agreed. She booked him for an appearance with Faye Emerson, "the first lady of television."

The buxom blonde actress and performer was married at that time to Elliott Roosevelt, the son of the late president, Franklin. Before rising to fame across the nation in the then-new medium of television, she had appeared on Broadway and as an actress in some two dozen lackluster Hollywood films. Bright and witty, she, nonetheless, had become famous on television for her *décolletage*. Behind her back, crew members on the show referred to her as "The Chest."

"Critical attention around the country, even national fame, came because of those God damn tits," Milton Berle once said. As "Mr. Television" himself, he seemed jealous that Faye was using her mammary charms to take some of the glory from the medium that he dominated at the time. Her son, William Crawford, would later tell the press, "When a cartoon showed a small TV screen containing only a V neckline, the reader knew it was dear old mom."

Throughout his entire first appearance on television with Faye, Marlon "all during the interview never once took his eyes off that monumental sight of Miss Emerson's cleavage," according to publicist Robert Condon. "Even

Faye Emerson

though Faye was noted for her poise under fire, she lost her cool that night. No matter where the TV camera moved, there was Marlon like a laser beam at the cleft just inches in front of his face."

"Is blonde the color of your real hair?" Marlon asked the astonished interviewer.

"Very frankly," she said, "I must tell the truth. My natural hair is brown. I tint it gold because blonde shows up better on TV."

"I think you sound sincere on your show," he said. "You don't put on airs. I don't like women who put on airs."

"I think glamour should be an integral part of a woman's personality," she said. "Not a superficial overlay."

"I agree with that," he said. "What I like is a woman with a high IQ in a low-cut gown. No dumb blondes for me."

"I'm glad you said that because most men are afraid of a woman with brains," she said.

"Women can be a lot smarter than men," he said. "I saw you on a show once with your husband. Elliott didn't recognize a quote from his own book on FDR. You did. You sure showed him up."

To that, Faye didn't respond but quickly changed the subject.

On the show, Marlon confided that he didn't expect to stick around with *Streetcar* when his contract ran out. "I don't want to disappoint Irene Selznick—one classy lady," he said. "But I've been suffering memory blackouts and forgetting my lines."

The ever-sharp Faye interjected, "Many actors in long-running Broadway shows go through the same afflictions."

"I feel it's time to move on," he said.

"What do you see coming in your future?" she asked. "A film career?"

"Oh, I just might make a movie," he said nonchalantly, breaking into what Bobby Lewis would later call a "shit-eating grin." "I'm sure Joan Crawford is in need of a new leading man," Marlon said. "She's already had John Garfield."

At that, Faye raised an eyebrow, noting that Marlon's comment could be taken two ways.

"Time for Crawford to turn to me and move on up in the world," he said.

After the show, Faye's chief rival in television, Arlene Francis, was waiting backstage to go on in another production. She later claimed that she overheard Marlon telling Faye: "Actually, I was just joking about making a film with Crawford. I hear she's just like Tallulah: insists that all her leading men fuck her!"

"Even though he'd brilliantly upstaged her," Arlene said, "Faye was obviously intrigued with Marlon. She invited him to join her for dinner. From what I heard the next day, Marlon became a weekend guest at her apartment. It was a good thing that Elliott was out of town."

Later Arlene said that "Faye's great success was merging sexuality with intellect. They called her both the 'Blonde Bombshell' and the 'Smartest Woman in Television,' depending on which newspaper editor was writing what headline. Of course, those commentators got it all wrong. I was the smartest woman on television. At least Faye was clever enough to walk off with Marlon when every woman in New York wanted a piece of the action. I envied her."

That Sunday night at a secluded inn on a riverbank in Connecticut, a sharp-eyed reporter spotted Faye arriving in a black, chauffeur-driven limousine. She emerged wearing an eggplant purple doeskin suit with mink accessories. As always, she was clad in her trademark alligator shoes. She signaled to someone in the back seat. The mystery guest remained in shadow and was driven away by the chauffeur.

Faye made a solo entrance into the main dining room. The manager of the inn grandly ushered her into a private dining room reserved for VIPs. Apparently, the mystery passenger made his entrance through the back door of the inn and was discreetly ushered into the same dining area where Faye was waiting. Members of the staff later said that the mystery passenger was none other than Marlon Brando himself.

The following week when Bobby Lewis encountered Marlon, he said, "I fucked the first daughter-in-law."

"I guess you mean the late president's daughter-in-law unless Harry Truman has a son stashed somewhere."

"As far as I'm concerned, FDR is still president," Marlon claimed. "Truman is just a caretaker carrying out Roosevelt's grand scheme."

"I see," Bobby said. "Faye Emerson. Not bad. How was it?"

"She gave me a rave review," he boasted. "She confessed to me that I went where no man has ever gone before and, most likely, will never go again."

The Poker Room evoking *Streetcar*

In spite of his mischievous performance with Faye Emerson, Condon prevailed on Marlon to make one other TV appearance, this time with Eve Hunter, a sort of clone of the former first daughter-in-law. Marlon agreed but only on one condition: that he be allowed to bring Wally Cox onto the show.

Condon later recalled that Marlon's second TV exposure was a disaster as well. "Wally sat with his legs crossed, his shoe pointing toward Marlon. The camera picked up Marlon as he leaned toward the shoe. 'Something smells awful!' Marlon told Wally in front of the TV audience and much to Hunter's horror. 'What do you think is on the bottom of your shoe that smells so bad?'"

With deadly seriousness, Wally looked at Marlon. "Don't know, Bud. What do you think it is?"

"I'd better get down on my knees and investigate," Marlon said.

"At this point, Hunter looked like she thought her show was going off the air," Condon said.

Kneeling before Wally, Marlon picked off the offending substance. "It's only chewing gum," Marlon proclaimed, beaming before the camera and holding up a wad of the sticky stuff.

Other friends came and went, but Marlon's relationship with Wally Cox survived not only that joint appearance on TV, but the "theft of every gal that Wally got interested in," according to Bobby Lewis. "If Wally liked some woman, Marlon always took her away from his buddy. How he found time to do that is still a mystery. He already had his steady stream of models, dancers, and aspiring actresses, even famous actresses. And those were just the females. God knows how many males, and not just Sandy Campbell, he fucked on the side."

Still a hawker of jewelry, Wally had begun to break into show business. His first gig came in December of 1948 at the Village Vanguard, a popular club on Bleeker Street in New York's Greenwich Village. Whenever Marlon wasn't needed on the stage as Stanley, he could be spotted in Wally's audience, laughing louder than anybody and applauding almost overly enthusiastically.

Since the night club had a late show, Marlon often showed up after performing earlier in the night in *Streetcar*. To anyone interested, and even to those not so interested, Marlon proclaimed, "Wally Cox is America's greatest comedian—you can forget about Jack Benny and Bob Hope."

Bob Condon never offered Marlon another interview on TV. But he did observe from behind the scenes when Marlon agreed to make *Come Out Fighting!*, a projected TV pilot, with him as the star. Filmed in a Brooklyn studio, Marlon played a boxer.

"He did a damn good job," Condon said. "But for some reason the series was not picked up. Marlon was furious at the rejection. At that time, his ego inflated by *Streetcar*, he thought that anything he did in front of the camera would be eagerly picked up by a major network, most definitely CBS or NBC."

"I saw him shortly after his last performance in *Streetcar*," Condon later said. "He told me that Irene had held out the offer of his appearing as Stanley Kowalski in the film version."

"There is no way that I'm going to do Stanley on screen," Marlon told him. "No way! I'm sick to death of Stanley Kowalski. Women I go to bed with want Stanley—not me."

"What will you do?" Condon asked. "Another stage play?"

"I don't think American audiences understand me," Marlon said. "I've had other offers from abroad. I'm off to Paris. I'm going to break into French films. Of course, I've got to work on my French a bit."

* * *

According to Phil Rhodes, a disturbing phone call to the theater brought out New York detectives who swarmed backstage. The stage manager reported to police that an anonymous caller warned that if "Tandy appears on the stage tonight, she'll be assassinated." Kazan was alerted and went to Tandy's dressing room to warn her of the call. "It's up to you?" he told her. "To perform tonight—or not." The consummate professional, Tandy opted to go before the lights and gave one of her more brilliant performances as Blanche, even though there were several detectives watching the audience. Nothing happened.

Karl Malden later said that he believed that Marlon, in a disguised voice, had made the death threat against Tandy. "Marlon especially loved it when he could pull off a prank in complete secrecy."

* * *

Nicholas Ray had directed Humphrey Bogart in the 1949 *Knock on Any Door*, casting John Derek in the part that both Ray and Bogie had wanted for Marlon. In spite of Marlon's original rejection, Ray still wanted to direct Marlon's screen debut.

Near Marlon's closing weeks in *Streetcar*, Ray arrived with yet another script for the actor's consideration. It was called *Rebel Without a Cause*.

The script had been created from a non-fiction work by Dr. Robert M.

Lindner, which had been published back in 1944. Ray was still struggling with the script, but thought there was enough on paper to interest Marlon into playing the reckless, rebellious, and misunderstood youth, Jim Stark. Ray was also aware that time was running out on a possible casting of Marlon. It seemed that as every month went by, Marlon was simply getting too old to play a teenager.

He agreed to study the script and was immensely intrigued with the character, especially the idea of street gangs. Irene Selznick would have been horrified to learn Marlon had taken to riding with a motorcycle gang in Brooklyn, known as "The Eagles," after his performance every evening in *Streetcar*. Unknown to him at the time, he was rehearsing for *The Wild One*.

The story is not completely clear as to how he was allowed to hook up with this tightly knit group of hoods. Fiore claimed that he had introduced Marlon to the gang leader, Tony Medina, who was skeptical at first about allowing Marlon to join in with his night-riding boys. However, when Marlon purchased for Medina the most expensive motorcycle in New York, the gang leader reluctantly consented. As it turned out, Marlon also became a steady supplier of young girls for members of the gang.

Ray was eager to learn all he could about gangs, and Marlon asked and won approval from Medina to allow the director to ride with The Eagles. Apparently, at no point was Medina informed that Ray was a film director and might one day film a movie involving street gangs. Later, in Hollywood, Ray would manage to hook himself up with a Los Angeles gang in his attempt to find inspiration for *Rebel Without a Cause*.

One night at a location in New York State, the exact spot not known, Ray witnessed an extraordinary test of daring. Two members of The Eagles raced their motorcycles toward a cliff in a game of "chicken." Both of the young men managed to brake in time, or else their bikes would have been plunged to the rocks below the cliff. Ray was so inspired by this scene that he later incor-

Nicholas Ray

porated it into *Rebel*, using cars instead of motorcycles.

Ray later said that Marlon, too, had wanted to play chicken that night, but that he had persuaded him not to. "It's too risky," he told Marlon. "If you do, there might be another Stanley Kowalski on the Broadway stage tomorrow night."

With script troubles mounting, *Rebel Without a Cause* simply did not go before the cameras in 1949, and it was not to become the vehicle for Marlon's screen debut. When the cameras rolled on *Rebel* preceding its release in 1955, it was James Dean who was cast in the star role of the rebellious youth. By then, Marlon was indeed far too old for the part. Ray later revealed, however, that after meeting Marlon he wrote what he perceived to be the actor's "personal character" into the role of Jim Stark in *Rebel*.

Carlo Fiore later remembered attending a screening of *Rebel Without a Cause* with Marlon in 1955. "Bud sat through the entire film with a stone face, not saying a word," Fiore said. "After the show, we drove to a drive-in hamburger joint, where Bud ordered two thick cheeseburgers with 'the works.' At this point he still hadn't told me what he thought of *Rebel*. Finally, the suspense was killing me. Losing my cool, I asked him, 'Well, what did you think of Dean? That kid is definitely living in your shadow.'"

"Marlon turned and looked at me like he didn't even know who James Dean was," Fiore recalled. "He didn't say anything at first. Finally, he turned to me and mumbled, 'I plan to fuck Natalie Wood. She's now the first on my list of possible conquests in Hollywood.'"

"You've already fucked Dean," Fiore chided him. "Why not Sal Mineo? I hear he's gay as a goose."

"Yeah, that Mineo boy might get lucky too."

"I hear that big tit Jayne Mansfield was originally tested for the role of Judy before it went to Wood. Have you had her yet? Or is she on your waiting list?"

"Mansfield is too blonde for me," Marlon said. "Besides I can have the real Marilyn anytime I want her. Why go for mock turtle soup when you can have the real turtle in the stew pot?"

"Good point," Fiore said. Nothing else was ever said between them about either James Dean or *Rebel Without a Cause*.

* * *

In spite of two turn-downs, Ray still pursued Marlon. In 1951, just as he was enjoying fabulous film success in *A Streetcar Named Desire*, Ray presented him with a two-page synopsis called *No Return*, a story of American gypsies.

From the very beginning, the director had only two stars in mind, Marlon Brando and Ava Gardner. He felt that each of them was a sensation. "Cast together they'll eat up the screen," he said. "Ava and Marlon are the two hottest properties in the business. Watch the screen catch fire!"

Ray managed to bring the two stars together at his home. He later said that he felt that neither one of them was particularly interested in playing gypsies on the screen. "I think they secretly wanted to meet each other, as both Ava

Ava Gardner

and Marlon were gorgeous sexual predators at the time, each in his or her own way the sex symbol of the Fifties."

"Marlon expressed some vague interest in *No Return*, although he warned me that there was too much focus on sex and violence," Ray said. "Instead of that, he said that the film should deal with the plight of the American gypsies and the abuse they have suffered in this country."

Ava's only response was, "I've always had the gypsy in my soul."

Instead of talking script, Ava and Marlon made sexually provocative comments to each other. Asked to recall exactly what the exchange was between the two super stars, Ray tried to reconstruct the spiciest of their dialogue.

AVA: Frank [a reference to Frank Sinatra] told me you were a real shit.

MARLON: Mickey Rooney told me you have big brown nipples. He also said that when aroused those nipples stand out like some double-long, golden California raisins. Is that true?

AVA: That's for me to know and you to find out later in the evening.

MARLON: At heart, are you still the li'l hillbilly Tarheel gal from North Carolina?

AVA: I'll always be that, honey chile. That's what attracts them, baby. Heaven knows, it's not my acting. Louis B. Mayer, that son of a bitch, once said of me: 'She can't act, she can't talk. She's terrific! Sign her!'

Ray remembered both Ava and Marlon disappearing into the Hollywood night together. "I just assumed they fucked each other's brains out before the rooster crowed. And neither agreed to commit to *No Return*."

Before *No Return* reached the screen, Ray made repeated calls to both Marlon and Ava, hoping to pitch the completed script to each of them personally instead of going through their agents. His calls were not returned.

No Return finally reached the screen in 1956. By that time, it had been more provocatively titled *Hot Blood*, and it starred another sex symbol, Jane Russell. Cornel Wilde, even though too old for the role, was more convincingly cast as the gypsy male star.

Eventually, Marlon saw *Hot Blood*, perhaps speculating what might have been if the film had starred Ava and him on the screen. His movie review to Fiore? "I thought Jane Russell and Wilde looked good in their costumes."

* * *

During the long run of *Streetcar*, Marlon was hailed by most critics as the most gifted actor of his generation. His interpretation of Stanley had changed how future actors would emote both on the stage and screen. Yet, long after leaving the role, he still doubted his interpretation of Stanley.

"I never nailed down the character of Stanley Kowalski," Marlon later said. "I am overly sensitive to the pain of others. Stanley never understood the pain of others, their emotional torments. That was especially true in the way he treated Blanche. I played him as big and lusty, a man who devoured blood-red steaks before eating pussy at night. But I never cracked below his surface. I never really understood what made Stanley Kowalski tick."

A Streetcar Named Desire ran for 855 performances, winning the Pulitzer Prize. The play moved Tennessee Williams to the foreground as the leading playwright of his day. It made a star of Marlon, and propelled Kazan into the top echelon of directors.

For all purposes, Marlon's appearance in *Streetcar* was his *adieu* to the stage, as reported in so many biographies. Actually in 1953 he would appear unspectacularly in a summer stock production of George Bernard Shaw's *Arms and the Man*. He toured with the play briefly, appearing as Sergius Saranoff at such theaters as the Falmouth Playhouse in Coonamesset, Massachusetts.

After this run, he would never appear on the stage again, telling a reporter in Ivoryton, Connecticut, "It wasn't that I disliked the experience. I hated it! I almost went out of my mind."

* * *

The ever-faithful, devoted, and loyal Shelley Winters continued her affair with Marlon throughout the rehearsals for *Streetcar* and even after opening night, although the competition for Marlon *après*-performance was far greater than she at first knew.

She proclaimed, "There was an electrical charge and almost an animal scent he projected over the footlights that made it impossible for the audience to think or watch the other performers on the stage. All you could do was feel, the sexual arousal was so complete. I don't believe that quality can be learned:

it's just there, primitive and compelling. The only time I experienced a similar reaction was when I saw Elvis Presley perform in Las Vegas."

Even though Shelley openly was aware that Marlon "flashed across the stage like sexual lightning," she could not believe "another extraordinary reputation" about him.

"That reputation was that he seduced everything on the hoof," Kazan said. "Both the stallion and the mare."

Shelley later claimed that "I figured the reputation couldn't be true because when did he have the time?"

Marlon agreed to let her sit in on his rehearsals for *Streetcar*, because she felt that "something big was about to happen on Broadway, and I wanted to be there learning everything I could." Often she became so mesmerized while watching Marlon as Stanley that she sometimes arrived backstage at *Oklahoma!* with only minutes to spare before she herself was due to go on stage. The stage manager docked her one dollar for every minute she was late.

Marlon had warned her to disguise herself, so that she wouldn't be spotted and ejected from the theater by Kazan. Shelley wanted to see Marlon act but also wanted to watch Kazan direct.

Slipping into the back of the theater, she covered her blonde hair with a dark scarf and wore an old black coat that made her look like an Apple Annie bagwoman. To conceal herself further, she sat behind a post in the auditorium. From that vantage point she couldn't actually hear Kazan's words to Marlon, because "Gadge," as she called him, spoke in a very soft voice to his actors, unlike another director, Otto Preminger, who always shouted at them.

Day by day she inched forward to hear more of the exchange taking place between Marlon and Kazan. One afternoon Kazan turned and looked at her. "If you're going to hang around the theater, you can at least go out for coffee for us, and let the stage manager stay on the book." She became the "gofer" during rehearsals, and Kazan, having found some useful purpose for her, let her stay.

She later wrote: "Marlon mumbled and stumbled around, and the other actors fluffed; then he would suddenly spark fire for himself and the others, and you could hear him clearly and articulately in the last row of the balcony. Gadge would rehearse one scene all day, and it seemed painful and agonizing. Then they would have a run-through of the scene at five or six o'clock, and the acting

Shelley Winters

197

would lift me from my seat. I knew I was watching theater history being made."

Shelley's hunch was right. Unable to attend the opening night of *Streetcar* because of her own stage appearance, she read the reviews over "two containers of coffee" the following morning. One male critic seemed to have developed a crush on Marlon. He wrote, "There has never been—nor will there ever be again—a performance like the one Marlon Brando gave last night."

Shelley agreed with only part of the statement. She later told Lee Strasberg, "But Marlon, as wonderful as he is, isn't the Second Coming. How can that guy say there will never again be a performance like Marlon gave last night? Maybe some time in the future Marlon III will rise up from the masses and dazzle the world." Later in life, however, she told a class at Actors Studio, "Maybe that critic was right. So far, no one has come along to equal Brando's performance. All we've had so far are clones—and bad ones at that."

Finally, Shelley got to see the actual play as performed on Broadway, not just a rehearsal, when she attended a benefit performance on Thursday when she herself didn't have to appear on stage. Marlon ordered that a ticket be set aside for her at the box office. The stage manager of *Streetcar* whispered to her that if she wished, she could get one-hundred dollars for that ticket. She turned down the money, even though in 1947 one-hundred dollars was worth five-hundred in today's coinage.

Backstage she encountered Marlon who was then inhabiting a big chorus dressing room on the third floor. Completely littered and cluttered, it contained a cot (at the time she thought it was for catnaps), blankets, and several barbells and weights.

There was a dressing table in the room as well. In front of her, Marlon stripped to the skin and headed for the shower, as he was sweat-drenched as the curtain fell. Taking advantage of his absence, she examined the objects on the dressing table, first picking up a Charles Atlas instruction book with tips on weightlifting.

What amazed her, as she'd later recall, were at least a hundred pieces of paper. On these sheets were written the names of various women, along with their addresses and telephone numbers. Some of the star-struck women, often girls, had left pictures of themselves in the nude. There was a collection of hotel keys from such places as the Waldorf Towers and the Plaza. She was shocked at the number of famous female stars who had left keys.

Emerging from the shower, Marlon caught her going through his papers. "Bud, what in the hell are you doing? Preparing for a play where you're a burglar?"

It was then that Marlon confessed that "every famous woman in films, theater, and café society who sees the play comes backstage to congratulate me and 'accidentally' leaves her key on my dressing table." He admitted that he'd already taken advantage of dozens of keys.

She was flabbergasted. "While you're performing this exhausting play eight times a week?"

"It's true: I'm exhausted but I'm doing my best. Some of them are knock-outs. And who knows? It's the kind of research I might need sometime when I'm playing the role of a roaming Lothario with a gleam in his eye, a part very different from Stanley Kowalski."

Faced with all those keys on the dressing table, Shelley that night decided to end her sexual relationship with Marlon, although it would be resumed later in Hollywood.

Later that night, over an inexpensive dinner in a cheap eatery operated by refugees from Hong Kong, he rushed to down his chop suey, claiming that he needed to get some sleep. She suspected that he was telling a lie and would soon be racing off to take advantage of one of those keys.

A normally outspoken woman, Shelley in her memoirs did not reveal that among the notes and propositions left behind were the names and contacts for an array of A-list actresses, many of them Oscar winners and among the most photographed and famous faces on the planet.

Although Shelley did not name these actresses, Marlon's agent, Edith Van Cleve, a friend of the author's, later recalled "every delicious tidbit."

Unknown to Marlon, Edith was also the best female friend of Tallulah Bankhead's. When Tallulah got up every morning and, over her first cup of black coffee and the first of the day's cigarettes, she called Edith for the latest report on "Brando's nocturnal adventures."

"What was the little fucker up to last night?" she always asked Edith, taking delight in hearing the latest report of the star Marlon was seducing now.

It is because of these two gossipy friends that some of Marlon's more notable sexual conquests were later revealed.

"There has never been a story of such famous women being serially seduced in the American theater," Kazan said. "I saw it unfolding before my eyes, and even I couldn't believe it. Surely, John Barrymore at the height of his virility and beauty, and wearing those revealing green tights, didn't seduce as many famous women as our Marlon Brando."

When journalist Joe Hyams, tried to compile a list of all the women Marlon had seduced, he gave up, claiming, "It takes a statistician rather than reporter."

Film critic David Thomson put it this way: "Many of the women seem reconciled to his infidelity. They may not even see it as something worthy of blame, or guilt. He is less fickle than mobile—the way of sperm, after all. He is entirely candid about the extent of his sexual appetite, and about his reluctance to settle. We do not have to agree that he is exceptional at sex; instead, he is unusual in that he pursues sex for its own sake, and is not often drawn into claims of love and eternity—the rhetoric that impedes so many of us. So lovers accept that they will be dropped and then reclaimed, depending on where he is, his mood, the chance of meeting. Never in love, he is never out of love. Liking sex with this woman, and that one, he is ready to repeat the experience. So in many cases women become fixtures in his life, only briefly in high fashion but never forgotten."

In spite of all the women parading through his life, Kazan startled Marlon by reminding him that "you are more dependent on your ties to men."

During the run of *Streetcar*, Marlon's sister, Fran, was quoted as saying: "Everybody wanted a piece of my brother, especially some of the leading female stars of the Golden Age."

Elia Kazan was blunt: "During the months he appeared under my direction as Stanley Kowalski, Marlon was a fuck machine. He became a phallic dream for both gay men and thousands of female theater-goers. Later he would become the wet dream for millions of film fans around the world. He was, in essence, the male sex symbol of the Fifties, with Marilyn Monroe wearing the crown for women. My greatest regret as a director is that I didn't have a chance to star both Marlon and Marilyn—the two Ms—in the same film.

After the opening night of *Streetcar*, the parade of famous actresses, most often from the film world, became a never-ending stream heading backstage. Ostensibly many of these stars expressed an interest in playing Blanche DuBois on the screen. However, many women who came to call were completely unsuitable for *Streetcar*.

"They came backstage for one reason only, and that reason was to fuck Stanley Kowalski," Kazan said.

Chapter Seven

Leading the parade backstage after a performance of *A Streetcar Named Desire* was the glamorous film star, Paulette Goddard. At one time she might have been married to Charlie Chaplin. Then again she might not have been.

This former Ziegfeld Girl, former Goldwyn Girl, intrigued Marlon for two reasons: she was brunette and attractive, of course, but he was mesmerized by the fact that Chaplin had been her Svengali. Upon meeting her, he told her, "Only for Charlie Chaplin would I consider appearing in film."

Regrettably, he would get his chance in the 1967 *A Countess from Hong Kong*, in which The Little Tramp would—disastrously—attempt to direct Marlon. Chaplin had been carrying around an idea for the script since the early 1930s, having originally intended to award star billing to his lover, Paulette, and to Gary Cooper. Eventually, long after passions had cooled between Chaplin and Goddard, the leading roles went to Marlon and Sophia Loren.

Perhaps from their first hour together, Paulette realized that Marlon was not her kind of man. He invited her out for supper. Instead of taking her to Sardi's, he took her to an all-night cafeteria near Times Square. Covered in jewelry and elegantly dressed, she attracted unwanted attention from the "dregs of the world," as she'd later describe the other patrons.

He told her, "Any old cheap cafe will do for me. I don't need to go to a fashionable night club or elegant supper club for food. In fact, I despise such places." He was saying that to a woman who'd spent most of her adult life at fashionable places. He attacked people who felt compelled to eat pheasant under glass, calling such ostentation "an affectation, an overindulgence, like decadent Romans who would kill an entire colony of pink flamingos to consume their tongues in a casserole."

Before the end of the evening, he told her that he'd never be seen driving around in a Mercedes-Benz or Rolls-Royce. "You can count me out, too, as a future buyer of one of those combination washing machines, iceboxes, and TV sets."

It is not clear at what point in the evening Paulette discovered that her rhinestone-studded purse, containing $65,000 worth of jewelry, was missing. In the excitement of meeting Marlon, she feared that she'd left it in his dress-

Paulette Goddard

ing room. In those days, Paulette was known for changing her jewelry two or three times in an evening. She always carried plenty of "spare gems" in her handbag.

Racing back to the Ethel Barrymore Theatre in a taxi with her, Marlon encountered a stagehand, who was closing down the house for the night.

Paulette rushed into Marlon's dressing room to discover that her purse was not there. She confronted the stagehand, demanding to know if he'd seen anybody come out of the dressing room after they'd left the theater.

"Just Igor Tamarin," the stagehand said.

She turned to Marlon, demanding to know who this Igor was.

"Oh, he often dances on tables," he told her. "Sometimes he appears nude or semi-nude at parties in the Village. He likes to impersonate Nijinsky."

Marlon claimed that he kept Igor in his dressing room to play soothing gypsy music to him before he went on stage as Stanley. "He's also my boxing partner, my wrestling mate, and my fencing instructor. When not doing any of the above, we play chess. He teaches me the finer points of the game."

"All very interesting," Paulette said sarcastically. "But is he a thief?"

"I wouldn't call Igor a thief," he said. "Perhaps sticky fingers would be a more apt description."

When Karl Malden shared a dressing room with Marlon, he was missing a silver cigarette case which he used on stage in an important scene every night opposite Jessica Tandy. He never recovered it. His suspicion centered on Igor.

One night Karl, pretending sleep, caught Igor rummaging through Marlon's pockets. Later Marlon admitted to Karl that Igor had indeed taken his cigarette case. "I've been trying to help my friend change his thieving ways," Marlon said, growing angry. "You're not helping Igor by embarrassing him by catching him red-handed."

After they left the theater, and in the early hours of the morning, Marlon managed to soothe the distraught Paulette. "My body heat and my hands—not to mention everything else—brought Miss Goddard some comfort in the night," he confided to Edith Van Cleve the next morning.

Waking up at eleven o'clock, he presented Paulette with her missing purse and the purloined jewelry, offering no explanation as to how the stolen objects had been found, much less delivered to her hotel room while she slept. She wanted explanations. He was mysterious. "Last night," he told her, "I shared my jewels with you. You tell me: which set of jewels do you appreciate the most, mine or those in that stupid beaded bag?"

Paulette's answer was never recorded for posterity.

* * *

When Wendy Barrie, the British actress of the 1930s, came backstage to meet Marlon, he was already familiar with her work, having seen her in Alexander Korda's *The Private Life of Henry VIII*, in which she'd played Royal Wife No. 3, Jane Seymour. He even knew that Wendy's godfather and future stage-namesake was none other than J.M. Barrie, the Scottish novelist and playwright. In his *Peter Pan*, there is a character called "Wendy."

None of these credentials particularly intrigued Marlon. He was more fascinated by her role as the girlfriend of the notorious gangster Benjamin Siegel, known as "Bugsy," a name he hated. He was reported to have killed three men who called him Bugsy to his face. Known as a lady killer, Bugsy was also called the handsomest gangster who ever lived. At the time Wendy came backstage to meet Marlon, Bugsy had recently been murdered. A notorious nymphomaniac, Wendy during her affair with Bugsy had to keep her libido under control. Men who showed her too much attention were fitted with cement shoes.

Having been born in Hong Kong in 1912, Wendy was twelve years older than Marlon at the time of their first meeting, but she was well preserved and exceptionally attractive.

In his dressing room, Wendy invited Marlon for a midnight supper in her suite at the Plaza Hotel. He gladly accepted.

As he'd relate in the morning to Edith Van Cleve, he peppered Wendy with questions about Bugsy, so many inquiries, in fact, that she grew impatient with him. She preferred that Marlon's attention be focused on her. She asked him, "Would you have preferred to go to bed with Benny instead of me?"

Marlon was enigmatic in his response. "He was one good-looking man, and I was told that he could go all night. Of course, you'd know more about that than I would. I'm sorry I didn't get to meet him before he was gunned down. I would have liked to have learned his sexual secret. If I could go all

Wendy Barrie in *The Private Life of Henry VIII*

203

night, I could get around to servicing more women lined up to meet me backstage. After my cannon has shot for the third time in a night, I'm usually so pooped I want sleep instead of more nooky."

He didn't sense her growing impatience with Bugsy questions but asked another one. "I thought all gangsters were Italian. My friend, Carlo Fiore, told me Bugsy was Jewish. Not only that, but that his middle name was Hymen."

"You're right on both counts," she said.

"My mother's name was Dodie. I wished she'd named me Marlon Hymen Brando. A cute name, for sure."

Benjamin "Bugsy" Siegel

Apparently, at some point in the evening the suave and sophisticated Wendy realized that the key to seducing Marlon lay in plying him with Bugsy stories. Bright and talkative, she had enough Bugsy tales to fill a large book, the size of one of the calzones so beloved by her late boyfriend.

So instead of discussing her favorite subject, which was herself, Wendy told Marlon little known Bugsy secrets. One was that Bugsy had discovered the obscure town of Las Vegas one scalding hot afternoon when he ordered his driver to stop the car. "While Bugsy was airing that big thing of his in the desert air, taking a long overdue piss, he got the divine inspiration to launch Vegas as the gambling mecca of the West."

"Benny," she said, "always felt that you could clear up almost any problem with a homicide. The boys in the mob called him 'the cowboy.'"

"Why cowboy?" Marlon asked.

"In the mob, a cowboy is a man who doesn't just set up a murder. He's the one who kills the victim himself instead of hiring someone else to do it."

"I see."

She enthralled him with Bugsy-in-Hollywood stories. "It's true," she said. "He was a total psychopath but what a charming one. He could charm the bloomers off anyone." She related the details of Bugsy's affair with the blonde bombshell of the Thirties, Jean Harlow, She also claimed that his best pals in Hollywood were actors George Raft, Clark Gable, and Gary Cooper. "Benny would round up the most beautiful gals in Hollywood and Vegas for his pals to seduce. He was a bit of a voyeur. Gable, Cooper, and Raft could fuck the cream of the crop, but Bugsy wanted to watch. He would sit at the foot of the bed and oversee all the action."

"Sounds a bit homosexual to me."

"I think he had a streak of that," she said. "Had you mentioned that to him, he would have shot you in cold blood. Cary Grant was one of his best friends. He always told me that he let Grant swallow his big cock any time he wanted, but that he never reciprocated."

"I've met Cary Grant," Marlon said. "I bet I could get him to suck my cock too."

Looking him up and down, Wendy asked him to remove his shirt. "I bet you could at that."

She told him that in addition to many random girlfriends, Bugsy had three other full-time mistresses. The Countess Dorothy diFrasso, Marie ("The Body") MacDonald, and "the cunty bitch," Virginia Hill.

"One time Benny registered all four of us at suites in the Flamingo in Vegas. When Hill ran into me in the lobby, she struck me so hard in the jaw that it became dislocated. I had to be taken to the hospital."

Wendy claimed that the blonde beauty, Marie, was relatively harmless but that Countess diFrasso, fresh from a broken romance with Gary Cooper, was serious competition. Holding Marlon transfixed, Wendy told of how the countess had taken Bugsy to Rome to peddle a revolutionary explosive device to Benito Mussolini, but that the invention fizzled out before Il Duce's eyes.

On that same trip, as related by Wendy, Bugsy, "the wild little Jew boy from the Lower East Side, was invited to join her at her country estate for a weekend. Once there, she introduced Bugsy to her fellow houseguests, Hermann Goering and Joseph Goebbels. Benny took such a dislike to Hitler's

Raw animal magnetism

two henchmen that he planned to assassinate them on the spot. DiFrasso finally talked him out of that."

The character that Marlon would later develop (the starring role in *The Godfather)* was created on the night Wendy plied him with Bugsy stories, claiming that her former lover had been guilty of hijacking, mayhem, narcotics trafficking, bootlegging, rape, burglary, bookmaking, robbery, the numbers racket, extortion, and "countless murders."

"It was Bugsy's role as a white slaver that intrigued me the most," Marlon told his agent, Edith, the following morning. "Bugsy, or so Wendy claimed, took orders from all over the world for only the most desirable women. This oil-rich sheik, for example, would want a gal who looked like Betty Grable. Bugsy would then have such a girl kidnapped and transported abroad, perhaps to Saudi Arabia. She'd end up in some harem never to be seen again. That really intrigues me. As I told you before, I always wanted my own harem. But if you're getting me only five-hundred dollars a week for *Streetcar*, it'll never happen. Not until you get me deals one day where I'll make millions."

Even though Virginia Hill—the sharp-tongued Georgia peach that Bugsy nicknamed "Flamingo"—was Wendy's rival in love, Wendy made her sound fascinating to Marlon. He learned that while in jail in Los Angeles, Bugsy was granted passes for conjugal visits with both Virginia and Wendy.

Behind closed doors, as Marlon learned, Virginia told members of the Kefauver Senate Commission in Washington that "mobsters think so highly of me because of my unmatched talent for blow-jobs."

Wendy believed that Virginia Hill knew some of the advance details of Bugsy's upcoming assassination which took place in her $500,000 Los Angeles mansion, a home that had once belonged to Rudolph Valentino.

At the time of his death, Bugsy was reading an unfavorable article about himself in *The Los Angeles Times*. Hill was not in California at the time, having flown to Europe to deposit mob money in a Swiss bank account. Two steel-jacketed assassins tore through a window and smashed Bugsy's face with the butt of an army rifle. One crashed through the bridge of his nose and tore into his left eye. The other blow pulverized his right cheekbone, sending bone fragments through the back of his neck, shattering a vertebra. The police later found his right eye fifteen feet away from the body.

"I think all this mob era stuff ended with Bugsy's death," Marlon told Wendy. "But I admire this Virginia Hill. She was the only one with enough spit, sass, and guts to stand up to guys like Al Capone, Joe Adonis, and even Bugsy himself."

Marlon's fascination with the image of Virginia Hill continued for years. Once on a trip to Europe, he hired private detectives to try to locate her cottage in the Alps, where she'd apparently settled. In the late Fifties, he'd heard that she was broke and was fleeing from both the mob and the Internal Revenue Service. The detectives were unable to locate her. In 1961 Marlon learned that she'd swallowed a bottle of sleeping pills and had gone out into a Swiss snow bank "for the big sleep."

He received the news with sadness. On the set of *The Fugitive Kind*, he told Tennessee, "I've been blown by some of the most skilled fellatio artists in the world, including yourself. But I'll always regret not getting a blow-job directly from Virginia Hill. From all reports, she was the best of the best."

Once Wendy started talking that night in her suite, it was hard to shut her up. It was her "gift of gab" that would soon lead to casting her on The Wendy Barrie Show, one of television's first talk shows which would make her the

206

Virginia Hill

rival of Faye Emerson, Marlon's recent conquest.

Later he would boast to Carlo Fiore, "There was only one way that I could shut Wendy up—and that was to stick my cock down her throat."

Until they drifted apart, Marlon continued to see Wendy on and off for a number of years, the way he did with a lot of his women.

Perhaps inspired by her depiction of Bugsy, he became obsessed at one point in the early Fifties of making a gangster picture.

He went so far as to have a Los Angeles tailor design "pimp gear" for him to wear in a gangster movie that was never made. Evocative of Al Capone, Marlon appeared in a banana yellow suit with shocking pink hosiery and alligator shoes dyed scarlet red. His wide-brimmed hat was dyed a flamboyant chartreuse.

Dropping the Capone dress, he decided to appear in his first gangster movie as Bugsy in dapper dress like George Raft. He'd seen all the Raft films and those of Edward G. Robinson. Because Bugsy was handsome, and Marlon was handsome, he wanted to make the life story of Bugsy Siegel. That dubious honor would go to Warren Beatty in 1991, who appeared in a highly fictionalized account of the gangster's life.

By then, Marlon had made a comeback playing a very different type of gangster. However, the character of Moe Green in *The Godfather* would be a rip-off of Bugsy's notorious life.

It was with a certain sadness that Marlon learned in the 60s that Wendy had had a stroke and that this once vibrant and talkative woman was mentally incapacitated.

* * *

Marlon later confided to Carlo Fiore that he'd fallen in love with the blonde sex symbol of World War II, Veronica Lake and her peek-a-boo bang, when he'd seen her emote in the 1941 *I Wanted Wings* with Ray Milland and William Holden.

On meeting her for the first time backstage after a performance of *Streetcar*, he was somewhat disappointed to see that she'd changed her hair style, eliminating her most striking feature which was what had attracted him

Veronica Lake

to her in the first place. The War Department had requested that she get rid of the peek-a-boo bang because too many women working in defense plants had imitated her hair style, getting their low-hanging bangs caught—sometimes tragically—in machinery on assembly lines. Like the Biblical Samson, the cutting of her hair diminished Veronica's standing at the box office. Her popularity was on the wane the night she met Marlon, her fame forever rooted in the war years of the 1940s.

Unlike many other actresses who came backstage to meet Marlon, pretending they were interested in playing Blanche DuBois, Veronica actually wanted the part. She was smart enough to know that she had little chance of being cast in the film version, but wanted to take the play on the road, appearing in playhouses from Kansas to Minnesota.

Although the idea of casting Veronica as Blanche DuBois may have appeared absurd to some, the papers of Irene Selznick later revealed that she had seriously considered casting Veronica in the film version. However, after giving it some consideration, Irene scratched Veronica off her list, favoring at one point Miriam Hopkins or Bette Davis instead.

Ironically, in the late 1960s, her film career but a memory, Veronica would play Blanche DuBois in England, cast opposite the muscled hunk, Ty Hardin as Stanley. It was not one of the more memorable productions of *Streetcar*.

Tennessee later told Marlon that he'd seen Veronica in the play. "She and that religious but good-looking freak Ty Hardin ruined my play. I don't think I'll ever allow it to be revived again. After seeing you and Vivien on the screen, I know now that there can never be another Blanche and Stanley to live in my memory. Your images are etched in my brain. Every other actor who follows in your footsteps will be a pale imitation."

"The night Marlon met peek-a-boo, he met his match," claimed Carlo Fiore. "One crazy meeting another crazy. I was with them on a few of their binges. That hot tamale was far more off her rocker than old Bud himself."

Kazan later claimed that the Brando/Lake affair "lasted for ten nights—if that. Most of the actresses who came backstage to fuck Marlon got only a one-night stand. But in Lake, Marlon found a female companion that he could take to those sex-and-booze orgies he still liked to attend in Greenwich Village. Marlon, of course, would go only for the sex—not the booze. Veronica liked both sex and booze—and plenty of both."

208

Veronica's reputation had already preceded her before she went backstage to meet Marlon. She didn't need to attend orgies in Greenwich Village for kicks. Back in the Hollywood of the Forties, she'd become notorious for her sex-and-booze parties.

She had another reputation as well. She was known to prefer heavily endowed men and had bedded some of the leading studs of her day, including such heavy hung players as Howard Hughes, Milton Berle, Gary Cooper, and the Dominican playboy, Porfirio Rubirosa.

"Maybe Bud didn't stack up so well against those other players," Fiore speculated. "That might explain how they quickly switched from bedding each other to bedding the cream of the crop at one of those orgies. I went twice to the Village with the new duo, and both Veronica and Bud were clearly the stars of the festivities. As for me, I took whatever decent leftover came my way."

After the first night, Marlon had taken to calling Veronica "Ronni," and she was seen riding behind him on his motorcycle as he made his way through the streets of New York.

"They were two kindred spirits," Fiore claimed. "She made sexual conquests as freely as he did."

One night at a party, Fiore heard her tell Marlon that when she was horny, she drove through the streets of Los Angeles at night on a stud search. "When I spotted a hot number, I'd pull up to the curb. 'Hi, I'm Veronica Lake,' I would tell them. 'Get in if you'd like to fuck a movie star. I'll let you play with my peek-a-boo if you let me play with yours.'"

From Veronica, Marlon learned a new breakfast menu: Coca-Cola mixed with milk. According to Carlo, "For about six very long weeks, Marlon insisted on sharing this drink with me. I preferred Scotch. Veronica also taught him that the best breakfast in the world was a cold slice of pizza resting in the refrigerator from the night before. When I told my own mamma mia about this, she threw up her hands in Italian despair."

At one orgy in the Village, Veronica witnessed homosexual activity occurring between two young men in the corner. She confided in Marlon that she found such sexual practices "revolting." He lectured her on tolerance, but it would take years for her to come around to his more enlightened point of view.

In the 1960s, her viewpoint about gays completely changed. She became known as "the Fag Hag of Miami." At that low point in her life, she socialized only with gay men—"and played a wicked game of pool with them indeed."

One afternoon Marlon escorted Veronica to the reading of a new play at Actors Studio. The star was Monty Clift doing a solo. At the end of the reading, Veronica walked up to Monty to be introduced by Marlon. At first, he seemed only vaguely aware of who she was. "You read that play like a fag with a hernia," she told him.

Looking startled for a moment, he shouted back at her. "You fucking Hollywood has-been. Let's face it, bitch, you're washed up. My career's just beginning. You're history. A footnote I might add." He angrily stormed off the stage.

"Now, now," Marlon cautioned her. "We'll have to learn to be more diplomatic around sensitive actors. Monty has enough troubles as it is."

"No one was sensitive to me in Hollywood," she said. "Everybody treated me like shit. You'll go there one day—sooner than later—and I'm sure they'll treat you like shit too if you let them."

"That will never happen," he assured her.

She advised that when he did go to Hollywood, he should become a rebel. "Don't let the bastards tell you what to do. You set your own rules. When you become the big star I think you'll become, they'll be forced to listen to you, especially when they count those box office receipts. Instead of you having to kiss their asses, they'll be lining up to eat your dingleberries."

Aggressively smoking a cigarette in a lawn chair in her backyard in Miami in the 1950s, Veronica reflected on Marlon. "I think he took my advice," she claimed. "But, even so, Marlon and I were never meant to be movie stars. I knew if I stayed on, the rat race would have killed me like it did my frequent co-star, Alan Ladd. In addition to alcohol, he was also battling his repressed homosexuality. Marlon was stronger than Alan or me. He told Hollywood to go fuck itself, and made the bastards take it."

Marlon sensed a dreadful loneliness in her. One night she told him that she was feeling blue and had gone to the phone to call someone. "I just sat there with no one to call, not a single, living, breathing soul. I ended up calling a liquor store to deliver me some more booze. At least I got to hear a human voice and got to see a living being at my door, if only a delivery boy."

As she related, he took her to Fire Island one day where both of them sat for hours, watching the sea in silence. Finally, she spoke, telling him that in the future she always wanted to live in a place by the sea. "I can sit for hours just listening to the sound the ocean waves make. More than anything on God's green earth, the sea gives me peace. Unlike us, it's eternal. On some very bad days, I imagine that I'm going to go to the sea where I'll just strip off my clothes and walk into it, letting it wash me away to a better universe."

That night over dinner on a terraced Fire Island restaurant opening onto the sea, she confided in him that her greatest ambition one day was to write *The Veronica Lake Cookbook*. "There will be nothing like it on the market. All the recipes will be easy to whip up—you know, when you come home exhausted or else too God damn drunk to fix yourself a decent meal."

He agreed with her that the book would be a good idea and urged her to write it. "I'll buy the first copy," he promised.

Back in New York, he kissed her good-bye for the final time. "I knew it was to be the last kiss," she said, recalling the affair years later in a Miami bar. "It was time for both of us to move on. Our romance was short but sweet. He was on the dawn of a brilliant film career, and I was in the twilight of one. Of course, my career could never compare with his, although Alan and I had a few good moments on the screen. At least we took millions of American minds off the dreaded war for an hour and a half every night."

"Victor Mature was the best performer I ever encountered in bed," she said. "And God knows, he had the equipment. Aristotle Onassis, of all people, gave me the most orgasms in a single night. But of them all, Marlon was the most sincere. When he was on top of you, looking deeply into your eyes with that poetic face he had, he convinced you, at least for a moment, that you were the most important woman in the world."

Years later, when Marlon read in the papers that a newspaper reporter had found Veronica working as a cocktail waitress in a Manhattan bar, he instructed his accountant to send her a check for a thousand dollars. Out of pride, she never cashed it, but kept it framed in her Miami living room to show her gay friends.

Facing death in 1973, Veronica Lake had long ago been diagnosed as a classic schizophrenic.

* * *

Anne Baxter came backstage to meet Marlon, and not because she wanted to join the parade of aging actresses seeking to portray Blanche DuBois on the screen.

Only a year older than Marlon, Anne wanted the juicy role of Stella when the film was made. The idea wasn't far-fetched. Months later, in one of the casting notes that went to Jack Warner's office, producer Charles K. Feldman proposed Olivia de Havilland as Blanche DuBois and Anne Baxter as Stella. The Indiana-born granddaughter of architect Frank Lloyd Wright had already won an Oscar as best supporting actress in *The Razor's Edge* in 1946 in which she beat out such veterans as Ethel Barrymore and Lillian Gish.

As they talked backstage, Marlon ignored all the other well-wishers, including "a gaggle of gals," waiting to see him. He told Anne that he admired the way she worked with Orson Welles, director of the 1942 *The Magnificent Ambersons.*

She laughed at the ordeal she'd suffered through with the director while filming this movie. "After devouring eight of Joseph Cotton's Machiavellian

Anne Baxter

martinis, he sent his chauffeur on his way and begged me to drive him home, all 250 pounds of him. En route, I felt six hands up my skirt. He kept repeating, 'Oh, the beauty of it, Oh, the beauty of it.' I finally managed to get him out of my car on a lonely corner of Sunset Boulevard. I threw my tattered bra in the gutter and headed home to Mom and a piece of her apple pie." She smiled at him. "I don't know about you and Orson working together," she said impishly. "You've got no tits, no bra to rip. Besides, Orson always says, 'The only thing wrong with The Method is the *The.*'"

After she'd said that, he knew he'd found a woman as irreverent as he was . . . well, almost.

He invited her to go for a ride in Central Park with him on his motorcycle, and she willingly accepted. As he was making his way up the alleyway after having exited through the stage door, a large woman with a thick Deep South accent accosted him. "Why, Mr. Brando, up there on stage you're Stanley Kowalski. But in person you're just like everybody else."

Excusing himself from Anne, he walked over to the nearest doorway. Once there, he unbuttoned his blue jeans and urinated against a brick wall.

Minutes later, with Anne hanging onto his muscled frame, he was zooming on his motorcycle through Central Park, coming to a stop in the parking lot at the Zoo.

"Isn't it a bit late for calling on the animals?" she asked.

"I have a friend here who lets me in at night," he said. "My friendship with him, plus fifty dollars. I've made a buddy out of this big baboon. I call him Weissmuller." He reached for a paper bag attached to his motorcycle. "I bring him his favorite treats every night. He's come to depend on me showing up with my bag of goodies. I think if I didn't come around, he'd just sulk in the corner and fade away."

Once the zookeeper had shown Marlon and Anne to Weissmuller's cage, he left them alone. Marlon reached into the paper bag and pulled out a large banana. "You won't believe this," he told her, "but Weissmuller here is a bit of a homosexual. He insists on kissing me every night."

As an astonished Anne looked on, Weissmuller wasn't feeling that amorous on this particular night. Catching Marlon by surprise, the baboon spat in his face.

"The blast hit him right in the kisser," she later remembered. "And we're not talking a dainty little spit but a big blast. Weissmuller must have been saving up all day to release that wad."

Stepping back in stunned amazement, Marlon recovered quickly. Wiping the spit from his face with the back of his hand, he went over to a nearby fountain and bathed himself as best he could. Then he filled his mouth with what appeared to be an amazing amount of water. His cheeks bloated with the liquid, he returned to the cage to confront Weissmuller.

"Marlon let go," she claimed. "Did he ever let that baboon have it. The animal recoiled in horror and ran to the rear of his cage where he covered his face with his hands, as if anticipating another attack."

"That will teach that God damn baboon some manners," Marlon said, taking her by the arm and leading her back to the motorcycle.

"That's it for me. I've had it. No more treats. No more visits. I knew I'd have trouble with that baboon one day. I don't want to admit this, but one night he mooned me. All those kisses didn't mean anything. He was just setting me up for the kill. How like a woman!"

Before getting on his motorcycle, she looked into his eyes. "Not this woman."

Later over cheeseburgers at a beer tavern in the Times Square area, Anne told him amusing stories about her career. She claimed that as a teenager she was fired from the stage production of *The Philadelphia Story* in pre-Broadway tryouts in 1939. "That damn dyke, Katharine Hepburn, thought I was too old for the part."

As regarded her marriage to actor John Hodiak, she told Marlon, "A marriage is happier when a man is more or less the sun and the woman's in the shadow. But what actress wants to be in the shadows?"

"I think you're sexy in sunshine or shadow," he said. "Very sexy. Sex and brains. What a winning combination, I've always said."

"Not in Hollywood," she countered. "The minute any woman is perceived as having a brain, it's supposed to cancel her sex appeal. Producers, and especially directors, don't know how to sell a star if they can't hype her sexually."

"I'm a bit short myself, and what I like about you is that I can tower over you."

"The question about any man with a woman is this? Can he be tall in the saddle even though short?"

"I've never had one complaint, and I don't expect any tonight," he boasted.

"What makes you think you're going to get lucky?"

"I think that was a foregone conclusion the moment you arrived at my dressing room door," he said. "But I must warn you, don't expect Stanley Kowalski. I'm not a rapist."

"I'll let you in on a little secret," she said, reaching for his hand. "I'll be the rapist!"

And so she was.

Two days later when he came by her hotel suite after a performance of *Streetcar*, he was looking for a repeat performance. He bribed a porter ten dollars to let him into her suite, as he wanted to take her by surprise.

He later related to Carlo Fiore what happened. "Anne must have been taking a shower. What I found wasn't her but a drunken Peter Lawford lying asleep and buck-assed naked on the sofa in her living room. I'm sure Peter would have liked it, but I wasn't into a three-way that night, so I tiptoed out. I went home to Russell, bedding down with my raccoon for the rest of the night."

* * *

Like Marlon himself, the glamorous and sultry Viennese actress, Hedy Lamarr, was one of Hollywood's most notorious bisexuals when she came backstage to greet him after his performance in *Streetcar*.

She was always frank about describing her affairs with both men and women in an age when such nocturnal adventures were carefully concealed. Most of the world knew she'd had affairs with Clark Gable, Errol Flynn, and Marlon's rival, John Garfield. What was not known at the time was that she'd also seduced Howard Hughes and a young John F. Kennedy.

She arrived backstage with a young blonde Viennese woman who was obviously in love with her. Hedy did not give the young woman the honor of a name, but introduced her to Marlon as "my hand-maiden." Marlon looked the rather voluptuous woman up and down. "Remind me tomorrow to call my agent and order one for myself." To the maid, he asked, "Got a young sister at home?" The young woman did not answer him.

Forever the provocateur, Marlon asked Hedy, "Is it true what I hear? That you slept with both Hitler and Mussolini?"

"I was married to Fritz Mandl," she said. "In case you are the only unenlightened person in the world, he was the famous Austrian munitions magnate. If he ordered me to sleep with one of those dictators, I did the bidding of my husband. That way, he could get fatter contracts. Hitler was all posturing. Out of uniform, he was not a man. Mussolini was the

Hedy Lamarr

most pompous ass I've ever known. Imagine stopping every minute to ask— in Italian, of course—how he was doing. A man secure in his sexuality would never do that. Mr. Brando, you strike me as a man secure in his sexuality."

"When you get lucky later tonight, you'll know just how true that is."

On the way to a late-night supper at Sardi's, with the hand-maiden tagging along, Hedy told Marlon that "Fritz taught me many things. He always said, 'A woman is a lady if she knows what jewels go with the right clothes.' Tell me, Mr. Brando, do you think I'm wearing the right jewelry with the right clothes?"

"In white ermine with a white satin gown and white ankle strap high heels with white diamonds, how could you possibly go wrong? At least no one will call you underdressed."

As the evening progressed, he seemed to want to etch every detail in his brain to report to Edith Van Cleve the following morning. She might not believe that Hedy actually came backstage to greet him.

Before getting out of the taxi, she took his hand and said to him, "If you use your imagination, you can look at any actress and picture her nude. I hope to make you use your imagination."

"That's fine with me," he said, "but I don't want to spend the entire evening imagining."

"You can at least spend dinner anticipating," she said. "I have learned that in sex the anticipation is almost as tantalizing as the actual conquest." She ordered a herring appetizer and a plate of cold salmon. "I must watch my fig- ure," she told him.

"You don't have to do that," he said with a smile. "I've been keeping watch over it ever since we came into the joint."

For some reason the hand-maiden ordered a large platter of shellfish— "heavy on the oysters"—which Marlon knew he'd have to pay for, as it was the most expensive item on the Sardi late-night menu.

Later the next day, when Edith pumped Marlon for "every word that Hedy said," he claimed he could not remember most of the dialogue. "Seated with Hedy Lamarr," he told her, "I can't listen to what she's actually saying. All I can do is look at the movement of her lips. As she talks, I watch the exquisite shapes made by her lips."

As they were drinking their coffee, Hedy had abruptly asked him, "Do you remember your first sexual experience?"

Taken aback for the moment, he finally said, "Not really. I'm not trying to be coy. It's just that I've told so many lies about my first experience, that I'm not sure what is real or imagined at this point. I think it was our family maid. Perhaps she was black, perhaps not. No, the first was milk-white. I just don't remember skin color at this point because the color of a woman's skin is not important to me."

Marlon was not being truthful at this point. He could recall in vivid detail his first sexual involvement with the family housekeeper, his beloved Ermi, a memory and a rejection that would haunt him forever.

"What color of skin do you think I have, Mr. Brando?"

"White porcelain."

She sighed. "Sometimes I find men tiresome, and that's why I carry my hand-maiden with me everywhere I go. Sometimes men have aroused me but proved to be impotent. No man should heat up a woman's body temperature and then leave her in a desperate situation. Don't you agree, Mr. Brando?"

"You will not have that problem later with me tonight," he promised. "My noble tool always does its duty."

"I certainly hope so," she said. "Tonight I'm feeling very horny." Hedy Lamarr was perhaps the only woman in Hollywood who uttered such a line, and, according to such lovers as Charles Boyer and Burgess Meredith, she uttered that sentiment frequently.

"Of course all the men in my life weren't impotent," she claimed. "Sometimes they were a bit kinky. One of my lovers was a whip-wielding sadist. He could only reach orgasm by tying my arms behind me and using the whip on me. I begged him not to mar my skin, which as you can see is perfect in every way."

"From what I can see, that's true," he said. "But I'll have to inspect your entire body to see if those whip lashes left any scars."

"That will be very difficult, Mr. Brando, because I prefer to have sex in rooms where only one small candle is glowing."

Back in her suite, the night began with Marlon ordered out of her bedroom until she could prepare herself for him. She summoned her hand-maiden to help her with full makeup. At the last minute the young woman brought ice cubes to rub across the nipples of Hedy's breasts to make them stand up straight. Only then did the hand-maiden summon Marlon into Hedy's boudoir.

The following morning he would report to Edith that Hedy was "the queen of orgasms," as she was already known in Hollywood. "She told me I was better than John Garfield, and that was music to my ears," he said.

Unknown to Marlon, he may have taken undue credit for his expertise in the sack. What the candid and outspoken Hedy later said was, "I experienced frequent orgasms when having sex with most men. With some men, I had uncountable orgasms." Marlon fell into the latter category.

Over morning coffee, Hedy reportedly warned Marlon not to fall in love with her. "All men I go to bed with fall in love with me. They also want to marry me and make a prisoner of me just like Fritz did when I married him and became Lady Mandl."

216

He promised her he wouldn't fall in love with her.

"One man, Ritter Franz von Hochstätten, son of one of Germany's most distinguished families, begged me to give up my career and marry him. When I wouldn't, he hung himself."

Dressing to leave her suite, he told her, "I've made love to women for most of a night. But in all my sexual history, I've never made love to a woman all night long. You were the first."

"I suspect I'll be the last, because there is no other woman like me on the planet."

"I agree with that," he said, bowing from the waist in the style of old Vienna. At her doorway, he must have realized he'd been too polite and courtly. "As a little boy growing up in Omaha, I never dreamed that the day would come when I would take sloppy seconds from both Hitler and Mussolini."

While she was still confused and pondering his words, he kissed her sensual lips and headed for the elevator to place his first call of the day to Edith Van Cleve.

* * *

Ingrid Bergman never entertained the slightest desire to play Blanche DuBois in *Streetcar's* film version. Ostensibly she went backstage after Marlon's performance one night in *Streetcar* to tell him that he was the most exciting actor on Broadway and to offer him the male lead in a future film she wanted to make. It was based on a story by Sigrid Undset, the Norwegian novelist and Nobel Prize winner. The role called for the male of the screenplay to be about ten years younger than the female lead. Having been born in 1915, Ingrid fit that profile of the older woman.

Ingrid Bergman

On learning that Ingrid would be in the audience that night, Irene Selznick cancelled a theater party of eight guests that she had planned to bring to the play. She was still furious at Ingrid for having had an affair with her husband, David O. Selznick, who had signed the exquisite, soft-spoken, and intelligent star to a seven-year contract.

Marlon told Carlo Fiore that he'd seen *Casablanca* three times and had "fallen for Bergman," and was eager to meet her.

At the time of their meeting backstage, Ingrid was viewed as a saint by most of the American public, or at least a nun. She'd worn the habit when teamed with Bing Crosby in *The Bells of St. Mary's*. But her leading men and her directors knew a very different Ingrid.

Alfred Hitchcock, who'd directed her in *Spellbound* in 1945, once said, "She'd do it with doorknobs."

Ingrid had even admitted to her first husband, the Swedish doctor, Petter Lindström, that she couldn't work effectively without being either in love with her director or her leading man—hence, her infamous affairs with Gregory Peck, Spencer Tracy, Gary Cooper, and even Crosby himself.

When Ingrid met Marlon, she was at the peak of her fame and popularity. The scandal of the still-married Ingrid giving birth to Roberto Rossellini's child had yet to erupt and earn her worldwide denunciation, including an attack for her "immorality" on the Senate floor. The more puritanical of moviegoers boycotted her films as she fled to Italy, her reputation shattered. All of that, however, lay in her future.

Over dinner after that night's performance of *Streetcar*, Ingrid pitched her idea of the film script to Marlon, who seemed vaguely interested. "I've had movie offers before. None of them seemed quite right for me. I think my image and your image would contrast brilliantly on film. Of course, you'd get star billing."

"Of course," said Ingrid.

"Hedy Lamarr visited me the other night," he said. "We'll never do a film together. Could you really picture Miss Lamarr and Mr. Brando on the screen?"

"Perhaps the two of you could go naked on camera," she said. "Lamarr earned her reputation in Europe by running naked on the screen. I would never get naked before a camera."

"But you do get naked when you go to bed with a lover?" he asked impishly.

"That I do," she said.

"I understand that in your native Sweden everyone—man, woman, and child—runs around jaybird naked while the sun shines."

"A gross exaggeration, but most Swedes aren't shy about nudity." She paused to light her own cigarette. "As for Hedy, did she want you to appear in a film with her?"

"It was never mentioned."

"Actually, Hedy was originally slated to appear opposite Bogie in *Casablanca*," Ingrid told him. "But MGM wouldn't lend her to Warners. They were hoping to repeat all that *Algiers* schmaltz—you know, thick cigarette smoke, music in the background, lots of exotic atmosphere, and cloudy, mysterious people in dark corners plotting shadowy deeds."

The teaming of Ingrid and Marlon in a movie was not as far-fetched as it

218

might have seemed. In the 1950s producer Sam Spiegel flew to the Rossellini/Bergman villa, Santa Marinella, in Rome, to pitch a script to her that would costar Marlon. She turned him down, claiming that Rossellini (then her husband) never wanted her to return to Hollywood.

Over dinner, Ingrid amused Marlon with stories of Hollywood, admitting that her private affairs were getting "dangerous" and might one day attract the attention of the press. "Many rumors about me are true, but not those about Cary Grant and me." She'd recently costarred with him in *Notorious*.

"Our kissing scene in that movie has already become famous," she said. "For more than two and a half minutes, we went at it. The lips, the neck, the ears. Since our voices weren't heard, Hitchcock told us to say anything we wanted. Actually Cary told me that he'd left a lot of dirty dishes in his dressing room when he'd had five members of the cast in for lunch. No one had come to clean up the mess. In our most cuddly scene, as we were trying to decide what to do with our noses, I told him I'd go and wash his dishes as soon as our on-screen 'romance' ended."

"True Method acting," he said, laughing.

In the months ahead, as Ingrid would go on to make scandalous headlines around the world, Marlon would vehemently defend her as she was branded "an apostle of degradation" for her adulterous love affair with Rossellini in the late 1940s. In defending her, Marlon would say, "She lives life by her own truth, and for that I respect her greatly."

Over dinner he'd been dismayed by her constant habit of excessive smoking, even though she claimed she suffered from chronic throat problems. Sensing a need for fresh air, he invited her for a long walk through the streets of New York.

Out in the cool night breezes, she lamented that she wasn't in Sweden. She told him of the long walks she used to take by herself in her native country. "There is no more beautiful place in all the world than Sweden in the summer. The sun shines brightly throughout the evening, and the skies are luminous. It's a magic time. Now we find ourselves in New York where the skyline is forever gray."

She didn't talk just about herself but asked about his career and his sudden fame. He told her that he hadn't changed at all since he'd appeared as Stanley Kowalski. "I still play the bongo drums and eat peanut butter sandwiches like I always did. If the world really wants to go crazy over me, that's the world's problem."

She took him to her suite at the Hampshire House on 59th Street at the edge of Central Park. She'd stayed here during her appearance in the play, *Joan of Lorraine*, which had opened on October 5, 1946 at the Alvin Theatre. "When I did that play, I sometimes had a gang of three hundred fans following me back to my hotel after the performance. During my twelve-week run, I called them the Alvin Gang."

She seemed genuinely curious about how he faced Broadway audiences every night. "Before the curtain went up on *The Maid*, I just seemed to break into little pieces. Once on stage, I had a hard time piecing myself back together again."

"I've had my mishaps," he said, without explaining what they were.

In her suite on the twenty-sixth floor, she stood holding his hand as both of them looked out onto an early morning view of New York. They were able to see all the way to the Brooklyn Bridge.

Dazzling good looks

Of all the women with whom he'd become momentarily involved during the time he appeared in *Streetcar*, Marlon had the least to say about Ingrid to the gossipy Edith the next morning.

"It is very easy for me to understand why she is America's most beautiful, most admired, and most beloved actress," he said, reporting on only the preliminary chitchat he'd had with the star.

"I felt he was protecting her reputation," Edith later claimed.

Apparently, on their first night together, Marlon had to settle for a demure kiss on the cheek from Ingrid.

She came back a month later to watch him emote in *Streetcar* once again. She also visited backstage and invited him back to her suite at the Hampshire House.

This time Marlon was a bit more forthcoming with Edith. "He made one enigmatic statement to me," she recalled. "Ingrid does not do what a whore does," he told me. "She's a lady yet also a woman with very strong desires. Yes, you might even call it lust. Even so, she maintains an aura of purity about herself. I think we'll make a great couple on the screen together."

"This time I got lucky," he admitted to Edith. "Unlike Rick in *Casablanca*, I got the beautiful but tormented Ilsa. But alas, it was for only one night. She didn't exactly say, 'Here's looking at you kid,' but she made it obvious that time was going by and it was time for me to move on. Play it,

Sam."

* * *

Arriving backstage to greet Marlon was Susan Hayward, known in Hollywood as "The Divine Bitch." Making a glamorous, stunning appearance, she was clad in a $10,000 ankle-length Labrador mink coat.

When he complimented her beauty, she said, "Honey, before flying to New York I decided to purchase this li'l old mink coat. A cloth coat can keep you just as warm. But if you have to go to a hock shop, you get more for mink."

In his dressing room, she reached into her purse and removed a shining red apple to present to him. "View this as your lucky red apple. Put it on your dressing table and don't remove it until you've given your last performance."

"Even if it rots?" he asked.

"Even if it rots. Let it stay there. To toss it in the garbage can spell disaster for you. Jess Barker, my creep of a husband, always presents me with a red apple at the start of every movie."

"If this magic works, I'll go for it." He placed the red apple on his dressing table, and in a much altered and decayed form, it was found there at the time of his last performance of *Streetcar*.

That evening he began to get to know this fiery redhead who lived her life in strict adherence to astrology. "If my astrologer warns me, I don't get out of bed, even if it means shutting down shooting for a day."

In her hotel suite, when he wanted to take her to bed, she insisted on listening to a song play until the end on the radio. "I hate that song!" she protested.

"Then why not switch to another station?" he asked.

"Bad luck will come to you if you don't listen for a song to play out."

"I see."

Under her mink, she wore a stunning yellow satin gown. "Yellow is my favorite color," she said. "But my husband hates it. That's why I always have to wear white, beige, or black around him. But he's not in New York with me, so I intend to wear yellow every day."

As he moved toward her to seduce her, she backed away. "Oh, no, buster!" she

Susan Hayward

221

said. "No man gets near me until he gives me flowers first."

"I'll be back." He left the suite and took the elevator to the lobby where he purchased three dozen tube-roses.

Back in her suite, he presented them to her and was rewarded with a kiss on the mouth. "How did you know that the tube-rose is my favorite flower?"

"I didn't," he said. "Just a lucky guess on my part."

En route to her bedroom, she informed him that a magazine article was coming out, naming her one of "Hollywood's Ten Most Exciting Women." "What do you think of that?"

He smiled and pulled her close to him, where he kissed her passionately on the lips. "Guess I want to find out what the excitement is all about."

Most of the famous actresses who came to visit Marlon during this notorious period of his life were one-night stands. Even though Marlon later told Edith that he virtually loathed every word that came out of Susan's mouth, "it was such a pretty and such a talented mouth that I wanted to extend my time with her."

Dressed in a yellow designer dress, she invited him to have lunch the following day with her at "21." Over a rare steak, she urged him to go to Hollywood "where the big bucks are. All this talk about how divine the stage is is pure bullshit." She informed him of this between sips of rum and Coca-Cola. "I can't stand any more of this crap that the real test of an actor is the stage. A stage actor has weeks or even months to create a role. Sometimes on camera we're not even given a day to pull off a big scene. I ask you, which is the greater achievement?"

He mumbled something but it wasn't a coherent answer.

Finally, she turned on him. "I'm tired of talking about myself. What do you think of me?"

"Well," he said leaning back, being the only diner at "21" who'd ordered a glass of milk with his lunch. "I woke up an hour earlier than you this morning. You had three magazine articles about yourself on the table. I think those writers said it all about you. 'A human goddess.' 'Cold as a polar bear's foot.' 'An actress who goes through life with her fists up.' And 'as resilient as a trampoline.'"

At the end of their meal, she urged, 'C'mon, big boy, we're going to Brooklyn."

In a limousine, they crossed the Brooklyn Bridge heading to the borough where she'd once lived in a tenement, becoming a friend to poverty. She showed him the corner where at the age of twelve she'd been the first female newsboy ever hired by the *Brooklyn Eagle*.

She ordered the driver to take her to Church Avenue and East 35th Street. "That's where Edythe Marrener was born. According to astrology I was a moon child, meaning I was born between June 22 and July 22. Moon children are emotional and creative. We're outwardly tough but sensitive at heart."

"My Irish father taught me to be tough," she said. "To fight for what I wanted. He told me to be like the rubber ball. The harder they hit, the higher they bounce."

Heading back over the bridge to her life as a movie star, she looked back at her native Brooklyn. "That's one of the places that's great to have been born in and just as great to leave."

At her hotel, he made an effort to get out of the limo with her but she opened the door for herself, jumped out onto the pavement, and shut the door quickly behind her, leaving him in the back seat.

"Tell my driver where to drop you off," she said. Standing on the curb as the long black car pulled away, she yelled to him, "See you in Hollywood, kid."

* * *

No more regal queen ever descended on Marlon backstage than "the lady of the shoulders," Joan Crawford. At the time, he was a young man, and she, in contrast, had been born at the dawn of the Edwardian era. Her first words to him were, "I've done everything a woman can do in life, but meet Mr. Marlon Brando."

No one had ever used such a line on him before, and he was immediately intrigued. When he fully understood who she was, he gently took her arm and directed her inside his dressing room, shutting the door to at least six younger women who looked like college coeds.

"You don't mind waiting in here while I get dressed for the street?" he asked.

"Not at all," she said, reaching into her purse for a cigarette.

"Forgive me, but I don't have a match."

"Never mind," she said, reaching for a gold cigarette lighter. "I prefer to light my own. Clark Gable gave me this lighter."

"I hear you two are quite good friends," he said, heading over to the rear of the large dressing room to change out of his Stanley outfit.

"Darling," she said, "I know exactly what you've heard. The whole world knows we're lovers and were from the first day we met. He's the only golden oldie I keep going with." She reached into her purse and removed a silver flask, downing a hefty swig. "Forgive my bluntness, but I don't believe in being coy. I always audition the new boy in town. By town, I mean Hollywood." She looked at him carefully, as he removed his tight blue jeans. "Don't be modest, darling. We stars are known for undressing in front of each other or in front of a director. I invited one director over and right in my living room pulled off everything. I said, 'Darling, you might as well see what you have to work with.'"

"In that case," he said, "the jeans are coming off. I must warn you I don't wear underwear."

"From your performance tonight, that was obvious. Anyway, there is no need for false modesty between us. Go on. Get undressed so you can get dressed. Don't worry yourself about a little male nudity in front of me. This is not my first time at the rodeo."

When he slipped into his street clothes, she looked a little astonished. He'd merely exchanged his Stanley stage jeans for a cleaner pair of street denim. "I have some advice for you. If you want to be a star, you've got to look like a star. I never go out of my house, even to buy a grapefruit, unless I look like Joan Crawford, the movie star."

"I'm not a movie star," he said. "Nor do I plan to become one."

"Don't kid a kidder, darling," she said. "All Broadway actors in spite of their protests secretly dream of becoming movie stars." She crushed out her cigarette. "On second thought, I'd love to go out with you to '21' tonight, with you dressed like that. Here I am dressed like a gilded lily. There you are still looking like Stanley Kowalski even though the curtain has gone down. I think we'd make a grand entrance. It will show the fucking New York press that Joan Crawford is still in touch with the new young generation of actors. The Method. Whatever bullshit you want to call it."

At "21," Marlon began to suspect that the entire evening had been carefully choreographed. Too many columnists had been tipped off about their appearance there that night. He later told Carlo Fiore, "The God damn bitch is trying to capitalize off my own fame and somehow link in with it. Here she is, the most famous face on the planet, and she wants some of my magic too."

In the middle of their dinner, a rather liquid one for Joan, except for a blood-red hamburger, he bluntly asked her. "You've got great eyes. Big eyes. A result of surgery, perhaps?"

"Not at all," she said. "A stupid rumor. I've always had big eyes, and I've got baby pictures to prove it. My teeth were too big and ugly, and I did have them capped."

For some perverse reason, he insisted on asking her rude questions as if hoping to penetrate the movie-star shell she'd encased her-

Joan Crawford

224

self in. "A lot of you famous ladies have shown up to seduce me and to 'audition' for the part of Blanche DuBois. Are you one of them?"

She burst into laughter. "Heavens no," she said. "I'm much too young and glamorous to play a faded Southern belle, even though I'm from Texas. I just heard from Irene Selznick that she's offering the part to Miriam Hopkins. Perhaps Bette Davis. It's a juicy part but not for me." She bolted down half of her martini. "There is a film script I've been submitted, and I'm seriously considering it."

"Is there a part in it for me?" he asked, not really caring.

"Indeed," she said. "The male lead. It's the story of an actress past her prime." She sighed. "I don't like the sound of that. She's still big box office, but spends an extra two hours at her dressing room mirror before making an appearance. In the film script, she falls for the young writer of her latest picture. She grew up in old Hollywood with the studio system. This young writer dresses sloppily and knows a new Hollywood she's never seen. He takes her out on dates on his motorcycle, stopping off at drive-ins for hamburgers. He invites her to a reading of bohemian poets. He falls in love with her."

"Do I get the girl in the final reel?" he asked.

"The script is not that far along," she said. "The star must make a big decision. Does she want to live in the old and fading world in which she'd been the queen? Or does she want to adapt and become born again with the young man who loves her, even though that would mean giving up a large part of her heart, things that she once thought sacred?"

"Seems like type casting," he said. "My God, a screenplay like that could be the real story of Joan Crawford and Marlon Brando, depending on how things go tonight."

Marlon reported on his one and only night with Joan to both Edith and Carlo Fiore. As he related to Fiore, he returned to her hotel suite with her after their dinner at "21."

"She did all the drinking and talking," he said. "Without any foreplay, about three o'clock in the morning, she pulled off all her clothes and eased herself down on her white carpeting. That's how she wanted to be taken."

"How it'd go?" Fiore asked.

"Not so good. She wanted to control the fuck, and I couldn't get into it her way. I never got past her bad breath. She must have been drinking since morning. My noble tool, as you know, rarely if ever fails me. That's why I call it 'ever-ready.' But with Miss Crawford, it let me down and couldn't do its job. All I remember after that was heading for the door and hearing the worst cursing I've ever heard from a woman in my life."

In spite of their ill-fated night together, Joan, in the words of Kazan, "still had the hots for Marlon," and she appeared three times on the set of *A*

Streetcar Named Desire when it was being filmed in Hollywood. "She still lusted for our muscled, T-shirted genius," Kazan said.

After the premiere of the film version of *Streetcar*, she sent Marlon a telegram, praising his performance and adding a footnote: "You can park your motorbike on my front lawn any time you so desire."

He did not respond.

When casting for the 1952 *Sudden Fear*, she requested Marlon but got Jack Palance instead. Ironically, he'd been Marlon's stand-in during his hospitalization with a broken nose. It was not Marlon but Palance who would introduce Joan to the theories of screen acting emerging from the Actors Studio.

She would encounter Marlon five more times in her life, and it was always at some public party or function. At one point, meeting him in the presence of Irene Selznick, she said, "I found Palance moody and confused," she said, "when working with him on *Sudden Fear*, and would much have preferred you in the part. His moodiness disturbed me. All this racing around the sound stages trying to incite some emotion. As for me, just turn the fucking cameras on and I'll give you all the God damn emotion you want. You want tears, baby. I can cry on cue." She kissed Marlon on the cheek.

Palance later commented on working with Joan. "After we made *Sudden Fear*, she praised my menacing performance. She also told all the big cheese in the industry that she'd never work with me again. She accused me of copying Brando. The cameras were rolling during one of our scenes when she brought everything to a halt. Getting out of character, she shouted, 'If I had wanted Marlon Brando to do this scene with me, we would have hired him.'"

Losing Marlon for *Sudden Fear*, Joan tried one final time to play opposite him in *Autumn Leaves*, produced in 1956 by William Goetz and directed by Robert Aldrich. Cast as a New England spinster, she marries a lonely man in his late twenties, only to discover that he is a psychotic. She felt that Marlon would be perfect for the part and sent him the script. He only glanced at the script before turning it down.

He sent word to her through his agent that, "I'm not interested in doing any mother-and-son films at the present time."

"Marlon Brando is now at the top of my shit list," she said. "Replacing Bette Davis."

Later, when a reporter confronted Joan and asked her if the rumors were true that she'd pursued Marlon for both *Sudden Fear* and *Autumn Leaves*, and even a number of other pictures, she flatly denied it. "I'm no great admirer of his acting," she said. "Or his looks for that matter. There's something flat and dead about his eyes. Brando doesn't really have the handsomeness of a Cary Grant or Clark Gable. They were well groomed and intelligent looking.

Brando looks like he changes his underwear about every two weeks."

* * *

Tennessee Williams had called Georgia-born Miriam Hopkins "our finest Southern actress." He was most receptive when Irene Selznick proposed her for the role of Blanche in the film version of *Streetcar*. Alerted that she was being considered for the part, Miriam rushed to catch Jessica Tandy's performance opposite Marlon.

Privately she told her friends that, "playing Blanche will bring me back bigtime. For my efforts, it's almost a foregone conclusion that I'll win the Oscar."

Racing backstage to meet Marlon, Miriam pointedly ignored Tandy. Before going backstage, Miriam had told Irene Selznick that Tandy "simply doesn't know how to play a fading Southern belle. For that, you need the real thing. I can't understand why Hollywood or Broadway keeps casting British actresses in the roles of Southern ladies. Damn you, Vivien Leigh! Damn you, Scarlett O'Hara! I should have starred in *Gone With the Wind*. I could have done the role better than anyone!"

At the time of her first meeting with Marlon, the sun was setting on both the film and stage career of Miriam Hopkins. Her star had shone the brightest in the 1930s when she was an aggressive leading lady in films. Marlon had seen only two of her films, both with Bette Davis: *The Old Maid* in 1939 and *Old Acquaintance* in 1943.

When Irene told Marlon that she was bringing Miriam backstage after the play to meet him, he was skeptical of ever working with her. At that point, he had not even committed to playing Stanley in the film.

He told Irene that he found the on-screen Miriam "compulsively viva-

Miriam Hopkins

cious, dashing about making little gestures and chattering endlessly. As for her acting, I think it's all flim-flam."

"Perhaps Miriam will convince you otherwise," Irene told him. "I think she'd make the perfect Blanche." She cautioned him not to mention to her that she was also considering casting Miriam's nemesis, Bette Davis, as Blanche. "If there's anybody Bette hates more than Joan Crawford, it's Miriam."

Backstage, Miriam made her intentions clear to Marlon without actually saying anything. It was obvious that she wanted not only the film role of Blanche, but to test the sexual prowess of its male lead.

She was a notorious seducer of both the elite of Hollywood, and some other major American celebrities as well. She'd bedded publisher Bennett Cerf ("great if you like the missionary position"); Maurice Chevalier ("a faggot if I ever saw one"); Bing Crosby ("he should stick to singing"); John Gilbert ("I can't believe what Garbo saw in him"); agent-producer Leland Hayward ("Katharine Hepburn could have him"); Fredric March ("rather skilled"), director Ernst Lubitsch ("as good a lover as a director"); Robert Montgomery ("he spends so much time denouncing homosexuals that I've begun to think he is one"); Franchot Tone ("ten inches and rock hard"), and director King Vidor ("he's more Bette Davis' type than mine").

Marlon was not completely captivated by Miriam, but agreed to have dinner with her. As he escorted her out the theater's back door, a small mob had assembled, mostly young women, each clamoring for an autograph.

At first Miriam thought the crowd wanted her autograph. But when she saw that none of the fans seemed to know—or care—who she was, she stood against the brick wall, letting Marlon ungraciously handle his adulation.

Later, he complained to her that, "I hate to be recognized. When people point fingers at me in clubs and restaurants and come over to annoy me, I just want to disappear."

"It's flattering for fans to single you out," she said. "In the 30s that happened to me a lot. When a performer is intriguing on film or on the stage, it's natural for people to want to know more about them. How they live. What they eat."

"And who they fuck?" he said sarcastically.

"That too," she said. "How else can you explain those silly movie magazines. I think your fame will grow, so you must learn to cope with the madness."

Almost using the more worldly-wise Miriam as an analyst, he told her, "My anxiety attacks are growing greater every day. Like Monty Clift, I have constant bowel trouble. I'm not sleeping at all. For the last three nights, I've had practically no sleep at all."

"When I can't sleep," she told him, "I don't count sheep. I count lovers. And by the time I reach thirty-eight or at least thirty-nine, I'm asleep."

"I'm frightened of myself," he admitted. "These uncontrollable rages come over me, and there are times I think I'm going to explode. I can't handle it. My greatest fear is that when I'm in one of my deepest rages I'm going to kill someone."

"Ever consider an analyst?" she asked. "One who specializes in psychosomatic illnesses."

"I'm going to such a guy right now," he said. "Bela Mittelmann."

"How's it going? she asked.

"He's a Freudian and the coldest man I've ever known," he said. "All I get from him is ice. He has no insight into human behavior and never gives me any help."

She urged him to drop Mittelmann and find another analyst more in tune with his perceived problems.

He told her he'd mull that over. "I could use Arthur Miller as an analyst."

"How so?" she asked. "He writes plays."

"He's been to see *Streetcar* three times," he said. "Of course, Tennessee claims that he's doing it because he's jealous of the play and wants to steal ideas from it. But I think he's really come to get a reading on me. I've gone out with him a few nights and we've talked. He's working on an idea for an essay. It's about penis envy, patricidal anxieties, incestuous yearnings, and suppressed homosexuality. According to Miller, I embody all those qualities. He claims that before the 50s end, particularly if I go to Hollywood, that I will become the symbol of a decade that will make guilt personal again."

Perhaps Marlon considered Miriam's suggestion to switch analysts. But he finally discarded the idea.

In the words of Elia Kazan, "Marlon kept lying on Mittelmann's couch for years. He used this effeminate Hungarian Jew as a substitute mother and father until Mittelmann mercifully passed on in 1959."

Kazan, also being treated by Mittelmann, claimed that the bald head and flab of the analyst evoked Moe in "The Three Stooges."

Breaking his patient's privacy, Mittelmann once told Kazan (who recounted the tale in his memoirs) that he suspected that Marlon's mother, Dodie, had molested her son when he was "just a little boy—and I think she did that frequently to make up for the inadequacies in her own life. I'm trying to break through with Marlon and to get him to recall those painful episodes with me. So far, no luck. These secrets are buried deep within him like the darkest of desires. But they are there. As long as they are buried, Marlon will be sexually confused."

"Have you ever been analyzed yourself?" Marlon abruptly asked Miriam.

"Never!" she exclaimed in horror. "Nor will I. I suspect that analysis might destroy the creative impulses that make me an artist. I think we're driven to perform as a means of working out our inner demons. Destroy the demon and you might also destroy our impulse to emote. It's the creative malady that keeps us going. To get rid of that would be like throwing the baby out with the bath water."

He looked at her in astonishment. "You've given me something to think about."

She was eager to steer the conversation toward *Streetcar*. Before praising the play, she admitted that "I'm a bad judge of a play or film. I turned down *It Happened One Night*. Of course, Claudette Colbert in my role went on to win an Oscar. To me, it was just another silly comedy."

"Bad judge of material or not," she said, "I think Blanche DuBois is the role of a lifetime. It would make up for me not getting to play Scarlett O'Hara, a part I was destined to play." She gently reached out for his hand. "I must warn you: You and I are being friendly and cozy now, but once the camera is turned on us, may the best actor win. I'll be competing against you in the way I did on the screen with Bette Davis."

Up close and personal

"Fair warning," he said. "But from what I've seen of you tonight, I think you may have too much vitality for us to work together. I also hear that socially you're a very fine person, but a bitch to work with."

"So it is said," she said, laughing. "Do you know those boys at the *Harvard Lampoon* once voted me 'the least desirable companion on a desert island?'"

"We have two different acting styles—like Tallulah Bankhead and I did," he said.

"You mean you're a Method actor and I'm not," she said. "I've often wondered. How can a motion picture star reflect real life experiences when she leads an entirely artificial life?"

"You've just scored a point over me there," he admitted. "Even so, Kazan keeps urging me to draw upon my real-life experiences. As he puts it, 'turn trauma into drama.'"

As she ordered her fifth cocktail of the evening, he bluntly changed the subject. "Are you married?"

"I don't remember exactly," she said. "I read in some fan magazine that I'd married this reporter, Raymond B. Brock, on October 23, 1945. But since

230

I haven't seen him since, I can't really verify that. If you're really asking if I'm free tonight, the answer is yes."

As the check was called for, Miriam reached for his hand and cuddled close to him, anticipating that he was going to invite her back to his apartment. "I can't wait to work in front of the camera with you."

"Perhaps that will never happen," he cautioned.

"Oh, but it will," she said. "I just know it. I can feel it in my bones."

Her feeling was right. Of course, she'd never play Blanche opposite his Stanley. She would have to wait until 1966 when she played a minor role in his film, *The Chase*, which also starred Angie Dickinson, Jane Fonda, and Robert Redford. "It's sad," Marlon told director Arthur Penn, "to find a former big star like Miriam playing a small role in this turkey."

Out on the sidewalk in front of Sardi's, Marlon hailed a cab. Miriam looked astonished when she realized that he was not going to get into the back seat of the taxi with her. Severe disappointment showed on her expressive face.

Instead of a royal screw, she got a demure kiss on the cheek and a goodbye. As he would relate in detail to Edith Van Cleve in the morning, "I told Miriam that some seductions are better to be dreamed than realized."

* * *

Along with a copy of the play, *A Streetcar <u>Called</u> Desire*, its working title, Irene Selznick enclosed a personal note to Bette Davis in Hollywood. It was dated June 20, 1947.

> *Dear Bette,*
> *Here it is, and I do hope you feel about it as we do. I am very eager to hear your reaction, and too, I want to tell you of our plans, as well as the changes contemplated. My home number is CR6-1911. Kazan will be working at my house all Sunday afternoon, but if you don't get a chance by then, do call me as early in the week as you can.*
> *Irene Mayer Selznick.*

Streetcar had not yet opened on Broadway, and Bette was the first on a list of possible actresses to star as Blanche DuBois. Other actresses would be considered, even improbable ones such as Ruth Warrick, Geraldine Fitzgerald, Constance Cummings, and Celia Johnson, but Bette was the number one choice for Irene. Although a New Englander, Bette had convinced Irene, thanks partly to the role she played in *Jezebel,* that she was the quintessential Southern belle.

Even though she needed a career boost at the time, as her film career was in shambles, Bette, exercising the worst of career judgment, turned down the play. She was furious when it became the hit of Broadway.

Bette Davis

She didn't want to make the same mistake twice when she heard that Irene might recommend her for the lead in the film. As she flew to New York to see the play, she also knew that her old friend, Olivia de Havilland, was also a contender and that Vivien Leigh was, at the time, a remote possibility as well.

Showing no loyalty to Miriam Hopkins, whom he'd praised, Tennessee shifted his alliance to Bette as soon as he knew the fading star was interested. "What perfect casting," the playwright told Irene, "a fading star playing a fading Southern belle."

In later years, Bette spoke of her trip to New York to writer Whitney Stine. "Tennessee promised me that if I did Blanche, he would see that I had it in my contract to do the film. Also, I was thirty-nine then, just the right age. Jessica Tandy did it brilliantly, but I thought Vivien Leigh wasn't good casting for the movie version."

She later added other comments to this statement. "Vivien got an Oscar for Blanche, just as she did for playing Scarlett O'Hara, a role that should have gone to me. Even though I lost that, I could have played Blanche DuBois opposite Brando. God, what an actor he is! I think Jack Warner sabotaged the deal. Ah, the lost causes. But I don't dwell on them. It was simply not to be!"

Years after Irene Selznick took Bette backstage to meet the rising young star, she revealed her personal reaction to the experience to Tennessee Williams and his companion. Frank Merlo, when she was starring in the stage version of *The Night of the Iguana*.

She also had observations for the general public, years later, about Marlon and Method acting, sharing her opinions in her memoirs: "They [meaning Method actors] have simply learned to express themselves, and I'm terribly happy for them. When they learn to express the character, I shall applaud them. Then there's the question of style. Without it, there is no art. As personal as these troubled actors are, there is—aside from much of a muchness—the same of a sameness. They are all busy revealing their own insides that, like all X-ray plates, one looks pretty much like the other. Their Godhead, the remarkably gifted Marlon Brando, may bring (as all true stars do) his own personal magnetism to every part, but his scope and projection are unarguable. He has always transcended the techniques he was taught. His consequent glamour and style have nothing to do with self-involvement but rather radiation."

Bette would later repeat these same sentiments to her old boss, Jack Warner, when she encountered him again in 1962. "I wouldn't hire Marlon Brando as a gateman," he told her.

Instead of a dinner at Sardi's, Bette invited Marlon to a celebrity party honoring Clare Booth Luce, who showed up with an entourage of gay young men who clearly worshipped her every pronouncement. As Bette and Marlon stood nearby eating small quiches, he could clearly hear Miss Luce rhapsodizing about him and his performance in *Streetcar*. "Look at that face," she exclaimed. "All youthful beauty. Have you ever seen anything so exquisite? Only Michelangelo could capture it in stone."

Before Miss Luce, Marlon contorted his face into a grotesque mask, sticking out his tongue at her like a gargoyle. Miss Luce turned her back to him.

Bette did not scold Marlon on the way back to her suite, even though he'd insulted one of the most powerful and influential women in America, who was, after all, only paying him a compliment.

As Bette would explain later to Tennessee, "By that point in the evening, I had discovered that Marlon was on the dawn of a nervous breakdown. Instead of scolding, he needed sympathy, even nurturing."

Bette Davis did not have any particularly well-developed motherly instincts, as was plainly revealed in *My Mother's Keeper*, a sort of "Bette Dearest," tell-all memoir by her estranged daughter. B.D. Hyman.

But although she was no temple of mental health herself, Bette could on occasion respond in a loving, supportive way, since she genuinely admired Marlon's talent. She had gone through many bouts of deep depression in her own life, and was sympathetic to other troubled artists, at least the few she admired. As for the others, she wanted to see all of them, especially Joan

Clare Booth Luce

Crawford and Miriam Hopkins, "on the next plane flying directly into Hell's Fire," as she once put it.

Bette claimed that after the Luce party, she invited Marlon back to her hotel suite. Once there, she found him visibly shaking. "He was sweating so profusely that his clothes were drenched," she said. "I suggested we call a doctor, but he claimed that these bouts were occurring frequently and that he had already sought medical advice. He also revealed that he was under the care of a psychiatrist."

During the course of the evening, if Bette is

to be believed, Marlon revealed to her that his mother, Dodie, had molested him as a young boy. "Many times she invited me into her bed," he is quoted as saying, "and I knew it wasn't right, but I didn't know how to stop it. Actually one part of me didn't want her to stop. I guess I was in love with her. She was always drunk—never sober—when she invited me to her bed."

Fran Brando later revealed that she had long suspected her mother of harboring an incestuous feeling "for young Bud."

At the same time that he was being molested by Dodie, Marlon also revealed that he was involved with the live-in housekeeper, whose name was Ermalene. He called her "Ermi."

Ermi was Scandinavian and had just turned eighteen when she came to live with the Brando family. Not a typical Danish blonde, she had silky dark hair because of her Indonesian origins. In his autobiography, Marlon admitted that, "We slept together. She was nude and so was I." He recalled fondling her breasts and crawling over her. What he didn't say was that she masturbated him, and also taught him to return the favor. When Ermi left to marry a young man named Eric, Marlon claimed that he was devastated, feeling that "my dreams had died with her going."

He told Bette that, "I felt abandoned. My mother had long ago deserted me for the bottle. Now Ermi was gone too. That's why in life I would always find women who were going to desert me; I had to repeat the process."

As Bette later told Tennessee, "Marlon spent the rest of the night suckling at my breasts like a little baby boy. It was like he was reverting to childhood and being with his mother again . . . or at least Ermi."

"He wanted to be masturbated," Bette revealed, "perhaps repeating the exact experience he'd had with Ermi and his mother. I felt sorry for him. Here he was night after night pretending to be this macho Stanley Kowalski. But in his heart he still was a lost little boy. Marlon and I would never again get together in private like that. He may not even have remembered what happened between us, blotting it from his mind. But it was a tender moment for both of us. Believe me, I've had very few tender moments with any man."

The day after his night with Bette, Marlon told Carlo Fiore, "I threw Bette Davis a mercy fuck. My noble tool felt obligated to do its duty because she's such an honored actress in films." Marlon's boast to his male companion may have been merely an attempt to cover up what really happened that night.

Marlon and Bette would meet again on the night of March 30, 1955 when he was awarded Hollywood's highest honor, the Academy Award for his appearance in *On the Waterfront*. After publicly presenting him with the statuette, she told him, privately "I named the darn thing Oscar myself. This statue's ass reminded me of my first husband, Harmon Oscar Nelson."

"That Oscar of yours had one fuckable ass," he told Bette, apparently astonishing her with such a homosexual reference. She later repeated what he'd said to Irene Selznick. "Imagine me, after all these years in Hollywood, being mildly shocked by Marlon's remark."

Before leaving the Academy Awards that night, Bette told reporters, "I was thrilled that Marlon Brando was the winner. He and I have a lot in common. He too has made many enemies. He too is a perfectionist."

* * *

After his contract for *Streetcar* expired, Marlon planned to sail for France. "After a long *shlunk* in Paris, I'll find myself," he told Stella Adler over a farewell dinner.

"You'll never find yourself," she warned him, "even if you search all your life. I'm not certain anyone ever finds himself." She paused. "Or herself."

Before sailing, Marlon told Wally Cox that he was forced to "abandon my two steadies, my only true loves." One of his girlfriends was Toni Parker, a beautiful brunette dancer appearing nightly at the Latin Quarter.

The other was Cecilia D'Arthuniaga, a Colombian working in New York as a fashion publicist. She was equally beautiful. He told Bobby Lewis, "Cecilia is the girl I'm going to marry. We'll raise thirteen snot-nosed kids." Even as he uttered those words, Marlon must have known that there was no truth in his declared intentions.

Bobby knew that even though Marlon abandoned women, he also tried to hold onto them. He was leaving Toni and Cecilia behind, but heading for Paris to contact two former girlfriends, Celia Webb and Ellen Adler, both of whom were temporarily living in France.

On at least one occasion, Bobby challenged Marlon, asking him why he didn't want to let go of a woman when he'd moved on to another one. "With women," Marlon said, "I've got a long bamboo pole with a leather loop on the end of it. I slip the loop around their necks so they can't get away or come too close. Like catching a snake."

Marlon was getting a free vacation, including round-trip passage by ship because he was afraid to fly, plus three weeks salary at $350 per week. Director Claude Autant-Lara, the most controversial figure in the French film industry, wanted Marlon to star in Stendahl's *Le Rouge et le noir* (aka *The Red and the Black*), even though he didn't speak French. Marlon was told that he could learn his lines phonetically.

As Edith Van Cleve arrived at the pier to see Marlon off on his ship, she noted that he carried a copy of the classic novel for shipboard reading. If he agreed to do the film, his role would be that of Julien Sorel. All Marlon had to do was "seriously consider" the part.

Carlo Fiore was also there to wish Marlon a *bon voyage*. Marlon was disturbed to see his longtime friend shaking and sweating, in dire need of a drug fix, but he seemed to appreciate that Fiore had at least tried to pull himself together for his departure. In Marlon's cabin, a small group of friends had gathered to drink champagne toasts to Marlon. Popping the first cork, Marlon said, "Let's drink this shit before it becomes domestic."

In June of 1949, Marlon was about to embark on one of the greatest homosexual adventures of his lifetime, enlivened with the addition of a beautiful French or Italian woman for variety. En route to France, word was passed around the ship that if a male member of the staff "wanted a great blow-job," all he had to do was "knock on the door to Stanley Kowalski's cabin."

Johnny Evans, a waiter in the dining room, later claimed that "Brando was insatiable. I think he went through all of us—at least many of us—including myself, more than once. He did it better than my girlfriend." In addition to the more virile male members of the staff, two or three young women on the ship's guest list were also seen leaving his cabin late at night, including one rather large woman who, according to Johnny, "looked like she was going to give birth before the ship reached its port."

When not offering his sexual services to the staff, Marlon read the works of the Existentialists, especially Albert Camus, Jean-Paul Sartre, and Simone de Beauvoir.

Before sailing, he'd told Edith, "I want to shake my Nebraska roots. It's about time I picked up some French culture after playing that dumb Kowalski character, which has nothing to do with me."

Celebrated on Broadway, even known by name in Hollywood, Marlon arrived in Paris as an unknown. Except for a select few, even the inner circle of French filmmakers and theater people had never heard of him.

In his autobiography, Marlon offered very few details about his weeks in Paris. "I was one of the wild boys of Paris," he wrote. "I did *everything*, slept with a lot of women, had no sense of time, and slept until two p.m. every day. Anything that was imaginable, I did in Paris."

The last line, intriguing with its lack of information, was certainly true.

At first Marlon and Autant-Lara, meeting for the first time in Paris, got along rather well. That is, until Marlon became better acquainted with the French director. Autant-Lara was flattered to hear Marlon say, "I don't think anybody working in Hollywood has ever made an effort to avail himself of their (*sic*) fullest potential the way French filmmakers do."

Autant-Lara came to his meeting with Marlon with impressive credentials. His father was the distinguished architect, Edouard Autant, a friend of the sculptor Rodin. His mother was Louise Lara, one of the most famous actresses to appear at the Comédie Française. In the 1930s he'd moved to

Hollywood where he'd worked on French versions of American films, notably Buster Keaton comedies.

Marlon was even pleased with the accommodations the director had obtained at the Quai Voltaire Hotel in the Seventh Arrondissement. The hotel had long attracted an artistic clientele, including Oscar Wilde, Richard Wagner, and Baudelaire. Marlon was housed on the fourth floor in a slightly seedy small bedroom in which Camille Pissarro had painted "Le Pont Royal" from his window.

On his first night in Paris with Marlon, Autant-Lara showed him his two most distinguished films, both made during the Nazi occupation of Paris during the war years. *Le Mariage de chiffon* (1942) and *Douce* (1943) were scathing satires on the class system. The director was the chief voice in France attacking the threat of "Hollywood imperialism." The hot-headed crusader was also the chief attacker of all forms of censorship. "My stands are not popular," he told Marlon. "I have no friends, but an army of enemies."

Autant-Lara found that Marlon, even though he couldn't speak the language, was a perfect mimic. "You speak French better than I do." The director thought Marlon would not have a problem learning his lines in French and repeating them in front of a camera.

The Brando/Autant-Lara honeymoon did not last long. The director's mistake was to an increasing degree turning to one of his favorite subjects, politics, as subject matter for his films. As an extreme liberal, Marlon was horrified by Autant-Lara's far right positions. He was opposed not only to blacks, but to Jews and even the North Africans living in French Algeria. When he launched into praise for Hitler, Marlon walked out. "If *The Red and the Black* is ever made," he told Autant-Lara, "it will not be made with me in it."

In 1954 Autant-Lara brought *Le Rouge et le noir* to the screen, starring Danielle Darrieux and Gérard Philipe, the latter appearing in the role originally intended as Marlon's film debut.

As the years went by, Autant-Lara's political stands grew even more extreme. In 1989 he was forced to stand down as a representative of France's far right National Front in the European Parliament after describing the Nazi gas chambers as a "string of lies."

As for his own career as a film actor in Paris, Marlon would have to wait until 1972 and his controversial appearance in Bernardo Bertolucci's *Last Tango in Paris*.

Marlon, who shortly after his arrival had orchestrated a few stray pickups in Paris, soon realized that his two girlfriends, Celia Webb and Ellen Adler, were romantically involved with other men. In fact, Ellen was so serious about her new companion, David Oppenheim, the American composer, that she planned to marry him.

His old friend, David Diamond, was also in Paris, so Marlon didn't have to be alone. In an attempt to explain his promiscuity to Diamond, Marlon said, "I have an inability to love because I feel inferior."

Marlon even encountered his former lover, James Baldwin, who introduced him to the expatriate American writer, Richard Wright. It was not a memorable encounter, and Marlon moved on. He wrote to Edith that, "I don't want to wander down memory lane in Paris, encountering everybody I knew in New York and spending all my time with Americans. I'm like a vampire. I want fresh blood!"

Finding himself in arrears at the Quai Voltaire, and with money running short, Marlon moved over to the Hotel d'Alsace, a fleabag. He occupied the exact room where Oscar Wilde had died penniless and in disgrace.

In the room next to him was Jacques Viale, an eighteen-year-old wannabe actor who'd been born in the agrarian Auvergne region of central France. He'd come to Paris to break into cinema, but was forced to work during the day as a waiter at La Coupole, a famous cafe once frequented by Ernest Hemingway and Henry Miller, among others, and scores of other American expatriates. Jacques was "out" before the term was coined. Once "liberated" in Paris from his provincial origins, he made no attempt to conceal his homosexuality. He later spoke about his relationship with Marlon during his "French exile."

"My friendship with Marlon later became my fifteen minutes of fame," he once said. "The acting career didn't work out, neither did my friendship with Marlon, but it was intense while it lasted."

"For a brief time I was Marlon's lover," Jacques claimed, "until I quickly learned that he didn't come to Paris to indulge in only one relationship, but sought many affairs with both sexes. Ultimately, I became his tour guide to Paris instead of his lover. Alas, alas! My time with him was the single greatest moment of my life. It was all downhill after Marlon."

* * *

His friends called him "the wolf from the steppes," because of his Russian ancestry. His name was Roger Vadim. A former stage actor and journalist, he dreamed of becoming a movie director.

On a pleasant mid-afternoon in June of 1949, he was sitting with his closest friend, the actor Christian Marquand, on the terrace of La Coupole, where much of the literary history of Paris in the 1920s had taken place. Jacques Viale was waiting tables that day.

Roger was sharing his latest adventures with Christian. In the heyday of the 1920s, Ernest Hemingway had been a regular patron of La Coupole, but he no longer came around. Roger claimed that at present, "Papa and I are currently sharing a mistress. Sometimes we take her out together. She has nothing but praise for me, but she constantly insults Ernest. He seems to find her taunts vastly amusing, roaring with laughter and tugging away at his beard."

The intense young actor/writer was also eager to share his recent adventures on the Riviera with Christian. Roger had just returned from the Hotel du Cap in Antibes, where he'd spent several days hanging out with a handsome young American from Massachusetts. "We became instant friends," Roger said to Christian." We became so close that he moved into my room because he soon learned that that was where the action was. Often we took the same woman in bed together, which as you know is one of my favorite things, having shared so many beds with you and some lucky girl or boy."

"What's your friend's name?" Christian asked.

"John Kennedy, but I call him Jack," Roger said. "He claims his father was ambassador to England and is really a big man in America."

Both Christian and Roger watched the slow-moving traffic along Boulevard Montparnasse. They noticed, in Roger's words, "an extraordinarily handsome young man—an Adonis, really—at the next table. He caught our attention. He had taken off his shoes and was massaging a naked foot, which he had placed on a table between a glass of Perrier and an ashtray. Groaning with ecstasy, like a woman about to have an orgasm, he kept saying, 'Shit . . . that feels good . . . Shit . . . that feels good.'"

Roger immediately introduced himself and Christian and started a conversation, learning that this charming and personable young man was an American named Marlon Brando. "I was fascinated by him, but Christian was mesmerized by this young American beauty," Roger said. "When Christian saw something he wanted, male or female, he went after it. I knew before the lights went on that night in Paris, Christian was going to have our new acquaintance. We had never heard of Marlon Brando before in spite of his success on Broadway. To us, he was just another out-of-work actor bumming around Paris."

Joining Roger and Christian at table, Marlon told them that he was staying in an uncomfortable fleabag. That revelation brought an immediate invitation from both Christian and Roger to come and live with them in their tiny studio

Christian Marquand and Brigitte Bardot
in *And God Created Woman*

on rue de Bassano. "We will guarantee you lots of amusement and much fun, but not much privacy," Christian assured him.

"That's fine with me," Marlon said. En route to Marlon's fleabag hotel in a taxi, the triple alliance of Brando, Vadim, and Marquand was formed.

"Of course, it was just assumed that all three men were heading for a sexual rendezvous," claimed Jacques Viale, who learned of this new friendship of Marlon's the next day. In his black suit and white waiter's apron, he had stood on the terrace of La Coupole, watching the three young men get into a taxi. "En route back to Vadim's studio, Marlon knew seduction was on the menu. Roger knew that. Christian knew that. Marlon told me that on their first night all three men 'hit the sack together.' How envious I was. How I would have liked to have become a fourth in that *ménage à trois*. Of course, then it wouldn't have been a *ménage à trois*. At least they could have let me watch if not join in their fun."

Jacques later became an intimate friend to both Christian and Roger, having been introduced by Marlon himself. He claimed that before Roger married three of the world's most beautiful women—Brigitte Bardot, Catherine Deneuve, and Jane Fonda—he "seduced pretty boys or handsome young men with almost as much frequency as he did nubile young women. Roger never admitted it in so many words, but left the distinct impression that he'd committed an act of fellatio on John Kennedy on more than one occasion. Later in life, Roger turned almost exclusively to women. Let's just say that before Bardot, Deneuve, and Fonda, he was discovering himself. Not me. I was gay when I popped out of the womb."

"From that first night, Marlon and I became brothers for life," Roger said. "To me, he was just a charming friend to add to my collection. To Christian, it was more than that. My normally heterosexual friend was falling madly in love, and he usually went for women."

That weekend Roger introduced Marlon to his "teenage sex kitten," as he called her. She was a stunningly beautiful young girl named Brigitte Bardot. Before meeting her, Roger told Marlon that, "My task is to ignite this schoolgirl's dormant sensuality." In that, he would succeed beyond even his own wildest speculations.

Brigitte was a frequent visitor to the studio at rue Bassano, although her father, Louis Bardot, had forbidden her to go there.

Brigitte and Jane Birkin directed
by Roger Vadim for *Don Juan*

Roger told Marlon that the first day he'd met Louis, "he took me to his desk in his study, unlocked a drawer, and showed me this pistol. 'If you lay a finger on my daughter, I shall not hesitate to use this on you.'" Risking his life, Roger ignored the threat, even though it seemed very serious.

Although after that first night in a three-way, Marlon had confined his sexual overtures to Christian, he was still fascinated by Roger. At the time, Marlon was reading a novel by Dostoyevsky. He compared Roger to a character in one of the Russian writer's novels.

Roger Vadim and
Brigitte Bardot

Roger's response was, "I have always modeled my life on literature."

Was there a romance between Marlon and Bardot, who along with Marilyn Monroe, would become the three reigning sex symbols of the Fifties? There has been much speculation but no concrete proof. And Brigitte has remained silent on the subject.

Roger said that Marlon often lounged around the studio with his magnificent physique in a state of undress when Brigitte came to visit. "But Marlon and Brigitte never felt any real rapport. They liked each other and were quite friendly and cordial, but that's all. At least from what I know. It seemed to me that two such spontaneous and profoundly sensual creatures would have understood each other. But Brigitte was not at all dazzled by Marlon's physique, and he found her charming but no more than that."

Frankly, Roger was disappointed, as he admitted to Christian that he wanted to have a three-way with Marlon and Brigitte. In various couplings, this was his favorite form of sexual pleasure. A future wife, Jane Fonda, would reveal in her memoirs that Roger often instructed her to bring a female prostitute to their bed, and she reluctantly complied with his wishes.

Roger later said that Christian, Brigitte, and himself learned what a genius actor Marlon really was late one night. It'd been a long evening, and all four of them had gone club hopping, first the Club Saint-Germain and later, Le Tabou, both on the Left Bank. Finally, they headed for the Right Bank and Les Halles where they ordered pig's feet and onion soup.

Walking back home as the early streaks of dawn came to the Parisian sky, they headed up the Champs-Élysées. Marlon stopped in front of a cafe, Fouquet's, a favorite hangout of American expats and the preferred watering hole of film people visiting from Hollywood. He spotted chairs and tables chained together so they wouldn't have to be taken in at night.

Without saying a word, he pulled on the chains and arranged the chairs on the sidewalk," Roger later wrote in his memoirs. "Then he began reciting the opening lines of *A Streetcar Named Desire*. He played all the parts—not just Stanley, but Blanche and Stella too."

"Marlon recreated the true magic of the theater with just a few chairs and two barroom tables," Roger said. "Grumpy men and women, half asleep on their way to catch the first subway train to work, stopped out of curiosity or amusement. But after watching Marlon for a moment, they were spellbound and fascinated. Even if they didn't understand English, they recognized pure talent."

Marlon told Jacques that one hot afternoon Brigitte came by the apartment to meet Roger, who was running two hours late. He quotes Marlon as saying, "As this sex kitten stood before me, she removed her blouse. She wore no bra."

"My waist is perfect," she allegedly told him. "Only nineteen inches. And my legs would pass inspection anywhere. But my bosom. I have twice more than I should have. With my tiny waist, they look even larger."

"I immediately asked Marlon if this little flirtation had led to a seduction," Jacques said. "He said it did not. That Brigitte put back on her blouse only minutes before Roger arrived in the studio. Frankly, I don't know if Marlon were telling the truth or not. Did that scene really take place only in his mind? For all I know, he was indulging in harmless day-dreaming. Yet it had the ring of truth. From what I knew of her, Brigitte would pull a stunt like that. As time would prove, she wasn't opposed to taking off that bra now and then, even if she didn't usually wear one."

Perhaps one reason Marlon never moved in on Roger's teenage girlfriend, as he had on almost any date of Wally Cox's, was that Brigitte had eyes only for her "steppe wolf."

"I can't take my eyes off Roger," she told Marlon. "He seems strange, of course, and talks as if the world were already his, which I'm sure it'll be some day. Everything he says, even the trivial, is fascinating. My mother doesn't feel the same way about Roger as I do. Every time she knows he's coming to visit, she locks up the silverware."

At one point, Roger asked Marlon

Brigitte Bardot

242

Brigitte Bardot in *And God Created Woman*

what he thought of Brigitte, revealing that he planned to marry her one day. "She's a child-woman," Marlon said, "on the verge of a great adventure. But she—not you—will be the author of her own script."

Roger would carry through on his commitment to marry Brigitte. In a stroke of genius, he also cast his wife in *And God Created Woman* in 1956, choosing Christian Marquand for the male lead.

"Brigitte became so big in the late 1950s," Christian said, "that everything about her persona—her tousled blonde bouffant, her crisp white man-tailored shirts, and even her cigarette pants—was imitated all over the world. The film's title said it all—*And God Created Woman*. It didn't say *And God Created Adam*. I don't know if any of the millions of people who flocked to see the film even noticed me. It was the Sex Kitten who sold the tickets."

On seeing the film years later, Marlon told his friends, "It doesn't hold up well. Looks like a pretty lame excuse to film Brigitte nude on a St-Tropez beach. But the movie sealed her reputation as the seductress of the age, although you couldn't prove that by me. Of course, there are those who say that Marilyn Monroe was the seductress of the age. At least I can verify that one from my own experience."

Although Roger continued to see Marlon on occasions, and Christian turned out to be one of his best friends for life, Brigitte and Marlon drifted apart.

She contacted him in 1984, hoping to enlist his support in her fight for animal rights—"not just the Indians, animals have rights too." He turned down her request to get involved in her cause but promised to make a contribution.

He asked her how she was. She repeated a line she'd used since her fiftieth birthday. "I have been very rich, very beautiful, much adored, and very famous, but very unhappy!"

"Only I could have made you happy, and now it is too late."

* * *

In the summer of 1949, Christian Marquand and Marlon Brando fell in love, in the words of Roger Vadim. "It was an unconventional love affair that would span the decades, and fidelity to each other had nothing to do with it. I don't think I ever saw a more compatible couple. While Brigitte and I would be indulged in a terrible fight, Christian and Marlon would be in my bedroom making mad, passionate love, just like I did with Brigitte when she wasn't mad at me."

Unaware of Marlon's recent success on Broadway in *A Streetcar Named Desire*, Christian later recalled, "Marlon and I had an instant rapport. We were two kindred spirits, in spite of the fact he grew up in the wild west of America, and I was forced up in seedy Marseille. I liked him from the very first time I ever laid eyes on him, and I never stopped caring for him. He was my all-time best friend, even more so than Roger."

Though on most occasions a heterosexual, Christian had been introduced to both homosexuality and the screen when the oh, so gay Jean Cocteau had cast him uncredited in his film debut in *La Belle et la bête* (The Beauty and the Beast).

Christian wasn't really French but of Arab and Spanish descent. Originally, he'd been a stage comedian. When meeting Cocteau, the director decided that "male beauty such as yours can only be captured on camera. You have a raw sexuality that only the camera can tame. You possess a male charm so powerful that you can command the wind to stop blowing." A gross exaggeration, of course. Perhaps Cocteau had had too much opium that day.

Three years younger than Marlon, Christian was already a household word in France when he met Marlon. He'd appeared in such French classics as Henri-Geôrges Clouzot's *Quai des Orfevres* in 1947. The name of Christian Marquand appears today in movie trivia questions. From 1962 until his death in Paris at the dawn of the millennium, Christian was married to the famous Tina Aumont, daughter of Jean-Pierre Aumont and Maria Montez. Maria reigns today as *Cobra Woman*, the queen of cinematic camp.

[Author's note: Even though he appeared in films for fifty-five years, Tina Aumont's father, Jean-Pierre Aumont, remained a second-tier star throughout his life. He was called to Hollywood on occasion for such films as the 1954 *The Gay Adventure* or the 1975 *Happy Hooker*. He is remembered today for his key role in François Truffant's valentine to moviemaking, *Day for Night*, released in 1973. Later in life, Aumont married actress Marisa Pavan. She was the sister of Sardinia-born Pier Angeli, who would carry on affairs simultaneously with both Marlon and James Dean before her death in 1971 of a drug overdose.]

At the time Marlon met Christian, the French star's future wife was only three years old and living in Hollywood.

Even before Marlon arrived in Hollywood to make his first film, the gossip colony was abuzz with news of his affair with the tall and craggy-handsome French star. Neither actor ever denied the rumors, even when blind innuendos about their close relationship appeared in the press. One columnist, writing in 1952, asked the question, "What Hollywood bad boy is spending romantic nights not locked in the arms of a beautiful woman, but in the arms of a handsome male French movie star?"

On Christian's subsequent visits to Hollywood, he was sometimes spotted with Marlon dining in out-of-the-way and darkly lit restaurants in the San Fernando Valley. He was seen holding hands with Christian. Later, when a reporter asked Marlon about these rumors, Marlon calmly replied, "I am not ashamed. One should never be ashamed of love for one's fellow man. Only hatred of one's fellow man."

Neither Christian nor Marlon, of course, were exclusively homosexual. "Even though their affair, which lasted for centuries, was intense, it did not preclude having sex with other people, often in three ways, with a handsome boy or a beautiful young girl," Roger claimed. "Christian also served as Marlon's pimp when Marlon flew in from Hollywood. Christian told me that, 'All I have to do is to speak to any girl and bring Marlon that girl if he wanted her.'"

Along with Jacques Viale, Christian signed up as Marlon's tour guide to show him "the real Paris."

Marlon definitely wanted to see the seedy underbelly of Paris, and his new friends were only too willing to share the city's secrets at night. At some point, Marlon tired of the frequent exhibitions, both homosexual and heterosexual, often staged for the benefit of voyeuristic tourists from London and New York.

Jacques Viale claimed that "Marlon wanted to go beyond mere girl/girl, boy/boy, and girl/boy sex. He once told me that Roger and Christian took him to the notorious House of Ducks. In French, we called it Le Canard Bleu. This was a hellhole near Place Clichy that flourished at the time. It was run by some scumbag named Monsieur Giscard Guichet. He always claimed he was a count but had run a boy brothel in Marseille. His duck house catered only to the most perverted and jaded of both Frenchmen and tourist creeps who were tired of devouring virginal young girls and virginal young boys. This seedy character knew the depths of human depravity. To his house, he brought only the fattest or pleasantly plump of female ducks. Once there, he would tie up the ducks for his clients to penetrate. Just before a man reached his climax, Guichet would slice off the head of the duck so that the client could enjoy the poor bird's death spasms. After his own night with a duck, Marlon started referring to himself as 'trisexual.' People often wondered what he meant by that. Well, now you know. Don't you have an expression in English, 'Fuck a Duck?'"

Beginning with that summer in Paris, Christian would remain one of Marlon's most cherished friends. Even when Christian's film career entered twilight, Marlon got him the role of the French plantation owner in

Apocalypse Now in 1979. Christian's biggest coup however, was before that when he got Marlon to agree to star in the ill-fated film, *Candy*, in 1968, a movie that Christian directed.

The two men saw each other whenever they could, and Christian was always Marlon's host during his visits to Europe. It was with a great sadness that Marlon saw Christian "slipping away from reality" as the century neared its end. The French actor died of Alzheimer's disease near Paris on November 22, 2000, sending Marlon into a prolonged period of mourning.

"First Wally Cox," Marlon said to friends. "Now my beloved Christian. *I'm next!*"

* * *

While Marlon continued his tour of the boudoirs of Paris and its low-life dives, Edith Van Cleve back in New York was besieged by film offers for him. Much of Hollywood, including MCA president Lew Wasserman, had been turned off by stories of Marlon's erratic behavior on Broadway. But when several directors, notably Stanley Kramer, began showing interest in starring the young actor in his first picture, Wasserman and others became turned on again. The question was, "Where was Marlon?"

"I don't have to tell you what a big city Paris is," Edith told Wasserman. "I'm sending my co-agent, Maynard Morris, to Paris to find Marlon wherever he is. Maynard is the guy, you may remember, who discovered Marlon in summer stock. Maynard knows a lot of people in Paris. I'm convinced that he can find Marlon and bring him to Hollywood."

Wasserman warned her that time was running out on Kramer's offer to Marlon for a starring role in his next film.

"Yes, I know, Lew," she said. "Fortunately, I have five other firm offers for even better parts for Marlon at a bigger salary also waiting on my desk."

Wasserman had no way of knowing if she were bluffing or not. "Get Brando!" he shouted into the phone. "Get his ass in those tight blue jeans back to America. We're going to make a big movie star out of the joker if we have to drag him kicking and screaming into stardom!"

Lew Wasserman

Chapter Eight

In today's terms, French actors Christian Marquand and Daniel Gélin might be called the Brad Pitt and Tom Cruise of their day. But as charming and as handsome as he was, Christian wasn't enough to satisfy Marlon's libido. Upon meeting Daniel, he wanted him too. And so it came to be.

When Roger Vadim and Christian moved into a larger apartment along quai d'Orléans, Marlon went with them. Since there were four bedrooms, another roommate was added to help meet expenses. Even though he'd married French actress Danièle Delorme in 1945, Daniel and Danièle were living apart in 1949, although their divorce wouldn't come until 1954.

As with Roger and Christian, Marlon formed a friendship with Daniel that would last a lifetime. Christian and Daniel had replaced Carlo Fiore and Wally Cox as Marlon's best friends.

Three years older than Marlon, and strikingly handsome, Daniel had been born in the Loire Valley of France, and he would take Marlon to his home turf to show him the region's fabled châteaux. Even though Daniel's career as an actor would span sixty years in French theater, TV, and films, international audiences know of him only for a small role he had in Alfred Hitchcock's *The Man Who Knew Too Much*, released in 1956. As Doris Day looks on in horror, Daniel appears before James Stewart in a Marrakesh souk with a dagger in his back. Daniel whispers to Stewart the revelation of an assassination plot.

In later years, Daniel would impersonate *Napoléon* on the screen in 1955 in a film of the same name. Marlon in the year before would pull the same stunt in *Desirée*.

Like Christian, Daniel, though basically straight (he would marry three women), had been seduced into homosexuality by the same man: Jean Cocteau. Daniel was an easy mark for Marlon's conquest.

"Marlon had Christian for love in the afternoon and Daniel at night, with lots of beautiful women on the side, each of them picked up and randomly discarded, whereas

Daniel Gélin

both Christian and Daniel stayed around almost until the end," Jacques Viale claimed.

Daniel was part of Paris' post-war St-Germain-des-Prés scene that centered around such writers and intellectuals as Simone de Beauvoir, Jean-Paul Sartre, Juliette Gréco, and Boris Vian. Daniel would introduce Marlon to each of these figures. Some of the meetings were successful, some were not, and one would lead to a seduction.

Sartre, the biggest name of all, ignored Marlon, telling Daniel that, "I have no interest in American actors. Also, no interest in this Tennessee Williams and his Southern decadence. All 'honey child' and dripping wax magnolias—no reality to it at all!"

Daniel called the chanteuse, Juliette Gréco, "my cellar friend," a reference to the fact that they met only in Left Bank cellars or boîtes where live music was featured. Upon meeting this beautiful brunette, Marlon was captivated by her. At first the attraction wasn't mutual.

Almost overnight, Marlon and Daniel were seen in Left Bank clubs hanging out with Boris Vian, who was one of the leading symbols of the post-war generation. Amazingly, he was an engineer, a poet, a novelist, a songwriter, a jazz trumpeter, and a record producer. Almost every night the trio shared a table at Tabou, a jazz joint.

Vian told Marlon that "only two things count in life: love, in all its many shapes, with pretty girls, and the music of New Orleans or Duke Ellington." Marlon didn't completely agree with that philosophy.

Vian called life "the foam of our days." In his broken English, he sometimes spoke in riddles to Marlon, who often didn't understand what he meant. "Because all this is not still nothing," Vian said enigmatically, "Boris Vian is prepared to become Boris Vian."

"I'm prepared to become Marlon Brando, but it might become a life-long struggle."

"I'm already Daniel Gélin. The one and only."

Sometimes Marlon and Vian would sit at tables twelve feet apart at Café de Flore and engage in fights with hard-boiled or even fresh eggs. When Sartre was hit one night, management asked Marlon and Vian to take their business elsewhere. Juliette Gréco remained a regular and acceptable customer. She said, "At the Flore, people are less ugly than anywhere else."

Even though kicked off the premises himself, Marlon still had a fond memory for the Flore. He claimed that "it was a great gathering place for artists of yesterday and of tomorrow, and the best place in Paris to take advantage of the first rays of the sun after a night of hell-raising with Daniel or Christian, sometimes Roger or Jacques."

Truman Capote, who had already known Marlon somewhat intimately,

248

showed up at the Café de Flore, spotting Daniel and Marlon at a nearby table. He told Tennessee, "They were so young and good looking and so unsuccessful at hiding their love. One afternoon I caught Marlon with his shoes off with his noble foot buried in Daniel's crotch under the table. Ah, if only I could find true love."

Daniel later claimed that the group of Frenchmen into which Marlon had stumbled was a "hot jazz generation" who had emerged in the closing months after the Nazis were run out of town. "We didn't just enjoy too much alcohol at night, we also overindulged in cocaine and heroin. Our main goal was not drugs but sexual freedom. That's where I stood when I first met Marlon, who seemed to want to be completely free sexually. Often the sex of our partner for the night didn't matter, and why should it? We were more concerned that the object of our affection for the night be good in bed and not whether they had a vagina or a penis. Both a penis and a vagina can bring sexual satisfaction if put to the right use, don't you agree? It was a new era in Paris, and all of us, including Marlon, were eager to break the sexual taboos imposed on us by our parents and a restrictive society. For example, I urged both Juliette and Brigitte to try lesbianism, but they had no interest."

Marlon quickly learned that Daniel had played the tom-toms in his film for Jacques Becker, a romantic comedy called *Rendez-vous de juillet (Rendezvous in July)*, released in 1949. On hearing that, Marlon began to practice the tom-toms with Daniel in the new apartment, driving Roger and Christian "insane."

Soon Daniel managed to get them bookings in Left Bank boîtes where both men entertained young audiences with their music. Marlon later wrote to Fiore in New York: "This, and not appearing in *Streetcar* on Broadway, is the most exciting moment of my life."

Ironically, in the films that lay ahead of them in the Fifties, both Marlon and Daniel, on different sides of the ocean, came to symbolize the youth of their generation, especially after Marlon made *The Wild One* and Becker made two more films with Daniel.

Even though married—Danièle Delorme had co-starred with him in *Rendez-vous*—Daniel in his own words devoted his life to "sex, drink, and drugs," candidly admitting later in life that the "lethal combination got the better of me."

A staunch, longtime socialist and political activist, Daniel inspired Marlon in his future fights to protect the rights of African-Americans and Native Americans.

As the years went by, Marlon watched as Daniel "squandered his great gifts, his remarkable talent," noting that his friend's personal life had become "a mess." After writing that, Marlon later admitted to Roger that, "I could be describing myself." Through all Daniel's stormy relationships, Marlon stood by him, even in the suicide attempts. He was there for the death of his one son, Pascal, who was only fourteen months old when he accidentally swallowed pills in 1957. Marlon wasn't physically on site when Daniel's second son, Xavier, whom Marlon knew well, lost a battle with cancer in 1999. But Marlon was on the phone almost every morning with Daniel, who was making his last threat of suicide.

In another irony, Marlon appeared with Daniel's illegitimate daughter, actress Maria Schneider, when they made *Last Tango in Paris* in 1972. She was the product of Daniel's affair with French model and bookstore owner, Marie Christine Schneider, whom he never married.

Upon Daniel's death in 2002, he won the praise of French president Jacques Chirac, who hailed him as "one of France's most enduring actors," claiming that he would be remembered for his "subtlety and sensitivity in his roles."

On hearing the news of Daniel's death, Marlon was devastated. "I have truly loved only three men in my life: Wally Cox, Christian Marquand, and Daniel Gélin. All the others were ships passing in the night."

* * *

The wild jazz club to frequent on the Left Bank was Le Tabou on rue Dauphine. Marlon started going there every night, often in the company of Roger Vadim, Daniel Gélin, Jacques Viale, or Christian Marquand, singly or in various combinations. Sometimes he brought his pickup for the night, which could be male or female.

The attraction was Juliette Gréco, the darling of Left Bank café society in the post-war years. Marlon, or so he told his new French friends, had fallen in love with her. This chanteuse had been dubbed "the high priestess of existentialism." Nightly she sang songs that were really poems, written for her by such stellar lights as Jean-Paul Sartre or Raymond Queneau, who had penned the extraordinary "*Si tu t'imagines*" just for Gréco. Jacques Prévert wrote the now classic "*Les feuilles mortes*" for her. The general French public still preferred Edith Piaf, but bohemian Paris adored Gréco, who had gained nationwide fame in France when Jean Cocteau cast her in his 1949 film, *Orphée*.

Born in Montpellier three years after Marlon entered the world, Gréco was the daughter of a Corsican policeman and a mother who later became a key figure in the French Resistance movement during World War II. Gréco herself was educated in a restrictive convent school before moving with her sister, Charlotte, and her mother to Paris. In 1943, all three of them were arrested by the Gestapo. Charlotte and her mother were sent to a prison camp,

Juliette Gréco

but the Gestapo released sixteen-year-old Gréco. She found herself wandering alone and penniless on the streets of Paris.

"I like this singer's mysterious dark looks," Marlon told Boris Vian. "A man could lose himself in a woman who looks like Juliette does. She's like a mysterious planet or a country in some remote corner of the earth waiting to be discovered."

Her tight-fitting black leotard added to her charm. At night she attended Communist meetings. With his more daring Left Bank friends, Marlon too attended some of these secret meetings, where he met poets, painters, writers, and musicians. Jean-Paul Sartre, who sometimes attended, told Marlon that Gréco's voice "encompasses millions of poems." He too was enthusiastic about Gréco, but never understood Marlon's appeal to his bohemian friends.

One night Marlon was seen at Le Tabou smoking marijuana with the jazz trumpet player, Miles Davis. Night after night, Marlon watched dawn break over the Paris skyline before heading back to his bed to sleep for most of the day.

The story may be apocryphal, but Marlon was said to have pursued Gréco in spite of her rejection of his often crude sexual overtures to her. She reportedly kept resisting him until one night, or so it is said, he climbed the wall of her apartment building. Somehow, it is believed, he climbed into the window of her second-floor boudoir, perhaps with the aid of a ladder. Once inside, he made his conquest of Gréco, as Left Bank rumor had it.

Roger Vadim and Christian Marquand claimed that Marlon was successful. Later, the romance between Marlon and Gréco was compared to that strangest of all desert plants, the Night-Blooming Cereus, called "queen of the night." Its exquisitely scented flower opens as night falls, then closes forever with the first rays of the morning sun. The fragrant, trumpet-shaped flower blooms for only one night at midsummer, evocative of Marlon's supposed conquest of Gréco.

She offered Marlon her debut single recording of "*Je suis comme je suis*" (I Am What I Am), which was written for her by Jacques Prévert. Marlon is said to have taken the record to Hollywood with him where he spent many a night during the Fifties listening to its haunting, evocative sound.

In later years, and perhaps unknown to Gréco, Marlon slipped into two or three of her concerts when the lights dimmed, disappearing before they went on again. He was especially impressed with her recording of "*Déshabillez-*

moi" (Undress Me). It became her most famous song, and she sang it in concerts around the world, often following in the footsteps of one of Marlon's other one-night stands, Marlene Dietrich.

Over the years, Gréco has had little to say on record about Marlon. She did find him intriguing, and, to an interviewer, remembered him as "a very polite and charming man with a great interest in everything. But I had the impression that he was not very strong. In performance, of course, he had enormous strength so that he had only to say something for you to believe it absolutely."

Back in New York after his return from Paris, Marlon told Carlo Fiore, "Of all the women I've met in the world, I thought Juliette Gréco was the one who truly deserved me. Obviously, though, she is a woman with a mind of her own—and quite a keen mind at that. It was her loss! She left a malicious blow like a knife in my heart."

He watched in surprise as her legend grew over the years, and she became the very symbol of *l'époque existentialist.*

In many ways, they would pursue the same politics in the years ahead, both becoming outspoken in their defense of oppressed people. He was, however, dismayed when Gréco "went Hollywood," becoming the mistress of Darryl F. Zanuck. The producer put her into a number of films in the late 50s and early 60s, including Hemingway's *The Sun Also Rises,* but she never caught on with American audiences, who preferred the likes of Doris Day, Marilyn Monroe, even Sandra Dee, in those days.

Shortly before Marlon's death, when world headlines announced that he was dying, Gréco gave one of her rare interviews, failing to mention her long-ago admirer. In bad translation from the French, she claimed, "I am rather insane than wise. I exist where truth lives and takes its form, where it becomes alive."

* * *

At the time Marlon flew into France, the magazine *Paris-Match* was the leading journal of Europe. Its director was Hervé Mille, a homosexual and an arbiter of Parisian taste and style. A cultured, elegantly attired Frenchman, he was the epitome of continental charm and grace, moving in the top echelon of Paris, his best friends including Coco Chanel, Jean Cocteau, Edith Piaf, and Charles Aznavour. In Paris, Hervé was called "the Richelieu of Jean Prouvost," a reference to the French press lord and wool magnate who owned *Paris-Match.*

Hervé's brother, Gerard Mille, was one of the leading decorators of Europe. He lived with Hervé at a sumptuous villa on rue de Varenne that was the major center of international Paris society in the post-Liberation era. As writer Marcel Haedrick once said, "Through the Mille home passed everyone who had talent, reputation, money, everyone who was of any importance, lasting or otherwise."

In February of 1949, Hervé had flown to New York to attend five performances of *A Streetcar Named Desire*. On his fifth visit to the play, he had gone backstage on the arm of Irene Mayer Selznick to meet both Marlon and Jessica Tandy.

The following morning, with Irene and her lawyer, he acquired the French rights to Tennessee's play, with a premiere production to be mounted in Paris. Before leaving New York, he called Marlon and invited him to visit him and his brother, Gérard, if he ever came to Paris.

Jacques Viale, who continued his friendship with Marlon, once tried to publish a small memoir documenting Marlon's adventures in Paris (on several trips), as well as recollections of Vadim, Bardot, Christian Marquand, Daniel Gélin, Jean Cocteau, and others. Poorly written, he could find no publisher for it. However, it provided a tantalizing glimpse of how Marlon came to have a friendship with such an unlikely pair as the Mille brothers, who lived in a world far different from his. Viale's account has no secondary source to back it up.

Marlon later told Viale that he "just arrived" at the doorstep to the Mille villa, remembering that it was still twilight and he couldn't resist the temptation to roll like a dog in their green grass. He claimed that Hervé later told him that when he looked out the window of his boudoir, seeing a young man in a T-shirt and tight-fitting blue jeans, he knew "at once that it was Stanley Kowalski shipped over from New Orleans."

It was true that Hervé had invited Marlon to call on him if he were ever in Paris, but the arbiter of protocol had expected a telephone call to precede Marlon's arrival at his door.

In spite of the intrusion, Hervé and Marlon became "instant friends," and Hervé is said to have taken him to a restaurant on the Left Bank frequented mainly by homosexuals and members of the French intelligentsia. When they returned to the villa, Gerard was still awake, having arrived home two hours earlier. He was reading in the library and listening to recordings of Edith Piaf. Even before Hervé introduced Marlon, Gerard "knew at once that it was Stanley Kowalski," having recognized Marlon from his photographs.

If Viale is to be believed, Gerard told Marlon that, "I'm an atheist, but on nights such as this I truly believe there is a God in heaven."

Whether true or not, Marlon claimed to Viale that he "moved in that night, and I've become their house guest on a rather intimate basis."

Gerard later told Vadim that he considered Marlon one of the most sexually liberated persons he'd ever met—"and that coming from a friend of Jean Genêt."

Three days later, Marlon arrived at the Mille villa on the arm of Christian Marquand, introducing the French actor to both Hervé and Gerard. The two brothers and Christian played a practical joke on Marlon, sitting through a lunch as if meeting for the first time. Actually, the brothers were friends of Christian, having known him for a number of years.

"We quickly brought Marlon into our circle," Gerard is quoted as having said. "Christian was already a permanent fixture."

Apparently, both Christian, called "the sexiest man in France," and Marlon, hailed as "the sexiest man in America," had free run of the Mille villa. The only time that Gerard got angry at them was when he went to his closet to select one of his six tuxedos for a formal dinner party and found all of them missing. Invited to a special premiere, his friends—Christian, Marlon, Daniel Gélin, Jacques Viale, Roger Vadim, and Frederick Brisson—had borrowed all his formal wear. A producer, Brisson was married to screen star, Rosalind Russell, whom Coco Chanel years later would denounce as a "big horse" when there was talk of casting his wife in a stage play based on Chanel's life, the part eventually going to Katharine Hepburn.

Marlon often wandered around the Mille household inspecting it as if it were a museum, looking on in awe at the calamander screens and the lavish

All dressed up

use of mirrors that seemed to give the salons a magic aura, that and the mammoth Chinese vases and the Venetian statues of blackamoors. Incongruously he encountered a lot of mounted deer.

Marlon became a fixture at the Mille dinner parties that often included Roger Vadim and Brigitte Bardot. Amazingly, with almost no credentials, Marlon had moved into the top echelon of *tout Paris.*

Hervé told Marlon that he had hired Jean Cocteau to stage the French production of *Streetcar*, and that the playwright, who had written *The Eagle Has Two Heads*, in which Marlon had appeared with Tallulah Bankhead, was eager to meet him. As of yet, they had found no French actor to play Stanley, although the celebrated but notorious star, Arletty, had been cast as Blanche DuBois.

At the time of his burgeoning friendship with the Mille brothers, Marlon spoke only a little bit of French. Gerard, or so it is believed, was the first to suggest that Marlon reprise his Broadway role as Stanley but in French. Vadim said that Marlon could speak the language with a perfect accent, even though he didn't understand the meaning of the words. "Your accent is better than mine," Vadim told Marlon. The Mille brothers agreed. Under Cocteau's tutelage, the brothers felt that Marlon could master the language and be a sensation at the Parisian premiere of Tennessee's play. Marlon agreed to at least consider the possibility, and a meeting was set up between Cocteau and him.

The brothers had already taken Marlon to hear their friend, Charles Aznavour, sing. Before Cocteau would arrive in Paris, Gerard wanted Marlon to meet "our other two dear, dear friends."

"Who might these 'dear, dear ones be?'" Marlon asked.

"They are so very different," Gerard said, "but forever alluring with a timeless charm about both of them. Coco Chanel and Edith Piaf."

* * *

Coco Chanel and Marlon Brando were certainly the odd couple. Only the Mille brothers would think of bringing this incongruous pair together for lunch. Marlon was not used to taking advice about his dress code from anyone, so he appeared in the garden in his blue jeans and a T-shirt.

When Coco arrived, the Mille brothers were shocked to see her also attired in blue jeans. Perhaps she'd been tipped off about Marlon's appearance on Broadway in *Streetcar*. At that time, no respectable woman in Paris wore blue jeans. But the *Grande Mademoiselle*, as always, was ahead of her time. In the years to come, women all over the world were wearing blue jeans. After all, Coco was the designer who got French women, and later the world, to shorten their skirts, bob their hair, and throw away their corsets. She also got them to wear her trademark Chanel No. 5.

Originally Jean Cocteau had been invited but had come down with a dreadful cold and remained at his home outside Paris, in the Île de France. Eager to meet Marlon, he sent a note instead. "Watch out for our little darling, Madame Coco," he wrote. "She has the head of a black swan but the heart of a little black bull."

Christian had warned him that Coco was a lesbian and had been a Nazi collaborator. Even though both of those charges contained a tiny grain of truth, they were hardly the full loaf of bread, as Marlon quickly determined for himself. In fact, he found her a bit flirtatious with him. He also took note of her independence, her strong will, and her sharp tongue. He further found her a self-made woman unashamed of her contradictions.

She inquired about his origins, and he told her Nebraska. Not quite sure where that was, she immediately thought he might be a native American Indian. "Perhaps you are the Last of the Mohicans," she said. Throughout the luncheon, she patted his hand fondly, referring to him as "*Mon petit Indien.* I'm so glad some American cowboy didn't shoot you down. You're far too beautiful to kill. Perhaps if you don't return to acting, I'll design men's clothes for you to model. Heaven knows somebody should design for men. All my rival male designers in Paris are pederasts, and I hardly need to name them for you."

When he invited her to come and visit America, she gladly accepted his invitation, having no intention of following through with it. "I should come and dress that dreadful First Lady of yours. Bess Truman. No wife of a head of state should dress like some washerwoman." Begun that afternoon and lasting throughout her life, Coco would attack the dress of American First Ladies, including Jacqueline Kennedy when she saw her photographed in a mini-skirt. "She wears her daughter's clothes," Coco proclaimed.

In the middle of lunch, an invitation arrived from Charles de Gaulle, who wanted to have lunch with her on the upcoming Sunday. She responded on the spot. "Tell your Mr. de Gaulle that the only invitation I'll accept is to his funeral," she informed a member of De Gaulle's staff.

Marlon was later to recall that "Chanel was the single most fascinating woman I've ever met. I detested every word that came from her mouth but was hypnotized by her. Even though she insisted on blowing the smoke of my Gitanes in my face, I still was held spellbound. Even when she blamed the Jews for the weakened franc, she continued to be mesmerizing. She complained that the blacks pouring into France had a bad smell but that she had been honored to have danced with some black prizefighter from America, with whom Marlon was unfamiliar.

He'd heard all the rumors about her, including her taking an aristocratic German officer as a lover during the Nazi occupation of France. He'd even heard about Operation Modelhut in 1943, when she'd volunteered to go to London as a representative of the Third Reich to negotiate the end of the war between Germany and England. Yet he could not believe that such a person, the most famous French woman of her time, could have entertained Nazi

Coco Chanel

256

sympathies.

Only that morning, he'd read an article that Gerard had given him, which wrote about Coco's life as an orphan, revealing that she had been born illegitimately in a poorhouse and was later raised as an orphan.

Telling a total lie, but perhaps trying to relate to her, he claimed that he too had been orphaned in Nebraska. He told her that gunmen had broken into his ancestral home on the American plains and had killed both his parents and his two sisters. He claimed that he had escaped by hiding out in the root cellar, the one used for riding out tornadoes.

She seemed to believe this distortion because it tied in with her vision of a gun-toting America. But she harshly reprimanded him for putting her into the category of an orphan, claiming she had "very rich and very loving parents." But despite her objections, the magazine article was right. She had been an orphan.

"I'm going to Deauville," she told him. "Perhaps you'll drive me there."

He kindly turned down her offer, gallantly kissing her hand.

"So sorry you're not free," she said. "I need protection in Deauville. Wealthy refugees there always buy my clothes, even right off my back. One time I found myself in only my lingerie hiding out in the women's toilet as I'd sold my gown and all the trimmings."

At the doorway to the villa, he gingerly kissed both of her cheeks. She returned his affection with a pat on the cheek. Her parting words were, "Fame is solitude. Don't let it happen to you."

* * *

Jacques Viale was not just a fan of Edith Piaf and her music, he worshipped her like a goddess. When he learned that Marlon would be spending some time with her, he demanded to know every single detail of his friend's meeting with the star, "even the times she got up to go to the bathroom, which I understand she will do with the toilet door open right in front of her friends so as not to interrupt the flow of conversation." Marlon agreed to tell Viale everything, "even when a mouse, or perhaps a cockroach, crosses the floor."

He was expecting a show business personality like Mistinguett, all in feathers and boas. Instead he got Edith Piaf in a simple black dress, even though it was designed by Chanel. Hand-kissing by the Mille brothers preceded a quick introduction to Marlon before Edith rushed up to the butler. "I need a drink. My saliva's so thick I could spit ten-franc pieces." That was a favorite line of hers.

Seated at table with her drink and Marlon, she told him, "I haven't slept for forty-eight hours. My doctor gave me a dose that would kill a stallion and still I am awake at night staring at my ceiling."

"I have found that one needs complete sexual release before sleep can come," he told her.

She smiled at him, patting his hand. "Thanks for the suggestion. I'll try it." She leaned back into the breeze, closing her eyes as if sleep might come after all. "I guess as a Broadway actor, with movie stars flying in from Hollywood, you're used to meeting only glamorous entertainers, beautiful women like Rita Hayworth or my friend Marlene Dietrich."

"I've met all kinds," he said. "Some not so beautiful."

Edith Piaf

"Now you're stuck with me, you poor dear, the one the press calls the little sparrow. Pale face, mousy hair."

"I think you're beautiful."

"Do you believe in reincarnation?" she abruptly asked, sitting up and opening her eyes.

"Of course, I do. Only a fool wouldn't believe in reincarnation."

"I do too," she said. "In a previous life I was Marie Antoinette dying a hideous death." She turned and gazed into his eyes as if demanding only the truth. "Who were you?"

"Napoléon," he answered almost without hesitation.

She looked even more deeply into his eyes to determine if he were mocking her. Finally, she decided he must be telling the truth. "I can see it in your face. You were Napoléon. I'm convinced of that."

Director Henry Koster, when he cast Marlon in the 1954 *Desirée*, would more or less tell him the same thing.

As lunch was served, with the Mille brothers hovering over Edith, she told the table that she'd had dinner with Pablo Picasso only two nights before. "He wants to paint me. A portrait like he did for Gertrude Stein. He calls my face poetic."

"It's not just poetic," Marlon interjected. "It's a book of poems."

"My, oh my," she said, looking Marlon up and down, beginning with his feet. "You must be a boxer.

"I do box as a matter of fact," he said.

"I just knew it!" she said. "I'm never wrong about these things. I adore boxers." She went on with her Picasso story. "He told me that I should hang onto the portrait once he finishes it. He claims that some day it will be like an old age pension fund for me when I sell it to a museum." She smiled. "He also made the most extraordinary statement. He said that he had a hope that his

258

paintings some day would cure toothaches."

As the lunch continued, Edith kept ordering more wine and urged Marlon to drink with her. Before that, he'd requested a glass of cold milk.

"Last month I also dined with Pablo," she said. "This time Jean Cocteau dined with us. All three of us made this agreement. We're going to write into our wills that our mourners show up at our funerals dressed in red. Anyone dressed in black will be kicked out. Would you write that same provision into your will, Mr. Brando?"

"I don't know," he said. "Death is so far from me at this point—surely the great occasion will occur for me sometime beyond the millennium—that I think it would be useless to put such a provision in a will. For all I know, people living on this planet won't even be wearing clothes post-millennium."

After lunch, she took him back to her apartment, where he just assumed she had seduction on her mind. As she was talking on the phone, he slipped off all his clothes and crawled naked under the sheets in her bedroom. After putting down the phone, she searched the apartment for him and seemed startled to find him naked in her bed.

"Who do you think I am, you bastard?" she shouted at him. "Some Pigalle whore? Get out of here!"

She chased his naked body from her bed and into the living room, holding open the door for him. Even though she was a virtual midget, she shoved him out the door, slamming it behind him.

Completely nude, he stood in the hallway, looking bewildered, not knowing what to do next. Suddenly, she opened the door and tossed only his blue jeans after him—not his T-shirt, not his shoes.

"I felt she definitely wanted to sample my noble tool," he told Viale later that night. "But she must have some mating ritual, the niceties with which I'm not familiar. I didn't play it right."

The next day, through the Mille brothers, she obtained his phone number and called him. Marlon picked up the phone. Instead of introducing herself, she sang *La Vie en rose* to him as an apology for her behavior.

She invited him back to her apartment that night. He somewhat reluctantly accepted her invitation. To his surprise, he found her dressed not in her little black Chanel but in tattered rags. She wanted him to take her back to Pigalle where she'd broken into show business by singing on the streets for a few francs a night. En route there in a taxi, she told him that she often performed this ritual. "It's important," she cautioned him, "to remember our roots."

On the streets of Pigalle, her haunting, evocative voice was raised in song once again. Marlon held the cap to collect the meager francs offered. Although one of the most famous women in France, along with Coco Chanel, Edith was not recognized. However, all the passers-by recognized the distinctive voice, seemingly figuring that she was a Piaf impersonator. Marlon found that highly amusing. One bagwoman came up to her and proclaimed, "Sweetie, you'll never sound anything like the real Piaf. You just don't have the voice!"

Later that night she took him to her familiar haunts at Pigalle and at Montmartre. She invited him to ride with her on a merry-go-round that stayed open all night, hoping to give drunken revelers a thrill. "I want to see the dawn come up with you," she told him as she purchased a gingerbread "pig" for him from a street vendor. Later she invited him to her favorite bistro, Lulu's. Over French onion soup, she told him, "Whenever I'm lonely I come here to pick up Joes." She actually used the word Joes.

Staggering drunk into her building at six o'clock that morning, she stumbled and fell against a bucket of dirty water that the washerwoman had left in her hallway. He easily picked up her frail frame. As he would tell Viale, "I removed the rags from her body, retaining only her panties, and put her to bed. Then I slipped out of the apartment."

A slightly hung-over Edith called him the next morning to invite him to go with her to the Lido that night to see "the most beautiful and long-legged showgirls in Paris. Most of them, my dear, are from London. They have everything I don't. Not just legs but breasts. Shapely asses."

At the Lido at the head table shared by Edith, Marlon gazed upon "the sexiest women I've ever seen in my life, all dancing bare-breasted," as he would relate to Viale. He was somewhat startled when Edith invited some of them to join her at table for champagne. All of the showgirls were eager to meet the great Edith Piaf. "I often come here when I'm lonely and invite some of the girls to go home with me to cook French fries," she told Marlon. "To his surprise," she did just that. After the show Edith, Marlon, and seven Lido dancers piled into two taxicabs and headed back to her apartment.

Once there, Marlon devoured the long-limbed beauties. He soon learned that of all the Lido dancers, a blonde from London made the best French fries.

The next day Marlon told Viale that he was hoping for an orgy. Roger Vadim had already told Marlon of Edith's lesbian tendencies and of her ongoing affair with Marlene Dietrich. But before dawn broke across the sky, Edith ushered the Lido girls out the door.

Apparently Marlon had proved his worthiness to her, and it was she who invited him to share her bed. He realized his mistake had been in getting into her bed on the previous night without an invitation.

Before taking off her clothes, she warned him, "I'm not a pervert. I noticed that the American men I sleep with think all French women are whores and will do all those nasty things their wives back home won't do for them. I believe in hygienic love. If you want dirty love, get yourself a whore from

Pigalle."

As she removed her final wardrobe, a pair of panties, he took in her small, frail body. "Also, I don't like men who get all sentimental with me and start crying for their mothers in the middle of the night. I want a man. Not a cry baby. And a final warning. If you want to go to bed with me, you must seduce Edith Piaf—not EDITH PIAF!"

The following day, Marlon told Viale, "Finally, I fucked her after days of foreplay. She was still asleep when I left her bed in the late morning. She looked deathly pale. In fact, she didn't even seem to be breathing."

Marlon became so concerned that he even called Gerard Mille and asked him to place a discreet call to see if Edith were all right. She informed Gerard that she viewed Marlon like a "meteor." This was the word she used for all her one-night stands. "He streaks across the Piaf sky and gives off a bright glow before falling to earth and turning into a cold piece of stone from outer space."

* * *

Jean Cocteau did not come to Paris to meet Marlon but sent an invitation for him to visit him at his country home at Milly in the Ile de France. Eager to meet Cocteau, Marlon arrived at the author and filmmaker's address where Joan of Arc had reputedly slept.

Marlon later told Jacques Viale and Christian Marquand that he'd been shocked at Cocteau's fakir-thin body with legs so willowy they evoked broomsticks. He extended a frail hand that looked as if it would be crushed if squeezed too tightly. The discolored yellow fingernails revealed his addiction to opium. To Marlon, Cocteau had a "slightly fish eyed look" which, even so, still managed to express an inner torture that suggested that all his dreams had

gone unfulfilled. "Those were the saddest eyes I've ever seen," he told Vadim. "They were so filled with pain that I felt I was looking into the doorway to Hell." When questioned how Cocteau's eyes could be so expressive and still fish-eyed, Marlon mumbled something and changed the subject.

In Milly, Cocteau put his delicate hand into Marlon's stronger grip as he proudly showed off his garden which was carved into oblongs like an herbarium from the Middle Ages. He was especially proud of his espaliered pear trees. Apparently, Cocteau and Marlon had made a silent agreement never to bring up the subject of Marlon's appearance with Tallulah Bankhead in *The Eagle Has Two*

Jean Cocteau

Heads. It was a distasteful memory for both of them.

Sitting on a bench in front of a bust of a sinister-looking jinni, Cocteau got to know Marlon. He'd seen him perform as Stanley on Broadway but had never gone backstage to meet him. Cocteau later told a friend, "the savage beast from the American Midwest in all his manly glory and with his muscles intact has arrived at my humble abode. Just as he raped Blanche DuBois, I know he will go even beyond that limit with me and rip my very heart from my chest."

Marlon seemed amused that on the day of their meeting, Cocteau was having a bad hair day which made him look like a crazed scientist from some 1930s film. His frizzy hair shot out in all directions, as if he'd just undergone an electric shock treatment.

Before lunch that day, Cocteau invited Marlon inside his house to show him to the guest bedroom. Marlon wandered about as if he'd entered a very eccentric museum. Surely the gilded imitation fruit trees were a bit much for his own taste. Certainly he must have received a jolt when gazing upon a mammoth ten-foot tusk of a narwhal. Art Nouveau wallpaper had been plastered on every wall, at one point forming a backdrop for Bérard's large painting of Oedipus and the Sphinx.

As Cocteau stood as close as he could to Marlon, measuring himself against Marlon's larger frame, he said, "I feel like a very old pretzel standing next to a slab of prize Grade A American beef."

Over lunch Cocteau introduced Marlon to "my protégé," Edouard Dermithe, whom he affectionately called "Doudou." The sexy Italian/Yugoslav appeared in the smallest and tightest bikini Marlon had ever seen, one obviously designed to show off his heavy endowment. To Marlon, it was obvious that Doudou was a pet toy. "Doudou is a painter of male nudes," Cocteau told Marlon. "Before you head back to Paris, you must pose for him, of course."

Marlon accepted that offer. Three days later, Cocteau's dear friend, Woodrow Parrish-Martin, an American artist, arrived from New York to spend a few days at Milly. He found Doudou painting a nude Marlon in Cocteau's garden. As Parrish-Martin later reported, Marlon was frontally nude but draped in a Roman toga with boots. Cocteau had placed a *faux* Doric pillar beside Marlon.

As ridiculous and preposterous as this scene may have appeared, it would be repeated by Marlon when he agreed to appear in the 1953 release of *Julius Caesar*, a film in which he would be half dressed but with his genitals concealed.

"I wasn't privy to all the secrets of the Cocteau household that summer," Parrish-Martin recalled. "But I do know that Cocteau, Brando, and Doudou were sleeping together in the master bedroom's four-poster with a lavish canopy. I was never invited to join them."

He also reported that Doudou and Marlon frequently sunned themselves in the nude in the garden, Cocteau making frequent appearances in a red silk Japanese robe. "He was deeply committed to his opium," Parrish-Martin claimed. "To me, this was a household of black orchids. Incidentally, the black orchid was Cocteau's favorite flower."

Parrish-Martin was still a houseguest at Cocteau's when Marlon departed for Paris. He turned a deaf ear to Cocteau's pleadings for him to appear as Stanley in the French version of

Woodrow Parrish-Martin

Streetcar. "There's no way in Hell that I'm going to play Stanley again in any language, including Finnish. I'm also turning down the film version if offered. Let Anthony Quinn do the role and fuck it up!"

During the course of Marlon's visit, Cocteau had learned that Marlon had studied dance, even the ballet. On several occasions, Cocteau promised to write a ballet in which Marlon would star, with a final scene danced in the nude. "It'll be a sensation in Paris." Marlon made it clear that he no longer wanted to be a ballet dancer.

Parrish-Martin felt that Cocteau found Marlon "sexually mesmerizing," but he completely misjudged Marlon's own fascination with him. "I think Cocteau was just a momentary diversion for Marlon. Marlon had a history of renting out his body—without pay, that is—to a number of famous men. Receiving a blow-job from some famous person meant very little to him. Certainly it didn't suggest an emotional attachment."

When Cocteau bade Marlon *adieu*, Doudou was conveniently taking his one-hour morning bath. Cocteau told Marlon, "My love for my fellow man has always involved the capitulation of myself. My love always leads to the forfeiture of myself and my own manhood. I have given everything and received so little in return. With you, it could have been so different. We could have been involved with each other on equal terms. It could have been so different with you."

Before heading out, Marlon enigmatically replied, "It would have been different all right."

* * *

Marlon went to see the 1945 French film, Marcel Carné's monumental

Les Enfants du paradis (Children of Paradise) three times. Later he called it "maybe the best movie ever made."

"I was mad about Arletty," he told Fiore. "I mean, I was really in love with her. My first trip to Paris, I asked to meet Arletty. I went to see her as though I were going to a shrine. My ideal woman. Wow! Was that a mistake, was that a disillusionment. She was a tough bird. Her feathers, and she'd covered herself with a lot of them, grew in all the wrong directions. She devastated me. It took a while for me to pick up the pieces."

Long before the arrival of Catherine Deneuve, Jean Cocteau had pronounced Arletty "the most beautiful woman ever captured on film." When he was planning to adapt *A Streetcar Named Desire* for the Paris stage, he naturally asked her to play the fading Blanche DuBois. In 1949, Arletty, though still in possession of her great beauty, was fifty-one years old, but looked much younger. She was the Marlene Dietrich of Paris. "Regardless of how deep I move into age, I will be the eternal *femme fatale*," she told Cocteau who agreed with her.

In post-war France, Arletty was at the nadir of her once-fabled popularity in French films of the 1930s. At the time Marlon arrived in Paris, Arletty was trying to live down charges that she'd been a Nazi sympathizer during the occupation of France. In 1945, she'd been sent to prison for having an affair with a German officer. "My heart is French," she told an astonished judge, "but my arse is international."

The partisan French referred to Parisian women who slept with Nazis as "horizontal collaboration." First thrown into the Drancy concentration camp, Arletty was later sent to Fresnes prison near Paris where she languished for 120 days. When released, she was put under house arrest for another two years.

When Marlon first met her, she was still under a three-year suspended sentence and had to report to a parole officer. The judge had forbidden her to appear on the screen until the Forties came to an end, although he had not ruled out stage work. When Cocteau offered her the role of Blanche DuBois, she accepted it.

Marlon attended the opening night of *A Streetcar Named Desire* in Paris. He would later write to Edith Van Cleve in New York that he found Arletty's Blanche "more authentic than that of Jessica Tandy." But overall he found the Parisian version of *Streetcar* "a vulgarization of Tennessee's work—a bastard child, really." He

Arletty

noted that Cocteau had included such bizarre touches as nude belly dancers undulating in the background.

Back in New York, Marlon told Carlo Fiore that the French actor playing Stanley—he couldn't remember "the joker's name"—was pathetic. "To show emotion, the fucker kept leaping over the stage furniture—not just the chairs but the table as well. He made me and the audience…well, 'jumpy.'"

After the performance, he eagerly went backstage to meet Arletty at long last. He had not shaved in three days, and his jeans were so dirty and smelly they could stand up on their own legs. His hair was a tangled mess. Biographer Charles Higham wrote, "Arletty came from a tradition in which stars dressed like stars, people got themselves up to go to the theater, and nobody came backstage without an invitation. She snubbed him, and he was mortified."

This is the "accepted gospel" as promulgated in other Brando biographies as well. However, Arletty's maid and longtime companion, Mme. Jacqueline Triolet, had a far different story to tell about her mistress and "this upstart young American actor." It was true that Arletty dismissed Marlon when she first saw him. However, Cocteau told her who he was and what a sensation he'd been on the New York stage playing Stanley.

Out of respect for his acting genius, Arletty contacted Marlon and invited him for lunch the following day. Cocteau had warned Marlon to appear in his one decent suit of clothing. On their second meeting, Arletty saw beyond the dress and found Marlon charming. Since the beginning of the war, she'd had a fondness for young men, especially handsome, virile young men. "I share that trait in common with Cocteau," she once said.

Far from rejecting Marlon this time as she had backstage, she invited him to spend the night in her boudoir. The following afternoon she took him to her tailor who hastily designed two suits for "my new protégé," as she referred to him. A dark suit was to be worn at night when he'd accompany her to chic parties. A lighter suit was made for daytime wear, especially long drawn out lunches in the Bois de Boulogne.

"She wanted to turn me into her kept boy," Marlon told Fiore. "Light her cigarettes at parties. Freshen up her drink. Fuck her silly all night and then have freshly brewed coffee waiting for her when she took off her satin domino the next morning. Arletty wanted a combination sex slave and manservant."

At one point during their short-lived and mismatched romance, Arletty asked him if he'd play Stanley opposite her. "I can easily get that jackal playing Stanley fired," she told him. She said that in just a week she could teach him all of Stanley's lines in French. "We'll be a big hit, far bigger than I am now. Later, we can take *Streetcar* on a tour of the provinces and really haul in the francs."

He never formally turned down the offer. Apparently, Arletty was not aware that both the Mille brothers and Cocteau had made a similar offer to Marlon, which also had been refused. Perhaps the offer was too much for Marlon to handle. Or maybe he was growing tired of *tout Paris*.

As he wrote Edith, he was heading south to Rome. "All the so-called intellects, like Sartre, spend their nights drinking and attacking America. There is a lot I don't like about my own country either. But I'm just tired of it. I'm heading for Rome to sample the climate down there."

Regrettably, he left no forwarding address, even though Edith was desperately trying to get in touch with him to present movie offers, especially one from Stanley Kramer.

Upon his return to America, he gave her more details about Arletty, though not many. "One morning when she removed her satin domino, she found that her 'boy' had fled the nest. I didn't even leave her a note thanking her for her hospitality and the use of her overripe pussy."

Over a dinner in Brooklyn with Fiore, he said, "Arletty might be an icon in French cinema, but to me she was just a vicious, devouring bitch. Whatever possessed this Nazi whore to think she could control the uncontrollable—namely me?"

* * *

Abandoning Paris, Marlon, along with Christian Marquand, took the train to Rome. Their compartment was so small that the two men practically slept on top of each other. Since they had to raise their bunk bed to use the toilet, they often held "pissing contests" out the train window to see which one could shoot the longest stream of urine.

Through some unknown friend in Rome, Christian had arranged a meeting for Marlon to meet Vittorio De Sica, the Italian actor and director. At some point during his stay in Paris, Marlon had convinced himself that he wanted to make a film debut after all, but only in a neo-realistic Italian movie directed by De Sica.

De Sica was one of the chief exponents of neo-realism in the Italian cinema, and of all the directors in Rome at the time Marlon most admired his work. On four different occasions, he'd seen *Ladri di biciclette* (The Bicycle Thief), released in 1948. It's the tender story of a working class man whose bicycle is stolen, and it had won a special Academy Award for best foreign language film before the category was created.

There was much that Marlon admired about De Sica, including his employment of nonprofessional actors and location shooting to make scenes as realistic as possible. He liked the way De Sica used social issues as a theme

266

Vittorio De Sica

in his movies. "Just the kind of movies I'd want to make myself," Marlon had told Roger Vadim before leaving Paris.

At the time of the arranged meeting between Marlon and De Sica, the director/actor was at the peak of his creative powers and a long way from his posthumous film in 1974, *Il Viaggio* (The Voyage) that told of a turgid romance with an unlikely pair of lovers, Richard Burton and Sophia Loren.

In 1949, De Sica had starred in a film, *Domani è troppi tardi* (Tomorrow Is Too Late), with a fragile teenage actress of unvarnished beauty, Anna Maria Pierangeli, who in short time would be sent to Hollywood and hailed as "The Little Garbo" and billed as Pier Angeli. At the Venice Film Festival the following year (1950) her film would be named best Italian movie of that year, and Pier would win the award as best performance by an Italian actress.

Though De Sica was aware of Marlon's performance as Stanley on Broadway, he had not actually seen the play himself. Many friends of his had seen it, and had only glowing reports to deliver back to Rome. De Sica told his associates that he was flattered that Marlon had expressed an interest in working with him, a desire rather evocative of Ingrid Bergman's wish to work with De Sica's rival, Roberto Rossellini. Even before Marlon and Christian arrived in Rome, De Sica was polishing a film called *Homecoming* in English. He envisioned Marlon playing the male lead, with Pier Angeli cast as his young Neapolitan wife.

According to Christian, De Sica started pitching his film to Marlon within an hour of their meeting. "I want you in my story to undergo an emotional transformation on the screen." Marlon would play a young Italian soldier returning in 1945 to his hometown, war-ravaged Naples. There he would painfully learn that his young wife, Pier Angeli, had been a prostitute to Nazi soldiers as means of putting food on the table for her two children, a boy and a girl. De Sica hoped that Marlon could dramatize the inner conflict he felt about his wife being a prostitute as part of a desparate move to keep her children from starving. At one point in the proposed film, De Sica wanted the young boy to say, "She did it for us, papa. So we would have food. When you went to war, you left us to die!" Marlon was tremendously intrigued with this neo-realistic film, and, according to Christian, considered it for one week as a possible vehicle for his film debut.

When De Sica learned that Marlon was a brilliant mimic and could imitate an Italian accent perfectly, he claimed that he would hire a voice coach for him. "No actor is needed to dub for you. Your Italian is perfect, if only you understood the words. But I will tell you what emotion to express."

"I have a commitment to examining the lives of the poor," De Sica told Marlon. "I'm devoted to Communism. If you have a true heart, you too will convert to Communism. You look well fed. Much of Europe, even today, goes to bed hungry, especially young children."

To illustrate his point, De Sica invited Marlon to join him on his nightly rounds across Rome where he called on what he labeled "the invisible ones." Marlon met a shoeshine boy only eight years old who wore rags and worked for meager tips. He met old women who lived by a lit fire at night near the Tiber and raided garbage cans outside restaurants for a few scraps of food. One pathetic old man begged for a few spare lire, claiming it was not for himself, even though he was starving. He wanted to purchase a saucer of milk for his dying dog whose flesh seemed eaten up with some devouring cancer-like disease.

The most pathetic case was a doe-eyed creature, slightly effeminate, but a boy of such great beauty that Marlon was awed by his looks. Since the age of eight, he'd been kept in a brothel where he was repeatedly raped by Nazi soldiers and members of Mussolini's Italian Fascist army, often at the rate of twenty men a night. After his ordeal, he could no longer utter sounds. De Sica paid an old woman to take care of the mentally damaged youth.

After the first week, Marlon was so impressed with De Sica that he told the director to draw up a contract. He would agree, or so he said, to sign for his first film role, although De Sica had only a six-page outline of the project.

"Good! Good!" De Sica said in the presence of Christian. "I am known for finding the unsuspected depths in an actor and bringing them out. Anna Magnani says I have an extraordinary sensitive touch with actors, especially children. You look like a man but I suspect you have the soul of a child. I will find your inner child and put it on film for all the world to see." Although not a homosexual, De Sica kissed Marlon passionately on the mouth in front of Christian. It wasn't a sexual come-on but a theatrical gesture to show his appreciation for this new talent who had mysteriously appeared on his doorstep.

De Sica introduced Marlon to his mistress, Maria Mercader. "I have lived with her since 1942 because my first wife, Giuditta Rissone, won't give me a divorce."

"Based on the success of his *Bicycle* movie, De Sica had raised $125,000 for *Homecoming*, $10,000 of which he pledged to Marlon with another $5,000 going to Pier Angeli. "Women should always make less than men," De Sica said. "We don't want to spoil them."

During Marlon's brief stay in Rome, the proposed movie advanced to the point where De Sica arranged a luncheon meeting between Marlon and "my brilliant new discovery," whom he called "Anna." He predicted that she would become the biggest female star in Italian cinema.

Only ten days after Marlon met Pier Angeli, De Sica called Marlon's *pensione* near Stazione Termini. Unknown to Marlon, the director was a compulsive gambler. To gain a bigger budget for *Homecoming*, he had bet all his bankroll on the roll of the dice in an illegal casino in a hilltown near Rome. He'd lost every lira.

Shortly before his death in France in 1974, De Sica recalled, "Instead of introducing Brando to the world in 1950, I made the world take note of Sophia Loren when I made *La Ciociara* (Two Women) and released it back in 1961. Perhaps making a world-class star out of Sophia was a far greater accomplishment than putting Brando in his first film. He would not have been well cast as the Neapolitan soldier returning home to his prostitute wife. And what audience would ever believe that that angelic Pier Angeli could ever, under any circumstances, have been a prostitute?"

* * *

Even before Marlon met Pier Angeli for lunch at De Sica's home, the director had warned him that the teenager had had a very sheltered and cloistered life under the "hysterical protection" of her overpowering mother, Enrica. The mother, according to De Sica, was mainly concerned with preserving her daughter's virginity until a suitable Italian—and Italian only—husband could be found for her innocent daughter.

De Sica had discovered Pier Angeli—then known as Anna Maria Pierangeli—while strolling along Rome's Via Veneto. He gave her his card, asking if she'd like to be in the movies. From some other man, that would sound like a sexual come-on, but Enrica, who had always wanted to be an actress herself, already knew the fame of De Sica. Within weeks, Pier was cast in a star part opposite actor De Sica in *Domani è troppo tardi*, in which she played a disturbed teenager on the dawn of her sexual awakening.

The role, as Marlon soon discovered, could have been based on Pier's own life. De Sica told Marlon that during the shooting of the film, Pier at one point refused to follow directions and kiss the young boy playing opposite her.

"Not even a kiss," De Sica claimed. "Anna thinks a kiss from a boy will make her pregnant. Even Shirley Temple, Little Miss Lollipop, has been kissed on the screen. We finally got her to kiss the boy. Anna fainted."

Although he would seduce older women, especially when he was in his twenties, Marlon had a special fondness for teenage virgins. He was immedi-

Pier Angeli

ately attracted to Pier, finding her frail, tiny, and undeniably lovely—"as yet unsullied by the probing of my noble tool," as he told Christian Marquand.

Even though innocent, Pier after her first movie had become slightly more sophisticated—"but not much," in De Sica's words. "She'd learned, however, to indulge in guileless flirting. She played the teenager coquette over lunch that day with Marlon. He fascinated her. She'd never met anyone like him. I told my friend, Anna Magnani, that it was 'only a matter of days before Marlon does what no man has ever done before: get the virginal panties off Anna's ass.'"

Instead of Pier Angeli, Anna Magnani suggested that De Sica hook her up "with this American big shot, this Mr. Marlon Brando. He'll see how fast my panties come off, though they won't be virginal."

Marlon began his seduction of Pier by first winning over her mother, Enrica. He brought her gifts and even took her for a motorcycle ride one night through the narrow streets of Rome. Although he seemed to be wooing the mother, his ultimate target, according to Christian, "was to pierce that tight little hymen of Anna's."

Marlon soon discovered that mother and daughter had an "almost frightening co-dependence" on each other. When most girls of Pier's age in postwar Rome were pursuing boys, Pier, in spite of her initial screen success, still played with her dolls. She also had a particular affinity for stray animals, especially the thousands of starving cats who roamed the streets of Rome looking for rats. She brought them food at night, which Marlon helped distribute to the hungry felines. He told her of his own devotion to stray animals, which did more than anything to win her trust. "He was just setting her up for the kill," Christian said. "Marlon always got a hard-on when he was around an innocent girl, some far too young."

Christian claimed that Marlon's seduction of Pier, when it inevitably came, was "tantamount to rape. He took her fighting, protesting body on a grassy knoll near the Colosseum. Apparently, Anna never told her mother, Enrica would have ordered Marlon killed. After the rape, from what I heard, Pier withdrew into a shell. Her mother thought she had come down with some rare disease which no doctor could detect. Marlon found Pier in such a despondent state that he quickly dropped her and pursued other nocturnal adventures, often with me at his side."

However, through De Sica, Pier contacted Marlon, sending him a note. He found the note "amusing," sharing it with both De Sica and Christian. "After that night with you," Pier wrote, "I belong to you—and just to you. No man in the world will ever do that to me but you! You are going to marry me! I just know it. I will become your beautiful bride. No one will ever know what happened between us. It will be our darkest secret. Even our children must not know what happened. I will tell them I was a virgin on my wedding night, and will insist that our own daughters go to their bridal beds as virgins."

Fleeing Rome, Marlon took the train with Christian to Naples where they sailed on to Palermo in Sicily. "Apparently, from what I learned, Pier desperately tried to get in touch with Marlon so that he could marry her," Christian said. "But more virgins and more trouble were already waiting Marlon in Sicily."

That seduction in Rome might have marked the end of Marlon's relationship with Pier. But it didn't. She was lured to Hollywood in 1950 at the age of eighteen. Once there, she would begin a meteoric rise to fame which would make her a household word in America.

Other actors, including Kirk Douglas, would temporarily enter her life. None was to become as famous as James Dean.

Only when Dean became involved with Pier did Marlon show a renewed interest. He didn't want Pier, and wasn't in love with her, but his plan—and it was a diabolical one—was to show Dean that he could take any woman—or any man, for that matter—from what Marlon increasingly called "my stalker and my clone," the way he contemptuously referred to his rival in Hollywood.

* * *

Vittorio De Sica had first met Anna Magnani when he'd cast her in *Teresa Venerdi* in 1941; it was released in America under the title of *Do You Like Women?* But it would be another Italian neo-realistic film director, Roberto Rossellini, who would make her famous when he cast her in *Open City* in 1944. That same year marked the launch of a tumultuous love affair between Anna and Rossellini.

At the time De Sica introduced this "volcanic earth mother" to Marlon, Rossellini had dumped her and had impregnated his new love, the already married Ingrid Bergman, causing a worldwide scandal.

Later, Marlon told Christian Marquand that he felt that Anna only inaugurated an affair with him to make Rossellini jealous. He might have captured the heart of the queen of Hollywood, virginal-looking Ingrid Bergman, but Anna wanted to show her former lover that she could run off with the newly crowned prince of Broadway, on the dawn of his becoming a major motion picture star. Rome was a small town in those days, and Anna was aware that word would soon reach Rossellini, whom Ingrid once claimed had been "the love of Anna Magnani's life."

The one quality that Marlon liked about Anna was her ability to look straight into your eyes "with all the emotion there ever was," he said. "Even if telling a lie, she had the look of absolute honesty on her face. Actually, she was not into telling lies."

As Tennessee Williams once said of his dear friend, "I never heard a false word from her mouth."

She inhabited a universe all her own, and for two very brief and fleeting weeks in Rome Marlon became part of her world. De Sica later recalled his introduction of the volatile star to Marlon over dinner in a trattoria on the outskirts of Rome. "From the moment she met Marlon, she seemed obsessed with him," De Sica said. "And Anna was not a woman to keep her feelings to herself. Right at the table, she was crawling all over Marlon. It was obvious she couldn't wait to get him back to her apartment."

Marlon later told Christian what had happened on the night he returned to her apartment. "She took me out on her terrace and told me that she never goes to bed until the sun comes up. She said that sunrise gives a lovely glow over St. Peter's dome."

"It's the same light that greeted Michelangelo when he was designing his dome," she told Marlon. "Maybe a little more pollution to deal with today."

Although she drank only wine, she kept a bottle of Johnnie Walker Red Label on her coffee table for her male visitors. She also kept pretzels and peanuts, quickly learning that Marlon hated pretzels and devoured peanuts.

As they were holding each other and kissing each other passionately on the sofa in her living room, a handsome young man appeared from her bedroom, looking as if he'd been awakened. He was attired only in a pair of white boxer shorts.

Anna later translated their exchange in Italian for Marlon. He had told her

Anna Magnani

that he had expected her to return home much earlier. She burst into fury at the sight of him. Rushing into her bedroom, she returned with his clothing, shouting at him in Italian. Without allowing him a chance to dress, she shoved him toward the door, kicking him out and tossing his clothes after him, evoking a scene in Marlon's own recent life in Paris.

Back on the sofa after the boy had left, she told Marlon that she'd given him a key but had demanded it back, telling him never to visit her again. "The trouble with men," she said, "is that they're hard to catch. But sometimes once you've caught them, and you decide you don't really want them, it's hard to get rid of them. Let the bastard go back to the street life! He'll see what life is like when denied the comforts I offered him. My reward from him was to find out that he'd been cheating on me with other women."

Other than that he'd seduced Anna, Marlon gave De Sica and Christian few details of his first night—rather, morning—of love-making with Anna. "It must have been successful," Christian recalled, "since the following night she was driving him all over Rome."

Marlon claimed that she was the best driver he'd ever met. "She could have raced a chariot through the narrow streets of Rome and never had an accident," he later claimed. "She definitely could have been the star of *Ben-Hur*. Behind the wheel, she was fearless. Other drivers knew to make way for her."

During their brief romance, every evening was the same. She'd take him to one or another of her favorite *trattorie* for dinner. But she always called and asked what he wanted to do that night. She was merely being polite, having already mapped out the evening in exact detail. Knowing that Marlon had no real taste for food, she selected charming restaurants serving the best of regional food and usually opening onto one of the hidden squares of Rome.

The owner of a particular restaurant would always come out to greet her, ushering her to the finest table in the house and hovering over her for the rest of the night. Anna, according to Marlon, never looked at a menu, but always told the owner what she wanted for dinner.

She would even tell the chef how she wanted a dish prepared. Veal Marsala was one of her favorites. One night, in front of Marlon, she lectured a chef for fifteen minutes, discussing in the tiniest detail exactly how she wanted her veal prepared.

He noted that she had an unusual custom. After espresso, she would gather up all the leftover food on their table and place it in one of two sacks she carried with her. Then she would go from table to table, seeking food "donations" from the other diners. When she'd filled the sacks, she drove to the Colosseum where she'd deliver the food to the hungry stray cats that roamed Rome at night by the thousands. He was surprised that he'd indulged in somewhat this same pastime with Pier Angeli, making him wonder if all Roman women displayed such kindness toward strays.

One night at midnight at the Café Paris on the Via Vittorio Veneto, Anna and Marlon were at a sidewalk table enjoying a final drink, both ordering mineral water. At the next table, a young blonde starlet, wearing a low-cut gown that hardly concealed her ample breasts, kept staring flirtatiously at Marlon, while breathing in deeply to expand the size of her already large bosom.

Finally, when Anna's jealousy could no longer be controlled, she got up and ordered Marlon to leave at once with her. Picking up a full wine glass, she walked over to the starlet and poured the red liquid over her exposed breasts. "I was a whore before you were born," she said, stalking down the sidewalk to her car with Marlon trailing behind her.

Roberto Rossellini

Later, Marlon described Anna to Christian as "an enormous boiling cauldron likely to explode in fury at the slightest provocation." Her close friend, a priest, Father Antonio Lisandrini, meeting Marlon, described Anna as "a phenomenon of nature, incredible in love and anger."

Marlon became even more convinced of that as Anna often told him stories of her five-year affair with Rossellini in the postwar, pre-Bergman years. Once when staying in a villa along the Amalfi Coast, she made his favorite spaghetti for him. She seemed to be preparing it with love, even though she'd found out only that day about his ongoing love affair with Bergman.

When the dish was whipped up to perfection, she asked him to bend over to smell the wonderful aroma. As he leaned his face over the scalding hot pasta, she took her hand, and showing great strength, plowed his face into the burning food, causing him to scream in agony.

"He deserved that and more, the bastard," Anna told Marlon. "He betrayed me, dishonored our love." She claimed that one night when they both were staying in a suite at the Hotel Excelsior along the Via Veneto, Rossellini volunteered to take her two dogs for a walk. Downstairs, he left the animals with the concierge, hailed a taxi to the airport, and fled on a plane to New York. "All night I searched Rome for him, going to all his favorite clubs and restaurants hoping to find him. No Roberto."

One night she drove Marlon to a small trattoria along Via Appia Antica, the ancient route into Rome. It was after eleven o'clock which he thought was a little late to be heading out for dinner, even by Roman standards. The restaurant looked nearly deserted as she pulled up her car and turned off the lights. She waited behind the wheel with him in the passenger seat for about thirty minutes as the waiters appeared to be shutting down the trattoria.

Shortly thereafter, a man and a woman emerged from the restaurant, holding hands. The waiters had turned out the lights by then, and Marlon could not make out their faces. After putting the woman in the passenger seat, the man got behind the wheel of a red Cisitalia convertible and headed back toward Rome.

Anna started her car and trailed them, refusing to answer Marlon's questions. On the highway, the convertible was speeding, as was Anna. In what looked like an attempt to pass them by, Anna sideswiped their vehicle. Marlon in the passenger side felt the greatest impact and called out to her to stop. Once his car was hit, the unknown driver of the other car seemed to recognize Anna. Stepping on his accelerator, he tried to escape from her vehicle. Clearly the better driver, she too chased him with her iron foot on her own accelerator. Racing her car toward the rear end of his convertible, she gained speed on him, slamming into his car.

The vehicle in front, though damaged, speeded up again and left them along the deserted highway.

Anna pulled her wounded automobile to the side of the road and slumped over the steering wheel.

"Who was that?" he demanded to know.

"That was Roberto Rossellini and his Swedish whore, Ingrid Bergman," she said bursting into tears. "I still love the son of a bitch. I should have killed him."

He shared her pain as he was forced to listen to her sobs, later telling Christian that "Anna's tears were not of the ordinary. They were more like monstrous cathartic outbursts. They came like thunderous torrents."

"I felt like such a heel when I left her the following morning while she slept," Marlon said. "I didn't even leave a good-bye note. But it was time for me to move on."

In a final phone call to De Sica, Marlon said that, to him, Anna is "like a bad verismo opera. Nothing but outpouring of grief. She's all about threats and recriminations. She's ready to indulge in violence between torrents of meaningless tears. I can't live this way. I fear I will be her next victim. There is no future for us. Please understand me and thank you for everything. One day we'll make a great film together. The greatest!"

Marlon would not meet with Anna again until she was cast opposite him in the 1960 *The Fugitive Kind*, based on a play by Tennessee Williams.

Both Anna and Marlon at that time would create their own disasters both on and off the screen.

* * *

In Palermo, Christian received a telegram to return to Paris at once for a film job. He left Marlon to roam Sicily at his leisure. Marlon was later to tell *Playboy* magazine that "the most peaceful moment of my life" occurred when he was lying in a field of aromatic wildflowers in a park to the east of Palermo. With his shirt off, he lay in the grassy field as the sunlight of Sicily—praised by the ancients—tanning the muscled body so recently ravaged by Anna

Magnani and others.

What Marlon didn't tell *Playboy* was that while he was enjoying such a peaceful moment, an angry father with mob connections in Palermo had sent a junta looking for him. Only the night before Marlon had somehow managed to seduce the gangster's convent-reared daughter, taking her virginity. Her father was almost insane, having once vowed that "even if her own husband attempts to fuck my daughter, I'll have his dick cut off."

Somehow Marlon got word that he was a hunted man and sneaked onto a night boat bound for Naples. From there, he booked train passage all the way back to Paris, arriving with almost no money, having spent every lira. He had about ten francs when he arrived at the train station in Paris.

Once back in France, he made an astonishing decision given his choices. He could have lived in luxury with Christian or Roger Vadim, even Daniel Gélin. The Mille brothers would have taken him in, and most definitely Jean Cocteau would have extended another "sing-for-your-supper" invitation to his villa at Milly.

Marlon didn't even contact his newly made friends. Instead he preferred to hang out under bridges and on the streets with the *clochards*, (drunken beggars) of Paris.

Amazingly, in spite of his meager French, Marlon was adopted by these homeless ones, and it was in their company that he ventured out onto the streets of Paris at night, searching for scraps of food in the alleyways at the back of restaurants.

Smoking a cigarette on
the set of *Streetcar*

Sent to Paris by Edith Van Cleve, her co-agent, Maynard Morris, had exhausted his hope of ever finding Marlon in such a large city with no address. Morris had called Roger Vadim and others who were known to have made friends with Marlon, but nobody in the film or theater world had heard from Marlon since he left for Italy. Christian thought he might still be in Sicily.

Maynard had booked passage on a flight leaving the next morning from Paris, heading to New York. He decided to take one final sentimental walk along the Seine before heading back to his hotel for the night.

What happened next was such a

coincidence that it might have appeared in a Charles Dickens novel.

Fred Zinnemann

As Morris was walking near a bridge by the Seine, he heard an American voice call out: "Hey, Maynard!" He was shocked and surprised. What Parisian beggar knew his name? Out of the shadows emerged Marlon, although Morris didn't recognize him at first. He looked like one of the *clochards* lurking in the background.

Marlon gladly accepted Morris' offer of a late-night dinner at a seedy bistro on the Left Bank. There Morris learned that someone had stolen Marlon's passport and that all his money was gone. Later Morris was telling Edith, "I couldn't believe it. Here every producer or director in Hollywood was clamoring for his services, and Marlon is out begging for food on the streets with the Parisian equivalent of the Bowery Bums."

Marlon's explanation was that he was "too proud" to visit his newly made French friends and that he wanted to test his survival skills by living on the street. Morris installed him once again at the Hotel Voltaire, paying his rent for one week. He gave Marlon about two hundred dollars in French francs, all the money the agent had left at that point. Marlon accepted it, promising to pay it back as soon as he got his first acting job.

Morris explained that as soon as he returned to New York the following day, he would have Edith send him a one-way ticket back to New York. Morris said that of all the offers that had come in for him, the most promising was a script called *The Men*, in which Marlon would be cast as the lead, playing a paraplegic. The film was to be directed by Fred Zinnemann. "Zinnemann's a rebel like me," Marlon told Morris. He'd seen the 1948 film, *The Search*, about Europe's displaced persons, and Marlon thought the movie had social significance." The producer of *The Men* was to be Stanley Kramer. "Kramer also has redeeming social importance," Marlon said, praising the movie the director had made, *Home of the Brave*, that explored racial prejudice in the U.S. armed forces.

"You're broke now," Morris said, "but you'll get forty thousand big ones for working on this film, after we take our cut, of course."

Three days later, Marlon received a telegram delivered to the Hotel Voltaire. It was from an ambitious young theatrical agent named Jay Kanter, who had moved to Hollywood and launched himself into a job in the West Coast office of MCA. He'd seen Marlon perform as Stanley in *A Streetcar Named Desire* three times but had never gone backstage to meet him.

Kanter enclosed a six-page outline of the script for *The Men*, and expressed his eagerness to let Marlon be his "go-between" in negotiations with Kramer and Zinnemann. "Forty-thousand dollars is a lot of money," Kanter added as a postscript. "Hope you'll seriously consider this."

Tired of searching for a living in rotting garbage, Marlon wired Kanter back. "I'm on my way to Hollywood."

Before leaving Paris, a freshly scrubbed Marlon called on all the friends he'd made in Paris, especially Christian and Daniel Gélin.

During one final visit with Jacques Viale, Marlon said, "Finally, a Hollywood director has found a way to get me. He's decorated a tree with one-hundred dollar greenbacks instead of leaves. I'm going to appear in a film. What else is there for me? Take up hustling again? Return to the stage? Help dad in the cow shit business? Movies sound like an easy way to make some quick money without much work. Actually, I have no respect for the medium at all. I'll be back in New York before the first snowdrop falls."

* * *

After all his philandering in Europe, Marlon came back to New York and sequestered himself for ten days and nights in the apartment of his mousy looking friend, Wally Cox. "They never went out, never saw anybody, and his other friends had to wait their turn," said Edith Van Cleve. "At that time rumors were rampant that Wally was handy with the gentlemen. I can only imagine what Marlon and Wally did for those ten nights. I do know that they called for take-out to be delivered."

Wally's career was just beginning to take off at the time with his first serious television role in *School House*. But it would be more than two years before he would become a household word with his *Mr. Peepers*, also on TV.

When these two actors emerged from seclusion, they could be seen on their motorcycles on the streets of New York. "Wally might have looked slight, with timid features, but on that motorcycle, according to all reports, he was a daredevil demon," Edith said.

She was invited to join Wally and Marlon for his final night in New York, although she ended up picking up the tab at a little Sicilian trattoria in Greenwich Village.

Over a plate of spaghetti, Wally told Marlon, "You're going to become rich and famous. You're going to have major status to go with that fame, which will be worldwide, not just Broadway. You're going to attract a horde of hangers-on, the likes of which you've never seen. You attracted dozens of hangers-on back in the days when you were nobody. When you returned from Paris, you learned that some of your so-called friends had stolen all your possessions, even the underwear you rarely wear. You will attract more friends like that in the days ahead."

"Don't worry your pretty little cocksucking head," Marlon said in front of Edith, flashing a smile to suggest he was joking. "I can handle whatever they throw at me. Those Nebraska winters are cold. It raises some tough boys. Tough enough to deal with those sun-kissed faggots with their orange-scented cologne water out there in Hollywood."

* * *

Crossing the vast American continent, Marlon read movie magazines. It seemed to him that the Hollywood he was heading to didn't seem too eager for new faces in the post-war years. The box-office champions remained Bob Hope, Bing Crosby, John Wayne, Cary Grant, Humphrey Bogart, Clark Gable, Spencer Tracy, Gary Cooper, Clifton Webb, Randolph Scott, and even Abbott and Costello. Tyrone Power, Alan Ladd, Robert Taylor, James Cagney, and Errol Flynn were also clinging to their fans. Hollywood already had an impressive array of new faces, including Burt Lancaster, Montgomery Clift, Gregory Peck, and Kirk Douglas, with Glenn Ford and William Holden fast emerging. Not only that, but the entire film industry was threatened with the growing menace of television.

It was Broadway who'd discovered "baby Brando," as he sometimes called his early days in acting. Marlon was already twenty-five years old on that hot, sultry September day he first stepped down onto the steamy turf of Los Angeles. The train station was called Alhambra, and it was a stopover east of Los Angeles for the Santa Fe railroad. He'd arrived on the Super Chief, which all the stars like Katharine Hepburn took when riding the rails between Los Angeles and New York via Chicago.

Waiting for him at the station was young Jay Kanter, who was not only handsome but looked like a model who had just stepped from the pages of *Gentlemen's Quarterly.*

Originally hired to work in the mailroom at MCA, Marlon's talent representa-

Brando and Jay Kanter

tives on the coast, Kanter was eventually assigned "to look after" Marlon. MCA's director, Lew Wasserman, had personally selected Kanter because he felt that Marlon could relate to someone his own age. "From all reports," Wasserman said to Edith in New York, "Brando needs a caretaker. You know, someone to wipe his ass after he shits, spoon feed him, put his dick into some starlet's pussy when he wants a good fuck."

The well-groomed Kanter quickly checked

Marlon's dress, as he'd heard stories, and was relieved to see that he wore shoes, or at least a pair of sneakers that looked as if they should have been retired to the back of the closet long ago. Kanter noted that his new star didn't wear socks, however. He was attired in a blue woolen suit which had a hole in the left knee, and the seat of his trousers had a wide rip.

All Marlon's clothing was crammed into a brown canvas handbag. Under his arm he'd tucked a copy of Spinoza's *Tractatus Theologico-Politicus*.

In spite of their differences, Kanter and Marlon instantly bonded, so much so that when Marlon went to MCA to meet Lew Wasserman, he announced that "Jay is my new agent here." Almost overnight Jay was promoted from the mailroom to his own office with a secretary to go along with it.

Marlon is credited with giving Kanter's career a big push. Not only did he become the agent for Marlon, but he signed, among others, two other stellar clients, Grace Kelly and Marilyn Monroe. Marlon even watched in happy surprise as Kanter rose even higher, becoming the production chairman of the combined Metro-Goldwyn-Mayer and United Artists.

After picking Marlon up at the train station, Kanter graciously invited him to move in with him, but Marlon wanted to be driven to Eagle Rock, a dreary working class suburb fifteen miles from Hollywood.

Even though she didn't want him and didn't have room, he was moving into the two-bedroom wooden cottage of Mrs. Betty Lindemeyer, Dodie's sister. The other bedroom was occupied at the time by Mrs. Elizabeth Meyers, Marlon's grandmother. Also occupying the cottage was Betty's husband, Oliver, who wasn't too happy to find Marlon sleeping on the sofa in the already overcrowded cottage.

Of the three occupants, Marlon preferred his feisty and good humored grandmother, whom he affectionately called "Nana."

En route to Eagle Rock, Marlon confessed his anxiety of having to face movie cameras with a broken nose. He pondered if he'd have enough time to have plastic surgery performed on his face before filming began. "You look beautiful," Kanter assured him.

That remark might have made Marlon wonder if Kanter was gay. He was not, but he was estranged from his wife, Roberta Haynes, although there was talk of the couple getting back together. Perhaps Kanter should not have confided that bit of information. If there was something Marlon liked, it was intruding into a marriage.

Kanter volunteered not his estranged wife at the time but a roster of available starlets, or even female movie stars who wanted to meet Marlon and were extending invitations. "I have no desire to go to Hollywood parties," he said, "and I prefer to date waitresses and secretaries instead of movie stars. I find female movie stars sticky, and I've known quite a few of them when I was appearing as Stanley on Broadway. I find that by the time a woman becomes a movie star, she's been on too many casting couches and her pussy is stretched out of shape."

Nana and Betty had not seen "Bud," as they called him, in several years. They found he'd developed some strange new habits, like eating a pint of peanut butter a day and sucking on at least a dozen pomegranates every afternoon. Often he'd try to spit the seeds on the ceiling. He had the disgusting habit of downing six raw eggs every morning. "He'd stand at my kitchen sink," Betty recalled, "cracking a raw egg and holding it over his mouth. Sometimes the egg would slide down his gullet but on a few occasions the slimy stuff landed on my linoleum floor."

Sometimes Marlon would be found sleeping on the sofa in the morning; at other times he'd be gone all night.

"A lot of guys on motorcycles came by to pick him up at night," Betty said. "They looked like an unsavory crowd to me." Again, Marlon unknowingly might have been in rehearsal for a future film, *The Wild One*. Betty expressed her fear in a letter to Dodie that her son might end up in San Quentin before he even became a film star.

Dodie wrote back that Marlon Sr. was anxious to invest Marlon's $40,000 earnings in a cattle ranch in Nebraska, and indeed he would in time, "losing every cent of Bud's dough," as Dodie would later put it.

In an attempt to improve Marlon's wardrobe, now that he was a movie star, Betty and Nana took him to a department store in Los Angeles where they purchased a pair of brown gabardine slacks for him and a Scottish sweater in mint green. "He looked real nice in his new clothes," Betty said.

Marlon put on the sweater before the two women boarded the elevator with him. On the way down, he took out a pack of matches and began burning off the sweater's fuzz. Before the elevator reached ground level, it looked like he was trying to turn himself into a human torch. Betty quickly took off her coat and smothered the flames. Amazingly, Marlon was not burned. "We never tried to dress him again," Betty said.

Sometimes Marlon would have supper with his family, and would shock his relatives with his bad table manner. "He'd lower his face right down to the food and slurp it down, making loud noises." Betty said "I liked Bud but, frankly, we were glad to see him go, big-time movie star or not."

When Betty asked if Marlon would give them his forwarding address, he reported that he'd be living from now on in the paraplegic ward of the Birmingham Veterans Hospital at Van Nuys. "You can visit me there," he told Nana and Betty. "But don't be surprised if you find me in a wheelchair with a urine bottle."

Originally entitled *Battle Stripe, The Men* was based on a screenplay by Carl Foreman. The director was to be Fred Zinnemann, with Stanley Kramer the producer. Marlon had been cast as Ken Wilochek, a former infantry lieutenant paralyzed from the waist down and sentenced to life in a wheelchair. A Nazi sniper's bullet had smashed into his spine in the closing days of World War II, according to the plot. A great deal of the film was to take place in a paraplegic ward, with actual victims cast in some of the parts, a touch of realism insisted upon by both Zinnemann and Kramer.

Cast in the sappy role of Marlon's devoted fiancée was Oscar winner Teresa Wright, who had gained nationwide fame in *Mrs. Miniver* and in another postwar film, *The Best Years of Our Lives*, which brought her a second Oscar, playing the love interest of Dana Andrews. Teresa, with her sad eyes and an aching vulnerability in her voice, was hoping to repeat this 1946 artistic and box office triumph with *The Men*, even though she'd be forced to deliver such corny lines as "I'm not marrying a wheelchair, I am marrying a man."

When he read the full script, including his own part of Ken Wilochek, Marlon wrote Dodie, "Here I am in Hollywood playing another Polack."

Zinnemann, a mild-mannered Viennese-born director, was eager to greet Marlon, and a meeting was arranged between the two by Jay Kanter. "I consider you and Monty Clift the two most adventurous actors of our time, and it's been a pleasure working with Monty on *The Search* and I'm looking forward with much anticipation of directing you in *The Men*," Zinnemann in his courtly way told Marlon.

Marlon's response startled Zinnemann. "I hope you're paying me more money than you paid Monty. He and I had an affair in New York, you know."

Zinnemann didn't know.

"I made him my bitch," Marlon claimed. "Now I guess you know who's the top gunner."

Assuming Zinnemann's role, Marlon rather arrogantly warned the director, "I refuse to be too much of a hero in this film. My character has to show his petulant, self-pitying side."

After he'd recovered from all that, Zinnemann told Marlon how he wanted the role played—"that of a young man whose body has betrayed him."

Zinnemann was somewhat surprised at Marlon's request but agreed to it. Marlon actual-

Teresa Wright

ly wanted to live for three weeks at the VA facility in a "rehearsal period" before shooting began. He didn't want the other paraplegics to know that he was an actor, since it was unlikely that any of them had seen *Streetcar* on Broadway. He planned to join in the same arduous exercises and therapy the other patients underwent, including extensive time spent in the pool. Zinnemann met with Pat Grissom, president of the Paralyzed Veterans Association, and he agreed to intercede on Marlon's behalf at the hospital. He also agreed at the right time to reveal Marlon's identity and to request permission from certain of the vets to actually appear as actors in *The Men*.

The hospital checked Marlon in as a patient, although he nearly blew his cover on the first day by scratching his crotch. "I don't understand, man," one of the patients said, noting Marlon's action. "You don't have any feeling there, do you?"

Marlon responded, "Old habits die hard."

Later, Grissom claimed that Marlon "must be a great actor. He was fitted for leg braces, and I received a report from the attendant that Marlon was paralyzed from the tenth dorsal vertebra down."

Marlon blended well with the other veterans, becoming "one of the guys." He later confessed to Zinnemann that he sometimes became so upset that he had to wheel himself into the bathroom "to throw up."

"These guys put up with a lot," he told Zinnemann when he came to visit one day. "Not being able to walk for one thing. Shitting their pajamas another. But I think the worse thing they have to face—and you should bring this out in your movie—is that they can never fuck their wives or girlfriends again. That's what is primary on their minds. They feel that even though their women are loyal now, they will eventually betray them with other men."

On another day Zinnemann brought the screenwriter, Carl Foreman, to meet privately with Marlon on the grounds of the hospital. "Imagine me making my screen debut playing someone impotent," Marlon said. "Me! Of all people. Me, whose noble tool has serviced half the world and is ready, willing, and able to service the other half."

"Surely, you exaggerate," a stunned Foreman managed to counter.

"I have no fear about your acting ability," Zinnemann said."I have complete confidence that you'll charge the role with erotic power though you're unable to get a hard-on. I saw you on Broadway. Even though the two characters of Stanley Kowalski and Ken Wilocek are entirely different, I want you to appear as the sexiest man the world has ever seen in a wheelchair."

During his confinement, Marlon became extremely attached to one handsome twenty-three-year-old veteran (his family has requested that his name not be revealed). He was not a paraplegic but a quadriplegic. "Not even able to light a cigarette," Marlon said.

Famous ass shot

After only a few days, the vet, who will be called "Steve," revealed himself to be a homosexual to Marlon and confided that he planned to commit suicide. "There is no life left for me," Steve told Marlon.

During the course of his stay, Marlon became very protective of Steve and had all his meals with him and helped him exercise as much as was possible for him.

As Zinnemann later learned, one night an attendant, checking the ward, discovered Steve performing "an act of fellatio" on Marlon in the men's room. The attendant asked Zinnemann if he should report this to the hospital authorities. The director urged him not to. "Don't you realize?" Zinnemann said, "Marlon was performing a noble deed, giving a poor wretched soul a little pleasure in a life where virtually all other pleasure has been denied. Please say nothing of this."

Before the filming of *The Men* ended, Zinnemann reported to Marlon that Steve had committed suicide, although it was never revealed exactly how a man without use of his arms and legs managed to kill himself. Marlon was very saddened and asked Zinnemann if he could take three days off from shooting to attend Steve's funeral and visit with his family. Already on a tight budget, Zinnemann agreed to that, feeling "I could not deny such a request although the studio was likely to yell at me for running over the budget."

The producer, Kramer, also anonymously visited Marlon at the hospital to introduce himself. Kramer told Marlon that he'd seen him in *Streetcar* but had also seen him perform opposite Tallulah Bankhead in "that turkey," *The Eagle Has Two Heads*. He laughingly recalled that when he was backstage he heard Marlon talking to Tallulah. Quoting Marlon to himself, Kramer said, "I'm going to go to bed with you tonight." According to Kramer, Tallulah didn't miss a beat and responded, "Indeed you shall, my dear boy, indeed you shall."

The day he met Kramer, Marlon made a strange request. He asked him to have one of his assistants deliver some porno movies to the ward so that the guys could enjoy them. "They've got to get their rocks off some way," Marlon told Kramer. "It's all harmless and might give the boys some pleasure." The very liberal-minded Kramer agreed that was a reasonable request and even privately bribed two night orderlies to allow the films to be shown. At nine o'clock, three porno movies from Kramer's own collection arrived to be shown to the paraplegics. Kramer later asked Zinnemann, "How did Brando know I collected pornography?"

Earlier that day, Marlon had asked Kramer to wheel him into the men's toilet. He didn't want the other patients to see that he could stand erect at the toilet and take a leak. When the coast was clear, Kramer signaled Marlon that he could stand up and piss. To his surprise, Marlon sat on the toilet seat.

"Listen, if you're going to take a crap, I'm out of here," Kramer told him. "I can't stand to watch anybody take a shit."

"No, I'm taking a piss," Marlon said.

At first Kramer thought Marlon was sitting down in case another paraplegic wheeled himself into the toilet.

"I always sit down on the toilet seat to take a piss," Marlon told him. "I have done that all my life, and I will continue to do it."

"You mean, like a woman?" Kramer asked.

"Exactly like a woman does it," Marlon replied. "A piss is always better sitting down. Women know best. I do many things a woman does. I can take a man's dick, and on occasion I even wear women's lingerie."

"I heard you go both ways," Kramer said, "but are you a total fag?"

Stanley Kramer

285

"Labels mean nothing to me," Marlon said, shaking himself off and pulling up his pants to jump back into the wheelchair. "Wheel me back to the ward!" he commanded an astonished Kramer, still trying to adjust to his male star's words. Finally, he broke into a laugh. "Elia Kazan warned me. You're a real kidder. Always trying to put people on. You're a good actor. I'm hard to fool, and for one brief moment back there in the crapper you almost had me believing you."

Even before Marlon started shooting *The Men*, two movie offers arrived for him, both delivered by Kanter. The first was to appear in a film noir boxing drama, *The Harder They Fall*, based on a novel by Budd Schulberg, who would later write the screenplay for *On the Waterfront*. Marlon turned down the role which would not be filmed until 1956, starring Humphrey Bogart and Rod Steiger.

Marlon also turned down the part of Raul Fuentes in *The Brave Bulls*. He told director Robert Rossen, who was under investigation by the House on Un-American Activities, that he was opposed to bullfighting and could not appear in a film about cruelty to animals. "Offer the role to Anthony Quinn," Marlon told Rossen. "He wants to be me anyway." Marlon still bristled at any report in print that Quinn was a better Stanley Kowalski on the stage than he was. To his surprise, Marlon's suggestion was taken. Quinn accepted the offer to play Raul Fuentes in *The Brave Bulls*, released in 1951.

Not all producers or directors were eager to hire Marlon. Alfred Hitchcock derided Method actors to the press. "As for Brando's Method acting," he said, "if I ever directed him in a film and he asked me what his motivation for a scene was, I'd tell him your motivation is your paycheck, sucker!"

Marlon had refused to sign a seven-year contract, and he would be free after he finished *The Men* to choose his next role. He was well aware that preparations were under way for the filming of *A Streetcar Named Desire*, and he knew that he'd be asked to repeat his role of Stanley on film. Even though he still publicly proclaimed he would turn down the role, if offered, he wrote to Dodie that, "It is almost an inevitable conclusion that I'll tell the fuckers yes. I am turning down all other offers and holding myself open to appear in *Streetcar* when the time comes—that is, if Irene and Tennessee can overcome all the censorship problems they'll have with this steamy drama. The way I figure it, the longer I appear as the reluctant debutante, the higher the final offer will be. If the shits want me to play Stanley, they'll have to pay my price. Fifteen thousand dollars for every inch of my dick." Marlon and Dodie never carried on typical mother-son dialogues.

Alfred Hitchcock

On his last night in the hospital, the ward was visited by

two Christian Scientists, Ethel Derrimann and Rebecca Hoover, both of whom appeared to be religious fanatics. Ostensibly to bring magazines and comfort to the men, the two zealots were actually there to convert. Derrimann preached to the cynical men in the ward, claiming that hospitals weren't the answer to their paralysis. "Only prayer and a belief in the Lord Jesus can save you!" she shouted at the men who were growing restless and hostile.

The only man in the ward who listened intently to every word was Marlon himself. Perhaps both Hoover and Derriman believed that they were converting him. Hoover added, "If your faith is great enough in the Lord, you can not only walk again but father children again."

At that false claim, Marlon jumped out of his wheelchair. Looking at him in horror, the two women did not at first comprehend what was happening, staring in disbelief.

Suddenly, deciding to reveal his true condition to the other vets in the ward, Marlon spun his chair across the room and stood proudly on his own feet. In front of his astonished audience, he performed a tap dance to rival Fred Astaire.

"I'm cured!" he shouted at the top of his voice. "I'm cured! He did a buck-and-wing as he raced toward the exit, crying, "It's a miracle! It's a miracle! I can walk!" He turned to the ladies for his exit line, "I can fuck again!" he shouted at the top of his lungs, sending three orderlies flying toward the ward to see what was happening.

The last these men saw of Marlon was a vision of him racing across the night-lit grounds of the hospital and jumping over an eight-foot fence with the agility of a pole vaulter.

* * *

Marlon became known for seducing many of his leading ladies in his films. Not so with Teresa Wright who had been cast as his fiancée in *The Men*. After meeting her on the set, he told Fred Zinnemann, "Have no fear you're going to be coping with an off-screen romance. After all, I'm not paralyzed from the waist down. Miss Wright is too squeaky clean for me. I don't think I could raise my noble tool for action with that one."

Speaking of their on-screen emoting, Teresa told Zinnemann, "there is just no chemistry between Marlon and me. As you know, I'm the only actress in Hollywood nominated for an Academy Award for each of my first three films. I'll not prepare my Oscar acceptance speech for *The Men*."

On the second day of shooting, Marlon told Zinnemann, "I suppose Miss Wright has ethereal talents, and that's why she doesn't pose in bathing suits or grant interviews with fan magazines. I applaud her for not sucking up to those

A scene from *The Men*

rags, but I'm not sure about this girl-next-door image of hers. I never liked the gal next door. I prefer women to be in my own house, in my own bed, not next door."

Teresa confronted Marlon during the first week of the shoot. "Some moronic columnist is promoting a romance between us. I hope it's not being planted by George Glass." She was referring to a movie publicity veteran who'd been hired to promote *The Men*. "I have it in my contract that there will be no leg art, no manufactured romances written about me by those two witches, Hedda and Louella, and no ermine-and-orchid settings for me. I also had my agent put in my contract that I'm not to be photographed running on the beach with my hair flying in the wind or looking insinuatingly at a Thanksgiving turkey. Samuel Goldwyn didn't always honor my contract. Most of his direction to me was, 'Let your breasts flow in the wind!'"

"Thanks for telling me this," he said. "I'll try not to be photographed with my hand in your bra."

"Don't be sarcastic with me, Mr. Brando," she said. "I have you know that Samuel Goldwyn paid me $125,000 a picture. For *The Men*, I'm getting only $20,000, half of what you're being paid."

"Even so," he said, "that's not too bad for a girl who didn't finish high school until she was twenty. Not me. I have a degree from Harvard University." He walked away, later telling Zinnemann, "Miss Wright's slightly warbling voice emerges from a steely core."

From the very beginning, and based on his experience living with the paraplegics in the V.A. Hospital, Marlon expressed his opinion that the film tended to avoid any issues graphically associated with his character's impotence. He clashed with both Kramer and Zinnemann. The normally mild-mannered Zinnemann responded in anger, "What am I supposed to do? Insert scenes showing you eating out Teresa's pussy? Without actually depicting it, the audience will be smart enough to know that by agreeing to marry you, Teresa has forever abandoned hope of penetration and will have to be satisfied with cunninlingus for the rest of her life."

"And what about a lifetime of changing my diapers?" Marlon said. "What about incontinence? We've got to work that in here somewhere. I mean, I lived in that ward. Every night the men pissed and shit all over themselves. I even followed their example. Every night I took a big crap in my hospital bed."

Teresa also complained to Zinnemann that "my best scenes have ended up on the cutting room floor." She was referring to a subplot which cast her opposite an actor, a healthy, full-bodied man, who was competing for her affection against Marlon. Zinnemann later said that the actor hired to play Marlon's rival was the son of one of the financial backers of *The Men*. "When Kramer and I saw the rushes, we realized he couldn't act at all. Instead of casting another actor in the role, and offending the backer, we dropped the subplot altogether and left it on the cutting-room floor. I figured this was the more diplomatic solution."

In later life, when Teresa started to grant interviews after her career was virtually over, she said, "Because of censorship problems, we never really came to terms with the unspoken problem in *The Men*. How was Brando, a paraplegic, going to make love to me when we got married? What kind of marriage were we going to have? What kind of love making? The issue remained relatively unspoken in *The Men*. If the film were being made today, perhaps it would be more graphic."

Teresa's husband, screenwriter Niven Busch, had warned her not to appear on the screen with Marlon. "I saw him on Broadway in *Streetcar*. He'll eat your heart for dinner. He'll upstage you at every turn."

At first Teresa didn't agree but after seeing the final cut of *The Men*, she admitted that her husband had been right. "I just cut my throat by agreeing to star opposite Brando."

Marlon sat between Kramer and Zimmenann when he saw the final cut of *The Men*. Kramer asked Marlon for his opinion. "I should have plowed my noble tool into Miss Sensitivity. After sampling that, I would have broken in this studio-era actress to The Method, made our scenes more effective. If my next film is *Streetcar*, I'm definitely going to plow it to Blanche DuBois, regardless of which pussy they cast in the part."

* * *

After the success of his war novel, *The Naked and the Dead*, Norman Mailer was summoned to Hollywood by Samuel Goldwyn. The script Mailer was working on seemed to combine *Day of the Locust* with *Miss Lonelyhearts*. "I want Monty Clift for the lead," Mailer told Goldwyn. "Brando is completely wrong for this part."

Mailer had hopes—soon to be deflated—of becoming a power broker on the West Coast. He decided to throw a big party for the Hollywood elite. Recklessly, he sent out invitations to all the big names of the industry—producers, directors, and top stars, both male and female. In those days of the Communist witch hunt, Mailer didn't realize that you didn't mix right wing

Hollywood with the "lunatic left." An impressive roster of big names accepted his invitation. At the time, Mailer was viewed as a possible rising star, and Hollywood didn't want to offend him. That would come later when he failed to deliver a picture with a huge box office gross.

Privately Mailer told close friends back in New York that Los Angeles was "the ugliest city in the world." But, when not making speeches for socialist presidential candidate, Henry Wallace, Mailer, in his own words, was "sucking up to *tout* Hollywood."

No longer hanging out with Marlon or James Baldwin, Mailer had acquired a new best friend, Mickey Knox, an actor from Brooklyn with whom Mailer was collaborating on a screenplay.

On the night of Mailer's party, it had been raining for two days and nights in Los Angeles. Even so, such big names as Fredric March and John Huston braved the elements to attend the party.

Having migrated back to the West Coast, Shelley Winters had been having a torrid affair with Burt Lancaster and wanted him to take her to Mailer's party. When he wasn't available, she impulsively called Marlon. How she was able to track him down is not known. She'd last seen him when their affair had ended abruptly upon her discovery that he was screwing around with "a hundred other women, including some big name stars."

After about fifteen phone calls and a lot of heavy negotiation between them, Marlon agreed to go to his first Hollywood party, after having attacked such gatherings in the press as "crass and commercial exhibitionism."

Spending his last twelve dollars on a taxi, Marlon showed up an hour and a half late at Shelley's door. He was soaking wet in the suit he'd borrowed from Jay Kanter. Shelley had already warned him that he couldn't wear jeans and a T-shirt to Mailer's bash.

"The suit was three sizes too small for him, since Kanter was a little guy," Shelley said. "I think the cuff of the pants came to Marlon's calf. Fortunately he wore high boots to conceal that a bit." After kissing him, she joked with him, "at least you didn't show up in a wheelchair. I hear you go everywhere these days in a wheelchair. Tonight you have to walk on your own two feet."

Behind the wheel of Shelley's battered old red Pontiac, Marlon got lost, and another hour and a half had gone by before they arrived at Mailer's house. He didn't have a valet for the night, and cars were parked way down the hill and into the street. Parking there, Shelley and Marlon raced without umbrellas up the steep hill to Mailer's house, arriving "like drowned rats." Miraculously having managed to arrive dry, and also late, Elizabeth Taylor and her escort, Monty Clift, were greeting Mailer in the hallway.

Marlon noted that Elizabeth and Shelley were wearing the exact same blonde sheared beaver coat, except Elizabeth's was intact and Shelley's was

Monty Clift

soaked and clinging to her body.

Marlon hadn't seen Monty since their affair back in New York, and there was a distinct chill between the two former lovers. Since Monty had gone to Hollywood before Marlon, and the press had hailed him as a conquering hero, he distinctly resented the arrival of Marlon on California turf. It was obvious to Marlon that Monty viewed him as severe competition. The press had already assumed that they would be competing for the same roles.

Overcoming Monty's stiffness, Marlon grabbed him in a bear hug and planted a wet kiss on his lips. Monty recoiled in horror at this public display of affection. Nonetheless, he managed to pull himself together and introduce Marlon to Elizabeth Taylor.

"The great Mr. Brando!" Elizabeth said, barely disguising a slight contempt in her voice. "We meet at last."

Aware of the condenscension in her voice, Marlon said, "You're so young you look like jailbait." He looked with a slight contempt at Monty. "But your virginity will remain intact with this one here."

"So, you're making a movie about some guy who's impotent," Elizabeth said. "Was that type casting?"

He countered, "Where's Lassie? I thought you'd bring him tonight. I've got to warn you, I don't make dog pictures."

"There are many ways a movie can turn into a dog, even without an actual dog," Elizabeth said.

Her words were prophetic.

John Huston was standing only ten feet from Monty, Elizabeth, and Marlon at the time. By 1967, he'd cast both Monty and Elizabeth in the screen adaptation of Carson McCullers' Southern drama, *Reflections in a Golden Eye*. When Monty died before filming began, Huston would grant the role of a homosexual to Marlon. Together this trio of talent would create "a dog of a picture," echoing Elizabeth's long-ago words.

In time, Marlon would come to respect Elizabeth as an actress and view her as a friend. But initially he wasn't impressed, although he would praise the movie that she and Shelley would do with Monty, *A Place in the Sun*. However, he told Shelley, "I could have played Monty's part

Elizabeth Taylor

more convincingly."

Marlon was rather snide in his late-night appraisal of Elizabeth to Shelley, claiming "she was dressed like she was attending a senior prom. That girl has no sex appeal at all. My prediction is that she'll never make it from child star into adult roles. Another classic case of what happened to Shirley Temple."

Marlon was angered by Monty's indifference. He felt the need to put him down before disappearing into the party. "It's true, Monty baby, I've finally succumbed to the jackals of Hollywood. Since I'm in town now, I might act you off the screen. Let's call it a friendly competition. I'll send you all the scripts I reject."

Monty took Elizabeth's arm and guided her away from Marlon. "Why not a wet one, Monty baby, for the road?" Marlon called out.

Monty didn't look back.

Shelley had disappeared into another part of the room, and Marlon turned around to accept an introduction from Mickey Knox. Marlon was not impressed with him either. Knox claimed that "my best buddy," Mailer, was hoping to sell the rights to *The Naked and the Dead*, for a film adaptation. "Listen, I saw you in *Streetcar*, and I thought you were terrific. There's a role ideal for you in *Naked*. I tried to convince Norman to offer it to you. But he wants Burt Lancaster instead."

Marlon turned and walked away, only to encounter Humphrey Bogart, whom he hadn't seen since backstage at *Streetcar*. "Hi, kid," Bogie said. "See that Adolphe Menjou standing over there. He and I just had a political fight. I nearly punched him out. He's definitely a neo-Nazi."

At that point, Ginger Rogers appeared. She already knew Bogie. "Ginger, are you still to the right of Hermann Goering?" he asked.

"Oh, you liberals!" Ginger said, jabbing Bogie in his stomach. Batting her false eyelashes, she turned and introduced herself to Marlon. "I didn't get to see you in *Streetcar*," she said, "but I hear you were terrific. All my gal pals told me you were just as sensational off the stage as on. Perhaps we'll make a movie together one day, and I can discover your talent for myself."

"I'm not a hoofer," he said, turning and walking away, having deliberately insulted an actress who'd won an Oscar for straight drama.

Seeing Marlon, Norman called him over and introduced him to Cecil B. DeMille. The director was lecturing the author on his dress code. "If you're going to succeed in Hollywood," DeMille told Mailer, "you've got to buy stockings that cling

Ginger Rogers

292

to your calves and don't fall around your ankles. Also your casual shirt and slacks need to be replaced with a dark suit. And learn to tie your shoelaces." Marlon quickly drifted away.

Charlie Chaplin

The real reason Marlon had attended the party was to meet Charles Chaplin. He discovered The Little Tramp standing alone in the corner. Marlon went up, introduced himself, and launched into praise of Chaplin's work.

Chaplin turned a somewhat deaf ear to Marlon's compliments. "I know, I know. Everybody from Albert Einstein to Sir Winston Churchill has called me a genius. But such talk bores me. What do you do for a living? A waiter perhaps?"

"I'm Marlon Brando, the actor. I starred on Broadway in Tennessee's *A Streetcar Named Desire*."

"Never heard of you," Chaplin said. "And I hate the title of your play. Too suggestive. No subtlety."

"I'm in Hollywood making movies now," Marlon said. "My greatest dream would be to make a film with you. I already know Paulette Goddard. Great gal! Sorry the marriage didn't work out."

"That's my business," Chaplin snapped.

"So, how about it?" Marlon asked.

"How about what?" Chaplin asked.

"Directing me in a film?"

"Mr. Brando," Chaplin said, before walking away, "that day will never come."

Chaplin was wrong. In *A Countess from Hong Kong*, released in 1967,

Sophia Loren

Marlon was cast in the lead opposite Sophia Loren. The long-delayed collaboration of Chaplin and Marlon would be a disaster. Instead of directing Marlon, Chaplin spent more time warning him not to pinch Loren's ass and not to stare too intently at her décolletage in close-ups.

By the time the picture was wrapped, Marlon would no longer hail Chaplin's genius. He had a different opinion. "Chaplin is the worst director who ever set foot in Hollywood. Not only that, but a fearsomely cruel man, an egotistical penny-pinching tyrant, and the most sadistic man I've ever met."

Back at Mailer's party, Marlon felt he was bombing with all the guests, and retreated behind the bar to help the bartender mix drinks for the remaining hour he was at Mailer's home. Shelley brought Marlon a small bowl of Mailer's bouillabaisse which Marlon tasted and found terrible. "This reminds me of the plate of the shit I was served instead of chicken on Broadway in *Streetcar*."

Mailer's Hollywood party was making Marlon nervous. He grabbed Shelley by the arm and headed for the hallway. Seeing them leaving early, Mailer chased after them. "The party's just getting going," he told Marlon.

"Fuck it, man," Marlon said. With a forceful display of anger, he turned on Mailer. "Just who in the fuck do you think you are? Elsa Maxwell? The queen of the Hollywood social set? You should be sitting on your ass in Brooklyn writing *The Naked and the Dead Jr.*"

Seeing two blonde beaver coats hanging in the hallway side by side, Marlon grabbed the dry one for Shelley, making off with Elizabeth Taylor's wrap. When Shelley opened the door, and Marlon saw that it was still raining, he also grabbed a trench coat for himself.

Shelley drove Marlon back to his aunt's house in the rain. In front of the house, still in her car, Shelley gave Marlon a good night kiss which turned into a wrestling match. He seemed to want to repeat the nocturnal adventures they'd enjoyed in New York. Aunt Betty turned on the porch light to discover "what the fuss was about." That ended Marlon's bout with Shelley.

Back at Shelley's apartment, a call came in for her at four o'clock in the morning. It was from Mickey Knox. "That fucking Brando stole my trench coat. My keys were in that coat. My car is blocking all the others in the driveway. The party has erupted into violent political arguments. Adolphe Menjou has called Norman a 'crypto-Communist.'"

Shelley provided Mickey with the details to reach the house of Marlon's aunt. It was not Mickey who showed up at Betty's doorstep, but two patrolmen with sirens blasting and dome lighting flashing. Betty got out of bed at five-thirty to return the trench coat and the car keys.

Throughout the ordeal, Marlon slept soundly. The next afternoon, he called Shelley to tell her that that was the first and last Hollywood party he planned to attend.

"You didn't get lucky last night," he told her. "Let's set up something for tonight."

* * *

Like Teresa, Marlon didn't plan to cooperate on any publicity for *The Men*. Nor did he plan to grant interviews. He did agree to meet with George

Glass, a movie publicity veteran. A short, stubby man, Glass won Marlon over with his sense of humor. "I'm the kind of guy if you ain't talking about me, I ain't listening," Glass said upon meeting Marlon, causing the actor to laugh.

Even though reluctant, Marlon agreed to talk to the reigning duennas of the gossip columns, Hedda Hopper and the even more powerful Louella Parsons, both of whom were capable of making or breaking careers. However, he demanded that these gossip mavens interview him at the studio. Hedda agreed, but Louella said no. Marlon would have to drive over to her home.

Louella Parsons

Marlon dubbed Hopper "the neo-Nazi lady with the funny hats." He was a liberal, Hedda was to the right of Atilla the Hun. He told her, "The only reason I came to Hollywood was because I didn't have enough moral character to turn down the money." After that, he shut up, only mumbling.

"Do you care to answer any more of my questions?" she asked.

"I don't believe I do," he responded.

"Fine with me," she said. "I didn't want to do this interview anyway. Your producer, Stanley Kramer, insisted that I come here to do it. You needn't submit yourself to further anguish. I'm leaving. Good day!"

In spite of his rudeness to her, Hedda praised Marlon's talent in her column. The rumor was that Kramer had bribed her to do that.

Marlon was seen driving down Hollywood Boulevard with a trick arrow in his head, giving the illusion that an Indian brave had pierced his skull. He arrived at the home of Louella Parsons with the trick arrow still "imbedded."

Opening the door for him, she didn't lose a beat. "I had no idea that *The Men* was a Western," she told him.

Unlike his experience with Hedda, Marlon did answer some of Louella's questions. He fed her misinformation, including the claim that he was born in Outer Mongolia where his father had been a civil engineer. As for his favorite food, he told her, "I eat the eyes of gazelles."

When Louella asked him about his mother, he bluntly told her, "She's a drunk!"

She wrote in her column, "He has the manners of a chimpanzee, the gall of a Kinsey researcher, and a swelled head the size of a Navy blimp, and just as pointed—as far as I'm concerned he can ride his bike off the Venice Pier."

Marlon continued to grant so-called interviews, none of which was successful. Even before the release of *The Men*, the press was calling Marlon the rebel, the goof, the oddball, and a crazy mixed-up kid.

Marlon could deal with that. What he hated was being referred to as "the next Valentino." He was also called a Dostoevskian version of Tom Sawyer. Many newspapers compared him to Greta Garbo, "wanting to be alone." He also scratched his genitals throughout interviews. He told one reporter that he found Hollywood "a cultural boneyard."

By this time in his career, Marlon had replaced Monty Clift as Hollywood's new *enfant terrible*.

Surprisingly, Glass even got Marlon to agree to some cross-country promotion to publicize *The Men*. Arriving in Chicago with his pet raccoon, Russell, Marlon was met by a studio representative. "Is there anything we can do for you, Mr. Brando?" the rep asked.

"Yeah," Marlon said. "Can you tell me where I can get my raccoon laid?"

After wrapping *The Men*, Marlon had greater respect for film acting, a sentiment not often heard at the Actors Studio. "Acting in films is the toughest form of acting," he claimed. "Anyone who can come through it successfully can call himself an actor for the first time. When you have to portray a shattering emotion while realizing at the back of your mind that if you move your head an inch too much you'll be out of focus and out of the frame—that's acting!"

Zinnemann found Marlon "a combination of idealism and shrewdness. He knows exactly what he's doing. And he's all that a director can desire in an actor. Yes, Marlon's not only a great character but he's a greater actor."

Even though he said this, Zinnemann would have far greater success directing Gary Cooper in *High Noon* and Monty Clift in *From Here to Eternity*. Yet in later life he always said he regretted never having had another opportunity to direct Marlon in a picture.

The Men opened at Radio City Music Hall in New York in the summer of 1950 at the start of the Korean War. Movie-going audiences at the time didn't want to see a film about paraplegics. Within two weeks of its release, it was pronounced "a dud" by movie distributors.

The movie-going public flocked to see other films at the time, especially *All About Eve, Cinderella, Samson and Delilah, Battleground, Annie Get Your Gun*, and *King Solomon's Mines*.

The reviews of *The Men* were respectful, especially about Marlon. René Jordan wrote, "Under the broken body and the childish tantrums, there is a vein of iron, a suggestion of a toppled God, a maimed Apollo."

John Mason Brown in the *Saturday Review* called Marlon "a seismograph of volcanic emotions." *Time* wrote of Marlon's "halting, mumbled delivery, glowering silences and expert simulation of paraplegics." The critic noted that Marlon's style didn't suggest acting at all but looked "chillingly like the real thing."

Marlon fought bitterly about the "happy ending" inserted at the last minute, which went against Foreman's original script. But in later years, his point of view about *The Men* softened. "Public sensitivity about the needs of persons with disabilities probably began in America with the release of *The Men*."

Still a best friend, in spite of his being a drug addict, Carlo Fiore had a different take on Marlon's first film, calling it "a sentimental, tear-jerking soap opera—the usual Stanley Kramer bullshit." He blamed Teresa Wright for her "essential prissiness" that ruined the movie for him.

Edith Van Cleve said, "*The Men* did not make Marlon Brando a movie star, and certainly not known in every corner of the world. That would come with a movie called *A Streetcar Named Desire*."

Some biographies have erroneously reported that Marlon was nominated for an Academy Award that year for his performance in *The Men*. The Oscar went instead to Jose Ferrer in *Cyrano de Bergerac*. Marlon wasn't even nominated.

He may have killed his chances when he told a reporter, "If I win the Oscar, I'll send a cab driver to pick it up for me."

When Marlon didn't even get nominated, Oscar winner Gary Cooper remarked, "That was the Academy's way of saving Brando cab fare."

After completion of the film, and with no immediate contract for another movie, Marlon boarded the train that would take him to Chicago and on to New York. As he traversed the American heartland, "he never tired of showing his buttocks at every station stop," the conductor noted. "Brando mooned himself across the United States."

Back in New York, he told Edith, "I made an ass out of myself in *The Men*. Before America sees that, I wanted them to look up close and personal at the real thing. I pulled down my pants and showed anybody who wanted to look between Los Angeles and New York what my two fleshy moons are like. I took a few public pisses too in case anybody's interested in what my noble tool looks like when it's asleep."

Chapter Nine

Six weeks after the Mailer party, Shelley read Mike Connolly's column in the *Hollywood Reporter*. To her horror, she learned that her lover, Burt Lancaster, was expecting a third child from his wife, Norma. For months, Burt had been assuring Shelley that his marriage was over.

Across the street at Victor's, a local dive with a bar so dimly lit it was said to conceal "every known indiscretion," Shelley tried to make herself forget her lovesick pain by downing three triple gin martinis.

She turned around to see who had taken the seat next to hers. It was Marlon.

She rushed to the women's toilet but didn't vomit. Then, she threw cold water on her face, as Marlon pounded on the door. When she didn't open it, he entered the women's room and wiped her wet face with a rough paper towel. "Burt, that bastard, is a liar," she shouted at him. "He's fucking his wife."

Marlon escorted her to a table where he'd ordered dinner for both of them. She could eat nothing so he finished her dinner too. Knowing her heart was broken, he told her, "Men have died from time to time and worms have eaten them, but not for love." She recognized the line from *As You Like It*.

Still drunk, and upset that he wasn't taking her heartbreak seriously, she slapped him, but instead of reacting with anger, he took her in his arms and kissed her instead. "I don't think I've ever seen Marlon so passionate," Shelley later recalled when she returned the blonde beaver coat to Elizabeth Taylor. "As we got more and more affectionate, there in the booth, the bartender suggested that we move to a rented hotel room."

Back in her apartment, as Shelley showered, Marlon lit every candle and every stick of incense he could find, placing the candles in makeshift holders that included a discarded bottle of Chianti. Then he assembled each of the pictures of Burt which Shelley had placed throughout the apartment. There were enough of them to spark a small bonfire. When she emerged nude from the shower, she looked even more beautiful by candlelight. The assembled studio shots greeted her, piled on a low-slung coffee table. "The best way to get rid of an old love is with a new love," Marlon told her.

She seemed to agree, telling him the incinerator was four doors down to the left.

Marlon had already taken off his blue jeans and T-shirt. He wore no underwear. Not bothering to cover himself, he gathered up the pictures and entered the hallway heading for the incinerator. It seemed that every tenant in the other apartments on the floor heard him as he smashed the glass and the frames around each individual picture, throwing the debris down the incinerator. Those tenants who actually opened their doors to see who was making the ruckus were greeted by the sight of Marlon, naked.

Shelley then dropped her robe on the living room floor and moved, naked, into the hallway to give him a passionate kiss. The Peeping Toms got a treat. Had even one of the tenants had a camera at the time, a memorable picture could have been snapped even before the term "paparazzi" was invented.

In her memoirs, Shelley remembered making love to Marlon all night long. Then, just before the sun rose over Los Angeles, there was a loud rapping on her door. Intuitively, she knew it was Burt Lancaster coming to make up with her. When his knocking didn't get any response, and perhaps assuming that she was sleeping too deeply to be easily awakened, he headed downstairs to a public phone.

Still wanting Burt back, in spite of his having misrepresented his allegiance to his wife, Shelley tossed Marlon his clothes and informed him of an escape route across her rooftop. Marlon wanted to stay "and duke it out" with Burt, but she insisted that he leave. Shelley was completely unaware that Marlon too had had a brief affair with Burt in New York.

Once she'd let him in, Burt immediately searched her apartment for signs that she'd had a liaison that night. In his haste to retreat, Marlon had left one of his sneakers. Seeing it, Shelley kicked it under her bed. As Burt roamed about ranting, she opened her curtains just in time to see Marlon, wearing only one sneaker, catch a streetcar, which vividly reminded her of all the brilliant rehearsals of the Tennessee Williams play that she'd witnessed in New York.

Two days later, when Shelley saw the final version of George Stevens's *A Place in the Sun*, in which she'd co-starred with Montgomery Clift and Elizabeth Taylor, she suffered something akin to a nervous breakdown because, in her words, she found the picture "so real." She had also been dieting rigidly, and taking pills to help her sleep, the combination of which was wreaking

Burt Lancaster

Shelley Winters and Brando

havoc on her nerves. On the advice of her doctors and friends, she was checked into Los Angeles' Cedars Medical Center.

That did not end her problems: Visits from Burt and Marlon had to be scheduled so that the two rival ex-lovers wouldn't run into each other. "Both men were athletes," Shelley said. "I don't know which one would have been declared the winner."

Elizabeth Taylor later remarked, "Poor Shelley. As always, the woman emerges the loser. Monty drowns her in *A Place in the Sun*, and she ultimately loses both a married man, Burt, and a man who will never marry, Brando."

After her release from Cedars, Shelley was seen boarding an airplane for New York with Marlon's chief rival and former lover, Monty himself.

When she returned to Hollywood, Shelley visited Marlon on the set of the film version of *A Streetcar Named Desire*, but it was clear that the affair was winding down. Unknown to Shelley at the time, he'd be involved in a secret affair with her new roommate, a blonde sex goddess being groomed to replace Betty Grable at Fox.

Alone in their new apartment, Marilyn Monroe confided to Shelley that she too was trying to get over a disastrous affair with a married man. "Why can't we be more like men?" Marilyn asked. "View seductions as just another notch in our belts. Why can't we sleep with just the most desirable of men and not get all emotionally involved with them? Certainly not fall for the louses who in the end always go back to their spouses."

Her comment echoed the famous number that she'd perform a few months later in *Gentlemen Prefer Blondes*.

There is a tantalizing reference in Marlon's autobiography, *Songs My Mother Taught Me*, that if read and investigated more fully would lead to rewriting episodes in biographies of Marilyn Monroe. Marlon writes that he literally bumped into Marilyn at a New York party after he'd made the film version of *A Streetcar Named Desire*. In reality, he'd already had a brief affair with her many months earlier, during the filming of *The Men*.

Even more tantalizingly, he admitted that, "I had first met her briefly, shortly after the war." Play that again, Sam? *Marilyn Monroe and Marlon Brando had met even before he went to Hollywood?* Typically, Marlon offered no details about the first meeting of the two up-and-coming sex symbols, male and female, of the rapidly approaching Fifties.

In all of the many exhaustive reports on the lives of Marilyn and Marlon, virtually no light has ever been shed on this strange encounter. The only insider to offer a clue about the historic first encounter between the film god and goddess is Carlo Fiore. Marlon told him that he'd first met Marilyn at a bar on Eighth Avenue in New York City, way back in 1946.

According to Fiore, he'd offered her fifteen dollars to come back to his rented room, where he claimed they made love all night. In the morning, Marilyn was gone, and he would not see her again until he filmed *The Men* in Hollywood.

Was Marilyn Monroe, for a brief period in 1946, hustling johns in New York City? It appears entirely possible. Marlon was not truthful to his girlfriends or mistresses, but he was not known to lie or exaggerate to Fiore.

Marilyn Monroe

"With me, Marlon didn't have to fantasize about encounters with broads." Fiore said. "I could see it taking place right in front of my eyes. Often it was my broad he was scoring with. Long before he became famous, he was plowing such big names as Marlene Dietrich. Why not Marilyn? When he told me he'd fucked Marilyn in 1946, I found that completely believable. Still do."

During the war, Marilyn, then known as Norma Jeane, worked in an aircraft factory during the week, and moonlighted as a model on weekends. Sometimes, while still married to James (Jim) Dougherty, she would disappear for a month or so at a time on a "modeling trip." One such trip involved an entire month spent in Washington State with a photographer named André de Dienes. De Dienes paid her two hundred dollars a month, the amount needed to repair the family's old battered Ford. De Dienes alleged that he not only took nude shots of her in the outdoors, but had an affair with her as well.

De Dienes is credited with teaching his nineteen-year-old model "variations on sex" that were unknown within the context of her relationship with her young husband.

At one point Marilyn told Sally Broye, with whom she'd worked at the aircraft factory, that she was slipping off to New York "to break into show business," perhaps to get a job dancing in a chorus line. According to Sally, Norma Jeane planned to tell Jim that she was seeking modeling work in Los Angeles, but that she claimed, privately, to have received an offer from a New York-based photographer for a modeling session. "The New York modeling job that Norma Jeane talked about apparently didn't pan out, and she found herself wandering penniless and broke on the streets of New York," Broye later claimed.

It was during this period in New York that Marlon apparently discovered Norma Jeane in a bar. Normally, he didn't go to bars unless he felt available pickups were there.

Lena Pepitone, Marilyn's maid in New York from 1957 until her death, revealed that Marilyn admitted to turning tricks for fifteen dollars in the Forties. Pepitone, author of *Marilyn Monroe Confidential*, claimed that she visited bars as a means of picking up men "for more pocket money."

Later, Marilyn admitted having worked as a hooker on the back streets of Hollywood, but denied that she ever actually accepted money for her favors. "I never took money. I only did it for food. Once I connected with a man, I'd negotiate for breakfast, lunch, or dinner, depending on the time of day."

Marlon's second encounter with Norma Jeane—now Marilyn Monroe—occurred in front of an apartment house in Los Angeles. Details are sketchy, but what happened between Marilyn and Marlon has been pieced together from remembrances of Fred Zinnemann and Carlo Fiore. Although their respective versions differed slightly, Marlon told each man essentially the same story about interchanges between Marilyn and himself. Marlon observed to Fred Zinnemann, "I wouldn't call her a rising starlet. Seems to me she spends more time on her back."

It is believed that at the time, he was waiting for Barbara Payton, who would become a scandalous movie star during the Fifties, but at that particular moment, he stood her up for Marilyn.

Rushing out of Payton's apartment building was a beautiful woman with a stunning figure, as Marlon later recalled to Zinnemann. Seeking a man (Marlon) in a car parked on the far side of the street, she apparently mistook him for her date for the evening. She was breathless when she peered inside the car. "You're not Sammy," she said, stepping back. "But you look familiar. You're Marlon Brando!"

"And who might you be?" Marlon asked. "Do I know you?"

"You don't recognize me with my new hair color," she said. I'm Norma Jeane, but now I'm known as Marilyn Monroe. You don't remember the time we got together in New York, and you invited me back to your place?"

"That could fit a thousand encounters," he said. "Get in the car. Perhaps you can do something to me to joggle my memory."

She giggled and ran around the rear of his car, wiggling her shapely butt onto the passenger's seat. "I didn't want to be with Sammy tonight anyway. He's fat and bald." As he started the car, she ran her hand across the back of his neck. "You're very good looking but not as pretty as before. Did you do something to your nose?"

"It was broken and not set right," he said.

"Adds character in my view," she said. "I don't like men who are too handsome."

"Thanks a lot!"

"What I mean is you're a handsome man now. When we met a few years back, you were just a pretty boy. I never go to bed with pretty boys. Of course, in my present situation I have to go to bed with almost anyone to get ahead. Get it? Give head to get ahead. But when I become a big-time movie star, I'll never suck another cock again—unless I want to, of course." Sexily, she looked over at him. "Unless I'm in the mood." She cuddled closer to him.

Zinnemann, according to reports, repeated this story at a number of dinner parties. Thanks to his repeatedly telling that story, the tale of young Marlon meeting young Marilyn as early as 1946 was, for a while at least, an oft-repeated topic of gossip in Hollywood.

"Forgive me, but I still don't remember you," Marlon is alleged to have said to Marilyn. "Perhaps if you'll go back to my place, you and I can repeat what you said we did in New York. I'm sure that will bring it all back to me."

"That would be fine with me," she said. "I hope you're not pretending that you don't remember because I've become too old for you. I mean I was young when we met. A teenager, really. Some men out here like only teenagers, not an old broad like me."

"You're not an old broad," he said. "In fact, with your sex appeal, your allure will be timeless."

"That's very flattering but you know yourself it's not true."

"Do I desire you?" he asked. "Put me to the test. Back at my place, we'll get naked together. If my noble tool rises to do its duty, then I still desire you. Fair enough?"

"The suspense is killing me," she said. "I can't wait." Leaning over him, she began to unfasten his trousers. As Marlon later told Zinnemann, "I practically had three accidents before we got there. Since that night in New York, someone had been teaching Marilyn new tricks. Maybe a lot of someones."

The next morning, Marilyn lingered over breakfast and stayed with Marlon "for a matinee performance," as she called it. Later Marlon recalled that, "I didn't think she had any place to go."

Marilyn said Sundays were very hard for her to get through in Los Angeles. "All the men I know are spending the day with their wives and families, and all the stores in Los Angeles are closed. You can't wander through looking at all the pretty clothes and pretending to buy something—not that I have any money to buy anything."

She shared her dreams about becoming a movie star with him. "I know a lot of gals arrive in Hollywood dreaming of becoming a movie star. But I have one up on them."

"What's that?" he asked.

"I can dream harder than they can."

After breakfast, she went to her purse and opened it, pulling out a lined slip of yellow paper. "I've written down all the names of the men I plan to seduce. Most are in show business, but some are not."

He read the list: Elia Kazan, Charles Laughton, Arthur Miller, Ernest Hemingway, Clifford Odets, Dean Jagger, Charles Boyer, Lee Strasberg,

The one and only Marilyn Monroe

Nicholas Ray, Jean Renoir, Harry Belafonte, Yves Montand, Charles Bickford, Eli Wallach, and Albert Einstein."

"I've only seduced one on your list," he said. "Better strike Hemingway, Charles Bickford, and Charles Laughton 'cause I hear they're faggots. But Einstein. You're not serious."

"I'm very, very serious," she said.

It has never been completely determined if Marilyn did indeed seduce Einstein. However, in 1985, director Nicolas Roeg made a film, *Insignificance*, about the alleged affair. Theresa Russell played the Marilyn clone opposite Michael Emil as "the professor."

Among Marilyn's possessions was discovered an autographed portrait of Einstein, signed: "To Marilyn, with respect and love and thanks, Albert Einstein." That evidence is often cited when biographers want to prove an affair between the scientist and the love goddess. Refuting that evidence is the claim of Eli Wallach. Regretting that he never became "the lucky victim" of Marilyn's sexual favors, despite the fact that his name was included on the list of her hoped-for seductions, Wallach claimed, years later, that he gave her a copy of Einstein's portrait as a joke, forging both the dedication and the signature.

Marlon's ongoing affair with Marilyn would stop and go, heating up in the mid-Fifties, but never completely disappearing, until her mysterious death in 1962.

Despite what he revealed to a handful of close friends, Marlon had very little to say "officially and on record" about Marilyn. He never demeaned her and spoke about her only in the highest regard. "Marilyn was a sensitive, misunderstood person," he said, "and much more perceptive than was generally assumed. She had been beaten down, but had a strong emotional intelligence—a keen intuition for the feelings of others, the most refined type of intelligence."

"Marlon lived through the whole Marilyn legend," Fiore later said. "The

Marilyn Monroe and Marlon Brando, sex symbols of the Fifties

nude calendar scandal, her lesbian relationships with such movie queens as Joan Crawford and Barbara Stanwyck, her tortured affair with the Kennedys—you name it. He was privy to her secrets and often gave her very good advice. She never seemed to heed Marlon's words, but still continued to call him for guidance she rarely followed."

Marilyn herself made few comments about Marlon, telling anyone who asked that, "He's very sweet and tender, not at all the Stanley Kowalski rapist people think he is."

Reporters clamored around her at an actors' benefit in December of 1955. She was escorted by Marlon. One reporter asked, "Miss Monroe, are you very seriously interested in Mr. Brando?"

"I'm not serious," she claimed, "but always interested."

Marlon kept Zinnemann up to date about his affair with Marilyn. He once told his director, "Marilyn's studio is claiming her bust measurement is 37. However, Marilyn herself disputes that. She says her bust measurement is 38. As for me, I have a built-in tape measure in my brain. I'm never wrong about these things. I'd put her bust at 35, and I should know!"

* * *

During a particularly tense moment of the Cold War, without letting his family or friends know, Marlon agreed to surgery on his knee for a long-ago injury suffered at the Shattuck Military Academy. The subsequent healing of the injury, and his complete recovery, had the unexpected result of making him eligible for military service in the Korean War.

To determine his draft status, he was asked to fill out a questionnaire. Under the question of race, he wrote: "Human." As for color, he listed: "Seasonal—oyster white to beige."

During his meeting with an army psychiatrist, he told the doctor that he was "psychoneurotic" and "suffered emotional problems." Although he was now physically able to be drafted and perhaps sent to Korea, he also checked off the box indicating that he had homosexual tendencies.

"That would do it for guys in those days," Edith Van Cleve said, "and Marlon had determined that he didn't want to sacrifice his life on the battle-fields of Korea, ending up like one of those paraplegics he'd worked with while filming *The Men* in Hollywood."

But despite his avoidance of military service in Korea, his life was threatened nonetheless, and in a particularly disturbing way. In the early 1950s, celebrity stalking was relatively rare, perhaps confined to some star-struck fans trailing Greta Garbo on the sidewalks of New York as she went window shopping.

But when Marlon moved into his small apartment on Sixth Avenue and 57th Street, he began to receive a series of mysterious late night phone calls. The person on the other end of the line would hang up without saying a word, although he could hear the sound of someone breathing. For three months, the calls came in regularly. For some reason, Marlon never changed his phone number, nor did he report the incidents to the police.

Perfecting his Method acting

Finally, one rainy night he heard a delicate voice on the other end of the line. It was that of a woman.

He engaged her in conversation, trying to learn as much about her as she was willing to convey. She claimed that her profession was that of a "stick-up artist." She robbed liquor stores in New Jersey at night, fleeing on a motorcycle piloted by another woman friend who, in the woman's own words, was "deaf and dumb."

"You can rob me," he told her, "but I never carry around more than a dollar or two."

That was not the point of her call. She had become obsessed with Marlon during his appearance in *Streetcar*. She admitted to having attended fifty performances of the play just to gaze upon him. She'd also stolen billboards advertising the play, using them to cover the walls of her bedroom.

She had also managed to steal an eight-by-ten glossy photograph of him from the theater, and placed it beneath her pillow. Every night, she informed him, she had a marathon talk with the photo.

He listened in amazement as she revealed her plan. She'd been stalking him many nights after dark, although he'd been unaware of her presence behind him. She admitted that she intended to kidnap him with the help of her motorcycle-riding pal. They planned to haul him, bound and gagged in a rented car, to a remote boathouse on Long Island. There, as she claimed, she was going to imprison him so that she could slowly cannibalize him. The scene would be eerily evocative of the future movie, *Hannibal*.

Any sane person might have put down the phone at that point and called the police. But not Marlon. Years later, as he recalled the event in interviews and even wrote about it, he stated that he believed the woman was "deadly serious." In spite of knowing that, he recklessly invited the woman to his apartment. Apparently, she already knew his address.

Arriving after eleven o'clock one night, she rapped on his door. He took the precaution of opening the door with the chain attached. Reaching out, he frisked her for a weapon. Slowly opening the door, he peered up and down the hallway to see if he could see her accomplice. The hall was empty, and the woman appeared to be unarmed and alone.

Inside the apartment, he invited her to sit down on his sofa across from his armchair. He studied her carefully, as if he were a police sergeant grilling a suspect. He also placed her under a harsh light from a standing lamp. She identified herself only as "Maria."

He found her extremely beautiful. She was an olive-skinned brunette with a very large bosom. She said that one of her greatest fantasies—other than cannibalizing him—was to be allowed to wash his feet in warm water. He said that was one request he could grant, and went into the kitchen to get a pan of water. Later he said that he suspected that Maria had a fantasy that he was actually Jesus and that she was Mary Magdalene.

Very tenderly she washed his feet and gently dried them with her long hair. During that act, he later claimed he became sexually aroused, inviting her into his bedroom.

As he was to tell Carlo Fiore, "Through some kind of bizarre thinking, or lack of thinking on my part, it became a thrilling idea to seduce the woman. I, as Jesus. She, as Mary Magdalene but also, secretly, as a potential cannibal."

The sex act, according to Marlon's later claim, came off beautifully until she broke into tears. "She must have cried for an hour after I committed the act on her," he later said. "I think she was a virgin."

He had a hard time of it, but he eventually managed to get her out of his apartment. As he remembered it, it was about three o'clock in the morning.

On the nights that followed, he said that he frequently encountered Maria waiting alone in his hallway when he returned home. "She never made a move toward me," he said, "nor did she do anything threatening. I had to get rid of her. Finally, I came up with the idea. As Jesus, I commanded her to go away and leave me alone. Since she thought I was Jesus, she obeyed me."

Before she left, she even gave him her phone number and address in Newark, New Jersey. Two weeks later, he left for Hollywood again. But he kept thinking about her. Then he called a detective in New York and had him track her down. The address proved valid. She lived in a rented home with her brother.

On an impulse, Marlon called Maria's

Getting all dolled up

house one night, getting her brother on the phone. He seemed aware of her obsession with Marlon and was thrilled to be speaking to a movie star. He revealed to Marlon that on the night he'd told her to go away, she'd arrived back at her house covered in blood. Apparently, she'd lacerated her body with shards of glass.

According to the brother, she went to her bedroom and tore down all the billboards advertising *Streetcar*. She also threw out all her Brando memorabilia. Outside in the backyard, she burned all the images. Back in the house, she announced to her brother, "Jesus is dead! He will not rise again."

Marlon put down the phone on the brother. He never heard from Maria again.

* * *

Marlon Senior was busy squandering Marlon Junior's earnings ($40,000) from *The Men* in a misguided investment in the Nebraska cattle business. But more money and bigger losses were on the way.

Warner Brothers finally met Marlon's demand of $75,000 to appear in the film version of *A Streetcar Named Desire*. Elia Kazan, who would direct the film, held out for the original Broadway cast. Consequently, Karl Malden and Kim Hunter were given the supporting roles that had made them famous on Broadway.

Jack Warner had preferred Burt Lancaster to Marlon, but acquiesced to Kazan's vision. Warner, however, definitely didn't want Jessica Tandy. "She's known on Broadway, but except for a few rotten movies, no one knows who she is," the studio chief said. "Olivia de Havilland should do it, but the bitch is demanding $175,000. I've got Vivien Leigh for $100,000. Her husband is making a movie in Hollywood, and the nympho wants to be with the cocksucker." Warner was referring, of course, to Laurence Olivier and his well-known homosexual proclivities.

Before this upcoming commitment in Hollywood, Marlon visited his family at Mundelein, outside Libertyville, Illinois. During his visit, Marlon Sr. showed him his archives of recorded conversations, claiming that he had audio recordings of the deals he'd made and the conversations he'd had with local businessmen. "That way, the fuckers can't cheat me later on."

Marlon Junior commandeered one of Marlon Senior's tape recorders, planning to put it to a different use. In New York, he was going to turn it on under his bed and secretly record the sounds and words uttered, most often in passion, during his love-making. He especially wanted to play back how women screamed when he climaxed in them.

* * *

In New York Bobby Lewis visited Marlon to congratulate him on his new-found movie stardom. Bobby recalled that Wally Cox was spending the night at Marlon's apartment. Cox was nursing a deep wound—the result of a bite from Marlon's pet raccoon, Russell, whom Cox detested.

Bobby remembered how he was shocked by Marlon's aggressiveness, even his crudeness. Later Bobby felt that Marlon once again was trying to work himself up to play the brute, Stanley Kowalski, in the screen version of *Streetcar*. "He wasn't Marlon that night, a man who had a gentle side, but a lager lout. He was insulting, even cruel to me, and he treated Wally like he was a doormat. But he still adored Russell."

He said that Wally had called for Chinese take-out to be delivered to Marlon's apartment. But before the delivery boy arrived, Marlon fell on the floor. "At first it looked like he was having a heart attack," Bobby said, "and I rushed to his aid, but Wally grabbed me and restrained me, shouting at me to 'Let him alone!'"

Wally pulled Bobby into the kitchen to explain that Marlon frequently suffered these "panic attacks." According to Wally, Marlon rolled on the floor with his eyes shut, often babbling. To Bobby, Marlon seemed to be going through an epileptic seizure.

"You know a lot about Marlon," Wally said to him. "Maybe too much. But there are secrets about him known only to me, secrets that will never be revealed."

"Such as?"

"I'll go to my grave and never tell," Wally said. "Marlon has a very, very dark side. Sometimes he can go for months and repress that side of him. But sometimes it comes out. You'd better leave the apartment. I think his dark side is going to be unleashed tonight. You wouldn't want to know what's going to happen in this apartment tonight. Good night!"

* * *

Five years younger than Marlon, and a native of Wichita Falls, Texas, Roberta Haynes was the estranged wife of Jay Kanter, who was not only Marlon's agent but to an increasing degree, his best friend. The relationship would last until Marlon's death.

A male friend was privy to the burgeoning romance between Roberta and Marlon. He didn't want his name used—call him "Hubert." "I still don't understand what was going on. Jay practically pushed Roberta into Marlon's arms, yet he told me he still wanted to get back with his estranged wife. When

311

Roberta Haynes

I asked him why, he said, 'I felt they would really go for each other.' If Jay was still married to her, and wanted to stay married to her, then why bring Marlon into the picture? Marlon always liked to intrude on couples, happy or otherwise."

At the time, Roberta was a curvaceous leading lady (measurements 35-24-34), who had appeared uncredited in *Knock on Any Door*, the Bogie picture that Marlon had turned down. Her Hollywood star would shine on her only briefly. In 1953 she would appear with Rock Hudson in *Gun Fury*, a routine western, and more memorably opposite Gary Cooper in *Return to Paradise*, a tale of the South Pacific.

When he met her in New York, Roberta reminded Marlon of a Polynesian beauty, the type he would seduce frequently during later decades in Tahiti. After breaking with Jay, Roberta had gone to New York to replace Leora Dana on Broadway in *The Madwoman of Chaillot*.

Roberta would later recall to Brando biographers that she first met Marlon at the Bird-in-Hand Restaurant along Broadway when he roared up on a scarlet-red motorcycle. In a black cap and leather jacket, he looked exactly like the motorcycle-riding hood he'd play in *The Wild One*. It was "love" at first sight.

Their romance was brief but intense, including a bout in the splashing fountain that stands regally in the square in front of New York's Plaza Hotel.

Although Marlon was seeing other women at the time, his romance with Roberta continued on and off whenever she was in town between road tour stopovers with *Madwoman*.

They were seen walking hand in hand down Fifth Avenue, buying fresh New Jersey strawberries from vendors, or shopping for a psychology paperback on Carl Jung in a Greenwich Village bookstore. He attended a performance of *Madwoman* at the City Center and then came backstage, exciting the cast. "At the time, every woman in New York wanted Marlon," said fellow actress Gwynne Betmann, "and Roberta walked off with the prize hunk. We were very envious."

Roberta recalled to one reporter that during her dates with Marlon, he was besieged with messages from Shelley Winters, which in front of her he tossed in the trash can. Whether he later returned Shelley's calls is not known.

He took Roberta to see *Play Me a Song*, in which Wally had a featured part. "The show opened and closed before it had even begun," Wally later said. "Marlon did everything he could to drum up interest with the press, but to no avail. My hour had not struck yet."

Sometime before the summer ended, Marlon wasn't seen with Roberta, but with Tamar Cooper, the daughter of Jack and Marie Cooper. In her mid-twenties, she could be seen holding on to Marlon "for dear life," as he raced on his motorcycle through the streets of New York.

When Jay Kanter learned of Marlon's affair with Roberta, he wasn't angry at his client but at his wife. When Marlon arrived in Hollywood to film *Streetcar*, Jay asked his wife to move back into their apartment. But since Marlon was already living there, along with his pet raccoon, Russell, Roberta didn't think that would be a good idea.

Fellow roommate and aspiring actor, Tony Curtis, once said, "For some reason Marlon always insisted that Russell sleep in our oven. It's a good thing I didn't come home one night and heat up the oven for a midnight supper."

Roberta soon learned that her affair with Marlon was winding down in spite of the lovely intimate experiences he'd had with her, including long walks in the country where he might take off his clothes for a nude swim. At the time Marlon was engaged in a number of other affairs, including one with a fifteen-year-old girl, which could have subjected him to a charge of statutory rape.

Whether Roberta learned about Marlon's temporary affair—conducted in Jay's apartment—with "Sister Elizabeth" is not known. But for a period of one month during the filming of *Streetcar*, a nun in black habit and stiffly starched wimple was seen coming and going from Jay Kanter's apartment. She was not coming to visit either Jay or fellow roommate Tony Curtis, but to have sessions with Marlon.

Sister Elizabeth, who later tried to hawk a "tell all" memoir to New York publishers, was born in Birmingham, Alabama. She'd come to Hollywood, like thousands of others, to break into films. But she always said that movie producers thought she was a dead ringer for Carole Landis, the 1940s star who committed suicide after a broken love affair with actor Rex Harrison.

Like so many other hopefuls, she took to prostitution to earn a living. When one client asked her to don a nun's habit—he had a closet filled with such costumes—she got an idea for future employment.

She began making the rounds of certain actors, mainly those born into the Catholic faith, who wanted to seduce a nun. In her unpublished memoirs, she claimed that the guilt-ridden Spencer Tracy was her chief customer, often employing her when Katharine Hepburn was

Tamar Cooper and Brando

313

Tony Curtis

away dating such women as American Express heiress Laura Harding or the more beautiful Claudette Colbert.

Sister Elizabeth was known for her 42-inch bosom, which she was quick to display since she wore nothing under her habit. "Often my clients wanted me to paddle them, perhaps evoking memories of their childhood. When Marlon got my number and began calling me, it was the reverse. He would pull up my habit and paddle me before we went on to other pastimes. I visited him for three weeks, and then he never called me again. Incidentally, I wrote about him in my memoirs. I call it *Confessions of a Kinky Nun*. If somebody would publish it, it would become a bestseller. I even sent a letter and my photograph to the White House when President Kennedy moved in. I thought, being born a Catholic, he might go for my nun's act. But he never wrote or called, even though I left my phone number. Guess he preferred Marilyn Monroe to me even though my bosom dwarfed hers."

In his own memoirs, Tony Curtis never revealed what he knew about Marlon's nocturnal adventures when they shared the same living space. He did reveal that a major turning point in his life involved seeing Marlon in 1947 on Broadway in *Streetcar*.

Jay's apartment in Los Angeles was on Barham Boulevard. When not living with Vivien Leigh and Laurence Olivier, Marlon stayed with Jay and Tony during the shooting of *Streetcar*.

At the time, Tony was filming the *Prince Who Was a Thief*. One night he asked Marlon, "What if you'd accidentally turned left down Barham Boulevard and went to Universal to be the son of Ali Baba, and I'd turned right and became Stanley Kowalski?"

"Then I'd have been stuck with 'Yondah lies the castle of my faddah,' and you'd have been yelling *STEL-L-A-A!*"

Cary Grant was Tony's favorite actor, and he could do a brilliant impersonation of him.

Unknown to Tony, his idol, Cary Grant, pulled up in his car one night in front of the Barham Boulevard apartment. He'd not come to see Tony but the other tenant. Earlier that day he'd made a "date" with Marlon himself.

* * *

"I can't stand the limey cunt!" Marlon shouted at Elia Kazan after the first three days of shooting *A Streetcar Named Desire*. "Miss Vivien Leigh. Miss Scarlett O'Hara. Now Lady Olivier. 'Good morning, Mr. Brando.'" He imitated her accent perfectly. "'Good afternoon, Mr. Brando.' She'll suffocate me with her politeness. I can't wait for the rape scene!"

"If the censors will allow it," Kazan cautioned.

The first time Marlon sat down to talk to Vivien, he found a vulnerable character, not the "prissy English bitch" he'd envisioned. She reached out and gently touched his hand, as she spoke of the first time she'd read *A Streetcar Named Desire* in 1948. "I was touched by the haunting quality of Blanche," she said. "The play seemed to speak to a woman inside myself that lives within my own heart. Blanche DuBois is the animus of my own being. Talk about Method acting!"

That remark seemed to win Marlon to her side. After that, and until the end of the eight-week shoot, he became almost inseparable from her.

He was full of questions about how she'd fared in the London stage production of *Streetcar*, which was directed by her husband, Laurence Olivier. He was also anxious to learn of the feuds Olivier had with Irene Selznick and Tennessee Williams over cuts Olivier had made before the play opened in the West End of London.

One Saturday morning he drove her into the desert so she could breathe the fresh air. She'd had a struggle with tuberculosis and was having a hard time breathing in Los Angeles. "It's been ten years since Larry and I were here. Now there's this bloody smog. You're used to it. I'm not. It's like a yellow blanket that hangs over everything and doesn't go away. It stings my eyes and fills my lungs with poison."

He told her he knew of an inn thirty miles away that was outside the smog's radius. She could rest there for the weekend.

"When I first came to Los Angeles to play Scarlett," she said, "I remember oranges everywhere. Now those orange trees have vanished like my virginity."

"From what I was told, you and Larry had to

Vivien Leigh and Brando as Blanche and Stanley

315

Ms. DuBois and sweaty Stanley

live as secret lovers the last time you were in Hollywood," he said. "Now you are the married Sir Laurence and Lady Olivier. The King and Queen of the London theater."

"It's a respectability I don't deserve, and a social responsibility from the throne I don't want. As you'll get to know me, and I hope you will, there is nothing respectable about me. In London I pick up taxi drivers and fuck them."

Startled, he looked at her. Had he heard right? Did she actually say that?

"Don't be surprised," she said. "I'm just as whorish as Blanche DuBois was, taking on all those soldiers at that army base."

She paused, lighting her own cigarette, as if remembering something he'd just said. "Forgive me, but you said Larry. Do you know my husband, Sir Laurence?"

"I met him a few years ago in New York when he came to see me in a play," he said. "I was very honored."

"I won't bother to ask you how well you knew Sir Olivier," she said, sucking the smoke deeply into her tainted lungs.

"It's just as well, because I won't tell you."

"Growing up in the theater, I am used to such things. I never quiz Larry about his private life. His first wife was a lesbian, you know. When he's with Richard Burton, Danny Kaye, Noël Coward, I ask no questions. Larry asks no questions of me either. I don't love him. We are only Sir Laurence and Lady Olivier in front of the press. When our pictures aren't being taken, we lead completely separate lives."

"If I ever get married, and I don't plan to, I will demand from my woman that I go on leading my separate life."

Driving through the desert with Vivien, Marlon arrived at a wayside motel that seemed to evoke that dreary place she'd seen in *The Petrified Forest* with Bette Davis, Humphrey Bogart, and her friend and lover, Leslie Howard, her beloved Ashley Wilkes in *Gone With the Wind*.

They registered as "Petticoat Blossom" and "Durango Canyon." Inside the best room, Vivien began to remove her clothing to take a shower. "Do you know," she said to him in the stifling heat of the desert bedroom, "I am part of the world's most beautiful, the world's most talented, the world's most admired, the world's most successful, and the world's most adored couple. If the world only knew the truth. Why don't you rape me like Stanley Kowalski raped Blanche DuBois?"

316

"An invitation I can't resist," he said, moving toward her.

After sex, he told her over a meal in a roadside diner that he hadn't liked her at first. "So fucking formal."

"Her Ladyship is fucking bored with formality," she said.

He broke into laughter before affectionately leaning over and kissing her on the nose. "I can't believe I've slept with Scarlett O'Hara. Rhett Butler's woman. You won't be the first woman that Clark Gable and I have shared."

"Trust me, Clark Gable never got into my pantaloons."

* * *

Marlon's relationship with Vivien would have gone unrecorded had he not confided in both Charles K. Feldman, the producer of *Streetcar*, and its director, Elia Kazan. The story of Marlon and Vivien was just too hot for these two men to keep to themselves. When Frank Merlo, Tennessee's lover, arrived with the playwright on the set of *Streetcar*, both Kazan and Feldman shared the news about Marlon's sexual adventure with the two men, who were each anxious to hear (and eventually repeat) the latest gossip.

Tennessee and Frank were also anxious to learn about Vivien's first meeting with Marlon. The playwright had predicted "fireworks." Kazan related the story.

Marlon had arrived at the Green Room at Warner Brothers on a buttercup-yellow motorcycle. He wore a tight-fitting Halloween orange T-shirt that showed off his muscles. But instead of his usual dirty blue jeans, he was clad in a pair of elephant brown slacks for the occasion. Later, Vivien remarked to her dining companion, Kazan, "I was surprised when he came into the dining room in shoes. I fully expected to see his bare feet."

As Marlon approached Vivien's table, he overheard an argument she was having with Kazan. She was demanding that she play Blanche the way her husband had directed her in London, and Kazan wanted her to do the role the way he'd directed Jessica Tandy on Broadway.

Not wanting to become part of the argument, Marlon

Frank Merlo, Elia Kazan, Tennessee Williams, and Charles Feldman

A captured scene of *Streetcar*

shook Vivien's hand and wandered over to join Feldman at another table. At the time, Feldman had the most notorious black book in Hollywood, and Marlon wanted his producer to fix him up with only the hottest names on the list of available starlets.

After Marlon's hasty departure, Vivien told Kazan, "I find him offensively rude. But it may be just the kind of Stanley vs. Blanche hostility that will play well before the camera."

"Before this movie began, I knew that Jack Warner had paired a gazelle with a wild boar," Kazan said. "But we're going to make a great film, and both you and Marlon are going to walk off with Oscars. His first, your second. Surely you want a brother to go with that lonely statue you won for Scarlett. *Gone With the Wind* was a long time ago. It's time you set Hollywood on its ass once again. With Marlon you can do it. I know you two are not matched socially, but in this case talent will be the great leveler."

"But he mumbles," Vivien protested. "I too have been accused of lack of projection on stage. It seems that no one can hear me in the upper tiers in those cheap seats."

"Marlon mumbles," Kazan said, "but believe it or not he can also speak with articulation." Catching Marlon's eyes at Feldman's table, Kazan summoned him over again. Marlon came over and sat next to Kazan. "I've got to get back to Charlie. He and I are in hot negotiations over my pussy line-up."

Vivien pretended she didn't hear him, feeling that he was deliberately trying to shock her.

Jokingly, Kazan claimed that after *Streetcar* was finished, he planned to take on a film version of *Henry V* as his next creative venture. Patting Marlon's hand, he urged him to give a quick audition in front of Vivien.

Without being asked again, Marlon launched into a perfect imitation of Olivier doing *Henry V*. He must have gone on for ten minutes before getting up from table and excusing himself once again.

"Now eat your fucking meal," were his departing words.

"I'm shocked, truly shocked," Vivien said when he'd departed. "If I'd closed my eyes, I could have sworn that that voice was coming from Larry himself."

"He's good," Kazan said. He looked at her as if he wanted her to forgive Marlon for his rudeness. As if sensing his request, she brushed such a thought aside. "Oh, fiddle-dee-dee, I can handle Mr. Brando." Her eyes had narrowed and she looked like she did when uttering her famous, "I'll never go hungry again" speech from *Gone With the Wind*. "Before *Streetcar* is wrapped, it'll be Lady Olivier who will shock Mr. Brando."

*　*　*

It is not entirely certain if Marlon had an affair with starlet Nancy Davis, later Mrs. Ronald Reagan. If he did, it was of short duration and occurred on the eve of her nabbing Reagan as her husband. Nancy left Marlon out of her autobiography, as she did other lovers. However, Marlon told both Charles Feldman and Elia Kazan that he'd made love to Nancy, whom he found "kinda cute with her brown eyes and hair just the color I like it."

In the early 1950s, Nancy was known to have composed a list of unattached marriageable males. At the top of her list was Ronald Reagan. Other men on the list included actors, producers, and directors. Surely Nancy knew enough about Marlon to know that he was "not marriage material." She allegedly told Ava Gardner, whom she encountered on the MGM lot, that "Marlon is just too wild and bohemian for me."

"But not for me, honey child," Ava was supposed to have countered. "Been there, done that."

Nancy had first met Marlon in New York when she was dating Clark Gable, a romance that never got off the launch pad. At the time of her reunion with Marlon in Hollywood, Nancy was in the throes of a torrid affair with Benjamin Thau, head of casting at MGM.

She had desperately wanted to appear opposite Cary Grant in the film, *Crisis*, and made a screen test, hoping to secure the role of the doctor's wife.

When Dore Schary saw the screen test, he pronounced it, "The worst screen test in the history of Hollywood." When *Crisis* opened later to no business, Grant told Nancy that she was lucky she didn't get the part.

Thau was deeply in love with Nancy at the time she was dating other men. He even wanted to marry her "in spite of my Jewishness and my age." No one ever accused Nancy of being anti-Semitic. Director George Cukor, who was dismissive of her, claimed, "If I had a nickel for every Jew Nancy was under, I'd be rich." The noted Hollywood biographer, Anne Edwards, once

Nancy Davis

said, "Nancy was one of those girls whose phone number got handed around a lot."

Peter Lawford had already spread the word that Nancy was skilled at fellatio. He alleged that she had kept not only himself but fellow actor Robert Walker (also Peter's lover) orally entertained throughout the course of a motor trip to Palm Springs.

One of Thau's assistants reportedly saw Nancy and Marlon dining at Chasen's, a restaurant that Marlon had never visited before, as he hated formal dining rooms. Nancy was elegantly attired in a black Coco Chanel dress, a large white hat, and a corsage of small orchids. Abandoning blue jeans, Marlon wore a sports jacket and slacks but no tie.

When Thau heard that the woman he loved had been seen out with Brando, he was furious, threatening that Marlon would never make a picture for Metro-Goldwyn-Mayer. "By trying to move in on Nancy, the cocksucking queer has ruined himself in this town—I'll see to that."

Whatever relationship existed between Marlon and Nancy fizzled quickly, because she was soon seen dating the handsome actor, Robert Stack, and was also seen with the playwright-producer, Norman Krasna, who wanted to marry her. Krasna had just signed a deal with Howard Hughes at RKO, and he promised to make her the queen of that studio if she'd marry him. She turned him down. Her eyes were still trained on Ronald Reagan, her dreamboat.

Marlon told Kazan that Nancy would never appear opposite him in one of his films—"that is, if I ever make another film. But if you know of any roles calling for 'the perfect wife,' then Nancy's your gal. She's the exception to every other actress in Hollywood. Instead of some big-time career, she wants to settle down in a rose-covered cottage, raise three kids, and greet hubbie with a Scotch and soda every night at six o'clock, as the smell of fried chicken wafts through the house."

Marlon may have accurately interpreted Nancy's feelings at the time. She later confessed to just such a dream, hardly knowing that the "cottage" would turn out to be the White House, where in 1981 she would suffer the highest disapproval rating of any First Lady in modern times.

When Marlon was informed of Nancy's marriage to Reagan, he sarcastically told Feldman, "A perfect match. I hear Reagan brushes his teeth every time he kisses a woman. I can even suggest a theme song for their marriage. Make it George Gershwin's 'Our Love Is Here to Stay.'"

Marlon in the years to come would always speak kindly of Nancy, "even when she was single-handedly running the Free World." On the other hand, he deplored Reagan for what he claimed was "his witch hunting of so-called Communists."

It wasn't Nancy but another brunette who had suddenly appeared in

Marlon's life. He was about to begin a hell-raising romance with a fiery natured Puerto Rican who called herself Rosita Moreno (later Rita Moreno).

Ten years into her future, her name would become a household word with the release of *West Side Story*. Twenty years into her future, she'd shock movie audiences by performing fellatio on Jack Nicholson at the end of *Carnal Knowledge*.

At the time Marlon met Moreno, she was seeing George Hormel, the famous heir to a meat-packing fortune. Ironically, Hormel had been a classmate of Marlon at the Shattuck Military Academy. When he learned that Marlon was in Hollywood, Hormel asked his former classmate to one of his parties, to which he often invited jazz greats, paying them if they requested money. Wanting to play his bongo drums with Stan Getz or perhaps Chet Baker, Marlon eagerly attended. It was there on one hot night that he met Rita Moreno.

As he'd done so often in the past, Marlon decided to "move in on Hormel's cattle ranch." As he boasted to Kazan the next day, "That fucker might think all the meat in America is being canned in one of his factories. But Marlon Brando's meaty noble tool is free and swinging in the breeze."

* * *

Tennessee, accompanied by Frank Merlo, arrived in Los Angeles for a screening of *The Glass Menagerie*. After that, he visited the set of *Streetcar* every day, telling Frank he was "mesmerized" watching "the chemistry" between Marlon and Vivien, something he said that he had always intended between Jessica Tandy and Marlon on Broadway but never elicited from her.

With Marlon and Frank Merlo standing in the background, Tennessee told Kazan, "Vivien has brought everything to the role of Miss DuBois that I intended, and much more than I ever dared to dream."

While Tennessee was watching Kazan direct Vivien and Karl Malden in a pivotal scene, Frank Merlo slipped off to Mushy Callahan's Gymnasium on the Warner Brothers lot. As he was undressing, he overheard two men laughing and joking in one of the shower stalls.

Hoping to get in on the fun, he stripped down and walked toward them. "Those two didn't even see me. I was all so very gay. To my surprise, I saw Burt Lancaster and Marlon showering together. Burt was soaping Marlon's back with one hand and probing his ass with the index finger of his other hand. Marlon was giggling like a school girl. I left those two love birds alone and seduced a well-hung grip that day instead."

Frank returned to the set just in time to hear Vivien tell Tennessee, "It's all your fault. Your character of Blanche DuBois is tripping me into madness."

"I can understand that," he replied. "Blanche has already given me three heart attacks."

* * *

As Tennessee and Kazan continued to battle the censors, filming continued on *Streetcar* during one of the hottest summers in recorded Los Angeles' history.

Except for Marlon himself, Jack Warner remained deeply dissatisfied with the cast. His dream had been to cast Olivia de Havilland in the role of Blanche, with her estranged sister, Joan Fontaine, playing Stella. When he couldn't get de Havilland, he asked Jane Wyman, recently divorced from Ronald Reagan, if she'd attempt the role. The answer was no.

Jane Wyman

At the urging of David O. Selznick, Warner briefly considered David's wife, Jennifer Jones. The veto on Jones came from Irene Selznick herself, who was still bitter that David had dumped her for the younger and more beautiful star.

One week before shooting began, and even after Vivien had been signed, Kazan still held out for Jessica Tandy. He urged Warner to pay off Vivien, who by then had a signed contract, and hire Tandy to replace her.

"No way!" Warner shouted back at his director. "If I don't want to fuck Tandy, I have to assume that other men in the audience will feel the same way. Not one man wants a piece of Tandy's ass. She's got the sex appeal of Lionel Barrymore. Case closed!"

Even at the last minute, Warner pushed James Cagney for the role of Blanche's almost boyfriend. But Kazan held out for Karl Malden.

Kazan and Warner clashed bitterly over Kim Hunter, the studio honcho claiming that Hunter had a "negative screen personality." Warner preferred Anne Baxter, Ruth Roman, or Patricia Neal, who was at the time in the throes of an ill-fated affair with Gary Cooper. "Even Donna Reed would be better," Warner claimed.

"If you cast one of those actresses," Kazan threatened, "I'm walking off the picture. Kim Hunter will be brilliant playing a girl who likes to get fucked by Stanley—and fucked regularly. She's the one. I should know. I've already auditioned her in that department."

While making *The Men*, Marlon had "screwed up" interviews with both Hedda Hopper and Louella Parsons, but he agreed to see columnist James Bacon on

Olivia de Havilland the set of *Streetcar*. The writer had been warned in

322

advance that questions about the actor's private life were off-limits.

But during the interview, Bacon later recalled, "Brando went into a detailed account of his personal life, one so raunchy that no publication could possibly have printed it in those days. He talked about fucking a girl in the ass with butter, and even made slight reference to a friendly romp with a goat back on the farm in Nebraska. Twenty-two years later when I saw *Last Tango in Paris*, in which Brando pretty much improvised the sex scenes, I realized I had been through this picture before, in Brando's own words back in 1950."

With other reporters, Marlon—and with good reason—continued to draw a curtain across any insights into his private life. "I have every right in the world to resist the insipid protocol of turning my life into the kind of running serial you find on bubble gum wrappers. You can't take sensitive parts of yourself and splatter them around like so much popcorn butter."

In contrast to Bacon, Louella Parsons and other columnists maintained an ongoing series of attacks against Marlon, deploring his manners and dress. Lolly called him "The Slob," and the label stuck.

But other members of the Hollywood elite found him dazzling, just as many A-list stars had when they came backstage to seduce him after his nightly performances in *Streetcar* on Broadway.

Gloria Swanson had no plans to seduce Marlon, but she later revealed that, "Although Monty Clift was offered the role of Joe Gillis in *Sunset Blvd.*, I secretly preferred Marlon Brando. I felt that the picture was so strong that I, as Norma Desmond, and Marlon as Joe Gillis, my gigolo, would have walked away with Oscars. Of course, the part went to the less charismatic William Holden."

In the middle of filming, Marlon's sometimes girlfriend, Shelley Winters, visited him on the set. Marlon took her by the arm and escorted her to his

Gloria Swanson

portable dressing room. Once inside, he locked the door for privacy. "Scream, Shelley scream!" he whispered to her. "We've got to shake the walls of this fucking trailer. I've got a reputation to maintain. Scream, Shelley, scream!"

She obliged.

In only two weeks, Kazan managed to remove each of the stage directions Vivien had learned from Olivier during the staging of the play's production in London. A new and different Blanche DuBois was recorded on film. Not only that, but Marlon was finding nuances in the role of Stanley Kowalski that he had not realized on Broadway.

"I made Vivien connect role with soul," Kazan later said. "She and Marlon were perfectly matched. A chemistry exploded on screen that didn't exist between Marlon and Jessica Tandy on Broadway. Before my lens were two highly charged actors exploding off each other."

Privately Marlon told Kazan, "That delirium and despair you're capturing on the screen is Lady Olivier herself. She's writing a textbook of the madness that lurks within herself. I fear, though, that she's going over the deep edge with Blanche. She'll never come back."

Other cast members took note of Vivien's tottering on the brink of a nervous breakfast. Karl Malden, though deeply devoted to Jessica

Karl Malden

Tandy, came to accept Vivien in the role of Blanche. "After all," he said, "she had star power. The film was riding on her. She was carrying all of us nobodies, including Marlon Brando himself. But she had a tenuous hold on reality."

In contrast to his ongoing struggles with Vivien, Kazan had no trouble directing Brando. He told Charles Feldman, "There was nothing you could do with Brando that touched what he could do with himself!" Feldman was surprised by the fact that Marlon had initially rejected the movie role of Stanley ("It'd be like marrying the same woman twice.") The producer was also surprised to learn that Kazan had originally refused the director's job, even when it was personally presented by Jack Warner. ("I don't think I could get it up a second time for *Streetcar*.")

Obviously, both Kazan and Brando eventually changed their minds.

* * *

Marlon was not necessarily known for getting along with producers. Charles Feldman, a canny Hollywood agent turned producer, was the remarkable exception. Marlon told Kazan, "Charlie is my kind of guy. We speak the same language." On the first day of their meeting, Feldman had won Marlon over by saying, "Welcome to Hollywood. I want you to make a picture about the three Fs—feuding, fighting, and fucking!"

In his mid-forties at the time, Feldman was often called "the Jewish Clark Gable," and many Hollywood insiders had told him that he should be in front of the cameras instead of directing operations from behind the scenes.

Feldman, as the New York-born president of Famous Artists, Inc., became the most famous agent in Hollywood, managing the careers of clients who included Tyrone Power, John Wayne, Marlene Dietrich, Ava Gardner, Gary Cooper, and eventually, James Dean. Not all of his clients liked him. Feldman once recalled that, "On the same day I was fired by Lana Turner, Rita Hayworth, and Marilyn Monroe."

Feldman told Marlon that during the filming of *Streetcar,* he would line up "the most fuckable pussies" in Hollywood for him.

"I'm ready, willing, and able," Marlon boasted. "Let the good times roll."

"To keep Vivien happy," Feldman said, "I'm seeing that she gets regularly fucked, too. So far, she's sleeping with anything in pants on the set. Kazan deflowered her when they took that long train ride from New York to Los Angeles. Through my friend Henry Willson, I'm keeping Olivier supplied with some of our better endowed young actors who want to be auditioned by Hamlet. You know that Olivier is gay, don't you?"

Not revealing his own sexual involvement with Olivier in the mid-Forties, Marlon merely said, "I'd heard that."

Just before he met Marlon, Feldman had divorced Jean Howard, a one-time MGM starlet, who had broken into films after working as a chorine and a Goldwyn girl. After retiring from show business, she became one of Hollywood's most famous photographers, shooting portraits of, among others, Tyrone Power, Gene Tierney, Richard Burton, and Cole Porter.

When his marriage "to the cactus flower of Texas" ended, Feldman became a "serial seducer" of Hollywood starlets, later offering some of them to his friends and clients. If it so happened that those friends and clients happened to be gay, he would call Henry Willson (discoverer of Rock Hudson) to supply what Feldman called "the man meat."

As he told Marlon, "When I got to Hollywood, I quickly learned that pussy won't always do it. To keep Monty Clift in line during the filming of *Red River*, I even let him suck my cock."

Feldman could also laugh at himself. "The first film I produced was in 1942. It was called *The Lady Is Willing*. Hot damn, did I ever learn that was true in Hollywood. Another film I produced two years later, *Follow the Boys*, also tells the story with me. I peddle flesh out here, male or female. It makes no difference to me as long as the money keeps rolling in. I'm one of those people who has no morals. That way, I never have guilt like that sickie, Spencer Tracy, who likes to have sex with teenage boys, then drinks himself into oblivion for a month over what he's done."

After the first week of shooting, Feldman called Marlon and offered him the use of his rented house in Beverly Hills for the weekend. He told Marlon that he was driving to Palm Springs "to fuck Hedy Lamarr for forty-eight hours straight."

"Did you provide me with some company?" Marlon asked, accepting access to the property.

"There's plenty of champagne chilling," Feldman told him. "There's lobster and a can of caviar. And beginning at ten o'clock tonight, the hottest blonde pussy in Hollywood will arrive. Her pussy is not actually blonde. But for you and for the occasion, I've asked her to bleach it for you."

"No need to do that," Marlon told him. "I actually prefer my pussy dark."

"Too late, baby," Feldman said. "Have fun pounding that thing. I've been doing it for weeks now, and I highly recommend it."

"I can't wait until ten o'clock."

* * *

The blonde starlet promised by Feldman didn't arrive on schedule at ten o'clock but at midnight. She was to embark on an agenda of being perpetually late—that is, if she showed up at all. Marlon had his night light on reading a story about Arthur Miller, who had told him that, "You should give up this Hollywood crap and return to Broadway where you belong!"

Letting herself into Feldman's house with her own key, this blonde beauty appeared at the door to Marlon's bedroom. Looking up at her, he noted that she had her eyes half closed and her mouth half open. She was clad in a red sequin dress two sizes too small for her and wore pink ankle-strap Joan Crawford fuck-me shoes. She spoke in a whispered voice that came out as if she were panting. "You know me. I know you. Uncle Charlie sent me over to entertain you."

He looked her up and down with great admiration. "How could I fail to recognize Marilyn Monroe? Come on in. Don't be a stranger."

She giggled, coming into the room. "I didn't tell Uncle Charlie we already knew each other."

"For God's sake," he said, "get out of that dress. Those tits of yours look like they need to be liberated."

As she slowly and tantalizingly began to strip in front of him, she said, "Don't get the wrong idea. I don't like sex all that much, as I might have led you to believe. I just do it to please men. Sometimes I even come."

"Tonight you will," he prom-

Marilyn Monroe

326

ised. "My noble tool always does its job with honor, respect, and dignity for the woman."

"Then let's get on with it," she said.

At the time, Johnny Hyde, her chief promoter, was still alive, but Marilyn was also hustling Feldman, fearing that Hyde with his weak heart would not always be around. She had volunteered her name as an entry for Feldman's little black book, promising the businessman and agent that she would entertain his clients, prospective clients, directors, and producers. Almost overnight she became the most requested starlet in the little black book.

Their passion, as Marlon was to report in great detail to Feldman the following afternoon, lasted for three hours. Both of them fell asleep around five o'clock in the morning and stayed in bed until nearly two o'clock the following afternoon.

Over orange juice in Feldman's kitchen, Marilyn told Marlon, "I think a girl should use sex like a weapon. I think this is the only way a girl can get ahead in a town ruled by men."

He was amazed at how bluntly she expressed herself, whereas many other women he'd known would have been more restrained.

"I like it when you make love to me," she told him. "I don't like many of Uncle Charlie's other clients."

"Thanks." He reached over to kiss her nose. "What's with this Uncle Charlie stuff?"

"I just call him that to tease him," she said. "He hates it. He says, 'So, now I've reached the Uncle Charlie phase of my life.' I told him that's what he gets for dating high school girls. 'If you don't like to be called Uncle Charlie, then go out with girls your own age,' I told him. Can you believe it? Uncle Charlie once fucked Greta Garbo. Now he desires *me*."

"Apparently, he doesn't desire you enough to keep you exclusively for himself," he said. "But sends you out to service other clients."

"Why not?" she asked. "After all, that's how I got my start in the business. I still remember the fifteen dollars you gave me in New York so long ago. I really needed the money. Thanks."

"You earned it."

"Uncle Charlie has big plans for me," she said. "Johnny Hyde's not going to be around for long. He's madly in love with me, but has a bad heart. He's also got a small penis and can't make me come. The one thing I hate about Johnny is that he thinks all women are tramps. Do you think that about women, Mr. Brando?"

"Not at all," he said, affecting grandeur. "I think you're enchanting. Far from a tramp. But you haven't yet unleashed your special magic onto the world. When you do, your name will rank with Helen of Troy and Cleopatra.

God had a talent for creating exceptional women: Dietrich. Garbo. And now Marilyn Monroe."

She giggled again. "I hope you really mean that. Men tell such lies. I don't know who to believe."

"Trust me." He slammed down his coffee and stood up. "Let's go for a walk in the garden. Breathe Uncle Charlie's fresh air." In the garden holding her hand, he asked her, "Have you ever been in love? Even once?"

She sighed and her lip quivered. "Yes, once. His name was Fred. A musician and a bit skinny for my taste. Unlike my husband, Fred could make me come. But he told me I was good for nothing but fucking. His only complaint was that my breasts were too big, too much like a cow. He said he preferred women with smaller breasts. He also found my clothes cheap. One night he told me I was too stupid to talk to, and I've been trying to improve my mind ever since."

"This Fred sounds like a total asshole," he told her.

Marilyn was talking about Fred Karger, a relationship that produced three of her pregnancies, each ending in abortion. He did not marry her because he did not consider her a suitable parent for his children from previous marriages.

Only the insiders of Hollywood knew how despondent Marilyn became when Karger slipped away to Santa Barbara on November 1, 1952 and married Jane Wyman, even though Ronald Reagan was still in love with her. Karger told friends that "Jane Wyman is the type of gal you marry. Marilyn Monroe is the type of gal you fuck."

Wyman would ultimately divorce Karger, charging that he had "an uncontrollable temper" and citing "grievous mental cruelty." But in 1961, to the surprise of Hollywood, she would remarry her musician. Until he died of leukemia in 1979 at the age of sixty-three, Karger maintained that "Marilyn stalked me throughout most of the 50s. She never got over me."

"Do you find me too stupid to talk to?" Marilyn asked Marlon.

"Not at all," he said. "I find you entertaining in conversation and the Miracle Lady in bed. Speaking of bed, my noble tool is rising to do its duty one more time."

She giggled, locking her hand with him as his hand enclosed one of her breasts.

After another round of sex, she jumped up from the bed and turned her naked ass to him. "Johnny tells me I have a behind like a nigger. What do you think, Mr. Brando?"

"I like nigger behinds," he said. "Get back in bed with me and I'll show you."

She smiled at him. "You've had enough for one morning. I don't want to spoil you. Don't tell anybody this, but I have nigger blood in me. Really, I do.

328

I'm not joking."

For reasons known only to herself, between 1948 and 1951, Marilyn insisted on telling confidants that she had "nigger blood" in her. There is no proof that she did. She told this same tale to Kazan and others. After 1951, she was never heard to make that claim again.

Rushing to the shower, she called back to Marlon. "I will let you fuck me three more times this afternoon. Then tonight I want you to escort me to a private party on the Fox lot. Tyrone Power will be there. I'll introduce you to him."

Marlon would later give a detailed report to both Kazan and Feldman about his night with Marilyn. Feldman was happy that, in his role as the producer of *Streetcar,* he'd pleased a hot new associate. Kazan had a different reaction. "I knew you'd eventually get around to Marilyn. I'm not jealous."

"Why should you be?" Marlon asked. He paused for a moment. "I know Uncle Charlie is fucking Marilyn. But you, Gadge. You and Marilyn?"

"In her busy schedule, she manages to fit me in. She's my mistress. I still love Molly but I like a piece on the side. I guess we'll have to work out an arrangement where you and I share her, with an occasional fuck going to Charlie."

"Let's not kid ourselves," Marlon said. "Where Marilyn is concerned, the lines form on the right and the left. What are you promising her? The lead in your next picture?"

"How did you guess?" Kazan said. "I told her the role is hers. But actually I just met with Darryl Zanuck. He's signing Jean Peters for the part."

"Better check with Howard Hughes," Marlon said. "I hear he's branded Miss Peters."

"It's okay with Hughes," Kazan said, "providing none of us ever get within ten feet of Miss Peters."

"What's this film about?" Marlon asked.

"Emiliano Zapata. He led a 1910 peasant uprising in southern Mexico. I've been in collaboration with John Steinbeck since 1948. Zanuck's going to produce it. He wants to star Tyrone Power in the lead."

"What's this fucking film called?"

"We're thinking of calling it *Viva Zapata,*" Kazan said. "I haven't run that by Zanuck yet."

"Why in hell haven't you told me about this script?" Marlon asked. "Power's getting a little long in the tooth to play a young rabble-rouser. Let me see the script. I've always wanted to play a revolutionary. If the script is good, I might even agree to come back to Hollywood for one more film role— mind you, just one more and that's it!"

Marilyn Monroe

* * *

That evening when Marlon and Marilyn arrived at 20th Century Fox, they headed for the Café de Paris, the studio's commissary, site of the party.

At the door, all conversation was interrupted as heads turned to feast on the stunning blonde starlet on his arm. Marilyn had poured herself into a low-cut strapless black cocktail dress with a décolletage that plunged toward hell. Wearing towering white high heels, she stood on shapely but wobbly legs, putting on a show for the eyes feasting on her. In the middle of a harangue to five of his assistants, all male, even Darryl Zanuck was upstaged and forced to take notice of this new arrival. No one seemed to notice Marlon.

Breathing in deeply, thereby accentuating the size of her breasts, Marilyn quickly deserted Marlon and began to work the room. Within minutes, Marlon had renewed his acquaintance with both Anne Baxter and Susan Hayward, whom he hadn't seen since his seductions of them during the Broadway run of *Streetcar*. Anne was polite and friendly, but it was obvious that her interest was now focused elsewhere. Susan chastised Marlon "for not calling me the moment you got to Hollywood." But when one of Zanuck's aides came to summon her to the studio chief, she moved on.

Jeanne Crain came up and introduced herself, telling him how much she'd admired his performance on Broadway in *Streetcar*. "I didn't know you were in the audience," he told her. "You should have come backstage. We might have had some fun."

She quickly changed the subject to herself, telling him that she and Claudette Colbert were going to make an exciting new picture called *All About Eve*. Ironically, neither actress would star in the film. The woman who would replace Jeanne in the role, Anne Baxter, was standing only ten feet away as Jeanne gushed, inaccurately, about her role in the upcoming film.

When Jeanne disappeared, Gregory Peck emerged, shaking Marlon's hands. "I'm such a slob," said the immaculately groomed Peck, "that I was offered the role of Stanley but I turned it down." He smiled at Marlon's startled look. "I'm joking," Peck said. "You and I will never compete for the same roles."

Suddenly, the blonde-haired June Haver was standing next to Marlon and chatting. He found her boring. However, the late arrival of Betty Grable attracted him. He headed for the door to introduce himself. As he did, Marilyn grabbed his arm. "I've been looking everywhere for you. Come on, I want you to meet my co-star, Tyrone Power." Marlon glanced over to the other side of the room, where Tyrone had joined the inner circle listening to Zanuck pontificate. When Marilyn tried to join the inner circle, with Marlon trailing her, one of the aides directed her away from the group.

"Oh," Marilyn said. "I guess we'll have to wait for His Majesty." Taking Marlon's hand, she led him to the terrace, then patted the seat next to hers. Sitting down, he took her hand. Marilyn's eyes drifted toward Betty Grable, whom everyone seemed to be ignoring. "Poor Betty," Marilyn said. "Everybody in the room knows that Zanuck is grooming me to replace her. Someday I'll get old, too, and he'll replace me."

"No one will ever replace you," Marlon assured her.

"There's talk I'm going to be loaned to another studio to make *Clash By Night* for Howard Hughes," she told him. "It's based on a play by Clifford Odets."

"I know Clifford," he told her. "Rather well, as a matter of fact."

"Barbara Stanwyck is the star," she said. "I hear she's a lesbian. I guess I'll have to sleep with her." She sighed. "First, Joan Crawford. Now, Stanwyck. Isn't there any big Hollywood female star who's not a lesbian?"

"Marlene Dietrich," he said jokingly. "Greta Garbo."

"Oh, I've heard about those two," she said.

"Work with Bette Davis," he advised her. "You'll be safe with that one. I know from personal experience she likes men."

Ironically, Marilyn would eventually be cast in *All About Eve*, starring Bette Davis.

As Marilyn sat talking with Marlon, waiting for Tyrone to become free, she started issuing opinions that he felt were only recently formed. She wanted him to know that she had opinions about many things, as she claimed she'd been improving her mind in the last few months. She spoke about acting, love-making, and politics. The interest in politics surprised him.

As she talked in her own distinctive style, he soon realized that he'd heard all these opinions before. Elia Kazan was the originator of these points

Betty Grable

331

of view, especially about radical politics. She was merely parroting Kazan's own ideas, and perhaps didn't even believe half of what she was saying.

Finally, he interrupted her. "When did you become interested in politics? Especially the doctrines of the Communist Party?"

"I'm not all that interested," she said. "Gadge is passionate about politics, and I guess some of his interest rubbed off onto me. I'd rather sleep with politicians than hear their rants. What about you?"

"I always make it a point to kick politicians out of my bed," he said. "I mean, if Harry Truman called me to the White House to sleep with him, I guess I'd go. After all, he is the president of the United States, the man who dropped the atomic bomb."

The one and only
Stanley Kowalski

She looked confused for a minute. "I didn't know Truman was gay." The word had only recently come into vogue.

Finding her charmingly gullible, he said, "Don't tell anyone, but he sleeps with his joint chiefs. Not only that, but Truman and Eisenhower were once lovers."

"Ike, too?" She looked distressed. "That leaves me out in the cold. It's about time they put a red-blooded heterosexual into the White House to give us gals a chance at them."

Freed from Zanuck, Tyrone suddenly appeared, kissing Marilyn on the lips before extending his hand to Marlon. "I haven't seen *Streetcar* yet," he told Marlon, "but I'm dying to. I hear you're terrific."

"There is a prediction that I'm going to become the king of Hollywood."

Tyrone looked surprised, as if he couldn't decide if Marlon was being supremely confident or merely jesting.

"You'll do something I couldn't do: Knock Gable off his throne."

"In time, in time, my good man." Marlon moved closer to Tyrone. "Did anyone ever tell you that you have the most beautiful eyes in Hollywood? The most sensual mouth?"

As Marilyn laughed, Tyrone appeared flabbergasted, still not able to determine if Marlon were a big put-on or if he were sincere.

"You certainly take a direct approach," Tyrone managed to say.

"Let's don't kid ourselves," Marlon said. "I hate pretense. All of Hollywood knows I sleep on both sides of the fence. Marilyn has had her

332

Tyrone Power

affairs with women. Stories of you and Errol Flynn, even Howard Hughes, are legendary. Since all three of us share the same bi-interest, I suggest we leave the party together and pursue those mutual concerns."

It is not known what happened next, but Anne Baxter, talking about that night years later at her home in Connecticut, said that she "was surprised to see Monroe, Tyrone Power, and Brando leaving the party together. All of us knew that Ty had engaged in a three-way with Hughes and Lana Turner. Why not with the new kid on the block? Brando. What Ty didn't know is that I had already sampled the charms of Brando before he got around to him. At that point, Marilyn Monroe and Marlon Brando were about to become the hottest ticket in town. Ty's star was fading. He'd long ago lost the male beauty he showcased in the Thirties. Perhaps he was trying to link up with the new stars of the future, hoping some of their magic would rub off. Whatever he was thinking, nothing would work out for poor Ty. Like Grable at that party, Ty was on the way out the door. Maybe in some weird way he thought some of their new dazzle would ignite his old dazzle. But in spite of his three-way with them, it doesn't work that way. Maybe it wasn't obvious to Ty, even though it was perfectly obvious to me: Marlon Brando and Marilyn Monroe do only solo acts."

A week later Marlon entered a night club where he was pursuing one of the performers, a Creole beauty fresh from Martinique. He'd made a date with the dancer for later in the evening. To his surprise, he found Marilyn wandering around alone.

Except she wasn't alone. She quickly informed him she was on a date with the seventy-one-year-old Joe Schenck, one of the founders of 20th Century Fox. Although Marilyn later maintained that her relationship with Schenck was strictly platonic, she told Marlon otherwise. "I can't stand it when the Jew shit puts his hands on me. I cringe all over, but a gal has to do what a gal has to do to get ahead in this rotten town."

Although initially surprised by her comment, Marlon was to learn later that Marilyn often riddled her private remarks to him with anti-Semitic references, a prejudice that would only grow as she got older. Her anti-Semitism, however, did not prevent her from later converting to Judaism at the behest of her Jewish husband, playwright Arthur Miller.

"The impotent bastard has asked me to marry him," she told Marlon, referring to Schenck. "He doesn't have long to live. He's already had a cerebral hemorrhage. But the old coot's a good dancer. He told me that if I marry him, he'll die soon. That way, as his widow, I stand to inherit fifteen million dollars. He knows that as my husband he can't be there for me in ways that are important to a woman. He says I can entertain men on the side, providing I don't rub his nose in it. Which means that even if I become Mrs. Schenck, you'll still get lucky with me."

"I'll take the job," he said with a smirk. "Filling in for stud duty for old man Schenck with someone as pretty as you is hardly work. You've got a deal." He reached over and kissed her on the lips.

She practically screamed at him, backing away. "A girl's got to look her best in this town. There you go messing up my makeup. It only took me an hour."

At that point, Schenck emerged from the men's toilet, still buttoning up. He walked over to Marilyn and kissed her on the cheek. He looked Marlon up and down. Just as Marlon extended his hand to introduce himself, Schenck backed away slightly. He didn't extend his own hand to Marlon. "I know who you are. You're Marlon Brando. I was telling Zanuck the other day that I don't care how big a star you become in this town. As long as I have anything to say about it, you'll never make a picture for Fox."

Taken aback, Marlon at first didn't know how to respond. Finally, he said, "Congratulations on getting out of jail. I hear President Truman pardoned you."

Marlon was referring to Schenck's sentencing to one year in jail for income tax evasion. He served four months until his pardon came in.

"Come on, Marilyn," Schenck said, roughly taking her by the arm and leading her away.

Turning her head as she departed, Marilyn smiled at Marlon.

"Until we meet again, Miss Monroe," Marlon called after her.

That future rendezvous would be sooner than either of them expected.

* * *

As one of the original backers of the Broadway version of *A Streetcar Named Desire*, Cary Grant had a vested interest in the film. He seemed to take an even greater interest in Marlon, although, as actor Stewart Granger revealed in his memoirs, Grant was simultaneously pursuing him at the same time.

Grant was hardly Marlon's most admired actor. But since he was such a big star, Marlon later told Kazan, "I think I'll go out with him to see how far he'll go with me."

Before the night of their first date ended, Marlon realized that Grant was

334

willing to go a great distance—or at least all the way to San Francisco. Driving Marlon to the Los Angeles airport, Grant announced that he'd arranged for them to have dinner in San Francisco. "It's safer and more discreet there," he assured Marlon. "Too many people know me in Los Angeles."

Marlon reluctantly went along for the ride. After he was airborne, he preferred to sit up front with the pilot instead of in the rear with Grant. From the pilot, Marlon learned that the aircraft belonged to Howard Hughes. Like virtually everybody else in Hollywood, Marlon already knew that Grant and Hughes had been on-again, off-again lovers since the 1930s.

Cary Grant

Checking into a suite at the Fairmont Hotel, Marlon noted that there were two bedrooms. He took the smaller one since Grant had brought more luggage with him. Grant appeared an hour later in the suite's living room. Marlon was wearing an ill-fitting blue suit, but Grant looked like a fashion model—an older one, admittedly—and was camera ready. Marlon was to say later, "I don't think I ever met a man as well groomed as Cary."

The clothes were perfect, but not the man himself. Physically, Grant was not the man he was on the screen. He looked years older. Finally, out of curiosity, Marlon asked him, "Is there something wrong? I mean, are you sick or something?"

"I'm getting better," he told Marlon. "While I was in London shooting *I Was a Male War Bride* with Ann Sheridan, I came down with jaundice. I lost thirty pounds, and I'm still weak, trying to get my energy back." That evening, Grant took Marlon to catch the "Pussy-Katt" revue at Finocchio's, the leading drag club in town. He confided that he and Hughes often went there when they were in San Francisco together. Marlon was famished and ordered two shrimp cocktails and a thick blood-rare steak, Grant preferring a simple piece of grilled chicken with some white rice.

Returning to their hotel suite, Grant seemed in a talkative mood, and Marlon was all ears. In spite of his health, Grant was drinking heavily, Marlon choosing to sip from a beer bottle.

By two o'clock that morning, Grant startled Marlon by telling him that he was going to retire from pictures. "I've saved my money. Howard Hughes has tipped me off to some good investments. I'm comfortable. I don't have to work a day in my life again if I don't want to."

"Man, I wish I could say the same," Marlon said. "If I had your money,

I'd find myself a Caribbean island somewhere and drift down there never to be seen again."

"I think it's time for us old guys like Jimmy Stewart and myself to step aside and make way for you younger upstarts, you and Montgomery Clift and God knows how many others there are waiting in the wings. I think the 1950s will see a very different type of male movie star than those of us who graced the screen in the Thirties and Forties. You will be up there leading the pack of the hot new young Turks."

"Perhaps," Marlon said, "and then again perhaps not. Unlike every other actor in Hollywood, I don't have a driving ambition to be a movie star. I'm keeping my options open."

"I don't enjoy making films anymore," Grant said. "Perhaps I never did. I feel my best films are behind me. Ben Hecht and Charles Lederer are working on something for me called, 'Darling I Am Getting Older.' I hate the fucking title. I think I'll turn it down. There's no way in hell I'm going to appear in a movie with a title like that."

When 20th Century Fox made the film, directed by Howard Hawks, the title was changed to *Monkey Business*. The female stars were Ginger Rogers and Marilyn Monroe.

By four o'clock that morning, Grant had confessed to Marlon that, "I came very close to killing myself in London. It wouldn't be the first time— I've tried to do myself in before."

"I don't understand it," Marlon said. "To me, you've got it made. Everything to live for, even if your career is winding down. There are other things to do in life than make movies."

"I'm sure there are," Grant said. "I just don't know much about those other things. It seems I've always made movies. I have had this dream of going around the world on a tramp steamer, with or without Betsy. Perhaps without her."

He was referring to his then-wife, actress Betsy Drake.

"I want to forget about this character I call Cary Grant. Take up my old name: Archibald Leach. My friends could call me Archie."

"To me, you'll always be Cary Grant," Marlon said. "The image is undelible."

"Directors haven't started offering me monster parts," Grant said, "but right this minute George Cukor is thinking about remaking *A Star Is Born* with Judy Garland in the lead. Guess what?" As he said that, he poured himself another drink. "I'd be cast as the drunken has-been, Norman Maine. Too close to home, I told Cukor. Imagine that Cukor offering me the role of a has-been."

"I hate growing old," Grant continued. He was still furious with the spinsterish columnist Hedda Hopper, rumored to be in love with Grant herself.

When the 46-year-old Grant married the 27-year-old Betsy Drake, she'd written: "When a man of forty falls in love with a girl of twenty, it isn't her youth he is seeking but his own."

After learning all the details about what Grant and Marlon talked about, Charles Feldman and Kazan waited for the climax.

"We stood out on the terrace to watch the sun rise over San Francisco, and I swear it was one of the most spectacular sights I've ever seen," Marlon said. "I think I'm going to move to San Francisco."

"And then what happened?" Feldman asked. "Did the old queer put the make on you?"

"We went to bed," Marlon said.

"Your bed or his?" Kazan asked.

"God forbid, separate beds?" Feldman said.

"I think whatever happened in that suite between Cary and me will be a secret I'll take to my grave," Marlon said. "I've already told you guys too much. I'm sure Cary will never tell what happened."

Although it's not known what transpired between Marlon and Grant during the remainder of the weekend, Marlon later reported that Grant repeatedly called him upon his return to Hollywood. "I'm not taking Grant's calls," Marlon told Kazan. "I've already got one limey to deal with. I don't need another one."

He was referring to either his co-star, Vivien Leigh, or perhaps to Larry Olivier.

Rebuffed by Marlon, Grant in the months ahead did little to conceal his disdain for the entertainment industry's new breed of actors. Without mentioning Marlon by name, he told the press, "It's a period of blue jeans, dope addicts, and Method—nobody cares about comedy any more."

Later, Grant would grow even more candid, telling an interviewer, "I have no rapport with the new idols of the screen, and that includes Marlon Brando and his style of Method acting. It certainly includes Montgomery Clift and that God-awful James Dean. Some producer should cast all three of them in the same movie and let them duke it out. When they've finished each other off, Jimmy Stewart, Spencer Tracy, and I will return and start making real movies again like we used to."

After filming on *Streetcar* was wrapped, Marlon called Feldman for a final good-bye. "Charlie, spending some time with Cary Grant has convinced me of one thing. Of all the possibilities for me in all the world, I don't want to be a fucking movie star. Let me out of this cage?"

* * *

Laurence Olivier

Back in New York, Wally Cox was not in the loop about Marlon's affair with Vivien Leigh. Wally shared one of Marlon's letters with Bobby Lewis. In the note, Marlon stated that, "Scarlett O'Hara has fabulous tits and a tight ass even at her age. I want to fuck her so much I walk around the set with a perpetual hard-on."

In his memoirs, Marlon claimed, "Like Blanche, she [meaning Vivien] slept with almost everybody and was beginning to dissolve mentally and to fray at the ends physically." He also falsely claimed that, "I might have given her a tumble if it hadn't been for Larry Olivier. I liked him too much to invade his chicken coop."

In spite of the five million dollars Random House had given him for his autobiography, Marlon wasn't being entirely candid. He not only invaded the Oliviers' chicken coop, he anchored there for a while as the chief rooster.

Day by day on the set, Kazan had seen the burgeoning romance between Vivien and Marlon unfold before his eyes. "Vivien's wild sexual craziness, her flirtatiousness, her faded Southern belle appearance turned Marlon on."

When not before the cameras, Kazan saw them constantly sitting with each other and smoking cigarettes. Sometimes Marlon would sing "Songs My Mother Taught Me" (the title of his autobiography). Vivien's two favorite songs from Marlon's mother-fueled repertoire were "Don't Fence Me In" and "Streets of Laredo," two odd choices for her.

Even Kazan was shocked to see exactly how Olivier intruded into the romance—and hardly as a jealous husband. In fact, he didn't seem jealous at all. "All Sir Larry wanted was a piece of the action. Or, should I put that differently? A piece of Marlon's ass. He'd long ago abandoned the bed of Lady Olivier."

One afternoon Olivier invaded the set. He'd been working that day, shooting the lackluster film, *Carrie*, based on Theodore Dreiser's bestselling novel, *Sister Carrie*. Vivien was telling Marlon, "Like Blanche, I'm a pathetic creature. An artist too sensitive for her own good. Too vulnerable. I am destructible. The world will soon do me in, I fear." Blowing out smoke, she looked at him in a new light. "Perhaps, for all I know, you will be my executioner. I may at this very moment be talking to a reincarnated version of Marie Antoinette's guillotine ghoul."

338

"No, not that. Anything but that."

At that point Olivier intruded, hugging Marlon into a tight embrace he'd not known since their last night in New York together.

Their reunion was followed by an invitation to dinner that night and a midnight swim. It would be the beginning of many dinners and many swims in the elegant Coldwater Canyon house with its egg-shaped pool which Charlie Feldman had arranged for them to live in during the shooting of *Streetcar*. It was the same house where the couple had stayed during the making of *Lady Hamilton* in 1941, and the same house where four years later Feldman would introduce Senator John F. Kennedy to by then-a-star Marilyn Monroe.

Although he'd lived briefly with Elia Kazan in a house nearby, and had "permanent quarters" with his agent Jay Kanter and roommate Tony Curtis, Marlon moved in with the Oliviers that night.

The Oliviers occupied separate bedrooms in the mansion. Olivier turned in first and was soon followed by Marlon. Vivien later told Kazan, "Sometimes I'd see a light on in Larry's bedroom, and I just assumed that he and Marlon were doing whatever two men do when they go to bed together. I never really understand that kind of love. But I must say this for Marlon. When it comes to couples, he's an equal-opportunity seducer. On many a night he rose from Larry's bed and joined me in mine. I never sleep. All my nights are sleepless. Sometimes he would find me in Charlie's garden wandering around like Ophelia in a see-through nightgown."

Another house guest who'd just arrived from London, actor David Niven, remembered walking into the garden to discover "Brando and Larry swimming naked in the pool. Larry was kissing Brando. Or maybe it was the other way around. I turned my back to them and went back inside to join Vivien. I'm sure she knew what was going on, but she made no mention of it. Nor did I. One must be sophisticated about such matters in life."

Niven later recalled that he felt that both Olivier and Vivien "were hopelessly in love with Brando. My God, he was so handsome I could have fallen for him myself, and I'm hopelessly straight. Marlon Brando was adorable. So unlike Stanley Kowalski that he was playing on the screen, he was so gentle, so kind. Of course, I saw only his gentler side. But from the sounds coming from Larry's bedroom, I also knew that Brando could be a brute."

Niven very accurately predicted that the so-called romance between the Oliviers and Marlon would not last beyond the shooting of *Streetcar*. The actor did think that his friend Olivier was "walking on thin ice in combining an affair with Marlon and the very jealous Danny Kaye. All Hollywood at the time was talking about Brando's romance with the Oliviers. There was no way in hell that Kaye couldn't have heard about it."

Even so, Kaye, along with Sylvia Fine, went along with his original plan to throw a grand party for the Oliviers in the ballroom of the Beverly Hills Hotel. The Kayes had worked desperately to trim their guest list to one hundred and fifty. Jack Warner claimed, "If someone didn't get an invitation to this bash, they either left town or turned off their lights at eight o'clock."

Danny Kaye

Without a specific invitation for him, Vivien and the Oliviers invited Marlon to join them for the event. Olivier even lent Marlon one of his tuxedos to wear for the occasion. Unknown to Marlon at the time, Kaye was deeply in love with Olivier.

Passing through the lobby leading to the ballroom, Marlon spotted Marilyn Monroe in plunging décolletage. A fellow male guest was introducing her to Errol Flynn. Marlon merely winked surreptitiously at her and walked on. Later, Marilyn would report that Flynn not only seduced her that night, but played "You Are My Sunshine" on his piano using only his erect penis.

At the head of the reception line and under glittering Austrian chandeliers, Kaye embraced both Olivier and Vivien, holding his hug with Olivier longer.

On seeing Marlon, Kaye looked shocked, staring first at Marlon and then at Olivier with a "how could you?" look. Suddenly, Kaye slapped Marlon. It was no stage slap but one using all the power and force in his body. Marlon was a boxer and could have clobbered Kaye. He chose not to.

"Like your hair color," Marlon said to Kaye before turning and walking away.

Kaye just stood there staring in defiance as he left. He'd dyed his hair bright red—almost orange—for a movie.

Vivien saved the night by linking her arm with Kaye, and, pretending a pride she didn't feel, grandly entered the ballroom where *tout* Hollywood was watching. Nearly everybody at that point knew that Kaye and Olivier were having an affair, and her fellow guests wanted to see how Vivien pulled off the evening.

"She was brilliant," Feldman later said. "What theatrics, entering the ballroom on the arm of her rival. She was gracious throughout the evening. No one could believe that she knew of the affair and secretly detested Danny Kaye. As for Marlon, I'm sure he found companionship later that night."

The following morning, neither of the Oliviers found Marlon in their beds.

Later, Vivien discovered a note addressed to both of them on their breakfast table in the Feldman garden.

Olivier seemed to know the contents. "Take it with us. We'll read it on the freighter."

After the thrill and excitement of Hollywood, Olivier felt that a long ride across the Atlantic on a small French freighter would be good for the both of them. The trip turned into a disaster.

Admitting that he and Vivien were hardly a honeymoon couple any more, he claimed that "the stark reality of our company plunged us both into depressions." He also said that "the idea of suicide had its attraction, and I found myself more and more drawn to the ship's rail and the fascination of the foam sweeping by."

As for Vivien, he recalled, "She was walking a stairway to a dark gulf. I knew she'd never climb back."

One night he invited Vivien to his cabin for a pre-dinner drink, telling her to bring the as-yet-unopened note from Marlon. "Please read it," he told her. "I can't bear to open it myself."

The note from Marlon read: "Dear Vivien and Larry. Thank you for your hospitality. You were both wonderful to me. I will treasure my memory of you for always. But it is time to move on now, and I'm heading back to New York to resume my life. My regret is never having gotten to know either of you. But, then, I have always depended upon the kindness of strangers."

Chapter Ten

When the candidates for the Oscars were announced in 1952, Marlon was nominated for an Academy Award for his portrayal of Stanley in *A Streetcar Named Desire*. His major competition came from the "sentimental favorite" Humphrey Bogart for his starring role in *The African Queen*. Also nominated was Marlon's former lover, Monty Clift, for his role in *A Place in the Sun*. The other contenders included Arthur Kennedy for *Bright Victory* and Fredric March for *Death of a Salesman*.

The same year, Vivien was nominated for best actress, her major competition being Katharine Hepburn for *The African Queen*. Marlon's girlfriend, Shelley Winters, was nominated for *A Place in the Sun*, as were Eleanor Parker for *Detective Story* and Jane Wyman for *The Blue Veil*. Karl Malden and Kim Hunter were both nominated for supporting roles in their performances in *Streetcar*.

On Oscar night, three of the contenders associated with *Streetcar*—Vivien Leigh, Karl Malden, and Kim Hunter—walked away with Oscars, Marlon losing to Bogie. Facing reporters, Kazan told the press, "Stick around, boys. Marlon's day will come."

A week later, Marlon told Kazan that he had spotted Katharine Hepburn sitting alone in a restaurant. This was a most unusual sighting, since Hepburn frequently maintained that her mere appearance in a public restaurant often caused her to faint. Since Hepburn and Marlon had been the big losers on Oscar night, he went up to her table to introduce himself and "to share our mutual loss of the nude statue."

"I'm Marlon Brando," he said. "But I'm sure you recognize me."

"Mr. Brando," she said to him, sounding like the aloof and aristocratic character she played in *Adam's Rib*, "I neither recognize you nor want to know you. Please leave me alone."

After that rebuff, he went into the men's toilet to take a leak. There were only two urinals. He stood next to a stranger who seemed to be observing him carefully as he pissed. Thinking it was a sexual come-on, Marlon turned angrily to stare into the face next to him. It was Spencer Tracy.

Tracy smiled at him. "You mopped up the screen, boy, with your Stanley

Kowalski." Stepping back from the urinal, Tracy buttoned up. "Keep up the good work, kid, and you'll make it some day." With those parting words, he exited. But then he stuck his head back inside the toilet. "Of course, you'll never make it as big as I am. But, what the hell! One star always burns brighter than the other." With that, he disappeared for the final time.

As Marlon told Kazan the next morning, "So that's how Oscar winners treat contenders. I want no part of it. By the way, I think Tracy's queer. Hepburn, too, from what I hear."

* * *

After the filming of *Streetcar*, Marlon returned to New York, making frequent appearances at the Actors Studio, claiming he wanted "to meet girls" more than he wanted to learn anything about acting from Lee Strasberg. Soon after, as it happened, Elia Kazan flew to New York to conduct some business with his attorneys, and in his wake, both Tyrone Power and Marilyn Monroe made it a point to be in New York too, perhaps to lobby Kazan for roles in his upcoming film, *Viva Zapata!*

At a party in Greenwich Village, Marlon was surprised to see Marilyn Monroe sitting alone, playing the piano. She hadn't told him that she was coming to New York. Before he could walk over and greet her, he was corralled by Tom Ewell and Wally Cox, who took him over to greet the playwright, William Inge, who would become the chief rival on Broadway of Tennessee Williams.

An hour later, Marlon was still talking with the men when Stella Adler entered the room, tapping him on the shoulder. In his autobiography, Marlon identifies Stella only as "someone." He claimed that he turned around quickly, in the process delivering a sharp blow with his elbow to someone's head.

That someone turned out to be Marilyn herself. "Oh, my God," Marlon quotes himself as saying, "I'm sorry. I'm really sorry. It was an accident."

"There are no accidents," she said.

Later in his autobiography, Marlon claimed that he sat beside Marilyn on the piano stool trying to teach her how to play. "You can't play worth a damn," he told her.

From that point onward, Marlon's autobiography, although admitting to an affair with Marilyn, drifts off into fantasy, not revealing what really happened during their next few days in New York.

He loved those
Guys and Dolls

Marilyn Monroe

Marilyn and Marlon were seen leaving the party together. It was later learned by Marlon's friends that she took him back to her hotel, where Tyrone Power was waiting for her. According to Carlo Fiore, Marlon, Marilyn, and Tyrone resumed what had been only a brief interlude together in Hollywood.

No one has ever recorded what happened in bed that night between Marilyn, Tyrone, and Marlon. But many of Tyrone's male lovers, including Errol Flynn, reported that he was a "bottom" so one can reasonably conclude what might have happened. Presumably both men serviced Marilyn.

But ironically, instead of spending time with Marilyn in New York, both Tyrone and Marlon ended up in the days ahead seeing her only rarely. She had a lot of "mysterious" appointments, and she didn't want to share the exact nature of her business with her lovers, considering it "too personal."

Soon, there emerged an understanding between the three of them about the desirability of a leading role in Kazan's upcoming film, *Viva Zapata!*. Marilyn claimed she would wear a black wig in the film and Tyrone felt that through the very clever use of makeup he could be transformed into a Mexican. "I'm already Black Irish," he told Kazan.

Although Marlon secretly wanted the lead in *Viva Zapata!*, he did not convey that desire to Tyrone, who continued to be Zanuck's choice for the role. In a pattern previously established with both Montgomery Clift and Burt Lancaster, Marlon continued a by-now familiar pattern of "seducing the competition."

Tyrone and Marlon—without Marilyn—were frequently seen together in New York.

Marlon was the latest in a long line of Tyrone's conquests: Howard Hughes, Errol Flynn, Noël Coward, Joan Crawford, Marlene Dietrich, Betty Grable, Rita Hayworth, Cesar Romero, Robert Taylor, Lana Turner, Loretta Young—and, yes, even the Argentine dictator, Evita Peron. "Why frustrate people?" he was fond of saying. "If I'm feeling horny at the time, and I like them, I'll oblige them. They meet me. They are curious. Sometimes we have to get the sex out of the way just to move on with our friendship."

Marlon invited several of his friends to meet Tyrone, including Stella Adler, Carlo Fiore, Wally Cox, Bobby Lewis, and James Baldwin. Tyrone was facing a crisis in his life and career, and he used this audience to speak openly about his conflicts.

Claiming he was fed up with costume dramas such as the recent box office failure of *The Black Rose*, he said he wanted to become a free agent in the summer of 1952 when his contract with Fox would expire.

"The days of my great vehicles—films like *In Old Chicago* or *The Razor's Edge*—are beyond me, I fear," he told Marlon's friends.

Tyrone hastened to add that before he relinquished movie stardom, he planned to make a final attempt to have a hit movie with *Viva Zapata!* "I'm being offered fewer roles," he told the group. "*Viva Zapata!* will put me back on top again. I have to reinvent myself. But I fear it's not in me. The world wants my youth, not my middle age."

"My new friend here has that Irish sense of doom and gloom," Marlon said. "His guilt is beginning to show on his face."

"I used to look like Dorian Gray," Tyrone said. "Now I look like the portrait in the closet. These bags under my eyes are real."

"All of us in time become the portrait in the closet," Stella said. "Right now our dear Marlon is arguably the most beautiful male animal in America. But what will he look like forty years from now? A grotesque, perhaps. Tallulah Bankhead once suggested to me that all of us become caricatures of ourselves."

"Tallulah should know," Marlon said sarcastically.

"I'm tired of talking about myself," Tyrone said. He turned to Stella. "What do you think about me?"

Perhaps she was being too kind, but she articulated her opinion very carefully. "I think you've embodied the Byronic hero in film. But I also think you were seduced by those jackals on the coast who turned you into their victim. Sure, they made you a movie star. Naturally, you were mobbed by screaming women and young girls at airports and train stations. Your face was young—beautiful, romantic, idyllic, more so than your nearest idols, Robert Taylor and Errol Flynn. But now that I see the post-war Tyrone Power, I feel a certain dissipation is showing. You are beginning to wear your disillusionment on your face. There is a cynical look there not obvious in your movies. I study face and body language in actors. I can't help but notice a downward curl to your perfect lips. You seem trapped in a career going nowhere. You must leave films. When your contract expires, go on the stage like your father. He did all right."

Stella was referring to the great stage actor, Frederick Tyrone Power or Tyrone Power II, who reached the peak of his success in 1905.

Tyrone claimed that he'd also discussed stage work with Kazan before leaving Hollywood. I told him, "'For anyone truly interested in the theater, it's a tragedy to be born handsome.' Kazan let me know that 'handsome is better than being born homely.' Then he thought for a minute. 'The greatest tragedy is to be born at all,'" he said.

Wally Cox told Tyrone that he felt that "like Marlon, Mr. Actor here, your incandescence can be transferred from screen to stage. So many other film actors would bomb on the stage—take Clark Gable, Greta Garbo. Tallulah Bankhead, however, as Marlon well knows, is the opposite. She's a stage actress, not a film actress. That's why Bette Davis has to play her parts on the screen."

"I fear I may be one of those filmic actors," Tyrone said. "Like our friend, Marilyn Monroe. She was surely invented for the camera."

Tyrone Power

"I'm not sure about that," Marlon said. "Only the other night Bill Inge said he would like to write a play for Marilyn and me." Ironically, after Elvis Presley turned it down, Marlon was offered the lead role in Inge's *Bus Stop* to star Marilyn and himself in the 1956 release. When he rejected it, Marilyn turned to the lackluster Don Murray to play the lead. Marlon's former girl-friend, Kim Stanley, would appear in the stage version.

Tyrone eventually took Stella's advice, opening *John Brown's Body* on February 14, 1953 at the Century Theatre in New York. The play was direct-ed by Charles Laughton, who fell in love with Tyrone, and it co-starred veter-an actors Raymond Massey and Judith Anderson. To make that appearance on stage, Tyrone turned down *The Robe* and half a million dollars, the role even-tually going to Richard Burton.

Stella later commented, "Power seemed at the crossroads. Marlon was about to become the hottest male movie star of his day, especially after he made *On the Waterfront* and *The Wild One*, and Marilyn Monroe was well on her way to becoming the chief star of the tabloids. I think by hanging out with those two, Power was desperately trying to connect himself with the new Hollywood that was emerging right in the bed he shared with them. In a way, you can say that Power was auditioning the new kid on the block, Marlon, and the new girl on the block, Marilyn, as if he could rediscover that special magic he once had when he was the world's most beautiful male animal back in the Thirties. Even *I* was gorgeous then."

At one point during their "dates" together, including late-night jaunts to Harlem jazz clubs, Tyrone reportedly warned Marlon not to fall in love with him. "Too many men and too many women like Lana have fallen for me. I love them but then I leave them without a formal announcement, the way I deserted poor Lana. I can't stand confrontations."

"Have no fear that I'll fall in love with you," Marlon is alleged to have said. "I have never loved anybody—maybe my mother. But that didn't work out."

"That's good to hear," Tyrone said. "I save my love for my women. My homosexual affairs are strictly physical—never of the heart."

"The heart is physical," Marlon countered. "The most important part of the body."

At a jazz club, where Marlon played the bongo drums, James Baldwin, the host, later reported an exchange between Marlon and Tyrone.

He heard Tyrone describing and then inviting Marlon to what he called "Esther Williams parties" in Los Angeles. In the early 1950s, the more liberated members of the Hollywood set, including married couples, were attending these booze-and-pool parties where no bathing suits were allowed. By midnight they usually turned into orgies, both gay and straight.

Tyrone claimed that he had become addicted to such parties in France when he attended a number of them. "The custom has now come to Hollywood," he said. "Since everybody is nude around the pool, you can see what you're getting before you take it to the bedroom. I've had some unpleasant surprises when men have dropped their trousers in front of me."

"I've had those occasions too," Marlon said. "With Princess Tiny Meat in particular."

"You mean Montgomery Clift?" Tyrone said. "Everybody's talking about how little his prick is."

"That's the guilty party," Marlon said.

"Try my good friend Rock Hudson," Tyrone urged. "Ten thick inches."

In the months ahead, Marlon, along with Tyrone, was in regular attendance at these pool parties, most often the mixed ones, although he and Tyrone, along with Rock Hudson, were also fixtures at some of agent Henry Willson's more notorious all-male pool parties.

Before any of that happened, however, Marlon "pulled a double-cross on Ty," according to Tom Ewell. "He fucked that poor guy in more ways than one. While romancing Marilyn and Ty, Marlon received a call from Elia Kazan. Gadge had overcome Zanuck's objections and had agreed to star Marlon in *Viva Zapata!* Marilyn's part went to Jean Peters. Since Marilyn and Ty—never together again—were still seen (separately) with Marlon in the months to come, I guess they forgave him. I would have been seriously pissed."

* * *

Puerto Rican born Rita Moreno was Marlon's classic type. His affair with her would stretch out for years. He moved in on Rita at the right time, just as her affair with George Hormel, the meat-packing heir, was winding down.

Hormel received bad publicity during a marijuana bust at his home. It was reported that Rita, standing only five feet two and weighing probably no more than ninety-eight pounds, attacked two burly policemen during the raid. "Rita was a fighter," said Carlo Fiore, "not just for herself but for social injustice. If someone crossed her the wrong way, she'd take them on. Of course, I learned all this from Marlon, not from personal experience."

Even so, Fiore was a bit dismissive of the relationship. "Rita could always amuse Marlon, like when she placed a basket of fruit on her head and imitated Carmen Miranda. Marlon always went big for that act."

Other observers took the romance more seriously than Fiore. When the romance first became known, one columnist claimed that the coming together of Rita and Marlon "must have been like two exiles stumbling on each other in a strange country."

"She was the woman Marlon should have married," Tom Ewell said. "That is, if I may speak for Marlon. She was smart, beautiful, talented, and a true blue friend. She was the woman Marlon always turned to 'when love goes wrong,' to quote the song from Marilyn Monroe. He should have married her instead of the three disasters he did wed. I once attended a party with Rita and Marlon when I saw them together for the first time. They didn't even know I existed. They sat in an armchair in the corner of the room. Rita plopped in Marlon's lap for the entire evening. I don't think they were even aware of others."

After Rita ended her tumultuous Hormel affair, Marlon began dating her on both coasts. At the time, she was not the star she ultimately became. She was appearing in such quickies as *So Young, So Bad* in which she played a juvenile delinquent who commits suicide after a sadistic matron makes her cut her hair. In that bomb, she was billed as "Rosita Moreno," her name changed to Rita for her next picture. That was *Pagan Love Song* in 1950, in which she

Rita Moreno

impersonated a Tahitian island girl, which was much to Marlon's liking and a portent of the dozens of young Tahitian virginal maidens who lay in his own future.

When she appeared as an Indian squaw in *The Yellow Tomahawk*, Marlon gave her the nickname "Honey Bear" in private, at least to his friends. If you didn't look quickly, you missed her in MGM's classical musical, *Singin' in the Rain*, released in 1952.

In her early days, Rita, according to Hollywood insiders, was a "neurotic, unhappy girl." Because of his constant failure to commit to the relationship,

Marlon did not necessarily add to her bliss. "They must have been dynamite in bed," Fiore said. "I can only guess. Marlon obviously liked what he was getting from her, because he returned to her time and time again. When not in bed, both of them shared a growing concern about social injustice and racial prejudice. So, they even had something to talk about."

Rita has commented publicly, only briefly, about her long-enduring romance with Marlon. She once explained their relationship this way, "You must know that dating Marlon in those days meant keeping your mouth shut. He would be furious with you, and would perhaps end the relationship, if you granted interviews. He was not only a private person, but wanted to keep his affairs away from the prying eyes of the press."

In later life, she said, "It's hardly a secret that Marlon liked fiery tempered, sexy Latin girls. I certainly qualified in that department. But that's for him to straighten out, really."

At the time, there was much press speculation that Rita was going to become the first Mrs. Marlon Brando. In one of the most highly publicized events of their affair, Rita flew to Tokyo where Marlon was filming *Sayonara*.

As the jealous Anna Kashfi (Marlon's first wife) remembered, "Evidently Rita materialized at the Miyako Hotel under an escort of photographers. Pictures of Marlon and her were soon available to all news bureaus, she smiling radiantly, Marlon looking discomfited."

Even as Marlon was preparing to marry Anna Kashfi, the presence of Rita hung like a black cloud over their marriage. On one occasion, as Anna was getting into bed with Marlon, she discovered a heavy black wig draped over an endpost of the headboard. In her words, "It hung there, tresses streaming downward, like an obscene trophy mounted to commemorate a conquest." She demanded to be taken home that night, but more fights over Rita loomed in Anna's shaky future with Marlon.

Brando and Rita Moreno

One night as Anna was in Marlon's bedroom, Rita arrived on their doorstep, pounding on the door and shrieking. "It's Moreno or me," Anna threatened him. "Make your choice—right now!" He went downstairs to calm Rita down and ask her to leave his house. Finally she did. But she would not be gone forever.

Rita's relationship with Marlon survived his short marriage to Anna, but her attempts to become the second Mrs. Marlon Brando failed.

"It's all my fault," Elia Kazan later said. "Even before Kashfi, Marlon had met the Mexican actress, Movita Castenada, on the set of *Viva*

Zapata! Like Rita, Movita was another fiery Latina. I guess Movita had something that Rita didn't. For my money, I would have stuck with Rita. Those two were perfectly suited for each other. Both devotees of Afro-Cuban rhythms on bongo drums at four o'clock in the morning."

Disaster almost struck when Marlon was filming *Mutiny on the Bounty* and met the Polynesian beauty who would become his third wife, Tarita Teriipaia.

At first Rita's reaction seemed subdued. "I was amazed to hear he was engaged," she told the press. "But he seems to be a lost soul, looking for a niche. Apparently, he's found what he's been seeking."

In private, Rita seemed to be growing more despondent over her failed relationship with Marlon. Thoughts of his two marriages drove her into such despair that in April of 1961 at Marlon's home on Mulholland Drive, she took an overdose of sleeping pills. Discovered by Marlon's secretary, Alice Marchak, Rita was saved by the arrival of an ambulance with a doctor who pumped her stomach.

There would be two more acts of self-destruction that followed within the next few months. Arriving at Marlon's house one night, Rita asked him to go for a ride in the Hollywood Hills with her so that they could discuss their relationship. At one point during a fierce argument, she lost control of her vehicle and plunged into a ravine, her beautiful face hitting the dashboard. She arrived "bloody and screaming," in the words of an orderly, at the nearest hospital.

Only eight days later, and still in recovery, she had another violent argument with Marlon. She ran into his bathroom and attempted to slash her wrists. Once again, she was rushed to the emergency room of the nearest hospital.

After a long hiatus, Rita came back into Marlon's life when director Hubert Cornfield cast her in a low-budget quickie film shot in France. An existential thriller, much of it in silence, *The Night of the Following Day* was released in 1969.

Brando in *The Night of the Following Day*

In it, Rita played a drug addict who sniffed cocaine in rolled dollar bills. Marlon was cast as a kidnapping chauffeur. Although the film was a failure at the box office, the role marked the last time his classic male beauty would be showcased on the screen. For the film, he'd lost weight and appeared "lean and mean," in the words of his director, wearing a black, form-fitting turtleneck and a bobbed blond wig.

Observers of the film being shot didn't know where the real life relationship ended and the reel

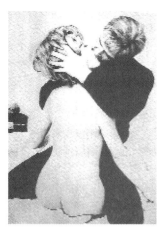

Rita Moreno and Brando in *The Night of the Following Day*

life of the two started. "I think their relationship on screen got messed up with their off-screen love affair," Cornfield said. Marlon delivered one line for his screen character that might have also been uttered to Rita in private. "I love you. Go on, cut my face if that's what you feel like—I deserve it." He smashes a bottle and offers her its jagged neck.

Critic David Thomson reported that the affair between Marlon and Rita resumed during the making of this unfortunate film. "The affair carries over into one prolonged, violent sexual scene in which people on the set were amazed to see Brando and Moreno losing their characters and becoming themselves," Thomson claimed.

The film would open and close almost immediately, just enough time for critics to attack it. Penelope Houston found that Marlon "was doing an imitation of Brando."

Another critic, Richard Roud, was so disappointed with Marlon's performance that he provocatively asked, "Would we, if we could see his earlier work again, decide he never was that good anyway?"

Marlon was glad to see filming come to an end on *The Night of the Following Day*. With the release of the movie, he'd discharged his final contractual obligations to Universal. He wrote the film's epitaph himself: "It makes about as much sense as a rat fucking a grapefruit!"

* * *

Up until the final hour, the producer, Darryl F. Zanuck, fought bitterly with Kazan over the casting of Marlon in the star role in *Viva Zapata!* Agreeing to abandon Tyrone Power, Zanuck pushed Anthony Quinn for the lead. "At least he's a God damn wetback spic, and we won't need makeup for that big-dicked fucker. I hear his dick is even bigger than mine, and I'm a legend..."

Rare for Marlon, he had even submitted to a screen test. Julie Harris played his wife in the test. When Kazan showed the screen test to Zanuck, he chomped down on his cigar. "You've got to be kidding!" he shouted. "Brando and Harris as Mexicans? Why not cast Betty Grable and Van Johnson in the part? There is no way in hell that Brando will ever be cast in *Zapata!*"

It was only at the last minute that Marlon's agent, Jay Kanter, could broker a deal, even getting a $100,000 fee for Marlon. At first, Zanuck appeared to be having a stroke when he heard the salary demand. "Fuck that!" he shouted. "I could buy every blonde whore in Los Angeles for that kind of dough." When Kanter held out a two-picture deal, and pointed out that Marlon was the hottest male star to arrive in Hollywood since the meteoric rise of Clark Gable, Zanuck capitulated. "Put a fucking drooping mustache on Stanley Kowalski, dye his hair jet black, tell Kazan to get him to stop mumbling, and let's pretend the fucker is a Mexican Indian. Movies are only pretense anyway."

Zanuck only green-lighted *Zapata!* because Kazan had directed *Gentleman's Agreement* for the studio in 1947, which had been nominated for eight Academy Awards, winning Best Picture.

After signing Marlon, Zanuck told Kazan what he really thought of his star. "He's nothing but a son of a bitch, and a surly one at that. Brando is even more of a bastard than I am. With the exception of Tyrone Power, a guy I've always wanted to fuck, even though I'm straight, I find all actors sons of bitches. I also hear Brando is a faggot. During the shoot, keep those Mexican boys away from our star. We don't want a fucking scandal on our hands with Mr. Macho. I hear he likes it up the ass."

Marlon also had utter contempt for Zanuck. "An absurd-looking man, Zanuck bore a striking resemblance to Bugs Bunny," Marlon claimed. "When he entered a room, his front teeth preceded him by about three seconds."

Before Kazan and crew departed for the hot sands of Texas along the Mexican border, Zanuck had one final piece of advice. "To make a film, there's only one thing to keep in mind. Will he fuck her or won't he?"

At the end of Zanuck's heated negotiations with Kazan, in which he got the director to lower his fee from $175,000 to $100,000, Zanuck shouted, "Now take your Jewish cowboys and get the fuck out of my office. Jayne Mansfield is waiting in the next room for me to fuck her."

The producer was referring to the Brooklyn-born actors Kazan had hired as cowboys. These included Irving Winter and Henry Silva.

As filming began, Marlon brought his magnetic presence to the set of *Viva Zapata!* But even his power as an actor could not escape the one-dimensional writing of John Steinbeck. The film attempted to focus on political issues such as democracy and dictatorship. But after reading the script, Zanuck had been dismissive. "I'm not impressed with John Steinbeck. I've met him. He's an asshole with dingleberries."

Zanuck was on target about the writing.

Darryl F. Zanuck

Steinbeck inserted such ponderous dialogue as, "A strong man makes a weak people." Kazan struggled to prevent *Zapata!* from becoming a left-wing tract. He knew that it was only a matter of weeks before he'd be called to testify in front of the Committee on Un-American Activities, in which he planned to reveal details about his Communist past in the Thirties. To "save his skin," he named "fellow travelers," earning him the undying animosity of Hollywood's more liberal members.

When Marlon watched on TV as his favorite director, Kazan, was "singing like a canary" in Washington before the right-wing investigators, he vowed never to speak to him again. He called Kazan's testimony "an act of terrorism" against his friends. But he genuinely liked Kazan and would, of course, in time forgive him. Another movie with Kazan, and with it an Oscar, lay in Marlon's future.

Throughout the filming of *Zapata!*, Marlon complained to Kazan that he'd been "snookered" into making a two-picture deal with Zanuck. He said that he had only done so because his agent, Jay Kanter, claimed that he'd lose his job if he didn't sign. Marlon wrote briefly about this in his autobiography, misspelling the name of his longtime friend and agent as Kantor (sic).

With the help of "that makeup genius," Phil Rhodes, Marlon worked on his own face to transform himself into a Mexican. He glued his eyelids together and put plastic rings in his nose. He also wore a two-way stretch plate inside his mouth. Even after all this hard work, cameraman Joe MacDonald privately remarked, "Brando looks like Charlie Chan in a sombrero."

What Marlon was actually trying to do was transform his own Midwestern look into an uncanny impersonation of Zapata. Marlon was inspired by Diego Rivera's famous portrait of the revolutionary.

Elia Kazan and Brando showing off the goods

Behind his stony Indian mask, Marlon's adopted mannerisms included a way of training his eyes into a fixed and unblinking stare. His fellow actors weighed in with their comments, Jean Peters claiming that "Marlon is deliberately trying to look cross-eyed." His rival, Anthony Quinn, cast as Marlon's brother, Eufemio Zapata, said that Marlon "was as inscrutable as an Aztec calendar." Fellow actor Joseph Wiseman, playing a venomous newspaperman in *Zapata!*, compared Marlon to "a Mayan statue."

Before filming began, Marlon went to Mexico and lived like a peasant in the little pueblo of Sonora. Here he studied the lives of the peasants—how they talked, moved, and sounded. He wrote Dodie, "As each day goes by, I become less and less a *gringo*. I'm thinking of finding myself a Mexican wife and settling forever south of the border. I'm also learning Spanish, and I think I have a good chance to become the biggest male movie star Mexico City has ever seen."

In yet another letter to Dodie, he wrote, "I have successfully transformed myself into a *mestizo* revolutionary. But Kazan says I'll have to wear brown contact lenses to disguise those slate gray eyes I inherited from you and Dad." Once he was given the lenses, Marlon buried them in his lower lip in a misguided attempt to keep them safe until one night he accidentally swallowed them. Kazan had to call a halt to shooting that day until the wardrobe department at Fox could fly in new lenses for Marlon.

Kazan had been forced to seek a location in Texas because the Mexican government objected to the script about their national hero. Zanuck had been warned that the safety of the *Zapata!* crew could not be guaranteed if filming actually took place in Mexico.

On a scouting trip, Kazan had discovered the dreary little border outposts of Del Rio and Roma in Texas. It was there that he sent his crew during the blistering summer of 1951, when desert temperatures often reached 120°F, causing Marlon's heavy makeup to "melt down." To cool off, Kazan and Marlon would go swimming naked in the Rio Grande after the shooting of the day ended.

In spite of the Mexican makeup, Marlon had only one thing in common with the hero Emiliano Zapata. The Mexican revolutionary had nearly two dozen bigamous marriages. Marlon would follow in his hero's footsteps—that is, if some of his more intense relationships could be called "marriages."

Throughout the filming, Kazan stuck by Marlon, calling him "the only genius I have ever met in the field of acting." During the shoot, Kazan gave Marlon free rein. Sometimes that worked, sometimes it didn't. In a scene in which Marlon was supposed to appear drunk, he consumed a bottle of tequila in his dressing room "for the purposes of authenticity." But when he was called before the cameras, he staggered and collapsed on the set. Two burly grips carried him back to his dressing room where he slept soundly until the following morning.

Kazan gave Marlon little guidance but did have a strong point of view about the character of Zapata. "Don't be misled by all that shit in Steinbeck's script about how the fucker loves his wife. In our hero's life, women are to be used, knocked up, and abandoned. Zapata loves his *compadres*. For these Mexican peasants, fucking is no big deal. Zapata's social concerns are his real concerns."

"Then I'm perfectly cast," Marlon said. "I'm like Zapata in real life!"

A scene from *Viva Zapata!*

The rushes Kazan sent back from Texas did not impress Zanuck in Hollywood. "It's just a big Mexican oater." Zanuck had produced pictures in the Thirties when Westerns were called oaters because of the grain fed to horses. "A *Scarlet Pimpernel* with a dignified motif—and no Carmen Mirandas!"

The more hostile the reaction from Zanuck, the more enthusiastic Kazan seemed to become about his picture and especially its male star. In a note to his boss, Kazan seemed carried away with Marlon's appearance on the screen. "Look at that face—that face! Its brooding sadness. The poetry of it. God damn it, it's the face of Edgar Allen Poe!" After reading that note, Zanuck called two of his male assistants into his office. "Is Kazan, like Brando, another faggot?"

When not chasing after women or having cute Mexican boys sent to his dressing room, Marlon found other amusements. At night he set off firecrackers in the tawdry, dust-covered lobby of the little Texas motel where he was staying.

Sometimes he captured deadly tarantulas and put them in the dressing rooms of the women working on the film. "One time that led to a virtual stampede," Kazan later said. "The women were nearly killing each other to see who could get out the door first. Marlon also discovered the joys of farting at the most inappropriate moments. Any time he met someone who thought he was important, Marlon would fart. He learned to fart on cue. I think he ate a lot of beans at night."

When not capturing tarantulas, Marlon appeared on the movie set dangling an imitation black widow spider on his left shoulder with his pet raccoon, Russell, on the other shoulder.

When Sam Stanley, a reporter from a Houston paper, arrived to interview Marlon, he amazingly granted the privilege. "My father is a great engineer," he told the gullible reporter. "Right now he's working on a secret plan coming out of Washington. Dad's designing a tunnel under the Atlantic to stretch between New York and Southampton in England."

He told another reporter that when shooting was finished on *Zapata!*, he was going to quit the movie business and become a geek in a circus. The lowest paid and most despicable job in all of show business, a geek is a guy who bites

Brando and Quinn, the best of friends

356

the head off live chickens. Marlon got the idea for this "new profession" by watching Tyrone Power play a geek in *Nightmare Alley*.

Marlon's water fights with the crew were harmless enough. But one of his pranks almost turned deadly. One hot afternoon, Marlon slipped real bullets into the gun of one of the extras during a battle scene. "Fortunately, I was a bad shot," said John Davidson, "or else I'm sure I would have mowed down three or four extras during the staged gun fight. Marlon's pranks were getting out of hand, and Kazan severely lectured him, telling him that 'little boys need to grow up.' Frankly, I wanted to plow my fist into the shithead's face. The next day he showed up on the set, pulling his stupid little pranks. He didn't even seem to give a fuck that he might have caused me to kill other guys."

Even more intriguing than the Mexican revolution and desert romance Kazan was depicting on screen were the real-life seductions going on off camera. In addition to a string of Mexican boys, who were each rewarded with a five-dollar fee for their services, Marlon was seducing female stars. Starring in his motel boudoir, as they appeared in his life, were Jean Peters, Marilyn Monroe, and Movita, the Mexican actress. Jean would quickly appear and disappear in Marlon's life. Marilyn and Movita would have a long run at his own box office. And Movita, eventually, after the passage of many years, would become Marlon's second wife.

Brando's multiple personalities

Years later, Kazan in front of Tennessee Williams and others said, "Practically every woman within a one hundred mile radius of Roma headed to town to fuck Marlon. But he ignored most of them. He had affairs with Movita, Peters, and Marilyn. But his warmest relationships were with men. He never seduced Tony Quinn, but I counted at least twenty guys who visited his bedroom over a short period of time. He particularly liked teenage boys, especially the really handsome, olive-skinned ones. He once told me, 'They have the smoothest skin—sometimes their asses are even smoother than a woman's creamy breasts.'"

* * *

Actor Anthony Quinn, according to Elia Kazan, arrived on the set of *Viva Zapata!* "with a chip on his shoulder—the first reason being that he wanted to play Marlon's role and not the brother."

From the very beginning, Quinn told Kazan that he was going to play the swaggering, lecherous, bullying brother with such power and force that "there's no way in hell that Brando is going to upstage me. Unlike Brando, I'll have no problem with a Spanish accent." Quinn was half Mexican, on his mother's side, with his father being half Mexican and half Irish.

Quinn had also taken over the role of Stanley Kowalski that Marlon had created. Under the direction of Harold Clurman, Quinn claimed that he'd received more critical acclaim in the role than Marlon had. That was not true, but Quinn always maintained that self-satisfying point throughout his life.

Quinn presented Kazan with an article containing a comment from actress Uta Hagen, who had also played Blanche in *Streetcar*. "Brando was too sensitive to play Stanley," Hagen charged. "Tony Quinn was better because in real life he is a brute. Except Tony doesn't know he is a brute."

The rivalry between Quinn and Marlon continued throughout the shooting of *Viva Zapata!* When Quinn complained to Kazan that the director was favoring Marlon in their scenes together, Kazan responded in anger. "That's a lot of shit! So eat it!"

To heat up the screen between Marlon and Quinn, Kazan went to each of the actors and told absolute lies. To Quinn, Kazan claimed that Marlon was spreading scandalous stories. Then Kazan would go to Marlon and tell him "outrageous libel" that Quinn was allegedly spreading about him. "I kept Marlon and Tony bubbling with hatred for each other," Kazan later claimed. "I really stirred up the pot between the two of them. But I was doing it for the good of the picture."

Even though Quinn never confronted Kazan again, accusing him of favoring Marlon, he continued to tell cast members he had contempt for Marlon. "I know Brando is a fairy," he told Jean Peters. "I'm sure he'd like me to stick my dick up his overused ass. But I have another suspicion. The way Kazan coddles Brando makes me think that our Commie director might also be a faggot. Kazan even walks like he takes it up the ass." Far from being a homosexual, Kazan at the time was having a torrid affair with Marilyn Monroe.

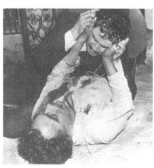

Quinn also revealed that at one point in the film, "my killing rage against Brando almost reached the danger point. I came very close to beating the shit out of the mumbling faggot. In one scene I lost control and started yanking his hair out of his conceited head. I wanted to stick my sword in him—and almost did. Can you see the headlines? QUINN KILLS BRANDO."

Anthony Quinn and Brando

During the second week of the shoot, Marlon and Quinn decided on a unique way to vent their

358

anger and to prove who was the better man. At the end of the afternoon's work in the blistering heat, the two actors staged pissing contests into the Rio Grande. The winner was the man who could piss the longest yellow stream.

On the first afternoon of the contest, three members of the crew watched as the two actors battled for supremacy. John Stacey, an extra, said, "The moment Quinn whipped it out, I knew he had Marlon beat. Quinn's dick was so fucking long that it practically stretched halfway across the river. It was no contest right from day one. Day after day we watched the pissing contest. Except for one afternoon, Quinn won every time. But we had to admire Marlon's tenacity. The one day he won, Marlon told us he'd been drinking beer all day."

Margo and Anthony Quinn in *Viva Zapata!*

After filming *Zapata!*, Quinn and Marlon didn't speak for fifteen years. One night while watching Quinn on nationwide television, Marlon learned for the first time that Kazan had deliberately invented lies to tell each actor. After the show, Marlon called Quinn. "Now I understand," Marlon told the actor. "Kazan was trying to make us hate each other, make our rivalry more realistic. I guess he didn't trust our acting skills. Kazan fed you a pack of shit. I never claimed that you couldn't act your way out of a paper bag. By the way, how does one act oneself out of a paper bag? I've had nothing but respect for your skill as an actor for years."

After that call, Quinn decided to bury the hatchet, as he put it. He believed Marlon's claim that Kazan had been the cause of the trouble between them.

"Marlon and I never became friends," Quinn later said. "We really didn't have much to talk about. We'd talk about whether a Mexican pussy is tighter than a *gringo* pussy. We talked about what a yellowbelly Kazan was to betray his Communist friends. Stuff like that. Not much else. I have always believed that I'm a better actor than Marlon. There's too much pretense with that one."

Quinn would later recall his last meeting with Marlon at a dinner party in Hollywood, in which Marlon confessed that "acting is a joyless burden—just a load of shit. I don't know how much longer I can stand it."

* * *

On his first meeting with Jean Peters, Marlon was captivated by the sultry brunette. Kazan warned him, "Stay away from her! Howard Hughes will have your balls. She's private property."

"I'm not afraid of Hughes," Marlon said. "What's he going to do. Swoop in on us in one of those old *Hell's Angels* planes and drop bombs on us?"

Marlon quickly learned that Hughes had sent a 24-hour "lady-in-waiting" to Texas to chaperone Jean during the shoot. "Since nothing ever energized my libido more than a well-guarded target, I was determined to have her," Marlon said. "We did a little casual flirting, but her chaperone was in watchful attendance, so I didn't get anywhere."

Nothing could be farther from the truth. Marlon was being too modest in his autobiography. Kazan always claimed that Marlon bribed the chaperone, seducing her and winning her devotion, which "cleared his pathway to Peters."

Once again Quinn found himself competing for Jean's affections. The actor also wanted to seduce her. "Both Marlon and Quinn were wooing Peters in spite of her chaperone," Kazan said. "One night both men, Marlon with a Mexican guitar, climbed up a tree outside her bedroom window to serenade her. I guess Peters found Marlon's warbling more enchanting than Quinn's 'Down in Old Mexico' songs. The next night Marlon got the invitation to visit Peters in her boudoir. Quinn was told to stick it somewhere else!"

On his first night with Jean, Marlon found her devastated and on the verge of tears. Seeing the first rushes, Zanuck had been horrified at the heavy make-up used on Jean's face. Marlon had always heard that Zanuck was "a bigot of the old Hollywood school," with contempt for blacks and Asians. He often gave such roles to white people.

"You're photographing Peters so dark skinned she looks like a nigger!" Zanuck had wired Kazan. "No one will buy a movie ticket to see a leading lady who doesn't look white," Zanuck also claimed. Time and time again Kazan was ordered to reshoot scenes with Jean "so that she'll come off white."

"In other words," Marlon told Jean, "our fucking producer doesn't want us to look like the Mexicans we're playing. I'm sending a wire to Zanuck myself and telling him, 'Miss Peters and I aren't in Kansas anymore.'"

The next day, the heat in Roma reached 120°F in the shade. To keep his pet raccoon cool, Marlon fed Russell strawberry milkshakes. "For some reason, Russell hates chocolate milkshakes and spits out vanilla ice cream," he told Jean.

At first she found Russell "adorable," until he pissed in the back seat of a new convertible Hughes had presented her. The next night, while Marlon was making love to Jean, Russell apparently

Jean Peters

360

became jealous. He took a bite out of Jean's ankle. The next day Hughes flew in a private doctor to treat the bite of his mistress.

As his days and nights deepened, Marlon found Jean a simple straightforward person. He couldn't believe she could "get involved with a nutcase like Hughes."

Born in Canton, Ohio, on October 15, 1926, Jean grew up with a dream of becoming an English teacher. Arlen Hurwitz, her roommate at college, shelled out four dollars and sent in Jean's picture, taken by a campus photographer, to the Miss Ohio State beauty contest.

Although at the time Jean felt that it was a waste of money, she emerged as the winner. Part of the prize was a Hollywood screen test which led to a $150-a-week contract at Fox. By the time of *Viva Zapata!*, Zanuck was paying Jean $6,000 a week.

Although she didn't think of herself as a "sex symbol" as envisioned by Zanuck, she was a stunning natural beauty, and it was this loveliness that had caught the attention of Hughes. Marlon was also taken with her "flawless and creamy skin," as he described it to Kazan.

He also liked the fact that Jean wore blue jeans as he did and didn't mind appearing without makeup. "Unlike Marilyn, who was the very cliché of a 50s movie star," Marlon said, "Jean dressed like a housewife from Ohio on her way to the supermarket. She also made the world's best Caesar salad."

Marlon confided in Kazan that after a third night of love-making, he'd asked Jean to become his wife and to give up her ongoing affair with Hughes.

Somehow Hughes, back in Los Angeles, learned of the affair and dispatched Jeff Chouinard, a former private eye and ex-fighter pilot, to Roma, Texas. Hughes felt (with good reason) that the woman chaperone had not been doing her job adequately.

Howard Hughes

Fearing that Marlon might be sexual competition for Hughes as regards Jean, Chouinard paid some of the extras working on the set of *Zapata!* to report on Jean's activities.

In his first dossier, the security chief wrote back to Hughes, "Brando has the sweet mind of a four-year-old and has no interest in chasing women."

Surely no private eye ever delivered a more ridiculous report to his boss than Chouinard sent to Hughes. For the time being, Hughes felt confident in the false belief that "Jean is not shacking up with Brando."

Later, Marlon found out that Hughes was

361

"spreading the word that I was a faggot. Howard Hughes is one to talk! Talk about the pot calling the kettle black."

It wasn't Hughes and his spying that ruined the blossoming romance between Jean and Marlon. It was "Montezuma's revenge," as Jean called it. She came down with "history's worst case of dysentery" and could hardly get through her final scenes without encountering "some potty emergency." Shot after shot was interrupted when Jean had to race back to her dressing room. On at least one occasion she didn't get there on time.

With Jean indisposed at night, Marlon wandered around looking for some action. Surprisingly for him, one Saturday night he didn't find anyone available. He wandered over to Kazan's cabin to talk over the film. He knocked on the door and heard a woman's voice calling out for him to enter.

In the half-darkened room, he made out the figure of a beautiful blonde in Kazan's bed. Under a flimsy white sheet, she appeared nude.

"Come on in, Marlon," she said in her most bewitching little girl voice.

He'd recognize that voice anywhere.

It was Marilyn Monroe.

* * *

At three o'clock in the morning, there was an urgent rapping on Marlon's door. Stumbling nude to answer it, he discovered it was Marilyn wrapped in a white terrycloth robe that probably belonged to Kazan. She rushed into his room, and, as he'd later relate to his director, she said, "Something dreadful has happened. Molly Kazan and Gadge's kids have arrived unexpectedly. They weren't due until next week but decided to come a week earlier. Gadge sent me to be your girlfriend while his family is here."

Marilyn Monroe

Pulling her into his arms, he told her, "We'll have a wonderful time pretending you're my girl-friend."

The next morning, Marilyn renewed her friendship with Jean Peters. Kazan later reported that neither actress showed any jealousy toward the other over Marlon. When Marilyn and Jean teamed with Joseph Cotten to make *Niagara*, released in 1953, there was an easy accord between the two actresses. "Jean must have known that Marilyn was also the on-again, off-again girlfriend of Howard Hughes, but this didn't seem to cause friction between the two women who genuinely seemed to like each other.

362

During the week Marilyn spent on the set of *Viva Zapata!*, Marlon got to know her as never before. She revealed to him that Kazan had introduced her to his longtime friend, the playwright, Arthur Miller, and that, "We're a threesome. I don't mean all three of us go to bed together. Sometimes I'm with Arthur, and on other nights when he's not with Molly I'm with Gadge. Gadge told me he doesn't think I'm star material, but Arthur has great faith in my talent and my future as an actress. He told me in time I might even become a modern day Sarah Bernhardt. To do that, however, I've got to stop playing all these dumb blonde parts."

Marilyn Monroe and Arthur Miller

While Kazan was sleeping with his wife, Marlon kept his director posted on what he and Marilyn talked about. They spent hours discussing acting, Lee Strasberg, and the Actors Studio. "Lee told me that I could do plays one day by Eugene O'Neill. *Anna Christie*, for example. He even told me that he'd like to direct me as Lady Macbeth one day."

"You're going to become a big star, Marilyn," Marlon told her. "But beware of Strasberg. You're his ticket to the big time. He'll just use you and exploit you, and take you for all you're worth."

Even though Marlon uttered those words, he surely could not have known how prophetic his comment was. Even post-millennium, Marilyn's estate, left to Strasberg, still brings in some eight million dollars a year in royalties and residuals for use of her celebrated image.

Every male member of the crew was captivated by Marilyn—all except one, Anthony Quinn, who called her "an empty-headed blonde with a fat rear. Oh, Monroe was pretty enough to look at, but there were hundreds of better-looking actresses poking around Hollywood. Even after she hit the big time, with *Gentlemen Prefer Blondes*, I never could see what all the fuss was about. All I knew was that she walked around our dusty Texas set in a slinky dress that showed the crack of her ass. There seemed to be precious little going on beneath her glorious blonde mane."

One hot afternoon, according to Kazan, Marlon "approached me with a deadly serious look on his face and asked me what my intentions were regarding Marilyn. Are you going to divorce Molly and marry Marilyn?" "Hell, no!" Kazan quoted himself as telling Marlon. "Marilyn Monroe will never be anybody's wife. She's not wife material. Girlfriend, yes. Even mistress. Wife, no!" He warned Marlon that Marilyn was "in a marrying mood." "I told him to watch out. She might lay a trap for even you, the world's expert at eluding a wedding ceremony."

Kazan also told Marlon that, "even as we speak, Marilyn is also trying to get Arthur Miller to divorce his wife and marry her. The woman is absolutely capricious. If some fool man marries her, he'll sit home at night wondering what man—or in her case, what woman as well—she's out fucking that night. Joe Schenck, Joan Crawford. Darryl F. Zanuck. Maybe even Rock Hudson, and he's gay. Marilyn told me she likes to fuck gay men for variety."

Not satisfied with any of these answers, Marlon again pressed Kazan to explain fully how he saw his own future with Marilyn. "You're going to keep fucking her? Is that right? Exactly what will she be to you?"

"Okay, if you must know, I can tell you," Kazan said. "A mascot—nothing more!"

On the fifth night in Roma, Texas, Marilyn confessed to Marlon that she was pregnant. She said that condition was "not unusual for me. I prefer natural sex, and I've had several abortions before. I don't remember how many."

He wanted to know if she knew who the father was. "I honestly don't know," she said. "I suspect one of four men in this order: Elia Kazan, Arthur Miller, Fred Karger, and Marlon Brando."

"Why do I come in last?" he asked. "My noble tool is as fertile as any of those jokers."

"I was a little more careful with you—that's all," she said.

A year or so later, Kazan confided in Tennessee Williams and his companion, Frank Merlo, "the most outrageous event that took place during the filming of *Viva Zapata!* You're not going to believe this." The director's claim was that some time during the shoot of *Zapata!*, Marlon and Marilyn slipped away from the set. Using assumed names, according to Kazan, they somehow obtained a license and were married one weekend in some Texas border town.

"Later on, when she was sleeping with me," Kazan said, "she called herself Mrs. Brando and told me that since I was married and since she was married we were committing adultery. I told her I had no problem with that."

No record has been found to show that Marlon actually married Marilyn, but it's entirely possible. Kazan later said, "It was amazing what a hundred-dollar bill could accomplish in those days in those little Texas towns. Both Marlon and Marilyn were two crazy mixed-up kids. They may have gone through a wedding ceremony on a lark, finding it an amusing thing to do. Marlon was a practical joker, and I could see him going along with that. Marilyn was so reckless she'd definitely do something like that. If they were telling me the truth, and I suspect they were, then Marlon's subsequent marriages to those three women, and Marilyn's marriages to Art Miller and Joe DiMaggio would make both of them bigamists."

After she returned to Los Angeles, Marilyn the following week placed an urgent call to "my husband," Marlon. "There will be no little Marlon Jr. No,

364

you're Marlon Jr. There will be no Marlon III. I've had a miscarriage. What a great little guy he would have been with Marlon Brando as his daddy and me as his mommie."

"How do you know it would have been a boy?" he asked.

"Don't be a silly goose," she told him. "Women have an instinct for knowing things like that."

"If you want a kid at some future date—I mean, one with me—just think of me as your sperm bank."

* * *

With all the affairs he had going on, Marlon also found time to launch a relationship with a Mexican actress named Movita, little knowing at the time that she would eventually become the second "official" Mrs. Marlon Brando.

Movita was an adopted name. Born perhaps in 1917 (various dates are given), Marie Castenada entered the world on a moving train traveling between Mexico and Nogales, Arizona. She was born into a family of two sons and eight daughters. Growing up in Los Angeles and attending Fairfax High School, she played "a mean guitar" and was also a dancer, playing bit parts that included a brief appearance in *Flying Down to Rio* with Ginger Rogers and Fred Astaire.

By the time Irving Thalberg cast her in *Mutiny on the Bounty* in 1935, with Clark Gable and Franchot Tone, she was billing herself as "Movita." *Mutiny* would represent the peak of her career, although other roles followed, including *The Hurricane* in 1937 and *The Girl From Rio* in 1939. She also appeared in a campy role as "Rosita del Torre" in *Rose of the Rio Grande* in 1938. Her career, however, was going nowhere.

Movita

In 1939, as war loomed in Europe, Movita married the Irish boxer, Jack Doyle, a tempestuous marriage that ended in divorce in 1944. Movita rode out most of the war years in England, suffering through nightly aerial bombardment from Hitler's Luftwaffe.

Marlon met Movita's husband, Jack Doyle only once. They even had a sparring match in the ring, Doyle generously providing Marlon with tips on how to improve his technique. Although he made a fortune from boxing and also did some acting, Doyle lost all his money through gambling and drink—in his own words, "on fast women and show horses." He died penniless in the 1970s, although Marlon once sent him a check for two thousand dollars when the ex-boxer had no place to live.

Returning to Hollywood from London after World War II, Movita could find very few roles—bit parts at the most.

Launched on the set of *Viva Zapata!*, Marlon's affair with Movita would continue on and off throughout the Fifties. He always left her for other women, then would return only to leave her again. That would also be the pattern of his married life to her as well.

Marlon told Kazan and his makeup man, Phil Rhodes, that Movita reminded him of a gypsy. "She's primitive and earthy," he said, "but what I like about her is that she believes everything I tell her." On the set of *Zapata!*, she worked with Marlon on his Spanish accent.

"Everybody else in the film except Marlon spoke like they'd been born in Brooklyn," Movita said.

Kazan found that Movita had a stabilizing influence on Marlon. "She was the mother figure, the Nebraska mommie Marlon never really had. Except she wasn't a prairie woman, but a Mexicali Rose. She reminded me of that old Mexican actress of the Thirties, the fiery, tempestuous, and volatile Lupe Velez, whose life ended in suicide. Actually I felt sorry for Movita. Marilyn Monroe and Jean Peters were a tough act to follow."

Although Marlon was fond of seducing teenagers, he found "the older woman," Movita, captivating in spite of their age differences. "I know my reputation for preferring jailbait, but I often throw a mercy fuck to older women," he told Kazan. "I think Movita is funny—she makes me laugh. She's also beautiful in her own kind of way. Just my type. She's also smart and very sympathetic to my problems when I lay my head on her breast at night. She's also the hottest piece of ass south of the border."

One week into her fling with Marlon, Movita appeared on the set of *Zapata!* with a large diamond ring, claiming it was an engagement ring from Marlon and that the two of them planned to get married upon their joint return to Los Angeles. She was seemingly unaware of any "marriage" between Marlon and Marilyn.

"Everybody laughed off Marlon's fling with his Mexicali Rose," Quinn said. "But I knew Movita very well. Very well, indeed! She was a very determined woman. I felt that she would survive all the Monroes and eventually get her man, and time proved me right. She even overlooked Marlon's tricking with dicks and stood by him, even though he treated her real awful. Yes, they would eventually marry—what a mistake!"

"I never understood Marlon's fascination for Movita," Jean Peters later recalled. "She was a bit too much of a Tequila Rose for me. She reminded me of Carmen Miranda, all in her bright colors. She was only missing a pair of castanets and a *Sevillano* polka dot dress in red and white. I think I contemptuously called her 'Carmen.' I thought Marlon was dating below his station in life."

First wife Anna Kashfi admitted that the dark-skinned and high-cheek-boned Movita "set Marlon's libido racing. For Movita—and for Marlon—it was sex at first sight," Kashfi claimed. "She accompanied him back to Hollywood to share his rented bungalow. They remained intermittent lovers for eleven years." Movita would also follow Marlon to New York on various occasions.

"She had incredible patience," Kazan said, "waiting and waiting and waiting to become Mrs. Marlon Brando. Considering what happened between them, her wait was in vain."

Quinn later said that unlike some of Marlon's girlfriends, or even his other wives, Movita "never tried to make hay out of her romance with Brando. She seemed content to live in the shadows of his private life, and that's probably why the relationship endured for as long as it did."

***

Tennessee Williams, in an indiscreet interview, once told a reporter, "Marlon Brando is just about the best looking man I have ever seen, with one or two exceptions. And I have never played around with actors. It is a point of morality with me. And anyhow, Brando is not the type to get a part that way."

Amazingly, the statement sent shock waves through the press, as if Tennessee were "outing" himself before the term was invented. At that time in the early 1950s, the world did not necessarily know that Tennessee was a homosexual. The only part of his statement that was true was the claim about Marlon being good looking. The rest was a total fabrication, since the playwright had long ago sampled Marlon's charms and had been plowed by the actor's "noble tool."

Tennessee's statement brought a laugh to fellow gay author, Gore Vidal. On hearing the comment, Vidal remarked, "Oh, that Tennessee! Don't you just love The Glorious Bird?" That was the way Vidal always referred to Tennessee.

Vidal would find himself on most lists of Marlon's male lovers. But in his memoirs, *Palimpsest*, Vidal tried to lay these rumors to rest. Once, when asked about Marlon's bisexuality, Vidal was a bit dismissive.

Gore Vidal

Kenneth Tynan

"Anyone with a great deal of sexual energy and animal charm is going to try everything."

Vidal encountered Marlon at a party in London when he was filming *The Countess from Hong Kong*, directed by Charles Chaplin. The writer claimed that Marlon arrived drunk at the party hosted by critic Kenneth Tynan, along with such guests as Richard Harris and Michelangelo Antonioni. During the course of the evening, Vidal writes that Marlon dared Tynan to go into the bathroom with him "for a full-on-the-mouth kiss as proof of our friendship."

Instead of embarking on an affair, Vidal said that he scratched his forehead when introduced to the actor. Marlon asked him, "Why are you scratching your forehead *like that*?" Vidal replied, "Would you rather I scratched *your* forehead?"

Antonioni, according to Vidal, was so impressed with the Tynan party that it inspired his upcoming film, *Blow-Up*.

Vidal would later claim that he "hardly knew" Marlon. Much more persistent were the rumors of an affair between Vidal and Paul Newman, Marlon's so-called clone. The friendship between Newman and Vidal would last for half a century.

In the aftermath of *Viva Zapata!*, Marlon installed himself once again in his apartment in New York on Fifty Seventh Street. Movita moved in with him, having accompanied him from Hollywood.

Leaving Movita to clean up his apartment, Marlon spent most of his days and a lot of his nights with Wally Cox. By that time, rumors of an affair between the two men were circulating on both coasts. But very few people knew who the actor/comedian Wally Cox was.

When he wasn't with Wally, Marlon renewed his friendships with Stella Adler and Bobby Lewis, among others. He was anxious to share his movie-making experiences, some quite humorous, with his theater friends. "I have utter contempt for the movies," Marlon claimed, contradicting earlier statements about how hard film-acting was.

Marlon introduced Movita to Bobby Lewis. "I think Marlon was smitten but not all that serious," Bobby later said. "I know that while he was living with Movita, he was seeing other people, including Rita Moreno and others, even some young actors on the side. There was some vague talk of marriage, and Movita continued to show off that diamond engagement ring, but I couldn't see Marlon settling down with some cha-cha bit actress. Or settling down with anyone as far as that goes. Marlon told me that the only real love in his life had been his pet raccoon, Russell, and that he'd even turned that critter loose in some forest in the Middle West."

Instead of spending all his time in New York pursuing seductions, Marlon was often lying horizontal on the couch of his psychiatrist, where he continued to maintain that, "I'm sexually confused."

"I don't know what the psychiatrist was doing for Marlon, but I found him the same as he always was," Bobby Lewis said. "Movie stardom hadn't changed him at all. He never took taxis, preferring the subway. He still liked to play the old water bag game out his apartment window, giving passers-by down below a sudden

Christian Marquand

spring shower, and he still took delight sliding down the banisters into the subway."

The novelty of being back in New York quickly wore off for Marlon. He also grew tired of Movita's Mexican dinners. "There's just so much chili a man can eat before the hot peppers burns his ass as you take a shit," he told Bobby Lewis.

Leaving Movita alone in the apartment, he flew to Paris. There he renewed his friendship with Roger Vadim and re-launched his sexual affairs with both Daniel Gélin and Christian Marquand.

"Although he abandoned women left and right, including his later wives, Marlon had a steadfast loyalty to Gélin and Marquand that was remarkable," Kazan once said. "He was in constant touch with both actors and spoke of them frequently. Was it love? In Marlon's case, I would hesitate to use the word love."

Tennessee, in his continental rambling, was introduced to Marquand by Marlon. "I never really got to know Monsieur Marquand," Tennessee later said. "Through all of our time together in Marlon's hotel suite, Marquand kept licking Marlon's body, paying particular attention to his neck. I think before the evening ended, Marquand had given Marlon at least three hickeys. Both men received me in their underwear. I have no objection to gentlemen callers receiving me in their underwear. I think Marquand, at least in those days, was a very handsome young man, and I applaud Marlon for his good taste in Frenchmen. As for Frenchmen in general, I think every male homosexual in America should have at least one interlude with a Frenchman at some point in his life."

Arriving back in New York, Marlon temporarily ignored the film offers being sent from Hollywood by Jay Kanter. He decided instead to make an appearance at the Actors Studio where he was requested to say a few words.

James Dean

His words turned into a long, drawn-out speech about stage acting versus screen acting.

At the back of the room sat a young man slouched down in his seat, so much so that his ass was hardly touching the bottom of the chair. Throughout Marlon's speech, the young man stared at him "so intently I felt my skin burning," Marlon later told Bobby Lewis. "I don't think I've ever been looked at that way before," Marlon said, "and I've been evaluated by the best of them, male and female."

From time to time, Marlon would steal a glance at the young man, whom he found was broodingly handsome, a severe intensity combined with an appealing vulnerability. Marlon immediately pegged the aspirant actor as a homosexual.

"He looked at me with such a childlike sincerity," Marlon later told Bobby, "that I knew it must be love. What else?"

After the session, and after the other students had filed out of the room, the young man remained glued to his seat, still slouching, and still staring at Marlon. As Marlon approached him, the young man rose to his feet and extended his hand.

"I'm your greatest fan," the young actor said to Marlon. "Some day I want to become an actor just like you. Your style, everything."

As he said that, Marlon still held onto the young man's hand, not returning it. "You can hold my hand all night long if you want to," the young man said.

"Indeed I shall," Marlon said. "Or should I have said, 'Indeed, I will.' I always confuse will and shall."

"I'm confused about a lot of things," the young man said. "Very confused. But not confused in my admiration for you."

"Since you seem to know who I am, who might you be?" Marlon asked.

"James Dean. But you can call me Jimmy. Born in Marion, Indiana on February 8, 1931. Died April 17, 1967."

"You know the date of your death?" Marlon asked. "How remarkable."

"I've always had this uncanny ability to predict deaths," Jimmy said.

"Do you know when I'm going to die?" Marlon asked.

"You'll die on December 24, 2010," Jimmy said. "A very old man."

"Do you really plan to die so young?" Marlon asked.

370

"I sure do," Jimmy said, snickering. "My motto is: live fast, die young, and leave a beautiful corpse."

"If that's your goal" Marlon said, "I'm sure you'll accomplish that loafy goal."

He stood looking into Jimmy's eyes for a long minute, maybe two minutes, maybe a lot more. As he would later recall the moment to Bobby Lewis, Marlon said he wasn't certain of the time. Finally, he spoke to Jimmy. "I hope you understand what I'm about to do. I sometimes do this with men. I'm going to take you in my arms and give you a long, deep kiss. It may be the first time in your life you've ever been kissed, really kissed. My kiss will be just the beginning of a lot of other deep kisses that I'm going to give you in the months ahead." As he moved toward the young actor, Marlon got so close he could smell Jimmy's breath. "All your dreams and fantasies about me are about to come true!"

* * *

In his autobiography, Marlon tried to conceal his romantically tortured involvement with Jimmy Dean, suggesting that he met his young admirer—six years his junior—much later than he actually did. Bobby Lewis often saw Marlon and Jimmy together in the winter of 1951.

At the time, Jimmy was being partially supported by an older television producer, Rogers Brackett, who was a homosexual. "If my relationship with Jimmy was a father-and-son type, it was definitely incestuous," Rogers later said. The producer wanted a monogamous relationship with Jimmy, but Jimmy refused to commit to that. Perhaps to punish Rogers, Jimmy described in intimate detail his various affairs with both men and women, including Marlon.

The composer, Alec Wilder, and also the television art director, Stanley Haggart, were also privy to the secret involvement of Marlon and Jimmy. Later, each of those three men, with additional information supplied by Bobby Lewis, relayed more or less the same accounts of the long-sup-

James Dean

pressed relationship between Jimmy and Marlon.

In his autobiography, *Songs My Mother Taught Me*, Marlon falsely claimed that he was introduced to Jimmy by Elia Kazan on the set of *East of Eden*. According to the autobiography, Jimmy told Marlon that he was "not only mimicking my acting but also what he believed was my lifestyle." In that statement, Marlon was accurate. Only the date and place of the introduction was wrong.

James Dean

Rogers Brackett claimed that according to Jimmy's own account, Marlon took him back to his apartment and seduced him on the afternoon of their first meeting at Actors Studio. "I got to make love to Marlon," Jimmy told Rogers, "which is something I've been longing to do ever since I first heard about him."

Actually, it was more like Marlon making love to Jimmy. "He was completely in charge of our love-making," Jimmy revealed to Rogers. He told me what he wanted, and I went along for the ride." Without Jimmy specifically saying so, it was obvious to Rogers that Marlon had sodomized his young friend.

As in previous years, Marlon had walked the streets and attended clubs and cafes with Clifford Odets or Leonard Bernstein. He was soon "spotted everywhere with Jimmy Dean," claimed Stella Adler. "I had many long talks with the two of them."

"They were a definite couple," Alec Wilder said. "Of course, the words, sexual fidelity, would be unknown in each of their vocabularies. Jimmy and I used to sit and talk for hours in my room at the Algonquin Hotel. He kept me abreast of the affair. I really believe that Jimmy fell in love with Marlon that year. As for Marlon, I don't think he ever loved Jimmy. I met Marlon only three times, and each time he was with Jimmy. In my opinion, Marlon was in love with Marlon."

"Jimmy tried to dress exactly like Marlon," Alec said. "With one notable exception. To keep warm in the winter, he wore a black bullfighter's cape slung over his shoulders."

Jimmy frequently visited Stanley Haggart, especially when he was broke. Stanley at the time was the leading art director in New York for television commercials, and Jimmy wanted Stanley to use his influence to get work for him. Rogers, too, helped Jimmy find work. But Jimmy would often disappear for weeks at a time, not returning at night to Rogers's apartment. "This would seriously piss off Rogers," in the words of his most intimate friend, Alec Wilder. "When Rogers cut him off from jobs, Jimmy would go over to Stanley's."

"Jimmy never had any money in those days," Stanley said. "Sometimes I would lend him fifty dollars with no expectation of ever seeing the money again. Believe it or not, fifty dollars could actually buy something in those days. Even when Jimmy had less than two dollars in his pocket, Marlon wouldn't lend him a cent. Jimmy said he felt that Marlon deliberately wanted him lean and mean on the streets, looking for a handout."

Stanley said that Jimmy never phoned in advance before dropping by his apartment in the East Fifties. "He just arrived on the doorsteps. He always wanted me to make tapioca pudding for him. It was sort of a comfort food for him. He never came to see me unless he was depressed or broke. His manners were horrible. He'd put muddy feet up on my new sofa and would flick ashes on my Oriental carpet, never bothering to use an ashtray. He talked frequently about Marlon and how frustrated he was in the relationship. I got the impression Jimmy was engaged in a cat-and-mouse affair with Marlon, with Marlon being the cat, of course. Marlon seemed to be toying with Jimmy for his own amusement. I think Marlon was sadistically using Jimmy, who followed him around like a lovesick puppy with his tongue wagging."

"I sensed a terrible loneliness in Jimmy," Rogers said. "Whatever he wanted or needed, I felt I could not really provide even though he shared my bed on many a winter's night. It was obvious to me that he preferred Marlon's arms to mine. Even though he must have known that Jimmy was hopelessly in love with him that winter, Marlon insisted on rubbing Jimmy's nose into his other affairs. Sometimes Marlon would invite Jimmy over to watch as he fucked some pickup from the street. Jimmy told me that he'd spent many a night at Marlon's watching like a voyeur as he made love to someone else. Jimmy claimed that Marlon often invited him for 'sloppy seconds' when the object of his lovemaking had retreated. It wasn't a very happy relationship for Jimmy, and I was as jealous as a bitch in heat, because at least momentarily I'd fallen—and fallen big—for Jimmy. When Marlon was out on one of his many dates, Jimmy would often stalk him, even following him home. On

many a night Jimmy would stand beneath Marlon's apartment house, looking up at his bedroom window as the lights went out, wanting to be in that bedroom himself. One very cold morning, Marlon came downstairs in his pajamas and invited Jimmy, shivering in the cold, to come upstairs with him. But, I fear, those acts of kindness were the exception—not the rule."

Stanley Haggart cited occasional acts of generosity on the part of Marlon. "When he found Jimmy half starved, Marlon would sometimes

James Dean

invite him to a steak dinner in the Village. But these were very rare occasions. When Jimmy had no money at all, he told me that he would consent to blow-jobs in a men's room in Central Park to earn a few bucks. When he got money, he lived on chocolate milkshakes for energy. He claimed he could survive on a daily intake of milkshakes, although he complained of a runny stool because of the lack of solids in his diet. I fed him when he came to me, trying to give him some red meat and a garden salad, followed invariably by my tapioca pudding."

Brando flips the bird at Dean

"Jimmy often spoke to me about his dreams of future stardom in Hollywood," Alec said. "He said he was going to keep imitating Marlon in his acting style. Then, when he actually got to Hollywood, he wanted to star in all of the movies Marlon turned down. 'I'm a natural for Marlon's rejects,' he told me. Even though I urged him to forge his own style as an actor, he never listened."

One night about two o'clock in the morning, Jimmy arrived at my apartment," Rogers said. "I hadn't seen him in days. He begged me to take him to an all-night diner where he could eat chili and beans like he used to when a boy in Indiana. Reluctantly I got dressed and went to the diner, even though I detest chili. He told me he was giving up his dream of a career as an actor. He said that Marlon had told him that he could never make it as an actor and that he had no talent. Jimmy was sobbing between the beans. He claimed that his relationship had deteriorated and that Marlon didn't want to see him again."

Ironically, at the time, Jimmy was hoping to land the role of Nels in the TV series, *I Remember Mama*. The same role, of course, had brought acclaim to Marlon in the stage play.

Back from the diner, Rogers felt that Jimmy was coming unglued. "He went to get his bongo drums. He always kept most of his possessions in my apartment. Back in the living room, he wanted to play the drums for an hour or two. At one point he pulled off all his clothing. I was shocked to see that he had burns on his chest. Jimmy told me that they were from cigarette burns by Marlon. I was practically ready to call the police on this brutal son-of-a-bitch

374

until Jimmy told me that he'd asked Marlon to do that to him. For the first time in my life, I came to realize what a masochist Jimmy was—or was becoming."

While filming *The Last Resort* in Key West in the 1970s, actress Barbara Baxley said that she knew both Jimmy and Marlon in the Fifties. "I remember seeing Marlon at a party in Greenwich Village. He knew that I was Jimmy's friend. I think these two guys had only known each other for a few weeks. Knowing of our friendship, he came up to me. 'You'd better get your boy to a psychiatrist right away,' he told me. 'He's an emergency case. One crazed sicko! If you only knew what he wants me to do to him.'"

Already aware of the S&M implications of the Brando/Dean relationship, Barbara cautioned, "You don't have to participate if you don't want to. You could just walk away."

"Just what I'm going to do with you right now," Marlon said before retreating to the other end of the room.

"Self-destructive or not, Jimmy continued to see Marlon even though I begged him not to," Barbara claimed.

* * *

The release of *Viva Zapata!* brought Marlon his second Oscar nomination. The first time he'd lost the award, bowing to a sentimental favorite, Humphrey Bogart. The second time he lost to another sentimental favorite, an aging Gary Cooper appearing in *High Noon*.

To Marlon's chagrin, Anthony Quinn won as best supporting actor. "I guess this Oscar shows Brando who's the better actor," Quinn told the press.

Although he always spoke contemptuously of the Oscar, Kazan revealed that Marlon seemed bitter at his loss of the award to Cooper. In a way, according to Kazan, Marlon felt betrayed by Fred Zinnemann, Stanley Kramer, and Carl Foreman, all of whom had worked on *The Men*.

"I should have made that fucking *High Noon*," Marlon told Kazan. "Instead Kramer offered the role to that little faggot, Monty Clift, and not to me. Clift turned it down and guess what? Kramer gets Cooper who's much too old for the part. If I'd made the film, I would have fucked Grace Kelly every night. I'm going to get the nympho bitch yet—just you wait and see."

Marlon, even at that time, was a bit of a prophet.

Zapata! gave Marlon a chance to show off his magnificent physique, winning him thousands of adoring new fans, both women and an increasing coterie of gay men of all ages who made him their new pinup boy.

However, audiences laughed at the wedding night in the film depicting Marlon as Zapata and his bride, as portrayed by Jean Peters. Instead of raping her like Stanley did Blanche in *Streetcar*, Marlon makes an unusual request.

"I can't read," he said to Jean on the screen. "Teach me. Teach me *now*. Get a book!"

The problem with Kazan's casting of Marlon was summed up rather devastatingly by critic Milton Shulman of the *Evening Standard*, "The ability to scowl, to shrug sullenly, and to shout without parting the lips hardly adds up to a Mexican bandit. Mr. Brando still has to prove he is good at something other than being Mr. Brando."

Marlon himself had serious doubts about his own portrait of Zapata. "I was too young to play the part," was his dismissive comment.

* * *

Back in Hollywood, the debate continued to rage over whether Marlon was "good in the sack—or not." Like his movies, Marlon was getting mixed reviews. "Some women found him gentle and loving," Kazan said, "and I should know because we both bedded Monroe. She was the one who found him gentle and loving. But a lot of the gals wanted Stanley Kowalski. If they got Marlon on the night he was playing Stanley, they gave him a good rating—that is, if they wanted him to be Stanley in bed which most of them did."

Some of these women went on to write memoirs, in which Marlon was evaluated sexually. Among these scribes were Liz Renay in *My Face for the World to See*. Actually the book shows more than her face, including a picture of her running nude along Hollywood Boulevard to the delight of the paparazzi.

Liz Renay is often hauled out to discount speculation that Marlon would not date blondes because they reminded him too much of his mother, Dodie. Liz enjoyed a brief affair with Marlon after filming ended on *Viva Zapata!*

"For a man who was supposed to avoid bedding blondes, Brando seduced more of these pale-haired ladies than I can count," Kazan said. "Shelley Winters, Liz Renay, Marilyn Monroe—and the beat goes on. Personally I think all this talk of Marlon not liking blondes is bullshit. He'd fuck a blonde one night, a brunette on the other night. One time when we were pissing together outside Roma, Texas, Marlon told me, 'What does it matter? All cats are gray at night.'"

Although born in Mesa, Arizona, to a family of religious zealots, Liz Renay abandoned her strict upbringing and became a "V-Girl" for World War II servicemen, praised for her beauty and her voluptuous figure. In time, she was one of the strippers along 52nd Street in New York.

A "gal pal" to mobsters, she eventually landed in Hollywood after winning a Marilyn Monroe look-alike contest. She was sentenced to three years probation for refusing to "be a canary" against mobster Mickey Cohen. When she violated probation, she went to jail for three years. Nonetheless, she was a survivor and went on to marry eight times and appear before more than a dozen grand juries.

En route were many lovers, including Marlon.

Some of her affairs were documented in her tell-all memoir. Many of her dates were with movie stars—not only Marlon, but Ray Danton, George Raft, Frank Sinatra, and Burt Lancaster. Sharing her memories, she wrote about Marlon and "exotic rum drinks in Polynesian hideaways, ending in his chaotic apartment." With Sinatra, she recalled a flight to Atlantic City for a champagne party in his private suite. During the filming of *Elmer Gantry*,

Liz Renay

she remembered Burt Lancaster and "steins of beer at Malibu Beach or in Yorkville's Germantown in New York." She claimed that if ten men gathered, eight of them would make a play for her. The suggestion was that the other two men would be gay. Liz even rated her conquests on a chart, with Burt topping the list for his Grade A performance in bed, although Marlon also scored high points, which his first wife, Anna Kashfi, found amazing.

Liz was one of literally thousands of girls who came to Hollywood to unseat the blonde goddess, Marilyn Monroe. The list most prominently included Jayne Mansfield.

William Ornstein, a writer for the *Hollywood Reporter,* was speaking of Liz but his comment could have included dozens of blonde hopefuls who arrived daily at Union Station, hoping to kick Marilyn off her throne. "Liz Renay was on the way to becoming a superstar. Add a few good breaks and

subtract a few bad ones, and she could have been Marilyn Monroe."

Marlon, however, was the one who got lucky, seducing both the wannabe and the real thing.

He didn't have time to get around to all the women who wanted him, however.

"I wanted to seduce Marlon Brando," actress Joanne Dru once said. "And, yes, I wanted him in bed to mumble, to be rough with me, even brutal, and definitely antisocial. I also tried to seduce his rival, Monty Clift, when I was the object of his affections in *Red River*. But that romance got nowhere. I never got Clift, I never got Brando. I guess I should have chased James

Joanne Dru

377

Dean. But, like Shelley Winters, I got John Ireland, and he ruined me for all other men. One night I encountered Tallulah Bankhead at a party, and we got into a fight over whether my husband, my John, had the biggest dick or her former John (a reference to John Emery) was the winner of the bull prize. I think my argument was more convincing. Tallulah finally capitulated, stalking away shouting, 'That John Ireland of yours is not a mere man—he sounds like a fucking horse!' John, I'm sure, had more than Monty, Marlon, and Jimmy put together. Of the three, I much preferred Marlon. He was the sexiest of the three bad boys of Hollywood. I'm sure Marlon would have gone for me. I'm a brunette and much prettier than Jean Peters!"

* * *

The summer of 1952 was coming to an end.

One afternoon as Marlon was in his apartment, sleeping nude next to a clothed Movita, a call from Hollywood came in from Jay Kanter. Director Joseph Mankiewicz and producer John Houseman had each seen Marlon perform in his long-ago stage appearance in *A Flag Is Born*.

Just as the rest of America, including comedian Milton Berle, was making fun of Marlon's mumbling on screen, Houseman and Mankiewicz knew he could speak with perfect diction and had a highly polished delivery—that is, if he wanted to. Kanter was fast and blunt with the offer. "Don't laugh," he said, "but these guys want you to join an all-star cast and play Mark Antony

in *Julius Caesar*. Read that, Shakespeare's *Julius Caesar*."

As Marlon took the train from New York to Los Angeles, a headline blared the news: ET TU, KOWALS-KI.

Arriving on the set of *Julius Caesar*, Marlon was presented with a bust of himself in the role of Mark Antony. It was the work of Constantine, the Hollywood sculptor. Marlon's reaction? "It makes me look as if I'm about to suck every cock in Hollywood."

Constantine's Marlon

378

Chapter Eleven

Producer John Houseman, Orson Welles' old collaborator at the Mercury Theatre, had conceived the "mad but brilliant idea" of casting Marlon as Marc Antony. In his autobiography, Marlon devoted only one cryptic paragraph to the film, *Julius Caesar*. "For me to walk onto a movie set and play Marc Antony without more experience was asinine."

Even before filming began, *Collier's* magazine called Marlon "The Neanderthal Man." Riding his motorcycle to the studio on the first day of rehearsal, he had seen a devastating comedy skit by Jerry Lewis on television only the night before. Lewis had practically gotten a standing ovation across the country by giving his impression of Marlon as Stanley Kowalski portraying Marc Antony doing his "Friends, Romans, countrymen" speech. Marlon detested such ridicule, which poured out not only from Lewis, but from Milton Berle as well. Before filming began, he'd already told Joseph Mankiewicz, his director, "I'm sick to death of being thought as a blue-jeaned slobbermouth."

Brando as Marc Antony

Before his return to Hollywood, Marlon had stopped off at Penny Poke Farm in Nebraska, which was continuing to sponge up every dollar he earned in films. His relationship with his father remained as tense as ever, but Marlon found Dodie warm and loving, delighted that her son was "tackling Shakespeare," as she put it, despite his earlier vow that he'd never do that. He spent a lot of his time in Nebraska shouting "Friends, Romans, countrymen" to the corn growing in the fields. But mostly he stayed in his bedroom listening to recordings of such Shakespearean actors as Laurence Olivier, John Barrymore, and John Gielgud. At times he became so absorbed in these melodious voices with their perfect diction that he'd refuse to come down for dinner with the Brando family.

To a persistent interviewer, Marlon was contemptuous of the film even before it was shot. "There were a lot of togas left over from *Quo Vadis?* So John Houseman persuaded MGM to do *Julius Caesar* for very little cost, including my own salary. I'm getting only $40,000, which isn't making my father too happy."

Although the casting of Marlon as Marc Antony had brought ridicule to both Houseman and Mankiewicz, their selection of the film's other actors generally met with approval. They assembled an impressive British and American cast, including the distinguished John Gielgud playing Cassius in his first ever American film. James Mason, rather contemptuous of Marlon, was cast as Brutus. Louis Calhern played Caesar, and Edmond O'Brien interpreted Casca. For the women, who were relegated to minor roles, MGM used contract players Greer Garson as Calpurnia and Deborah Kerr as Portia.

Marlon approved of the male actors, but was a bit dismissive of Kerr and Garson as characters in a Shakespearean play. "Their names were added just for box office," Marlon told Mankiewicz. "I'm trying to decide which one to fuck first. If I proposition Deborah Kerr, and I don't think I will, I fear it will not be a match made in heaven. But I hear Garson likes young guys. I think I'd like to fuck Mrs. Miniver. Why not? Another notch in my belt. Garson wouldn't be the first aging movie queen who has sampled by noble tool."

Even up until the final minute, the front office at MGM remained skeptical about casting Marlon as Marc Antony. Houseman, however, continued to lobby for Marlon until the eleventh hour, referring to him as "one of the very great actors of our time." Amazingly, the front office wanted to give the role to "the most wooden actor in Hollywood," gun-toting Charlton Heston. Throughout his life, Marlon always held Heston in deep contempt, and especially loathed his right-wing advocacy of gun control.

Before leaving for the West Coast, Marlon, accompanied by his pal, Wally Cox, had gone to a recording studio and crafted a recorded version of his dialogue in *Julius Caesar*. Once that was completed, he invited Mankiewicz

Clad in Roman attire,
but what's underneath?

to "that filthy pad on 57th Street that bore the remnants of many broads."

Mankiewicz sat in a broken-down chair that still smelled of Russell the raccoon's urine, even though the animal was by now running wild through the forests of Nebraska. Finally, when the recording came to an end, Mankiewicz rose from his chair. "For God's sake, Marlon, you sound like June Allyson."

Mankiewicz carried the recording over to John Houseman. After listening intently to it, the producer told his director, "You've got your work cut out for you. We need a voice like Orson Welles has. There's a soft, feminine side to Brando's voice. He also has a slight lisp like Bogie. His thin voice doesn't match his rugged face or his powerful physique. Maybe we could keep him in the film but get Olivier or Paul Scofield to dub his voice."

Our hero

Instead of becoming paralyzed, Marlon continued on an almost day-and-night schedule to perfect his role. Two months later he approached both Houseman and Mankiewicz with another recording, this one far more powerful. "My God, I think he's got it!" Mankiewicz shouted.

When Mankiewicz sent the recording to Dore Schary at MGM, the production chief at first refused to believe the voice was Marlon's. "I don't have time for your silly games," he wired Mankiewicz. "Any fool would know that was the voice of Olivier."

Still objecting to casting Marlon, Schary proposed one final choice for Marc Antony. "What about Stewart Granger?" The British actor was an MGM contract player at the time.

Both Houseman and Mankiewicz felt that Granger "was just another pretty English boy, great for a gay man's fantasy but lousy for Marc Antony."

Marlon had already protested against a portrait bust by the artist who went by the name of Constantine. Then, on the set, he was shown Kenneth Kendall's oil painting of him as Marc Antony wearing a scarlet toga with gold laurel leaves. Marlon shouted, "That painting's shit!" MGM had wanted to hang it in the lobby of the Four Star Theater in Los Angeles where *Julius Caesar* was scheduled for its West Coast premiere.

Suddenly, Marlon's old friend from Rome, director Vittorio De Sica, arrived unexpectedly on the set. De Sica wanted to wish him luck and to express his regret that so far they had not been able to work together. As a courtesy, Marlon walked him up and down the Roman streets constructed by

Joseph Mankiewicz

MGM prop men. At the end of the tour, De Sica proclaimed, "Ah, what realism! It looks exactly like modern day Ferrara."

When shooting began, Marlon was rooming once again with his agent, Jay Kanter. When Movita flew in from New York to join him, Kanter rented a home for the two of them in Laurel Canyon. But Marlon was rarely home, as he continued to pursue his other affairs.

Years later, Mankiewicz recalled, "Marlon had Movita stashed up in some canyon somewhere. But she had to wait her turn. Even though I had an all-star cast in front of the camera while making *Julius Caesar*, Marlon had an all-star cast off camera. You name it. Greer Garson, Pier Angeli, Rita Moreno, Jimmy Dean. Marilyn Monroe on a few occasions. Ursula Andress. Katy Jurado. John Gielgud. Even Stewart Granger. Stewart Granger! You heard that right. How in hell did he make the list? Our boy Marlon was one busy boy. He must have used starch on his noble tool to keep it stiff at all times."

Marlon confided to Mankiewicz, "I don't want any of the motley crew I'm dating to pin me down." The director was astonished to hear such a distinguished group of actors and actresses referred to as a motley crew. "If a person wants an affair with me, he or she will have to learn my ground rules. I don't want to sound immodest, but I am, after all, Marlon Brando, a fucking movie star. That means I can have any star or starlet in Hollywood I more or less want. I can't really remember getting turned down. In relationships, I do the turning down. I'm the one who walks. No one walks out on me!" But even as he made that claim to Mankiewicz, Marlon must have known it wasn't true.

Marlon held back during rehearsals, delivering lines *sotto voce*. In contrast, during rehearsals, John Gielgud gave full performance-level readings with a musical speaking voice that never harmonized with the rest of the cast. "I had to pump blood into Marlon and take a quart or two from Gielgud before they faced the cameras," Mankiewicz said.

Brando practices sword fighting

Though stating that, he presented a different point of view to his producer, John Houseman. "Marlon is working his ass off," Mankiewicz claimed. "And it's a very talented and much fucked ass."

During the first week of shooting, Houseman showed up frequently on the set. Although originally, it had been his idea to cast Marlon as Marc Antony, he later confided his bitter disappointment to Mankiewicz. "I think our boy is awed by all this talent, especially Gielgud's," Houseman claimed. "He's a stuttering bumpkin only remotely acquainted with the English language."

Gielgud overheard the remark. Not wanting to interfere with Mankiewicz's direction, Gielgud modestly sought and obtained the director's permission to tutor Marlon in Shakespearean speech patterns at night.

When Gielgud departed from the set, Mankiewicz turned to Houseman and said, "That British faggot wants to get into Marlon's blue jeans. Or at least see what's under the toga. I think he views these upcoming lessons as his golden opportunity. Gielgud has developed a lovesick crush on our boy Marlon."

* * *

In the privacy of Gielgud's dressing room, Marlon found the English actor "cadaverously thin with the features of a hooded falcon." He later told Mankiewicz that Gielgud was "perfect casting for the lean and hungry Cassius."

Although Gielgud maintained a steely reserve in most social encounters, Marlon liked him at once. In spite of their very different backgrounds, the relationship became confidential from the first hour. Gielgud even confided in Marlon that he was afraid to appear before a camera—"at least at close range because I fear I'll photograph like an effete homosexual."

Gielgud came to his lessons in Shakespeare with Marlon following his long string of seductions of young actors—notably Richard Burton and Laurence Olivier. Like these two English actors before him, Marlon found Gielgud highly astute and intelligent—"brilliant at Shakespeare and brilliant at direction. He could seduce you with the sound of his voice, not his body," Marlon later told Mankiewicz.

When Marlon complimented Gielgud on his voice, the actor said, "It is all I have. All my life I've been surrounded by actors who have marvelous bodies. Take Larry Olivier. I adore his voice but he has it all over me in vitality and looks. He can play Romeo in love scenes that become intensely real and tender on stage. As for my Romeo, I fear I'm very cold aesthetically compared with Larry."

"How do you think we'll compare when this damn film is made?" Marlon asked before answering his own question. "You'll provide the spirituality, the abstract, and I'll come in with earth and blood. I will bring realism to Shakespeare. You, especially with your voice, will provide the lyricism."

"What about our bodies?" Gielgud asked.

The question did not surprise Marlon, who later told Mankiewicz, "John had been drinking in my looks ever since I came into his dressing room."

"I will provide the male beauty, and you can go for the sublime," Marlon said.

On the third night of rehearsal in Gielgud's hotel suite, he asked Marlon to remove his clothing. "I've made that same request of beautiful young actors such as yourself before. I feel that if you are nude, I can better evaluate you as an actor. When you read your lines in the nude, you get closer to the essence of a character."

Marlon was never afraid to take off his clothes in front of anyone, and he quickly met Gielgud's request, knowing exactly what the older actor's motive was.

Later, Gielgud was cautious and respectful in recalling his lessons with Marlon. "I went to Marlon's caravan," Gielgud said, "and went through his scenes and showed him where the phrasing and the color should be different. The next day he came down and played it using everything I'd given him."

Privately Gielgud never revealed his feelings for Marlon. Publicly, he lauded him. "He was very self-conscious, nervous. He used to come on the set looking perfectly wonderful in this sort of tomato-colored toga and straight bangs with a cigarette in one corner of his mouth. Then he'd take it out and put it behind his ear to show he wasn't being posh. He was awfully afraid of looking silly in that costume."

Gielgud's lessons paid off for Marlon. Within days, his on-camera performances improved remarkably. Mankiewicz felt that Marlon's "Friends, Romans, countrymen" speech had rarely been delivered "with so much intensity, with the passion of his soul in it."

Most biographers claim that after a few lessons, Gielgud bowed out of his role of teaching Marlon how to perform Shakespeare. But Mankiewicz later recalled that that wasn't so. "Gielgud was in there until the end lusting for our boy."

Gielgud was so taken with Marlon performing Shakespeare that he invited him to go back to England with him, where he had been asked to appear opposite Paul Scofield in repertoire at Hammersmith. "I personally will direct you in *Hamlet*."

Marlon turned down Gielgud's offer. "I can't play London or anywhere else. I've promised Jimmy Dean to go scuba diving with him in The Bahamas. But thanks for the blow-jobs."

Gielgud was deeply insulted but when asked put a good face on the

John Gielgud

rejection. "I actually begged Marlon to play *Hamlet*, and he seemed flattered as that was the role that had brought some attention to me. He vowed, though, that he'd never act in the theater again."

As time went by, however, Gielgud grew a bit bitchy about Marlon. "In *Julius Caesar*, Marlon was merely imitating Olivier. An actor imitating another actor acting. Sad, really."

After Gielgud finished his role in *Julius Caesar*, Mankiewicz approached Marlon and asked, "Forgive the intrusion, but I've got to ask the million-dollar question."

Marlon immediately sensed what Mankiewicz wanted to know. "It was the least I could do for John to express my gratitude for those lessons in Shakespeare. I felt I owed him one."

* * *

From the first moment Mankiewicz introduced them, actor James Mason took an instant dislike to Marlon. Mason knew that he was the central character in *Julius Caesar*, but he told Mankiewicz that "like he did in *Streetcar*, stealing the play from Jessica Tandy, Brando as Marc Antony is taking the film's sympathy from me. I'm coming across as colorless. Any actor who could make such an antihero as Stanley Kowalski sympathetic can walk away with this picture. You've got to stop him, and put the focus back where it belongs. Namely, on me!"

Mankiewicz agreed to do that and for the next few days attempted to shift the sympathetic focus back to his friend, James Mason, with whom he'd bonded during the making of *Five Fingers* at Fox.

The ever-sharp Marlon was the first to catch on to his director's motivation. His immediate response was a violent denunciation of Mankiewicz, with whom he'd had a fine working relationship up to that point.

In front of fellow actors Edmond O'Brien and Louis Calhern, Marlon threatened to walk off the picture if Mankiewicz "threw one more scene to Mason." When tension between the actor and his director reached the boiling point, Marlon took the low road. "All of fucking Hollywood knows you're plowing it to Mason and his beloved wife, Miss Pamela, every night. You're the hottest ménage à trois in town. But that's no excuse for you to favor your fuck boy here over me. It's not professional."

At this outburst, Mankiewicz was horrified, shutting down the set for the day. What Marlon had confronted him with was true. Mankiewicz was indeed locked in a three-way embrace with both Pamela and James Mason, and their affair was the gossip of Hollywood.

"All of us were tense about performing Shakespeare on camera, and when Marlon came out publicly with that little secret, all of us knew privately that it made it so much worse," Calhern said. "I adored Marlon but wish he hadn't gone that far. He'd embarrassed Mankiewicz in front of all of us. Frankly, I don't care if he embarrassed Mason or not. I detested that cold-blooded sucker."

Amazingly, Mankiewicz forgave Marlon for his outburst, although it must have been painful to have been humiliated in such a public way. Mason never spoke to Marlon again unless he had to within camera range.

Mason was on target with his perceptions about Marlon even before seeing the film. Writer Kenneth L. Geist nailed it: "James Mason as Brutus compounds the problem because his personality is not inherently good-natured, and his bitter, unsympathetic quality, though muted, continually works against the domestic pathos of his scenes with his wife [Deborah Kerr]. The qualities that made Mason a star in the Forties—the arrogance and coldness that made him 'the man you love to hate'—are wrong for Brutus, and Mason rightly suppresses them. But the result is a performance restrained to the point of self-effacement."

Matters grew worse between Marlon and Mason when another director, George Cukor, appeared on the set. He was approaching Marlon to costar opposite Judy Garland in *A Star Is Born*. Cukor was frank with Marlon, telling him that, "Cary Grant was my first choice, but he turned me down."

"A fading, alcoholic has-been," Marlon said sarcastically. "Too close to home for Cary, I guess. What I don't understand is why would you come to me with the role. I'm in the prime of my life. A has-been? My greatest roles are yet to come. Your casting of me in this film sucks. Really sucks!"

He looked across the set to where Mason was sitting clearly within earshot of Cukor and Marlon. "If you're looking around for some actor to play an alcoholic has-been, he's sitting right over there." Marlon pointed to a startled Mason, who abruptly got up from his chair and walked off the set.

Ironically, Cukor did offer Mason the role opposite Garland. Whatever reservations he had about accepting the role, Mason overcame them. As for Marlon, Mason was not diplomatic when a member of the press asked him what he thought about working with

John Gielgud, Brando, and James Mason mingle during breaks

Marlon. "He's an asshole, a son of a bitch, and one of the dwellers in the lower circles of Hell. He's like some grotesque baboon who delights in showing his ass to the world, and is so wrong in thinking we want to gaze upon its fleshy mounds!"

Louis Calhern

Just as his relationship with Mason collapsed completely, a friendship developed between Marlon and veteran actor Louis Calhern. The younger actor and the older actor quickly became confidants. Calhern confided in Marlon that he had been having an affair with Marilyn Monroe ever since John Huston had cast the two of them in *The Asphalt Jungle*. "She was my mistress on screen, and I guess I wanted to duplicate our roles off screen," Calhern told Marlon.

Then he delivered his bombshell. "But lately I've become impotent with Marilyn. I've gone to doctors. I don't know what to do. The way I see it, when a man becomes impotent with Marilyn Monroe, he's no longer a man. I know you and Marilyn come together on occasions. You're so much younger than I am, but I'm turning to you for advice. What can you tell an old man who's suddenly impotent with Marilyn?"

Marlon looked Calhern squarely in the eye. "I wouldn't worry about it if I were you. Even if I, who's known for his always reliable noble tool, had ever been impotent with Marilyn, I wouldn't let it bother me. I think it's only a phase that you're going through. It will soon disappear, and you'll be a stallion again. In the meantime, take up with a brunette or redhead before tackling a blonde again. You just may need a change of flavors."

After early doubts, Mankiewicz became so thrilled by Marlon's performance as Marc Antony that he asked him to appear in a filmed version of another play by Shakespeare, *Macbeth*. For some reason, Marlon chose to insult his benefactor. With deadly seriousness, Marlon said, "Only if I get to play Lady Macbeth." He turned and walked away.

As he was heading for his dressing room, he encountered Fred Zinnemann who had directed him in *The Men*. In Marlon's dressing room, Zinnemann also made him an offer, informing Marlon that a screen play would soon be ready. "It's based on the life of Van Gogh. I can't envision anybody else but you in the role of Van Gogh."

Marlon stood up, as if to dismiss Zinnemann. "Then I guess Van Gogh won't be cutting off his ear any time soon on the big motion picture screen."

Back on the set, Mankiewicz chose to ignore his star's latest rejection. Mankiewicz's day was brightened when word came in that the front office of MGM was "thrilled" with the rushes of *Julius Caesar*.

"Marlon clearly surprised all those Doubting Thomases," Mankiewicz said. "In spite of a somewhat abrasive personality off-camera, he was great as Marc Antony. So much so that the front office was planning a follow-up vehicle. I was asked to develop the film version of yet another play by Shakespeare, *Antony and Cleopatra*, although I would have preferred to do *Macbeth*. It was already decided that Marlon would be ideal as Antony once again but in the different setting of Egypt. When Dore Schary told me who he wanted to cast as Cleopatra, I collapsed. Instead of rounding up 'the usual suspects,' an Olivier or Vivien Leigh, Schary sent over Ava Gardner to talk to me. Ava's very beautiful, and I know Frank likes her pussy. But Cleopatra? Ava Gardner in Shakespeare? I told Ava I was busy and sent her to talk over the film with Marlon. At that time, he didn't even know that MGM was planning to develop *Antony and Cleopatra*. He certainly didn't know he was going to be asked to play Antony once again, this time opposite Ava Gardner. What a cruel joke! I watched in amusement as Ava made her way across the set to Marlon's dressing room. Oh, if only I could have been a fly on the wall to see what was about to take place in that dressing room. Thinking it might be one of the many women at the studio wanting to seduce him, I fully expected Marlon to open the door with a hard-on."

* * *

"Honeychild, I hear that I'm about to barge down the Nile as your Cleo," she said, startling Marlon with her sudden appearance and perhaps evoking a sexy memory of their previous time together. "The last time Tallulah Bankhead attempted such a thing on Broadway, her barge sank. Do you think me and you can keep the fucking thing afloat?"

At this point Marlon kissed Ava hard on the lips and ushered her into his dressing room, shutting the door. For what happened next, Mankiewicz would have to rely on whatever information he could get out of Marlon.

"We'll never know what went on in that dressing room," Mankiewicz recalled, "but Ava and Marlon spent at least three hours in there getting reacquainted. I had to shoot around my Marc Antony."

The director remembered that when Ava did leave Marlon's dressing room, she looked a little worse for wear. "You can tell Dore Schary the deal is off, sugar," Ava said to Mankiewicz. "Right from the horse's mouth, Marlon told me there's no way in hell he's going to play Marc Antony again on the screen. Once was enough. 'More than enough,' he told me."

"Too bad," Mankiewicz said, lighting up his pipe. "I think I could have come up with some real screen magic between the two of you. The combination of Gardner and Brando might have set off a demand for a series of films starring the two of you sexpots. Spencer Tracy and Katharine Hepburn are my good friends, but I find them sexless on the screen. You and Marlon exude sex appeal from every pore. Hell, with the two of you on the screen, guys will go to the movies carrying their overcoats. You know what they'll be doing under those overcoats."

"Honeychild, it's been a long time since I fell off the turnip truck from North Carolina," she said.

"As Cleopatra, I could truly have turned you into the enchantress of the ages," he told her.

"What a joke!" She lit her own cigarette and provocatively blew smoke in his face. "Ava Gardner quoting Shakespeare. Honeychild, when I landed in Hollywood, I couldn't even speak the king's English. My Tarheel accent was so thick it could cut molasses pie."

Even though he quickly abandoned hopes of bringing Ava and Marlon together spouting Shakespeare, Mankiewicz had other plans for them. He was working on an original story, *The Barefoot Contessa*, which he had originally planned to publish as a novel, but was turning into a screenplay. It was still in the early stages of development.

In his scenario, his heroine, a performer he called Maria Vargas, becomes a glamorous Hollywood star who lands a titled European aristocrat for a husband. The Vargas character was clearly based on Rita Hayworth, who in 1947 had married Aly Khan, son of the Aga Khan one of the wealthiest men in the world, and spiritual leader of the Shia Imami Ismaelian Muslims. The marriage would end in divorce in 1953. Mankiewicz called his scenario a *drame à clef*. In one of the early versions of the project, he'd centered the male lead around the character of a Texas tycoon modeled on Howard Hughes.

Right on the set of *Julius Caesar*, Mankiewicz began negotiations with one of his costars, Edmond O'Brien, to play the third lead, that of a smarmy publicist.

For the female lead, in addition to Ava, Mankiewicz considered both Joan Collins and Elizabeth Taylor. Out of embarrassment, and perhaps the fear of

an outraged reaction from Aly Khan, Mankiewicz was hesitant to offer the role to Rita herself.

Mankiewicz pitched the leading male role of Harry Dawes to Marlon, claiming that he wanted to expose "the Cinderella myth of movie stardom."

Marlon flatly rejected the role. "I'm not into making pictures about movie stars this year. I'm not into even being a movie star myself."

After Marlon turned him down, Mankiewicz went to Humphrey Bogart, who told him he'd be delighted to

Ava Gardner appear in the film. Later Mankiewicz would regret the use of Ava and Bogie. "They had no chemistry on the screen. Perhaps my fantasy cast would have been Marlon with Rita Hayworth. Who could play herself better than Rita?"

In the days ahead, and during the final weeks of shooting *Julius Caesar*, Ava continued to slip around and see Marlon in private. They didn't avoid the prying eyes of Mankiewicz, however.

One night after work, Marlon became very confidential, as he often did on certain occasions. He had a remarkable revelation to make about Ava, although Mankiewicz recalled that he did it with "great understanding and sensitivity."

Talking about it years later, Mankiewicz tried to quote Marlon's exact words. For the first time Marlon learned of Ava's peculiar "pastime," a revelation missed by her biographers but not by Anthony Summers in *Sinatra the Life*.

Ava, according to Marlon, was fascinated by prostitution. Marlon quoted her, "Fucking's a great sport. The shitty part is all the talk you have to put up with from the man before the dirty deed is done."

During their first week of intense love-making, Ava told Marlon that what really turned her on, other than their own sex together, was picking up female prostitutes along Santa Monica Boulevard.

"She's not a dyke," Marlon assured Mankiewicz. "But she likes to pick up these ladies of the night and spend the rest of the evening smoking and drinking with them as she listens to their low-life tales of lust in the dust. Life on the hustle, the raw edge."

Mankiewicz at first found this story unbelievable, suspecting that Marlon was playing one of his many practical jokes. However, he cautioned, "I don't know why I wouldn't believe it. I've lived in Hollywood long enough to know that any one of the denizens out here is capable of anything."

In bringing Mankiewicz into his confidence, Marlon revealed his big plan for Ava that coming Saturday night. He was going to escort her to a bordello which specialized in offering "movie stars" to its male clients, and to a few female clients as well.

"The madam of this bordello claims that if you can't fuck the real thing, she's prepared to offer you the mock," Marlon said. "A look-alike. A man gets to spend the night with his screen favorite: 'Joan Crawford,' 'Marilyn Monroe,' 'Elizabeth Taylor,' 'Jane Russell,' or 'Judy Garland.' Would you also believe 'Margaret O'Brien?'" Mankiewicz himself had patronized the bordello on certain occasions.

Marlon claimed that Ava wanted to be taken to the bordello to meet the madam. "That's not all," he said. "With the permission of the madam, Ava wants to exchange places this coming Saturday night with her stand-in."

"That's wild!" Mankiewicz said. "It's incredible. May I be the first male customer to hire the real Ava for the night?"

Marlon pondered that request for a minute. "If you showed up as Ava's first client, I would just shit my pants. I don't know what Ava would shit."

At this point, Mankiewicz, a normally brilliant storyteller, drifted off and was skimpy on details. He did admit that after Marlon and Ava entered the bordello that Saturday night, he came in about an hour later and requested Ava's services from the madam. After a one-hundred dollar fee was paid, Mankiewicz was escorted to Ava's small bedroom, while Marlon drifted off "to do my duty with 'Betty Grable.'"

"Here I want to end my story like one of those old movies where the shade is drawn over the nocturnal activities of a man and his wife as 'The End' flashes across the screen," Mankiewicz said. "I will tell you this much: I spent two hours in Ava's whorehouse bedroom that night. But I've told you enough. The lady, and she is a lady, deserves her privacy."

The next day, as Marlon reported to Mankiewicz, an angry call came in from Frank Sinatra. "Listen, creep, and listen good. I know all about you and Ava. Stay away from her. Don't ever come within twenty feet of her even at a party. You got that? First offense, broken legs. Second offense, cracked skull. If you live through all that, cement shoes. One more false step and you've had it." He slammed down the phone.

* * *

"Mrs. Miniver, I presume," Marlon said, walking up and extending his hand to Greer Garson upon their first meeting. He didn't know how the relationship would go. In what was an obvious catty remark made about him to the press, Garson had recently said, "On the whole I do not enjoy actors who seek to commune with their armpits, so to speak." Instead of taking that remark as an insult, Marlon chose to view it as a challenge.

She was courtly and gracious to him in spite of what she might have privately thought. She even invited him for tea the following afternoon in her dressing room.

With an amused eye, Mankiewicz watched the so-called romance develop between the established "great lady of the MGM war years" and the upstart young stage actor from New York.

Marlon didn't generally accept invitations to tea from leading female stars, but he decided to honor Garson with his presence. The woman whom film critic Pauline Kael would denounce as "One of the most richly syllabled queenly horrors of Hollywood" seemed in the flesh like "a rather nice lady if you like motherly types," Marlon said.

Marlon, with a certain self-satisfied amusement and a twinkle in his eye, kept Mankiewicz posted on his developing relationship with the red-haired Garson. Alone in her dressing room, Marlon told her, "We've both made movies with Teresa Wright, and I must say she was more successful costarring with you in *Mrs. Miniver* than she was with me in *The Men*."

Greer Garson

"You're far too kind," Garson said, pouring him tea.

"Teresa told me, and I quote, 'There are actors who work in movies. And there are movie stars. Greer Garson is a movie star.'"

"I guess that's a polite put-down from the bitch," Garson said. "I loathed her smugness."

That candid comment won Marlon to Garson's side, and he would remain a devoted fan until the end of the shoot. She told him that when she invited him to her dressing room, she "didn't want him to get the wrong idea."

"Don't worry about that," he assured her. "I'm getting the right idea."

She smiled and told him a story about his former rival, John Garfield. She said that he misunderstood a note she'd sent him, inviting him to tea. "As I turned my back on Garfield to make the tea, he grabbed me saying, 'Let's not fool around, Greer. I want to fuck you right now!' I broke free of him and chased him from my dressing room. What's it going to be with you?"

"I'm not going to be chased out if that's what you're getting at. You invited me here, and I'm going to do my duty and perform like a gentleman should."

"Even if that lady is married?"

"Especially if that lady is married. The way I view it, if a woman is married, she's tired of that same old dally-whacker night after night."

"Dally whacker?" she asked, confused. "What an odd word."

"Don't bother to look it up," he told her. "I made it up."

"I guess dally–whacker is just as good a word as any." She poured his tea. "Let's have a sip of my brew and take it from there."

"Miss Garson," he said, "in America that's called winging it."

Mankiewicz claimed that he was "left hanging," and didn't get any more details on the Garson/Brando affair. However, he did claim it was "of short duration." During their time together, Marlon discovered that Garson had fucked Louis B. Mayer, and even a few electricians and grips on her films. "She was oh, so discreet," Mankiewicz said. "But beneath all those Academy Award nominations for playing a lady beat the heart of a siren. Garson and I

Greer Garson, Brando, and Deborah Kerr

even got it on one night. I asked her if she'd ever fucked Walter Pigeon, who played her husband in a million movies. She denied it. But she did admit to me that she got it on with Clark Gable and Errol Flynn—not at the same time, of course. She said she turned down a proposition from Joan Crawford. Garson was quite passionate in bed in spite of her screen image. After getting to know Garson in a very private way, I think she showed Marlon a good time in their roll in the hay."

The director claimed that most of the sexual liaisons between Garson and Marlon took place in his dressing room. "I had to talk to Marlon one hot afternoon. As I approached his dressing room, I saw Garson leaving. I was almost certain he'd been banging her that day. When Marlon came to the door, he was wearing a pair of purple bikini-style underwear. At long last I found out what he wore under that Roman toga."

"Marlon admitted to me that one weekend Garson managed to slip away from her house and go with him to the Riverside Inn in Riverside," Mankiewicz said. "That's where Ronald Reagan between marriages—and sometimes during marriages—used to take his bitches. Marlon told me that he and Garson registered as Lord and Lady Greystoke. You know, Tarzan's ancestral relatives."

Mankiewicz claimed that Garson was only on the set of *Julius Caesar* for a short time. She told Mankiewicz that, "I've been a devotee of Shakespearean roles ever since I made my debut in a school play portraying Shylock, complete with beard. I wanted to be in it even if I were only carrying a spear! Deborah Kerr received a similarly small role as Portia. Kerr and I were just there to dress up the story. Our parts are so small that we felt like the producer's girlfriends while making it."

After the end of filming, Marlon would not be close to her again. However, "like a voice from the past," she called him one day to star opposite her in the screen adaptation of the original Broadway play, *Sunrise at Campobello*, which had opened at the Cort Theatre in New York on January 30, 1958, with Ralph Bellamy cast as Franklin D. Roosevelt and Mary Fickett as Eleanor Roosevelt.

Jack Warner had acquired the screen rights for half a million dollars. Garson was cast as Mrs. Roosevelt. Surprisingly, she campaigned for Marlon to get the part of her on-screen husband despite Jack Warner's strong objections.

Garson went so far as to call Marlon with her idea, but he laughed off the suggestion. "No more wheelchairs for me." He was referring, of course, to his first picture, *The Men,* and to FDR's confinement for many years in a wheelchair. He later reported that Garson sounded very disappointed. Privately he told friends, "Greer and I would have been laughed off the screen." Later, he read with dismay that shooting had begun with her cast as Eleanor, and with Ralph Bellamy reclaiming the role he'd originated on Broadway.

"Leave it to Hollywood," Marlon said. "They've got an Eisenhower Republican playing Eleanor Roosevelt. First, they should cast a Democrat as Eleanor. It's an insult to the grand old lady of the Democratic Party. Secondly, they should cast a lesbian as Eleanor. Personally, I don't think straight women should ever be cast as lesbians. There are many fine lesbians in Hollywood who could impersonate Eleanor. Garson's not one of them!"

* * *

Even though Movita was sitting at home waiting for him, and Marlon was also seeing Rita Moreno on the side, he still found time to call the Mexican beauty, Katy Jurado. He'd been captivated by the actress ever since he'd seen pictures of her when Fred Zinnemann had cast her in *High Noon* opposite Gary Cooper and Grace Kelly.

Katy's reputation as a femme fatale in Mexico had preceded her arrival in Hollywood. In her native country, she was already known on the screen for portraying sultry home-wreckers and mysterious women with a past. Marlon said he felt that she was going to become the Dolores del Rio of the Fifties. He told Mankiewicz that he was attracted to "her enigmatic eyes, black as hell, pointing at you like fiery arrows."

As Katy once said in an interview years later in Cuernavaca, "Marlon called me one night for a date, and I accepted. I knew all about Movita. I knew he had this thing for Rita Moreno. Hell, it was just a date. I didn't plan to marry him."

She did admit, however, that their first date stretched into an affair that extended for a number of years, climaxed by their last times together on the set of *One-Eyed Jacks*, a picture Marlon would direct himself for release in 1961.

Katy Jurado

394

After one night with Katy, Marlon henceforth called her, "my sultry Mexican wildcat. I've never had sex like that with any woman. Frankly, I don't think I'll ever top Katy, though I may roam the world far and wide. She does everything. She even makes love to your lungs."

Future husband Ernest Borgnine would call her "beautiful, but a tiger." In time, her future costar Elvis Presley would dub her La Chula [an affectionate moniker that roughly translates as "female pimp"] as a nickname.

In 1954 Katy was nominated for an Academy Award for her appearance in *Broken Lance* opposite Spencer Tracy, the first Mexican actress ever to be so honored. After the nomination, Tracy told his good friend, Pat O'Brien, "That Katy is too much woman for me. Better go back to my other Kathie [a reference to Katharine Hepburn] who makes no demands on me. And, I mean none, except that I give up drinking."

All Mexicans Marlon had met or read about were born South of the Border into poverty. Not Maria Christina Jurado Garcia. She came into the world "with a gold spoon in her mouth" [her words], having been born the same year as Marlon to a rich family in Guadalajara.

Her world of wealth and privilege ended when the federal government confiscated the family lands for redistribution to the landless peasantry. All her life Katy exploded into almost violence whenever the subject of that takeover came up.

"As a woman, she's a stunning beauty," Marlon told Mankiewicz. "She has a more assertive personality than Rita Moreno, and that is really saying something. Katy calls her image on the screen a 'distinguished and sensuous look.' I don't know how distinguished she is but that is one sensuous woman. She's the same dangerous seductress cum man-eater in real life that she's been in all those Mexican movies, which she has made me sit through one by one."

Marlon was startled to learn that to support her family she'd once worked as a bullfight critic. She'd met John Wayne one afternoon at a bullfight. With Wayne as the director, Budd Doetticher, who was also a professional bullfighter. He cast Katy in his 1951 film, *Bullfighter and the Lady*, shot in Mexico, even though she knew only a limited amount of English and had to speak her lines phonetically.

She confided to Marlon that she'd had an affair with Wayne, who wanted to marry her. "Unlike you, Marlon, this so-called Duke is no Duke in bed. He's on and off you in no time and doesn't possess the adequate equipment to satisfy a woman." Marlon seemed delighted at Katy's put-down of Wayne's sexual technique.

"If there is one person in all the world that Katy truly detests, it's Rita Hayworth," Marlon told Mankiewicz. "Katy feels that she should be receiving the same acclaim that Rita is getting and is seriously pissed off. One night when she went to a theater in Hollywood to see Rita perform in *Gilda*, Katy jumped up and cursed the screen at Rita's performance. Ushers had to haul her from the theater. That's how jealous she is."

When Marlon, accompanied by Katy, went to see her performance in *High Noon*, he burst out laughing when she delivered her line, "It takes more than big, broad shoulders to make a man." She was so furious at him for laughing at the line that she slapped his face.

"What a spitfire!" he told her.

"Don't call me spitfire," she said in anger. "Why must all Mexican actresses be called spitfires. Why not hot tamale?"

"But you are one."

"Latina women can be more than sexpots in American cinema. You have nothing in this country but racist cinema."

"Actually, I agree with you on that point."

Two years before his own death in 2004, Marlon learned that Katy had died in Cuernavaca on July 5, 2002. "How will I get through the rest of my life without Katy Jurado somewhere in the world?" he said. He hadn't contacted her in years. "Oh, my memories," he said when challenged about how long he'd been out of touch. "To Mexicans she was what Anna Magnani should have been to the Italians but wasn't." He never explained exactly what he meant.

When queried, he said, "Oh, I had a point there somewhere. But these days when I go to make my point, I don't find I can get there. It's like my noble tool. For the first time in my rotten life, it's beginning to fail me. Louis Calhern had that problem when he tried to fuck Marilyn Monroe in some forgotten decade I've lived through."

* * *

During the filming of *Julius Caesar*, Jay Kanter kept Marlon abreast of movie offers coming in for his rising young star. The one that intrigued him the most was from Columbia, an offer to star in the musical *Pal Joey*, with Billy Wilder directing. Marlon would be cast as a hustler and a womanizer.

"Marlon was only tempted by the project because his costar was to be Mae West," Mankiewicz later said. "I'm not sure he had any intention of actually making the film. He flirted with the offer just to meet Mae West. He told me he'd always been fascinated by her. 'We're both sexual rebels,' he said."

"Ever since I was a kid, I've heard stories that Mae West isn't a woman at all. But a drag queen. For once and for all time, I'm going to get to the truth of this."

An invitation from Mae was forthcoming. Marlon even put on a suit before arriving at her Ravenswood apartment. Ushered into her all-white living room by some bodyguard he suspected was her lover, Marlon found Mae sitting on the sofa carefully arranged in a nest of white boas. She did not normally rise to her feet to greet visitors, but on this occasion she did stand up. It was obvious that she wanted him to inspect her entire figure. "Might as well see what you've got to work with as your female star."

Mae West

"And what a stunning figure it is," he said hoping his compliment would win her favor.

"As you can plainly see, my hour-glass figure hasn't shifted yet," she said, taking her hands and rubbing them along her hips to emphasize her slimness. "My measurements are the same as Venus de Milo's. Only I got arms." She sat back down on her white satin sofa, carefully rearranging herself in a field of boas. "So, you're Marlon Brando. Stanley Kowalski in the flesh. That's how I like my men. In the flesh!"

"It's an honor to be here," he stammered. "I must admit I'm overcome with Mae-mania."

"Don't let it worry you," she said in that famous voice of her. "I'm addictive."

To him, Mae looked different bare-headed, without her trademark picture hat. She was also a lot shorter than he'd envisioned. She wore a full-length pink gown and a tiny jacket of scarlet red. Around her neck she'd placed a heavy-laden diamond necklace. Noticing him staring at it, she said, "They don't call me Diamond Lil for nothing."

He was a bit awed by her, and, as he'd later tell Mankiewicz, "Mae did most of the talking. I sat there with my tongue hanging out. But I think that's the way Mae wanted it."

"So Columbia wants me to star in this flicker, with you as my leading man. A sort of Diamond Lil meets Stanley Kowalski drama. Are you game?"

"I'm mulling it over," he said.

"Me, too, but I've got problems with the script," she said. "First off, I write my own lines. Let's face it: This country has only three leading playwrights: Eugene O'Neill, Tennessee Williams, and me. They want me to come aboard this project because of all the publicity I'd generate for *Pal Joey*. Not only would they be getting me, but millions of dollars of free publicity. They'd clean up at the box office. But I'm not so sure I'll be willing to give them this Christmas present. I've spent years building up my reputation as a fabulous entertainer, and I don't know if I want these boys cashing in on my fame. I am, after all, an institution."

"That you are, Miss West," he said. "Vivien Leigh and I, in my humble opinion, had a certain dynamic on the screen. I'm sure Marlon Brando and Mae West would heat up the screen in a different way."

"Watch that billing, duckie!" she said. "The way I see it on a marquee is like this: MAE WEST STARRING IN *PAL JOEY* WITH MARLON BRANDO."

"I bow to your greater box office appeal and your legendary name," he said, perhaps not meaning a word of it.

"You'd better be careful before signing to do a picture with me," she cautioned him. "When I'm on the screen, no one in the audience looks at any other performer. You can have your own scenes by yourself or with that other gal in the picture. But I fill the whole screen when I'm on."

"That's completely understandable," he said, showing her the greatest respect despite her egomaniacal pronouncements.

"No disrespect intended, Brando," she said, "but I sorta envisioned my return to the screen with this good-looking guy I met the other night. The new boy in town. Rock Hudson. I think me and him might start a heat wave on the screen. Give 'em fever. He's got muscles in all the right places, or so I hear. Do you get my drift? A man's gotta have a long loaf in the bread basket or else I'm off the staff of life."

Still in full possession of her show business savvy, Mae seemed to realize even then that she and Rock Hudson appearing together might cause a sensation. At the 1958 Academy Awards, the duo did just that. Mae verbally caressed Hudson's body as they sang, "Baby, It's Cold Outside." The audience at the Pantages Theater whistled, shouted, stamped their feet, and cheered. "We brought down the house," Mae later claimed. "Too bad Hudson is one of the boys. I discovered Cary Grant and made him famous too. Too bad he's a fairy like Hudson. Fairy boys have always been attracted to Mae."

"Would you feel comfortable playing your character in *Pal Joey*?" he asked.

"I always play ladies of no character," she said. "Who wants to go see a movie about a lady with morals? Morality and me never met up with each other on the screen."

At one point in her monologue, she interrupted herself. "Perhaps you're unaware of it, and I understand, of course, but you're not just staring at me, but looking at me like I'm a big juicy apple, the kind the serpent handed to Eve, and you want to take a big bite."

"Maybe that's true," he said. "But I'm awed by you. Your skin. It's peaches and cream."

398

"And my teeth are my own too," she said. "What did you expect? Some wrinkled old fossil? I'm timeless."

"I see the evidence before me," he said.

"I'll let you in on the secret of my youth and beauty," she said, "and I've never told anyone this. It's because I inherited this double-thyroid. It's responsible for my powerful sex drive, my boundless energy, and my youthful look. I inherited it from my three-breasted grandmother."

"What a great gift!" he said.

"I was also born with my cherry intact," she said, laughing at her own comment. "But I gave that up before I reached puberty. I still believe in sex at least once a day. How about you?"

At first he looked puzzled. "Oh, of course. At least once a day, maybe a lot more."

"My kinda man," she said. "I like a man with some life in him."

"Don't get married," she cautioned him. "A man like you will always want to have a lot of harmless fun, and marriage will only hamper you. I got hitched one time. But I used to lock up the old goat in my broom closet and go out on the town, returning before the rooster crowed. The geezer got used to it."

Midway into his visit, she rose from the sofa once again and invited him on a tour of her apartment. "I keep the curtains drawn at all times except night," she told him. "My perfect skin could never tolerate the harsh light of Los Angeles."

Everywhere he looked, he saw gilt and cream colors, along with white fur rugs and gilded Louis XIV chairs. Photographs of Mae in her show business prime were everywhere. Seeing him looking at a photograph of her on Broadway in 1928, she asked, "Don't you think I look the same?"

"The same," he said.

Some of the pictures of her were taken during the heyday of vaudeville. One was of a very young man. With a quizzical look, he stared at it.

"You won't believe this but that photograph is of me," she said. "I got my start in vaudeville as a male impersonator."

"What horrible casting!" he said.

Back in her living room, she had her bodyguard bring both of them a glass of chilled cranberry juice. "I'm a teetotaler," she said.

"You're welcome to spend the night," she said, "but I must warn you about something. I keep men around only as long as they serve my purpose. When I'm done with them, out the door they go. I'm too busy being Mae West to take too much time with any man. For a gal like me, men are meant to satisfy me—not the other way around."

Marlon spent the night at Mae's apartment, the intimate details of which he did not make available to Mankiewicz, except to say that the action took place under a mirrored ceiling in her bedroom. "I like to see how I'm doing," Mae had told him.

Despite their off-screen activities, they never faced the cameras in *Pal Joey*, their roles going years later to Frank Sinatra and Rita Hayworth. "Such a shame," Mankiewicz said. "With Mae West and Marlon Brando, *Pal Joey* would have become the camp classic of all time."

Even though Marlon was skimpy on boudoir details, Mankiewicz did demand to know the answer to one gnawing question. "Ok, spill it! Is Mae West really a man in drag?"

Marlon's reply was a bit enigmatic. "She's a male chauvinist pig but all woman!"

* * *

When *Julius Caesar* opened in New York on May 8, 1953, Dodie wired her son: "You've proven you can do the classics. I'm so proud of you. Your devoted Dodie."

Although *Julius Caesar*, when viewed today, is a disappointing film in many respects, Mankiewicz always defended Marlon's performance. "He plunges into acting the way a deep-sea diver goes overboard. He keeps his eyes shut for hours to see what it's like to be without sight—in case he ever has to play a blind man. He practices using only his left hand for days so he'll know what it's like to play the part of a character who's lost his right hand."

Many critics were kind to Marlon. One critic for the *Observer* in London suggested that to appreciate Marlon's versatility "one should try to imagine John Gielgud portraying Stanley Kowalski."

Laurence Olivier was asked if he thought Marlon playing Marc Antony was doing an imitation of him. "I thought, God, that's me up there on the screen, and God am I awful! Is that all I've given to the world?"

When the 1954 Academy Award nominations came out for the films of 1953, Marlon once again was nominated as best actor. He found himself competing

Marlon visits Monty Clift on the set of *From Here to Eternity*

400

against two of his former lovers for the prize, Montgomery Clift and Burt Lancaster, both nominated for their roles in *From Here to Eternity*. *Eternity*'s director, Fred Zinnemann, who had directed Marlon in *The Men*, had briefly toyed with the idea of casting Joan Crawford with Marlon playing the role that eventually went to Lancaster. Marlon's co-star in *Julius Caesar*, Deborah Kerr, took over the role that Crawford rejected. Also nominated for best actor was Marlon's future rival, Richard Burton, for his performance in *The Robe*.

Deborah Kerr

All of these actors lost out to the heavy favorite, William Holden, who walked away with the trophy for his role in *Stalag 17*.

Privately Marlon told friends that if he ever won the prize, instead of being nominated, "I'll get up on the stage, pull out my dick, and piss on the front row. No prizes should be awarded for acting. Actors shouldn't compete against each other like it's a boxing match. How can any sane person compare my performance in a Shakespearean play with Holden's war prisoner drama? Hollywood's insane. They can take their Oscar and shove it where the sun don't shine!"

* * *

Since Russell the raccoon was wandering wild in some Nebraska forest, hopefully with a playmate, Wally Cox moved back in with Marlon upon his return to New York after *Julius Caesar*. Wally had been forced to move out because Russell had taken such a dislike to the actor that he frequently bit him, often severely.

Wally and Marlon once again picked up the thread of, in the words of Tom Ewell, "a relationship that was about as close as two men could ever get."

Bobby Lewis was a frequent visitor to their apartment. "It was a dump, really, with a toilet that looked like it was scrubbed every fifth year," Lewis said. "But Wally and Marlon didn't mind living in this squalor. Wally wanted Marlon all to himself, and I think Marlon was faithful for about ten days. Then he slipped back into his old habits. He even urged Wally to settle down and get married. After all, Wally was bisexual. For Wally's homosexual needs, Marlon assured him that 'I'll always be there for you.' Or at least that was my understanding of the situation from long talks with both men."

With *Julius Caesar* wrapped and with no other film contracted for, Marlon was an "artist-at-large." Through Jay Kanter, offers continued to pour in from Hollywood.

An intriguing prospect came in from Marlon to star in *Prince of Players*, based on the life of Edwin Booth (1833-1893), the famous American actor who became notorious as the brother of John Wilkes Booth, the man who assassinated Abraham Lincoln. The ensuing scandal forced him into temporary retirement.

Richard Burton

Philip Dunne, the director, wanted Marlon to star in this bio/drama based on a scenario by Moss Hart. Dunne had already lined up some of the great actors of the day, including Raymond Massey, Charles Bickford, and Eva Le Gallienne, with lesser-known younger players who included Maggie McNamara. Pretty boy John Derek was cast as John Wilkes Booth which Marlon found "an amusing conceit."

After briefly considering it, Marlon turned down the leading role, deciding, "I don't want to play an actor, and certainly not a classical actor." The studio, 20th Century Fox, briefly considered turning it into a vehicle for Laurence Olivier, finally offering the role to Richard Burton, who accepted it.

At a party in Hollywood, in front of witnesses, Marlon derided the script and the casting of *Prince of Players*. "It's just a showcase for Burton to show us how bad he is in a Shakespearean role. I turned it down because the film had too many staged portions of Booth's most famous plays, especially *Hamlet*. I wanted it to be a probing study of Booth's fascinating and tragic life. When Fox couldn't get a top-rate actor like Olivier or me, they settled for Burton, a third-rate performer with even worse skin."

The remark eventually reached Burton, who was furious, threatening to physically attack Marlon if he ever encountered him. That critique from Marlon marked the beginning of a suppressed but simmering feud between the two men that lasted throughout their lives. The war between them accelerated when they made the disastrous film, *Candy*, released in 1968 and directed by Marlon's long-time lover, Christian Marquand.

Christian Marquand

The great director, Fritz Lang, who had directed Marlene Dietrich in *Rancho Notorious*, wanted Marlon to star in *Human Desire*, based on a work by Emile Zola. The tagline for this film noir was, "She was born to be bad...to be kissed. . .to make trouble!" After reading the script, Marlon wrote the Viennese director, "I cannot believe that the man who gave us the über dark *Mabuse*, the pathetic child murderer in *M*, and the futuristic look at society, *Metropolis*, would stoop to hust such crap as *Human Desire*."

Lang eventually cast a very wooden Glenn Ford in the role. Marlon continued to make appearances at the Actors Studio where he was treated like a celebrity. Aspiring actors and actresses adored him, and were only too willing to make themselves available to him. Sometimes he gave them actual advice on acting. "You've got to get into a part to the point that you're no longer acting but living the character. In movies don't let the director tell you you've got it right on the first two or three takes. Demand at least ten different takes."

It was during this period between jobs that Marlon and Wally Cox posed for the most notorious photograph ever taken of an A-list movie star. In the photograph, Marlon is committing fellatio on his friend. Charles Higham in his book on Marlon wrote: "A vicious forged photograph of Marlon in a sexual encounter with Wally Cox gained wide underground circulation in Hollywood; the faces had been cleverly superimposed on other people's bodies in a studio lab. The forger of this piece of smut was never identified."

The photograph was real, however, and was no forgery. Wally's face does not appear in the photograph, only Marlon's. Marlon himself later admitted to posing for the candid shot. Only Wally's penis is shown, and it's fully erect.

Later Marlon admitted to friends that he did indeed pose for the photograph, but dismissed it by saying, "It was only done as a joke at a party. It's not to be taken seriously."

The picture gained such notoriety that it came very close to being introduced as evidence of "Mr. Brando's perversity" in the bitter divorce proceedings that flared between Marlon and Anna Kashfi, his first wife.

Woodrow Parrish-Martin, who had met Marlon when he stayed with Jean Cocteau in the Île de France, always claimed that the photograph was taken at a party in Harlem staged by Phil Black.

"All of us used to go to his parties in the Fifties," Parrish-Martin said. "They were the talk of New York. Completely outrageous and totally gay. Of course, you had to cough up ten dollars for all the food, drink, and sex you wanted. But that was cheap for what you got."

There were two Phil Blacks operating in Harlem at the time, and their identities were often confused. Phil Black was also known for staging the greatest Harlem transvestite ball of the year, which drew many luminaries such as James Baldwin or even the "snow white" Anaïs Nin, the celebrated

movie stars from Hollywood, including Lana Turner and Ava
ʳed up at these infamous balls, one of which was raided by the

id to have dared Marlon to pose for the photograph, and that
_.. ᵤm up on his dare. "Wally went along with it," Tom Ewell said.
"I wasn't at that particular party, but I attended Black's orgies when I was in
town. In addition to the sex going on in his back bedrooms, Black staged the
best entertainment for the voyeur. He also spread out the best buffet in New
York City. I attended just for the food." Ewell then smiled. "Yeah, right!"

The photograph must have mass produced, because within weeks it was
in wide circulation on both the East and West coasts. One of James Dean's
male lovers said that he remembered the young actor having the picture taped
to the wall over his bed.

"I think every gay male in America at the time had a copy of Marlon's
candid shot," said gay actor Roddy McDowall. "When I went to Paris one
summer I found the picture being sold openly at kiosks along the Seine. Any
American tourist who wanted to see Brando's skill at fellatio could smuggle a
copy back into the United States."

The author of *Hollywood Babylon*, Kenneth Anger, once told an interviewer for the Australian publication, *Campaign*, that he too possessed a copy
of the picture of Marlon giving head.

"It was taken in 1952," Anger very accurately said. "He is going down on
his roommate, Wally Cox, the television actor. I've tried to publish it a couple
of times, but publishers have always refused."

Although the photograph is available today to anyone who can surf the
web, newspapers and magazines in 2004, upon the occasion of Marlon's
death, once again refused to publish the salacious photograph, which looks a
bit tame by today's standards. However, by 2004 the photograph had gained
such notoriety that many obituaries and follow-up stories in the wake of
Marlon's death felt compelled to mention this long ago "outrage."

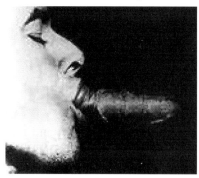

Getting intimate with Wally

According to Fiore, Marlon never
seemed overly embarrassed by the picture. "Throughout his life," Fiore said,
"Marlon never had any false modesty
about showing his genitalia. In fact, when
he made *Last Tango in Paris*, Marlon was
willing to have himself photographed letting it all hang out. Any big-time male
movie star who would do that wouldn't
get unduly upset over some long ago, stupid photograph showing a little cocksuck-

ing. Most actors at one time or another do that in their career. Sometimes we had to drop trousers in those days just to get a stinking part."

No one was happier than Marlon when Wally was cast as the school teacher, Robinson Peepers in the 1952 sitcom TV series, *Mr. Peepers*. The show made its debut as a summer replacement. Because of its high ratings and rave reviews, it moved quickly to a regular line-up. The sitcom that starred Wally was about a mild-mannered high school science teacher, the epitome of a "Casper Milktoast." Soon Wally's nerdy voice became familiar to millions of households throughout America. One TV reviewer at the time added a personal note to his interview with Wally, calling him "quite a ladies man."

"That brought a laugh to the hip denizens of the Actors Studio," Bobby Lewis later said.

After *Mr. Peepers* was cancelled, Wally was given another sitcom—*The Adventures of Hiram Holiday*, which ran during the 1956 and '57 season. His longest running "gig" was as the voice of the lead role in the cartoon "*Underdog*," which lasted for nine seasons, running from 1964 until his death in 1973. "There is no need to fear! Underdog is here!"

For more than six years, from 1966 until his death, he was the upper left square on "*The Hollywood Squares*" game show.

Brushing aside the fellatio portrait, Wally once filmed a commercial that studio executives considered "too indecent" for broadcasting on TV. In the "offending" material, Wally on camera opened his dress shirt to reveal a small segment of his undershirt. In the days before Janet Jackson showed the world her breast, this was considered "exposing underwear on a live model," which was strictly forbidden, and the commercial never aired.

Marlon's comment? "I'd like to show the fuckers something that can't be aired!"

* * *

Back in California, Marlon rented a ranch house near the Pacific Palisades. Movita soon followed, although Marlon, as usual, continued to pursue various other affairs. He rarely, if ever, appeared in public with Movita. For several months, he made no appearance with any other woman.

When seen in a public place, such as a Los Angeles restaurant or a movie house, he was invariably alone. There were two reasons for this: Movita threatened him that if seen out with another woman, she'd leave him and return to Mexico. Not only that, but Marlon was leading a secret life at night, far from the prying eyes of the media.

Unknown to many of his friends at the time, Marlon was doing research for a new movie, *The Cyclists' Raid*, with shooting slated to begin early in

Movita and Marlon's silly faces

1953. Just as he'd entered a ward of paraplegics to research his first film, *The Men*, he now took to hanging out with motorcycle gangs, including the notorious *Hell's Angels*, named after the first big movie ever shot by Howard Hughes.

The scenario of Marlon's new film was based on an incident that happened on the weekend of July 4, 1947, in Hollister, California. An estimated four thousand motorcyclists hit the little town and virtually took it over before departing the next day after wrecking the place.

Marlon was an old friend of the motorcycle. Almost daily he and Wally Cox had ridden their motorcycles through the canyons of New York. In Los Angeles, to prepare for the movie, he took to motorcycle riding with a vengeance. He also took to patronizing mainly gay-oriented shops and appeared at night dressed in black leather and silver chains, his face partially hidden by a cyclist's cap which he wore at a jaunty angle some described as "feminine."

He was frequently spotted around Los Angeles at night with what was called *pachucos*, Latino juvenile delinquents. He often attended a tough bikers' joint, Tequila Maria's, with its sawdust floors. Drug dealing went on behind its barn-like structure.

It was here that he met Luís Ramon, a twenty-three-year-old, well-built Latino who had slipped into the country illegally by crossing the Mexican border and heading for San Diego when he was only fourteen. He'd become a hustler, eventually acquiring enough money to move to Los Angeles on a new motorcycle he'd recently purchased.

It is because of Luís that we know anything at all about Marlon's life with the bikers. "I had been gay since I was six years old and my uncles in Mexico used to play with me," Luís said. "When I first met Marlon, I already knew who he was, although I didn't recognize him at first. I thought he was an amazing look-alike. On the first night, I took him back to my place. We fucked all night. Before the morning, I was telling him—in Spanish, no less—that I loved him. That was decidedly uncool, but I just blurted it out."

Luís claimed that he introduced Marlon to all the members of his motorcycle gang, and they eagerly accepted him, even answering his detailed probing questions.

"Marlon wanted to join our culture," Luís said. "That meant lots of liquor, lots of drugs, occasional violence, and creamy nights of testosterone."

One night, Luís recalled, the police swept into Tequila Maria's, arresting *pachucos* caught with drugs. Luís and Marlon were forced to strip to the waist so their arms could be tested for needle marks. The policeman, according to Luís, didn't realize he was man-handling both Stanley Kowalski and Marc Antony. Before releasing Marlon, the cop frisked the well-built actor.

Brando in *The Wild One*

"Everything would have gone smoothly," Luís said, "if Marlon had kept his trap shut." As he was being frisked, Marlon told the cop, "All of us have to get our kicks some way." That suggestive remark so infuriated the cop that he hauled Marlon to jail where he was booked for the night.

"I was waiting outside the jail when Marlon was released the following morning," Luís said. "Marlon told me that he was thrown into a cell with about ten other men. He said they taunted him and called him 'pretty boy.' He told me in graphic detail how he was held down and gang-raped by all the men in the cell. I didn't know if he was telling me the truth or not, but he sure looked like something had happened to him. I sorta believed his story. A lot of cute young guys were gang-raped when they were thrown into these cell blocks with the dregs of the night."

Luís admitted that he soon realized that Marlon "wasn't going to be my mate for life. He had sex with a lot of the other guys I introduced him to. Marlon didn't want a commitment to me. He was not only having sex with the men, but he had some Mexican bitch stashed away somewhere, and he often disappeared to ball her. Marlon played the field."

"He used to help me out financially, but our break came when he refused to hire me to play one of the bikers in *The Wild One*," Luís said. "A lot of guys, even some of my friends, were hired, but for some reason Marlon didn't want me around. Maybe I knew too much. I was bitterly disappointed and wanted to get back at him."

Luís took his amazing story to the editors of *Confidential*, the leading scandal magazine of the time, and he thought he had a deal made. "At the last minute, they were bought off," Luís claimed. "They practically kicked me out of their offices."

In those days, *Confidential* was willing to suppress a story for the right bribe. There were rumors that Harry Cohn, studio chief at Columbia in charge of production, sent $50,000 in one-hundred dollar bills to the editors of the magazine to squelch the story.

Actual bikers, mixed in with actors, were used in the filming of *The Wild One* to give greater authenticity to the movie. Many were straight and brought their "motorcycle mammas" to the set. Others were gay. One biker, in fact, erroneously reported to a journalist that Marlon had a "twelve-inch dick that had to be taped to his stomach so that it wouldn't bulge in his jeans and distract film-goers." That revelation was never reported, but *Time* magazine suggestively made the point in a cover story entitled "Too Big for His Blue Jeans."

Marlon and co-star, Yvonne Doughty

With a little help from artist Andy Warhol, Marlon, as a leather-jacketed, motorcycle-riding hood, became an icon of the 20th century. Marlon later referred to this image as "my curve ball. I became the poster boy for attitude, angst, and anomie."

Producer Stanley Kramer thought he had a hit with Marlon's new film. He'd been disappointed in his famous *Death of a Salesman*. Released in 1951, it had registered only a marginal profit at the box office. Kramer had read a magazine article about the infamous Fourth of July weekend in northern California. Motorcycle-riding hoodlums, known as the Nomads and the Boozers, invaded the hamlet of Hollister and took it over, drag-racing up and down the main street. To cope with the unrest, squad cars from three neighboring towns roared in to maintain law and order, although they could not completely control the beer-drinking mobs.

Based on this incident, Marlon was cast as one of the gang leaders, Johnny. From the beginning, Marlon found much to object to in the script, beginning with the title of *The Cyclists' Raid* He demanded unsuccessfully that the title be changed to *Frenzy*. For a week, that's what the film was called until studio publicists changed it to *Hot Blood*. Eventually, Harry Cohn at Columbia called the shots, renaming it *The Wild One*.

"I'm playing a sexual outlaw," Marlon wrote Dodie back in Nebraska. "But the Breen office is demanding a lot of changes in the script. Those shit-heads think the plot is Communist and are afraid it will incite young America to rise up against their elders. Bullshit!"

The first meeting with László Benedek, the Hungarian director, went off well. "That's probably because we talked about everything but the film," the director later recalled. But by the end of the first week of shooting, Marlon was at war with Benedek, insisting on rewriting many of his lines. Kramer had given Benedek only twenty-four days to shoot the film, and the director was literally on the verge of tears throughout most of the shoot.

With contempt, Marlon told Kramer that Benedek should devote his future "to keeping Doris Day a virgin in her films."

Marlon derided Benedek to fellow cast members, claiming "Mr. Goulash has no balls. Why in the fuck did Kramer hire a Hungarian to direct a film about American biker hoods? Beats me!"

Marlon hated the director's continental manners which seemed inappropriate on the set of such a picture. Benedek didn't help matters when, on seeing the first of the rushes, he commented, "If you've seen one American biker, you've seen them all—and that goes for Marlon Brando."

Marlon told anybody who was interested that he'd turned down the film script when first offered. "I told Kramer I wasn't doing any motorcycle movies that year. 'Get Jimmy Dean,' I told him. 'He also rides a bike.'" As the script was continually weakened by mandates from the censors at the Breen office, Marlon grew more and more disillusioned with the movie, becoming increasingly inarticulate, finally resorting to mumbling.

Marlon drew mixed reviews from his costars, Mary Murphy and Lee Marvin. Mary was thrilled at "meeting Mr. Gorgeous" and reportedly developed an instant crush on him. He was seen flirting outrageously with her and on a few occasions took her for long rides on his bike. Apparently, the romance never blossomed because of the sudden appearances on the set of two women.

Marlon had told his biker buddies that he planned "to deflower" Mary, whom he suspected of being a virgin. But his plans were put on hold when his sister, Jocelyn, showed up on the set. "Marlon was at his best when she came around," Mary said. "He was real sweet around his sister."

During the final moments of the film, Marlon hands Mary a stolen statuette. Reviewers likened it to a phallus.

Regrettably, Mary's future in films, which stretched out for two decades, would not be bright. Her role as the good girl to Marlon's bad boy would be her only standout film role. "She had her one brief shining moment," Benedek said, "in what became a cult film."

Murphy later ended up running an art gallery.

Mary Murphy and Brando

At the time of his sister's visit, Marlon had formed a close bond with actor Sam Gilman, who played a minor role in the film. Like Wally Cox, Gilman soon became Marlon's "sidekick," as he called it. Except for one "bust-up" the two men would remain close friends until Gilman's death.

"After Jocelyn left, Movita showed up," Gilman claimed, "so I guess Marlon never got around to plowing Murphy, assuming that a nice gal like her would have given in to him."

Jocelyn and Brando on the set of *The Wild One*

Gilman remained with Marlon throughout the shoot and in the years to come. "He hovered over Marlon like a mother hen," claimed Kramer. "Frankly, I think Marlon abused Sam. In front of other cast members, Marlon would order Sam to bring him a quart of banana ice cream, or Marlon would demand that Sam shine his shoes. The actor always seemed willing to do Marlon's bidding just to remain in his company."

During the shoot, Marlon himself took credit for inserting the movie's most famous lines. When a waitress asks Marlon what he's rebelling against, he responds, "Whaddya got?"

When Lee Marvin came together with his co-star, the meeting was a disaster, according to Gilman. "Marvin wanted to be Marlon."

Marvin was cast as Chino, the leader of a rival gang. In the film, Marvin says, "Hi ya, sweetheart. Johnny, I love you." One reviewer likened Marvin's lines to his playing Mercutio to Marlon's Romeo. Those lines were all the love expressed between the two rivals, who hated each other as much off screen as on screen.

Off-screen exchanges between Marvin and Marlon were kept to a minimum. Marvin chided Marlon, claiming that he was going to change his name to Marlow Brandy. Marlon replied, "I'm going to change my name too. My new moniker will be Lee Moron."

Mary, reportedly, later tempered her enthusiasm, claiming that "Marlon was a little too plump to play Johnny. At twenty-nine he was also too old. The role called for an eighteen-year-old."

"Marlon was deeply depressed at the way the movie was going," Gilman said. "He ordered me to bring him more and more food. His ass broadened toward the end of the shoot."

Lee Marvin

A rough-riding cyclist himself, Marvin was all too aware of the homosexual element among the bikers cast in the film. He called the gay bikers "pussies." Not only that, but Marvin mocked the "sensitivity" that Marlon displayed as an actor. "When Marlon wasn't on the set, Marvin imitated him, employing a girlish lisp and placing his hands on his hips and prancing around like a fairy," Gilman said. "Personally, I found Marvin disgusting and reported to Marlon the shit going on."

At the end of the shoot, one reporter asked Lee Marvin what it had been like working with Marlon. "He's the biggest piece of shit on a stick in Hollywood, where the competition is keen for that title."

When asked about Marvin, Marlon responded, "An asshole! A sadist both on and off the screen. As an actor, about all he can do is toss a cup of scalding coffee into poor Gloria Graham's face." Marlon was referring to the 1953 *The Big Heat*, which contained just such a scene which has now entered the pantheon of all-time screen portrayals of a sadist.

Marlon himself admitted that *The Wild One* was a failure, and many years after the film was released claimed that it "doesn't hold up well today," although it inspired an array of biker pictures, including *Easy Rider*. Audiences today often laugh at certain sequences in the film.

Marlon said that the original script was one of social significance, but that the message of the film had been impossibly diluted. "It had been our intent to make a film that showed why young people tend to bunch into gangs, including motorcycle gangs, to express themselves in violent acts."

But upon viewing the finished product, Marlon felt that, "If anything, the film made motorcycle gangs fun." He told Kramer that *The Wild One* was the "biggest disappointment of my career."

"Don't worry about that," Kramer said. "If you stay in pictures, you'll have far bigger disappointments." Incidentally, Harry Cohn has delivered a one-line review after seeing our film. 'I hate it!'"

Marlon claimed that "the only good thing to come out of the film was its help in releasing some of my inner violence. Before *The Wild One*, I thought of going home and killing my father. After *The Wild One*, I decided that I shouldn't actually kill him, but pull out his corneas."

Marlon vowed never to work with Kramer again, even when the producer called him and offered him the starring role in *The Defiant Ones* in 1958, opposite Sidney Poitier. Marlon slammed down the phone on Kramer.

The Wild One was widely denounced for promoting "anti-social behavior

A scene from *The Wild One* with Marlon and Mary Murphy

among the young." It did become a cult film among teenagers, many of whom dressed as Marlon did in the film, in leather jackets and blue jeans. No one did that more than James Dean, who suddenly appeared on his own motorcycle, dressing and talking exactly as Marlon did in *The Wild One*.

One fan who saw the movie claimed that Marlon's "sideburns, overt sexuality, and grooving to the jukebox invented Elvis Presley."

British censors were so horrified at the violence depicted in the movie that they refused to allow it to be shown in their country. It languished in vaults until 1968, when it was released throughout the British Isles with an X rating.

Fleeing Hollywood, Marlon returned to New York. With him, he carried a book on the life of Gauguin. He told friends like Wally Cox and Edith Van Cleve that he wanted to retire and go to an island in the South Pacific.

"I'm going to make one more picture, then spend the rest of my life like a lazy lizard in the sun, eating, sleeping, and reproducing the race. Before my noble tool relaxes for the final time, I plan to father at least twenty-eight dark-skinned island children with at least that many women."

Thinking he was joking, the reporter did not record Marlon's comment.

However, there was a grain of truth in what Marlon was saying.

* * *

In the spring of 1953, mainly as a means of providing jobs for out-of-work friends, Marlon astonished his agent, Edith Van Cleve, by suggesting that he was available for the straw-hatted summer theater circuit. He agreed to appear in George Bernard Shaw's *Arms and the Man*.

When the deal was set, he called all of his friends, including Carlo Fiore. "Listen, playboy," Marlon told him. "How'd you like to come on the road with me and get your ass off the streets this summer?" Fiore agreed, providing he could find a connection to keep him supplied with drugs.

Marlon told Fiore that he wasn't serious about the play but just wanted "to fuck around and have some fun." He rounded up the rest of his gang, including Marie and Philip Rhodes, Janice Mars, Valerie Judd, and Sam Gilman.

During the previous month, Marlon had been seeing a handsome young actor, William Redfield, who had become an almost constant companion. Marlon was hanging out more with this Manhattan-born stage actor than he

412

was with Wally Cox. Marlon chose the lesser role of Sergius, the aristocratic Bulgarian major with Bryonic pretensions. The more important role, that of the pragmatic, anti-romantic Bluntschli, he graciously conceded to Redfield. Among Marlon's friends, Redfield was the only one lucratively employed at the time. But he gave up a profitable job on TV to follow Marlon to New England.

As one of the original members of Actors Studio, Redfield had befriended Marlon. "Befriended isn't really the word," Fiore said. "I think he worshipped him. That summer the two men got to know each other on intimate terms."

"I'd known Redfield for several months before finding out he had a gay streak in him," Fiore said. "Of course, I think most actors have a gay streak in them, even the straight ones. One night on the road I walked into Marlon's bedroom and found them going at it. Redfield was on top. Seeing me, Marlon shouted, 'Get the fuck out of my room. Can't you see I'm busy?' Redfield was so intent on riding it to the finish line that he didn't even seem to notice my intrusion."

"Redfield and Marlon were virtually inseparable that summer," Fiore said, "although both of them got some female ass on the side. But always together. They even fucked chicks together like Marlon and I had done in that long ago summer. Redfield followed Marlon around like he was a lovesick puppy. I think he really fell in love with Marlon. I warned him to keep the relationship physical—not emotional—but the fool wouldn't listen to me. Like a bitchy queen, he accused me of wanting Marlon for myself. He claimed I was jealous. I was jealous of their friendship, as I wanted to spend time with Marlon, but only as a friend, not as a fuck buddy. Redfield didn't believe me. Since he wanted to fuck Marlon, he just assumed that I did too."

(Top left to bottom right) William Redfield, Herbert Ratner, Janice Mars, Lydia Westman, Carlo Fiore, Ann Kimball, Marlon, Sam Gilman, and Phil Rhodes

A lot of biographers have reported a romance between Marlon and Janice Mars, a cabaret entertainer and a friend of both Tennessee Williams and William Inge. "I don't call going to bed a few times with someone a serious romance," Mars later recalled. "As I remembered it, Redfield and Marlon were cutting a swath through all the waitresses and apprentices along the route.

There was plenty of heterosexual activity going on beside the male bonding between Redfield and Marlon. I didn't learn about their own affair until after the run of the play. Fiore spilled the beans. I wasn't surprised. In the theater, you're used to such things."

When not "fucking around," as Fiore put it, Marlon spent a lot of time with his new friend, Sam Gilman. They had met on the set of *The Wild One* with Gilman in a bit role. "The friendship lasted longer than mine with Marlon," Fiore claimed.

As co-stars, Marlon and Redfield began their romance during the run of the play in early July of 1953 at the Theater-by-the-Sea in Matunuck, Rhode Island, before going on to Falmouth on Cape Cod and Ivorytown in Connecticut, winding up in Framingham, Massachusetts. Redfield claimed, on most nights, that Marlon just walked through the part. When Redfield challenged Marlon about this, he said, "Man, you don't get it. It's just summer stock."

He impressed a sixteen-year-old teenager, Tammy Grimes, who was to become a star in her own right. Janice Mars felt that Marlon wanted to have an affair with this under-aged actress, but that speculation cannot be confirmed. In spite of Marlon's bad acting, Tammy was very supportive of him. She found Marlon "mesmerizing onstage, even when he was improvising hilarious monologues of double talk."

Professional reviewers were not so kind. One critic in Connecticut wrote that "In *Arms and the Man*, Marlon Brando is making a fool of himself."

Janice Mars remembered only the good times. She recalled Redfield and Marlon taking lot of nude swims together. "All that was missing in those chilly New England waters was Katharine Hepburn."

"Marlon seemed adrift that summer," Gilman recalled. "He was thinking of going to Europe, maybe Mexico. He often spoke of going to a place in Mexico where beautiful girls put fireflies in their hair at night to illuminate their beauty in the moonlight."

"He told me that one of his joys of traveling the New England circuit was to piss in some of the same places where George Washington whipped it out."

At the close of the show in early August of 1953, Marlon had become so passionate in his relationship with Redfield that he invited him to sail to France with him aboard the Liberté. The trip would last two months.

Movita was left to fend for herself in Marlon's apartment. As the two men sailed away, Movita stood on the docks, waving good-bye and suppressing her tears. It is not known if she was realized that Redfield was having an affair with her future husband.

In Paris Marlon renewed his affairs with Daniel Gélin and Christian Marquand. On many a night on the continent, Redfield was left alone to amuse

William Redfield stares as Marlon waits for his flight

himself until Marlon and he headed to the south of France "and the fleshpots of the Riviera."

Seven years later, in 1961, as Redfield sat in the townhouse of Tallulah Bankhead, he provided only a brief sketch of his involvement with Marlon. Like Marlon did years before him, Redfield was appearing in a play starring Tallulah: in Redfield's case, the ill-fated *Midgie Purvis.*

Marlon, Redfield claimed, had been very grateful to him for helping to create the *Mr. Peepers* television sitcom that had brought fame to Wally Cox.

That evening in 1961, Redfield spoke of his own career and his hopes and dreams when he'd started out on Broadway at the age of nine, making his debut in *Swing Your Lady.* Two weeks after that drunken night at Tallulah's, far from her listening ears, Redfield confided, "Marlon and I have many things in common, mainly that both of us appeared in plays with Tallulah Bankhead and survived. No small accomplishment."

At that time, he spoke with great affection for Marlon, and felt that "our friendship will last to the grave. We're bonded at the hip.

But in reality, the friendship wouldn't last as long as Redfield prophesied.

* * *

Even though Marlon dumped Redfield as his lover after their two-month sojourn on the continent, the friendship endured, although they would go for months without seeing each other.

In 1965, Marlon persuaded director Bernhard Wicki to hire Redfield for a role in *The Saboteur: Code Named Morituri,* to be shot on Catalina Island, off the coast of Southern California. Marlon was slated to co-star with the British actor, Trevor Howard. Marlon even secured a role for Wally Cox as an alcoholic doctor.

Although not normally a heavy drinker, Marlon took to "heavy boozing during the shoot," said Sam Gilman, who'd also obtained a job as "dialogue coach" on the film because of Marlon's influence. "Marlon shared a two-bedroom villa with both Wally Cox and Redfield. One night he'd share Wally's bed. On another night he'd sleep with Redfield. Personally, I think Wally was his favorite."

Gilman claimed that in addition to this male-on-male activity, "there was

Yul Brynner

a steady flow of anonymous pussies parading in and out of Marlon's villa or dressing room. I don't know how he managed to service everybody. I asked him if he'd let me take on some of them. At least his discards. He said he'd throw me some action."

Wally frequently appeared on the set drunk, but Marlon was very tolerant. He told Sam Gilman that "my old buddy is in a bad marriage. He's troubled."

Other than Trevor Howard, Marlon's other co-star was Yul Brynner, filmdom's first bald star, born in Russia of Swiss-Mongolian extraction. This former trapeze artist and café guitarist fascinated Marlon.

Both men were notorious bisexuals who had seduced many of the same partners. Both had had affairs with Jean Cocteau, with whom they'd smoked opium. But mainly they'd seduced the same women: Tallulah Bankhead, Anne Baxter, Ingrid Bergman, Joan Crawford, Marlene Dietrich, Marilyn Monroe, and even Nancy Davis, so they had a lot to talk about.

Marlon was clearly bored during the making of the film, and he devised a way to shock the crew. One afternoon between takes, he put on a record and danced with Brynner. "It was a real bumping of the crotches," Gilman said. "At the end of the dance, Marlon kissed Brynner long and hard on the lips. For Marlon, that was not an unusual occurrence."

"What started out as a joke just to shock the bored cast turned into something a little more serious," Redfield claimed. "To relieve their mutual boredom, Marlon and Yul started spending long hours together in his dressing room. I just assumed they were having an affair. What else?"

Also appearing in the film was a pretty, demure-looking actress, Janet Margolin of New York. She was cast as a Jewish refugee. She had gained fame in the film, *David and Lisa*, released in 1962.

"Marlon taunted me throughout the film," she said. "He was very cruel. He frequently attacked my acting and undermined what little self-confidence I had. He told the director that I was completely miscast and was ruining the entire film on which everybody else was working so hard. Time and time again his attacks drove me from the set in tears.

Yul Brynner, Janet Margolin, Wally Cox, and Brando

416

His quicksilver nature practically pushed me to the point of suicide at one time. It was a dreadful experience working with him. Don't add me to his list of conquests. When the picture bombed, I even called him in New York to shoulder all the blame myself. The son of a bitch pretended he didn't even know who I was."

Marlon's temper continued to be frayed throughout the shooting. At one point he physically assaulted the director, Bernhard Wicki, an act of violence rare for Marlon.

Morituri died a painful death at the box office, opening and closing in two weeks in August of 1965. Critic Pauline Kael suggested that a great actor—meaning Brando—had become fortune's fool.

Marlon in *The Saboteur: Code Name Morituri*

"Marlon Brando, a once-promising actor, has begun a downward drift," wrote James Roberts. "In a few years, I predict the question will soon be, Marlon who?"

Critic Kenneth Tynan, Marlon's sometimes lover, was delighted by the film. "Brando shows his true quality for the first time in a decade, with a perfect German accent, a silky smile, a flair for deadpan ironic comedy, and miraculous timing that explains every pause and hesitation as exhaustively as a footnote. Outside the masterworks, one seldom encounters screen acting as subtle as this."

Upon seeing the movie, Elia Kazan claimed, "Marlon seems hell-bent on destroying what could

Kenneth Tynan

have been a career as the greatest male movie star of the 20th century!"

* * *

After *The Saboteur: Code Named Morituri* was released in 1965, Redfield wrote a famous book on acting, *Letters from an Actor*, eventually published in 1966. The *New York Times* ran an excerpt of the book. In it, Redfield claimed that Marlon had "dishonored himself" by appearing in so many trashy movies. The actor built a case that Marlon should give up films and return to the stage, where, as Redfield generously suggested, "he could be our finest Hamlet."

Although it was not a vicious critique of Marlon, Redfield's *New York*

Times article produced an avalanche of protests from Marlon fans who defended their star. One reader asked, "If Marlon Brando has William Redfield for a friend, he need look no further for an Iago."

An infuriated Marlon told Fiore, "Billy has betrayed me. The Brutus to my Caesar. I can't believe that I ever trusted him."

Even though he'd never speak to Redfield again, Marlon did delight in the success Redfield eventually had while co-starring with Marlon's own friend, Jack Nicholson. The two actors appeared together in the Oscar-winning *One Flew Over the Cuckoo's Nest*, released in 1976.

When Redfield died of leukemia the following year, Marlon uttered the following pronouncement: "Even though I banished him as a friend, his death causes me great pain," Marlon said. "Like so many other friends in life, he tried to cash in on his association with me, and that is wrong. He should have stood on his own accomplishments, and be judged as a man that way. Regrettably for him, his epitaph and his only claim to fame will be one achievement: FRIEND OF MARLON BRANDO. Those words should go on his tombstone."

* * *

Flashback to 1953: Upon his return to New York with Redfield from France, Marlon rested in his apartment. Movita, although threatening daily to leave and go back to Mexico, was still there. Jay Kanter continued to send scripts to Marlon, often with firm offers, but he just wasn't interested and sometimes wouldn't even bother to read them.

Then a call came in from Elia Kazan. He wanted Marlon to star as Terry Malone in a drama about organized crime in New York's dockyards. "I'm not doing any crime pictures this year," Marlon told his former director. In spite of all his pleadings, Marlon flatly rejected the role.

A month later Kazan contacted Marlon again. "Frank Sinatra is calling me daily to cast him as Terry Malone. I'm going to be forced to sign him on unless you agree to come aboard."

"Baby Frankie wants to play the role?" Marlon asked as if he hadn't heard right.

"He's got his heart set on it," Kazan said.

"I'll do it!" Marlon practically shouted. "I'm your Terry Malone."

"You'll do it?" Kazan couldn't believe his ears. "I'll send the script over right away."

"Fuck the script!" Marlon said. "Just send the contract, and I'll sign it. You can tell me what to say on the first day of shooting, and I'll do it."

Chapter Twelve

From his apartment in New York, Marlon toyed with scripts sent to him by Jay Kanter in Hollywood. One film, to be called *Stazione Termini*, would have him playing opposite Ingrid Bergman. David O. Selznick acquired that property for his wife, Jennifer Jones, changing the title to *Indiscretion of an American Wife*, casting Montgomery Clift opposite her.

Jack Warner finally overcame his long-held objections to Marlon and offered him the lead in a pirate movie, *Black Ivory*. His co-star would be Vivien Leigh. "Scarlett O'Hara alias Blanche DuBois and Stanley Kowalski playing Caribbean pirates," Marlon told Jay Kanter. "And Hollywood thinks *I'm* crazy!" Fortunately, the film was never made.

Before producer Sam Spiegel and a reluctant Elia Kazan agreed to cast Marlon in *On the Waterfront*, other actors were considered.

Unknown to all but a few movie trivia experts, Kazan arranged a screen test with the handsome, blue-eyed Paul Newman, whom Marlon used to call "another one of my clones." Newman had made a hit on stage in *Picnic* and was successful in his test. Delighted with the results, Kazan offered him the role of Terry Malloy, but had to back out when both Frank Sinatra and Marlon wanted the part.

Actually, it was Spiegel who went after Marlon and finally got him to accept the role of Terry Malloy. From the beginning, Kazan had wanted Sinatra, who had just scored such a major comeback in *From Here to Eternity* with Burt Lancaster and Montgomery Clift. One Sinatra biographer wrote that the singer turned down the project. "Bullshit!" Budd Schulberg later recalled. "Frankie would have given his left nut to play Terry Malloy."

As proof that Sinatra really wanted the role, he unsuccessfully sued Sam Spiegel for half-a-million dollars for breach of contract when he learned that Marlon had been signed to play the part.

Still holding out for Sinatra, Kazan and Spiegel almost came to blows over casting. Kazan said, "I don't want that son of a bitch in my film, and he's not right for the part anyway." Kazan had been deeply offended at Marlon's remarks that he'd never work with him again "for turning canary and exposing all his Commie friends."

Although Kazan still wanted Sinatra, he later admitted that "I had to eat shit" and, despite his objections, offer the role to Marlon when Spiegel insisted that "I can get my investors to double the bankroll with Brando instead of Sinatra."

"Privately, I felt that Frankie, even though a bit scrawny, could have portrayed a more credible boxer than the easy-going Marlon," Kazan later admitted.

To add insult to injury, Sinatra—almost as a consolation prize—was offered the role of the priest, later played by Karl Malden. Sinatra rejected the role in fury, telling Kazan

Frank Sinatra

that "your darling little mumbler is the most overrated actor in the world."

Even though Marlon accepted Spiegel's offer, he showed contempt for the role from the very beginning. "I'm just doing it for the money," he told the press. Actually he did need the money, a total of $125,000—"cash up front." Marlon Sr. had been consistently mismanaging the cattle ranch in Nebraska and had been running up huge debts in his son's name.

Both Kazan and the film's scriptwriter Budd Schulberg were working for percentages of the gross. Jay Kanter urged him to accept such a deal as well, but Marlon flatly rejected it. When *On the Waterfront* went on to make millions, Kanter stated that "Marlon really screwed himself—what a mistake! He should have listened to me."

As part of his deal with Spiegel, Marlon insisted that "my new best friend," Sam Gilman, be hired as his dialogue coach. Fiore signed on as Marlon's stand-in, although warning Marlon that he was still hooked on heroin.

Eventually, Marlon agreed to work with Elia Kazan "for one more time", although he was still disappointed that his former director had "squealed" to the House Committee on Un-American Activities, identifying as Communist sympathizers individuals who had once been his friends.

"I'm getting tired of calling Kazan a canary," Marlon told Fiore. "Got another word?"

"Why not rat? Stoolie. Cheese-eater."

Ironically, all of these epithets for an informer were used in the script to describe the character that Marlon was playing in the film, Terry Malloy.

420

Because of a schedule conflict, Marlon turned down a star turn in *Mister Roberts*, the part going to Henry Fonda, Dodie's former lover. This was no great loss for Marlon, since he wasn't the right actor for the part anyway.

In 1949 Kazan had read a series of Pulitzer Prize-winning articles by Malcolm Johnson in *The New York Sun* documenting corruption among the unionized dockworkers in New Jersey and New York. Soonafter, he decided to transform these stories into a screenplay. In a collaborative effort with Arthur Miller, he had already worked on similar material, naming their rough draft *The Hook*, which was never purchased by any studio.

Inspired by *The New York Sun's* treatment of the Malcolm Johnson exposé, Kazan turned once again to Arthur Miller for help. This was somewhat amazing in that Kazan had named Miller as a Communist before the House on Un-American Activities. Angrily, Miller rejected Kazan's peace offering, calling him a "stool pigeon." Another of the names exposed by Kazan was Marlon's old rival, John Garfield.

Critics have suggested that Kazan used the film as an "affirmation of the nobility of turning informant," thereby justifying his own controversial stance of "ratting on his left-wing friends."

One day Kazan discovered that Budd Schulberg had been inspired by the same series of news articles crafted by Malcolm Johnson. On learning of this, Kazan drove down to Schulberg's farm in Pennsylvania and before two o'clock the following morning had agreed to a collaboration on the project, fully aware that many studios would consider the material too drab for the screen. There was also fear of union violence when shooting began. Kazan anticipated that there would be attempts to disrupt filming.

Like Kazan himself, Schulberg had also "named names" before HUAC. "Those two squealed like pigs on castration day," Marlon said.

Lee J. Cobb was cast as Johnny Friendly, the mob boss of the waterfront. The name was apt for Cobb, who had also been a "friendly" witness before HUAC.

Cobb had exposed the left-wing involvement of such actors as Sam Jaffe and Lloyd Bridges. On learning this, Marlon suggested that the film be retitled *The Three Collaborators*.

After completing the script, Kazan and Schulberg had shopped it to all the major studios, finding nothing but rejections.

In rejecting *On the Waterfront*, Zanuck told Kazan and Schulberg, "People today want to see

Carlo Fiore and Brando clowning around on a tractor

films about the rich and glamorous, not some grainy black-and-white flicker about sweaty longshoremen. Besides, it's too depressing for CinemaScope."

"But what about those Okies in *Grapes*?" Kazan asked, referring to the 1940 Henry Fonda movie, *Grapes of Wrath*.

"That was long ago and this is now when movies are facing a triple threat from television." But when *On the Waterfront* walked away with all those Oscars, Zanuck later admitted, "I made a mistake. Bigtime."

Finally, the independent producer, Sam Spiegel (calling himself S.P. Eagle), green-lighted the project "but only in black and white and only for a low budget."

Spiegel was fresh from his success with *The African Queen*. He was telling anyone in Hollywood willing to listen, "I personally saved the careers of two potential has-beens, Bogie and Hepburn. Their careers were nose-diving until Sammy boy came along."

Harry Cohn at Columbia finally agreed to distribute the film, after having already rejected it twice. Cohn claimed, "I still hate the script but I'd cast Brando reading the phone book. I can make big bucks on Mumbles."

Fiore claimed that before filming began, Marlon haunted the stevedore bars along the New York and New Jersey docklands. "Sometimes I'd go with him to these joints," Fiore said.

"At other times he wanted to make the nightly rounds by himself. I know that he picked up some of these burly boys for rolls in the hay, just as he'd seduced the bikers before making *The Wild One*. Marlon once told me that he got closer to understanding the character of Terry Malloy by actually fucking with these stevedores. 'You don't get to know them by hanging out with them swilling down beer as they brag about how many bitches they fucked last week. You only get to know them when they take off their clothes and are alone with you in bed. That's where they really reveal themselves. They're so vulnerable then. They'll let you get inside their heads and inside something else to boot.'"

Evoking an incident that happened to him while researching bikers' bars for *The Wild One*, Marlon with his *faux* Bronx accent was caught up in a narcotics raid one night at a waterfront dive in Hoboken. Marlon later told Fiore, "I was just doing some people-watching when all these cops burst into the joint. I was forced into a line-up against the wall. I had to strip off my shirt while a copper searched me for those tell-tale puncture marks of a heroin addict. This time I passed the test and kept my mouth shut so I wouldn't be thrown into the Tombs for the night."

After the casting of the male actors, Kazan set about to find a suitable female lead to play opposite Marlon.

Joanne Woodward was a strong contender for the female lead. But she lost the part the day Marlon showed up for Eva Marie Saint's audition with Kazan. "Marlon asked me to dance and then took me in his arms and we twirled around the floor. There was so much at stake for me, and it was so emotionally powerful, I burst into tears."

"At the end of the dance, Marlon kissed me and went over to Kazan who was standing nearby intently watching us," Eva Marie said. "We've found our gal," Marlon told Kazan.

Eva Marie Saint had made a name for herself on the stage and in TV drama. Marlon had seen her in Horton Foote's *A Trip to Bountiful*, and was impressed with her cool detachment and acting skills.

Elizabeth Montgomery had also been a "heavy contender" for the part, but Kazan finally went with Eva Marie for the role of Edie Doyle because he felt that Montgomery came off too much "of a finishing school dame" to play a woman reared on the waterfront in Hoboken.

With Marlon's cooperation, Kazan decided to make Eva Marie a supporting actress instead of a lead actress. His ploy was that she would stand a better chance of winning an Oscar as supporting actress than as a lead player. At Oscar time, Kazan's ploy worked, and Eva Marie walked off with an Oscar.

Marlon had only one major objection to the casting of Eva Marie in the role. When he chided Kazan, Marlon may have been joking. "I hear our star is involved with someone—I mean, really involved—and there goes my chance to fuck her unless I can figure out a way."

Marlon was referring to Eva Marie's husband, Jeffrey Hayden, the television director. Once he met Marlon on the set, they became "instant friends." Hayden told Kazan that it was "harmless" for Marlon to have lunch every day with his wife. "He's just building up her confidence," Hayden said to Kazan, who wasn't so sure about that.

Kazan once noted that Eva Marie's marriage to Hayden "lasted longer than most people's lives."

Kazan later denied rumors that Marlon and Eva Marie had an affair during the making of the film. She

Brando and Eva Marie Saint
in *On the Waterfront*

had only fond memories of working with Marlon. "He had a wonderful sense of humor," she said. "It was cold and I wore red flannel long-johns. When it got bitter, I'd pull up my skirt and do a can-can for him. He always loved that. When it got really cold, he'd look at me and say, 'I think it's time for the can-can.'"

The only trouble between Eva Marie and Marlon came one day when he didn't like the way she was emoting with him in a scene. It called for viciousness on her part, which she wasn't delivering. He began to taunt her, to criticize her acting, her appearance, and her delivery of lines. As the camera rolled, he had her in a frenzy and in tears. She later recalled, "I came at him screaming, kicking, and clawing; I really wanted to kill him. It was only after the scene was shot and he broke up laughing that I knew he'd tricked me into delivering a performance I might not otherwise have been able to pull off."

On a cold, windy day in Hoboken, with a wind chill factor of below zero, shooting began on *On the Waterfront*. Members of the mob, acting as spies for their gang bosses, observed the proceedings carefully. Kazan used a quasi-documentary style of direction. Boris Kaufman came up with a bleak monochrome cinematography. The net result, especially when real dockworkers were used to be stationed around Marlon, was a film of chilling realism.

Marlon later admitted to Fiore that ten minutes before he was to shoot his first scene as Terry Malloy, he didn't know how to play the character. "Should I play it as Mutt? Jeff? Perhaps Falstaff?" But when the camera was turned on him, he instantly fell into character, coming up with a believable person that would become one of the great post-war screen portrayals.

Kazan had been a former dockworker himself, and he knew the milieu well. He also knew that mob reprisals against him were a distinct possibility. He hired a bodyguard to be with him at all times. It helped that the bodyguard was the brother of the local police chief.

Marlon felt no need of any protection—in fact, he took the subway to work, dressed as a dockworker. "I wanted to feel like one of the blue collar workers."

That democratic attitude didn't extend to hanging out with the stevedores around the big bonfires they lit in steel drums to keep warm. Fiore and Marlon retreated to a warm hotel room in a local dive ridiculously called the Grand Hotel. "There," according to Fiore, "we had lots of hot coffee, mama's apple pie from room service, and we soaked in hot baths, occasionally knocking off that odd piece of ass."

Although Marlon's relationship with Eva Marie went smoothly, he frequently conflicted with Steiger, evoking his feud with Anthony Quinn on the set of *Viva Zapata!* Marlon told Kazan, "This Steiger creature likes to cry in every scene. What a cry baby! What a ham!"

A scene from *On the Waterfront* with Rod Steiger

Spiegel showed up on the set to chastise the freezing crew for not working faster on the thirty-day shoot. Wearing a vicuna coat and $125 alligator shoes, he always arrived in a limousine, with two well-stacked blondes waiting for him in the back seat to rush back to "21."

Marlon viewed Spiegel as a "dazzling con artist." It was Marlon who provided a characterization for Spiegel that would become part of his legend. "Place Spiegel in a foreign country—buck-assed naked—and in 24 hours he'd be in bespoke tailoring, living in the penthouse suite in the best hotel in town, as a chauffeured limousine pulled up with the three hottest, big tit blondes in town."

Marlon was racing against a time clock and didn't need Spiegel to tell him what time it was. In a "moment of madness," he'd signed a two-picture deal with Darryl F. Zanuck. He was soon due in Hollywood for costume fittings on *The Egyptian*, based on Mika Waltari's best-selling novel. Marlon was intrigued with the possibility of playing Sinuhe, a surgeon who treated the poor in the era of Ramses.

Both Marlon Sr. and Dodie showed up at the docks to watch some of the scenes being filmed. Marlon's relationship with his father remained as chilly as the Hoboken winter. But Marlon was warm and loving to Dodie, perhaps sensing that she was in failing health that might lead to her death. Fiore admitted that "I almost fell in love with her all over again." Chain smoking, Dodie shocked Marlon with her physical appearance, even though she'd tried to hide her deteriorating condition by using heavy makeup.

In the filming Dodie watched, Marlon plays Terry Malloy, an ex-pug, longshoreman. His ties to the mob come from his brother (Rod Steiger) who works for the boss of the docklands, Lee J. Cobb playing Johnny Friendly.

Unwittingly, Marlon lures a workmate to his death. "I just thought they were going to lean on him a little," Terry later said. The dockworker is tossed from a roof to his death.

The action brings in the crime commissioners, as played by Lief Erickson and Martin Balsam. A dedicated local priest, Karl Malden, Marlon's old friend from his *Streetcar* days, was cast as the priest, who fights corruption. He is joined by the sister of the dead man, Edie, as played by Eva Marie Saint.

Charley (Steiger) is sent by the gangland boss to persuade Marlon not to testify against the mob, which leads to their memorable taxicab scene.

Charley's failure to secure Terry's cooperation in keeping his mouth shut leads to Charley's murder. Marlon finds him dead hanging on a baling hook used by dockworkers to remove cargo.

The death of his brother, however, only increases Terry's resolve to testify before the crime commission. After his testimony, Marlon is severely beaten. But in a fake Hollywood-style ending, he is seen leading the dockworkers through the yard doors, having successfully dealt with Johnny Friendly's goons. The workers, like docile sheep, shift their alliances from Friendly to Terry when he proves to be the stronger man.

Karl Malden, bloody Brando, Eva Marie Saint and an extra on the set of *On the Waterfront*

The most famous scene in the movie takes place in the back of a fake taxi-cab between Steiger and Marlon. In that scene, Steiger attempts to persuade Terry not to testify before the crime commission. Marlon reminds his brother of the days when he'd been a boxer and had a good chance at the title bout until he'd been ordered by Friendly to throw the fight.

In the scene, Steiger threatens him with a gun. Marlon's response is, "Oh, Charley, Charley, I could have had class. *I could have been a contender*. I could have been somebody, instead of a bum, which is what I am." Terry turns accusingly toward his brother. "*It was you, Charley, it was you.*"

This is the most anthologized of all of Marlon's movie scenes, and the source of millions of Brando imitations.

Kazan later admitted that he didn't really direct this memorable scene but "let Rod and Marlon work it out in improvisation. Marlon showed *me* how the scene was to be performed."

It was ironic that Marlon walked out at four o'clock that afternoon on what was to become his most famous scene in films. In his contract, he had written that every afternoon at four o'clock he was to leave the set for sessions with his analyst, Bela Mittelmann.

Steiger was furious that Marlon had walked out on him during his big moment. For his close-up, Steiger was fed Marlon's lines by Kazan himself.

Marlon never liked his most famous scene. He always protested that Charley would never have drawn a gun on him. "Brothers don't do such things," Marlon falsely claimed. "The mob boss would have sent someone less involved to kill me." On that point, Marlon was possibly right. Behind the scenes, Fiore had goaded Marlon into challenging Kazan by telling Marlon, "The gun-pulling bit hits a bullshit note."

In his autobiography, Marlon admitted that he and Steiger changed "the one-way ticket to Palookaville" scene completely. Steiger too claimed that "Brando and I did a lot of improvising in that scene."

But despite the eyewitness testimony, including statements from Kazan, that Marlon improvised the taxi cab scene, Budd Schulberg later denied it. "Marlon did not improvise it. That is a grand myth. During the film he would improvise a word here and there, but he didn't change lines. Much later, Brando said he had improvised the cab scene. That's absolutely nonsense. The scene was intact before we sent him the script."

Steiger went through the movie "throwing shit fits," in the words of Marlon. Steiger clearly detested the real star of the picture and made that obvious. At one point he confronted Kazan, accusing him "of throwing every scene to Marlon. The way you kiss his ass is sickening. Next thing I know you'll be rimming his ass. I know what's going on in that Grand Hotel room of his."

Of all the actors in the film, only Lee J. Cobb, cast as Johnny Friendly, the mob boss of the dockworkers, overacted, his scenes veering close to caricature. "He's seen too many Edward G. Robinson movies," Marlon told Kazan. Nonetheless, Cobb, along with Karl Malden and Rod Steiger, were each nominated for best supporting actor. Of course, with three actors in the same film competing, they cancelled each other out, paving the way for a dark horse winner like Edmond O'Brien in *The Barefoot Contessa*.

In a scene with Karl Malden as the priest, Marlon spits and says, "Damn!" This marked the first time that a four-letter word had been uttered in American cinema since Rhett Butler said farewell to Scarlett O'Hara in *Gone With the Wind*.

Rod Steiger and Brando in the famous taxi cab scene

The most poignant scene in the film occurs when Eva Marie drops her glove. It wasn't in the script. It was an accident. Impulsively Marlon picks it up and puts it on his hand. As Kazan later said, "By holding onto the glove, Marlon symbolically was holding on to her. He transfers his sexual or loving feeling toward her onto the glove. He was able to express through the glove something he couldn't express to her directly, because he was held back by the knowledge that he'd been an accessory to her brother's murder."

When the film was wrapped, Kazan told Spiegel, "This time Hollywood can no longer delay granting Marlon his overdue Oscar. Marlon is a bisexual the way an artist should be: He sees things both as a man and as a woman."

Working for a fee of $15,000, Leonard Bernstein created background music to give the film a melodramatic *West Side Story* punch and lyricism. One-time lovers back in the Forties, Bernstein and Marlon shared memories of their early days in New York, but whatever passion had existed between the two men belonged to their yesterdays.

Leonard Bernstein

Amazingly, Marlon did not realize he'd created another defining role in the history of American cinema as he had done with the role of Stanley in *Streetcar*. When Kazan showed him the final cut of the film, Marlon sat through it in silence. At the end of the film, he was so depressed with his performance that he left the studio without saying another word to Kazan. He later told Fiore, "Kazan and I have made our last picture together." He meant those words.

Kazan, however, wasn't finished with his attempts to cast Marlon in films. On four different occasions in the future, he would approach him with offers—*East of Eden*, *Baby Doll*, *A Face in the Crowd*, and *The Arrangement*. In each instance, Marlon turned Kazan down, claiming, "The roles are not right for me. After you and I brought Stanley Kowalski and Terry Malloy to the world's attention, I think we've given it our best shot."

In spite of these rejections, Kazan in later years told interviewers, "Marlon's performance in *On the Waterfront* as Terry Malloy is the finest thing ever done by an American film actor."

As for his own interpretation of his role, Marlon later said, "*Streetcar* was just as effective, but then I had more part under me."

Alan Frank, in his review of *The Screen Greats*, put it accurately, "Brando was completely under the skin of his character. Malloy was a mass of impeccably integrated contradictions—tough and yet capable of moments of great tenderness and sensitivity, self-willed and far from articulate, although still succeeding in conveying deep emotion."

On the Waterfront grossed six million dollars, but was made for less than $900,000.

Kazan found only forgiveness in Hollywood once *On the Waterfront* was a success. "It was full–blown cinema art," claimed Bosley Crowther in *The New York Times*. Overnight, Marlon's salary tripled, and Kazan also could write his own ticket.   ·

Parading into Jack Warner's office in Hollywood, Kazan informed the studio chief that he wanted to film John Steinbeck's *East of Eden*, an update of the ancient Cain and Abel story. Warner immediately okayed the project. "Cast whatever actors you want in the part," Warner told him. "Anybody but Marlon Brando. I can't stand the shit on a stick."

"But Marlon's the one I want," Kazan said.

"Okay, okay, offer the fucker the role, but get out of my office. I'm gonna cry!"

Having made six good movies in a row, Marlon had now stretched the bounds of credibility. Even though Kazan had called him "the only genius I've ever met in the field of acting," Marlon upon his return to Hollywood was about to show the world that even geniuses have their bad hair pictures.

* * *

Wandering the streets alone at night, Marlon sometimes called on the actress Barbara Baxley long after midnight. She was appearing on Broadway at the time in *Camino Real* by Tennessee Williams.

"Marlon felt great despair," she said. "One night he collapsed sobbing in my arms. 'I'm not good enough for the role,' he cried out. 'I'm no good! I'm making a fool of myself.' I offered him what comfort I could. The next morning he refused to leave my hotel room and go to work. Kazan sent Carlo Fiore over to get Marlon when I called Kazan to tell him what was happening. 'I'm not going to make the picture!' Marlon shouted at Fiore when his friend came into my room. Fiore virtually had to haul Marlon back to the set. I thought Marlon was experiencing a total nervous breakdown and would never make it through the filming."

Stella Adler blamed the psychiatrist, Bela Mittelmann, for reducing Marlon "to a jelly-like state emotionally." She said that on one cold night he arrived at her apartment building and stood in the hallway bellowing "Stella! Stella!" until she came to the door to let him in.

Barbara Baxley

Movita lived in Marlon's apartment on 57th Street across from Carnegie Hall while he was shooting *On the Waterfront*. Sometimes he'd come home; sometimes he wouldn't. Only once did she show up on the set herself, amusing the crew with a certain ability she had to assess the size of a man's penis by fondling and examining his left hand. Movita claimed she learned "this trick from the gypsies."

"A lot of men on the crew were insulted by

her findings," Fiore said. "She had me right down to the very inch. 'What about Marlon?' I asked her. "He compares his hands to those of a syphilitic dwarf."

"Marlon and I are extremely practical in bed," she enigmatically told Fiore. "We have a very passionate sex life. I want to marry Mr. Marlon."

Thinking she could win Marlon's hand in marriage by making a better nest for him, she set about to redecorate their apartment, spending five thousand dollars of her own money. She ripped out the worn cabbage rose linoleum and hauled off the ripped couches and chairs which still smelled of raccoon urine.

Fiore had encouraged her in this interior redecoration. When Marlon found out that Fiore was behind the scheme, he confronted him, "Fuck man! Fixing up my apartment with her own God damn money is going to make it harder for me to kick her out."

In spite of her redecorating efforts and her attempts to provide a proper home for Marlon, he sent her packing to California to pursue an acting career going nowhere. Their eventual marriage loomed years into the future.

Out with Movita. In with Rita Moreno. Fiore never liked Moreno, although admitting that "she was one sensual woman." He also confessed that he "never liked Marlon's women." Kazan even speculated that there was an unfulfilled sexual attraction between Marlon and Fiore. "I doubt if those two ever hit the sack," Kazan said. "Each had too much macho pride to ever do that. But I bet they wanted to."

* * *

Although he loudly and frequently proclaimed that he hated parties, Marlon was seen at quite a few of them, especially those in Greenwich Village during the making of *On the Waterfront*. Norman Mailer threw a party and invited Marlon, who showed up with Rita Moreno. "If a woman was married, you could almost guarantee it that Marlon would make a pass at her, even with Miss Moreno looking on. My wife was no exception."

James Dean, the lover

One night at a party in Brooklyn, Marlon brought as his "date," James Dean.

"How Marlon Brando could later proclaim he didn't meet Dean until he was starring in *East of Eden* for Kazan is beyond me," said Jimmy Schauffer, an out-of-work actor at that Brooklyn party. "All of us along Broadway knew that Dean and Brando were carrying on. It was the worst-kept secret. From what I observed that night, Brando was definitely in charge of the relationship. If he wanted something, perhaps a drink, he sent Dean to get it. When Brando was ready to go, he got up and without saying a word Dean tagged along like a puppydog after its master. We'd also heard rumors that there was more than a little S&M in that relationship. Guess who the S was?"

Instead of hopelessly pursuing Eva Marie Saint during the filming of *On the Waterfront*, Marlon chased Anne Ford, a twenty-four-year-old blouse designer. He met her at a party that his new friend, Sam Gilman, threw in his honor.

Two nights later, when Marlon was alone in the Gilman apartment, he called Anne to come on over. At the time she had dinner guests and claimed that she couldn't get away. He told her that all she had to do was announce to her guests that she had "a sudden need of her ear trumpet and would have to pick it up." She found that amusing but made up some more urgent excuse for her guests and headed out of her apartment building to Sam Gilman's. Later she would remember, "We watched old movies in Sam's living room, ate hot dogs, and went to bed."

The coupling was apparently successful because Anne and Marlon were seen eating more and more hot dogs and frequently "wandering off to dreamland after all that mustard," as Fiore put it. Since Movita had left, Marlon didn't have a nagging woman at home to greet him at night.

On nights for whatever reason that he didn't want to see Anne, and was too tired to pursue a woman on his own, he called Gilman, commanding him to "get your ass out of bed and bring me a woman. I don't much care what she looks like as long as she knows how to fuck and suck!"

Fiore called Gilman "Marlon's faithful lapdog. Sam would get out of bed and go out on a gal hunt. He always turned up with something. Almost any gal in Manhattan in those days wanted to fuck Marlon Brando, so the pickings were easy for Sam."

After what Fiore called "Marlon's strange piece of ass," he'd be seen escorting Anne again. She sometimes showed up on the set of *On the Waterfront* where the dockworkers called her "Marlon's piece." She remembered searching for shiny, juicy apples on Seventh Avenue for Marlon and buying frozen chicken breasts to reheat in his oven for their dinners.

"At night we watched *Mr. Peepers* on TV starring his friend, Wally Cox, whenever he was on," Anne said. "Sometimes Marlon would strip nude and play the bongo drums for me. On other evenings, he'd introduce himself as Count Von Huesen to headwaiters, speaking with a thick German accent."

At one of the dingy movie houses on 42nd Street, he took her to see *The Wild One*. He'd never seen the picture before with a real audience. Sitting in the front row, he wore his Bad Ass cyclist's cap from *The Wild One*. Anne recalled that at several points during the screening, he covered his eyes to avoid certain scenes. "He just groaned," she recalled. "It was painful for him. He thought he was awful. 'It's so bad,' he said to me. 'I just can't watch it. How could I have done it?'"

Finally, when one scene came on showing him on a motorcycle, he whispered he couldn't take it any more. Standing up in the theater, he shouted at the audience, "Look at Marlon Brando's fat ass!" After that, he stormed out of the theater with Anne chasing behind him.

The romance ended quickly after Anne gave an interview to *Glamour* magazine. She recalled one bizarre night with him. "He came through my front door shirtless, danced the entire length of the room, made a demi-disappearance behind the opposite door and exited with a graceful Arabesque kick—without a word of greeting or a glance my way. His conversation, often over the phone, consisted of abstract flights of fancy. Once he was a crow and about to take off on his midwinter flight to Florida. 'I'd like to drop you a postcard.' he said. 'but these claws make it so difficult to hold a pen.'"

* * *

Dodie had written to Marlon that she was traveling by train to Los Angeles, where she planned to visit with her sister, Betty Lindemeyer, with whom Marlon had stayed when he first came to Hollywood to make *The Men*. He had been increasingly concerned about her health ever since she'd showed up on the set of *On the Waterfront*, suffering from hypertension as the result of her long-term alcoholism.

One night Betty called Marlon in New York to tell him that Dodie had collapsed and had been rushed to the Huntington Memorial Hospital. Leaving within hours, Marlon took an emergency flight to Los Angeles and arrived at the bedside of Dodie. The doctors told him that she was suffering from a disease of both her kidneys and liver. All of her years of hard drinking and chain smoking had caught up with her.

For three weeks in that hospital bed, Dodie slipped in and out of a coma. Marlon Sr. had also flown in to be at her death bed, as had her other children, Jocelyn and Fran.

Marlon was at her side at five o'clock on the morning of March 31, 1954 when she came out of her coma and reached for his hand. She issued a warning. "Don't fight with the big boys in Hollywood. They have the power to destroy you, and they always win. Go along with them, Bud. Take the money and run."

She drifted back into her coma but rallied about twenty minutes later. "I'm not scared," she said, "and you don't have to be." She drew her last breath which was more of a gasp. In death, he kissed her silent lips.

She had died at the age of fifty-five, three days before his thirtieth birthday.

Very calmly, Marlon went to the night nurse to report his mother's death. He also asked to borrow a pair of scissors. Back in Dodie's hospital room, he snipped a lock of her hair. For a souvenir and remembrance, he took the pillow from her head and also removed an aquamarine ring from her finger, which he would later wear himself after having the band extended.

He later told Fiore that he wandered for hours during the rest of that morning along the beaches of Santa Monica. "I felt at one with nature," he said. "I ran after some seagulls trying to join their colony, and for a brief moment I imagined that I could fly away with them. Over the rainbow, as Judy might say. I merely succeeded in frightening them. Dodie gave me life and taught me to like the wind, to listen to it, to learn from it. To appreciate the spring green pushing its way up in the Nebraska soil. To love nature. To love animals—not just Russell. She taught me that we are all creatures of this God's earth from which we'll return when it's all over, as it was for her." In front of Fiore, Marlon burst into deep sobs. Fiore took his friend in his arms and held him tightly.

Tributes from friends and acquaintances from all over the world poured in for Marlon. In New York, Stella Adler told the press that, "Dodie Brando was a very heavenly, very beautiful, very girlish, but lost soul."

The very small, very private funeral was attended only by Marlon, Marlon Sr., Fran, Jocelyn, and Betty Lindemeyer.

There is some doubt and dispute about what Marlon did after the funeral. Most of his friends say, "He just disappeared from the face of the earth," whereas others challenge that claim.

Stella denied that Marlon "fell apart—he was remarkably pulled together throughout the ordeal." Her claim was not supported by others, including Fiore. His friend said that Marlon tried to kill himself in Los Angeles by swallowing a whole bottle of sleeping capsules.

Fiore was unable to provide specific details, but his claim was that Marlon was rushed to a hospital where his stomach was pumped. In an unconfirmed report, Marlon attempted to jump out of the window on the upper floor of his hospital room. A nurse entered the room at that opportune moment and prevented his fall, screaming for orderlies to come to Marlon's rescue. Again, Fiore admitted that this information did not come from Marlon himself, who didn't want to discuss the matter with him.

What is known is that Bela Mittelmann, Marlon's psychiatrist, flew to Los Angeles to be at the side of his patient. Marlon's sister, Fran, claimed that "with the aid of Mittelmann, Bud confronted some awful truths. One, that he was in love with Dodie. Another, their relationship was incestuous." The other sister, Jocelyn, apparently never spoke out on this matter.

At one point during his psychiatric counseling with Mittelmann, Marlon became so furious at Marlon Sr. for his treatment of Dodie, that he confessed that he'd purchased a gun. According to Fiore, Marlon told Mittelmann that he planned to kill his father.

Sam Gilman related somewhat the same story. "The fact that Marlon told several friends of his that he planned to murder his father indicated to me that he was not going through with it," Gilman claimed. "He wanted to be talked out of it. I, among others, did just that, urging him to throw away the gun. I think the buying of that gun and the threat were just part of Marlon's healing ritual, following Dodie's death."

Fiore said that, "I loved Dodie too and my own grief was intense. But Marlon's grief was unlike anything I'd ever seen over the loss of a relative and even a parent. He didn't bathe. He didn't eat. It was like he wanted to die, to go and join Dodie. At times, though, he would blame her 'for my own life being so fucked up—it's because of her that I have never been able to commit to another woman.' At one point he even accused Dodie of trying to control his life from the grave. Then on another night he came up with a different story, blaming himself for the mutual failure of their lives. The most astonishing remark Marlon ever made to me came about a month after Dodie's death. It was about two o'clock in the morning. I'd been drinking heavily all night but Marlon hadn't touched one drop. He looked at me with that kind of sincerity that only Marlon seems to possess. In a voice so soft it was almost a whisper, he said to me, 'Dodie should have divorced Dad and married me. I should have been the only man in her life. Marlon Jr., not Marlon Sr., was the man for Dodie. I could have made her happy.' I made no comment on his remark. I didn't dare. Why? I think he was not talking to me but conversing with the darkest, deepest reaches of his own soul. He was carrying on a debate with himself. His dark side speaking to his more rational side. His words were not meant for human ears."

Dancer Sondra Lee, who was rumored to have been a girlfriend of Marlon's back in the Forties, said, "I continued to see Marlon over the years, and I knew him very well. I think he became more cynical after Dodie died. There was a new and razor-sharp edge to him that had never been there before. He seemed less vulnerable. In time he would develop great compassion for the Indian or the downtrodden black. But in individual relationships, I think he lived more for himself and didn't pay quite the attention to other people's feelings that he used to. That was especially true in the case of his lovers. It was a leaner, meaner Marlon that settled his dispute with Fox and reluctantly consented to make that turkey, *Desirée*."

In the weeks following Dodie's death, one reporter cornered Marlon and asked him if he felt that her excessive drinking hastened her death. Marlon turned violently on the reporter. "Don't you dare say that! My mother never touched a drop in her life."

* * *

In New York, Stella Adler threw a party for Marlon at her apartment. Even though passion's fire had been put out between them, he had remained her loyal friend and still thought of his former teacher and lover as his mentor.

At the party he was dazzled by a petite, raven-haired beauty who was only nineteen. She stood barely five feet one. Ignoring the other guests assembled in his honor, he spent the rest of the evening monopolizing Josanne Mariana-Berenger.

She had a certain toothy gamin quality that eventually led to comparisons with French actress Leslie Caron. "I didn't know Josanne very well when I invited her to my party, but she possessed a sharp Gallic wit that appealed to Marlon," Stella said.

Assuming that she knew all about him from reading movie magazines, he stood close to her, looking deeply into her eyes and asking probing questions. By nine o'clock he learned that she was working as a governess for the family of a New York psychiatrist, who ironically turned out to be a close associate of Bela Mittelmann, Marlon's own analyst. By ten o'clock he found out that her stepfather was a French fisherman who lived with her mother in a small hamlet on the French Riviera. By eleven o'clock he knew that she had been a model and that her dream was to become an actress. By midnight he'd proposed marriage to her. Telling Stella good night and thanking her for the party, he left the apartment with his arm around Josanne's trim waist.

Josanne Mariana-Berenger

If Josanne thought that the road to romance with her newly discovered Prince Charming would be a smooth ride, she was sadly mistaken. The following night—he had invited her to dinner—he showed up with another girlfriend, Betty Schoffield, a wannabee actress.

"Betty was pretty but dumb," Fiore said. "I should know. When Marlon wasn't balling her, I was taking those sloppy seconds. Marlon not only took Betty to dinner with Josanne, but over the meal devoted all his attention to Betty, ignoring Josanne. Although he'd made love to Josanne the night before, and had proposed marriage, he

435

ignored the object of his affection over dinner that night. He went home with Betty."

On the following evening, he showed up for dinner with Josanne, and he was alone. After his success on TV with his sitcom, *Mr. Peepers*, Wally Cox had moved out of the apartment he shared with Marlon across from Carnegie Hall. As a replacement there, Marlon installed Josanne.

She became a fixture in his life, even accompanying him back to Hollywood, where he faced contractual duties with Darryl F. Zanuck at Fox.

Rumors of an impending marriage were published in the press. At first reporters were dismissive, having been tricked by Marlon before. As a practical joke, he once told a reporter that he was engaged to the French actress, Denise Darcel, and that they would be married soon. When the story broke, the actress denied the report and threatened to sue the newspaper. When the angry reporter confronted Marlon, he merely shrugged off the attack. "I thought you were too smart to fall for a ridiculous story like that."

When confronted with the charge of having staged a publicity stunt with the announcement of his engagement to Josanne, Marlon responded in anger. "Why does Marlon Brando need publicity? If anything I avoid it. Besides, if it were a big publicity stunt, I would be stupid to admit it. If it's not a stunt, then our engagement speaks for itself. Write what you want. People will think what they will."

In Hollywood, Josanne rented a modest apartment, found work as a sales-clerk, and took acting lessons. She also found time to make the rounds of various studios, hoping to cash in on her publicity with Marlon. There were no offers.

Finding no legitimate work in Hollywood, Josanne, unknown to Marlon, posed for some skin magazines, using a different name. Living in a foreign

country, she was forced to earn money however she could, because Marlon offered her nothing. On a few occasions, he would go out for dinner with her, forgetting to carry any cash with him. Although he promised to pay her back, he never did.

To keep expenses down, she rented a room within her apartment to a beautiful aspirant actress, Ursula Andress, who was then unknown. This turned out to be a mistake. Marlon met the stunning actress and began dating her behind Josanne's back. He had another reason to date Ursula. She was also going out with James Dean, and Marlon, as he said to Fiore, liked "to move in on Jimmy's territory." There was a certain irony here, as Marlon was also dating Dean himself.

Josanne Mariana-Berenger and Marlon

By June of 1954, Josanne found Marlon so moody and depressing that she announced that she was returning to France to stay with her parents. Marlon claimed that he would follow her to France as soon as he "took care of some business," which, unknown to Josanne, meant resuming his affair with Rita Moreno.

Kissing Josanne good-bye, he promised, "I'll soon be there." As the weeks dragged by, he began by writing her two or three letters a week. But soon there were no letters coming in from him.

In late October he sailed on the *Île de France* to Paris, where he would resume his friendship with Roger Vadim and re-launch his affairs with "my old faithfuls," Christian Marquand and Daniel Gélin.

In Paris, he stayed with Hervé Mille, of *Paris-Match*, his longtime friend. To Marlon's surprise, he found that Hervé had entertained a famous house guest, the handsome young senator from Massachusetts, John F. Kennedy. Although registered at a deluxe Paris hotel, Kennedy was actually staying with Hervé. "What's going on here?" Marlon demanded to know.

"I'm saving the exclusive for *Paris-Match*," Hervé said. He was only joking. He had no intention of exposing Kennedy's private life in his publication or in any other.

It came as a total surprise when Marlon sent Josanne a telegram. She didn't even know that he was in Paris. He asked her to join him. Racing to Paris on the train, she resumed her affair with Marlon. He told her that the engagement was still on, and that he wanted to go to Bandol to meet her parents who lived over Henri's Bar. Bandol is a fishing village west of the naval port of Toulon along the French Riviera.

A few days later Marlon was seen roaring into Josanne's hometown on a motorcycle. By October 29, a newspaper in nearby Toulon reported that, "Madame and Monsieur Paul Berenger of Bandol are happy to announce the engagement of their daughter to the American film star, Monsieur Marlon Brando."

After that announcement, seemingly "half the press of the world" descended on the little fishing village of Bandol. In Paul Berenger's fishing boat, Marlon escaped with Josanne to a little island off the coast where the two of them went into seclusion in a rented fisherman's cottage.

Reporters soon tracked them down, and Marlon and Josanne were forced to flee back to the mainland. At one point, in an almost unprecedented move, Marlon held a press conference, begging the reporters to leave him alone and to stop hounding Josanne. He explained that he was in Bandol to get to know his future in-laws. "I also want to live for a while under this beautiful blue sky where my fiancée grew up." He refused, however, to announce a date for their wedding.

After the press conference, Marlon was besieged with doubts about a possible marriage. Weeks later he would tell Fiore that he suspected that he'd been tricked into a marriage proposal. "Those doubts didn't go away," Fiore said. "If anything, they only intensified when the shit hit the fan in Paris."

The French press had been digging into Josanne's past life, even though she was only a teenager. It was learned that at the age of seventeen she'd posed nude for the Polish artist, Moïse Kisling. Buying the pictures from Kisling, a Paris department store devoted a window to the nudes, causing a near riot among shoppers. The charms of Marlon's bride-to-be were displayed for all the world to see.

The manager of the store announced to the press that Marlon had called and offered to buy Kisling's nudes "at any price," but the offer was refused. "The pictures remain in the window," the manager said. "No fire sale could attract the attention my store is getting."

Even though Marlon was dismayed at the nudes, he continued his romance with Josanne. He especially liked to pig out on Madame Berenger's bouillabaisse—in fact, he developed a lifelong addiction to this dish. Josanne's mother prepared the soup daily from fish caught by her husband.

In boat-necked, striped jerseys that matched, Josanne and Marlon were photographed on the Riviera shopping for fresh fruit at vendors down by the waterfront or else going for bike rides. One night they dressed up and showed up at the grand casino in Monte Carlo where Marlon gambled away five thousand dollars.

There was a growing perception in the press, which was very critical of Josanne, that she was no more "than a gold-digging French hussy."

"Back in Hollywood, I didn't know what was going on," Sam Gilman said. "Later when Marlon and I hooked up again, I learned that during his engagement to Josanne he'd had at least twenty affairs with various genders. Although he professed to be 'head over heels' in love' with this French gal, I had my doubts. My fear was that she was just using Marlon to carve out a career for herself in films, although she didn't seem to be doing a good job of that."

At first it appeared that Josanne was unaware of Marlon's bisexuality. However, when Tennessee Williams arrived in Paris and invited the two of them for dinner, he learned that someone had filled her in. The playwright was en route to Rome. Tennessee

Brando and Josanne
Mariana-Berenger

438

reported that over dinner Josanne accused Marlon of having an affair with Christian Marquand and stormed out of the restaurant. "Like Frankie and myself [a reference to his lover, Frank Merlo], Josanne and Marlon fought a lot."

For some unexplained reason, Marlon sent Josanne to Paris while he remained on the Riviera. He promised to join her there soon. In Paris, Josanne lost some of her shyness. As Marlon, with a hint of disappointment in his voice, later told Fiore, "She was only too willing to pose for pictures. Too willing to grant an interview. She seems to want to promote her own career as an actress." In Paris, Josanne announced that she planned to marry Marlon that coming June.

When cornered by a reporter on the Riviera, Marlon refused to confirm the June date. He was vague, claiming "maybe we'll be married in a year. The wedding might take place in New York. Then again it might be in Bandol. Everything depends on whether Monsieur and Madame Berenger want to travel to the United States. We'll work it out. Why don't you back off and give us time to sort things out for ourselves?"

Fiore later claimed that Marlon "got to know a few olive-skinned Provençal boys" while Josanne went alone to Paris. "From what he later told me, he was particularly captivated by a seventeen-year-old son of a fisherman in Bandol. From what I heard, the kid was a stunning beauty with that incredibly dark hair that Marlon always liked on either a man or a woman."

In spite of sleeping nightly with this boy, Marlon told another reporter that, "My life depends on joining Josanne in Paris."

Marlon wired Josanne in Paris to sail back to New York without him. He claimed urgent business in Rome where he had received a number of film offers. Hopping aboard the Nice-Rome express, Marlon sped south.

* * *

Somewhere between the French border and Rome, Marlon picked up a beautiful blonde. She was Italian but from the Tyrolean part of Italy. Perhaps she was really of Austrian stock. Nothing is known about her. By the time he checked into the Excelsior Hotel, he was alone. But not for long.

Tennessee Williams had already arrived in Rome to meet with Luchino Visconti. The playwright was in the midst of writing some dialogue for the film, *Senso*, in which Visconti wanted Marlon to star opposite Ingrid Bergman. Marlon was particularly interested in the film, set in Venice in 1866, because Christian Marquand had also signed to play a supporting role. Marlon met with Visconti in the presence of Tennessee, and Marlon expressed great interest in the project. But unable to raise the financing required for a

Brando/Bergman vehicle, the director settled—at far lesser salaries—for two other stars, Farley Granger and Alida Valli.

Tennessee later claimed that Marlon showing up in Rome when he did solved a major problem in my life. "At the time, I was seeing a very beautiful young man, Guido Arnella. A stunning creature, a sort of Italian version of the French star in the years to come, Alain Delon. My romance with Guido was suddenly interrupted when Frank Merlo called to tell me that he was arriving in Rome. I had to get rid of Guido and fast. At the meeting I had between Marlon and Visconti, I took Guido along with me. When Guido and Marlon met, it was love at first sight. Marlon thought he was taking Guido away from me, but it was time for him to go. Marlon didn't know this, but he got me out of a tight spot, as Frankie's plane was about to land in Rome."

Almost overnight, Guido was installed in Marlon's suite at the Excelsior. Tennessee also reported that Marlon, Frankie, Guido, and he had dinner together. Frank was unaware of how the group's romantic liaisons had so recently shifted.

Tennessee also claimed that even at this early date he had communicated with Marlon about a play he was working on. It eventually was to be called *Cat on a Hot Tin Roof*, and would open on Broadway in 1955, starring Ben Gazzara, the gritty Italian actor born in New York City.

"I assured Marlon that *Cat* would be an even bigger role for him than Stanley," Tennessee said. "He expressed great interest but ultimately turned down the role, even when I called him to tell him that Elia Kazan was going to direct."

Encountering Elizabeth Taylor at a party in Hollywood one night, Marlon told her that he'd read that she had just signed to do the screen version of *Cat on a Hot Tin Roof*. "I never liked the fucking play," he told Taylor.

He had also learned that Paul Newman had signed to co-star with her. "Too bad you're having to play opposite Newman," Marlon told her. "Compared to me, he's a mere pipsqueak. It's sad to think you're not getting to sample the real thing."

One night back in Rome when Marlon was spotted at a trattoria by a reporter from the United States, he was pointedly asked why he didn't bring Josanne to Rome with him. He was also asked if he'd broken off the engagement. "That's spittoon rubbish! If you must know, I still love Josie."

In another part of the world, Josanne was also asked about her romance with Marlon. She told reporters, "I love Marlon and he loves me. There is nothing else to say."

While lying in bed with a nude Guido, Marlon read his mail from Jay Kanter in Hollywood. Other film offers were coming in. Marlon foolishly turned down the lead in an explosive movie, Otto Preminger's *The Man With the Golden Arm*, the coveted role going to his archenemy, Frank Sinatra.

Marlon also turned down *War and Peace*, and told director Vincente Minnelli that "there is no way I'm going to appear in *The Four Horsemen of the Apocalypse*. Didn't Valentino do that? I don't dance the tango."

While in Rome, Marlon also received offers from European producers. Director Marc Allegret wanted him to star in the French version of *Lady Chatterley's Lover* by D.H. Lawrence. Learning of Marlon's refusal, Guido contacted the director and volunteered himself as its star. Allegret turned down Marlon's lover, casting actor Erno Crisa instead.

Irene Papas

Tennessee claimed that Guido kept Marlon so busy during his Roman sojourn "that he didn't have the time to sample the local Pier Angeli types that he was so fond of doing."

Tennessee was wrong. After Marlon's death, the Greek actress, Irene Papas, admitted that she launched an affair with Marlon in Rome during this period. In fact, in an interview with *Corriere della Sera*, the Italian daily, she called Marlon "the great passion of my life."

The revelation came when a journalist approached her, hoping to get a comment from her about Marlon's death. "A comment? What can I say? That I esteemed him, but I want to add something. I loved Marlon Brando. I really cared for him. We had a love story. Let's call it a long relationship. Perhaps I'm doing wrong to speak about it now that he's not around to contradict me, but I'm confessing precisely because, as of today, he's in the absolute, far from anybody, belonging to everyone."

She claimed that neither she nor Marlon ever wanted to talk about their relationship because "we didn't want to share with anyone this love that wasn't a true secret but a private one, belonging just to us." She said that she first met Marlon when he was thirty and she was twenty-four.

"I have never since loved a man as I loved Marlon," Papas said. "He was absolutely the man I cared about the most and also the one I esteemed the most, two things that generally are difficult to reconcile."

The interview was granted at the ancient Greek theater in Epidavros, 110 miles southwest of Athens. She recalled that her last meeting with Marlon was five years before his death. It occurred in Greece when he was there to attend a conference. "In spite of the burden of time that showed on his body, in spite of so many things, even family tragedy, he was still magnificent in the way he used his head and how he would reply to you. I remember our good-bye kiss."

Leaving both Papas and Guido in Rome, Marlon took the train all the way to Paris. As he later told Roger Vadim, "I got on the train alone, a cabin all to myself. But during the course of that long journey, I did some entertaining. Very entertaining. The gender was of no importance to me."

As winter deepened in Europe, Marlon decided it was time to return to America for film commitments. For the final lap of the train journey into Paris, he was sharing his cabin with a handsome but unknown young man, whom Marlon introduced as "my secretary." He arrived with this young man at the St-Lazare station in Paris. There he was greeted with a bevy of inquiring reporters and thousands of wildly cheering French teenage girls, whom Marlon labeled "the screamers."

After rounding up his friends, Marlon was seen with Roger Vadim, Hervé Mille, Christian Marquand, and Daniel Gélin. Somehow in the confusion of seeing his friends and/or lovers again, the young man, "the secretary," had seemingly disappeared from Marlon's life.

Marlon sailed into New York harbor aboard the S.S. *United States*. He was nattily dressed, wearing a dark blue suit raffishly set off with a Tyrolean hat with a peacock feather. He refused to give a date for his wedding, although claiming he still planned to marry his French beauty.

As expected, he was asked what he called "the stupid question of the day."

A reporter shouted at him, "How do French girls compare with American girls."

"I don't see what nationality has to do with choosing a wife, unless she's Joe Stalin's cousin," Marlon said. "Comparisons? The French have Brigitte Bardot, and we Americans have Marilyn Monroe. How do you choose between these two love goddesses? It's a matter of personal taste."

Marlon seemed in no rush to fly back to Los Angeles, although telling friends, "I can't wait until I'm with my Josie again."

* * *

Once in New York, and in spite of his talk to reporters, Marlon resumed his affair with Rita Moreno. When not with her, he was seen dancing the mambo—taught to him by Katherine Dunham—with a Spanish flamenco dancer, Carmen Amaya, who was reported to be "Marlon's latest flame."

"Before rushing back to the arms of that Berenger dame, Marlon was also seen about town with any number of exotic beauties," Fiore said. "Marlon was also seeing a lot of beautiful boys on the side, mostly aspirant actors who hoped that some of his magic would rub off on them. Instead of a movie contract, these losers left Marlon's apartment the next morning with a sore ass.

442

When one of these actors would try to hold Marlon to his promise, he would merely laugh at them. 'You fell for the oldest casting couch routine in Hollywood,' he would tell them. 'Let that be a lesson to you if you actually ever raise the train fare to Los Angeles.'"

As a cynical joke, Marlon often hooked up some of these aspirant actors with a "Hollywood producer friend of mine." Actually Bob Salser was a photographer of male nudes who did highly illegal male pornographic movies on the side. "What Marlon did in helping me cast dirty gay movies in the Fifties should have won him an award," Salser later said.

Before heading back to the West Coast, Marlon launched another "scandalous" affair, which got him exposure in *Confidential*, the leading scandal mag of the Fifties. He began a "torrid romance" with Jerri Gray, a Broadway dancer who would later appear with Sammy Davis Jr. in *Mr. Wonderful.*

Fiore said that Gray would strip down and do an interpretative dance "that would make Rita Hayworth's *Gilda* look like it was danced by a Mother Superior."

"Was Brando a great lover?" Gray was asked by a reporter.

"Enthusiastic would be a better word," she said.

What made the story scandalous at the time was that Gray was a black woman. In those days, A-list white movie stars did not openly date black women. Interracial liaisons were forbidden. Although they were going on back then, they were discreetly kept from the prying eyes of the press. Marlon, however, seemed to flaunt his romantic involvement with Gray.

"It wasn't just black women—and on a few occasions black boys—it was also Asian women," Fiore said. "If a woman had sloe eyes and the inscrutable face of the Orient, you could count on Marlon to be banging those tom-toms and lighting that incense. I lost count of the broads."

Josanne, of course, never became Mrs. Marlon Brando. Back on the West Coast, Marlon reunited with her. "But not really," Sam Gilman said. "His affair with James Dean was at its peak. He was also involved with Dean's girlfriend, Ursula Andress. Pier Angeli, now in Hollywood, came back into Marlon's life as well. It was all very incestuous. Rita Moreno was there, Katy Jurado. Movita in and out. Dozens of others. Two big movie stars—one male, the other female—lay in his future. Marlon was one busy boy. He and the French dame just drifted apart."

Following his breakup with Josanne, she refused to talk to the press. Finally realizing that her dream of a married life with Marlon was "only to be dreamed," she returned to France and the arms of her childhood sweetheart, whom she later married. Years later, she granted an interview to the press in which she claimed, "Marlon is far too independent a man to submit to the bonds that would tie him down in a marriage. I know that now. I didn't back then."

As was the case with many a girlfriend or boyfriend, Marlon remained friends with Josanne. When he visited France, he sometimes went to Bandol to renew his acquaintance with Monsieur and Madame Berenger—"my in-laws that never were." He was also spotted bouncing Josanne's new baby upon his knee.

During his marriage to first wife Anna Kashfi, she asked him what went wrong in his love affair with Josanne. He shrugged his shoulders. "She had bad breath."

* * *

In Los Angeles it was the night of March 30, 1955 at the Pantages Theater. Seemingly half the world would be listening to the Academy Award presentations, where Marlon had been nominated as best actor of the year for his performance in *On the Waterfront*. In fact, the picture had been nominated for eight Oscars, putting it up in the *Gone With the Wind* category. Even composer Leonard Bernstein had been nominated for an Oscar for his music score.

In addition to having three actors nominated for one picture—Lee J. Cobb, Rod Steiger, and Karl Malden—Eva Marie Saint was up for best supporting actress, ironically competing with Katy Jurado, Marlon's girlfriend, for her performance in *Broken Lance*. Other nominees that night included the picture itself, Elia Kazan for best director, Budd Schulberg for best screenplay, and Boris Kaufman for best cinematography.

Marlon later admitted that he was "in great conflict" about attending the ceremonies. Even at this early date in his career, he didn't believe in the granting of awards for acting. He recalled that on the night of the ceremony itself, as he was being driven to the presentation, he was still pondering whether he should put on formal wear.

Marlon was not the only one concerned that night about what he should wear. Backstage at the theater, Sam Spiegel was in a semi-hysterical state pacing up and down. Earlier in the day, he'd called Kazan. "I feel like a whore with flu in a World War II cathouse in Honolulu, with two hundred sailors waiting for their turn at me. What if the fucker turns up in a ripped T-shirt and dirty jeans?"

Right before the beginning of the ceremonies, Marlon emerged from his dressing room looking immaculate in black tie and tux. "You've got class, boy," Spiegel told him.

"If only I could say the same for you," Marlon responded in an insult to his producer.

Brando with his Oscar

Spiegel remained "the nervous nelly," as the ceremony

began, still pacing up and down. To anyone who'd listen, he asked, "What if Brando tells the audience to shove it?"

Backstage, Marlon encountered Bob Hope. "This is such a terrible competition," he said to a somewhat flabbergasted Hope. "There's such a hysterical feeling to win. It makes actors lose sight of the real objective. I feel like I'm being shipped off to Devil's Island to get my ears chopped off."

"Crosby did that to me years ago," Bob Hope quipped before walking off. Later he'd stage a mock fight on stage with Marlon, pretending to try to grab the Oscar from his hands.

Marlon was once again pitted against that sentimental favorite, Humphrey Bogart, to whom he'd lost for *The African Queen*. This time Bogie was nominated for *The Caine Mutiny*. Marlon's other competition was Bing Crosby, another sentimental favorite. The "boys in Vegas" were betting on Crosby, who had starred in *The Country Girl*. Ironically, the author of that screenplay was Clifford Odets, Marlon's former lover and still friend.

In another touch of irony, Marlon was competing against James Mason for *A Star Is Born*, a role Marlon turned down although it would have given him a chance to play opposite Judy Garland whom he admired. Marlon didn't expect much competition from Dan O'Herlihy in *Adventures of Robinson Crusoe*. Marlon was pissed at director Luis Buñuel for having made the film in the first place. Marlon had always wanted to play Robinson Crusoe himself.

Spiegel thought things were going his way when Eva Marie was announced as an early winner. She'd arrived pregnant at the theater. Earlier in the evening, Marlon had jokingly told reporters that he—not her husband—was the father. Accepting the award, the actress gasped, "I think I may have the baby right here." A few titters could be heard across the room. The next morning some puritanical members of the press reproached Eva Marie for her statement. Louella Parsons found the remark "tasteless," and Hedda Hopper thought "it cheapened the ceremony."

Finally, Marlon's big moment came, as Bette Davis walked across the stage in the very same way she'd done in *Beyond the Forest*, which had ended her long career at Warner Brothers. She was wearing a skull cap to cover her bald head, which had been shaven for her role in *The Virgin Queen*.

Taking the white envelope from Price & Waterhouse, she opened it. Reading it, she let out a whoop in a cracked voice: MARLON BRANDO!

On stage, Marlon's speech was short. "Thank you very much." Holding up the Oscar, he noted, "It's much heavier than I imagined. I had something to say and I

Oscar anyone?

445

can't remember what I was going to say for the life of me. I don't think that ever in my life have so many people been so directly responsible for my being so very, very glad. It's a wonderful moment, and a rare one, and I am certainly indebted. Thank you."

In front of the audience of his peers, Marlon appeared young and awkward, but sincere—"not the arrogant prick he'd been portrayed in the press," said Kazan.

Backstage Marlon was kissing everybody in sight, beginning with Bette Davis whom he hadn't seen since the night she came backstage to "mother him" when he was appearing in *A Streetcar Named Desire*.

He walked over to congratulate Grace Kelly, reminding her that if he'd accepted the role he would have co-starred with her in *High Noon*. "Too bad you didn't," she said flirtatiously. "We would have had a good time."

"So it's true what they say about you and your leading men?" he said with a mocking tease to his voice.

"That's for you to find out for yourself, Mr. Brando," she said. At some point in the evening he slipped her the phone number where he'd be later that night.

"You were great!" he told Grace when reporters surrounded them. "Personally I thought Crosby and Garland would beat us out."

One member of the press shouted at Grace, "Kiss him!"

"I think *he* should kiss *me*," she demurely responded.

Marlon happily obliged, kissing her again and again until the photographers were satisfied.

Privately he told her that he should never have made *On the Waterfront*. "I hold the film in contempt. I was awful in it." He held up his Oscar. "Look at how Hollywood rewards mediocrity!"

Some members of the press had been disappointed. Hoping for hot copy, reporters had wanted Marlon to behave outrageously. Instead he told them, "I'm sick to death of having reporters stand around staring at me as if I'm about to throw my raccoon at them. I no longer own Russell. His heart belongs to Mrs. Russell these days. If I know Russell, he probably has eight kids by now."

Louella Parsons came up to Marlon to congratulate him. He almost kissed her before realizing it was his archenemy who had written all that unflattering copy about him when he'd first arrived in Hollywood. He shook her hand instead, then whispered that he was going to give her an exclusive "for old time's sake."

"The other night I was fucking Katy Jurado up on the roof of a house in Laurel Canyon," he told Lolly. "As you know, she was one of the nominees tonight. Now Katy is a Latina woman who likes to give voice to her passion.

As we were deep into the dirty deed, she started screaming, 'Fuck me! Fuck me! Fuck me, Marlon Brando!' As I plunged all of my twelve inches into her, she shouted at the top of her voice: 'MARLON BRANDO MARLON BRANDO! I'M CUMMING!' I clapped my hand over her mouth and hissed at her, 'For fuck's sake,' I told her, 'don't use my God damn name.' Now print that!" He turned and walked away from Lolly.

"I left her with her mouth open like she was catching flies," he later told Fiore.

As Grace was leaving the theater, she walked back over to Marlon. This time she gave him a kiss on the lips. She explained that she was rushing off to Romanoff's to celebrate with Bing Crosby. At the time she was having an affair with her co-star in *The Country Girl*. "I feel embarrassed," she said. "After all, I got my Oscar but you took his."

Marlon went to the home of Jay Kanter, his agent, who had assembled an array of well-wishers, each wanting to congratulate Marlon. The French champagne flowed, Marlon preferring to take his bubbly in a souvenir mug from the city of Los Angeles instead of in one of Kanter's crystal goblets.

Pulling off his dinner jacket and loosening his tie, he plopped down on Kanter's sofa. Before him on the coffee table he placed his newly won Oscar. In front of the other guests, he addressed his Oscar. "I hope you're gay," he told the statuette.

"Why do you want him to be gay?" Fiore asked.

"Because I'm going to win a companion for him, and they don't make female Oscars," Marlon said.

Fiore warned him not to get too carried away, pointing out that the hock-shop value of an Oscar, just for its metal, brought only eighty dollars.

Grace Kelly and Brando
at the Oscars

"But you're forgetting one thing," Kanter said. "It can mean added millions at the box office and a hefty bank account for the star if he'd taken my advice and opted for a percentage. Even so, you'll find that your salary has been tripled for your next picture."

Many observers of the Hollywood scene made predictions that night about Marlon's future. At post-ceremony parties all over the city, insiders predicted that Marlon's "wild years are over."

"He's become part of the Hollywood establishment," pronounced Sam Spiegel, who apparently never became a member himself.

"The Oscar has pacified Marlon," Hedda

Hopper told the gathering at one party. "Now he's a major star. Take it from Hedda, Brando will start acting like a star."

How wrong she was.

Back at Kanter's gathering, a call came in at one-thirty that morning for Marlon. Getting up from the sofa, he seemed to know who was on the other end of the line.

After taking the call, Marlon confronted Fiore in the hallway. "Make my excuses, would you? I've got to bug out. A rendezvous with a fellow Oscar winner."

Fiore demanded to know where he was going at this hour.

"I've got a date with a blonde," Marlon said. "And there are still those people who spread the rumor that I don't like blondes."

* * *

The paths of Grace Kelly and Marlon had almost crossed several times in recent years. Looking like a highly polished product of a finishing school, Grace had only just departed from the offices of agent Edith Van Cleve in 1951 before Marlon arrived. His agent told him that she'd just signed "a girl I flipped over after talking to her for only fifteen minutes. Her name is Grace Kelly. I think she's going to become a big Hollywood star. She's not only serenely beautiful but talented." Edith was instrumental in getting Grace cast in a small role in Henry Hathaway's drama, *Fourteen Hours*, released by 20th Century Fox in 1951.

Working in theater in Colorado during the summer of 1951, Grace fell in love with Gene Lyons, a good-looking Irish actor with a "brooding charisma" that many critics likened to Marlon. In New York, Edith kept Marlon posted on the emerging career of Grace. She often said she'd like to have both Grace and Marlon cast in the same film together.

Grace Kelly

"When I heard that Grace had fallen for Lyons, I was a bit dismissive," Edith said. "Another would-be Method actor, I thought. I told Grace this." Edith even told Marlon about Grace's affair with Lyons, since Lyons was often compared to Marlon.

"Oh, no, not another Brando clone," he said.

"I mentioned this very point to Grace," Edith said. "And guess what she told me? Grace said she'd 'rather have the real thing.'"

Marlon smiled smugly. "Glad to know that,"

448

he said. "I'll have to put Grace Kelly on my ever-growing list of stars and starlets to seduce."

Marlon's MCA agent in Hollywood, Jay Kanter, had also been an early promoter of Grace. In fact, Kanter was the agent who brought Grace to the attention of Stanley Kramer and Fred Zinnemann when they were casting *High Noon*.

It had been Edith's dream to see her two favorite clients, Grace Kelly and Marlon, cast in *High Noon*. Both Zinnemann and Kramer, who had produced *The Men* with Marlon, found Grace "very straitlaced and very virginal." She got the part, along with Marlon's girlfriend, Katy Jurado, playing the third lead. The film, of course, would bring Gary Cooper his second Oscar. To win it, he had to beat out the closest runner-up, Marlon for his role in *Viva Zapata!*

The affair between Grace and Marlon might have happened months before it actually did. In addition to such rejects as Joanne Woodward and Elizabeth Montgomery, Kazan had briefly considered casting Grace Kelly in the Eva Marie Saint role in *Waterfront*. "But I finally decided that was ridiculous," Kazan confessed. "Who would have believed Grace Kelly as the girl who grew up in the wilds of the Hoboken waterfront?"

In her dainty white gloves, Grace's rivaled the poise of Jacqueline Kennedy. But Grace's image was deceiving.

Before their respective Oscar winnings brought them together, Marlon was well aware of Grace's reputation for seducing the A-list stars of Hollywood, of which he was now an exclusive member.

In the short span of a few years, the objects of her affection would include not only Gary Cooper, but Clark Gable, Cary Grant, William Holden, Ray Milland, David Niven, Frank Sinatra, James Stewart, Spencer Tracy, and such pre-Prince Rainier royal seductions as another playboy prince, Aly Khan, and even Mohammed Reza Pahlavi, the Shah of Iran.

"Despite her lady-like poise, and her somewhat aloof air, Grace had the mentality of a streetwalker," Edith later said. Author Gore Vidal once called her "an easy lay—she was notorious for that."

Don Richardson, a theater instructor who'd had a brief affair with a teenage Grace, said, "She screwed everybody she came into contact with who was able to do anything good for her. She screwed agents, producers, directors, and certainly all of her leading men, even the gay ones."

After making *High Noon* with Grace, Cooper said, "She looked like she was a cold dish with a man until you got her pants down. Then she'd explode."

As director Henry Hathaway once said, "She wore those white gloves but she was no saint."

Marlon was to find that out for himself on Oscar night. But before the dawn broke, he also came to realize that Grace had used him for more than just a roll in the hay.

Only five years older than Grace, Marlon was a bit young by her standards. She was known for her preference for older leading men. During her Hollywood career, the average age of her leading men was forty-six.

Bing Crosby

When Grace met Marlon, she was already deep into her affair with crooner Bing Crosby, her co-star in *The Country Girl*. He was twenty-six years older than she was. Actually their affair had begun a year and a half before they'd made a film together.

As his wife, Dixie Lee, lay dying of cancer, Bing was falling in love with Grace. Their affair was often conducted at the home of actor Alan Ladd, a close friend of the singer. Before heading for bed, he often turned out the lights in the living room, leaving the pair on his sofa. "Just lock the door when you guys leave," Ladd would often tell Bing and Grace.

Edith remains the main source of information about the affair between Marlon and Grace. But she regretted that Marlon provided only scant details, "although he used to keep me regally entertained with a lot more information about his affairs with famous actresses, especially those he seduced when appearing on the stage in *Streetcar*. I once told Marlon that listening to his tales of seduction was tantamount to my getting off. So he used to call and say, 'I've got another conquest to report to you. This one is going to make you cream your bloomers.'"

Apparently, during Marlon's first hour with Grace, he had to listen to her complaints about Bing Crosby. Although she'd just won the Oscar for *The Country* Girl, he claimed that Bing had almost denied her the role, since he had approval of his leading lady. "He thought I was too beautiful," Grace told Marlon. "Not drab enough."

"Bing Crosby has a point there," Marlon said.

Unknown to Marlon at the time, Bing had fallen deeply in love with Grace and wanted her to marry him since the death of Dixie had left him a widower. "But I'm not in love with him," Grace had told her friends. She also told the same friends that Bing was refusing to take no for an answer.

What happened in Grace's suite around three o'clock that morning is still not known in exact details, but Bing arrived for a showdown with Grace. Instead of that, he found a nude Marlon in her bed.

"That must have been doubly difficult for Bing," Edith said. "Earlier in the evening he'd been denied the Oscar by Marlon, his last chance. Now he finds the same young nude stud in Grace's bed. Reportedly, there were fisticuffs. What chance did an aging, drunken singer have against a well-built young actor who was also a boxer? Marlon was a bit vague, but I gathered that he knocked out the voice behind *White Christmas*."

From what Edith gathered, Grace called both the house doctor and the hotel manager. A drunken Bing was removed to another suite as Grace and Marlon resumed their affair.

Edith speculated—and it was pure conjecture on her part—that Grace knew that Bing was going to drop in on her after he'd made the round of Hollywood parties where well-wishers tried to console him for his loss of the Oscar to Marlon.

"Frankly, I think Grace wanted to dump Bing and just used Marlon to help her do just that," Edith said. "Since he wouldn't listen to her refusals of marriage, and since he kept begging her to marry him, the drama queen in Grace came up with a way to make her point. What better way to tell a man that you're not going to marry him than to dramatize it with a nude Marlon Brando in your bed with a full erection raring to go."

After Oscar night, Bing Crosby joined Frank Sinatra in developing a lifelong hatred for Marlon.

Before the dawn broke, Grace was interrupted by another Hollywood legend, marring her night of bliss with Marlon. A phone call came in for her around five o'clock that morning. Somehow the caller had obtained her phone number.

In a drunken but famous voice, the intruder said, "This is Judy Garland, Judy FUCKING Garland. You bitch! You took what was rightfully mine. Tonight was my last chance for the Oscar. You'll have many more chances in your future. This was it for me. I'll never forgive you." Judy then slammed down the phone on Grace.

She reported to Marlon what Judy had said. "She's got a point," Marlon countered. "You'll probably go on to win seven more Oscars."

"What the hell!" Grace said, not disguising the anger in her voice. "Why don't you take my Oscar over and give it to Judy? Before Judy, I had to deal with a very jealous Jane Wyman."

Vying with Judy for *A Star Is Born*, Grace also faced competition from Wyman, who had been nominated for her role in *The Magnificent Obsession* opposite Rock Hudson.

"When I ran into Wyman, she told me that she'd seen *The Country Girl* but had walked out on it," Grace told Marlon. "'Isn't it terrible when these Hollywood directors miscast us in a role,'" the bitch told me "Grace did a perfect imitation of Wyman's distinctive voice.

"That's true," I told Wyman. "If they'd wanted someone drab and mousy, they could have cast you, my dear."

"Meow!" Marlon said. "Wyman must have wanted to slap your face."

"There's more," Grace said. "Before she stalked off, I told her, 'if you lose the Oscar to me, and I'm sure you will, you can rest on your laurels. After all, you've had Ronald Reagan, and I haven't had time to get around to him yet. But he's next on my list.'"

"Grace may have intended to use Marlon as a mere pawn," Edith said, "but after their first night together I think she developed a genuine affection for him. Perhaps I should call it passion. I know for a fact that Marlon and Grace slipped off together to spend at least two secret weekends together on the French Riviera when she was reigning over Monaco."

In public, he was usually very respectful of Grace. When she became Princess of Monaco, Marlon said, "In Hollywood only Audrey Hepburn could have moved so effortlessly from movie star to royalty."

***

"Seducing a princess is an experience every man should know at least once in a lifetime," Marlon told Edith after he'd made the *Countess of Hong Kong*, with Charlie Chaplin directing him in London. He'd made that remark after completing the film for Pinewood Studios outside London in 1966. At the time he'd lost a lot of excess tonnage.

Uncharacteristically, he'd hobnobbed with the aristocrats of Britain, and was even seen dining one night with Princess Margaret and her husband, Lord Snowdon.

Princess Margaret Rose

"Apparently Margaret Rose was really taken with Marlon," Edith said. "He was a bit lean on giving me details of that affair. I think it took place at something called Strand House in Winchelsea, a hamlet outside Rye in Sussex."

As for the sexual attraction of Margaret Rose to him, Marlon smugly said, "Lesbians are always attracted to me."

Although the royal princess was hardly a lesbian, several of her affairs with women were revealed following her death. In referring to her as a lesbian to Edith, Marlon must have been privy to some information not known to the general public at the time. "Whatever streak of lesbianism she might have had was cured by me," Marlon smugly told Edith.

452

Bob Dylan

Bianca Jagger

Faye Dunaway

One night, Marlon, perhaps in jest, told Edith, "I'm tired of princesses. Why not a queen? As my agent, you're ordered to get me the private phone number of Liz. I hear Philip leaves her alone many a night in that drafty palace. I've also heard that she's seen two of my movies and thinks I'm hot. Who knows? She might divorce Philip and marry me. My noble tool might become responsible for a number of royal princes running around London."

"I'll get onto it first thing in the morning," Edith said. "I'll call the Archbishop of Canterbury. I think he has her number."

"Edith poured herself another hefty Scotch and sprawled across her sofa. "I need to get off again," she said. "Tell me about your affair with Irene Papas. While you're at it, fill me in on all the gory details about those rumors of affairs with Faye Dunaway, Bianca Jagger, and, while we're on the subject, all the dirt on Bob Dylan. That *Forever Young* song really grabs me!"

* * *

What happened to Marlon's Oscar?

Over the years it disappeared, eventually turning up for sale at a London auction house. Marlon protested that it was stolen merchandise and that it was his personal property. The auction house called off the sale, but the possessor of the *Waterfront* Oscar refused to return the prize.

It is not clear if the holder of the Oscar was male or female. The London auctioneers informed Marlon that the owner of his Oscar was claiming that it had been a gift and refused to return it. Marlon staunchly denied that he'd ever given away his Oscar.

* * *

One night at two o'clock in the morning in New York, Marlon placed a call to Fiore. "Get your ass out of bed and get over here to help me pack."

"What in the fuck is going on," a sleepy Fiore asked.

"I'm going to Hollywood to appear in a camel opera."

"You on a camel?" Fiore asked in astonishment. "In Nebraska, they ride horses, not camels. What role is this latest bullshit from Hollywood?"

"They want me to play Cleopatra."

Chapter Thirteen

As part of a two-picture deal that Marlon had foolishly signed with Darryl F. Zanuck at Fox, he was assigned the role of a doctor in *The Egyptian*, a multi-million dollar extravaganza shot in CinemaScope and Technicolor. Initially, he'd been intrigued by the project until he finally got around to reading the script. After he'd read it, he called Jay Kanter. "I'm going to find a way out of this Egyptian pile of camel dung." His agent warned Marlon of severe complications—"perhaps the destruction of your screen career"—if you don't go through with it.

Two days before he was to report for work on *The Egyptian*, his costar, Bella Darvi, showed up unannounced at his doorstep. All of insiderish Hollywood knew that she was Zanuck's *inamorata*. The Polish-born actress claimed that she was "just paying a friendly call" on her upcoming male costar. Darvi had failed in the first role that Zanuck had assigned her, *Hell and High Water* (1954), but he persisted in casting her for the important role of the Babylonian whore in *The Egyptian*. Earlier, Marlon had told Kanter, "What typecasting for Miss Darvi!"

Later Marlon would claim that "the only thing I liked about Darvi was her brunette hair." Patiently he listened to her long tale of past misfortune, as she spilled out her life to him, going from the tortures of World War II concentration camps to the glittering palace casinos of Monaco. During this long recitation, he kept refilling her glass with Scotch.

As Marlon learned, Darvi by the age of eighteen was gambling heavily in the casinos and running up big debts. The source of her money remains unknown, some observers suggesting prostitution.

It was in Monaco that movie mogul Zanuck, accompanied by his long-suffering wife, Virginia, discovered Darvi, then known as Bayla Wegier. In a foolish move she'd later regret, Virginia suggested to her husband that Darvi might have "the same appeal as Ingrid Bergman."

Paying off her gambling debts, the Zanucks shipped her off to Hollywood, installing her in their guest cottage. Zanuck began to groom her for stardom. After arriving unexpectedly on Marlon's doorstep, Darvi was invited to spend the night in his bedroom. She left early the following morning for the studio.

At ten o'clock, Sam Gilman came by with eight pairs of new shoes for Marlon to try on. He didn't want to go to a shoe store "just to be stared at," so he ordered Sam to select various shoes in his size. Painstakingly Marlon tried on each pair, rejecting each of them. He suggested to his ever-faithful Sam that "you go back to the store and try again to come up with something I like. Also, a pair that actually fits would help."

Bella Darvi

Over breakfast with Gilman, Marlon revealed details of having spent a night with his prospective leading lady. "I know Zanuck has the hots for her, but she can't act. We pretended to do a scene together. She's a hopeless case. I can't believe Zanuck is so smitten that he hasn't noticed this, but the bitch is cross-eyed. Not only that, she speaks with a lisp and has a foreign accent to boot. The American public won't be able to understand a word the cunt says. Her speech is slurred. Of course, that could be from all the scotch she put away. One mumbler—namely me—in a picture is enough."

"After our so-called rehearsal together, my noble tool did its duty," Marlon told Gilman. "I fucked her. Once was enough. After all that alcohol, the bitch just lay there flat on her back, leaving me to do all the hard work. Not only that, she has the worst drunken breath since I got close to Joan Crawford. There's no way in hell I'm going to play opposite her. I'm telling Zanuck first thing tomorrow that I'm off the picture. Rabbit Tooth can put his girlie in some other movie. I want him to cast Elizabeth Taylor in the role of the whore."

Gilman offered a mild protest, suggesting that Taylor worked for another studio and was already involved in a movie.

"I guess you didn't hear me, Sammy boy," Marlon said with contempt in his voice. "I have long suspected the wax buildup in your ears. It's Elizabeth Taylor—or else I walk!"

The next morning, Marlon met Michael Curtiz, his director. The Hungarian was still dining out on his fame for having directed Humphrey Bogart and Ingrid Bergman in *Casablanca* during the war. The meeting between Curtiz and Marlon lasted for less than fifteen minutes.

"I'm told you're a tough pisser to work with," Curtiz told Marlon. "I have my own way of dealing with tough pissers. Remember who I am! I stood up to Mr. Tough Guy, Bogie himself. If I can handle him, I can certainly handle some faggot from the New York stage. Any time an actor gets out of line with me, I know how to deal with them. I have this bull whip on the set with me. I take it out and zing it across their buttocks. You're an easy target, Brando. That ass of yours seems to be growing bigger every day. I'm going to round

456

up one of Marie Dressler's old girdles and fit it on your fleshy mounds."

Giving no oral response, Marlon rose from his chair and walked out of Curtiz's office. Behind the wheel of his car, he drove it off the lot without one good-bye wave at the security guards.

"It was the talk of the town," Gilman later said. "Marlon just up and disappeared. I was certain he was on his way back to New York. Plane, train, I knew he didn't drive."

On hearing that his star had bolted, Zanuck screamed so loudly his bellows could be heard across the Pacific all the way to Japan, or so a secretary at Fox later claimed.

"I frantically called for Marlon, searching everywhere for him," Kanter said, "But as it turned out, he walked out on a full-blown disaster."

Marlon's hasty evaluation of Darvi and *The Egyptian* turned out to be deadly accurate in spite of the fact that Zanuck had assembled an all-star cast. "Victor Mature and I would have supplied the beefcake," Marlon said, "with the two Jeans—Gene Tierney and Jean Simmons—coming in with the cheesecake."

When it became obvious that Marlon wouldn't relent, Zanuck secretly approached James Dean, offering him the role of the doctor in *The Egyptian*. "I figured if I couldn't get Brando, go for the clone."

James later said, "I didn't do Biblical epics. Besides, I was afraid I'd be standing in back of a camel just at the moment he decided to dump the big load. Speaking of shit, that's *The Egyptian*."

Edmund Purdom replaced Marlon in the role of the doctor. Marlon had met Purdom briefly when the British-born actor appeared as James Mason's servant in *Julius Caesar*. "I'm not impressed with him as an actor," Marlon told John Gielgud.

"Neither am I," Gielgud said. "But as a male beauty, Mr. Purdom can put his shoes under my bed any time."

As in the case of Darvi, all attempts to make a star out of Purdom failed. Even Zanuck was finally forced to admit that both his male star and *The Egyptian* itself "turned out to be a pile of shit. Even ten Brandos couldn't have saved this turkey."

Despite growing evidence that it was a bad idea, Zanuck continued to try to make a star out of his mistress, casting her in *The Racers* in 1955. And although he starred her opposite some of the leading men of her day—Victor Mature, Richard Widmark, Kirk Douglas—Zanuck couldn't transform the Polish beauty into a convincing star. When his wife Virginia discovered that their *protégée* was having an affair with her husband, she sent her packing.

After a few more unsuccessful films abroad, Darvi returned to her heavy drinking and even heavier gambling at Monaco. The years were unkind.

Mounting debts from gambling and increasing despair over her failed career led to several suicide attempts. She attempted a memoir, *Why I Never Worked with Marlon Brando and Other Tales of Hollywood,* but never got beyond the first chapter. Finally, on the morning of September 11, 1971, she succeeded in killing herself by turning on the gas in her apartment in Monaco.

Marlon was hardly saddened. "I hear that while making *The Egyptian*, Darvi took a pounding twice a day from Zanuck's big dick, but also managed to fuck Victor Mature, Peter Ustinov, Michael Wilding, and even Michael Curtiz himself. How did Jean Simmons and Gene Tierney ever keep their pussies intact from that insatiable whore? Thank God I bolted from El Stinko. I don't do sword-and-sandal epics."

As late as the early 1960s, Marlon was turning down "sand pictures," although he obviously relented when he agreed to do a western, *One-Eyed Jacks*, released in 1961.

Later, he rejected what he called "another camel dung opera," *Lawrence of Arabia*. He turned down David Lean's offer. The director cast Peter O'Toole instead, and, upon the film's release in 1962, the replacement for Marlon became an international star. Years later when O'Toole encountered Marlon, Marlon said, "My rejection of that Lawrence sod made a star out of you. But damned if I wanted to spend two years of my life out in the desert on some fucking camel."

Lawrence of Arabia wasn't the only classic film Marlon rejected, as he made his way through the Sixties as the featured actor in one horrible, ill-chosen film after another. He refused to play the Sundance Kid opposite Paul Newman's Butch Cassidy. "Too bad," Elia Kazan said upon hearing the news. "The idea of Marlon on the screen in a picture with Newman makes me drool. Who knows? I might have even gotten the two of them to fuck each other off screen so I could watch."

After he fled Hollywood and the set of *The Egyptian*, Marlon landed in New York, exactly as Gilman had predicted. His flight made front pages around the country. Those same newspapers reported that Zanuck was suing him for two million dollars for breach of contract. Marlon asked his psychiatrist, Bela Mittelmann, to write Zanuck, explaining that Marlon was under his constant care—"a very sick and confused boy." Zanuck was not impressed and continued with his suit.

Afraid to stay at his own apartment, Marlon moved in with actress Barbara Baxley at her small Murray Hill studio.

Baxley later claimed that Marlon wasn't just pretending to Fox that he was in the throes of a nervous breakdown. "He *was* breaking down, and I've seen enough cases of that, including in my own life, to know a basket case when I see one. His career in Hollywood had become white heat—too hot for him to handle. He was the biggest thing in Tinseltown since sliced bread. But his career was taking a toll on him. His father had just squandered all his hard-earned money on bad cattle investments in Nebraska, and was demanding $150,000 more in immediate cash. And his mother, the love of Marlon's life, was dead. His own love life was in chaos. Of course, we shacked up. But it wasn't love between us. I felt that Marlon was just getting his rocks off—nothing more."

The actress said that Marlon would endlessly sit in her little studio, not listening to television or even the radio. "He just sat there for hours staring at a blank wall. He was definitely entering the most paranoid part of his life. He began to distrust even his closest friends, and I suspected he might turn on me. He especially suspected Carlo Fiore. He expressed doubts about the loyalty of Sam Gilman, who was virtually his faithful servant. He even came to suspect the loyalty of Phil Rhodes, his faithful makeup man. One night he attacked Wally Cox. Surely no man on earth was a more loyal friend than Wally. But Marlon falsely claimed that 'I know for a fact that Wally is writing a book about me.' But Wally was doing no such thing."

Baxley, who had spent a good part of her own life in the offices of psychiatrists, tried a bit of amateur analysis on Marlon. "He hated being under legal obligation to anyone, much less a Hollywood studio, and especially Zanuck. Big salaries from Hollywood simply didn't impress Marlon although, God knows, he needed the money. Even though he'd become a big star, Marlon still remained the Hollywood bad boy with the Bad Ass cyclist's cap riding a motorcycle. He didn't want anyone to be his master. A sad paradox. The truth was, Marlon couldn't even be his own master. He wanted love but spurned it once he found it. He sought fame but hated what he'd seen of it. He wanted to be a great actor but at the same time claimed that acting was a silly and stupid profession. He was an extremely complicated character who didn't know anybody else, because he didn't know himself. As for Bela Mittelmann, Marlon should have thrown that quack off the Empire State Building long ago."

One afternoon, Marlon slipped out of Baxley's studio to buy some yogurt at Max's Deli. Recognizing Marlon, the owner alerted the press. When reporters descended, Marlon fled.

He appeared two hours later at his own Carnegie Hall apartment. Somewhere he'd managed to secure a disguise, appearing as a United Nations diplomat with a false mustache, striped pants, and a walking cane of ebony and pearl.

He called Baxley that night to tell her where he was. "This is the obvious place for me to go. My own apartment. No one will think of looking for me here."

A U.S. marshal was trying in vain to serve Marlon with legal documents.

Suspecting Marlon might be holed up in his own apartment, the marshal came up with a scheme. Pounding on Marlon's door, he announced that he was from the Academy with an announcement of Marlon's nomination for an Oscar.

The door swung open, and Marlon was served his subpoena.

Only the previous day, Marlon Sr. had informed his son that all their investments in cattle had failed and that he needed that $150,000 at once. "You're broke!" Marlon Sr. bluntly told his son.

Weighing his position, Marlon called Jay Kanter in Hollywood, begging him to come up with some settlement. An agreement was hammered out between Kanter and Zanuck.

Marlon agreed to appear in the historical romance, *Desirée*, for Zanuck "if you'll call off your legal hound dogs."

In one of Hollywood's worst casting mistakes, Marlon was cast as Napoleon.

"In some ways I'm perfect for the role," he told Fiore. "I'm short enough. Napoleon was short. I've been eating so much junk food lately that my ass would look fat in a pair of silk breeches, like Napoleon's ass did. In doing research for the part, I read that Napoleon was a 'phallic, narcissistic type suffering from a castration complex and had an organ inferiority, with sado-masochistic tendencies.' The character fits me to a T. But how embarrassing to be playing a man with a small dick. My reputation will suffer."

* * *

Before flying to the West Coast to film *Desirée*, Marlon, at Stella Adler's urging, had gone to see Eugene O'Neill's long-running Broadway drama, *Long Day's Journey into Night*. Stella was convinced that Marlon would be ideal if cast in the film version.

He sat through the whole play, watching the deteriorating condition of a mother hooked on drugs. Later, he told Stella that the play was "too close to home," a reference to his having survived the alcoholism of Dodie. "Besides, it's a lousy play. I won't do it. I've turned down O'Neill plays before. Shitty playwright."

After Dodie's death, Marlon attempted a reconciliation with Marlon Sr. One biographer wrote that Marlon Sr. was "an astute businessman" in oil wells and cattle, and had, in fact, made so much money for his son that he "could live comfortably for the rest of his life." Nothing could be farther from the truth.

Marlon Sr. was completely incompetent as a businessman and had squandered all of Marlon's money. He was flat broke during the making of *Desirée*, and had to borrow $25,000 from his costar, Merle Oberon, to pay expenses.

460

According to an agreement worked out between Kanter and Zanuck, Marlon would surrender all of his $175,000 salary to Fox for having run up such huge costs for the studio when he bolted the set of *The Egyptian* and fled to New York.

Despite his father's disastrous handling of Marlon's finances, beginning with the first $40,000 he was paid for his role in *The Men*, Marlon agreed to go into business with him again. Together they founded a film company, Pennebaker Productions, named in honor of the maiden name of Marlon's mother.

* * *

German-born Henry Koster was selected by Zanuck to direct *Desirée*, because the movie mogul had been pleased with the way he'd handled Richard Burton in *The Robe*.

The mild-mannered director would prove no match for the temperamental and arrogantly stubborn Marlon.

Koster had assembled an all-star cast, with the British beauty, Jean Simmons, cast as the eponymous Desirée. The veteran beauty of the screen and boudoir, Merle Oberon, was cast as Napoleon's errant wife, Josephine. Michael Rennie was to play Napoleon's trusted general, Bernadotte, with Cameron Mitchell cast as Napoleon's brother, Joseph.

Marlon also wanted some of his friends hired for the picture, insisting that Sam Gilman be cast as Fouché, the French minister of finance. Phil Rhodes was hired as makeup man. Florence Dublin, the wife of one of Marlon's best friends, Darren Dublin, was hired to play Elsa Bonaparte, Napoleon's scheming Corsica-born sister.

Marlon wanted Darren as his stand-in. But James Dean, perhaps playing a competitive game with Marlon, had already hired Darren as his stand-in on *East of Eden*. Marlon was furious at James, finally insisting that Zanuck lure Darren back to the set of *Desirée*. Darren acquiesced, but during his subsequent time there, he found Marlon increasingly hostile and resentful that "I had betrayed him."

Eventually, during the filming, Marlon broke off his relationship with his former friend, claiming falsely that Darren was "banging" his girlfriend, Josanne Berenger. During their confrontation, Marlon spat in Darren's face. Because he needed the money, Darren stayed on the set for another three weeks. But the friendship was never repaired.

Carlo Fiore had become hooked on heroin again, and was not asked to get involved in the production of the film. But despite that, he arrived on the set right after shooting began in need of money. With some reluctance, Marlon lent him money out of the loan Merle Oberon had given him, warning him not to spend it on drugs.

He didn't get around to reading the script until after shooting had begun. And after reading it, he was dismissive of its merits. Upon meeting costar Jean Simmons, he told her that "the film is ridiculous. But I didn't want to be in debt for the rest of my life, so I showed up." He also claimed that the casting of him as Napoleon was "Zanuck's sick joke on me."

The screenwriter was Daniel Taradash. "At least they got Taradash's surname almost right," Marlon said, no doubt referring to the word "trash."

Marlon in *Desirée* attire

Holding the script up in front of Koster, Marlon dropped it at his feet. "Do you actually plan to shoot this crap? To me, it reads like Barbara Cartland's rewrite of *Das Kapital*."

Koster considered himself an expert on Napoleon. He noted that Marlon had read only a book or two about the French dictator "and overnight had become an expert, clashing with me." In contrast, Koster said that he had been a Napoleonic scholar, an interest inherited from his father, who had filled their house in Germany with Napoleonic artifacts, including uniforms, flags, and helmets. "Brando simply didn't have it in him to play Napoleon. I did the best I could with him. But Stanley Kowalski was no Bonaparte, not even a distant cousin."

Marlon called Koster "a lightweight who was much more interested in uniforms than in the impact of Napoleon on European history."

When commenting on the accent that Marlon adopted for *Desirée*, fellow actor Cameron Mitchell delivered what became a famous comparison. "Instead of Claude Rains or even Sir Cedric Hardwicke, his voice was a cross between the nasally, comically aristocratic Hermione Gingold and the meltingly husky Joan Greenwood."

In the film, Jean Simmons, playing Desirée, is still in love with the Little Corporal. But in a plot line that reflected the bizarre power structure of Europe in the early 19th century, because of her status as the wife of one of his generals (Bernadotte), she eventually becomes Queen of Sweden. During an emotional reunion with Napoleon after her move to Sweden, she tells him of her dislike of that country. He asks her why. "It's too cold." At that point in the filming, as a gesture of rebellion against a plot line he despised, Marlon unexpectedly broke into song, jokingly delivering a historically inappropriate version of "Baby, It's Cold Outside."

462

"Koster completely lost his temper with that one," Mitchell said. "Of course, the line was ridiculous, but Marlon deliberately ruined the scene and wouldn't shoot it again."

Koster recalled that for some reason Marlon froze in certain scenes. "On one occasion, all Marlon had to do was to deliver a simple command to an officer, as played by Michael Rennie," Koster said. "He flubbed every take. Finally, he said it right on the twentieth take. I didn't like the scene but ordered it printed anyway since I didn't think I'd get anything better out of him."

At one point, when Marlon didn't like a scene, he pulled down his pink silk Napoleonic breeches and demanded that Koster come over and inspect him for crabs.

One afternoon, Marlon denounced Koster in front of the entire crew. "You're superficial!" Marlon shouted at his director. "You can't direct shit. Who in the fuck do you think you're trying to direct? Deanna Durbin?" Koster had directed the demure Canadian teenager with her beautiful soprano voice in some of her musicals.

Imitating Durbin, Marlon burst into his own rendition of "Ave Maria." Storming off the set, he went to his dressing room and called Zanuck, threatening to walk off the picture unless Koster was fired and replaced with another director.

However, by the following morning, Marlon's temper had cooled. He was back shooting the final scenes of *Desirée*, but refused to take any more direction from Koster. If Koster tried to direct him, Marlon would turn to the person nearest him and engage in a conversation, making indiscreet remarks about Koster, including speculation about how small his penis was.

One day Zanuck sent word that Haile Selassie, the emperor of Ethiopia, would be visiting the set to watch the filming of *Desirée*. Privately Zanuck had learned that Selassie had admired Napoleon.

Hoping to impress Selassie, Zanuck invited him to witness the scene in which Napoleon crowns himself emperor in front of at least a thousand fancily dressed extras pretending to be at the cathedral of Notre-Dame in Paris. According to Mitchell, Marlon deliberately set out to sabotage the shooting by giving many of the extras water pistols. "He got a reluctant Sam Gilman to hand out the weapons and to instigate the water duels."

When Emperor Selassie arrived on the set, Marlon spoke to him in French. The Ethiopian dictator wore a chest of medals, of which he was obviously proud. As Napoleon, Marlon wore only one medal.

Marlon as Napoleon with
Emperor Haile Selassie

463

"It looks to me like you won more battles than I did, and I conquered Europe!" Marlon said. Selassie appeared stone-faced in front of Marlon and ten members of his Ethiopian palace guard. "Selassie was furious, insulted, whatever," Mitchell said. "After that, he pointedly ignored Brando. But there was more fun to come."

Just as Koster called for action, Marlon signaled Gilman for the war to begin. Suddenly the male dress extras, and a few of the women too, pulled out their water pistols and began squirting each other.

Henry Koster

"Getting completely carried away, the actors reverted to their childhood, as they squirted every target in sight," Mitchell claimed. "The game just escalated. At one point Marlon picked up a fire hose and aimed it right onto the set. The antiques were ruined. So were the costumes. So were the wigs. If Koster had kept the cameras on, the scene would have been more interesting than anything actually shot in *Desirée*. The whole day was a disaster. Zanuck threatened to sue Brando once again, but nothing ever came of it. Up until then, Brando had nearly reduced Koster to tears. On that day, Koster cried like a baby. As for Selassie, he got the hell out of there. I bet that was the last movie he wanted to see being shot."

Throughout the entire film, Mitchell claimed he was horrified at how Marlon repeatedly humiliated Koster. "At one point Koster was reduced to getting down on his knees and begging Brando to get up out of his chair and face the cameras. Finally, Brando agreed to be filmed but only if Koster personally went to the commissary and bought him a chocolate ice cream soda 'extra thick.' The director was forced into this humiliating act, and he dutifully held up production until he could go and buy that soda. Actually Brando didn't need Koster. Brando as Napoleon was his own director. At one point Brando argued with Koster for about an hour over how a scene should be shot. I was amazed when Brando finally gave in to his director. It was a full frontal shot with Brando in his pink silk breeches. After one minute of filming, it was obvious why Brando had given in. He was sabotaging the scene. Brando was

pissing in those pink silk bloomers he wore. That yellow stain around his crotch grew as big as Australia before Koster called cut."

Mitchell was a ruggedly handsome actor, and on several occasions he suspected that Marlon was coming on to him. "I'd heard that he was bisexual, and I could tell he had the hots for me. Whenever he was around me, he always made up some excuse to put his hands on me or his arm around me. One day he confessed to me that he

Cameron Mitchell

464

was trisexual. But he didn't explain what that meant. The second week into the shoot, he whispered to me that he and I should indulge in a little brotherly love to make our scenes as brothers more vivid on screen. 'What exactly does that mean?' I asked him. 'Come on, you know,' Brando said to me. 'Come back to my dressing room for a little suck. The other day when I was pissing at the urinal with you, I was impressed with what I saw.' Unlike some straight actors who went with Brando just because he was Marlon Brando, I didn't go that route and turned him down. After that, he refused to speak to me off screen."

At the end of shooting, Koster was ready for a nervous breakdown. He told Zanuck, "Back in the Thirties, Greta Garbo and Charles Boyer might have pulled off *Desirée*. But I had pieces of wood for actors, especially one Marlon Brando who has taken ten years off my life."

Having fulfilled his obligation to Fox on *Desirée*, Marlon announced to a reporter that he was leaving on a world tour that would last at least two years—"maybe forever." He claimed that he planned to find some secluded hideaway, perhaps in the South Pacific. "I'll eat two quarts of ice cream a day, get awfully chubby, and fuck brown-skinned teenage gals until I've doubled the island population."

He had expressed similar sentiments before. Each time he made such a pronouncement, he put it more colorfully than before. The truth of the matter was that he had emerged penniless after shooting *Desirée*. He told Kanter that to meet his obligations, he needed another job—"and be quick about it." In a coincidence, he claimed that he would "even play a song-and-dance man."

When MGM refused to let Gene Kelly star as Sky Masterson in the Damon Runyon classic, *Guys and Dolls*, Marlon won the part by default.

* * *

Film industry insiders had predicted "fireworks" between the very proper Merle Oberon, *doyenne* of Hollywood, and Marlon when they met on the set of *Desirée*. She was a woman known for her impeccable manners, and he was still called "the rebel," although he'd taken to wearing a better wardrobe. James Dean was now dressing as Marlon used to.

Merle had already heard all the gossip about how cruel Marlon could be to aging movie queens. The story of his rejection of Joan Crawford was frequently cited. Merle went to her old friend and former lover, Zanuck himself, and expressed her grave reservations about working with a Method actor like Marlon, who was just the opposite of her "Old Hollywood" style of emoting.

She desperately wanted to play the role of the

Merle Oberon

465

Empress Josephine, the wife of Napoleon, but feared that her screen dynamic with Marlon wouldn't work unless Zanuck hired a more powerful director to keep Marlon in line. "Just endure," Zanuck told her. "All things come to an end, even Marlon Brando!"

Although intimidated by his reputation, Merle was pleasantly surprised when she actually met Marlon. "He seemed absolutely fascinated by me," she claimed. "He told me that he had much admired my previous work on the screen. We became very close during the filming, and he was a frequent guest at my house. One time in my dressing room he broke down and poured his heart out to me over the pain he was suffering from the loss of his mother. I felt great sympathy for him. He even let me make some suggestions as to how he should play Napoleon." She chuckled. "I told him that an emperor like Napoleon wouldn't chew gum. He parked the glob under his throne."

Years after *Desirée* was filmed, Merle said that Marlon was "very cooperative with me but not with the others. They had a terrible time with him. But I found him fantastic. He used to come to my house for dinner—and if I said eight o'clock, he would be there right on time and dressed in his blue suit and tie. I remember he met Noël Coward at my house, and they got on very well." When she said that, Merle was unaware that Marlon and Coward had met on intimate terms in the mid-Forties. Neither man chose to enlighten her on the nature of their previous encounters.

Merle was later credited with transposing her own accent—neither French nor British—onto Marlon. Her voice was a bit clipped, with overly enunciated vowels. "God damn it to hell!" Fiore later said. "Even though I was sometimes hired as Marlon's dialogue coach on a picture, he went for years speaking in that Merle Oberon voice of his. He sounded like a lisping Boston faggot with terminal lockjaw!"

Throughout the shooting of *Desirée*, Marlon was kind to Merle, knowing that at her age she was sensitive as to how she was being photographed. "You're the best thing in the picture," he kept reassuring her, and he was right.

"No one could believe that Marlon was putting on a suit and tie for Merle and attending her fancy dinner parties," said Sam Gilman, who was living with Marlon at the time. "Marlon never checked to see if any of the women he was balling had a husband stashed away somewhere. He always managed his seductions even if there were a husband hidden in a closet somewhere."

Marlon bragged to Gilman that, "I've never fucked a Tasmanian aristocrat before. By the way, does Tasmania have aristocrats?"

Actually Merle had deceived Marlon. She wasn't from Tasmania, but had been born in India as a "half-caste," a term widely used at the time. (In Merle's case, she was the product of an English father and an Indian mother.) She had spent a great part of her career trying to keep the world from knowing her origins. Actually, her bloodline wouldn't have mattered to Marlon. He liked Indian women in saris. In fact, he was to marry his first wife, Anna Kashfi, thinking she was Indian, only to be horribly disappointed when he found out she wasn't.

No one had a tape recorder under Merle's bed when Marlon arrived to seduce her. But many of her former lovers gave her ten points on a scale of one to ten, including Zanuck himself. Although Prince Philip always remained tight-lipped about his affair with Merle in Mexico, Clark Gable, Leslie Howard, and Gary Cooper all praised her charms in bed, as did a whole array of other stars, including David Niven, Ronald Colman, George Brent, Brian Aherne, Maurice Chevalier, James Cagney, Richard Harris, Rex Harrison, Robert Ryan, and countless others. On hearing a recitation of all the stars she'd successfully seduced, Marlon seemed impressed. "She did better than Scarlett O'Hara," he said. "She managed to seduce both Rhett Butler and Ashley Wilkes—not bad."

Many women detested her, including Marlene Dietrich who was offended by her pseudo-ladylike affectations. "A common piece," Marlene called her. Cecil Beaton claimed that Merle was "almost a nymphomaniac—as promiscuous as a man enjoying a quick one behind the door."

"Such a lady!" Marlon told Gilman after the first night he'd spent with Merle. "I can't imagine that she ever sweats. Do you think she needs to go to the can? Or has she evolved beyond that messy deed? She even has her chef prepare hamburgers *en croûte*. And Napoleon himself never ate with better silver."

When Marlon became the latest in her long list of movie star bedmates, he made only one complaint to Gilman, claiming that she once interrupted him while they were having hot sex.

"Just imagine," she whispered in his ear, "I'm in bed with Stanley Kowalski. *The* Marlon Brando!"

"My hard-on deflated at hearing that," Marlon told Gilman, "but soon I was back in the saddle again, my noble tool doing its duty."

Gilman claimed that although Marlon didn't fall in love with Merle, he had a real empathy for her. "Merle knew her star was fading," Gilman said. "Apparently, she had long talks with Marlon about the twinkle in her star growing dimmer and all the feelings that aroused within her, knowing that her career was near its end. After *Desirée*, she made only sporadic appearances, one of which was a small role in *The Oscar* in which she was type-cast as an actress past her prime."

"The only roles open to me in the future will be that of a rich old lady involved with a much younger man," Merle told Marlon.

If Gilman is to be believed, Marlon told her, "Come over here and join me in bed. We can start rehearsals on that role right now."

In the years to come, Marlon watched with a certain melancholy as Merle fulfilled her self-prophecy. Her last film appearance was in a vanity production, *Interval*, released in 1973. In it she played an older woman involved with a much younger man. The actor was Robert Wolders who became her last husband. Marlon had been at a party in Hollywood in the late 1960s when Merle met the handsome actor. He later jokingly (or perhaps not) told Gilman, "I wanted that hunk for myself until Merle made off with him instead."

After seeing Wolders emote with Merle in *Interval*, he sent her a kind note in Mexico, knowing how hostile the critics had been to her. Instead of praising her acting, he complimented her "timeless beauty."

She responded by extending an invitation to him to sail with Wolders and her on an around-the-world cruise aboard the old vessel, *Kungsholm*. He sent his apologies, pleading other commitments.

The affair of Merle and Marlon hardly survived the shoot of *Desirée*. Gilman knew what went wrong. He claimed that Merle made the mistake of inviting Rita Hayworth to one of her dinner parties. The two stars had become friends when Rita was cast with Merle in the romantic triangle, *Affectionately Yours*, released in 1941, co-starring Dennis Morgan.

"At the end of Merle's little *soirée*, she asked Marlon if he'd drive Rita home," Gilman said. "The love goddess had arrived at the dinner without an escort. Marlon too readily agreed. After that night, it was out with Merle, in with Rita."

* * *

"The poor little rich girl," heiress Gloria Vanderbilt, was about to enter Marlon's life, if only for a one-night stand.

Gloria, as she confessed herself in her romance memoir, *It Seemed Important at the Time*, had seen *On the Waterfront* and was mesmerized by Marlon—"that inarticulate sensitivity. So feminine—and yet so masculine." Right then and there she decided, "Yes, that's for me."

Gloria Vanderbilt

Very early one morning, she called her best friend, Carol Marcus, in California. Carol not only knew Marlon, but had dated him and had been seen riding around New York City on the back of his motorcycle.

After an almost constant busy signal, Gloria finally got through to Carol. Coincidentally, Carol's line had been tied up talking to Marlon. Carol's plan involved having dinner with him that night. In response, Gloria arranged a seat on the

468

next available plane winging its way to the West Coast . . . and to Marlon. Amazingly, she arrived in Los Angeles in time for dinner.

At "Chez Brando," Gloria was attired in a scarlet sari with gold threads.

She wrote of "instant gratification" when she first laid eyes on Marlon. If she defined her husband, Leopold Stokowski, as God, then in her view Marlon must be Zeus . . . at least.

Gloria dined with Carol and Marlon's aunt, Betty Lindemeyer, in the kitchen of Marlon's house. But Gloria stayed on after the other two women had left for the night.

Before midnight she'd been delivered to his bedroom where she remembered seeing a framed photograph of him dressed as Napoleon that had been shot on the set of *Desirée*. Although his phone was switched off during his lovemaking to her, she recalled the phone's lights going on and off throughout the night. She suspected these unanswered calls were coming in from other women.

Carol, who apparently wasn't jealous, came to pick up Gloria the next morning.

Carol was throwing a party that night, and Gloria waited in vain all day for Marlon to call. She anticipated that he'd show up at Carol's party but he didn't. Instead Gene Kelly danced in the door, and Gene and Gloria ended up kissing as the husky sounds of Lauren Bacall singing "Little Girl Blue" drifted in from the living room.

Marlon never showed up, but called the following day, reaching Gloria shortly before she boarded her plane back to New York. He thanked her for "tender feelings."

Although she pined for Marlon in New York, listening to the Nat King Cole recording of "Unforgettable," she never heard from him again. After that "tale of enchantment," she decided she'd never again give her secret heart completely to anyone—"not even to Zeus Marlon."

Other lovers were waiting to fill the vacuum—an aviator, Howard Hughes, a crooner, Frank Sinatra, and even an unidentified man from Chicago. She called him "the Nijinsky of cunnilingus."

The details associated with each of these love affairs, as noted above, were revealed by Gloria herself in 2004 in her "romance memoir," *Gloria Vanderbilt: It Seemed Important at the Time*. And until she revealed the details of her brief affair with Marlon, as noted above, their short-lived romance wasn't known except among intimate friends.

* * *

Previous biographers of Marlon and Rita Hayworth were in for a shock on March 1, 2003 when *Harper's* magazine published an article "Last Tango in

Rita Hayworth

Westwood: On Not Sleeping with Marlon Brando." The piece was written by Phyllis Raphael.

The article described a dinner at a Westwood restaurant, where Phyllis, along with her husband, Bob, "the young Turk," joined Rita and Marlon at table sometime in 1968, before Marlon's body became shrouded in fat. During the course of that evening, Marlon shamelessly flirted with Phyllis—"his knuckles light as a firefly's wings—tracing the upper flank of my left arm," out of sight of her husband Bob. This was not a revelation. Marlon routinely flirted with other men's wives.

But during the course of that dinner, despite his flirtations with Phyllis, Marlon directed most of his charm toward Rita. At that point in her life, Rita no longer looked like the dazzling Love Goddess of the Forties, the stunning Latina beauty, who'd married film genius Orson Welles and Prince Aly Khan. Phyllis found "no trace of the glamorous actress who looked out from the covers of fan magazines I read in high school under the hair dryer in my Brooklyn beauty parlor. Her face is puffy, her hair is pulled back in a severe bun, and she's dressed in a strict buttoned-up glen plaid suit and laced-up oxfords. She doesn't look so much like a movie star as like a woman who, if she even had a film career, would have spent it playing the matron in British orphanages. But Brando is treating her as if she's still the luscious Gilda, her silken leg extended from the slit in a long, strapless black gown."

At the table, as witnessed by Phyllis, Marlon confessed that he and Rita were "old, old friends. She's always been there for me," he said. "She saved me from myself, and we had some great times together."

This would come as a revelation to the readers of *Harper's* magazine and certainly to Hollywood insiders, who had up until then never known of any links between Rita and Marlon.

During the course of the dinner, as related in Phyllis' magazine article, Marlon went on and on with his lush tribute to Rita. He kissed her fingertips in tribute for "How much you've taught me, the Stanislavsky side of you, the degree which your insights have shaped my performances."

Was Marlon a bit drunk? Had he confused Rita Hayworth with Stella Adler?

Under the sunlight of Marlon's praise, Rita leaned her head on his shoulder and, in Phyllis's words, became "suddenly younger, even glowing."

She said, "No, not really!" But it was obvious that she welcomed his compliments.

Marlon was engaging in a "courtship dance" with Rita as he must have done at one time or another in some distant past. He talked of the times they'd spent together. "No one—no one—was more fun than Rita," Marlon said. "We shared plenty of laughs." He paused provocatively. "But there was more . . . so much more. Rita here was a rare lady. A pure soul! A class act."

Phyllis wasn't alone in corroborating the long-standing relationship that thrived, virtually unknown to the public, between Marlon and Rita Hayworth.

Rita's close friend, Jane Sinclair, who lived in Paris during the last seven years of her life with a very young French husband, shed some light on the Brando/Hayworth romance shortly before her death in 1993. A woman not known for her discretion, she was also a close friend of Roger Vadim and Christian Marquand.

Jane Sinclair revealed that Rita and Marlon conducted a secret romance within the confines of a home that "one of my husbands used to own in Beverly Hills. Rita and Marlon were never seen in public. It was all very private, very hush-hush. They went to bed together the night Marlon brought her back from a dinner party thrown by Merle Oberon. I don't think it was love, but the romance had a certain passion in it." Privately, after a few drinks in the bar of the Ritz Hotel in Paris, Sinclair confessed her reason for promoting a romance with Rita and Marlon: Behind their backs she was secretly dating Rita Hayworth's husband, the singer, Dick Haymes. A toothy, slick-haired singer from Argentina, his eager-to-please baritone had enchanted radio audiences during the 1940s.

Sinclair admitted that when Dick couldn't get money from Rita, he got it from her. "I was forced to pay by the inch, darling."

Sinclair attempted to explain Rita's fascination with Marlon. "It wasn't just about sex. I went to bed with Rita's other husband, Prince Aly Khan. He could send a woman into ecstasy, the greatest lover since that Dominican stud, Porfirio Rubirosa. I also went to bed with Marlon one night. But he was no Prince Aly, no Porfirio."

Until she met Marlon, Rita often complained that, "Every man I've known fell in love with Gilda and woke up with me." Marlon was different. He claimed that Rita looked her prettiest without makeup. He found a good, gentle person behind all the lipstick, satin gowns, and black hosiery.

"Unlike many of her lovers, Rita had plenty to talk about with Marlon after the sex was out of the way," Sinclair said. "Actually, I think Rita used Marlon as her analyst, and he always liked to meet and listen to people in trouble. Rita told him all her secrets, things she'd buried inside herself for years. Like surrendering her virginity to her father, Eduardo Cansino."

Cansino was a Spanish vaudeville dancer, and Rita danced with him on stage in the "Sin City" of Agua Caliente, Mexico, the patrons thinking they were brother and sister.

Rita also told Marlon that her first husband, "that god damn con man," Edward Judson, had forced her to sleep with powerful men in Hollywood who would further her career. He ordered her into the bed of Harry P. Cohn, then head of Columbia Pictures. Rita always privately referred to Cohn as "that shithead." She claimed that Judson threatened to mutilate her face if she didn't sleep with the man he'd selected for her.

Rita confessed to Marlon that her husband, Dick Haymes, was just "using me for a meal ticket. After all his drunken sprees and all those ex-wives, he's blown four million dollars. He's also left with a bagful of kids to support."

Marlon, according to Sinclair, was always willing to listen to Rita's woes, both marital and romantic. "He also wanted to hear all the details of her love affairs," Sinclair said, suspecting that Marlon might be a voyeur.

According to Sinclair, Rita's list of lovers was long, including such "usual suspects" as Kirk Douglas, Charles Feldman, Glenn Ford, Errol Flynn, Howard Hughes, Tony Martin, Victor Mature, Robert Mitchum, David Niven, Gilbert Roland, Tyrone Power, and James Stewart.

Some of her romances weren't successful. Peter Lawford pronounced her the "worst lay in Hollywood—always drunk, and she never stopped eating." Marlon learned that she'd had a serious affair with the Spanish bullfighter, Luis Dominguin, when he was not in the arms of another Forties love goddess, Ava Gardner. There was a surprise or two for Marlon, as Rita revealed details about her affair with Caryl Chessman, California's "Red Light" bandit, accused of impersonating a police officer who robbed and sometimes sexually assaulted his victims. From his cell on Death Row at Folsom Prison, Chessman wrote four separate books, each of which generated public sentiment against capital punishment. After eight stays of execution, he went to the gas chamber on May 2, 1960.

But the biggest surprise for Marlon came when he learned the horrors of her "storybook romance" with Prince Aly Khan. She described some of his endless affairs. Before meeting Rita, Marlon thought that she had vast wealth as a result of that marriage. Rita revealed to him that even though her father-in-law, the morbidly obese Aga Khan, the hereditary Iman (spiritual leader) of the Shi'a Imami Ismaeli Community, was worth his weight in diamonds, he didn't share those riches with his playboy son, a womanizer and a gambler. She claimed that she often had to pay her husband's debts until she too ran out of money. "The bastard owes me $18,000 in child support," she told Marlon. She also told him that even though married to Aly Khan, she was pursued by other royals, especially the endlessly decadent king of Egypt, King Farouk, and the persistent Shah of Iran.

"Marlon was shocked to learn that Rita was broke and having a hard time surviving," Sinclair said. "I think he gave her money to help pay her debts. Like Judy Garland, she came within a few inches of getting evicted."

In one of the most despicable acts that Harry Cohn ever did, he placed secret recording devices both in Rita's dressing room and also within her house. Howard Hughes had pulled the same trick on Ava Gardner. One night Cohn made a recording of Rita and Marlon in bed. He kept it in his office, frequently playing it for his friends. He thought it was all one big joke. "Mumbles and Gilda making love," he called it.

Without revealing his true feelings, Marlon once told Carlo Fiore that "there is one thing that I think about a lot when I'm pounding Rita. I hate to admit this, but it gets me extra excited."

"You think of her as Gilda?" Fiore asked, stating the obvious thought in most men's heads.

"No, not that at all!" Marlon said. "Rita's likeness was stamped on the first atomic bomb dropped on Hiroshima. I think about that right before I'm about to erupt inside her with my own explosion!"

According to Jane Sinclair, Marlon continued his friendship with Rita "even when passion's flower wilted," in her words. He only stopped coming to see her when she had moved deeper into Alzheimer's, the disease that was to dominate the remaining twenty-five years of her life, and she no longer knew who he was.

Marlon was watching television on May 14, 1987 when news broadcasts announced Rita's death. Friends said he wept unashamedly.

* * *

Marlon found his *Desirée* costar, British-born Jean Simmons, "my kind of woman." An actress of effervescent talent, with delicate traits and mannerisms, she reminded him of Audrey Hepburn or Deborah Kerr. Critics called their teaming in *Desirée* "dreary," but that was on screen. Off screen they became friends. On meeting Marlon, Jean called attention to the fact that they

Stewart Granger

had been slated to appear together in *The Egyptian* until he bolted. "It was the script—not your casting," Marlon assured her.

When he met her, Marlon was aware of Jean's ongoing feud with Howard Hughes. The aviator had developed an obsession with her and had urged her to dump her husband, Stewart Granger, and marry him. When she refused, he retaliated against her, threatening to destroy her career. Such an action drove Stewart to plan "how to murder the bastard," as he confessed in his autobiography, *Sparks Fly Upward*, published in 1981.

Four years younger than Marlon, Jean did not have a reputation for being promiscuous when she met Marlon, although she was rumored to have seduced two of best friend Elizabeth Taylor's husbands, Nicky Hilton and the producer Michael Todd. Speaking of Elizabeth Taylor husbands (at least future ones), Richard Burton and Jean were also rumored to have had an affair during their costarring turn in *The Robe*. There were also rumors of affairs with the studly Robert Mitchum and Laurence Harvey, who actually preferred black men to white women.

Marlon claimed that he "held back in my desire for *Desirée*" because Jean was married to Stewart. That pronouncement came as a surprise to Marlon's friends. Never in his life had he held back on the seduction of a woman because she was married or had a steady boyfriend. If anything, he seemed to prefer women already in a deep commitment to another man instead of what he termed "free-range vaginas."

Before Jean introduced Marlon to her husband, Marlon contemptuously referred to the British actor as "the great white hunter," because of such previous adventure films as MGM's blockbuster hit of 1950, *King Solomon's Mines*. Stewart also held Marlon in contempt, or so it seemed. In his autobiography, Stewart admitted that even though Jean liked Marlon, he found him "fairly insufferable."

When Jean told Marlon that Stewart was dropping by the set to meet him, he admitted that he was looking forward to "sizing up the competition." His remark could have been interpreted in two different ways. One, that he viewed Stewart as a roadblock to his moving in on Jean. Two, that he wanted to evaluate an actor who was often "spoken of in the same breath for the same roles in movies."

Considering how different Stewart and Marlon were as both men and actors, it now seems a bit of a stretch to think they could have played the same roles. But for years the word in Hollywood was, "If you can't get Marlon, go for Granger." MGM, in fact, had originally wanted Stewart for the role of Marc Antony instead of Marlon.

As improbable as it seems today, Stewart was asked by director Laurence Olivier to play Stanley Kowalski in the London production of *A Streetcar Named Desire*, opposite his wife, Vivien Leigh. Granger turned down the offer, which had originated directly from Irene Mayer Selznick, claiming that "Brando is a tough act to follow."

Eventually, both men were offered, and both of them refused, starring roles in such soon-to-be classics as *From Here to Eternity* and *A Star Is Born*.

One critic wrote that suave Stewart Granger, instead of appearing in costume epics and adventure films, "would be better suited for drawing room comedies, lounging about in a smoking jacket, swilling martinis, and making

474

Michael Wilding, Elizabeth Taylor, Stewart Granger, and Jean Simmons

bedroom eyes at the ladies." The critic was right on target. As Stewart himself would readily admit, "I'm not the type to play a peasant in New Orleans calling for Stella."

The 1962 *Sodom and Gomorrah* had first been offered to Marlon who turned it down, Stewart going for it. In the film Stewart played opposite Pier Angeli, girlfriend of both Marlon and James Dean. When Marlon learned that Stewart had been cast in the film instead of himself, he sarcastically remarked, "I wonder which role he's playing. Sodom or Gomorrah? If I know Stew, he's definitely going to play Sodom."

Like Marlon himself, Stewart not only had already led a life of high adventure, but many of his greatest episodes lay in his future. He'd had love affairs with the two richest women in the world, Barbara Hutton and Doris Duke. Like Marlon, he'd been involved in a three-way with Laurence Olivier and Vivien Leigh. In time, he would chase a nude Vivien around and into her swimming pool, trying to force tranquilizers down her throat.

Like Marlon, the swashbuckling MGM star was a bisexual, his most enduring romance being with another British actor, Michael Wilding. When Elizabeth Taylor was planning to marry Wilding, columnist Hedda Hopper summoned the couple to her home. Once there, in front of Wilding, Hopper declared that Wilding was a known homosexual and that Taylor would be "throwing away your life" if she married him. At the time, Taylor and Wilding were house guests of Stewart and Jean. After their return to the Granger-Simmons house, Wilding told Stewart about the confrontation.

In anger, a drunken Stewart called Hopper, denouncing her as a monumental bitch. "How bloody dare you accuse a friend of mine of being queer, you raddled, dried up, frustrated old cunt." He slammed down the phone on the powerful columnist, who attacked him repeatedly throughout the remainder of his and her career.

Years later, when appearing in New York in the play, *Chameleons*, an older and mellower Stewart admitted that Hopper had been right. He revealed that he had indeed had an affair with Wilding, claiming "it was something men did during the war."

When Marlon met Stewart on the set of *Desirée*, both men were prepared to take an instant dislike to each other. Marlon had been difficult and temperamental with his director and the rest of his crew, except costars Merle Oberon and Jean Simmons. But Sam Gilman claimed that "Marlon turned that old black magic on Stewart the moment they shook hands. Marlon absolutely captivated *Scaramouche*," he said, referring to the MGM costume epic in which Stewart had starred in 1952.

In contrast to the brash, swashbuckling image he projected on the screen, Stewart was completely different in person, a caring, articulate, educated, sensitive actor with a bisexual background to equal Marlon's own adventures. As John Gielgud once said, "Stewart is adept at bringing the greatest pleasure to both men and women."

Apparently unknown to his wife, Jean, an intimate relationship quickly developed between Marlon and Stewart, according to Gilman. He said that the friendship was conducted in total secrecy and lasted "at least" through the filming of Marlon's next picture, *Guys and Dolls*, in which he was cast once again opposite Jean Simmons.

During the filming of *Guys and Dolls*, Stewart admitted that he was having anxiety attacks about his marriage, as Jean faced "the triple menace of Brando, Frank Sinatra, and Joseph Mankiewicz," who was directing the picture. If rumors are to be believed, Mankiewicz succeeded where Sinatra and Marlon struck out. Although not admitting to an affair with Jean, Mankiewicz years later recalled that Marlon and Sinatra "may not have gotten Jean, but they did at least get to share Ava Gardner so I don't feel that sorry for them. Having sampled the charms of Ava myself, I know what a treat that must have been for my boys."

Both Marlon and Sinatra surely would have been horrified to have the director speak of them as "my boys."

After that fateful meeting with Stewart, Marlon called off his chase of Jean. "He went for the handsome hubby instead," Gilman said. "Why not? Virtually every horny woman, bisexual male, or gay boy had the hots for Stewart back in those days. Cary Grant pursued him for years."

Gilman, who was living with Marlon at the time, saw the affair between the two men unfold before his eyes. "Slipping around so as not to alert his wife, Stewart was a frequent visitor at Marlon's. I know they disappeared into Marlon's bedroom on many a night. I don't know for sure, but there was no television in that bedroom. Not even a radio. Those two boys must have been up to something, unless they settled for holding hands. Knowing Marlon as I did, he never settled for that, not even some passionate kisses. Marlon had to go all the way."

In front of Gilman, who poured their drinks and often cooked meals for the two actors, Stewart kept Marlon constantly amused with stories from his life. He claimed that he once tested for the lead role in *Quo Vadis?* with a seventeen-year-old Elizabeth Taylor. John Huston was called in to direct that day, instructing Stewart to play his part "like a drunken buck nigger!" The starring roles eventually went, of course, to Deborah Kerr and Robert Taylor.

Marlon learned that Stewart lost his virginity to "Josette," a young French prostitute he met in Paris while he was there for a rugby match. He spoke of his first wife, the British actress, Elspeth March. Stewart claimed that he seduced a female French friend of hers only to "come down with history's worst case of gonorrhea."

He also told Marlon that Doris Duke had such a large vagina, that "even Porfirio Rubirosa, the world's heaviest endowed playboy, couldn't fill it." Stewart was obviously not aware that Marlon had already had an affair with the tobacco heiress. "I practically fell in when I seduced Duke," Stewart told Marlon and Gilman. "And as you already know," Stewart said, directing his comment just to Marlon, "I'm very well hung." In fact, when the wardrobe department at MGM first put a pair of tights on me, for *Scaramouche*, I bulged so much they had to tape my equipment to my belly."

For weeks, Stewart amused Marlon with his stories. Both men had seduced Hedy Lamarr and shared stories about their respective adventures with the Austrian beauty. "When I fucked Hedy, she was late for her hairdresser. Nonetheless, she instructed me, 'Now don't come too fast!'"

"That had Marlon doubled over in stitches," Gilman said. Marlon also took delight in the impersonations that Stewart did of his fellow British actor, Cary Grant. He always referred to Grant as "the leader of Hollywood's pansy brigade."

One night Stewart, in front of Gilman, told Marlon that Elizabeth Taylor was number one on his list of future conquests. "I've always wanted to fuck her," he said. "I've had the groom. Why not the bride?"

Marlon admitted that he, too, would get around to "fucking Liz when the time is right." Richard Burton always maintained that "my Elizabeth and that Brando creature had an affair" when they costarred in *Reflections in a Golden Eye*, released in 1967.

In front of Gilman, Stewart told Marlon that when he came to Hollywood, he found out that Englishmen had a reputation for being stuffy and condescending. "That's just an act we put on. Deep down we're bawdy and raunchy."

"You're not stuffy at all," Marlon said. "And I should know. If it weren't for the accent, you could be an American."

Stewart arched an eyebrow. "Should I take that as a compliment?"

"What reputation do Americans have in London?" Marlon asked.

"Frankly, they're known as cocksuckers whereas British men are famous for being sodomites."

"Well," Marlon said, getting up and motioning Stewart toward the bedroom. "Reputations are about to be tested tonight."

Gilman took that as proof that Marlon and Stewart were engaged in a sexual liaison—"or else liked to have pretty hot dialogue."

And then one day after *Guys and Dolls* was wrapped, the relationship between Marlon and Stewart ended. "To my knowledge, they didn't have a falling out," Gilman said. "Marlon had a brief attention span. He once told me that nothing captured his attention for more than seven minutes. Stewart had a good track record. He stayed around until weeks turned to months. I know it's an odd coupling. Stewart Granger and Marlon Brando. But so was Marlon Brando and Wally Cox an odd coupling. Stewart and Marlon took real delight in each other's company for as long as it lasted. Real male bonding. I overheard them making plans to go on a big trip to India together. Marlon even urged Stewart to settle down with him one day and purchase the ranch next to his in Nebraska. Marlon claimed they could ride on horseback together and watch the wildflowers burst into bloom on the plains—shit like that. They even compared notes on what it was like to fuck Ava Gardner. In the long run, there was no love lost between the two men. But for one brief moment they ignited passion in each other. Both men had a great gusto for living. They came together, however briefly, and a good time was had by all except me. I didn't go that route."

* * *

Sam Gilman was on the set of *Desirée* the day Marilyn showed up. He later learned the details of what transpired between the two stars. She was

Marlon as Napoleon
with Marilyn Monroe

working on a nearby set, filming *There's No Business Like Show Business*, a frothy tribute to Irving Berlin. In the film, she performed her now infamous "Heat Wave" number, in which she seemed to be doing a caricature of Carmen Miranda.

Encountering Marlon, she giggled when she saw him dressed as Napoleon. In a formal gown, she posed for pictures with him. On the surface, everything seemed all right. One major star calling on another major star.

But in his dressing room she showed him where makeup concealed black and blue marks on her right arm. "Marilyn abhorred violence of any kind," Gilman

478

said. "Marlon was furious to learn what a mean shithead DiMaggio was in private, in contrast to his public image. He'd come home drunk and accused Marilyn of continuing her affairs with both Marlon and Frank Sinatra, and countless others, even though married to him. That may have been true. Even so, violence was not the answer. Marilyn told Marlon that DiMaggio had started beating her and that she'd run into their bedroom and locked the door. He broke down the door and continued beating her, avoiding her face so that she could still appear before the camera. At least he knew enough to do that. He didn't want the press to learn what a shit America's hero really was. Marlon became incensed when he learned of this. He wanted Marilyn to move out, and he told her she could come and live with him until she found a place of her own. He also advised her to file for divorce. Two nights later, he told me that Marilyn's marriage to DiMaggio wasn't legal anyway, because technically she was still married to him and had not gotten a divorce. I still don't know to this day if Marlon was actually married to Marilyn—or whether he was just putting me on."

Somehow, Marlon broke through to Marilyn. Standing nearby as if on security watch for Marlon, Gilman heard Marilyn singing "After You Get What You Want You Don't Want It," which was one of her numbers for *There's No Business Like Show Business*. Gilman later learned that Marilyn was auditioning the number for Marlon, seeking his approval.

Marilyn was no dumb blonde. She had a reason to visit Marlon other than to say "Hi."

"She must have been fucking Joseph Mankiewicz, because she'd learned that the Damon Runyon musical, *Guys and Dolls*, was about to be cast," Gilman said. "Mankiewicz had wanted Gene Kelly for the role but MGM said no. Frank Sinatra was lobbying for the role of Sky Masterson. Ever since he'd cast her in *All About Eve*, Mankiewicz and Marilyn had had a sometimes thing. Perhaps over pillow talk, she'd learned that the director was going to offer the role of Sky Masterson to Marlon, even though Sinatra would have been the more obvious choice."

Marlon later told Gilman that he thought Marilyn was joking when she revealed that. "Me, a song-and-dance man? That'll be the day!"

Marilyn desperately wanted to play one of the two female leads. She would do either one, but preferred to portray Miss Adelaide, although she said that if she agreed to the part, the role would have to be greatly expanded.

Marlon promised to lobby for her, because he was still a friend of Mankiewicz, but said he would refuse

Joe DiMaggio

479

the role himself. "If Joe Mankiewicz is crazy enough to offer me the part, I'll tell the fucker to go fly a kite." The role of Miss Adelaide eventually went to Vivian Blaine, who had originated the part on Broadway.

According to Gilman, Marilyn told Marlon that DiMaggio wanted to turn her into a simple housewife. Her first husband, James E. Dougherty, had tried to do that back during World War II.

"You know, a home-cooked dinner by the fireplace where I prepare his favorite pasta as he watches baseball on TV, or big-time boxing, perhaps a Roger Rogers movie," Marilyn said. "He even insists that I iron his white shirts, using lots of starch." What Marilyn failed to tell Marlon was that at the time, she and DiMaggio had three servants.

Publicly, she was informing the press, especially her favorite columnist Sidney Skolsky, that, "Marriage is something you learn more about while you live it." Privately, she told Marlon that the marriage to DiMaggio was all but over except the formalities.

"I think Marlon and Marilyn seriously discussed marriage—the real thing for all the world to see, not that fake ceremony, or whatever in the hell it was, that they had on location with *Viva Zapata!*" Gilman said. "Marlon told me that Marilyn agreed to the marriage, providing that she would not be expected to have children."

Three nights later, when Marilyn came over for a dinner cooked by Gilman, Marlon said, "DiMaggio's going to be a tough act to follow if I take up with Marilyn."

"What do you mean?" Gilman asked.

"Marilyn told me, 'Joe's biggest bat is not the one he uses on the baseball field.' She also told him that, 'If sex is what it took, I'd stay married to Joe.'"

"I've never heard any woman complain about your noble tool," Gilman said to reassure his friend.

One week later, as Gilman recalled, a new and different Marilyn fled to the set of *Desirée* to see Marlon. "Instead of a formal dress, she wore a tattered bathrobe that was last washed in 1913," Gilman said. "She wore no makeup and looked awful. At first I didn't recognize her. Marlon later explained to me that Marilyn Monroe was just a show business concoction. The real girl wasn't anything like Monroe."

To illustrate his point, Marlon related an incident that had occurred along New York's Fifth Avenue several months previously. "We were just strolling along and chatting. She wore a scarf and no makeup. Suddenly, she turned to me and asked, 'Do you want to see what happens when I become Marilyn Monroe?' She took off the scarf, applied lipstick, did something to her hair, gave me her raincoat to hold, and then walked like the sultry bitch she'd played in *Niagara*. Within moments, she was mobbed by adoring fans. It seemed that everyone forgot me. Me, fucking Marlon Brando. The biggest movie star on the planet."

On her second visit to the set of *Desirée*, Marlon saw at once that Marilyn was in serious trouble. "He just walked off camera," Gilman said, "and headed for Marilyn. Wrapping a strong arm around her, he led her once again to his dressing room where he put out the DO NOT DISTURB sign. All shooting had to be suspended for the day. The director was furious. I hung around in case Marlon needed me later. I never knew exactly what drove Marilyn in such a condition to the *Desirée* set. Later Marlon quoted her to me. 'My brains are leaving me just like they did with my mother,' Marilyn told Marlon. 'They're going to come for me. Lock me away in some hospital.' Perhaps without knowing it at the time, Marilyn was having a prophetic vision of her future."

Marlon said that Marilyn begged him to run away with her. "Any place in the world," she told him. "Just a place where we can hide out forever."

"I fucked her," Marlon told Gilman. "That was the only way my noble tool knew how to calm her down."

"Marilyn did hide out for several days with Marlon before everything blew up between Jumpin' Joe and her," Gilman claimed.

"I like a gal like Marilyn," Marlon later told Gilman. "She can take it in three different holes—my kind of woman."

Suddenly, without even leaving a note for Marlon, Marilyn disappeared.

"I told Marilyn good-bye," Gilman said. "I even saw the man who had come to take her away. It was Frank Sinatra. I told Marlon that Marilyn had left in a taxi. If I'd ratted that it was Sinatra, he would have exploded on me. God, did he hate Sinatra."

"Believe me, the feeling was mutual," Gilman claimed. Not only was Sinatra seriously—and even dangerously—pissed over Marlon's moving in on Ava Gardner, but Sinatra had just learned that Marlon, after holding out, finally told Mankiewicz that he was willing to sign to play Sky Masterson. Sinatra needed film work, and with great bitterness eventually agreed to accept the minor male role of Nathan Detroit.

Gilman claimed that during Marilyn's filming of *The Seven Year Itch*, Marlon forgave her for running out on him without a good-bye.

"They would be close until the day of her death," Gilman said. "But never again did I hear talk of marriage."

* * *

At the Fox studio, Marlon took Carlo Fiore to see a screening of *Desirée*, explaining that "I used a lot of nose putty and layers of makeup. Since I was forced to do the picture, I walked through the part. I tried to get some humor in my characterization, but the final result merely depressed me instead of amusing me."

When Anna Kashfi, who became Marlon's first wife, went to see the film with her neighbor, Marilyn Monroe, Anna claimed, "I was appalled by the awkward expository dialogue and by the camera angles that emphasized Marlon's fat buttocks bulging against snug, silk breeches."

Marlon winced when he saw how Zanuck was advertising the picture for its 1954 release with the somewhat confusing slogan, "Before Josephine there was *Desirée* . . . and some say there was always . . ."

A preview audience in Pasadena laughed at some serious parts of the movie. In one scene, Marlon, playing Napoleon, asks the question, "When did you stop loving me?"

A heckler rose up in the audience. "When you made this shit-kicker."

The audience burst into derisive laughter. The years of unprecedented ridicule for Marlon had begun.

Paul Holt, writing in the *Daily Herald*, summed it up: "This is probably the worst performance of any star asked to play a character role in costume that Hollywood has ever offered us in a long and dogged assault upon our credulity."

Normally critical of Marlon's acting, Sir Laurence Olivier said, "I adored his performance. The best screen Napoleon ever!" Whether Olivier was being serious or else indulging in subtle ridicule is not known.

Vivien Leigh had a different opinion, calling it "a burlesque walk-through by a zombie. I think Audie Murphy would have been better cast as Napoleon."

When Jay Kanter told Marlon that *Desirée* had outgrossed *On the Waterfront*, Marlon made his comment by quoting H.L. Mencken, "No one ever lost money underestimating the taste of the American public."

Marlon delivered one final comment about *Desirée* and then refused to speak of it ever again. "It was a serious retrogression and the most shaming experience of my life."

Privately, Carlo Fiore expressed his dismay about Marlon's career to Bobby Lewis in New York. "This is the end for Marlon as an actor. He should have been born years earlier when he could have played in adult movies. Now we're going to get such freak things as Marilyn Monroe's ass splashed nine feet across the screen in CinemaScope. Stuff like that. Next thing I know, Zanuck will ask Marlon to take over for Raymond Massey and play Abe Lincoln. I'm sure he'll be asked to play Douglas MacArthur. It's a certainty he'll get the next remake of Valentino's life story. My prediction? He'll end up like James Stewart and Gary Cooper, certainly Henry Fonda, playing some old Gabby Hayes codger in a sagebrush oater!"

* * *

In the 1950s, Swiss-born Ursula Andress, who styled herself as "the female Marlon Brando," was struggling to learn English with some vague hope of making it as a Hollywood star. She had the beauty and the physical assets, but lacked talent and never wanted to work hard enough to master the King's English, preferring her native German tongue.

James Dean with girlfriend number two, Ursula Andress

Marlon had met the Swiss bombshell—often called Swedish in biographies—when she was temporarily sharing an apartment with Josanne Berenger, Marlon's "one true love," or so he said.

When Andress moved into her own ivy-covered cottage overlooking Sunset Boulevard, Marlon was a frequent visitor.

Still living with Marlon at the time, Sam Gilman said that Andress was a true *femme fatale*. "If Josanne wanted to hold onto Marlon, she made a fatal mistake in introducing him to her roommate. No woman on the face of the earth should introduce a boyfriend or husband to Ursula. When Marlon met her, she could have any man on the planet she wanted, providing he wasn't gay. No, I take that back. She could have any man she wanted, including the gay ones. If I know Ursula, she'd convert them to heterosexuality."

"Marlon told me that he was dating two young women, Ursula Andress and Pier Angeli, and he was going to marry one of them and keep the other one as his mistress," Gilman said. "But I haven't decided which one is going to be cast in the role of the long-suffering wife and which one is going to be cast as the lucky mistress who gets the diamonds, the mink coats, and me," Marlon said.

"But isn't James Dean dating Andress and Angeli," Gilman protested. "Aren't they, in fact, his girlfriends, maybe with a little Terry Moore thrown in between sessions with the boys."

"Yes, Jimmy is dating both Pier and Ursula," Marlon said. "That is precisely why I'm interested. I have to keep showing Jimmy boy who's the real man in our relationship. I'm practically driving that boy to suicide. When not with Ursula or Pier, or running off

Ursula Andress

483

to Mexico with that shit-kicker from Texas, Howard Hughes, Jimmy boy can't seem to get enough of my noble tool."

Unlike James's affair with Pier Angeli, Marlon did not take the month-long romance with Andress seriously. "She's more woman than Jimmy can handle," he told Gilman.

Andress remembered her courtship with James. "He came by my house late. He came in room like wild animal, and smell of everything I don't like. We go hear jazz music and he leave table. Say he go play drums. He no come back. I don't like to be alone. I go home. He come by my home later and say he sorry. Ask if I want to see his motorcycle. We sit on sidewalk in front of motorcycle and talk, talk, talk, until five. He go home."

On other nights, she was seen riding around Hollywood on the back of James's motorcycle. She was also spotted in fast-moving cars driven by James—in fact, she was with him on the day he purchased the car that would cost him his life.

On the times she did go out with him, she said that they "fought like cat and dog—no, two monsters. But we make up and have fun."

She more or less followed the same pattern with Marlon. They too argued and made up. Apparently, they got into a row over American music on their first date, and the arguments continued. "That Ursula had a mind of her own—I'm sure she still does," Marlon once said. "She doesn't depend on a man to make up her mind for her. She's got opinions about everything."

Marlon was particularly interested in finding out from Ursula who the better lover was: James Dean or himself. "I don't think Ursula ever revealed that secret to him," Gilman said. "It drove him crazy. She probably took delight in that. Marlon might have thought that Ursula was too much woman for Dean. Personally, I think she was too much woman for Marlon as well."

When Marlon was "dating" James during the filming of *East of Eden*, he found that the young actor would often arrive at his house on a motorcycle with a German-language phrase book tucked up in his jacket. Marlon asked him why he was trying to master German. "I want to be able to fight with Ursula in her own language. She's not making much progress learning English, and I want her to comprehend how vindictive my insults are."

"Sounds like love," Marlon said jokingly.

Soon the press was referring to Ursula as "the paramour of Marlon Brando." One columnist predicted a combustion when "the female Marlon Brando hooks up with the one with the testosterone."

Marlon was influential in getting Andress a contract with Columbia. Nothing much came of that, and she later bought her way out of it, even though she hadn't made a film for the studio.

After Marlon, and after James, Andress met her John. He was the hand-

John Derek

some matinee idol John Derek, or "Derrick" as some Dean biographers erroneously put it. She would marry Derek in 1957, divorcing him in 1966. Derek went on to marry two younger beauties, Linda Evans and Bo Derek.

Waiting in the wings to grab Ursula were Warren Beatty, Ryan O'Neal, Harry Hamlin, and even Jean-Paul Belmondo and Fabio Testi. By then, Marlon had long faded from the picture.

However, when *Dr. No*, the first of the James Bond thrillers to reach the screen, was released in 1962, Marlon went to see it three times. Like the rest of the world, he was mesmerized by the now-famous white bikini scene of Andress emerging from the sea. Cast in the role of Honeychile Ryder, she brought a smoldering presence to the screen. Becoming an almost overnight legend, she was launched as one of the most desirable women on the planet. Her role also launched the Bond movies as a Hollywood staple, even though she was paid only ten thousand dollars for her effort. She later sold the bikini at auction for $61,500 to an anonymous buyer. *Dr. No* propelled her into a minor screen career where she became a 1960s pop icon, appearing with everybody from Frank Sinatra and Elvis Presley to Woody Allen and Peter O'Toole.

In the Nineties, when Marlon was writing his "tell-all" autobiography, he placed a two-hour call from Hollywood to Rome to speak to Andress. At first he flattered her, calling her "the ice maiden of forty wet dreams." But then he insulted her by asking her if she'd ever had an affair with him. He wanted to get it right for his memoirs.

It comes as a surprise that he was doing such personal research, because his memoirs became famous for leaving out details of his affairs, excepting Marilyn Monroe, of course.

When Andress's former husband, John Derek, heard of this phone call, he was astonished. "Who wouldn't remember fucking Ursula Andress? Marlon Brando must be coming down with Alzheimer's disease."

In a quote attributed to Andress (she may not have said it), she summed up her emotions about her affair with Marlon. "Marlon Brando can't love any woman because he never stopped having an affair with himself."

* * *

Pier Angeli had arrived from Rome to make her way toward stardom in Hollywood. Marlon had not seen her since his rape of her in Italy.

When not debating whether to make a film of *Antony and Cleopatra*, MGM executives were also considering filming *Romeo and Juliet*. The stars?

485

Marlon as Romeo and Pier as Juliet. Marlon decided to call Pier and discuss the project with her.

Pier was that curious "mixture of child, waif, and minx." When she'd first met Marlon in Italy she was—in her own words—"greedy for life, romance and emotion."

"What she got was rape, then abandonment," said director Vittorio De Sica.

When Pier arrived in Hollywood, on the rebound after a heart-breaking affair with Kirk Douglas, she was ripe for a new romance.

Marlon showed up at the Pierangeli house, and Pier agreed to see him despite of the brutality of their past in Rome. Her mother, Enrica Pierangeli, insisted that her sister, Marisa, go along on their dates.

With loud honking, Marlon arrived for his first date in front of the Pierangeli home. He was driving a large truck filled with bales of hay. He invited Pier and Marisa to join his friends, who included Rita Moreno, Jerome Robbins, and Phil Rhodes, his makeup man. Setting out on a picnic, Marlon, using an old map, got lost and never found the lake where he was headed. It had long since dried up.

Nonetheless, he became a fixture around the Pierangeli household that summer, and was finally able to date Pier without a chaperone. Sometimes he'd show up for dinner with the family, loving Enrica's pastas and bringing not-yet-released movies for the family to see.

At the end of the summer, Enrica claimed that Marlon was "the adorable son I never had, full of love, sensibility, and great compassion." Apparently, she didn't have a clue as to what was going on between her daughter and Marlon.

On their frequent dates, Marlon and Pier were spotted on the beaches of Malibu, strolling along the sands hand in hand. They were seen riding horses in Griffith Park. They often stopped at one of those 1950s diners, with waitresses on roller skates, to order hamburgers. Or else he'd take her to a movie in Pasadena. Marlon claimed he never patronized movie houses on Hollywood Boulevard "because too many fuckers know who I am." When not with Marlon, Pier would repeat, more or less, the same dates with James Dean.

Marlon drove Pier around Hollywood in a bullet-riddled car that had once belonged to Bugsy Siegel, the gangster whom he continued to admire and whose life story he wanted to film one day. "I'd go over big in a gangster movie," he once told Fiore.

Although Marlon dated Pier, who was twenty-two years old at the time, he told Sam Gilman that she was still a child at heart. "Sometimes as I'm driving her around Los Angeles, she sucks on a lollipop. She often hums nursery rhymes, and she still collects stuffed animals. Anytime I fuck her, I give her a

James Dean with girlfriend number one, Pier Angeli

teddy bear. She likes pink ones, not black or brown ones."

Whereas Pier's mother, Enrica, eventually approved of Marlon, she objected violently to her daughter's romance with James. Her first problem was that he was not a Catholic. Even when he promised to convert, she still disapproved of him because of his bad boy image. She'd also heard stories of various homosexual liaisons. According to Enrica, "Dean was always dirty. He was utterly self-centered. He used to come into my house and not even say hello. He'd head for my living room and play loud music, often until four o'clock in the morning. I doubt if he'll ever amount to anything."

At the time, Pier was filming that cinematic disaster, *The Silver Chalice* that starred the young newcomer, Paul Newman—the actor who James most admired after Marlon. James had met Pier when he strolled over from the *East of Eden* set to watch Newman perform in *The Silver Chalice*, one of that engaging young actor's worst roles. Originally Newman was to have played James's brother in *East of Eden*. "I want to check out the competition," James told Kazan. "This Newman baby is hot!"

Hand holding in the Warner Brothers commissary led to hotter dates. Soon Pier was giving James a gold wrist watch and even a miniature gold frame with her picture in it. Referred to as "Romeo and Juliet" in the press, Pier and James began their star-crossed affair, most of it carried out secretly in hideaways along the Pacific Ocean.

Pier claimed—falsely or not—that their love was so great that they once seriously contemplated holding hands together and walking into the Pacific Ocean. "That way, we knew we'd be together forever."

Marlon told Gilman that he felt that Enrica's objection to James only drove Pier into his arms. Apparently, Marlon was right on this call. Conducting an affair in secret only seemed to add spice to the Angeli/Dean affair, especially since she was also slipping around having an affair with Hollywood's other bad boy, Marlon himself.

"To capture the two bad boys of Hollywood at the same time, both of them men with an ambiguous sexuality, was no small accomplish-

Paul Newman

ment for Pier," said Virginia Mayo, who was the actual star of the 1954 *The Silver Chalice* at Warner Brothers.

Occasionally, James might get out of his Brando drag and dress formally, as when he escorted Pier to the premiere of *A Star Is Born* in 1954, a night when Judy Garland was clearly the star.

Pier Angeli and Vic Damone

The romance between Pier and James lasted from late June until the end of September, 1954.

Unknown to James, Pier was also secretly dating not only Marlon, but the singer, Vic Damone. She was having affairs with all three. Although publicly professing to be hopelessly in love with Pier, James behind her back mocked her as "Miss Pizza Pie."

Gilman later claimed that it was Marlon himself who ended—at least temporarily—Pier's affair with James, an act that drove her into the arms of Damone.

Unknown to either of the other parties, Marlon arranged dates with both James and Pier on the same night. James was invited to arrive an hour earlier. Two hours previously, Marlon had called Pier, telling her that he'd injured his leg in a fall. He asked her to enter his living room through the garden, telling her that the door would be open.

When she arrived, Marlon was nude on the sofa with James. "It was a hot sixty-nine the boys were having when innocent, impressionable Pier walked in on them," Gilman said. "I was in another room but I heard her scream and saw her racing out through the garden and back to her car."

James left the following morning, flying alone to New York. Someone tipped off reporters that his romance with Pier was off. In New York, journalists asked him what had happened.

"Something," he said enigmatically.

James, Marlon, Pier, and certainly Gilman knew what that "something" was.

James was still in New York when he heard over the radio an announcement from Louella Parsons that Pier was going to marry Damone.

Avidly, Marlon read press comments about the unhappy end of the romance between Pier and James, his own two lovers. "I am normally contemptuous of the press because of all the shit they've written about me. But in reading about Jimmy and Pier, I now know that most columnists live in a fantasy world. They're not only vindictive, they are fools. All these stories are a lot of bullshit—nothing more!"

Legend has it that James, astride his motorcycle, waited across the street from St. Timothy's Catholic Church at Beverly Glen and West Pico, in Los

James Dean

Angeles, during Pier's marriage to Damone.

"The press continues with its fantasies," Marlon told Gilman. "That shit story about Jimmy waiting across from the chapel! While Pier was getting married, our boy was probably somewhere taking something up the ass. I should know."

Far from being heart-broken over Pier's marriage to Damone, James had launched a hot and torrid sexual affair with Rock Hudson. Other than Marlon himself, the handsome actor had always been James's fantasy male and one of the imagined passions of his life. Alongside pictures of Marlon in his bedroom, James had posted three pictures of the well-built Hudson posing without his shirt. The romance with Hudson would endure until they were cast opposite Elizabeth Taylor in Edna Ferber's *Giant* and went on location together in Texas. The strain proved too much for their affair.

Biographers have claimed that James and Pier never met again, and that each mourned the loss of the other until their dying days.

Other, far more knowledgeable sources maintain that the affair between Pier and James continued until his untimely death. These same sources also claim that Marlon continued his affair with Pier for another eighteen months into her marriage to Damone. Always contemptuous of Pier, Gilman said, "She wanted Marlon's dick, Dean's pecker, and Damone's Italian sausage."

As shocked as she might have been witnessing Marlon having sex with James in the Brando living room, Pier eventually recovered from the experience and continued her affairs with both actors even during her marriage. "It was all very sick," Gilman claimed. "Everybody knew that Dean was one disturbed little boy. In time, when Pier took her own life, the world learned how mentally unbalanced she was too. Compared to Pier and Dean, Marlon looked sane—and that's one hell of an accomplishment for him."

When Hollywood reporter Joe Hyams once arrived at James's house, he encountered Pier in tears fleeing from the same premises. Even though married to Damone at the time, she'd come to tell James of her pregnancy. Hyams later reported that he found Dean looking distraught. "I held him to my chest and rocked him." The distinct impression Hyams gathered was that Pier believed that James was the father of her baby, not Damone.

By coincidence, Damone encountered James at the Villa Capri restaurant in Los Angeles on the night in August of 1955 when Pier gave birth to a son. "Come on, let's drink a toast to my son."

James raised his glass to the singer. "I'll drink a toast to my son any time," James said. The head waiter had to pry the two combatants apart.

When Marlon heard about these fisticuffs, he said, "Both Damone and Jimmy are full of shit. I'm the father!"

After James's death, Marlon's days with Pier were numbered. As Marlon found other interests, and Pier continued to stay with Damone, "the noble tool spoke for the last time," in the words of Gilman.

In a surprise development, which infuriated Marlon, Pier became close "gal pals" with Anna Kashfi following Kashfi's bitter divorce from Marlon in 1958 and the subsequent custody battles over their son, Christian.

Marlon told friends that he felt Pier had betrayed him by providing a sympathetic shoulder for Kashfi to cry on and spill out her bitter recriminations against him. Whether Pier ever told Kashfi about her brutal rape by Marlon in Rome is not known.

In her later years, Pier claimed that "Jimmy Dean is the only man I ever loved deeply as a woman should love a man. I never loved either of my husbands the way I loved Jimmy."

Privately she confided to friends, "I was never in love with Marlon Brando. In fact, today I hate him. Of all the men in my life, of all the brutality I suffered, even the fights with Vic Damone, I detest Brando the most. He used acts of violence on me, both physically and mentally. He's a sadist! I never want our paths to cross again. I will be bitter toward him until the day I die."

Even though Marlon came to view Pier as "the enemy," he still followed the rise and fall of her career in Hollywood. In her final years, after two unsuccessful marriages, she drifted from Hollywood to Rome, accepting what bit parts she could find during her descent into alcoholism and drugs.

When Susan Strasberg encountered Pier in Rome, she reported to Marlon that, "Pier's still beautiful in a fragile, battered sort of way. But a heavy drug addict. A hopeless creature."

Elia Kazan, Marlon, Julie Harris, and James Dean

In Los Angeles, it was the night of September 9, 1971. Troubled by the collapse of a once promising career that had her hailed as both "the new Ingrid Bergman" and, absurdly, as "the new Rita Hayworth," Pier swallowed a massive dose of Phenobarbital. Her lifeless body was discovered the next morning. She hadn't quite reached her fortieth birthday.

Her family claimed it was "accidental." Marlon told his friends that "Pier killed herself because she never got over me." That assessment appears highly unlikely.

As a description of her tragic suicide was splashed around the world, James Dean was long dead, of course, and Marlon was indifferent, at least according to Elia Kazan. "I knew Pier from the time she hung out with Jimmy on the set of *East of Eden*. I'm not sure he was that much in love with her. He was carrying on countless other affairs with both men and women when he was dating Pier. Marlon told Pier he loved her, but he deceived her. As for Pier, I think she was so mixed up she didn't know from hour to hour who she loved. I doubt if she loved Damone, but she was sure as hell fascinated with Jimmy and Marlon. Personally, after Jimmy died, I think she used him for publicity purposes, hoping to revitalize a dead career. She claimed to be the love of Jimmy's life. Sorta Romeo and Juliet crap. Jimmy was no longer around, but I spoke to Marlon about Pier's suicide, and he didn't give a fuck. His only remark to me was, 'All of us have to go sometime, somehow, some way.'"

* * *

Even though Marlon had rejected Elia Kazan's offer to star in *East of Eden*, he visited the set of that film to renew his relationship with the director. He wanted to see its star, James Dean, at work in front of the camera. After watching James emote for a while, Marlon privately told Kazan, "It looks like our boy here is wearing my last year's clothing and employing a style of acting I abandoned after my first six months on Broadway in *Streetcar*."

Kazan told Marlon, "I'm directing him in this movie, and he'll probably be a big hit. The boy does have something. Call it star quality, I don't know. My deepest regret is that I'm not directing you in the film. Come on, fucker, it's the story of your life. You could play it brilliantly. You've lived it. The story of a confused and angry young man abandoned by his mother—read that Dodie—and starved for the love of a rigid, puritanical bastard of a father—read that Marlon Sr."

When Kazan called a break for lunch, James invited Marlon to his dressing room. Once there Marlon warned James that by appearing in *East of Eden*, "You're courting fame, and nothing is more destructive than being famous. I can't walk down the street any more but what I'm followed. I can't go see a movie any more but what a line of girls follows me into the theater. The other day I went into a deli to order a hot pastrami on rye and a cream soda, and at least five faggots were suddenly behind me, yelling, 'Marlon, can we have your autograph!' You know what I did? I pulled down my jeans and mooned them. I told them, 'Autograph this, boys. Write Marlon on one cheek, Brando on the other.'"

Paul Newman and James Dean

Marlon was vastly intrigued to learn that Kazan had originally tested James with Paul Newman, who was up for the part of James's brother in *East of Eden*. "I'm very attracted to Paul," James confessed. "On some days I'm in love with you. On other days in love with Paul. At the end of the test, I asked Paul to give me a kiss. Real deep and dirty. He pinched my ass instead. But I wished he'd done more than pinch my bottom," James said. "I always wanted Paul Newman to fuck me and make an honest woman out of me."

Years later when Marlon told this story to Gilman, Marlon said, "Jimmy wasn't the only one who wanted to fuck with Newman. Frankly, I did too. When he worked with Pier Angeli on a picture, she wanted Newman's tool too. Frankly, I don't think any of our horny trio ever got our man."

Back on the day of Marlon's first visit to the set of *East of Eden*, and in the privacy of James's dressing room, he told Marlon of a recent visit from Tennessee Williams, who was in town, working on the outline of a new play, *Cat on a Hot Tin Roof*. "He came by the set to talk to Kazan about directing the play on Broadway," James said. "But once he laid those eyes on me, he didn't have much time for Kazan. Tennessee told me he originally wanted you for the lead. It's the story of a repressed homosexual. Think you can handle it?"

"There's nothing repressed about me," Marlon said.

"Perhaps," James said enigmatically. "I invited Mr. Williams to come back to my dressing room. I know he went down on you several times during the war when you boys were on Cape Cod together. He was a bit drunk when he showed up here. But I took down my jeans and let him blow me, perhaps like he'd done to you at one time. I guess I'm the better man. After that blow job, Mr. Williams offered me the lead role in the Broadway production. I hear Kazan thinks *Cat* is going to be a major success. Bigger than *Streetcar*. Out with Brando. In with James Dean. The new boy on the block."

If James thought he was going to anger Marlon, he didn't succeed. Marlon had already turned down the play and told Tennessee that he never planned to venture to Broadway again, especially with one of his plays. "We did it fine the first time, and once was enough for one life."

Kazan later suspected that James remained deeply in love with Marlon, but when he arrived in Hollywood he tried to prove how macho he was by dating Ursula and Pier. "Frankly, Marlon was ready to dump Jimmy at one point," Kazan said. "But, suddenly, on hearing that he was going out with Ursula and Pier, Marlon's interest in Jimmy was piqued again. Up to then,

492

Marlon had shown no interest in Ursula. Suddenly, Marlon began calling her for dates. I guess he had to prove to Ursula that he was a better lover than Jimmy. Or, maybe, prove something to himself. When it comes to Marlon Brando and Jimmy Dean, who can figure those two out? I mean, Marlon was also dating Marilyn Monroe, and I was too. That would go on for some time. Did it really matter that she would marry some baseball player along the way? Joe DiMaggio was fucked up. So was Arthur Miller. So was Marilyn. So was Jimmy. I guess I was the only sane one in the lot even though my liberal enemies still called me 'the canary.'"

James wanted to date the same women that Marlon did, according to Gilman, including not only Pier Angeli and Ursula Andress, but Katy Jurado too. Marlon exploded when he learned about the Dean/Jurado affair. "That fucking Jimmy doesn't want just to imitate me, he wants to be me!"

During the filming of *East of Eden*, columnist Sheila Graham called James "the poor man's Brando." Even though James worshipped Marlon, he told Elia Kazan, "I want my worship of Marlon to remain private. Public comparison of the two of us as actors is an unfriendly gesture."

After his visit to the set, Marlon began to see James on a regular basis, but not as often as he liked. According to Gilman, James wanted to date Marlon every night. "He torched for Marlon," Gilman said.

"Even when Marlon was out on a date—most often with a woman—Dean stalked his prey," Gilman claimed. "On his motorcycle, Dean often followed Marlon and his date. If they went—say, to a Mexican restaurant—Dean would show up and sit there all night at the bar drinking Tequila Sunrises until Marlon left. I was in the house and know for a fact that Dean often called at three or four o'clock in the morning. Marlon told me that he was sitting in his car one foggy night at a lookout point on Mulholland Drive. He was in the car, with of all people, Natalie Wood. Suddenly, the face of James Dean appeared at the window, staring in at them. I would have been spooked by Dean. But Marlon felt that it was just 'harmless child's play—he's got a crush on me. But so does half the rest of the world, both male and female, so I can't blame Jimmy for that. Once they get a taste of my noble tool, they want to own it. But it belongs just to me. I will decide where to put it to use.'"

Natalie Wood

James kept Marlon entertained with a puckish series of tricks. Like a Houdini he would disappear into the bathroom and lock the door from the inside. Then he would escape through the lone window but also leave it unlocked from the inside. Marlon would rush to the front door. There was James smiling sheepishly. Marlon could never figure out how he did that

James Dean

trick. Sometimes he would put both a cigarette and lit match in his mouth and put his lips together. He'd then open his mouth and the cigarette would be lit. Also the match would still be burning.

"I think Dean and Marlon shared one bad boy characteristic in common," Gilman said. "When either of them had to piss, they found the nearest wall and pissed to their heart's content regardless of who was looking on. When a wall wasn't available, they used a fire hydrant or a tree like a dog."

James revealed to Gilman in Marlon's presence that during his struggling days as an actor he was the kept boy of Rogers Brackett, a TV producer. Later when Rogers fell on hard times after losing his job in advertising, he appealed to James to lend him some money.

"Sorry, Pops," James said. "I didn't know it was the whore who had to pay."

"I thought the story rather sad, really," Gilman said. "But Marlon laughed for a good ten minutes, like it was the funniest thing he'd ever heard in his life."

In spite of their differences, Marlon and James had a lot in common—and not just their Midwestern origins. Both had fathers who claimed that all actors were "faggots and fairyboys."

"Both had a sexual ambivalence," Carlo Fiore said. "Both had sides so dark that no flashlight would ever be strong enough to penetrate those dark recesses."

One night James told Marlon that the turning point of his life occurred back in Marion, Indiana, when he went to see *The Men*.

Gilman sat on the sofa, listening to James, seated on the floor of Marlon's living room praise the older actor. "You were terrific," James told Marlon. "I didn't know what acting was all about until I saw you in *The Men*. You conveyed so much with minimalism. Suddenly, I knew how to do it. Through you I learned to show anguish. Unlike Bette Davis in constant motion, you taught me the power of stillness. The use of outward serenity to convey internal turmoil, the complete opposite of screen acting until you came along. Even the tiny flicker in your face conveys something, an emotional byproduct, an unrealized dream, an unfulfilled passion. After *The Men*, I decided to become a serious actor. It was the greatest moment of revelation in my entire life."

"All these pronouncements from Dean struck me as a lot of ass-kissing," Gilman said. "I think there was also a lot of ass-kissing of another kind going on in the bedroom as well."

Friends back in New York were startled to get notes from James signed: "From James-Brando-Clift-Dean."

After seeing *The Wild One*, James adopted a new dress code that focused on jeans, black leather jackets, and white T-shirts. As his adulation of Marlon reached a fever pitch, he purchased a motorcycle.

One night James parked his motorcycle and took Marlon for a spin in his new Alfa Romeo. Marlon returned two hours later, his face white. "He's a daredevil on the road," Marlon told Gilman. "I think he has a death wish. He drives like he wants to die and take me with him. If I ever get in a car with him, I'm going to take the wheel. Behind the wheel of a car, Jimmy boy is absolutely fearless."

Marlon always confused Gilman when he made pronouncements about James. "Jimmy wants to be loved but he doesn't," Marlon told him one night, leaving Gilman to ponder that remark for himself.

"Don't fall in love with me," James warned Marlon, in front of Gilman. "When emotional demands are made on me, I collapse."

"Don't worry your pretty head," Marlon told him. "But at least you've revealed to me how to get rid of you in case that's my desire in the future."

"There is a toughness about him that's only pretend," Marlon told Gilman when James had left. "Actually he needs to be nursed like a baby. Sometimes when he's in need of a mother, I let him suckle at my breasts."

Dore Schary was talking of casting James in *Somebody Up There Likes Me*, the story of middleweight champ, Rocky Graziano. Because Marlon fancied himself a boxer, he and James often worked out in the ring. "Frankly, I think Marlon threw some killer punches at Dean when he wanted to punish him," Gilman said. "There was always an undercurrent of latent hostility between Marlon and Dean. It made me uncomfortable to be around the two of them."

James, of course, never made the film. It was given to newcomer Paul Newman. Cast opposite him was none other than Pier Angeli.

After filming *East of Eden*, James showed up at the gallery of Kenneth Kendall to admire a sculpted head, inspired by Marlon, that the artist had crafted. Kendall later revealed that James was so impressed with the sculpture that "he almost devoured it, fondling it, loving it. He was totally fascinated."

While there, he also wanted to see all the pictures of Marlon that Kendall had in his files. "He went through them one by one," Kendall said. "At the end, he was very hesitant, but he managed to blurt out a request."

"Would you sculpt me like you did Brando?" James asked.

At first Kendall wasn't impressed with Dean, who had shown up slovenly dressed at the studio. When the artist went to see *East of Eden*, he became impressed

Dean Memorial Head

and later did a sculpture of James which was placed in Griffith Park. By that time, James was dead.

Gilman claimed that Marlon's affair with James continued until the young actor's death. "Marlon didn't seem jealous or to mind that Dean at the same time was also dating Rock Hudson. The boy's affair with Hudson lasted at least until they shared that rented house in some Texas hicktown during the shooting of *Giant*. When that happened, I think things really soured between Hudson and Dean. Hudson later said some very unkind remarks about Dean."

Midway into the shoot, director George Stevens caused real hysteria in James when he informed him that he had originally offered the role of Jett Rink in the Edna Ferber drama to Marlon.

"Marlon turned me down," Stevens told James. "I then went to Montgomery Clift. He turned me down too."

"Guess you're left with sloppy seconds," James said. Before storming off the set in anger, he told Stevens, "Or should I say sloppy thirds?"

"Hudson and Dean were thick as thieves for a few weeks there," Gilman said. "Marlon merely found their affair amusing, but he warned me that the romance between the two men would not last. 'Rock is so too square for our kinky boy,' Marlon said."

"Late one drunken night I asked Marlon if he'd ever had an affair with Hudson," Gilman said. "I knew he'd attended all-male parties at Hudson's house. In those days, Marlon showed up with Tyrone Power, who was also having an affair with Hudson."

"No, I never fucked The Rock," Marlon said. "Quite the opposite. Rock fucked me. If there's one thing more delectable than my noble tool, it's my rosebud!"

"During his final months with Marlon, Dean was out of control," Gilman said. "Dean arrived about three o'clock one morning. I let him in the house. He was threatening to kill himself if he didn't see Marlon. I woke up a sleepy Marlon who wandered downstairs naked. He conferred privately with Dean. Somehow Dean managed to persuade Marlon to drive away with him in the middle of the night. I hope Marlon was doing the driving."

"I noticed that Dean would get drunk by having only two glasses of vino. And he was one mean fucking drunk. Marlon would just sip a coke observing Dean like a boa constrictor sizing up a chicken to deep throat. Marlon needed to keep his sanity in order to control Dean later in the night. Under the influence of alcohol, Dean reverted from Dr. Jekyll to Mr. Hyde. He physically tried to assault Marlon on more than one occasion. Marlon never fought back. A much stronger man, he could have physically restrained Dean."

Rock Hudson

"I shouldn't mention this, and God will get me for it, but Marlon and Dean engaged in some very sick games together, especially near the end of Dean's short life," Gilman claimed. "Very S&M stuff. Marlon on occasion did engage in violence with some of his girlfriends, as has been widely reported. To my knowledge, he never got violent with any of his male lovers except with Dean. They played their dirty games with each other. It was like the two rivals brought out only the darkest side in each other. Many a night I heard Dean sobbing yet begging for more."

"The thing that I found the most disgusting was that the men engaged in fist-fucking," Gilman said. "In the last months of Dean's life, it was widely rumored that he liked to be fist-fucked. I think Marlon turned him on to it. I don't think Marlon ever fist-fucked any other person in his life but Dean, and I think he did that only because he was begged to do so. Frankly, when Marlon first told me about it, I had never heard of such a practice. I didn't even understand how it was physically possible. I mean skin stretches only so far. Later on, I heard reports that Dean frequented bars on Santa Monica Boulevard where he'd pick up two, maybe three, or perhaps on some occasions five bikers willing to fist-fuck him."

Some of James's female dates, such as Betsy Palmer, thought he was not "all that interested in sex. I just assumed that he was almost asexual."

Gilman differed with that opinion. "He had a whole string of seduction mates. To Marlon, I called them Jimmy's little girlfriends and his little fairy-boys. I can't speak for his whole life, but during the time he was dating Marlon, he also had a whole harem, both male and female, each one of whom seemed willing to do his bidding. He was banging some bitch one night, and the very next night getting fucked by some biker. I hear he liked only bikers who dressed like Marlon did in *The Wild One*."

Betsy also used to accuse James of "being queer but this didn't seem to bother him. I once heard Dean on the phone. Apparently, he was being propositioned by Liberace who offered him a thousand dollars to come to Las Vegas with him. That was a hell of a lot of money back then. Liberace told Jimmy that he'd already seduced Rock Hudson, and wanted Jimmy next. Apparently, if Jimmy is to be believed, Liberace also told him that he wanted to go to bed with him even more 'than I want to seduce Marlon Brando, although I'll get that one too.'"

Another Dean girlfriend at the time, Arlene Sachs, claimed that she had just turned seventeen when James took her virginity. "There was blood all over. I know a lot of people were claiming that he wasn't interested in sex but I think he was very interested. He devoted every night to its pursuit."

Liberace

497

James Dean in his Porsche

One night, James invited aspirant actress Rachel Evergreen to an orgy. "Everybody knew why they were there, but nobody knew how to get the orgy to begin," Evergreen said. "Jimmy dropped his blue jeans—he wasn't wearing any underwear—and began jerking off in front of everybody. That got the action started."

"Later he told me that Marlon Brando got orgies started just like that in Greenwich Village in the Forties," Evergreen claimed. "If it's good enough for Brando, it's good enough for me," Jimmy told me.

James, according to Evergreen, was rather upfront about his homosexual affairs. "When he moved back in with Rogers Brackett after the producer found a job, James was always complaining to me that his ass was sore from having been fucked all night."

Marlon and James in front of witnesses engaged in what was called "a cat fight" at an all-male gay party in Malibu only days before James's death. In front of amused witnesses, Marlon accused James of dating women such as Ursula Andress just to mask his homosexuality. "You and Tab Hunter are doing the same thing," Marlon shouted at James. "Taking out beautiful women and giving them a peck on the cheek at the door. You claim to hate all this manufactured Hollywood publicity crap, yet you indulge in it like every-one else in this cesspool—that is, everybody except me. I've got nothing to cover up. Nothing to be ashamed of. I am what I am, and I'm proud of it."

According to the gay men at the party, James ran from the house and tried to get on his motorcycle but Marlon prevented him from doing that.

Ronnie White said that "Dean might have been killed that night if Brando had let him get on that motorcycle. He'd been drinking heavily all afternoon. At my party Brando had only a cranberry juice cocktail. Brando drove Dean home in Brando's car. The next afternoon a hung-over Dean arrived at my house and rode off on his motorcycle without even coming inside to thank me for the party. What a bitch! I don't care what has been written about Dean and Brando. From what I observed, they were just two bitchy queens going at it. Not macho studs. In fact, I think both of them were just drama queens."

The sun was starting to go down on the afternoon of September 30, 1955. During the making of *Giant* in that "drought-stricken whistle stop" of Marfa, Texas, director George Stevens had forbidden James to go car racing. With filming behind him, he was driving his Porsche Spyder to Salinas to compete in a race there. With him was his mechanic, Rolf Wütherich.

With the afternoon sun blinding him, James raced to an intersection along Route 41.

498

Also approaching the intersection was Donald Turnupseed, a student from Polytechnic Institute at San Luis Obispo, who was driving a black and white Ford sedan. He was rapidly approaching Route 41 at its Y-shaped junction with Route 466. Convinced that he could see his Porsche, James accelerated. Inexplicably, Turnupseed's car began to cross 466. The Porsche smashed into the heavy sedan.

James was killed instantly on impact. His neck was broken, his chest crushed. He was only twenty-four years old.

Dazed, Turnupseed stepped from the wreckage of his car. He had only a slight bruise, but would live for the rest of his life under the burden of "the man who killed James Dean." There were even death threats against him from James's most devoted fans.

Thrown clear and landing in a ditch, Wütherich survived, although he faced several subsequent operations. He lived until 1981, dying at the age of fifty-three in his native Germany. The cause of death was another car accident.

With Sam Gilman, Marlon drove to the site of the wreck a week later. Gilman stayed in the car at Marlon's request. Getting down on his knees, Marlon surveyed the ground. Only a few feet away, Gilman heard his words.

"Jimmy, I loved you more than I told you."

Chapter Fourteen

Although Marlon had avoided Cary Grant since his early days in Hollywood, he did agree to accept a call from that actor one lazy afternoon when he was lounging in the sun in his garden. Sam Gilman brought the phone to Marlon.

"Hey, kiddo," came a distinctive voice familiar to movie audiences the world over. "Thanks for the memory."

"I thought Bob Hope owned exclusive rights to that line," Marlon said.

"It's a show business tradition to steal from each other," Grant said. "Just ask Milton Berle."

"What's up?" Marlon asked, obviously not eager for another one of Grant's propositions.

"I just read a script sent over by Joseph Mankiewicz. He wants me to play Sky Masterson in *Guys and Dolls*."

"You'd be great in the role," Marlon said.

"I turned him down. I suggested you for the part."

"I don't get it," Marlon said. "This is Stanley Kowalski from *A Streetcar Named Desire*. Everywhere I turn someone seems to think I can be a song-and-dance man. I don't even know how to sing, much less dance, except for Katherine Dunham routines. You're not the first person who wants me to appear in this musical."

"Frank Sinatra desperately wants the role," Grant said. "I heard you don't like Sinatra. Take the role just to piss him off."

"It's a deal!" Marlon said.

Grant hung up the phone without a good-bye.

* * *

Even before filming began, the award-winning *Guys and Dolls* was viewed as a hot property in Hollywood. Since its 1950 opening on Broadway, it had run for three years. Shelling out a million dollars for the film rights, Samuel Goldwyn, then seventy-two years old, purchased the property in 1954.

In a surprise development, Goldwyn contracted with Joseph Mankiewicz to direct *Guys and Dolls*, even though he'd never done a musical before. It took Goldwyn several weeks to decide on the male star, the role of gambler Sky Masterson. Sinatra kept badgering Goldwyn for the part, but the aging producer turned a deaf ear.

After Grant rejected the role, Goldwyn wanted Gene Kelly. The dancer was eager to restore his box office clout after the fiasco of *Brigadoon* and his shelved ballet film, *Invitation to the Dance*. Metro's corporate chief, Nick Schenck, refused to release Kelly. Schenck had a long simmering feud with Goldwyn, and told him, "Go fuck yourself!"

Undaunted, Goldwyn continued his search for a male star, approaching Burt Lancaster. He too turned down the role. At one point, Goldwyn flirted-with the idea of casting Bob Hope and Jane Russell in his costly musical. Tony Martin was briefly considered. That casting was one of Goldwyn's better ideas. Even Bing Crosby was a candidate. Goldwyn then toyed with the possibilities of casting Kirk Douglas, Robert Mitchum, and Clark Gable.

Finally, the producer decided to cast against type and sent the script over to Marlon. Within days, Marlon rejected it. But Goldwyn persisted, appealing to Mankiewicz, who'd had an easy working relationship with Marlon during the filming of *Julius Caesar*.

The director wired Marlon: "UNDERSTAND YOU'RE APPREHENSIVE BECAUSE YOU'VE NEVER DONE A MUSICAL COMEDY. YOU HAVE NOTHING—REPEAT NOTHING—TO WORRY ABOUT BECAUSE NEITHER HAVE I. LOVE, JOE."

Marlon's closest friends, including both Gilman and Carlo Fiore, urged him to take the part to show the world that he could be effective in something other than a heavy drama. Finally, after Mankiewicz assured him that his singing voice would be dubbed, Marlon wired Goldwyn with his acceptance

Brando in *Guys and Dolls*

But finding an accomplished singer to match Marlon's rather high-pitched speaking voice proved difficult.

Going back on his original promise, Mankiewicz then decided that Marlon would have to use his own voice. Frank Loesser was brought in. He had created the music and lyrics for the Broadway version of *Guys and Dolls,* following a script by Abe Burrows and Jo Swerling, who'd based their musical on the Damon Runyon story, *The Idyll of Sarah Brown.*

After working with Marlon for two weeks, Loesser recorded his voice, telling Mankiewicz and Goldwyn that

Marlon had a "voice that was of a pleasing, husky baritone quality." On hearing a recorded version of his own singing, Marlon declared that it "sounded like the mating call of a yak." Later, he changed his appraisal, lamenting that his voice "sounded like the wail of a bagpipe through wet tissues." Goldwyn saw great possibilities in Marlon using his own voice. "I can just see the headlines," he told Mankiewicz. "BRANDO SINGS!"

The Italian vocal coach, Leon Ceparro, was brought in to teach Marlon how to sing. The usually testy, finicky, and highly critical coach was kind to Marlon's voice. He claimed that Marlon "has an opera singer's palate. He can sing a top B flat without effort. This is a tremendous feat after only a few weeks of training."

At one point Ceparro made an uncharacteristic and preposterous statement, claiming that Marlon could "make the Met if he studied hard enough."

Marlon told reporters, "Up to this time my singing has been confined to the bathtub. But my voice coach tells me I'll be quite a dramatic tenor."

Marlon knew that the press was making fun of him for accepting a role in a musical. One day he confronted some other reporters. "When I was a rebel, you boys portrayed me as an asshole. I was the hot copy boy who scratched his ass and pissed on the rug. What am I now to you boys?" Without waiting for an answer, he stormed off.

With a few exceptions, almost the entire cast was poised to ridicule Marlon behind his back. But he found an ally in Francis, Goldwyn's wife. She'd listened to a recording of his voice and claimed, "Marlon sounds like a young Fred Astaire. Not only that, but he taught me the proper way to do barbecue, Nebraska style."

Actually sound engineers had to work for weeks, splicing together pieces of various sound tracks before getting a complete song as recorded by Marlon.

After the film's release, Marlon's singing voice didn't cause shock waves in America. But it did in Germany. Up until then, Marlon's movies had each been dubbed into German by a gravel-voiced baritone. Upon hearing Marlon's high-pitched singing, audiences booed. By the thousands many didn't go to see his future movies, since his macho image had been destroyed by the high register of his voice in *Guys and Dolls*.

Marlon knew that his dancing would also be a problem, even though he'd performed with the Katherine Dunham troupe in New York. "But that was a different type of dance," he told Fiore. "This *Guys and Dolls* shit is difficult hoofing and hard to pull off."

The brilliant dance director, Michael Kidd, was brought in. Marlon's dancing didn't annoy Kidd as much as his constant gum chewing. Kidd brought a bucket to the studio and carried it around, telling Marlon to "spit it out." Later, Kidd said, "I wish Marlon would get his oral gratification some-

Michael Kidd choreographs
Marlon for his role
as Sky Materson

where else, if you get my drift. He's certainly no dancer but he's musical. And he loves to hoof it."

After working with Marlon, Kidd continued his kind appraisal, regardless of what he might have personally thought. "Marlon moves like a prizefighter—very light on his feet. A little heavy for ballet, but audiences will be agreeably surprised when they see him on the screen."

Marlon's fans were surprised to hear he'd be singing and dancing in a musical, and they wondered why their idol had accepted such an unconventional role. Unknown to his legions of admirers, Marlon desperately needed the money, and Goldwyn was offering him $200,000 for starring in *Guys and Dolls*.

Marlon would later tell author Truman Capote, "I wanted to do something bright, something yellow. Up to now the brightest thing I've ever done was red—red, brown, gray, down to black."

* * *

Mankiewicz dreaded the morning that Frank Sinatra arrived on the set to confront his costar. Although Sinatra had lobbied for the role of Sky Masterson, he'd accepted the lesser role of Nathan Detroit, who ran "the oldest established permanent crap game in New York." Sinatra's role called for a Jewish borscht belt comedian, an actor like Sam Levene, who had been perfectly cast in the part on Broadway. Ironically, there was little singing associated with Sinatra's role, since he'd have been perfectly suited to sing Loesser's rapturous songs.

Angry for having been cast in the minor male lead, Sinatra was still fuming over Marlon's affair with his beloved Ava Gardner. He was also still resentful that he'd lost the role of Terry Malloy in *On the Waterfront* to Marlon.

Marlon was contemptuous of Sinatra, telling Mankiewicz that, "He's a great talent on stage but a shithead off stage. He thinks he's god and parades around with a string of henchmen following him. The crooner can't act. I think he peaked when he was a bobby sox idol back in the war years."

In spite of their differences, Marlon tried to befriend Sinatra on the first day. He even asked him if he could come to his dressing room for some acting tips. "Look, Brando, don't give me any of that Method acting shit!" The two actors rarely spoke during the rest of the shoot.

Sinatra was known as a one-take actor. In no less than two takes, he'd get it right. In contrast, Marlon often required twenty to twenty-five takes.

In their first scene together, Sinatra had to eat a slice of New York deli cheesecake, as he attempted to con Sky Masterson into a sucker bet. After going through almost two cheesecakes, Sinatra stood up in rage. "These fucking New York Method actors! How much cheesecake do you think I can eat?" He turned to Mankiewicz. "Don't put me in the game, coach, until Mumbles here has finished rehearsing." He stormed off the set.

The next morning, Sinatra's temper had cooled, and he resumed eating that cheesecake. This time Marlon required only three takes. Even though Mankiewicz wasn't satisfied with the scene, he decided to print it anyway.

Fiore had been hired as Marlon's stand-in and was a close observer of what was happening. "Marlon had traditionally seduced his competition like Burt Lancaster and Monty Clift. But Marlon's charm was wasted on Sinatra. There was no way that Marlon was going to get to suck Frankie's big dick. That Hoboken WOP liked pussy too much. Ol' Blue eyes detested Marlon and often looked like he wanted to have him killed. Perhaps do it personally."

As had been defined before he accepted the role, Sinatra was supposed to both speak and sing with a Bronx Jewish accent. But breaking out of character almost from the first day, Sinatra launched into his smooth balladeer's voice, singing flawlessly and without any accent. When Marlon heard Sinatra's first number, he was livid with anger.

Behind Sinatra's back, Marlon went to Mankiewicz to protest. "Sinatra's singing is all wrong. Where's the Jew? The Bronx accent? He's supposed to clown it up. But he's singing like he's been cast opposite Judy Garland and is competing against her 'Over the Rainbow' voice. You can't have two god damn romantic leads in *Guys and Dolls*. I'm the fucking romantic lead, and you've got to do something about it!"

"Why don't you go tell Sinatra how to sing a song?" Mankiewicz asked sarcastically.

When Mankiewicz refused to redirect Sinatra, Marlon exploded in fury in his dressing room in the presence of Fiore. "I'll never work with that fucking Mankiewicz

A captured scene from *Guys and Dolls*, though similar to what Brando would like to have done to his co-star, Frank Sinatra

505

again. What a weak nelly he is not to stand up to Sinatra. At least Mankiewicz has stopped sucking James Mason's prick now that he's lusting after Jean Simmons."

Sinatra also had complaints about Marlon's singing. Speaking privately to the director, he said, "Don't you see how humiliating it is for me to be stuck in the chorus backing up Brando in 'Luck, Be a Lady tonight?' The guy can't even carry a tune, and I've had to be on camera for a total of fifty takes already. The fucker still hasn't got it right. I'm the world's greatest interpreter of that song, and I'm hearing its worst rendition from Mumbles."

Frank Sinatra

Marlon refused to watch the takes. Sinatra sat through every session in the studio. After watching Marlon and Jean Simmons perform on screen in one scene, Sinatra told Mankiewicz: "If nothing else, *Guys and Dolls* proves how much Brando is out of his depth in anything but serious drama. Critics call him a tiger of an actor. Tell tiger tail to work only in feline parts in the future." Before leaving, he turned to the director a final time. "Tough shit for Brando! There aren't that many tiger parts around these days."

The camera picked up some of the hostility and tension between Marlon and Sinatra. After three weeks, Marlon was reduced to calling Sinatra "that WOP from Hoboken. Did you know his fat mother, with her unwashed ass, was really an abortionist?" Marlon never explained why he thought Mrs. Sinatra had a butt none too clean.

When Sinatra heard this, he threatened to personally "beat the cocksucker to a pulp." Aware of Marlon's bisexuality, Sinatra countered Marlon's growing criticism of him by calling him a cocksucker—not to his face but loud enough on the set that Marlon could clearly hear him.

Marlon's nerves were reaching an explosive level. Before filming began, he'd reduced his one hundred and ninety pounds down to one hundred and sixty-five by keeping to a diet of steak, salads, and fresh vegetables. But as his agitation increased, Marlon's overeating began in earnest, and his weight shot up again. "The heavy drape jacket you see him wearing in the movie was meant to cover up his expanding thighs which were growing elephantine at one point," Mankiewicz claimed.

As confirmed by actor Regis Toomey, cast in the role of Arvide, "The entire cast was sharply divided into two warring camps: pro-Brando and anti-Sinatra, or pro-Sinatra and anti-Brando. Sinatra was snotty and very difficult. It was obvious to the cast that he hated both Brando and his own role as

Joseph Mankiewicz

Nathan Detroit. He could be a prick. He gave Mankiewicz a hard time. If there was a need for communication between Sinatra and Brando, Sinatra sent one of his henchman. To communicate with Sinatra, Brando sent Fiore."

Toomey also noted that it didn't help relationships between the two stars when Marlon won the Oscar for his role in *On the Waterfront*, the announcement coming in the early days of filming for *Guys and Dolls*.

One day Marlon told Fiore, "Sinatra is the kind of guy that when he dies he's going to heaven to curse God for making him bald."

"Meow!" Fiore said. "If I didn't know what a macho heterosexual stud you were, I'd swear that you were a queeny bitch."

"Get the fuck out of my dressing room," Marlon told him. "Or else I'll stick my noble tool up your ass, and you'll scream like a stuck pig! You know you've always wanted it."

"I hope you're joking," Fiore said.

"Don't test your luck," Marlon told him.

Fiore reported that one scene with Sinatra called for endless retakes. In the scene, Marlon was supposed to put his hand at Sinatra's throat and cover his bow tie to see if Sinatra could describe its color. "It appeared at one point that Marlon actually wanted to choke Sinatra instead of covering his bow tie," Fiore said. "It got so bad that I felt Sinatra was going to order his goons to beat up Marlon. Then a surprise. Marlon seemed to be fed up with Brando himself. His nerves frayed, he walked off the picture.

"Get someone else," he told a startled Mankiewicz. "I'm through. I'm leaving the studio. *Guys and Dolls* is a piece of shit, the smelly kind."

By the next morning, Mankiewicz had stayed up half the night persuading Marlon to come back to the studio. He showed up on time and completed the scene with Sinatra in one take.

Off camera, neither actor spoke to the other, not even a good morning.

The worst was yet to come.

* * *

One afternoon when Sinatra wasn't needed on the set of *Guys and Dolls*, Ava Gardner showed up. According to Fiore, she spent the rest of the day in Marlon's dressing room. Fiore himself delivered the message to Mankiewicz that Marlon would not be available for an appearance before the cameras until the following day.

Ava's motives, to put it mildly, are suspect here. She liked Marlon, but it was clear that she never had any abiding passion for him. Their affair was a sometimes thing, as the two of them pursued other interests.

Fiore speculated, perhaps accurately, that Ava wanted to make Sinatra jealous. "Her appearing on the set that day, with Sinatra out of the picture, both figuratively and literally, was her fuck you to Ol' Blue eyes," Fiore said. "Since the crew was equally divided into Sinatra and Brando camps, she knew that word would get back to Frankie boy before the rooster crowed. And it did."

Years later, Mankiewicz claimed that he felt "Marlon was playing with fire. He'd already antagonized Sinatra to the point that I suspected any day Sinatra would call up two henchmen from Hoboken to pay a call on 'Mumbles.' To mess around with Ava like Marlon was doing was asking for it. I knew Marlon very well, but I didn't tell him how to run his private life just as I refused, even though I was the director, to tell Sinatra how to sing. I'd directed Ava in *The Barefoot Contessa*. She had a will of her own. I could hardly tell her what to do on camera, much less off camera. I didn't want open gunfire on the set of *Guys and Dolls* but I clearly anticipated it. The next day I told Marlon that if he wanted to have an affair with Ava, he should do it in private. Not on the set. He seemed placid about the whole event, acting like there would be no repercussions from Frankie boy. I knew otherwise."

"When a woman as beautiful and sultry as Miss Tar Heel comes to get serviced by my noble tool, only a cad of a man would turn down a lady in distress," Marlon told Mankiewicz. "It was my duty to rise to the occasion, and that is exactly what I did."

Mankiewicz was surprised the next day when he encountered Sinatra. "Far from being enraged, he seemed relatively cool," Mankiewicz said. "That is, relatively cool in Sinatra's terms. He was always a bundle of energy. He reminded me of a firecracker about to go off at any moment. I knew that at least ten people had told him about Ava's visit to Marlon's dressing room. Sinatra even had a scene on camera with Marlon that day. Even though he didn't speak to Marlon, the scene went easily. Sinatra performed brilliantly on the first take. It took Marlon ten takes but he finally got it. Instead of showing his usual impatience with Marlon blowing the scene, Sinatra willingly suffered

Frank Sinatra and Ava Gardner

through every retake until Marlon did what I wanted. Then Sinatra got up, excused himself, and went to his dressing room, where he was constantly surrounded by his flunkies. When not on the set, he was on the phone to Chicago, New York, Las Vegas, Miami, and especially Havana for some reason. I figured that guy had a lot of far-flung business interests and deals going on that I wasn't privy to and didn't want to be."

Producer David Dexter once said, "Handling Sinatra is like defusing a ticking bomb." Mankiewicz agreed with that assessment. He just wanted to wrap *Guys and Dolls* and get it in the can before any eruptions occurred.

He was not to get his wish.

Sinatra had married Ava Gardner on November 7, 1951, but their divorce would not come through until July 5, 1957. Long before that, Ava had confided in Marlon that the marriage "was all but over."

Marlon told Fiore, "What Sinatra doesn't know is simply put: Ava Gardner is through with him. She's moved on to other dicks. Not dicks as big or as impressive as that dangler Sinatra carries between his legs, but nonetheless other tools. Sometimes tools not as noble as my own. He's still carrying the torch for her. It's sad, really. I've never had his problem. My problem is trying to get a woman to move on when I'm through with her. I would never carry the torch for any woman. With my pick of all the beautiful women in all the world, do I need to carry the torch for just one woman? No way! Sinatra is a fool. I heard he even had Lauren Bacall deliver a coconut cake to Ava. Did that swooner—so beloved by the 1940s bobbysoxers—really think a coconut cake would do it? Ava hates coconut. She told me so herself. Now if Sinatra had sent her favorite, chocolate fudge, he might still be getting some North Carolina pussy."

Two days later, Sinatra got his revenge, or so it appeared. Fiore is the only source of the revelation of what happened to Marlon, who later wanted to cover up his humiliation and keep the news from Mankiewicz and other members of the crew. Marlon certainly had no intention of going to the police.

In Fiore's own words, here is what happened.

"Marlon often rode his motorcycle home from the studio. On the days he did that, I would return to his house maybe an hour or so earlier and get everything ready for him. That often meant lining up the 'entertainment' for the evening. Sometimes it would be one of the cast members, male or female, from the set of *Guys and Dolls*. With Marlon, you never knew who he would show up with for the night. When Marlon failed to arrive at the appointed time, I didn't think anything of it. He was often late. Sometimes if he met some meat along the way, he didn't show up until the next morning. For a month I had been staying over at Marlon's place, although I lived elsewhere. But that's another story."

By midnight when Marlon didn't show up, I went to bed. Around two o'clock, I heard Marlon calling for me from the living room. It was a real distress call. I jumped out of bed buck naked and headed downstairs. What I saw horrified me. Marlon wasn't beaten and bloody like he appeared on the screen in *On the Waterfront*. But there was something wrong. First, he looked like shit. But it was more than that. He looked like he'd just visited hell and had escaped with his life."

"As the morning wore on, and I tended to him, I learned only a little bit of the story. For reasons of his own, Marlon chose to spare me some of the details. It seems that he was accosted by three men while he'd parked his bike at some remote garage and had gone inside to use the men's toilet. One of the guys entered the men's room. He had a gun with him. Marlon was forced into some big black car and driven somewhere. He wasn't sure. The men threatened to kill him. Marlon was told that before they killed him, he was going to be castrated. It was sort of like the Chance Wayne role that Marlon turned down in Tennessee Williams's *Sweet Bird of Youth*."

· "Marlon claimed that he suffered an agonizing two-hour ordeal with these men who held him at gunpoint in the back seat of a limousine. 'They kept talking about killing me and castration', Marlon told me. 'One of the goons told me that he was going to offer me a choice: He could kill me, a quick and easy death with a bullet in the heart. Or else he'd let me live. If he let me live, he'd castrate me and then carve up my face so that no plastic surgeon could ever repair it. He said that he'd let me make the choice of these two evils.'"

"Marlon told me that he had never been so frightened in all his life. 'If those guys were actors, all of them should receive Oscars,' Marlon said. 'I thought they were the real thing. From the way they talked, they sounded like they were from back East. If anything, they sounded like some of the stevedores I worked with in Hoboken. They meant business. I was sweating blood. I also shit my pants. They put the fear of God in me. Don't you get it? God! *One* Frank Sinatra.'"

"I seriously questioned Marlon," Fiore said. "At no point during his torture was Sinatra's name mentioned by the goons. No 'stay away from Ava Gardner' shit—nothing like that. No warning from Sinatra that the next time would be fatal. I'm sure Sinatra was behind this whole thing. He threatened and intimidated other people in his life—or so I heard. Why not Marlon? His arch-enemy number one."

Marlon said that at one point he realized that the men were not going to kill him or use a knife on him. Somewhere in the Hollywood Hills, he was kicked out of the car. He remembered rolling down a steep ravine. His body was bruised but his face bore no damage. He could complete work on *Guys and Dolls*. He said he climbed back up the ravine and hailed a passing car about thirty minutes later. It was a man and his wife. They recognized him at once and were only too glad to drive *the* Marlon Brando wherever he wanted to go. He told them that he'd had an accident while riding on his motorcycle, and had run over the edge of the highway. He lied that his motorcycle was wrecked somewhere down the ravine, and that he'd send one of his staff to rescue it in the morning. "Marlon stayed up all night," Fiore said. "I doctored him, even gave him a bath. When morning finally came, he was too weak to go to work. It was a Friday. I called Mankiewicz to tell him that Marlon was sick. He slept all weekend. He didn't even want to get up to go to the bathroom. He had me bring him a pan. I even had to help him take a crap, something I don't relish doing. But Marlon insisted."

"I was with Marlon on Monday morning when he showed up for work. Amazingly he looked terrific, like he'd had a long vacation. No one could tell, I'm certain, that anything had ever happened to him. He went ahead and finished the picture on time. But he gave Sinatra wide berth. Marlon even hired a bodyguard."

* * *

Samuel Goldwyn's first choice for Marlon's costar in *Guys and Dolls* was Grace Kelly, but she turned him down. The producer then offered the role to Deborah Kerr, Marlon's costar in *Julius Caesar*, but she had other commitments. Finally, he awarded the role to Jean Simmons, who had starred with Marlon in *Desirée* where they had become friends. Like Marlon himself, she was an untrained singer.

Jean Simmons and Brando
rehearse for *Guys and Dolls*

Jean showed up on the set, and she and Marlon resumed the marvelous camaraderie they'd developed while filming *Desirée*. Apparently, Jean was not aware of Marlon's secret involvement with her husband, Stewart Granger. "That certainly would have put a strain on the relationship," Fiore said. Jean quickly fitted into her role as Sister Sarah, a mission sergeant who falls for a two-bit gambler, as played by Marlon.

After working with Jean for only two weeks, Mankiewicz was like a lovesick schoolboy telling

Goldwyn, "In terms of talent Jean Simmons is so many heads and shoulders above her competition. So much so that I wonder why she didn't become the great star she should have been."

What Mankiewicz didn't tell Goldwyn was that he'd fallen for Jean and would pursue her throughout the picture. The director had deserted the still-warm bed of James Mason and his outspoken wife, Pamela, and had moved on to other interests. When Marlon learned that his director was smitten with Jean, he told Fiore, "At least it's better than sucking a prick's prick!" Marlon was referring to James Mason.

Despite his ongoing feud with Sinatra's boys, Marlon worked smoothly with Jean once again. Of course, where were the usual embarrassing moments. As Sarah, Jean had to deliver a disastrous piece of dialogue when she was talking about a song, "A Women in Love." Before the camera, she was forced to say, "But now it's playing inside me all true and honest as though my heart were beating the drum." On hearing this, Marlon broke into hysterical laughter on camera.

Mankiewicz fought bitterly with Goldwyn over the casting of the second female lead, the role of Adelaide, who in the script has already lived through a fourteen-year-old engagement to Nathan Detroit. Goldwyn wanted Betty Grable to play the aging chorus girl. Mankiewicz wanted Vivian Blaine to re-create her Broadway turn as Adelaide.

When Grable learned that she wasn't going to get the role, she called Goldwyn and thanked him for his support. Then she burst into tears. "My last chance to do a really big musical," she sobbed.

Unknown to Goldwyn, Marilyn Monroe, then the hottest female property in Hollywood, pestered Mankiewicz for the part. She could do that over pillow talk, as she was sleeping with him at the time and had been carrying on an on-again, off-again affair with him ever since he'd directed her in *All About Eve*. Finally, he told her that he was going to let Vivian Blaine re-create the role of Adelaide that she'd done so successfully on Broadway.

Marilyn even called Marlon and asked him to intervene on her behalf. But he told her that his contract did not allow for his approval of leading ladies. "Very well," Marilyn said. "Then it's over between Joe [Mankiewicz] and me. No more nooky for him!"

Firmly maintaining his position, Mankiewicz finally got the green light to cast Vivian Blaine.

Unusual for Marlon, he did not sexually pursue either Jean or Vivian. In contrast, Fiore claimed that Marlon "fucked almost everything else on the hoof, including the extras." He claimed that he didn't know from day to day the target of Marlon's affections.

Fiore remembered one extra who looked "fifty-five if she was a day. Her black hair was obviously dyed, and her large breasts sagged so low they fell to her navel. Her legs were so thin in proportion to the bulk above that she seemed top-heavy. I couldn't believe it when Marlon asked me to get her telephone number."

"That broad is old," Fiore told Marlon. "She's also ugly as sin."

"You fuck your broads, and I'll plant my noble tool in mine," Marlon told him. "Get her phone number for me."

Fiore got the woman's number. "The next morning he told me that the old bag came over to his house."

"She fucked my brains out," Marlon told Fiore, "and later the bitch thanked me for giving her a chance to fuck *the* Marlon Brando."

Marlon's sexual expressions on the set weren't limited just to women. One of the handsome extras on *Guys and Dolls*, Mickey Gayot, a Broadway dancer, claimed he had an affair with Marlon during the shoot. "Marlon often called me to his dressing room where he'd fuck me. No love making. Just down to action. I really enjoyed it but wanted more, of course. I didn't get it. When the job ended, I gave Marlon my phone number in New York and asked him to call the next time he was in town. One night I read in Winchell's column that Marlon was back in New York. But he never called. I'm still waiting, Marlon!"

Fiore more or less confirmed Gayot's account. "Marlon fucked half the girls in the chorus and a lot of the male extras as well, especially the good-looking or well-built ones. The parade in and out of his dressing room was amazing. Everybody was talking about it. I don't know how he could fuck so many and still have time to get around to service his 'regulars' with that always reliable noble tool of his."

* * *

While working as a stand-in for Marlon on the set of *Guys and Dolls*, Fiore rented a poolside studio on a beautiful Beverly Hills estate that was itself rented to the actress, Barbara Payton. She charged him only forty dollars a month.

A brassy blonde with a black, whoring heart, Barbara Payton flashed on the screen as a bombshell before becoming an alcoholic, drug-addicted hooker.

Years later, Fiore recalled his experience with Payton and Marlon's involvement with her. "The bitch was Hollywood's number one trollop," Fiore claimed, "and I should know. But you can also ask Bob Hope, James Cagney, and Gregory Peck, among countless others for confirmation."

Still young and beautiful at the time she met Fiore and Marlon, Payton had come from the cold winds of Cloquet, Minnesota, to the warm beds of some of Hollywood's most famous players, including Howard Hughes. She was blessed with blue eyes and a fair complexion that revealed her Norwegian ancestry.

Hollywood's most sexually motivated attorney, Greg Bautzer, once said, "You have never been given a blow-job until you've been on the receiving end of Barbara's skilled mouth and tongue. I've been blown by the best of them—Lana Turner, Judy Garland, Joan Crawford, Marlene Dietrich—you name 'em. Barbara takes top prize."

Hughes once told his pimp, Johnny Meyer, "Payton will do anything in bed—and I mean anything. If you want to piss in her mouth, that's okay with blondie."

Before meeting Marlon, Payton had been the Queen of the Tabloids between 1950 and 1952. The single most scandalous movie star ever to emerge from the placid 1950s, Payton dumped her husband in the late 40s and headed for Hollywood determined to make it big. "If a blonde with absolutely no talent like Lana Turner can become a movie star, then I know I can too," she announced to anyone interested.

When her test at RKO didn't work out, she ended up as a carhop at Stan's Drive-In at the corner of Sunset Boulevard and Highland Avenue. Hustling tips and peddling chocolate milkshakes and blood-letting hamburgers, she also did another type of hustling on the side.

The riches from her nocturnal activities allowed her to buy an expensive wardrobe. Soon she was seen at all the posh clubs, including the Trocadero, Ciro's, and El Mocambo. She was hailed as "the Queen of the Night."

Her love nest on Cheremoya Avenue was paid for in 1949 by none other than the much-married Bob Hope. When the comedian refused to give her an additional $5,000 a week in "spending money," she threatened to blackmail him in exchange for her silence. Hope settled what was called "a huge sum of money" on her, but she went through all her new loot in just three months, claiming, "I have expensive tastes."

A.C. Lyles, the movie producer, once claimed that "Payton never had an itch she didn't scratch." Minor actor Mickey Knox recalled that she'd kept him in bed for three days and nights, all in one stretch. "I had to crawl out of that dump on my hands and knees. What a workout! What a pussy!"

She even got involved with James Cagney, who secured her a contract at Warner Brothers for $5,000 a week. He put her in *Kiss Tomorrow Goodbye*. The film had hardly been released before she was swallowing Gary Cooper's mighty sword near the sound stages of *Dallas* while taking in $10,000 a week. Suddenly, she was seen around town with the classy New York actor, Franchot Tone, who had been married to Joan Crawford in the 1930s. Tone was twenty-two years older than Payton, and he lavished expensive gifts on her, including jewelry.

During her affair with Tone, Payton also fell for rock-jawed Tom Neal, a sort of dime store John Garfield. Almost sadistically, Payton played one man against the other and would eventually marry each of them, thereby creating two of the shortest marriages ever recorded in Hollywood history.

Neal learned about Payton's involvement with Tone, and on the night of September 13, 1951, emerged from the bushes outside Payton's apartment and attacked Tone, smashing his nose and breaking one of his cheekbones. Tone was

Barbara Payton

rushed to the hospital with a brain concussion and remained in a coma for eighteen hours. Morning newspapers headlined this "Love Brawl" across the world.

Marlon wanted Fiore to keep him posted on any "suspicious activities" transpiring within the Payton estate in Beverly Hills. One day Fiore reported to him that he'd seen Payton in her living room going down on her latest lover, a black man who arrived every afternoon on a motorcycle. Seeing Fiore, she acknowledged him with her eyes but continued at her specialty.

Fiore reported to Marlon that the next morning at two o'clock, Payton arrived in his apartment, using her landlady's key, and asked if she could perform oral sex on him, like she'd done with her black lover. He turned her down, or so Fiore claimed.

After hearing this, Marlon told Fiore that he was interested in being fixed up with Payton so that he, too, could enjoy her specialty. He remembered that he'd had a date with her before he encountered another blonde, Marilyn Monroe, leaving the same apartment building where Payton had been living at the time.

During the three months that Fiore lived on Payton's rented estate, Marlon was a frequent visitor. "He said he felt that Payton was only interested in oral sex, although that doesn't appear to be the case."

Marlon learned that Payton liked to perform oral sex while dressed in black fishnet hosiery, a garter belt, and revealing black lingerie.

"No one will ever know the exact details of what went wrong between Payton and Marlon," Fiore said. "He only liked to give me the dirty details of his triumphs, rarely his failures. Payton was a known blackmailer. She'd blackmailed Hope, Cagney, and so I hear, Gregory Peck, although I'm not so sure about Peck. Through some guise that I don't know about, she managed to get compromising pictures taken of her male victims. Somehow pictures of

Payton giving both Tone and on a different occasion Tom Neal a blow-job were circulated all over Hollywood. Don't ask me how, but she managed to get pictures of herself performing a blow-job on Marlon. All that I know is that one day Marlon called me to his dressing room. 'Thanks but no thanks for fixing me up with our fellatio artist, Miss Payton,' he told me. 'Getting away from that bitch has cost me fifty thousand dollars, and you're to blame.'"

Fiore said that earlier, when he had warned Marlon not to get hooked up with Payton, Marlon had brushed him aside.

"Don't you know enough by now not to talk back to the biggest movie star in the history of the fucking world?" Marlon told Fiore. "This is Hollywood. Underlings don't talk back to big stars. Get out and I don't want to see you for the rest of the day unless I need a shit and run out of toilet paper and need you to come and lick me clean."

Fiore continued to live on the estate until one morning Payton announced that she was broke and would have to abandon the property. For the remainder of the filming of *Guys and Dolls*, Fiore moved into the apartment of a Parisian hooker. "Hell, Marlon had to have her too," Fiore said. "He couldn't let me have a girl, even if a hooker, all to myself. He too had to get in on the act. By that time, I had resumed my fondness for heroin, and really didn't give a fuck what he did. Or what the hooker did."

Marlon, according to Fiore, was Payton's last A-list seduction. After he'd extricated himself from her life—all at a price—Payton was headed for Skid Row. She moved deeper and deeper into heroin addiction and—among other professions—became a lesbian-for-hire. She ended up a broken down and snaggle-toothed whore working Santa Monica Boulevard, jumping inside the cars of strangers and giving fast blow-jobs for ten dollars while her clients kept the motor running.

In February of 1967, Payton, unconscious, was found in the parking lot of Thrifty's Drug Store in Hollywood. At first, sanitation workers thought that her reclining body was a bag of trash. She'd been living on the streets for the past three months. She was rushed to Los Angeles County General Hospital.

Marlon learned of her plight in the morning newspapers and had Sam Gilman deliver five hundred dollars in cash to her hospital bed. With the money, after her release from the hospital, she went to stay with her parents, both of whom were also alcoholics. In May of 1967 her mother found her slumped over a toilet. Her daughter was dead. An autopsy revealed that she'd died of a heart attack and liver failure just six months shy of her 40th birthday.

Later in life, Fiore said that, "Marlon Brando, my former friend, had more affairs with movie stars, male and female, than any other star in the history of Hollywood. But his affair with the very sleazy Barbara Payton—the most hot-to-trot hoyden who ever graced the silver screen—has to rank as the tawdriest of his seductions."

* * *

At the end of the filming of *Guys and Dolls*, Goldwyn presented Marlon with a shiny new black Thunderbird, a car that back in the mid-Fifties was all the rage. When invited to the New York premiere of *Guys and Dolls* at the Capitol Theatre on the night of November 4, 1955, Marlon felt obligated to attend, even though he hated film openings. He agreed to pick up Jean Simmons and ride with her to the premiere.

As their limousine neared the theater in the Times Square area, Marlon remembered screaming fans, mostly female teenagers. He likened them to "a horde of Mongol warriors screaming hysterically."

The fans overran the barricades and descended on the limousine, pounding the windows and trying to break in. Marlon recalled two members of New York's finest in blue arriving on horseback to chase away the mobs. Their pathway cleared, Jean and Marlon were practically carried into the theater. "All I remember that night were hands everywhere on my body," Marlon said. "I must have been groped fifty times before getting into that god damn theater. I felt like Sinatra back in the Forties when he appeared there."

Years later, he still shuddered when he remembered the incident. "It was the most terrifying moment of my life. I thought surely I was going to die."

Otherwise the night went smoothly. The premiere of *Guys and Dolls* was a big event, attended by such notables as New York governor Averell Harriman, along with Mary Martin, Audrey Hepburn, Margaret Truman, William Holden, and Humphrey Bogart.

All the major participants in the film, including Mankiewicz himself, later admitted that *Guys and Dolls* was a great triumph as a Broadway play, but a dud as a movie. Yet despite the cast's cynicism, critic Andrew Sarris hailed it as "the most entertaining musical from Hollywood since *Singin' in the Rain*."

In 1955 it became the second biggest movie attraction in America, grossing thirteen million dollars and eventually receiving four Oscar nominations, although none went specifically to Marlon. That year, only *Giant,* starring James Dean, Elizabeth Taylor, and Rock Hudson, earned heavier grosses.

Even so, Marlon claimed, "This is the last time I'm going to try to take over for Gene Kelly."

* * *

When he first met Anna Kashfi in the Paramount commissary in October of 1955, Marlon would later tell George Englund, his partner in Pennebaker Productions, that she "was the most beautiful woman in the world."

Anna Kashfi

At the time of their first meeting, Marlon was entertaining Eva Marie Saint who was on the lot filming *That Certain Feeling* with Bob Hope. Over lunch, Marlon, according to Kashfi, was "nibbling" at the nape of Eva Marie Saint, his costar in *On the Waterfront*. Distracting himself from Eva Marie's neck, Marlon turned to a nearby luncheon guest, asking, "Who is that good-looking broad in the red sari?"

And thus was launched an ill-fated union that would be played out before the world.

Kashfi said that at first Marlon did not reveal to her that he was a movie star. Instead, according to her, he claimed to be the author of "Twinkle, Twinkle Little Star." She said that it took Spencer Tracy, her costar in *The Mountain*, to explain to her who Marlon actually was.

Although a film actress herself, Kashfi maintained that she'd never heard of Marlon Brando at the time of their meeting. Nor, according to her claim, had she seen any of his films. At the time, Marlon, of course, was the most publicized movie star in the world. Other journalists have maintained that Kashfi knew exactly who Marlon was and had arrived in Hollywood deliberately to seduce him and form a relationship with him, having already heard of his penchant for liking exotic women. Marlon Sr. at one point called Kashfi a "gold-digger."

Their first date had been in that black Thunderbird that Goldwyn had presented to Marlon after the filming of *Guys and Dolls*. Since Kashfi demanded a chaperone, Marlon brought along George Englund, another bachelor. Subsequent dates were in a battered old Volkswagen in dire need of a muffler. Kashfi remembered it as "Marlon's rattrap strewn with beer cans, stained hamburger wrappers, and discarded newspaper sheets that smelled of urine."

Marlon's first seduction of Kashfi may have been tantamount to rape, as he picked her up and carried her into his bedroom without her permission. He told her that rape was "just an assault with a friendly weapon." She would describe his lovemaking as "a well-rehearsed, polished performance—selfish, without warmth or naturalness." She also claimed that he "is not well appointed," adding that, "he screens that deficiency by undue devotion to his sex organ, calling it 'my noble tool.'"

While working with Spencer Tracy on one of his dullest movies, *The Mountain*, Kashfi was touted in the press as "Calcutta born to a fine Hindu family." It was claimed that she could speak eight languages. A talent scout had spotted her at a dance recital in London and had brought her to the attention of Hollywood director Edward Dmytryk.

518

The affair began on a slow note since Marlon left for Japan shortly after it began to film *The Teahouse of the August Moon*. When he returned, he learned that Kashfi had been hospitalized for tuberculosis. Placed in the City of Hope Hospital in Los Angeles, Kashfi would remain there for three months in recovery. Since the final scenes of *Teahouse* were actually shot within a studio in Los Angeles, Marlon—protected by a surgical mask—became a frequent visitor to her hospital room. He most often showed up in the costume of the Japanese character he played in *Teahouse*. "Herro, herro," he'd greet her. "Raff if you must. I'm just a doctor making one of my house cawrs." To look Japanese, he wore a rubber lid around his eyes and was given protruding teeth, a wig, and layers of yellowish greasepaint. He began to bestow gifts on Kashfi, including Dodie's jewelry, even the pillow he'd removed from under his mother's head only minutes after her death.

At one point in their courtship, Marlon told Kashfi, "If my mother, Dodie, had lived, I could not have married you. She wouldn't have let me go. She loved me too much."

Up until then, the word "marriage" had never been mentioned.

* * *

Kashfi appeared in a small role opposite Rock Hudson in *Battle Hymn* in 1956. They had not become friends. But when she met his wife, Phyllis, the two women instantly bonded. Hudson was a homosexual, and his marriage to Phyllis had been forced onto him in an attempt to prevent an exposé by *Confidential* magazine. Phyllis had worked for the notorious Henry Willson as his secretary. Willson, a homosexual, had "created" Rock Hudson, even inventing his name.

As the Hudson marriage was falling apart, Kashfi frequently stayed with the couple at their beach house in Santa Monica. Marlon became a frequent visitor too, but seemed more interested in disappearing with Hudson than visiting Kashfi.

Marlon needed no introduction to Hudson, who at the time was the number one box office star in the world. Tyrone Power, one of Hudson's many male lovers, had introduced them long before at one of the all-male gay parties that Hudson threw at his home.

On some nights Marlon didn't even drive by the Santa Monica house, but had Hudson come

Rock Hudson

to his place. Friends of both actors always claimed that Hudson and Marlon "were never close."

Sam Gilman had a different point of view. "Just what do you mean by close? Is sucking someone's cock close? Is taking Rock's ten-inch dick up your ass close? I would say that Marlon and Rock rocked while Phyllis and Kashfi sat somewhere wondering where the boys were. What friends should say, if they want to be more truthful, is that Rock and Marlon never fell in love. They just fucked each other's brains out."

During the time he dated Hudson, Marlon, according to Gilman, "was in great shape. For *Teahouse*, he'd dieted himself down to one hundred and seventy-five pounds. Rock used to come by and the two of them would soak pairs of blue jeans before putting them on. Then they would go out and lie in the noonday sun for the jeans to dry. That way, the jeans would be molded to their bodies."

Gilman claimed that he often served the men drinks at Marlon's home, where both of them talked about the difficulty of "being the two most famous movie stars in the world" while trying to maintain a secret life. One day Gilman heard Hudson telling Marlon that he was "ninety-five percent homosexual, five percent bi." In contrast, Marlon claimed that he was "seventy-five heterosexual, only twenty-five percent homosexual."

"Let's work on that twenty-five percent," Hudson said to Marlon, flashing his by now world-famous smile.

When Hudson turned on the charm, like he did with Marlon, he ridiculed himself by calling himself "Charlie Movie Star."

Hudson confided to Marlon, "For me, my wife doesn't exist. She repulses me. It's getting so I can't stand to be in the same room with her."

According to Gilman, Hudson strongly advised Marlon not to marry Kashfi. "I don't even know her, but I sense a deeply troubled individual," Hudson claimed. "There are emotional problems. If you marry her, I think you'll live to regret it. It'll be a fast ride to hell. Trust me, I know about bad marriages."

When Hudson and Marlon got bored, Hudson would do something wild like call up Judy Garland who would sing "The Trolley Song" to them, even "Over the Rainbow."

One afternoon in front of Gilman, Marlon sat in the garden nursing his drink. "We can't fuck any more this afternoon," Marlon told Hudson. "I've

Rock Hudson and Phyllis Gates

had my fill. I don't want to see Anna tonight. Not even Rita Moreno would interest me. I'm sure you don't want to go home to Phyllis. God, how could you have married her? She looks like something a pimply faced boy would take to the senior prom. Let's think of something exciting we can do tonight."

Stark naked, Hudson rose from a chaise longue beside Marlon's pool. "I've got it!" he said. "I'm calling Liz Taylor to come over for dinner. Who knows? We might even have a three-way. After all, the three of us are the biggest God damn movie stars in the whole fucking world!"

* * *

Marlon didn't want Kashfi living with him, so he installed her in a 1930s-era apartment complex in West Hollywood. Marlon Sr. lived in the same building. Later, Kashfi claimed that she'd been moved there so that Marlon's dad could spy on her. The relationship between Marlon Sr. and Kashfi remained cool. She found him a brooding old man "with the residue of debauchery etched across his face."

With Kashfi moving into an advanced state of pregnancy in September of 1957, Marlon decided that he had to get married as a means of legitimizing their child. Both parents accurately predicted that the baby would be a boy. Fiore urged that Marlon seek an abortion for Kashfi.

At the time of their first meeting, Fiore had been impressed with Kashfi. But as he got to know her, he spoke of her "frightening rage." The first time he saw her in a temper fit, she rushed from the bathroom with a large bar of soap which she hurled at Marlon. "It got him between the eyes and cracked in half," Fiore claimed. "Stunned, Marlon staggered back and fell."

Consistently, Fiore warned Marlon not to marry her. Kashfi, according to some reports, suspected that the relationship between Fiore and Marlon was "homoerotic." Many observers close to Marlon came to the same conclusion.

Although admitting many revealing secrets about Marlon's life, as well as his own, including heroin addition, Fiore always denied that he and Marlon

Brando and Carlo Fiore

ever engaged in sex. After their visits to Los Angeles, both of Marlon's French friends, Christian Marquand and Roger Vadim, privately revealed their suspicions that the relationship between Marlon and Fiore was sexual. Upon hearing this, Fiore dismissed their suspicions. "Both of those queer French frogs want to get into Marlon's pants themselves."

But Gilman once told friends that one morning when he was serving coffee, he discovered that Marlon and Fiore, both of them naked, had fallen asleep in each other's arms. And Fiore did admit that one morning, he woke up to the sensation of Marlon playing with his [Fiore's] genitals.

Kashfi not only found the intimacies between her husband and Fiore suspicious, but she also began to suspect that there was something going on between Marlon and Christian Marquand. When he came from Paris to visit Marlon, Kashfi noted that the two actors "displayed an affection toward each other that far overreached the usual expression of friendship."

Marlon didn't want to alert the press to news of his upcoming marriage. However, to buy the wedding ring, he showed up in

Brando and wife number one, Anna Kashfi

the center of Pasadena wearing a flowing saffron-colored Hindu robe. Within minutes, his disguise was discovered, and he was mobbed by fans.

Marlon had intended to marry Kashfi in Arizona, but at the time that state barred interracial marriages. Instead the wedding took place at the modest home of Marlon's aunt, Betty Lindemeyer.

Before she could go through with the ceremony, Kashfi demanded a nosegay of Madonna lilies. Surprisingly, no Los Angeles florist had them for sale. The flowers had to be flown down from San Francisco. That took hours.

While waiting, "We sat around drinking champagne until the flowers arrived," Kashfi said. "By then everyone was understandably drunk. At that point I would have married a baboon."

Finally, the ceremony began. On wobbly legs, Kashfi appeared in a sea green sari with a white brocade blouse embroidered with gold. Marlon wore an opera cape with a shocking pink lining and a classic Homburg. Conducting the ceremony was not the Buddhist priest as requested by Kashfi, but a Presbyterian minister, the Rev. J. Walter Fiscus, pastor of the Little Brown Church in the Valley in North Hollywood.

At the time of his marriage, Marlon was thirty-three years old. His bride was twenty-three. She was also two months pregnant.

Marlon told Fiore that he had no intention of staying married to Kashfi and planned to divorce her a few months after the birth of their child. "I married her only to legitimize our boy. In other words, I got married to get divorced."

Marlon had made no plans for the honeymoon. Driving around aimlessly, he came to the house of Jay Kanter in Beverly Hills. His agent hastily moved out, and the recently married couple spent the first night of their honeymoon in this borrowed house. "There was no sex," Kashfi later said. "It was not the most memorable of honeymoon nights."

Marlon later told Fiore that he didn't like to "touch women when they are in a family way."

Having made no plans, Kashfi suggested to Marlon that they drive out to stay with her newly acquired friends, the Western writer, Louis L'Amour, and his wife, Kathy. They lived in Palm Desert in a house filled with memorabilia of the Old West.

L'Amour later recalled that "Marlon amused us by crushing out cigarettes on the back of his hand. He claimed that he'd learned the trick from James Dean."

"Leaving the gals to clean house," L'Amour practiced target shooting with Marlon. For lunch he drove Marlon to his favorite barbecue joint eighteen miles away, where the two men would always forget to bring food back to their women.

L'Amour said that he found Marlon's habit of public urination amusing. "The first time I got him to the barbecue joint, Marlon had to go," L'Amour said. "We'd been drinking beer in the car. He couldn't wait to get to the crapper. Right in front of the open-air tables, Marlon whipped it out and pissed all over the place, arching the yellow stream high. The diners were shocked at their first up-close exposure to a genuine movie star."

Marlon's habit of urinating whenever he felt like it had gotten him in trouble before, notably at some unknown girl's school where he was nearly arrested, and again in the waiting room of a Boston train station.

Louis L'Amour

At night, Marlon and L'Amour sat on a cowhide sofa in the Western-styled living room, as the writer would regale him with stories of the Old West. In a short time, L'Amour would become one of the most prolific of all Western writers, following in the footsteps of Zane Grey. U.S. presidents such as Dwight Eisenhower would cite L'Amour as their favorite writer. Although Marlon listened attentively, he was more interested in stories of L'Amour's own life.

The writer spoke of his "hobo-ing it cross country" on freight trains with bums, some of whom had been riding the rails for fifty years or so. "I came to know all the hobo jungles, wheat bins, and gaps in piles of timber," L'Amour said. He remembered sleeping on the beach in San Pedro, California, one summer where he said that one night he was held down by "three drunken truckers who raped me. It caused me to have a new appreciation of women. I don't see what fun they get out of having a man stick it to them. To me, I felt like a pig probably does when he's getting castrated. Such pain! Only having a baby must be worse. No one can accuse me of being gay. I hated it!"

Brando and
George Englund

Marlon didn't respond exactly, merely stating that, "Pleasure comes in many forms."

L'Amour told of circling the globe when he was a merchant seaman and visiting the bordellos of "Persia," Egypt, Borneo, and the Dutch East Indies, reciting at great length some of the "specialties" he'd encountered among foreign prostitutes. Marlon seemed intensely interested. Not caring if his new wife were within hearing distance or not, he told L'Amour that he too planned to sample the bordellos of the Far East "in my immediate future."

Before the week-long visit came to an end, Marlon told L'Amour that he wanted him to "jot down all your most intense experiences in a film treatment." He promised that his newly formed production company, Pennebaker, would seriously consider filming his world travels. Marlon promised the writer that, "I'll play Louis L'Amour myself."

"Who else?" L'Amour asked.

George Englund recalled L'Amour arriving at Pennebaker months later not to sell his own scenario, but a hard-boiled Western novel *To Tame a Land*, "a sodbuster oatie," as L'Amour put it. Englund later wrote that L'Amour didn't look the part of a Western novelist. "He was a large man with wavy black hair that suggested a Greek Mafia don whose boats ran hashish out of North Africa," Englund said.

Although Englund expressed doubt about L'Amour, he felt that Marlon "as a Western hero seemed a strong commercial idea."

The project eventually led to Marlon starring in and directing *One-Eyed Jacks*, released in 1961.

During their first month of married bliss, Marlon informed Kashfi that he intended to lead the same life he'd led before their wedding.

He was true to his word. After their marriage, Kashfi claimed that she saw even less of him than when they were dating. Much to Marlon's horror, she began to talk to the press, including one of his chief critics, columnist Hedda Hopper. Kashfi's remarks, by anyone's standards and especially for the 1950s, were extremely candid, "Living with Marlon is like an afternoon at the races—short periods of orgiastic activity followed by long periods of boredom and anticipation. He's almost never home. He attracts women like feces attract flies."

It was music to Hopper's ears, which rested beneath a large picture hat. Hedda, taking copious notes, learned that, "Marlon leaves a lot to be desired as a romancer. He's just plain clumsy—and that's the truth. If he weren't a film star, he wouldn't get to first base with a woman."

The reporters who trailed after Kashfi discovered that her parents weren't from India but were British, living in Wales. Until Anna's marriage to Marlon, Mr. and Mrs. William O'Callaghan hadn't even known the whereabouts of their daughter.

Mrs. O'Callaghan protested that, "There is no Indian blood in my family or my husband's family," but she did agree that her daughter had indeed been reared in Calcutta when her husband found overseas work there.

Kashfi stuck by her Indian parentage story, claiming that William O'Callaghan was her stepfather—not her real father. She cited David Kashfi, an Indian architect, as her real father and said that she had been the byproduct of an "unregistered alliance"—a demure way of declaring that she was illegitimate. According to her, her mother had married O'Callaghan two years after her birth.

Mrs. O'Callaghan claimed that her daughter, Joanne O'Callaghan, had been born in Darjeeling, India, on September 30, 1934.

In spite of all these revalations about her origins, Kashfi continued to deny she was British. At one point, she claimed, "I have never even heard of the couple," referring to the O'Callaghans.

Publicly, Marlon maintained that reports of his wife's mysterious racial

Louella Parsons, Debbie Reynolds, and Hedda Hopper

525

origins were "just so much garbage rooted out by a pack of vultures." Even so, the press continued to put the word "Indian" in quotes when referring to Kashfi.

When members of the press moved in on Marlon for his reaction to reports that Kashfi had faked her background, he brushed them aside. He uttered a snappy, "No comment!" Privately, he had plenty to say to his friends, and the issue led to violent fights between Kashfi and himself.

He even hired private detectives to look into Kashfi's claims about her background. One of Marlon's detectives concluded in his report that Kashfi "was about as Indian as Queen Elizabeth of England." Marlon felt he'd been victimized and betrayed. The world press in its blitzkrieg of the story was making him out to be a fool. At one point he called his attorney, asking if he could have the marriage annulled on the grounds that Kashfi had given false information on her marriage license. He became extremely bitter about how the press was invading his privacy with each new exposé. He denounced reporters as, "All scum, just hired buffoons, character assassins. Men driven by brains as aggressive as a hungry Tyrannosaurus Rex."

Kashfi's marriage to Marlon was of the "Stormy Weather" variety. "Even before they got married, they started fighting," Fiore said. "The fighting continued on their non-honeymoon and for every day thereafter. Marriage did not deter Marlon from sleeping with other people."

Launched into married life, Marlon hauled Kashfi around Hollywood to show her off, spending evenings, for example, at the home of Humphrey Bogart and Lauren Bacall in the Holmsby Hills where Marlon and Bogie played "sadistic chess" until late into the night.

It was during this "marriage from hell," that Marlon became a "porno star." Making use of a camera attached to the foot of his bed, he taped sexual encounters with various women, some of them famous. He also taped certain sexual encounters with men, including at least three movie stars. It was later revealed that one of those movie stars was Rock Hudson.

Kashfi, years from that time, claimed that when her son discovered these homosexual porn movies, it drove him insane, eventually leading him to commit murder. Such claims, of course, were dismissed by the courts. At one hearing before a judge, Kashfi charged Marlon with "unspeakable sexual acts." Accusing him of lapses in morality, she claimed that he "degraded himself and his family in society."

As tensions between Marlon and herself increased, Kashfi reverted to the bottle and pill popping, relying heavily on Nebutal and Seconal.

A baby boy was born to Marlon and Kashfi on Mother's Day, May 11, 1958, at the Cedars of Lebanon Hospital in Los Angeles. Marlon wanted to name him Christian, after his French lover, Christian Marquand, Kashfi preferred Devi which means "goddess" in Hindu. The child became known as Christian Devi Brando, Marlon calling him "Chris," Kashfi stubbornly sticking to "Devi." He was slated to grow into a tragic life.

Christian Brando
and Anna Kashfi

After the fight over a name, their next big battle was over whether to have Christian circumcised or not. Kashfi favored circumcision, Marlon opposing it. In his view, an uncut penis was far more sensitive, and men "who are intact enjoy sex far more." He had repeated that same sentiment to others as well. In retaliation, she publicly claimed that Marlon's opinion was "based on his own undistinguished pudendum." After becoming a senior citizen, Marlon himself would one day undergo the circumcision operation.

In June of 1958 Marlon Sr. married Anna Frenke Paramore, the daughter of Gene Frenke, a real estate investor. She was only thirty-eight. Kashfi claimed that she had to insist that Marlon pick up the phone and talk to his father, who had not invited him to his wedding. "Hi, Pop, I hope you'll be happy," Marlon said before slamming down the phone. He turned to Kashfi. "Why did you make me talk to him? That God damn son of a bitch. I can't stand him. And the way he treated my mother. . .to hell with him."

Likewise, son Marlon had not invited his father to his wedding to Kashfi. "I'll bury him dead before I do!" he had proclaimed.

Anna Frenke Paramore
and Marlon Sr.

In spite of saying that, Marlon entertained his father and his new wife frequently when they arrived in Los Angeles. Sometimes Wally Cox and his wife, Betty, joined them for dinner. Rumors were circulating at the time that Marlon's only reason for marrying Kashfi was to camouflage his homosexual relationship with Wally. That gossip appears to be unfounded. The hostilities between Senior and Junior remained intense. Marlon Sr. once denounced his son for his "nonstop screwing."

Upon his return from Japan and the filming of *Sayonara*, Marlon demanded that Kashfi wear kimonos and attend to him like a geisha.

While Marlon was dating other women—or,

more secretly, men—Kashfi went on a house hunt for them, finding a Japanese style home on Mulholland Drive that had originally been built for Howard Hughes. Marlon fell in love with the place. At long last he'd found a home. Mulholland Drive was to be the place where he'd end his days.

The home at 12900 Mulholland Drive was a single-level structure with two bedrooms that stood on four acres of landscaped grounds opening onto panoramic views of the San Fernando Valley. At first he rented it for $1,500 from its owner, "a Buddhist monk." Marlon came to love the privacy afforded by the property and the owner's rock garden and Japanese temple. The house lay at the termination of a winding private driveway. At the beginning of the drive, Marlon posted a sign on the gate. "Unless you have an appointment, under no circumstances disturb the occupant."

After they moved into the house on Mulholland Drive, Dean Martin dropped by to take acting lessons from Marlon, and Maureen Stapleton arrived to occupy the spare bedroom. Fed up with Stapleton's extended stay, Kashfi kicked out this talented actress and longtime friend of Marlon's from the 1940s.

It was only ten days before their first wedding anniversary that Kashfi announced that she was divorcing Marlon, claiming she could no longer tolerate "his strange way of living."

Kashfi fled Marlon's home, moving in with Pier Angeli, who had also separated from her husband, Vic Damone. Some thirty days later Kashfi filed for divorce. In papers read in court, she claimed "grievous mental suffering, distress, and injury."

The Brando/Kashfi divorce became final on April 22, 1959. The terms of the divorce called for Marlon to settle half-a-million dollars upon Kashfi, to be paid out over the next decade, plus one thousand dollars a month in child support, as she'd retained custody of Christian.

* * *

If their marriage was stormy, their post-divorce was a tornado. The battles over the custody of Christian began on November 18, 1959, and continued into the 1970s, revealing details of Marlon's heretofore secret life never presented to the public. "Kidnapping," raids on each other's homes, lurid court testimony, and even violence characterized their battles. No divorced couple in the history of Hollywood fought each other longer and harder—and more notoriously—than did Anna Kashfi and Marlon Brando. A pawn in their fights, Christian himself ultimately became the victim of his parents' endless battles both in and out of the courtroom. This troubled youth would one day make scandalous headlines around the world.

Anna Kashfi attacks Marlon

In their continuing battles over Christian, Fiore claimed that Marlon and Kashfi "were fucking up the kid's life, shuttling him back and forth between Marlon's home and Kashfi's rented houses. The kid became confused. He seemed completely disoriented. Ultimately he grew up to be impossible to handle."

In 1960 Marlon hauled Kashfi into court when she refused to grant him visitation rights to see his son. He asked the court to hold his former wife in contempt and grant him full custody of Christian. Kashfi countered that she had refused Marlon because he showed up at her doorstep with "an unidentified girlfriend." Kashfi was referring to Marlon's latest flame, actress Barbara Luna.

Kashfi also claimed that Marlon "brutally beat me and struck me, and once threw me to the floor of the bedroom while the baby was in my arms." In her testimony, she also maintained that Marlon had taught her son, only two and a half years old, to say "fuck you."

In a stern warning, Judge Benjamin Landis told Marlon, "You are an artist, and you have a certain right to your eccentricities, but the child has rights too."

Four months later they were in court again, Marlon claiming that he had been denied thirteen consecutive visits with Christian. In counter testimony, Kashfi said that she did not want her son exposed to "an immoral man" like his father.

Marlon's attorney requested that Kashfi be held in contempt. Furious, she loudly denounced Marlon in court, calling him a "God damn slob." When the judge ordered a recess, Kashfi, in front of photographers, waited for Marlon to leave the courtroom. She slapped Marlon in the corridor, her violence being recorded on film.

Kashfi wanted to prove that Marlon was unfit to have Christian in his custody. She claimed that Marlon "flaunted his mistresses and illegitimate children" in front of their son.

In court, Marlon attempted to show that Kashfi was often under the influence of drugs, such as barbiturates. He once obtained the key to her apartment. Entering it, he discovered Kashfi "out cold."

"I scooped up Christian and made a hasty retreat," Marlon said.

Flying back from Tahiti on June 29, 1961, Marlon once again battled Kashfi in a Santa Monica courtroom. It was at this hearing that Marlon for the first time publicly announced that he was secretly married to his old girlfriend, Movita.

529

In the courtroom, Movita made faces at Kashfi as she testified. After hearing both Kashfi and Marlon denounce each other, Judge Eric Auerbach lectured them, declaring that their battle over Christian had become a personal vendetta. He said that the young boy had "become an instrument of vengeance" between the divorced couple.

The portrait Marlon always painted in court was that of Kashfi as a violent woman. "While I was home in bed, she came in and flung herself on the bed and bit me three times and slapped me. I tried to restrain her and get her out of the house, but she went to get in her car and tried to run over me. I went back in my house and locked the doors. She threw a log through one of the windows and came back into the house through the windows. I held her down on the bed and tied her with the sash of my dressing robe. I then called the police. I told them I would not press charges and asked them to escort her home. She refused but the police persuaded her."

Once when an angry judge shouted at her, she stormed out of court. The judge had reprimanded her for not answering questions on the witness stand. "Isn't that too damn bad!" she told reporters in the hall.

* * *

Kashfi seemed hell bent on embarrassing Marlon in every court session. In one of her more lurid custody suits, she claimed that she found the door unlocked at Marlon's home and entered it. According to her testimony, she said that she came into the house and went to his bedroom where she discovered him in bed "with a certain Asian beauty who shall remain nameless."

Surprisingly, since there was nothing illegal about that, Marlon was nonetheless asked in court, "Do you have ladies into your home for sexual reasons?"

Marie Cui with baby

"I have ladies in my home for many purposes," he responded, "including sexual."

The unknown woman was actually Marie Cui, with whom Marlon was having an affair.

While filming some scenes in Manila for *The Teahouse of the August Moon*, Marlon went to a club where he spotted an eighteen-year-old dancer, Marie Cui. He was immediately captivated by her beauty. Their romance began that night.

In counter testimony, Marlon claimed that Kashfi "broke into my house and jumped up on the bed and started pulling the girl's hair out. The girl, terrified, beat it. Then Anna started wrecking the house. When she heard the taxi drive up, Anna ran down to try to catch the girl before she left. I followed along, with Anna biting me, hitting me, scratching me, and swearing at me. Finally, I said, 'Anna, this is enough. Go home.' She refused, so I took her and turned her over and spanked her as hard as I could."

Kashfi tried to refute that claim, saying that when she discovered the nude girl, that both Marie Cui (not naming her specifically) and Marlon had "jumped on me. Furniture started flying. I'm not strong enough to fight two people, so I ran."

Kashfi said that she broke into Marlon's home to "get back at him for breaking into my house and poking holes in my diaphragm with an ice pick. In a further charge, she stated before the court that on the night of her unannounced visit to Marlon's house, he "tackled me in his front yard and knocked my head against a stone."

Her charges were greeted with skepticism by the court.

Marlon was vague about this particular encounter, putting the date as "sometime in 1961 or perhaps 1962."

The judge ruled against both Marlon and Kashfi, granting temporary custody of the six-year-old Christian to Frances Brando Loving, Marlon's sister, who lived in Mundelein, Illinois, with her husband and other children.

In time, Marie Cui would have her own court battles with Marlon.

On February 27, 1963, Cui gave birth to a daughter, which she named Maya Gabriella Cui Brando. Later, when she filed a paternity suit against Marlon, she claimed that he had refused to see her when he discovered that she was pregnant. Cui steadfastly maintained that Marlon had urged her to have the baby and that, "I deliberately got myself pregnant."

She also claimed that she fully expected to receive financial support when she returned to Manila to be with her family. But no money ever came from Marlon, according to her later court testimony.

When she returned to Los Angeles, Cui said that she went directly from the airport to Marlon's house, entering it when she found the door unlocked. She claimed that "I walked right in and slapped him in the face."

Marlon entered St. John's Hospital in Santa Monica, suffering from a kidney infection. There he was served with a subpoena from Cui on July 19, 1963.

As Marlon appeared before Judge Edward Brand on August 1, 1963, he learned that Cui was seeking $775 a month financial support. Five days later, when the blood tests came in, Marlon was discovered not to be the father. Judge Brand dismissed charges against him, although Cui steadfastly maintained that "the child is Brando's."

Astonishingly, Marlon and Cui were reported to have continued with their sometimes love affair over the course of the next few years, and reportedly Marlon contributed to the financial support of the woman's daughter. "Maya always claimed that Marlon Brando was her father," a friend recalled. However, in spite of his financial contributions to her education, he always insisted that Maya was not to use the name of Brando.

Marie Cui would be in the vanguard of a number of Asian beauties that Marlon seduced. Fiore estimated that it may have added up to nearly three hundred. Reporter Joe Hyams once headlined an article: "Brando, As a Great Lover He Seems to Be Without Equal in Contemporary Film History."

* * *

On the afternoon of December 6, 1964, Kashfi passed out and was found comatose. Rushed to UCLA Medical Center, she was carefully examined. The determination was that she'd overdosed on barbiturates. In the aftermath, Marlon was granted temporary custody of Christian.

When she was released from the medical center, Kashfi broke into Marlon's home, kidnapping her own son against court orders. Backed up by his attorney, Allen Susman, along with two private detectives, Marlon arrived at the Bel Air Sands Hotel where he broke into Kashfi's suite and reclaimed his son. He was armed with a court order.

Barefoot and in her nightgown, Kashfi chased Marlon and the men into the hotel lobby. Once there, she assaulted three people who tried to restrain her. One of them, Sergeant Ed Hall, was also a policeman. He arrested her and charged her with assault and battery of a police officer.

Marlon was forced to appear in court before Superior Judge Laurence Rittenband. In his testimony, Marlon claimed that his former wife suffered from "psychoneuroses which at times causes hysterical blindness." He also reported that she kept a loaded revolver and that he feared she "might harm herself and my son."

In October of 1965, the judge allowed Kashfi, in spite of the testimony, to regain custody of Christian. Marlon called the decision "barbarous."

For her assault on the policeman, Kashfi was fined two hundred dollars.

* * *

Court testimony over the years about Marlon was damaging, but Kashfi came in for her share of hits. A friend of hers testified that she found Kashfi in her apartment, unconscious in a puddle of her own vomit. Outside, baby Christian played unattended at the side of a swimming pool.

On another occasion, Fiore maintained that Kashfi left her young son alone in a car parked on Wilshire Boulevard, while she stormed Marlon's office "in a frenzy of rage, beating him with her fists." After observing the romance, marriage, divorce, and subsequent legal battles, Marlon's close friend, George Englund, finally concluded, "If you're in love with Marlon, you're in rough company."

Except for Christian, Marlon's other children stayed out of the limelight. When a reporter asked him how many children he actually had, he said, "Several. My children are flowers in the great meadow of love!"

Having spent the half-million dollars awarded to her by a judge, Kashfi went back to court, asking for a continuation of payments. She was turned down.

During filming of *The Godfather*, Marlon was back in court where he and Kashfi were awarded joint custody of Christian. By now, the boy was twelve years old. Learning that Christian was consuming alcohol and taking drugs, the judge ordered that he be enrolled at Ojai Valley School.

Weeks later Kashfi arrived in Ojai and checked her son out of school. Her motives for doing so were unclear. Perhaps she feared that Marlon's attorneys were going to legally take her son away from her again. With two "unknown men" in the car with Kashfi, Christian was driven to a remote fishing village in Baja California, Mexico, south of the California state line. Kashfi then attempted to return to Los Angeles on a bus, but along with a woman companion, was taken from the vehicle and booked in a Calexico jail on a charge of being disorderly. Kashfi claimed that her son had been kidnapped and that she feared for his safety.

Mexican agents managed to locate the thirteen-year-old boy at a so-called hippie campsite in Baja. He was hiding under a pile of dirty clothing and appeared to be suffering from bronchitis. Apparently, during his captivity, Christian had been subjected to homosexual advances by one of his captors.

One of the "hippies" at the campsite claimed that Kashfi had promised to give them ten thousand dollars for hiding Christian. Eventually the teenager was returned to Los Angeles. Mexico deported the eight Americans at the campsite, labeling them "undesirables." Back in Los Angeles and in court again, Marlon was allowed to take Christian to Paris where filming resumed on *Last Tango in Paris*. Kashfi fumed but was powerless to do anything about it.

Christian was returned to school at Ojai, but was later expelled when he set fire to his dorm.

Anna Kashfi

Desperately searching for a case against Marlon, Kashfi used the scandal of the Academy Awards against him. When Marlon refused to accept the Oscar for his role in *The Godfather*, she filed a petition in Superior Court. Before a judge, she claimed that her son had been humiliated and embarrassed by Marlon's "blatant disregard for conventional social decorum" on Oscar night.

When *Last Tango* was released, sparking an international controversy and blaring newspaper headlines, Kashfi went back to court again. She claimed that Marlon's appearance in the film made him unfit to be a father, and she wanted a judge to remove the joint custody provision of the court, returning Christian solely to her. She maintained that he portrayed "a sexually maladjusted and perverted person who utters obscene, foul, shocking, and distasteful profanities." Her former husband, she claimed, was appearing in a pornographic movie, said to be evocative of the private videos he'd taped at his home with various sexual partners.

Attorneys at the time tried to introduce the notorious photograph of Marlon performing fellatio on Wally Cox, depicted earlier within this book, but the judge refused to allow it and dismissed other charges as well.

Finally in April of 1972, Marlon gained full custody of his son.

Even after Kashfi's marriage to salesman James Hannaford, her legal wrangles with Marlon continued. She sued Marlon once again for custody. In her petition, her attorneys maintained that Marlon, on a ski trip to Idaho's Sun Valley, pushed Christian onto the terrace. After his shower, according to the petition, he was clad only in a towel. The temperature on the freezing terrace was 15°F.

The allegation was that in front of the terrace window, Marlon had "dropped his pants, pressed his buttocks to the glass, and yelled, 'Here, climb into this!'" Kashfi eventually dropped the suit.

In 1979, Kashfi got her revenge on Marlon by publishing *Brando for Breakfast*, a shocking tell-all memoir. Heretofore, no wife in Hollywood history had written such a revealing book. In it, she ridiculed not only his lovemaking but his sexual organ, exploring what she called his "kinky sexuality and sexual compulsions." Crown Publishers, hoping to reach a large audience, claimed that in the memoir, "Anna Kashfi shows the ability to admire Brando's greatness even as she rails against his imperfections. She also shows an understanding of her own failures, which drove her, almost fatally, to seek solace in drink, drugs, and madness."

"He can be brutal," Kashfi told her readers. "He has punched photographers who had the temerity to request a pose. He's slapped and beaten women and shown callous unconcern at the death of a friend or employee. Within his being lurks the unregenerate soul of a Cro-Magnon."

Chapter Fifteen

One could borrow the title of the Eugene O'Neill play, *Strange Interlude*, to describe Marlon's brief affair and continuing relationship with the beautiful actress, Susan Cabot. Three years younger than Marlon, this Bostonian was reared in a series of eight foster homes, evocative of the young life of Marilyn Monroe.

The details of the Brando/Cabot affair remain sketchy even today. He apparently saw one of her movies and became intrigued with her black hair and sultry good looks. She was a B actress appearing in B movies with such actors as Tony Curtis, John Lund, and Audie Murphy. A former roommate of Marlon's, Tony Curtis, may have introduced them.

Marlon was obviously more impressed with Susan the woman than Susan the actress. She'd appeared in such forgettable films as *Ride Clear of Diablo* (1954) and *Flame of Araby* (1951). At the time Marlon met her, she was working for the "King of the Bs," Roger Corman, playing the lead in the melodramatic rock 'n roller, *Carnival Rock* (1957).

Susan told Marlon and other friends that she was tired of appearing as a "prop" in sagebrush westerns and Arabian Nights fantasies.

Susan Cabot

In 1959, while still dating Marlon secretly, Susan launched herself into a highly publicized affair with King Hussein of Jordan. Again, the circumstances of their meeting are unknown, no doubt arranged by one of the king's assistants. Hussein had told several of his associates, including reporters, that his all-time favorite film was *Son of Ali Baba*, in which Susan co-starred with Tony Curtis. Perhaps he fell in love with Susan's screen image and set out to pursue her.

"At that time Marlon was getting ready to dump Susan," Carlo Fiore claimed. "But when he heard that the king was fucking her, Marlon got interested all over again. I guess he figured if Susan was good enough for Hussein's bed, she was also worthy of Marlon's."

Susan continued to maintain very secret relationships with both Marlon and the king as she moved deeper and deeper into the 1960s. Perhaps deciding that neither suitor would ever marry her, she wed Michael Roman in 1968. Subsequently she gave birth to a son, Timothy Scott Roman, who suffered from dwarfism. At the time, she told Fiore that she didn't know if the father was Marlon Brando or King Hussein. Fiore found that pronouncement "totally awesome—why not name her husband as the suspected father?"

Fiore was never certain if Marlon believed that the boy was his or not. Marlon admitted to having had unprotected sex with Susan during the first stage of her marriage.

As an act of generosity, he privately contributed to the child's support. A medical researcher had told him that some hormone could cure dwarfism. This was all highly experimental based on "a substance" that was said to be taken from cadavers. Some medical authorities maintained at the time that injections of this mysterious substance could make dwarfs grow taller. Fiore felt that "all this crap sounded like some Frankenstein movie, and I stayed out of it."

"Marlon at the time had lost all sexual interest in Susan but seemed fascinated with the subject of how to make dwarfs grow tall—it was too bizarre for me," Fiore said.

On December 10, 1986 Marlon received a call from someone, informing him that Susan had been bashed to death by a weight-lifting bar. The fatal blows were delivered by her own son, Tim, in their Encino home. At the time Tim was twenty-two years old.

Before confessing to the crime himself, her son maintained that his mother had been killed by unknown assailants using Ninja methods.

At his trial, Tim's defense attorneys maintained that he was "an emotional wreck because of an overly protective and disturbed mother who lived like Norma Desmond did in the movie, *Sunset Blvd.*, but in a home seething with filth and decay." The conditions were said to be so horrible that "they constitute child abuse," in the words of the defense attorneys.

These same attorneys also maintained that at the time Tim caved in his mother's head, he had "become temporarily unglued" because of all the various experimental hormones he'd been forced to take. Marlon's worst fear did not happen. At first, he'd feared that his name would be drawn into the courtroom proceedings. All his financial contributions to Susan had been paid in cash so that he would not leave a bank trail of canceled checks.

In a surprise development, Tim received a suspended sentence and was placed on probation instead of a conviction for murder.

536

Breathing a sigh of relief, Marlon told Fiore that he had finally concluded that the young man was not his son, even though he had privately provided money over the years. "Any child born to a woman and impregnated by my noble tool would have been born perfect—not a dwarf."

* * *

"If a beautiful young woman ever had a penchant for suicide, she dated Marlon," Fiore once said. Of course, he was exaggerating, but Marlon throughout his life romanced many women who later either attempted or else succeeded at suicide—Rita Moreno, among them.

At the time of his marriage to Anna Kashfi, he was secretly dating her friend, the green-eyed, tempestuous Gia Scala, who had been born in Liverpool, England, although she was descended from an aristocratic Italian family and had grown up in Messina, Sicily. Moving to the United States to live with her aunt in Long Island, she developed into a stunning beauty. One night she caught the attention of an ex-Marine, Steve McQueen, who fell in love with her and wanted to marry her, although she turned down this future film star.

She was first discovered as a professional "quiz kid" on "The Arlene Francis Show," which led to a contract with Universal International. During the making of *The Big Boodle*, she claimed that a heavy-drinking Errol Flynn raped her, but she didn't press charges. She was seen around town dating handsome actor George Nader, later learning that he was a homosexual involved in an affair with Rock Hudson among others.

In 1957 she was cast in *Don't Go Near the Water*, opposite Glenn Ford, who had completed filming *The Teahouse of the August Moon* with Marlon. Both actors had become blood enemies for life.

In the original casting and in a bit of irony, the female lead had gone to Anna Kashfi. Kashfi later wrote of her horror in working opposite Ford. "His vendetta with Marlon apparently enveloped anyone close to Marlon. He flaunted his dislike for me early in the shooting schedule. In shots with his back to the camera, he would wave his hands in front of my face. In our close-up two-shots, he would whisper obscene limericks in my ear. He never passed up an opportunity to carp at me."

At one point tensions mounted between Ford and Kashfi to the point

Gia Scala

Glenn Ford

that he could no longer tolerate her. "You're out!" he screamed at her. "Out! Out! Out!" He strode off the set. The role was given to Gia Scala. Apparently, there was no jealousy between the two actresses, who became close friends.

Ford could tolerate Scala, not Kashfi. Once again Ford was cast opposite Scala in the film, *Cowboy*. Before shooting began, Scala told the director that she wouldn't be able to shoot on location in Texas and New Mexico because she had to remain near the bedside of her mother, who was dying of cancer. In another one of those twists of fate, Kashfi was assigned the role to replace Scala.

Ford was horrified but learned that he did not have casting approval, so he was forced to make the film with Kashfi in the lead. As he told the casting director, "I can't even stand to be in the same room with anybody who fucked Marlon Brando. That means, I'm a lonely man."

"Marlon and Ford detested each other long before they made *The Teahouse of the August Moon*," Fiore said.

Fiore claimed that the feud between Ford and Marlon arose when Ford was cast in *Human Desire*, a role Marlon had rejected. Fiore attended the movie with Marlon, who loudly denounced Ford's "wooden" performance. Marlon told a reporter, "Glenn Ford is the kind of movie star tailor-made to smile on camera for publicity eight-by-tens. He's hopelessly boring on the screen. In this corruption of the Émile Zola book, Ford just stands there on camera waiting for accidents to occur."

Word of this critique immediately got back to Ford in Hollywood. When the hottest—and some said the best—male actor in America criticized another, that made news.

When Daniel Mann cast both of these actors—sarcastically called "the male version of Joan Crawford and Bette Davis"—in *The Teahouse of the August Moon*, it was inevitable that the two men would clash.

Marlon soon tired of Scala and dropped her. Despondent over her mother's death from cancer, Scala sailed to England to film *The Two-Headed Spy*. There she threw herself over Waterloo Bridge and into the Thames. But she was pulled to safety by a passing cab driver. When Fiore told Marlon of this, he said, "If a woman wants to kill herself, she should be allowed to do so."

In May of 1971, Marlon learned from his son, Christian, that Scala was undergoing psychiatric observation at a hospital in Ventura County. He was disturbed to learn that she was later released into the custody of Kashfi and was staying with Christian and her. Scala learned that her ex-husband, Don Burnett, was going to marry TV actress Barbara Anderson. Despondent and still in love with her former husband, Scala swallowed roach poison and was rushed to the hospital where a priest administered the last rites of the Catholic Church. Miraculously she survived.

But on April 30, 1972, she finally succeeded in killing herself by taking an overdose of drugs. She was found dead at her home in the Hollywood Hills. She was only thirty-eight years old. "She didn't like the world and wanted to go to another place," Marlon said. "And that's the opinion of an atheist."

* * *

When Marlon signed to do *The Teahouse of the August Moon*, his luck in film scripts was running out. A popular novel by Vern J. Sneider, it had been adapted by John Patrick into a Broadway success. Marlon claimed that he'd attended the play four times and had "laughed so hard the first time I farted three blasts in a row," much to the chagrin of the other members of the audience sitting near him.

At first when Marlon expressed an interest in the play, executives at MGM thought he wanted the lead of the bumbling Captain Fisby, later assigned to Glenn Ford. Not so. Marlon wanted to play Sakini, a comically sly Okinawan interpreter and handyman to post-war American occupation forces, a role that had been played rather effectively by David Wayne on Broadway.

Complete with "Jap makeup," as he called it, and a *faux* Japanese accent, Marlon told Fiore that, "I'm going to play Sakini as gay, and naïve America will never know the difference."

The theme of the movie was a cultural clash between U.S. servicemen stationed in Japan and the post-war natives. Wayne, who had appeared with Spencer Tracy and Katharine Hepburn in *Adam's Rib*, was bitterly disappointed to learn that Marlon had stolen the role from him. Dore Schary, chief of production at MGM, had been set to go with Gene Kelly as Fisby, with Wayne repeating the role of Sakini that

Brando in *The Teahouse of the August Moon*

539

he'd done so successfully on Broadway. His hopes were dashed when he learned that Brando wanted his role. Wayne was told that he didn't have the "star power" to carry the picture.

Marlon personally selected Daniel Mann to direct. His credits included *Come Back Little Sheba* with Burt Lancaster and *I'll Cry Tomorrow*, with Susan Hayward. Both these movies stars had gone to bed with Marlon.

Arriving in Tokyo, Marlon lectured reporters on the evils of the American occupation of Japan, claiming that it was tantamount to the American treatment of their native Indians. "I always threatened to punch out John Wayne if I ever met him. I'm really pissed off at the way Indians are treated in his movies. But I met him only one time in my whole life. It was at a restaurant in Los Angeles. I was dining with Jane Greer trying unsuccessfully to get into her panties. Wayne came over to my table. He introduced himself. All smiles and soft-shoe charm. He told Jane and me that he hoped that we enjoyed the food. That was it. The first and last time I laid eyes on the fucker. We'll never do a movie together, although he'd be better in this role of a U.S. serviceman than that shit-kicker, Glenn Ford."

In Japan, Marlon revealed that he had just returned from a trip to Bali where he'd happily observed naked Balinese women bathing in a river. In his view, all the women of the world should appear in public bare-breasted. "There should be no shame. After Bali, I have decided to spend the rest of my life on an island somewhere surrounded by a bevy of beautiful cinnamon-colored girls. Cinnamon is my favorite color. In the future, I will drink only cinnamon-flavored coffee."

Marlon spent the first week hanging out with veteran character actor Louis Calhem, with whom he'd bonded during the filming of *Julius Caesar*. He found Calhern deep into alcoholism and depression over the breakup of his affair with a much younger woman. MGM had cast Calhern as Colonel Purdy.

After five weeks in Japan, Calhern suffered a heart attack and died. Marlon wired John Patrick: "Lou died in his sleep last night, and I'm glad. He was so lonely and unhappy that he really didn't want to live." Calhern was replaced with Paul Ford, who'd done the role on Broadway. All scenes that had been filmed with Calhern had to be re-shot.

The day before he met Marlon, Glenn Ford had complained bitterly to Daniel Mann about his salary. He'd just learned that he was being paid far less than Marlon, even though Ford's role was much larger. "I'm the fucking star of the picture!" Ford shouted. "Not Stanley Kowalski."

Marlon's attempts to bond with Ford turned out to be clumsy overtures. His questions, perhaps deliberately so, were too provocative. "Tell me, Glenn. You and I have fucked some of the same stars. Bette Davis, Joan Crawford. But what is it like to fuck Judy Garland? Also, Barbara Stanwyck? Stanwyck comes as a surprise. I hear she's a dyke." Ford turned and walked away.

540

Marlon later blamed Ford for ruining the movie because he was "too absorbed in himself to give a good performance. He refused to work in concert with me," Marlon said with a certain bitterness. "It was a horrible picture and I was miscast."

Marlon and Ford clashed, as Ford reverted to all the tricks he'd learned in the movie business to steal scenes, such as backing up two steps so that the camera would have to follow him and he'd wind up full faced in the shot, eliminating the other actor—in this case, Marlon.

Marlon later claimed that "Ford took scene-stealing to Olympian heights." But Marlon also told Ford that he was aware of all his manipulative tricks. He cited the case of Olivia de Havilland who, to steal a scene, breathed in deeply to make her breasts swell out. But he reminded Ford that he had no breasts to swell. "If you've got anything else that swells under your uniform, we don't want to see it on camera. Save it for Rita Hayworth."

Marlon denounced Ford's performances beginning from the first day of the shoot, calling him "a second potato William Holden, but without Holden's hard-on on camera. Ford stumbles and stammers, and his performance means nothing, says nothing, goes nowhere."

When this was reported to Ford, his only comment was, "I despise Marlon Brando. Always have. Always will."

One reviewer wrote, "*Teahouse* is Brando's chance to impersonate Charlie Chan. Casting Marlon Brando and Glenn Ford in the same movie is as mismatched as having Marjorie Main play a love scene with Tab Hunter. It just doesn't work."

Brando on Ford: "A stick-in-the-mud."

Ford on Brando: "A vain showoff."

One night Marlon, drunk on too much sake, told Carlo Fiore, "I hope Glenn Ford doesn't wake up in the middle of the night, think I'm *Gilda*, and try to fuck me."

Fiore countered that Marlon need have no fear of that from the very macho, very heterosexual Ford.

On film, Marlon's accent was sometimes incomprehensible, as he tried at every turn to sabotage the performance of Ford. When Marlon became aware that Ford was trying to steal scenes from him, Marlon proved himself the master of the game. From that day on, he set out to wreck every scene in which Ford appeared, driving that studio system actor into virtual tears. At one of Ford's biggest scenes in the film, Marlon suddenly appeared on camera swatting flies. Although he'd selected Mann as his director, Marlon soon conflicted with him because of the way he was performing on camera.

Teahouse stands as one of the three worst pictures Marlon ever made. One critic claimed that, "It was the most appalling movie made in the 1950s by any actor." Marlon delivered such smarmy lines as, "Pain makes man think, thought makes man wise, wisdom makes life endurable."

Mann and his assistants finally concluded that Marlon could not play comedy but was a great tragic actor. "In comedy, he is the worst kind of ham," Mann said. "A real clumsy technique."

After *Teahouse*, Marlon would not attempt such a wily impersonation and character role until he signed to make *The Godfather* sixteen years later.

After filming *Teahouse*, Ford apparently tried to forget having worked with Marlon. But, according to Fiore, Marlon developed an obsessional hatred of Ford. Marlon tried to round up or hear every negative comment ever made about Ford.

Marlon took delight one night when he encountered Bette Davis in a restaurant after she'd made *A Pocketful of Miracles*, released in 1961. Referring to Ford, Davis said, "That son of a bitch is telling everybody in Hollywood that he helped me have a comeback. That shitheel wouldn't have helped me out of a sewer."

David Swift, who directed Ford in *Love Is a Ball* in 1963, said, "Ford approaches his craft like a twelve-year-old temperamental child." Marlon agreed.

Marlon's friend from the 1940s, Clifford Odets, told him, "It is an easily won bet that in a few years Glenn Ford will get just like the other movie people: bored, sprawling, careless, an overly relaxed fallen angel—they are all affable boys out here, almost tramps."

After Joanna Copeland Carson divorced Johnny Carson in 1972, Ford started dating her. The comedian made several cracks about him on *The Tonight Show*. Ford was so infuriated that he considered suing Carson. But Carson's biggest fan was Marlon himself, who stayed up at night to watch *The Tonight Show*, hoping to hear more mockery of his nemesis.

"Not since Frank Sinatra, have I hated a fellow actor this much," Marlon said. "His first wife, Eleanor Powell, claimed that it was sheer hell living with Ford because of his inferiority complex. I bet he's got a lot to be inferior about!"

* * *

Marlon's next film, *Sayonara*, marked his return to Japan, a land for which he felt great affinity. "American women should be subservient like Jap women," he told Carlo Fiore, whom he'd hired as a dialogue coach for two hundred and fifty dollars a week.

The film was based on that sprawling mess of novel by James A. Michener, a romance and tragedy in modern Japan. In signing to do the film,

Joshua Logan, Brando,
and William Goetz

after turning it down three times, Marlon wanted the picture to have a message and expose the Air Force's official policy of opposing inter-racial marriage. Before *Sayonara* was filmed, American occupation forces were opposed to its men marrying Japanese women, and made it illegal for them to take their wives back to the States. Marlon hoped that *Sayonara* would be a plea for greater racial tolerance.

Or at least that was what he said. Driving him forward was a $300,000 salary, plus a return of ten percent of the gross. That turned out to be another one-million dollars for him at a time he desperately needed the money to fuel his production company, Pennebaker.

Marlon hated the script that Logan and producer William Goetz presented to him. Privately, Marlon told Fiore, "I could piss a better script in the snow than this shit." When Marlon complained to Logan about the script, the director generously suggested that he could rewrite any part of it he wanted to. With Fiore's help, Marlon practically rewrote the entire script. However, only eight lines of the revised dialogue actually appeared in the final cut.

Marlon, however, insisted on a complete new ending, objecting to the "Madame Butterfly finale." As originally intended, Marlon falls in love with a Japanese dancer but must leave her at the end of the picture. He demanded that at the end of *Sayonara*, he marries his beloved, thereby negating the title. "There is nothing inherently wrong with racial intermarriages, even black and white," he told Logan. "Love does not follow a color line. I want to marry the object of my affection at the end of the film."

Amazingly, Logan and scriptwriter Paul Logan agreed to this change, which completely distorted Michener's original concept.

When he met Marlon for the first time, Logan had expressed his regret that Elia Kazan instead of himself had directed Marlon in *Streetcar* on Broadway. "I got the script from Tennessee and read it before Kazan," Logan said. "Your interpretation of Stanley was the greatest male role on Broadway in the Forties. Under my direction we would have made it even better." Logan also revealed that he'd wanted to cast Marlon in the film lead of *Mister Roberts*. The director felt that Henry Fonda, Dodie's former lover, had been creditable playing the lead on Broadway "but is too old for the film." Fonda, nevertheless, got the movie role after all.

After meeting his director, Marlon told Fiore, "At last I've met a man more high strung and quixotic than I am. He's driven by demons, maybe bigger ones than I am. Fits of depression descend on Logan like summer rain." Sometimes the rain turns into hurricane gales."

Although their initial meetings had been pleasant, Marlon clashed with Logan on almost every scene once filming began. Marlon wanted a message picture, whereas Logan saw *Sayonara* as a more commercial venture. Once he expressed his concept of making movies to Marlon. "Films are about making money at the box office. To do that, you have to have an almost nude Marilyn Monroe trying to scale a twenty-foot wire fence to escape from about a dozen would-be rapists, all of whom are hardened criminals and haven't gotten their chance at a real woman—only boy ass—in years."

Marlon later reported to Fiore that he thought Logan's "concept for making movies is very quaint."

Logan also cast two actors, James Garner and Ricardo Montalban, in the film. Both men, of course, later became stars in their own right. Marlon thought Garner, in spite of "his incredible nervousness," performed well in the role. But he seriously questioned the casting of Montalban. "A Mexican in the role of a Kabuki performer?" he asked Fiore.

When he signed for the picture, Marlon was looking forward to playing opposite Audrey Hepburn. But two weeks into production, Logan informed him that Hepburn had turned down the role, fearing, "If I play an Oriental, I'll be laughed off the screen."

Logan discovered Miiko Taka, a Nisei-American working for sixty dollars a week in a travel agency in Los Angeles. He introduced her to Marlon, even though she had had no acting or dancing experience. Marlon met privately with her and told Logan that "Taka has great sensitivity and would be ideal in the role."

Logan later regretted his decision to hire Taka, telling Marlon, "I tear my hair out trying to get a decent performance out of her. After *Sayonara*, she's going nowhere in films."

Brando and James Garner in *Sayonara*

Marlon made no attempt to seduce Taka, as he'd done with so many of his leading ladies in the past. "She was definitely Marlon's type," Fiore recalled, "but we were too busy to get around to her." He claimed that "Marlon and I must have fucked every Japanese girl involved with *Sayonara*."

544

One girl was a deep-throat kisser, biting Marlon's tongue and causing it to swell so badly he couldn't enunciate on camera. "Mumbles was really Mumbles that day," Fiore said. "Logan was furious."

Marlon insisted that he play his character with a Southern accent. "As everybody knows, Southerners are the most bigoted people in America. If I'm a Southerner, it'll make my character's about-face on racial prejudice more compelling."

When the movie was released, Marlon's southern accent often drew a negative reaction from critics. One critic labeled it "Brando's cornpone and chitlin' accent." Always negative toward Marlon's performances, *Time* magazine found that his Southern accent appeared to have been "strained through Stanislavsky's mustache." C.A. Lejeune in the *Observer* suggested that subtitles should have been used to make Marlon's words comprehensible.

Even though Marlon was difficult with Logan during the shoot, the director nonetheless pronounced his star "a genius—the best actor I've met since Garbo."

Marlon was highly critical of Logan during the filming. At one point he told Truman Capote, who'd come to Japan to interview him, that, "In one scene, I did everything wrong I could think of. I rolled my eyes, grimaced in the wrong place, and used irrelevant gestures. When I finished the scene, Logan smiled at me and said, 'It's wonderful Marlon. Print it!'"

Marlon may have been misleading Capote. In the final print, no such outrageous scene appeared as described by Marlon.

Marlon also admitted to Capote that, "I just walked through the part—nobody knows the difference anyway."

Considering how casually Marlon began his filming of *Sayonara*, Hollywood insiders were surprised when he was nominated once again for an Academy Award for best actor. He lost to Alec Guinness in *The Bridge on the River Kwai*. Marlon could take some comfort in knowing that his long-time rival, Anthony Quinn, nominated for *Wild Is the Wind*, also lost.

Fiore said that Marlon felt some embarrassment when his co-stars won for supporting roles, Red Buttons, playing Sgt. Joe Kelly, and Miyoshi Umeki, his Japanese wife. In the film, Buttons chooses to die rather than leave his Japanese wife behind. The plot bordered on soap opera.

Marlon and Fiore sat through a showing of the final cut together. Logan sat alone ten rows behind them. Neither party said a word during the long screening. When the end flashed on the screen, Marlon rose to his feet and headed for the door. "Not my cup of sake," he called back to Logan.

In a sarcastic remark, Fiore said, "A lot of pretty Jap gals crossed a lot of pretty bridges."

The world did not agree with Marlon or Fiore. *Sayonara* grossed millions around the globe and became Marlon's most successful film until his appearance in *The Godfather*.

As he was leaving Tokyo, a call came in from Twentieth Century Fox, reminding him that, according to his contract, he owed them one more picture. "How would you like to play a Nazi officer with an ash-blond dye job?"

* * *

In a disastrous move that he'd regret for the rest of his life, Marlon agreed to meet with the author, Truman Capote, in January of 1957 at the Miyako Hotel in Kyoto. Capote had been assigned to write a piece on Marlon for the *New Yorker*. Marlon hadn't seen the writer since he'd performed in *A Streetcar Named Desire* on Broadway. At that time, he'd shared an erotic moment with Capote and his friend, Cecil Beaton.

Marlon learned that Beaton was also in Kyoto with Capote, but he invited only Capote to dinner at his hotel—not Beaton, even though he'd posed nude for him. Before the meeting, Capote had told Marlon that the first part of the interview would be on the record, followed by the candid remarks later "of two old friends getting together to share a memory or two." It sounded innocent enough.

But the director of *Sayonara*, Joshua Logan, didn't fall for Capote's reassurances and had, in fact, barred him from the set of the picture. Horrified to learn that Marlon had granted the interview, Logan called Marlon's suite to warn him, "The vicious queen will destroy you."

"Don't worry your sweet noggin 'bout this little tadpole one bit," Marlon said, using his exaggerated Southern accent he'd adapted for his character in *Sayonara*. "I can't go into details, but Capote worships me. The piece he'll probably write on me will sound like that silly fodder printed in *Photoplay* magazine."

"I'm not so sure," Logan said. "I've heard this guy talk at parties. He's not that kind to you. He tells everybody that he and Cecil Beaton seduced you. He even claims that you posed nude for Beaton. I've heard him describe your dick to enraptured audiences. Personally, I think he's got it in for you. He knows you're one of the most powerful icons in America. Capote likes to shatter icons. To expose them for having clay feet. He'll do the same to you."

"Before the night is over, I'll have Capote sucking on my noble tool."

Truman Capote

546

"So you think," Logan told Marlon. "I have just read the little fucker's *The Muses Are Heard*. He treats human beings like bugs to be squashed underfoot." *The Muses Are Heard* was Capote's non-fictional lampoon of the *Porgy and Bess* troupe traveling in Russia.

"I know Capote," Marlon assured Logan. "I can handle the little Southern faggot just fine. I will speak only the usual crap to him. Stuff fit to print. He will not get a look into my soul. My soul is a very private place."

Carlo Fiore remained in Marlon's suite during the first hour of what became an infamous encounter between the author and the actor. Arriving with a bottle of vodka under his short arm, the diminutive Capote—"slim and trim as a boy"—minced into Marlon's cluttered suite.

With his high-pitched, nasal voice, he greeted Marlon with a kiss on the lips and a handshake for Fiore. Although not a teetotaler, Marlon rarely drank much alcohol. In front of the suspicious Fiore, Capote started pouring the liquor for Marlon, preferring a "courtesy sip" for himself. Fiore later recalled that Capote used "his eccentric charm and sly manipulation to get Marlon to drink that vodka."

The interview began at 7:15pm, with Fiore departing an hour later. Privately in the bedroom, Fiore told Marlon that he'd call him "every hour with an emergency. This will allow you to escape from the pansy's clutches." Marlon agreed to that. Fiore kept his promise, but Marlon refused to respond to the so-called emergency calls and kept talking nonstop to Capote until 12:30am the following morning.

Sitting with pages of a script piled around him, Marlon opened up to Capote as he'd done to no other journalist. He revealed very personal moments about his mother, Dodie; about his private views on friendship, love, and marriage; about what a lousy director Joshua Logan was—and on and on, one personal revelation piling up on top of another.

Marlon said that he was working on a script for his newly formed production company, Pennebaker. It was to be a Western, and improbably titled *A Burst of Vermilion* because of the red handkerchiefs the cowboys in the movie would wear around their necks.

During this long ordeal, Capote took no notes as he was known for his "unfailing memory."

Capote later claimed that Marlon, throughout his long ramblings, "sounded like an educated Negro using big words only recently learned."

Later the writer revealed the secret of his interviewing techniques. "You make the victim think he's interviewing you. I told Marlon some of my most personal secrets, even about my mother. Naturally, we shared homosexual secrets with each other. Slowly, ever so slowly, I began to spin my web. By opening myself up to Marlon, I got him to open up like a flower petal facing

Yukio Mishima

the dawn. He began to reveal himself as he never had before. The more he talked, the more confessional he became. By the first hour, I knew I was on to a big story. My victim was trapped. I came for an interview but went away with insights that no other writer had ever gotten."

As his opening gamut, Truman described his recent rendezvous with Yukio Mishima, the successful Japanese novelist and playwright who would commit hari-kiri, publicly, on November 25, 1970, as a samurai-inspired act of defiance against the modernization and corruption of the Japanese psyche. "As a lover, he found me inadequate," Capote claimed. "But in exchange for his own hospitality in Japan, he told me that when he comes to New York he wants me to arrange for him to suck a big white cock."

Having seduced each other before, Capote and Marlon were frank in talking about their homosexual affairs. They spoke at length about the young actor and friend of Capote's, Sandy Campbell, whom Marlon had seduced when he'd worked on stage with him in *Streetcar*. Marlon told Capote of his involvement with Clifford Odets, Tennessee Williams, Laurence Olivier, and their mutual friend, Leonard Bernstein.

Capote finally left a drunken Marlon in his suite. The next morning, Marlon told Fiore that his hours with Capote had been better than any session he'd ever had with his analyst. "And it didn't cost me a fucking cent."

Having had no sleep all night, a gleeful Capote called Joshua Logan, who'd come to work early on the set of *Sayonara*. "Oh, you were so wrong about Brando," an ecstatic Capote informed the director. "Last night your star talked my head off. I got my man." He paused for dramatic effect. "In more ways than one!" Capote hung up the phone on a bewildered Logan.

Capote was being sly, but Logan, no stranger to homosexual affairs himself, got the message. He was convinced that Capote had seduced a drunken Marlon, as the author once did with Errol Flynn. Later in the day on the set, when a hung over Marlon showed up for work, Logan confronted his star. Logan wasn't concerned with the morality involved in the Capote seduction of Marlon, but about any bad publicity that might be generated for *Sayonara*.

"Did you go to bed with Capote?" Logan demanded to know.

"If you call 'going to bed' getting a mere blow-job from the little monster with the succulent mouth, then OK, I went to bed with him. I've gone to bed, as you call it, with lots of other men, too. But I hardly consider myself a homosexual, given my long track record with women. Gays are attracted to me. I let them seduce me. I'm doing them a favor. They want it so much. Why deny them the privilege? It's nothing for me to get a blow-job. When you're horny, any port in the storm will do."

While Capote was in Marlon's suite, Cecil Beaton in another part of town had picked up two American sailors. After giving each of them a blow-job, the two young Navy men robbed Beaton, making off with his wallet, an expensive watch, and a valuable camera.

Over breakfast that morning, Beaton told Capote, "If I had it to do over again, I would still have taken them back to my suite. As you well know, I'm not at all enchanted by Americans, Truman Capote excluded, of course. But I must admit that your sailors have tasty cocks. But I have a question for you. Why are all American men circumcised? That's a very cruel cut to us lovers of foreskin."

In the weeks ahead, Marlon began to fear exposure by Capote in the *New Yorker*. In May, Marlon sat down and wrote Capote a three-and-a-half page, single-spaced, handwritten letter. The letter, later released by Truman, was filled with an odd choice of words, misspellings, and unusual grammatical constructions.

"It is, indeed, discomforting to have the network of one's innards guy-wired and festooned with harlequin streamers for public musing, but, perhaps it will entertain. I am sorry, in a way, that you didn't complete your plans for the full travesty you had planned to do because it has come full upon me, that there are few who are as well equipped as yourself to write, indeed, the comedy of manners."

This letter was written before Marlon had actually read the interview. But the gossipy Capote had told "everybody I know about it" even before publication. Word had traveled back to Marlon who was aghast.

Entitled "The Duke in His Domain," the Capote profile of Marlon appeared in the *New Yorker* in November of that year. In the article Marlon was depicted as an overweight, self-indulgent movie star pretending to be on a diet while stuffing himself with French fries, spaghetti, and apple pie. And that was just for openers.

"The interview could have been so much worse in print if I had wanted to reveal all I knew about Brando," Capote later recalled. "If I'd written about the homosexual liaisons of Marlon's, I could have destroyed his career. As it was, I was kind to him. Of course, my profile was not just a journalistic revelation. More of a celebrity exposé. But actors should be exposed for what they are: mental dwarfs."

New York gossip columnist, Dorothy Kilgallen, called it "a real vivisection." Her rival columnist, Walter Winchell, wrote that the article was "the type of confession usually confined to an analyst's couch." Marlon's sister, Jocelyn, called the article "a well-written, bitchy hatchet job!"

Enraged, Marlon called Joshua Logan to apologize for having been so critical of him in the article. "That little bastard spent half the night telling me his problems," Marlon said. "I felt the least I could do was tell him a few of my own. If I ever run into the pissy queen, I'll kill him!"

Logan chided Marlon that, "You should have done that before you let him come into your room."

Capote never responded to Marlon's heartfelt plea to suppress the profile. But the author did have a post-publication comment to make to a reporter.

"Brando apparently felt that my profile of him was an unsympathetic, even treacherous, intrusion upon the secret terrain of a suffering and awesome sensibility. I thought it was a sympathetic account of a wounded young man who is a genius at acting but not markedly intelligent."

Seething with anger but also painfully humiliated, Marlon called on George Glass and Walter Seltzer to press a lawsuit against Capote, seeking the advice of two savvy Hollywood insiders. Glass had first met Marlon when he'd been working as a publicist for Stanley Kramer. A one-time publicist himself, Walter Seltzer had turned producer.

When the men got Marlon to confess that he actually did make the revelations as reported by Capote, they advised him to drop the lawsuit.

Feeling dejected and powerless to fight back, Marlon sighed before getting up to leave their office. At the door, he paused and looked back at the men.

"I was sandbagged!"

* * *

Marlon often assumed the role he was playing on screen off screen. When filming *Sayonara*, he wanted his women to behave like Geishas. Cast as a Nazi officer in his next film, *The Young Lions*, released in 1958, "Marlon became Little Hitler," in the words of Carlo Fiore, "very imperial and very domineering."

Fiore should know. He'd just married Marcia Hunt, but was having marital troubles almost from the beginning. Since he needed the money and also wanted to "escape from America," he gladly agreed to accompany Marlon to Germany and France as a "hired hand" during the shooting of *The Young Lions*. Marlon told his buddy, and Fiore agreed, that "we don't want our women following us to Paris."

The script by Edward Anhalt, who'd won an Oscar for his screenplay, *Panic in the Streets*, in 1950, had been adapted from the best-selling novel by Irwin Shaw about World War II. Marlon owed 20th Century Fox another picture as part of a two-picture deal. Having walked out on *The Egyptian*, he'd made only one picture, *Desirée*, for producer Darryl F. Zanuck. Zanuck asked Marlon to play the role of an idealistic but disillusioned Nazi Wehrmacht officer, Christian Diestl, in *The Young Lions* to complete his contract. The script centered around three soldiers: Marlon as the Nazi officer, a Broadway singer turned soldier, and an American Jew.

Budgeted rather modestly at two million dollars, Fox had devised a shooting schedule of less than fifty days. The first meeting between Marlon and his new director, Edward Dmytryk, took place at Marlon's residence. He was already familiar with the director. It was Dmytryk who had discovered Anna Kashfi in London and brought her to Hollywood for a role in the Spencer Tracy movie, *The Mountain*. Later, after his divorce from Kashfi and the bitter custody battles that ensued, Marlon sarcastically thanked Dmytryk "for that dubious achievement."

Dmytryk immediately realized what an unconventional star he'd be facing. Only thirty minutes into a debate over the script, Marlon got up and announced, "I've got to take a leak." Thinking Marlon would excuse himself and go to the toilet, Dmytryk was astonished to see Marlon toss out some flowers from a Japanese vase. Wearing a kimono, Marlon opened his robe. He was nude underneath. "In front of me, he took a horse piss into the vase," Dmytryk said.

After urinating, Marlon sat down to tell Dmytryk of the "serious reservations" he had about the script. "I want you to understand something before I sign on," Marlon said. "I can't play villains. I won't play a villain. If I walk into a room filled with a hundred people, and just one of them hates me, I have to leave at once. That's how sensitive I am. Playing a Nazi as a villain, and getting millions of audience members around the world to boo me, is more than I can take. It's more than I will do. Either you allow me to play Christian with humanity and sympathy, or I'm off the picture."

Marlon went on lecturing his director. "We must make Shaw's clumsy novel into a World War II version of Stendhal's *The Red and the Black*. I foolishly turned down that classic. Here's my chance to play Julian Sorel in another version, a character struggling between the black robe of the priest or the scarlet red of Napoleon's troops."

Edward Dmytryk directs
Marlon in *The Young Lions*

The director reminded Marlon that Nazis were inherently evil. "They killed millions of people," he protested, "and not just Jews."

Since Marlon had script approval, and since Zanuck was demanding Marlon for the part, Dmytryk had little choice but to go along with Marlon's "rewrite" of the lead character in the film.

Zanuck had an ulterior motive for wanting Marlon in the film. At the

A scene from *The Young Lions*

time, Marlon was one of the world's reigning box office champs. In return for Zanuck not pressing "for millions" in a court of law when Marlon walked out on *The Egyptian*, Zanuck agreed to pay him only $50,000 for his appearance in the film. Eager to put his legal and financial fights with Zanuck behind him, Marlon agreed to those humiliating terms.

In contrast, Montgomery Clift, Marlon's co-star, was earning $750,000. Even Maximilian Schell, in his first American movie, was pulling in $200,000. Dean Martin, the other co-star, told Marlon "not to fret too much—that fucking Zanuck is paying me only $25,000."

In Paris, Marlon, with Fiore's help, began to rewrite his scenes in the film. When the author of the novel, Irwin Shaw, arrived in Paris, Marlon arranged to meet with him at the bar of the Hotel Raphael.

There, Marlon lectured the embittered novelist. "No race, no nationality has the market on evil," Marlon told Shaw. "You wrote the character of Christian too villainous. I will have to search for his humanity which is missing from your novel."

The hot-tempered Shaw disagreed so violently with Marlon he almost struck him in the face. Later, Shaw told Dmytryk, "It serves me right for sitting down with the stupid fucking actor. I knew he didn't have any fucking brains. If he had any brains, he wouldn't be an actor in the first place. An actor is an empty fucking inkpot. You have to pour ink into the god damn fool to get anything out of him."

Before landing in Paris, Marlon had been shocked to learn that his co-star was none other than Montgomery Clift. The press was already predicting "the battle of the century" as the two famous Method actors battled it out for acting honors in the film.

Having been lovers in the 1940s, Marlon and Monty had remained "acquaintances and occasional friends over the years." Most often they had been portrayed as rivals, which they were. They were often up for the same roles.

552

Dean Martin and Monty Clift in *The Young Lions*

After James Dean's death, the press had hailed Marlon and Monty as "the only two bad boys left in Hollywood." Marlon had no objection to the casting of Monty in the film, and told Dmytryk that he'd be "most interested in seeing Clift work up close," even though they had virtually no scenes together.

Although he had no objections to Monty, Marlon violently objected to the casting of Tony Randall in the role of the Broadway entertainer. Dmytryk anticipated objections from Marlon when Dean Martin was cast in the role, but there were none. Marlon and Martin liked each other.

Following an acrimonious break with his partner in comedy, Jerry Lewis, Martin was trying to establish himself as a straight actor in his first "dramatic part."

"Any performer who would have the good sense to break from that Lewis creature can't be all bad," Marlon said.

Dmytryk cast other top-flight actors in the film, which turned a projected B picture into an A movie. Playing along with Marlon, Monty, and Martin were Hope Lange, Barbara Rush, and May Britt, as well as Maximilian Schell, who was having a hard time with English lines. Once again, Marlon secured a small role in the film for his ever-faithful Sam Gilman.

On the first day of shooting in Paris, Marlon told Dmytryk, "I've got to play somebody else in this film other than Brando. Monty, as usual, will be playing Brando. I've been giving Dean Martin acting lessons, so he too will be trying to play Brando. Having my identity stolen, I've got to come up with some new characterization."

Arriving in Paris to begin filming, Marlon told the press, "The picture will try to show that Nazism is a matter of mind—not geography—that there are Nazis, and people of good will, in every country. The world can't spend its life looking over its shoulder and nursing hatreds. There would be no progress that way."

In Paris, Marlon seemed to resent his newfound celebrity, remembering fondly the days when he could roam the streets without being recognized. "It's a nightmare for me," he told Fiore. "Everywhere I go people mob me. They rip my clothes. They tear my shirts. They try to swallow me whole. I feel countless hands on my crotch. At times I feel the fucking world wants to rape me. My tool, noble as it is, can't service the entire world!"

553

Back in his beloved Paris, Marlon resumed his long-time relationships with Christian Marquand and Daniel Gélin. He told Carlo Fiore, "The years have gone by and my love for these French froggies is as strong as ever. A bond never broken. Sometimes I think I like to fuck these men more than I like to bang Anna's pussy." He was referring, of course, to Anna Kashfi whom he'd left behind. Marlon also threw parties at his suite at the Hotel Raphael, inviting his friends from the late Forties, Roger Vadim and "sex kitten" Brigitte Bardot.

In later years, Fiore admitted that he was jealous of Marlon's friendships with other men, especially Christian Marquand. Fiore was also stood up for Sam Gilman and Gélin, Marlon wanting to spend his evenings with those men instead of Fiore.

Fiore was always quick to point out that his jealousy was based entirely on hating to share Marlon as a friend "but not as a lover. When it came to love-making, Marlon and I didn't go there." Over the years, Fiore continued to deny that any sex took place between Marlon and himself. "I must admit that when Marlon insisted on watching me fuck my girl of the moment, I became a little suspicious. I think, if I recall, his eyes were glued to my hard dick instead of the woman in question. If Marlon and I ever had any sexual contact, it was at one of the drunken orgies we attended when you didn't know who you were getting unless you felt specific body parts."

Speaking privately to Fiore one night at a party, Vadim confided that he'd noted "many, many changes in Marlon since our last reunion. He's no longer the shy American boy Christian and I picked up in that café on the Left Bank and brought home to live with us. He no longer has that marvelous vulnerability he had back then. He's far more self-assured, even a bit arrogant in his demands. He's become his own man. I doubt if he can be manipulated. He seems to be saying, 'You should not pity me. It is I who should pity you.'"

The director wanted Marlon blond for the movie. After trying on a dozen wigs provided by wardrobe, Marlon gave up. "My God, I look like a drag version of Marilyn Monroe. If I appear on the screen in one of these wigs, men will go to movie houses with an overcoat over their laps. Underneath, they'll be jacking off watching me emote."

Marlon invited Fiore to join him at the Parisian hair salon, Carita-Alexandre's. "I'm going to bleach my hair." When Fiore arrived at Marlon's suite to accompany him to the hairdresser, he was shocked to see Marlon attired in the Nazi uniform he'd wear in the film.

"There was Marlon all in his jackboots, peak cap, and battleship gray breeches," Fiore said. "His uniform was set off by an Iron Cross. Marlon had taken to going across Paris and speaking with a German accent. I warned him not to appear on the street in full Nazi regalia, reminding him that Parisians were still suffering from the wounds of the war. Marlon wouldn't listen and paraded down the Champs-Elysées as a Nazi to the beauty parlor. I feared a sniper's bullet. We did get one old lady who spat at him. Nothing more serious than that."

Marlon emerged from the hairdressing salon into the bright sunshine of a Parisian afternoon. "His hair wasn't just blond," Fiore said. "It was the color of a bright lemon with just a touch of lime-green chartreuse in the right light. It was the strangest color I'd ever seen."

Observing it in a mirror, Marlon claimed that he liked the dye job. In his reflection, he gave the Nazi salute, then goose-stepped up the Champs-Elysées.

Marlon asked Fiore to accompany him to the first fast-food emporium ever to open on the Champs-Elysées in the post-war years. "There Marlon downed three different entrecôtes along with heaping mounds of *pommes frites*. His weight had already shot up to one hundred and ninety-five pounds. I asked Marlon if he wanted to reach two hundred. I told him, 'When we get back to the Raphael, we can call room service for dessert. How about a chocolate milkshake and a banana split?'"

"Don't trouble your overfucked ass about it," Marlon shot back sarcastically at Fiore. "We're in Paris, god damn it. Froggies don't know how to make desserts like that."

Marlon bonded with co-star Dean Martin, although he was prepared not to like the man. But that was only during the first week. By the end of the second week, Dean was spending all his time with Monty Clift. "What an unlikely pair," Marlon told Fiore. "What does a macho man like Martin want with a repressed homosexual like Monty? There's only one thing Dean must be getting out of this relationship. Monty was always good at cocksucking. Martin's Italian sausage must be getting quite a workout."

Whenever Marlon did meet with Dean Martin, the exchanges were pleasant enough. "I certainly can't talk theater with him," Marlon told Fiore. "Dean and I talk about pussy, agreeing and disagreeing about the various actresses in Hollywood who have the tightest pussies. I'm sure Dean doesn't indulge in pussy talk with Monty."

On the nights that Fiore, not Christian Marquand, accompanied Marlon out on the town, Fiore felt that his friend was "a time bomb waiting to go off." Coming out of the Lido night club, Marlon was accompanied by a handsome twenty-year-old male dancer from Brazil, not one of the long-legged showgirls. When a Parisian cameraman tried to photograph Marlon and his date for the night, Marlon lunged at him, trying to choke the photographer and smash his camera. "I had to pull Marlon off the guy," Fiore said, "or else he might have been slapped with a multi-million dollar lawsuit."

As the days rolled by, Marlon spent more and more time with Marquand, even bringing him to the set. Fiore was often ordered to wait in Marlon's dressing room until needed. When Marlon started asking Marquand to coach him with his performance, the real director, Dmytryk, felt threatened. He ordered Marquand off the set. He later told Fiore, "I don't like gays or switch-hitters like Marquand."

* * *

Marlon liked to befriend his leading ladies and often seduce them. On the set of *The Young Lions*, there was an impressive array of beautiful actresses: Hope Lange, Barbara Rush, and May Britt.

Marlon struck up a relationship with a hot-tempered, Paris-born entertainer, Liliane Montevecchi, who was also appearing in the film in a small role as a French prostitute. A *prima donna* from Roland Petit's ballet company, she was in the tradition of Leslie Caron and Zizi Jeanmaire. Marlon was immediately captivated by her delightful mangling of the English language.

When the July rains descended on Chantilly, north of Paris, Marlon sought and got permission to go for a few days to visit the Costa del Sol, settling into the emerging resort of Torremolinos. Montevecchi had made it clear that she didn't want to become another one of Marlon's girlfriends, but a friendship did ensue.

In his post-*Sayonara* period, Marlon wanted his women to be subservient like those he'd known during the filming. Montevecchi had no intention of being that. She was very outspoken and held very strong opinions.

Back in Paris to complete the filming, Marlon and the French dancer were having a heated argument in the bar of the Hotel Prince de Galles on the Avenue George V. After that disastrous interview with Truman Capote in Japan, where Marlon had gotten drunk on vodka, he had sworn off liquor. Instead of a cocktail, he ordered a large silver pot of boiling water to be placed on the table so he could make his own tea.

To make her point with Marlon, Montevecchi slammed her fist down on the table, upsetting the silver pot of scalding water.

Liliane Montevecchi

Marlon screamed in agony as the water burnt his groin. Pulling down his pants—he wore no underwear that day—he ran into the reception area. Flashing his injured genitals at the reception desk, he demanded an ambulance to take him to the hospital at once. The reception desk personnel didn't seem unduly concerned to see a half-naked American movie star with scalded genitals. At the Prince de Galles, this veteran crew had seen it all. They quickly called an ambulance.

Marlon suffered second-degree burns, and his body was shaved. When Fiore rushed to his hospital room, he found a doctor rubbing a stinking yellow sulphur-like salve over Marlon's genitals.

"The doctor's gay," Marlon called to Fiore. Marlon didn't know if that were true or even if the doctor spoke English. "He loves getting to play with my dick and balls," Marlon said. "Can you believe that this has happened to me? Here we are in Paris of all places. I had so many pussies and so many tender rosebuds lined up to fuck. Now I'll have my noble tool in a sling!"

When Fiore returned the following afternoon, bringing flowers, Marlon invited him in. "The hospital, I've learned, is staffed by nuns. Every time the bandages on my genitals have to be changed, every nun in this hospital makes it a point to come into my room with some made-up excuse. These gals have never seen a man's dick before. The way I look at it, if they want to get a glimpse of my noble tool, even though it's burnt, let them feast their eyes and enjoy themselves. Later on, they can resume their lives as brides of Christ."

Back in California, when Kashfi heard the news, she suggested the following day's headlines: BRANDO SCALDS BALLS!

In Paris at the Hotel du Palais-Royale, Marlon went at once to Monty's suite to greet him and to tell him how much he was looking forward to co-starring with him in *The Young Lions*. He even apologized for taking star billing, claiming, "The studio demands it."

Having not seen Monty in several months, Marlon discovered a wreck of a human being following his auto accident. Monty was also suffering from phlebitis and downing tranquilizers like Ronald Reagan scarfed down jellybeans. Monty was also suffering from a bad cold, for which he was taking belladonna "because my nose is so stuffed I can't breathe."

Although Marlon was later highly critical of Monty's pill popping, Carlo Fiore said, "Marlon should not have been so critical of Monty. Marlon himself was relying heavily on Seconals and amphetamines to get through another day."

Throughout the Fifties, Marlon had taken somewhat of a paternal interest in Monty, even though competing for roles with him. "It was a case of if you can't get Brando, go for Clift," Darryl F. Zanuck once said. Their love affair, in the Forties, such as it was, was almost a forgotten encounter when Marlon and Monty reunited in that hotel suite in Paris.

Although Marlon took little notice of the careers of any other actor, except James Dean, he journeyed to Broadway to see Monty appear in *The Sea Gull* in 1954. Marlon was in illustrious company, joining old friends Harry Belafonte and Marlene Dietrich. Arthur Miller even sat with Marlon, although the playwright had been disturbed to learn of Marlon's love affair with Marilyn Monroe.

All of these legendary names went backstage to congratulate Monty on his performance. Marlon approached him first, taking the emaciated actor in his arms and planting a wet kiss on his lips. "That was a genius I saw on that stage tonight," Marlon told Monty in the presence of the other famous guests.

Later, when Monty was exiting through the back door, reporters cornered him to ask about Marlon. "Mr. Brando is continuously creative even with shitty material," Monty told the press. Privately Monty confided to their mutual agent, Edith Van Cleve, that he "absolutely detested" Marlon's performance in *The Teahouse of the August Moon*. "First he was a joke cast as a Jap," Monty said. "Also Marlon played it far too gay."

"Poor Monty never lived long enough to see some of Marlon's future travesties on the screen," Edith said.

Monty attended a dinner party at the home of his close friend Elizabeth Taylor on the night of May 13, 1956, while they were filming *Raintree County*. Drunk and drugged, he left the party and started down the hill in his car but ran over a ravine, smashing his vehicle into a telephone pole. He came close to death. Screaming as she raced down the hill, Taylor climbed down into the ravine and opened Monty's smashed car door. Seeing that he was choking, she reached into his throat and removed five of his teeth.

Up all night and unable to sleep, Fiore at his apartment had the radio on when a bulletin came over the wire announcing Monty's accident. Ignoring the time, Fiore called Marlon, awakening him.

"Freddie," Marlon said with growing impatience. That was his nickname for Fiore. "Do you know that it's four o'clock in the morning? Thanks for the news about Monty. So bad. But I'm going to look like Monty does right now if I don't get my own beauty sleep." He hung up the phone.

Weeks after the accident, Marlon visited Monty when he was released from the hospital, discovering that Monty was losing his battle with drugs and booze.

According to Fiore, Marlon went to see Monty, hoping to save him. After only one hour, Marlon concluded that there was no hope for Monty. He was too far gone.

At one point, and again according to Fiore, Marlon told Monty, "I should hate you because you've always been viewed as my competition. But I don't hate you. You've been good for me. You've made me a better actor because I want to be better than you. That makes me work harder. You're my touchstone. My challenge. Ever since I saw *A Place in the Sun*, I knew you could take the screen from me. But, after that, you've just gone downhill. You never lived up to your promise."

Marlon's words angered Monty. "At least I didn't make *Guys and Dolls* singing and dancing with Sinatra," Monty said.

"Touché!"

"You don't know this," Monty said, "but I was offered the role of Napoleon in *Desirée* before you."

"You've got to be kidding," Marlon said in astonishment. "Montgomery Clift as Napoleon? You could never have done it. Never have donned those pink silk breeches. Besides, your ass is far too skinny to play Napoleon. They would have had to pad your butt."

"Wardrobe didn't need to pad your butt for *Guys and Dolls*," Monty said. "That was one big, *big*, big fat ass up there on the screen—and in color too. You all but mooned us!"

Before he left Monty's suite, Marlon urged his friend to join Alcoholic Anonymous. "You're going to die if you don't stop this!"

"I can't stop!" Monty said, his eyes showing the same emotion and tenderness he'd revealed in his final scene with Elizabeth Taylor in *A Place in the Sun*. "I've got to go on until I can't go on any more. Only now the end is much sooner than later for me."

Later that night, Marlon called Fiore to his hotel suite to talk about his encounter with Monty. "All I could do was to look into that shattered face and shed tears with Monty. We cried in unison."

Monty Clift

"The structure of that once beautiful face has been forever altered by the beauty butchers," Marlon told Fiore. "It was once the most sensitive face ever to appear on the silver screen. No more! His once-tender lips are marred by a vertical scar. His features are so altered that he looks like a cadaver that someone dug up two years after it'd been resting in some dark crypt."

"He looks like a zombie," Marlon went on. "He's drugged day and night from what I gather. There is such a neurotic fragility about him that it makes it painful for me to be in the same room with him. He reminds me of an eggshell. Easy to crush in my hand at any moment. But I have no desire to destroy yesterday's competition. He's no longer a rival to me in spite of what the shitheads in the press claim. The only thing we still have in common at this point is that we have the same two agents—Edith Van Cleve in New York and the ever-loyal Jay Kanter on the West Coast. Both good people unlike the fuck-ups they have to deal with in the theater and the film industry."

"Monty can no longer convey that bewildered deer-caught-in-the-headlights look of his," Marlon said. "If anything, his present face is an expressionless wraith. After all that plastic surgery, his face is immobilized. As I spoke to him, those incredible eyes of his were still alive but the face is a mask concealing a dead brain long ago buried by the numbness of booze and pills. Monty is enveloped in a fog of anesthesia."

In later years, Fiore said that "Marlon's relationship with Monty was always off base. During the making of *The Young Lions*, it entered the twilight zone."

"It was important for Marlon to prove that he was superior to Monty, and he clearly was," Fiore said. "Marlon was fucked up. But compared to Monty, Marlon was actually sane and in control. Marlon had to be *the man* in their relationship. Back in the Forties he had to show their friends that he was the one in charge. How else to explain why he forced Monty to go in drag with him to a party hosted by Kevin McCarthy at his home in Bedford Village. From the beginning, Marlon wanted to be top gun. That was what happened during the entire filming of *Lions*. The movie marked the end of their troubled and very strange relationship. It was painful to watch from a front row seat like I had."

Fiore shared the limousine that drove Marlon and Monty to Chantilly, north of Paris, where the filming began. "I remember it rained a lot of the time. When Monty and Marlon learned there would be no work for them, they would take the train to Paris. I often went along with them."

Increasingly, Monty was out of control, whereas Marlon held back on his drinking, nursing one cocktail all night. Fiore remembered one night at the bar of the plush George V Hotel. In the course of two hours, Monty downed fifteen gin martinis—"extra heavy on the gin."

In front of the hotel, he broke loose from Marlon and Fiore and climbed onto the roof of a limousine. On top of the car, "twitching like a paralytic," Monty danced a jig before collapsing and sliding down onto the hood. Both Marlon and Fiore rescued Monty, putting him into a taxi and going back to his hotel suite where they undressed him and put him to bed.

Back on the set the following morning, Monty was terribly hung over but still drinking alcohol from a thermos. He wanted to watch Marlon act. After one scene, he came up to Marlon. "Please stay in character," he said. "Don't play Christian like he was Jesus Christ. You're not Jesus Christ, you know."

When Monty later learned that Marlon at the end of the film wanted to roll down a hill, ending on the ground with his arms outstretched like a crucified Christ figure, Monty threatened to bolt the movie. "If he does that," Monty told Dmytryk, "I'm off the picture. I mean that!"

Monty prevailed, but even so he complained to the director almost daily, attacking Marlon's performance. "He's sloppy," Monty said of Marlon. "He uses only one-tenth of his talent."

One afternoon Irwin Shaw appeared on the set to see "what Hollywood is doing to my novel." Still infuriated at Marlon, the novelist pointedly ignored him, but bonded with Monty. After seeing the rushes, Shaw told Dmytryk, "I detest Brando's performance. Who does he think he is? Only Monty is true to the character I wrote."

One day Monty didn't report to work at all. From a young French boy Monty had been sleeping with at the Hotel du Palais-Royale, Marlon and Fiore learned that night that Monty had gone to a gay bar on the Left Bank. It was called Tabou. Arriving at the club, Marlon and Fiore didn't spot Monty among the patrons, although Marlon attracted a lot of attention from the gay men.

Fiore led Marlon to the backroom where, to their horror, they discovered a nude Monty lying on a pool table. He was being fucked by a young man who wore only a leather jacket. At least ten other gay patrons of the backroom had lined up to sodomize the American movie star.

Much to the anger of the other gay men, Fiore and Marlon forced Monty to get off the table. They dressed him and took him in a taxi back to his hotel, where they undressed him and put him to bed.

The one-day disappearance was but a prelude to an even larger vanishing the following week. Dmytryk was horrified, threatening a lawsuit. Marlon did not seem unduly disturbed. He told Fiore, "I heard that Spencer Tracy used to disappear and go on a big drunk before every picture. Tracy's a big star. *Was* a big star. If Tracy can get away with that shit, why not Monty? It's what queers like Monty and Tracy do. It's all because they can't come to terms with their homosexuality. As for me, I've never had any sexual regrets. Why should I? Life is too short for all that guilt crap."

A posse sent by Dmytryk found Monty in Rome. Apparently, the actor had left a paper trail. He was discovered in a seedy bordello that hired both male and female prostitutes. Underpaid Italian sailors on leave rented their bodies to gay johns to make extra money. Monty had heard of the bordello and had gone there "hungry for seafood," as he put it. The aging woman owner of the brothel, who looked like Lotte Lenya on a bad night, told the studio posse that Monty had hired at least a dozen sailors during his brief stay in the brothel.

Marlon greeted Monty when he was returned to France by the posse.

Neither man spoke of what Monty had been up to in Rome. Later that night, Marlon told Fiore, "Monty is deeply horrified at his own homosexuality. Even though he's plagued by it, he returns to it time and time again like he did in Rome. I suspect that he hates the homosexual acts he indulges in so much that he's a homophobe himself. There is no acceptance of who he is. His sexual guilt is even greater than that of Cary Grant, and I know of which I speak."

After the final scene was shot, Marlon bid a final farewell to Monty. In front of the entire cast, Marlon walked over to Monty and embraced him, putting a kiss on his lips. "Take care of yourself for my sake," Marlon said. "Without you around to challenge me to do better and better work, there would be no one left." He kissed Monty on the mouth again. There were tears in Monty's eyes as Marlon departed from the set.

When the picture was presented at an Actors Studio benefit at the Paramount Theater in New York months later, publicist John Springer virtually had to force Monty to go. En route to the theater in a limousine, Monty put up a brave front, telling Springer that, "I've already written my Oscar acceptance speech."

During the screening of *The Young Lions*, Monty's brave façade collapsed. When his image appeared on the screen in a close-up, a young woman rose from her seat in the balcony. "Is *that* him?" she shouted so loudly that all the patrons, including Monty, could hear her.

After the screening, Monty retreated in disgrace from the theater. But instead of focusing on his own performance, he chose to attack Marlon in front of Springer. "That God damn Marlon Brando! He's turned Christian into a fucking Nazi pacifist."

After *The Young Lions,* Monty still had a few major movies in him, including the 1959 *Suddenly, Last Summer,* but privately he "was on the road to hell," as his lover, Roddy McDowall, said. Later, Elizabeth Taylor used her box office clout to get Monty cast opposite her as a homosexual in the film, *Reflections in a Golden Eye.* But he died of a heart attack on July 23, 1966.

Marlon agreed to stand in for Monty and take over the starring role. When he encountered Taylor during the first day of shooting of this 1967 release, he spoke kindly of their mutual friendship for Monty and the waste of a great talent. "Monty's gone to a far and better place," Marlon said. "He did not belong in this world."

* * *

The Young Lions opened to mixed reviews. Marlon's scenes with Monty were viewed, in the words of one reviewer, as a "boxing match" in which Marlon was "the only contender," drawing more favorable reviews than his rival. The picture evolved into a commercial success worldwide. It would be Marlon's only success for nearly fifteen years.

David Watts of the *Financial Times* gave Marlon credit for turning "a third-rate bestseller into a second-rate box office hit."

Although world audiences, including those in the United States, generally accepted Marlon's sympathetic portrayal of a Nazi, it ran into trouble with Israeli censors who at first would not allow it to be shown in their country. Surprisingly when Egypt banned the film, Israel relented, allowing it to be shown to record-breaking crowds of Jewish movie-goers.

Egyptian censors had a different reason for banning the film. *The Young Lions* portrayed an American Jewish soldier, as interpreted by Monty, in a favorable light.

Reacting to the Egyptian ban, Israeli censors rescinded their position. "The Jew is so lovable that we decided to overlook Brando's sympathetic portrait of a Nazi," one censor told the press. "By now, the whole world knows what monsters the Nazis were. One screen portrayal by Brando could hardly change global perception."

* * *

Back in 1940, Tennessee Williams wrote a play which he called *Battle of Angels*. Biking over to the dressing room of Tallulah Bankhead, he offered it to her, his favorite star. Two weeks later she read it and turned it down with a certain violence. Even though he eventually persuaded Miriam Hopkins to appear in its key role, it had always been viewed as a disaster. Nonetheless, it remained one of Tennessee's favorites.

During one of his many dry spells as a writer, he took the play out of mothballs to rewrite. Finally, he mounted a Broadway production of it, retitled  *Orpheus Descending,* in 1957. Although he'd wanted Marlon and Anna Magnani to star in it, both actors turned him down. Maureen Stapleton and Cliff Robertson headed the cast instead.

Tennessee set this soapy Southern melodrama in the bigoted little Mississippi Bayou backwater called Two Rivers. The main character of Val Xavier was a former hustler and café entertainer who appears in a snakeskin jacket with a guitar and a line: "You're not young at 30 if you've been at a party since you were 15."

Tennessee promised Marlon that his character would be "full of sexual exoticism and poetic

Tennessee Williams

yearnings." Marlon's response was "this Val Xavier character strikes me as a hustler who used to sell it by the inch."

"We all have to do what we must to survive," Tennessee said.

"The line I like best is when you have Val classify people into three types—'the buyers, the bought, and those who don't belong to no place at all,'" Marlon said.

"I'm sure I don't have to tell you which type of people we are," Tennessee said.

Marlon as Val Xavier in *The Fugitive Kind*

Even with several rewrites, when Tennessee struggled to make Marlon's part larger, the playwright's revised scripts were still rejected by Marlon.

Annoyed by the rejection, Tennessee told Marlon's agent, Edith Van Cleve, "I made the character of Val Xavier a possible bisexual so Marlon should feel perfectly cast."

Orpheus Descending was only one of five plays that Tennessee had offered to Marlon, each one rejected by him. In Japan, Marlon had told Truman Capote, "There are beautiful things in *Orpheus*, some of Tennessee's best writing, and the Magnani part is great. She would wipe me off the stage. This boy Val never takes a stand. I didn't really know what he was for or against. Well, you can't act in a vacuum. And I told Tennessee. So he kept rewriting. I had no intention of walking out on any stage with Magnani. Not in that part. They'd have to mop me up."

Marlon's bank account had been drained dry following his divorce settlement with Anna Kashfi. His father had called him to tell him that all of his money invested in the Nebraska ranch had been used up. His new studio, Pennebaker, was running into financial disaster with Marlon's debut as star/director in *One-Eyed Jacks*. When Sidney Lumet, the director of *The Fugitive Kind*, offered Marlon a million dollars to appear in the film, he agreed.

Anna Magnani signed on for $125,000, the same salary as the director, Lumet. Joanne Woodward, who'd won the Oscar in 1957 for her portrayal of the psychotic heroine in *The Three Faces of Eve*, was hired for $30,000.

Until Marlon signed on, the part of Val Xavier had been cast with Anthony Franciosa, the husband of Shelley Winters, Marlon's former girlfriend,

564

Joanne Woodward

Franciosa had agreed to do the role for $75,000. During the making of *Wild Is the Wind* in 1957, Franciosa had been Magnani's lover both on and off the screen. "Hollywood is nothing if not incestuous," Lumet said.

Marlon later told the press that the only reason he agreed to do *The Fugitive Kind* was "because I needed the money and in a hurry, and it was the best role I could find overnight."

When Marlon showed up on the set, he was greeted by Lumet, who at the time was married to Gloria Vanderbilt, one of Marlon's "one-night stands." The director may not have known of his wife's involvement with Marlon. Both director and star assumed a professional relationship with each other. Marlon was "somewhat fascinated" that Lumet had been one of the original "Dead End Kids" and also the former son-in-law of Lena Horne. Ironically, Lumet, a former actor, had replaced Marlon on Broadway in *A Flag Is Born*.

There was a certain awkwardness when Marlon greeted Joanne Woodward, whom he'd dated for a month back in 1953. The Georgia-born blonde had married Paul Newman in 1958, an actor often unflatteringly described as "Brando's clone." There were rumors at the Actors Studio that Marlon and Woodward had had an affair. Friends of Woodward's claimed that Marlon was not her type and that she was dating him only to make the already-married Newman jealous.

In *The Fugitive Kind*, Woodward was cast as a rich, wild, and exhibitionistic nymphomaniac-dipsomaniac, with white makeup, black-ringed eyes, and bleeding nose. In one scene she was asked to kneel before Marlon as Xavier. She says, "I want something to hold the way you hold your guitar." She makes it rather clear to film audiences what it is that she wants to hold—and in her mouth at that.

Reportedly, Woodward later said—rather astutely—that Tennessee, Marlon, and Anna Magnani were performing "in a self-parody of their past glories."

Joanne Woodward and Paul Newman

At the end of the filming, Woodward would also claim that she'd never work with Marlon again. "I hated working with him because he was not there. He was somewhere else."

* * *

Lumet dreaded the day when Magnani would encounter Marlon in Milton, New York, a small town eighty miles north of Manhattan that had been disguised to look like something in Mississippi. He feared that the meeting would be "like two hydrogen bombs waiting to explode." Lumet was unaware that the younger and sexier Marlon had had an affair with the younger and sexier Magnani on her home turf in Rome years before.

Almost from the first hour he'd reunited with Magnani, Marlon knew that "there was no spark between us," as he'd later tell his friend Sam Gilman. "The chemistry just wasn't there."

In a phone call the night before, Tennessee told Marlon that, "Anna told me she's in love with you, Marlon. You're in for a hot time!"

Later that afternoon Marlon responded to a question from the press. "Magnani is the explosive type of woman I like to play opposite. She is real. Of course, she is crazy like me and we have our differences."

Still believing that she could seduce Marlon as she had back in Rome, Magnani at first was enthusiastic about him. "When I work with him," she said, "it is like I work with a strange animal ready to pounce." Of course, that was not necessarily a compliment. She softened her words, "Yet it is a wonderful experience to see him be so realistic. So completely *all* man."

After only a few days, Marlon called Tennessee. "When I encountered *La Lupa* [her nickname], I found that she has turned into Tallulah Bankhead. An older creature for sure, but one even more sexually aggressive. She is that kind of woman, like Tallulah, who makes me flinch. Nothing but a sexual predator and a caricature of the actress she used to be. She is fierce for all the wrong reasons. She is intimidating to others. She once possessed a certain raw beauty. She has now reached the borderline of ugly."

At the age of fifty-one, Magnani was horrified that the cinematographer, Boris Kaufman, was making her look old. She brought in glam-

Anna Magnani

Anna Magnani and Brando

orous pictures of Sophia Loren and Gina Lollobrigida with instructions that she wanted to be photographed as they were, forgetting they were much younger and more beautiful than she was.

Sadly, Lumet watched her struggle as she faced the cruelty of the camera that seemed to pick up every wrinkle and crevice. "A great talent with a great problem," Marlon said. "She drove us crazy worrying about the way she looked. Her looks fit her character. After all, she was playing an aging woman lusting after a hot young stud—namely, me."

Marlon confessed in his autobiography that Magnani on several occasions tried to see him alone. He finally paid a call on her at her hotel suite. "She started kissing me with great passion," Marlon said. "I tried to be responsive because I knew she was worried about growing older and losing her beauty. As a matter of kindness, I felt I had to return her kisses. To refuse her would have been a terrible insult. But once she got her arms around me, she wouldn't let go. If I started to pull away, she held on tight and bit my lip, which really hurt.

"With her teeth gnawing at my lower lip, the two of us locked in an embrace, I was reminded of one of those fatal mating rituals of insects that end when the female administers the coup de grace. We rocked back and forth as she tried to lead me to the bed. My eyes were wide open, and as I looked at her eyeball-to-eyeball, I saw that she was in a frenzy, Attila the Hun in full

attack. Finally the pain got so intense that I grabbed her nose and squeezed it as hard as I could, as if I were squeezing a lemon, to push her away. It startled her, and I made my escape."

Anna Mugnani in
The Fugitive Kind

Having escaped her clutches, Marlon had to play a love scene with her the next day. "It was downhill after I rejected her," he said. "I don't know how we ever finished this cornpone drama. What made our love scenes worse was her furry upper lip."

At the end of the shoot, Magnani told Tennessee, "I do not wish to work with Mr. Marlon Brando ever again."

567

Maureen Stapleton

On the other hand, Marlon said he would work with Magnani again "but only with a rock in my fist."

Tennessee was nervous about the conflicts between two of his friends. He claimed that "Brando and Magnani engaged in a clash of egos never before known in the history of the cinema."

Advertisements for *The Fugitive Kind* falsely claimed that, "The Screen Is Struck by Lightning."

"All the lightning was off camera," claimed Maureen Stapleton, Marlon's talented friend from the Forties. On Broadway, she'd played Lady Torrance but was forced to take the minor supporting role of the sheriff's wife in the film. "Talk about humiliation. But I'm a trouper and I did it. In the theater, a paycheck comes sometimes before pride. I'm sure Marlon himself would agree. We were both working for paychecks."

* * *

Tennessee made the mistake of attending a sneak preview of *The Fugitive Kind* at the RKO Theater on 58th Street in New York. He was accompanied by his longtime companion, Frank Merlo. The audiences—at least those who did not walk out on the showing—booed the screen.

After the screening, Tennessee and Frank were slipping out of the theater heading for a get-away taxi. A member of the audience spotted Tennessee and hissed at him. Other patrons also saw the playwright and began hissing him as well. "I just hissed back," Tennessee later said.

The next day the reviews started to come in. Writing in *Time and Tide*, Clancy Sigal said, "Watching Brando imitating Judy Holliday's impersonation of him in *Bells Are Ringing* is, at its most serious, like seeing a scratchy old film of Duse or Bernhardt; surely someone is kidding someone?"

The film opened officially in April of 1960, playing to nearly empty movie houses across the country. Exhibitors reported that many members of the audience walked out in disgust before "The End" flashed on the screen.

Regrettably, the failure of the play, *Orpheus Descending*, and its film version, *The Fugitive Kind*, marked the funeral rites for Tennessee's fashionable reputation. But for the rest of his life, on and off during those dry spells as a writer, Tennessee would get out the script and dust off the play. His "bail-out" rewrite never came.

In New York, Tennessee and Frank called Marlon and asked if they could

568

drop by his apartment one night. Arriving early, Tennessee and Frank greeted Marlon like old friends.

"Hon, the old faggot has come back into your life," Tennessee said to Marlon, warmly embracing him.

"You never left," Marlon said.

Over drinks—far too many for Tennessee—he told Marlon that he feared he was going to become a library author instead of one whose plays are performed on Broadway.

Marlon countered that he was going to become an actor written about in film schools instead of one seen on the screen. He told them that while making *The Fugitive Kind*, he'd taken a plane back to Los Angeles every weekend to cut his directorial film, the western movie, *One-Eyed Jacks*, in which he also starred. "The God damn thing drove me into bankruptcy and ran up to eight hours."

He said that the other day, a college student had sent him his thesis. As part of an academic study, the student had maintained that *One-Eyed Jacks* was a homosexual movie. The paper claimed that Sam Gilman, Marlon's best friend, who was also cast in the film, performed with "sexual innuendo" when playing opposite Marlon's character of Rio. "In fact, the conclusion was that Sam Gilman and I, along with the other cast, had made a homosexual movie."

"Welcome to the club," Tennessee said. "Everyone writes that about my plays."

Marlon told his guests that variations on the Horatio Alger story were the wrong reading material for America's youth. "Fame is a fraud and a gyp," Marlon said. "The biggest disappointment of my life."

At the door, Tennessee and Frank kissed Marlon on the lips. They did not know when they would see him again.

Tears welled in Tennessee's eyes when he told Marlon that "on some glorious morning I'm going to create another Stanley Kowalski character for you to play."

"I'll be there for you," Marlon said.

Before heading down the hall, Tennessee looked back at Marlon.

Marlon in *One-Eyed Jacks*

"I'll race you to hell. Bet I'll get there before you do."

Marlon would later claim that "he encountered Tenn deep into drugs and pills—but not quite as bad as Monty. Tenn was clearly coming apart. Success is a deadly game, especially when you can't live up to your earlier successes. Just ask me."

Tennessee Williams died on February 25, 1983, after choking on a bottle cap in a New York hotel room.

* * *

Tennessee seemed to have predicted his own demise as a playwright. And Marlon lived to see the twilight of his own career, as he limped from one bad movie to another. "I never seem to get it right," Marlon said, remembering his films of the 1960s. The decade saw him stumble from one box office disaster to another. But unlike Tennessee, Marlon made a brief comeback with the release of *The Godfather* in 1972.

When his stage and screen performances thrust him into the public arena in the 1950s, he was part of an exclusive ten-member club whose films earned more than any other actors' in the entertainment industry. But by the 1960s, times had changed. The American public was growing tired of Marlon's "poetic hooliganism." The subsequent decline of Marlon Brando as a film star remains one of the great tragedies in film history.

The kids who had flocked to see *The Wild One* in the 1950s had grown up and sired rebellious children of their own. Now, they could even scoff at the idol of their teenage years.

To his new best friend of the 1990s, Michael Jackson (of all people), Marlon confided, "My good-bye has been the longest good-bye in the history of show business. My tragedy was I didn't know enough to get off the stage when the play had ended."

THE LONG GOOD-BYE

THE STARS OF *ONE-EYED JACKS*: From left to right, Katy Jurado, Marlon, Karl Malden, and Pina Pellicer converge for their shooting of this disastrous Western in Death Valley. The original director, Stanley Kubrick, who was fired by Marlon, had wanted Spencer Tracy to play Malden's role of Sheriff Dad Longworth. In the film, Malden with a twelve-foot bullwhip savagely beats Rio (Marlon). In objecting to Tracy, Marlon said, "I don't want that closeted queer getting his jollies sadistically beating me. The old faggot would probably develop a boner, his first in years. Poor Kate Hepburn. But I hear she's dyke-oriented anyway."

"NO TITS!" was Marlon's demand for his leading ladies, both Mexicans, Katy Jurado, his former lover, and Pina Pellicer, cast as her daughter. "I don't want my leading ladies heaving big boobs on the wide screen while I'm trying to get an important point across." Jurado jokingly presents Marlon (during an early costume fitting for his upcoming role in *Mutiny on the Bounty*) with a *faux* Oscar, complete with genitals. She jokingly said, "You deserve the Oscar for seducing more women, including me, than any other actor in the history of Hollywood. A noble tool, indeed!"

GERONIMO! The Indian chief known as "Red Arrow" was hired by the crew of *One-Eyed Jacks* to teach Marlon how to use a bow and arrow. These lessons were said to have launched his interest in the plight of the American Indian. In his classic story of revenge in the Old West, Marlon set out to "storm the citadel of Western cliches." In poker, two one-eyed jacks are usually wild cards. "Brando was the only wild card during that filming," said leading lady Katy Jurado. "He was also too old to play Billy the Kid."

HOLLYWOOD'S NEW CINDERELLA: On location for *One-Eyed Jacks*, Marlon launched an affair with his leading lady, the emotionally fragile Mexican actress, Pina Pellicer. Calling her "Pigeon," he became her Svengali. Marlon fired Carlo Fiore from the film but not before he found Pellicer "like an exposed nerve--thin, frightened, and full of anger." When a beautiful older Mexican actress appeared on the set, Pellicer dropped Marlon. The lesbian relationship didn't work out. Returning to Mexico, Pellicer committed suicide in December of 1964.

EN ROUTE TO THE TICKLED PINK MOTEL: On the set of *One-Eyed Jacks*, Marlon faced his leading lady, Pina Pellicer. When he took her back to his Monterey motel, she said, "it wasn't sex, it was a devouring." After sex, Marlon, "dieting" for the film, called room service and ordered two apple pies à la mode and a quart of cold milk before bedtime. "He went to sleep but I felt unfulfilled, used by him," Pellicer told her costar Katy Jurado, cast as her mother. Ironically, at the beginning of the film, Katy had been Marlon's motel bedmate.

DIRECTOR OUT OF CONTROL: Under Marlon's direction, the budget for *One-Eyed Jacks* zoomed from $1.6 million to $6.5 million. An extraordinary one million feet of film was exposed. The first so-called "director's cut" ran for an astonishing eight hours. Paramount executives took the film back from Marlon, and studio editors cut it to a length of 141 minutes. At its official premiere on March 30, 1961, Marlon called what was to have been "the greatest Western ever filmed" a potboiler.

THE BLIND DIRECTING IN EXPENSIVE VISTAVISION: "I don't know how this film is going to end," Marlon told his startled cast. "But I want a scene where someone gets shot in the back. Who wants to be the shooter? Who wants to be the shootee?" Chico Day, his assistant director, pointed out to Marlon that he was looking through the wrong end of the range finder. "Holy shit!" Marlon said. "Little wonder we're so way behind schedule on this fucker! What the hell? Tell the executives at Paramount they can go fuck themselves."

WAITING FOR THE CLOUDS TO ROLL BY: During the filming of *One-Eyed Jacks*, Marlon spent hours waiting for clouds to roll in. "I've go to have clouds, not a clear sky, before we can go on shooting." Howard Hughes, while filming *Hell's Angels*, had done the same thing. "Only difference between Marlon and Hughes waiting for those clouds is that that Texas drill bit could afford to waste weeks with the cast getting paid overtime," Sam Gilman said. "Marlon didn't have the money. I knew before its release that *One-Eyed Jacks* would never pay back its cost. But I danced all the way to the bank."

MARLON HOLDS OPEN THE DOOR FOR FRANCE NUYEN: Born in Marseilles in 1934, the beautiful but hypersensitive Eurasian model and actress, France Nuyen entered Marlon's life when she appeared as a young girl in the stage version of *South Pacific*. The introduction was arranged by Joshua Logan, the play's director, who had clashed with Marlon on the set of *Sayonara*. Even though engaged to Anna Kashfi at the time, Marlon launched himself into an affair with this somewhat näive young actress. "It is my job to show her the way," Marlon told his friends, one of whom, Carlo Fiore, recalled Nuyen sitting at Marlon's feet 'looking up at him adoringly." The Franco-Chinese actress of exotic charm traveled in disguise with Marlon to Haiti. "He just wanted an excuse to be a big little boy and dress up and be someone else and see how long he could fool everybody," she said.

THE WORLD OF SUZIE WONG: Starring on Broadway in this production, France Nuyen was engaged in a torrid affair with Marlon. He told Carlo Fiore, "In our relationship, I'm the top, France the bottom." "I might have imaged such," Fiore told his friend. At one point Marlon urged his then director, Stanley Kubrick, to write in a part for a Chinese girl in *One-Eyed Jacks*. He even suggested France Nuyen for the part. Kubrick shot back, "She can't act." After that exchange, Kubrick was out of a job and went on to greater glory. In the end, though, France never got anybody to write in a role for her.

BARBARA LUNA IN BUTTONS, BOWS, AND GARTER BELT: Making her debut on Broadway at the age of six in Rodgers and Hammerstein's *South Pacific*, Barbara Luna was a "mixed breed." She had Italian blood flowing through her veins along with Hungarian, Spanish, Portuguese, and Filipino plasma. Over the years she appeared in films with Marlon's "lovers and enemies," including Frank Sinatra, Vivien Leigh, Spencer Tracy, and Lee Marvin. She ended up in the daytime soap opera, *One Life to Live* (1968), playing Maria, "the bitch everybody loves to hate." Luna, as she preferred to be known, was the first choice to play Anita in *West Side Story* in 1961, but the producers cast Rita Moreno, one of Marlon's girlfriends, instead. During the making of *One-Eyed Jacks*, Marlon launched an affair with Luna. He told Karl Malden, "I was working only fourteen hours a day directing this fucker, and I still had a lot of sexual energy to use up."

"MY MEXICAN TAMALE" That's how Marlon referred to his second wife, the Mexican actress Movita, whom he married in 1960 in the wake of his divorce from another exotic actress, Anna Kashfi. Before getting hitched, Marlon and Movita had been lovers for years. In spite of Marlon's reputation for preferring underaged "jailbait," Movita was an older woman, born in 1917 (Marlon was born in 1924). Marlon told his friends that he'd married Movita in a secret ceremony because she was pregnant at the time. Installing her in a fine home in Coldwater Canyon, Marlon supported Movita but never lived with her. With Marlon, she had two children--a son, nicknamed "Miko," and a daughter, Rebecca.

HOLLYWOOD IS NOT A FIT PLACE FOR CHILDREN: Tired of Marlon's constant womanizing, Movita announced in April of 1962 that she was returning to Mexico. Pictured above is Movita with her stepson, Christian (left), and her own son, Miko (right). Anna Kashfi, Christian's mother, did not want Christian to associate with Movita's children. After her return to her homeland, Movita remained married "in name only," but stayed on friendly terms with Marlon. In a surprising legal twist, Judge Harry Brand in a Santa Monica courtroom in 1968 granted Movita an annulment from Marlon in spite of the fact that their marriage had produced two children.

"THE NADIR OF MY CREATIVE RESOURCES HAS BEEN REACHED" was Marlon's lament at the end of the shooting of his role as Fletcher Christian opposite Trevor Howard's Captain Bligh in a remake of *Mutiny on the Bounty*, released in 1962. This contradicted an earlier statement, "I had some of the best times of my life making the film." At least he discovered his Shangri-La, a coral atoll in the South Pacific, Tetiaroa, which he purchased in 1966. Making headlines around the world, *Bounty* became one of the most controversial and costliest films in cinema history, skyrocketing to a final tab of $18 million. Marlon suffered through five separate versions of his character in a staggering total of 30 different screenplays, as costs mounted during the long eighteen-month shoot. Marlon used ear plugs to keep him from hearing director Lewis Milestone's commands. Because of "the disaster," Marlon would forever be known as "profligate" and "undisciplined." Flying back to Los Angeles after filming, he lamented, "My bankability, even my career, are threatened. It's shit roles for me from now on." Milestone called Marlon "a ham actor, a petulant child."

578

POLYNESIAN "LOVE SONG": During the making of *Mutiny on the Bounty*, Marlon launched a relationship with Tarita Teriipaia, the daughter of a Bora-Bora "papa" and a Chinese "maman." In *Mutiny*, she'd been cast in the minor role of Maimiti, the Tahitian girl in love with Christian Fletcher, as played by Marlon. Life imitated art as the pair became involved. She remembered Marlon living in a beachside hut and playing the bongos all night when not sleeping with local island girls. After the long, arduous filming, he flew her back to Los Angeles

where she discovered that he was still married to Movita, who ironically, had played the same role (Maimiti) in the original 1935 version of *Mutiny* with Clark Gable and Charles Laughton. When Tarita became pregnant, Marlon urged her to abort the child, but she refused. A son, Teihotu, was born on May 30, 1963, and Marlon denied fatherhood. Enraged, he flew to the atoll where he severely beat Tarita with his fists and a belt. Heading back to Los Angeles, he abandoned her in "a pool of blood," according to her memoirs, published in French.

THE "SLEEPLESS MARRIAGE": Amazingly, if Tarita is to be believed, Marlon rarely slept with her during their long affair and their common law marriage that produced two children. In custody battles with Marlon in Los Angeles, first wife Anna Kashfi referred to Tarita and her brood as "Brando's mistress and his illegitimate children." While filming *Mutiny*, Marlon often spoke of Tarita's "Rousseau-like innocence." He claimed that he delayed seduction of her for six entire

months, a record for him. The real reason for the delay may have been a bad case of gonorrhea he'd contracted from all his womanizing with the beauties of the South Pacific, often at the rate of three per night, sometimes all of them in the same bed with him.

"AND WE ALL LOSE OUR CHARMS IN THE END": Marilyn Monroe sang those exact words when she was filming *Gentlemen Prefer Blondes* with Jane Russell. This photograph of her was secretly taken following her autopsy when she was the victim of a suicide (perhaps a murder) on August 5, 1962. As has so often been said, her image evoked, and continues to evoke, all that is good, bad, ugly, glamorous, 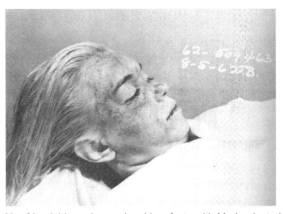 phony, and tacky about Hollywood. Her friendship and occasional lovefests with Marlon lasted up to a point close to her death. Marlon was one of the last people, other than Peter Lawford, that Marilyn spoke to just before her untimely death. Throughout the rest of his life, he claimed that she was murdered and had not committed suicide. He also maintained that hours before her death, Marilyn confided in him "a story so shocking that it would blow the lid off this town and lead to a rewriting of all those Marilyn and Kennedy biographies."

THE NOT SO UGLY AMERICAN: When *The Ugly American* was released in 1963, Marlon's radical-ization" had begun and was making world head-lines. Marlon allowed his close friend and Pennebaker partner, George Englund (husband of actress Cloris Leachman) to direct the two-hour film. His sister, Jocelyn, was granted a supporting role but most of the key players were relatively unknown. With a mustache inspired by Ronald Colman, Marlon played a U.S. diplomat, "a pig-headed man of good intention." He flew to Tahiti after filming. While on his island, he heard a radio broadcast announcing that Marilyn Monroe had died. At first it seemed unreal, as he'd so recently spoken to her in such a confidential manner.

ODE TO THREE WAYS: Being a Democrat, Marlon had supported John F. Kennedy in his bid for the presidency, but as JFK's campaign evolved, the Massachusetts senator was far too much of a moderate for Marlon's left-wing politics. Marlon had two major reasons for disliking the young president when they met together in a Los Angeles hotel suite a few months before the president's assassination. Marilyn had already related her stories to him about the "abuse" she'd suffered, both from the president and from his brother, the attorney general, Robert Kennedy. Marlon also resented the President's close association with Frank Sinatra before the two men went their separate ways. The President liked Hollywood gossip, and welcomed his meeting with Marlon. The President viewed Marlon as "the greatest womanizer who ever set foot in Hollywood," with conquests whose numbers surpassed even those of Sinatra. According to Carlo Fiore, Mr. Kennedy and Marlon "wanted to indulge in some serious pussy talk," evocative of Kennedy's friendship with Sinatra, who had arranged for JFK to meet beauties who enjoyed seductions that carried the presidential seal. Fiore claimed, "Marlon later told me that the first question Kennedy wanted to know was, 'Is Shirley MacLaine's pussy really red?'" Marlon later said that he was embarrassed at not knowing the answer to that, having never seduced her. Kennedy and Marlon talked for about two hours. The President seemed fascinated as Marlon told him about his A-list seductions. Both Kennedy and Marlon agreed that they were "never finished with a woman until they'd had her three ways."

A FLIGHT TO NOWHERE: The 1964 silly froth, called *Bedtime Story*, might have been filmed in the 1930s with Cary Grant and James Stewart. Instead, it starred Marlon and David Niven. Marlon was much too fat to appear in a beach scene with Shirley Jones, but that didn't stop him from showing a lot of flesh--too much, in fact. Playing two adventurers, both Niven and Marlon actually played themselves. As two Riviera-based gigolos, Marlon and Niven join up to con wealthy women, most often widows and divorcées. Penelope Gilliatt, in the *Observer*, wrote: "It makes you feel that civilisation might as well leave it to the amoebae again."

THE WIDOW AND THE CONTENDER: Separated from his wife, Cloris Leachman, George Englund, Marlon's close friend and partner, was spending a lot of time with Lee Radziwell. She, of course, was the sister of the former First Lady, Jacqueline Kennedy. Lee invited Englund to visit with Jackie and her in Washington, and he was specifically asked to bring Marlon too. The two sisters were staying at the home of Ambassador Averell Harriman, who had lent Jackie his house as a refuge following the assassination of her husband in Dallas.

At the house, guarded by the Secret Service, Englund introduced "the two best known people in America," Mrs. Kennedy and Marlon Brando. Fueled by an excessive consumption of martinis, the quartet agreed to dine at the Jockey Club, Jackie's favorite French restaurant in Washington. It was the night of January 29, 1964. At the restaurant, the party was ushered to a private table. But someone spotted them and called the press. Within the half hour, paparazzi and reporters descended to record Jackie's first social appearance since JFK's funeral. Escaping like "fugitives" in Englund's words, the famous quartet fled through the kitchen. Later, Lee and Marlon cooked omelettes as Jackie and Englund sat in her living room, describing the recent, traumatic events in Dallas.

Three weeks later, Marlon received a thank you letter from Mrs. Kennedy, claiming she found "the omelettes wonderful and the conversation even more wonderful." She asked Marlon to tell no one, but invited him for a secret weekend away from the prying eyes of the press. Marlon told Carlo Fiore that his time with Mrs. Kennedy was "far too brief," and he eagerly looked forward to getting to know her better. Their secret rendezvous took place in New York at the Hotel Carlyle, where Mrs. Kennedy's late husband had enjoyed trysts with Marilyn Monroe.

Back in Los Angeles, Marlon refused to tell Carlo Fiore the details of his affair with Mrs. Kennedy. Marlon revealed only one tantalizing detail. According to Marlon, Mrs. Kennedy revealed that on a visit to India, Nehru himself had taught her how to stand on her head and meditate. In New York, she taught Marlon to do that. Fiore claimed that Marlon stood on his head for the next three weeks, at various times meditating. But, complaining of headaches, he eventually abandoned the practice.

After his brief interlude with Mrs. Kennedy, Marlon wrote to her, proposing marriage. He claimed that his own marriage to Movita was in name only. He said that he could easily get a divorce. He also promised to provide privacy and comfort for Mrs. Kennedy and her children on an island in the South Pacific. She found his proposal "amusing" and filed it with some 2,000 others she'd received, including one from a Greek shipping magnate that looked promising.

In 1974, after Mrs. Kennedy had become Mrs. Aristotle Onassis, Marlon had a violent run-in with Ron Galella, America's most famous *paparazzo*. He was known to all tabloid readers for his consant harassment of Mrs. Onassis. After his release from the hospital, Galella sued Marlon for half-a-million dollars. The lawsuit was settled out of court for $40,000. Mrs. Onassis reportedly was "thrilled that Marlon was still out there, looking out for me."

THE SABOTEUR: CODE NAME--MORITURI: In this old-fashioned melodrama, released by 20th Century Fox in 1965, Marlon teamed up once again with Trevor Howard, his *Mutiny on the Bounty* costar. Also appearing in the film were Marlon's old friends, William Redfield and Wally Cox, along with Yul Brynner, with whom Marlon bonded rather intimately. *Newsweek* called the film "patent claptrap." Both Marlon and Brynner needed the money, and that's why they did the film. The bald-headed Brynner detested 20th Century Fox so much he dubbed it "16th Century Fucks."

THE DEATH OF MARLON SR.: The love-hate relationship between Marlon Sr. and Marlon Jr. ended in 1965. Despite their outward show of affection, as depicted below, "the two men hated each other," in the words of Sam Gilman. Early in June of that year, the doctors for Marlon Sr. diagnosed a melanoma growing on the back of his hand. After radium treatments, it was determined that the cancer growing in him was not operable. Death came on July 18, 1965 at St.

Vincent's Hospital in Santa Monica. A few months months before Marlon Sr. died, he'd engaged in a bitter fight in Pennebaker offices, denouncing his son as a "God damn fool." Marlon Sr. had even slapped Marlon Jr. in front of witnesses. "Marlon took it like a man, but stormed out of the office," Sam Gilman said. "When Marlon Sr. died a few months later, there was no funeral. After hearing of his father's death, Marlon told me, 'I loathed the bastard, and I'm glad he's out of my life. Fuck him.'"

Later, Marlon journeyed to Nebraska and spread his father's ashes in the fields of Penny Poke Farm. Marlon Sr. was described, in his obituaries, as a "successful businessman" even though he had squandered enormous amounts of his son's money in foolish investments.

THE CHASE-- HOTHOUSE, SOUTHERN, AND GOTHIC: In her steamy drama about a hard-drinking Southern backwater, playwright Lillian Hellman let it rip. In a screenplay inspired by both *Peyton Place* and *High Noon*, it focused on wife-swapping, racism, megalomania, arson, and murder. The cast was gold plated, and included Marlon, an extraordinarily handsome Robert Redford, and legendary beauties Angie Dickinson and Jane Fonda. Fonda later described her part as "Barbarella comes to small-town Texas." Even the infamously narcissistic movie star of the 1930s, Miriam Hopkins, found herself wandering into the film. Its producer, Sam Spiegel, said, "Brando sleepwalked through *The Chase*. The only chase occurred when Brando ran from process servers sent by Anna Kashfi." Director Arthur Penn later declared that Brando "looked like a baby Orson Welles. He was good at seduction. All off camera." After it was released in 1966, the film bombed at the box office.

DON'T GIVE ME THAT FUCKING BULLSHIT!: That was Marlon's opening line to the Canadian director, Sidney J. Furie, when he said that he was looking forward to working with Marlon on the 1966 release, *The Appaloosa*, a Mexican western. The simple plot has Marlon, cast as Matt Fletcher, setting out to recover a horse stolen from him by John Saxon, playing a Mexican bandit. From the beginning, Marlon wanted to send "more messages" in the picture about the harsh treatment of Indians. When Alan Miller, the producer, retitled the film *Southwest to Sonora*, Marlon threatened to walk. The British, however, released it with the *Sonora* title. Miller was horrified when Marlon insisted on his hiring of Christian Marquand, his French friend. "Marlon wanted top salary for Marquand, even though he had nothing to do with the picture," Miller claimed. "From what I gathered, Marquand earned the salary I was paying him by hanging around naked in Marlon's dressing room all day. They put more energy into sodomizing each other than Marlon did playing his part on camera."

584

TWILIGHT FOR THE LITTLE TRAMP:
"In one of the worst mistakes of my life,"
Marlon signed on to be directed by
Charles Chaplin, whom he'd always idolized. Approaching the end of his life,
Chaplin was not what he used to be when
he cast Marlon and Sophia Loren in the
1967 disaster, *A Countess from Hong
Kong*, an idea that had originated in
Chaplin's head back in 1931. Set in the
stateroom of a luxury ocean liner, it was a
typical 1930s "comedy," though improbably and wrongly placed within a 1960s
setting. The director combined his usual
mix of farce and sentimentality. Chaplin
had never been duller and more unimagi-
native. The little tramp ended up detesting
Marlon. "I would have whipped the horses
harder leading his cortège to the ceme-
tery if he'd died midway into production,"
said Chaplin.   Marlon responded, "A
nasty, sadistic asshole from hell. And I'm
being kind. Ernst Lubitsch might have
pulled it off. Not Chaplin!"

**"LISTEN, YOU SON OF A BITCH, YOU'RE
WORKING FOR CHAPLIN NOW!":** Marlon
rarely agreed with reviewers. But he pasted
Time magazine's review of *A Countess of Hong
Kong* over his bathroom mirror. *Time* wrote: *"A
Countess from Hong Kong* is probably the best
movie ever made by a 77-year-old man.
Unhappily, it is the worst ever made by Charlie
Chaplin." As a screen team, Hollis Alpert, of
Saturday Review, found that Marlon and Loren
had "about as much passion as that of a pair of
love-wracked halibuts." "It was the swan song
of a great silent screen talent who last had a
grand design for a film back when I was shitting
my diapers in Nebraska," Marlon said. "At the
end of the shoot, Marlon told Chaplin, "You can
take this fucking film and stick it up your ass.
Frame by frame!"

"HER TITS AND ASS ARE TOO BIG": Marlon, at least when he was still speaking to his director, Charlie Chaplin, had an unkind appraisal of his costar, the Italian bombshell, Sophia Loren. He taunted her at every turn. When Chaplin directed them in their first love scene, he whispered--not sweet nothings in her ear--but an insult. "Did you know, you've gotten black hairs growing out of your nose which is too big?" Loren was upset from day one, having lost her battle for top billing on the film. Many a morning Marlon showed up late to work as Loren--made up and fully dressed--waited for him. He'd been carousing all night with his lover, Christian Marquand, even in his hotel suite when a startled reporter from a London newspaper came to interview Marlon and caught him "slurping Marquand."

ELIZABETH TAYLOR AT HER MOST FLAMBOYANTLY VULGAR: When Monty Clift died of a heart attack, Marlon signed on to play the repressed homosexual, Major Weldon Penderton, in *Reflections in a Golden Eye*, directed by John Huston and released in 1967. It was based on a bizarre Southern drama by Carson McCullers, a story of infidelity, perversion, and murder in an Army camp in Georgia. The film included Julie Harris, playing a next door neighbor who cuts off her nipples with a pair of garden shears. Richard Burton had turned down the role because he was nervous about playing a homosexual. He later overcame that prejudice

when he signed on as Rex Harrison's lover in *Staircase* in 1969. Burton visited the set every day, ostensibly to watch Marlon act. But privately he told friends that he suspected "Liz has the hots for the boy. I have to see that she doesn't get into trouble." What did Marlon think of the Burton/Taylor romance? "Loved her, hated him!"

CANDY "ON AN ABYSMALLY LOW AND TASTE-LESS LEVEL": Marlon later claimed that it was only because of his friendship with Christian Marquand that he agreed to appear in *Candy*, released in 1968. Marquand, as the film's director, lined up Charles Aznavour, James Coburn, John Huston, Walter Matthau, and even Sugar Ray Robinson for what came to be called "the ultimate dirty movie." The film was freely adapted from the best-selling pornographic spoof by Terry Southern. Richard Burton was signed to star opposite Marlon. He played a debauched Welsh poet (type casting?). Ringo Starr was improbably cast as a Mexican gardener. Also miscast was Marlon, who played a phony Jewish guru. Taking a page from the *Kama Sutra*, Marlon has to teach Candy, as played by Ewa Aulin, the seven stages of sexual mysticism. The joke is, he's exhausted before reaching the seventh stage.

Before the end of the filming, Burton blamed Marlon "for leading me astray and getting me to appear in this stinker." Marlon responded: "My suggestion is for you to remake the Laurel and Hardy series. Based on your domestic life with Liz Taylor." Later a reporter asked Marlon what it was like to appear on screen with the *great* Richard Burton. "It was like working with the Seven Deadly Sins," Marlon shot back.

QUEIMADA! **RELEASED AS** *BURN!***:** In this 1970 release, Marlon played an English spy, Sir William Walker. In Cartagena, Colombia, where the picture was shot, he remembered nearly killing his director, Gillo Pontecorvo, so bitter were the clashes between the two hot-tempered men during filming in 1968. Marlon claimed that the motley crew were stoned most of the time, enjoying a strong variety of marijuana known as Colombia Red. Mostly he remembered the women, many from Brazil. "Dozens of them showed up, mostly upper-class women from good families, and they wanted to sleep with everybody," Marlon said. "After they went home, some told me, they intended to see a doctor who would sew up their hymens so that when they got married their husbands would think they were virgins."

587

"LOOKING LIKE A SLIGHTLY MAD BEN FRANKLIN": That's how the *New York Times* described Marlon's appearance in the 1971 release of *The Nightcomers*. It was shot in England and directed by Michael Winner, who based the script on the Henry James short story, *The Taming of the Screw*. Cast opposite him was Casablanca-born, Stephanie Beacham. Critics wrote of her "icy beauty, withering stare, and a British accent wielded like a poison dart." She was nervous about her nude scenes with Marlon. She need not have been. No one went to see the picture. After languishing in a vault for a year, it was finally picked up by an American distributor, who played it to empty houses across America. The smart money boys in Hollywood predicted, "Brando is finished in pictures."

THE GODFATHER--
THE COMEBACK OF MAR- LON BRANDO: After a series of critical and financial disas- ters, Paramount executives were leary of casting Marlon as *The Godfather* in Mario Puzo's best-selling novel. Director Francis Ford Coppola wanted Sir Laurence Olivier, who was not available, to play Don Corleone. Although he needed the work, Marlon at first turned it down, claiming that he would not make a film glorifying the Mafia. But after reading the script, he said, "I don't think the film is about the Mafia at all. I think it is about the corporate mind." Years later, Marlon blamed Coppola for his mas-

sive weight gain. "Coppola not only makes the best pictures but the best spaghetti in the world." At the time he was cast into *The Godfather*, Marlon was otherwise virtually unemployable. His weight had ballooned--and he was constantly depressed.

YOU WANT BRANDO AFTER TEN BOX OFFICE FIASCOS?: Executives at Paramount discouraged best-selling author Mario Puzo in his campaign to cast Marlon in their film version of *The Godfather.* "Brando is troublesome and uncooperative," said Paramount Production chief, Robert Evans, "And not only that, he'll fuck your wife or mistress behind your back." Refusing to change his mind, Puzo, a tough product of Manhattan's Hell's Kitchen, sent Marlon galleys of *The Godfather,* his epic story of a crime family that would soon capture the attention of the world. In addition to the book, Puzo was also writing the filmscript, and still holding out for Marlon. Marlon didn't read the book, but called Puzo to thank him for sending over the galleys. "Paramount will never hire me," Marlon told the author. "So let's forget it. I'm sure George C. Scott will get the nod." Puzo would go on to write all three *Godfather* movies (the latter two without Marlon), for which he'd receive two Oscars. When Puzo died on Long Island in 1999, he was writing a fourth *Godfather* movie, the film script of which he was going to send to Marlon, hoping that he'd agree to appear in a cameo.

"I'M PAYING BRANDO ONLY $50,000. BUT IF THE PICTURE IS A SUCCESS, HE'LL MAKE A FORTUNE: That was Robert Evans talking, the chief of production at Paramount. In addition to his base salary, Marlon was also given five percent of the gross of *The Godfather,* with a ceil-

ing of $1.5 million. In a financial mistake, and strapped for cash, Marlon sold his points back to the studio, ending up with only $300,000.

When Evans finally agreed to cast Marlon, he sent him Mario Puzo's film script. Marlon finally got around to reading it, finding it "cheap pulp fiction in the tradition of Harold Robbins." But after reading the complete novel, he agreed to sign on. Later, Marlon told Sam Gilman that he was fascinated by their producer, Evans, because, "I understand that he's fucked Ava Gardner, Lana Turner, and Grace Kelly. Having sampled the charms of a couple of these ladies, I'm impressed with his choice of bedmates. Even more, I'm impressed with his judgment. He got an invitation from Sharon Tate the night she was murdered, but Robert said no." (Later, Sharon invited Jay Sebring instead, who, with Sharon, ended up as part of the Charles Manson blood-bath.)

TOP HEAVY WITH OSCARS: Director Francis Ford Coppola was the heavy winner in 1972 as he collected Academy Awards for *The Godfather*, one of the highest grossing pictures in the history of films. It brought him an Oscar for the screenplay he fashioned with Mario Puzo. The film also won a Best Director Academy Award for Coppola as well as a Best Picture Oscar. Coppola was launched on his way as one of the country's most erratic and controversial filmmakers. Coppola was working on *Godfather IV* with Puzo at the time of the author's death. After Puzo died, Coppola abandoned the project, saying, "I can't do it without my friend." Coppola suffered the indignity of both Marlon and George C. Scott turning town their Oscars for films written by him--Scott for *Patton* in 1970 and Marlon for *The Godfather* in 1972.

"A FAUN TRAPPED IN THE HEADLIGHTS OF AN ONCOMING CAR": That's how Al Pacino described his feelings during his first meeting with Marlon. Cast as Michael Corlone, Pacino once said, "Jeez, every time I'd run into Marlon Brando on the set, my face would turn red and I'd start laughing." Originally Marlon was unhappy with the casting of Pacino as his son. "I want Robert Redford," Marlon demanded, but didn't get him. Coppola recalled a dinner when members of the cast were introduced to Marlon. "Immediately everyone started relating to him as *The Godfather*. Jimmy Caan started telling jokes. Al Pacino looked tragic, and every time Brando turned his face, Bobby Duvall started to imitate him." Pacino was nervous in his first scene opposite Marlon as Don Corleone. The scene depicted a bedside vigil Michael keeps for the Don following an assassination attempt. "Have you any idea what it was like to do a scene with Brando?" Pacino later asked Coppola. "I sat in movie houses when I was a kid watching Brando in *Streetcar* and *Viva Zapata!* Now I'm playing a scene with him. He's *God*, man."

"BRANDO IS STRICTLY TABOO. LOOK WHAT HE DID TO *MUTINY*": The Paramount casting director who said that is living today in a seedy motel off Social Security. Financed in part by the breathtaking box-office returns on the sappy *Love Story*, *The Godfather* eventually emerged as a spectacular box-office success. Prior to his being cast in the film, Marlon submitted to the humiliation of a screen test, which took place in the privacy of his home. For the test, Marlon stuffed his cheeks with wads of tissue paper. When Robert Evans at Paramount saw the test, he proclaimed: "He certainly looks Italian. Fine! But who is he?"

"He's an actor named Marlon Brando," Coppola told the studio chief. Charles Bluhdorn, the sometimes-visionary chairman of Paramount, on hearing who the actor was, jumped up from his seat. "Oh, no, no, no! Anybody but Brando!" Dieting before filming began, a thinner Marlon was confronted by Robert Evans. "You're too thin to play the Don," Evans warned him. Throughout the rest of his life, no producer would ever utter such words to a bloated Marlon ever again. That very night Marlon resumed his diet of spaghetti, potatoes, three beefsteaks, two apple pies, a quart of ice cream, and a large jar of milk.

"THE WINNER IS...MARLON BRANDO": Those words came from Liv Ullmann on March 27, 1972, after she opened the envelope in front of millions of people during the selection of the year's best actor in a motion picture. Marlon, for his role in *The Godfather,* had vanquished such once and former friends as Sir Laurence Olivier, who had been nominated for his role in *Sleuth.* But Marlon didn't show up to receive his award.

Marlon had sent, on his behalf, Sacheen Littlefeather (alias Maria Cruz) to reject the Oscar if presented. She arrived minutes before the announcement, looking like an Apache princess and robed in white buckskin with turquoise beads. Heading her off when he learned what was happening, the producer of the Academy of Motion Picture Arts and Sciences event, Howard Koch, encountered Littlefeather and threatened to cut her off the air if she read Marlon's long-winded refusal speech.

Appearing as the most newsworthy event during Hollywood's most glamorous night, Littlefeather was forced to speak extemporaneously, as titters erupted across the auditorium. Littlefeather informed the otherwise shocked audience worldwide that Marlon was turning down the Academy Award as a protest against filmdom's misrepresentation of Native Americans.

Littlefeather was both a Yaqui and an Apache, but many press reports the following day called her a Mexican. It was also revealed in the press that in 1970 she'd won the Miss American Vampire Contest.

The attacks on Marlon began that very night. The following day, columnist Rona Barrett went on television, challenging Marlon to "put your money where your mouth is and build hospitals and schools for the American Indian with his riches from *The Godfather* and *Last Tango* instead of squandering the money on a Tahitian paradise for yourself."

By the thousands, other attacks came in, including versions from both Rock Hudson and Clint Eastwood. The Columbian Coalition, a lobbying group for Italian-American rights, also blasted Marlon. "Frankly," the organization said in a written statement, "we see a blatant contradiction between your reasons for refusing the award and your participation in a film that defamed the Italian-American community. You should be ashamed of yourself."

Marlon responded, "I am not ashamed!"

592

LAST TANGO IN PARIS (1972): The young Italian director and poet, Bernardo Bertolucci, had come up with an intriguing idea for a film destined to become one of the century's most daring and controversial. He was fresh from his success in making *The Conformist*, which had starred Jean-Louis Trintignant, the French actor, along with Dominique Sanda. The basic plot of *Last Tango in Paris* revolved around an expatriate, middle-aged American who meets a reckless young girl for a series of sexual encounters, without ever revealing their names to each other. Bertolucci approached Trintignant to star in it, but was turned down when he learned that the role called for frontal nudity. Sanda had no objection to appearing nude, but she was pregnant. Ironically, the father of her baby was none other than Christian Marquand, Marlon's longtime lover. Bertolucci's second choice for the role was Catherine Deneuve, but she, too, was pregnant.

With Trintignant out of the picture, Bertolucci thought of casting Marlon, an actor he'd idolized since he was eleven years old and sat in a dark movie house watching him emote in *Viva Zapata!*

In Paris, Marlon was taken to see *The Conformist*, by his longtime lover, a Chinese lady named Anita Kong. She'd seen the film seven times and admired it greatly. Marlon too was impressed with *The Conformist*, and agreed to meet with Bertolucci at his suite at the Hotel Raphael where Marlon had stayed during the filming of *The Young Lions*. "I felt shy and in awe of Marlon when meeting him for the first time," Bertolucci recalled. "And then he started talking in Tahitian French. I spoke normal French. In time, I learned much of my English from Marlon. He mumbles a lot. That's why nobody understands me when I speak English."

Marlon was looking for some daring and provocative project as a followup to *The Godfather*. As Bertolucci pitched the story idea of *Last Tango in Paris*, Marlon became more and more intrigued with the possiblities. Of course there were problems. The producer of *Last Tango* was none other than Alberto Grimaldi, who was suing Marlon for $700,000 for his "inappropriate behavior" during the filming of *Burn!* By coincidence, Grimaldi felt that the script of *Last Tango* had "infinite possiblities" with Marlon in the lead. If Marlon would sign for the picture, Grimaldi agreed to drop the lawsuit. He even offered Marlon a salary of $250,000, plus ten percent of the world gross. Marlon signed on.

During pre-production, Bertolucci took Marlon to an exhibit at Le Grand Palais in Paris to see the gruesome paintings of Francis Bacon. He claimed that these paintings had inspired him to film *Last Tango*. Looking at the paintings with Marlon, Bertolucci waxed enthusiastically about "the burnt browns and blood reds of a homosexual's palette." He told Marlon, "In Bacon's paintings you see people throwing up their guts and doing a makeup job with their own vomit. You are like one of the figures in a Bacon painting. Everything shows up in your face. You have the same devastated plasticity."

"BRANDO IS AN ANGEL AS A MAN, A MONSTER AS AN ACTOR": Those were Bertolucci's words uttered after only a week of contact with Marlon. The director had flown to Los Angeles to spend long hours with Marlon in his house on Mulholland Drive. During these sessions, Marlon and Bertolucci took turns playing Freudian analyst with each other. For one brief moment, it was seriously considered that *Last Tango* should be written as a homosexual drama between a middle-aged man and a young man, both doing nude scenes with each other depicting actual anal penetration on the screen. That idea hardly survived an afternoon. When he

would later see the film, the Swedish director, Ingmar Bergman, said that *Last Tango* would have been more powerful if it had been about two men.

In Los Angeles, Bertolucci issued a challenge to Marlon. "Let's talk about ourselves, about our lives, about sex. That's what the film is going to be about."

In the film, Marlon is cast as Paul, a forty-five year old American expatriate living in Paris. He'd lived for the past seven years as the parasitic husband of the *patronne* of a Parisian flophouse. At the beginning of the film, Paul's wife has committed suicide.

Cast as a nineteen-year-old girl opposite Marlon, Marie Schneider was the illegitimate daughter of Daniel Gélin. There was a certain irony here. Along with Christian Marquand, Gélin had been Marlon's French lover for years.

Maria claimed that she got along with Marlon "because we are both bisexual." When asked about this by a reporter from a French film magazine, Marlon admitted that he was bisexual. "I am not ashamed. I've never paid attention to what people said about me. Deep down, I feel ambiguous. Sex somehow lacks precision. I say sex is sexless."

During the filming, Christian Marquand was a frequent visitor. "Forty years of Marlon's life experiences went into that film," Marquand claimed. "It was Marlon talking about himself. His relations with his mother, father, children, lovers, friends--all come out in his perfect performance as Paul."

"THE MOST POWERFULLY EROTIC MOVIE EVER MADE": The word was out for the world press, even two weeks into the filming. Paramount executives told Bertolucci they did not want Marlon cast in the lead, figuring that the relatively modest budget of one and a half million dollars might balloon as it had during the filming of that "nightmare, *Burn!*" At the time *The Godfather* had not yet been released as "box-office dynamite." Bertolucci turned instead to United Artists, which granted him partial financing, even though fearful that the *Last Tango* might be "too pornographic."

On Marlon: "I have at my disposal a great actor, with all the technical experience any director would require," Bertolucci said. "But I also have a mysterious man waiting to be discovered in all the richness of his personal material."

Sounding like a character created by Norman Mailer, Marlon at one point in the movie's dialogue says, "What the hell, I'm no prize. I picked up a nail in Cuba in 1948, and I got a prostate like an Idaho, but I'm still a good stick man. I don't have any friends. I suppose if I hadn't met you, I'd probably settle for a hard chair and a hemorrhoid."

Marlon later admitted to *Rolling Stone* magazine that he never actually knew what *Last Tango* was about. "Bernardo went around telling everybody that the movie was about the reincarnation of my prick. Now what the fuck does that mean?"

Upon the release, Bertolucci flew to New York to promote *Last Tango*. Once there, a reporter asked him about rumors of an affair with Marlon. "I fall in love with all the actors in my films. Both actors and actresses. They are the prolongations of my penis. Yes, my *penis*. Like Pinocchio's nose, my penis grows!" As the journalist noted, the director didn't exactly answer the question.

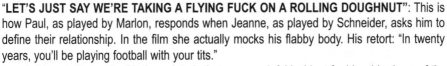

While in New York, Bertolucci received a secret communication from the White House. President Richard Nixon wanted a private screening of *Last Tango in Paris*. With his strong leftist leanings, Bertolucci was no admirer of Nixon. He refused the presidential request even though he was a guest in what was at the time known as "Nixon country."

"LET'S JUST SAY WE'RE TAKING A FLYING FUCK ON A ROLLING DOUGHNUT": This is how Paul, as played by Marlon, responds when Jeanne, as played by Schneider, asks him to define their relationship. In the film she actually mocks his flabby body. His retort: "In twenty years, you'll be playing football with your tits."

In his autobiography, Marlon related what was a painful incident for him: *I had one of the more embarrassing experiences of my professional career when we were making this film in 1972. I was supposed to play a scene in the Paris apartment where Paul meets Jeanne and be photographed in the nude frontally, but it was such a cold day that my penis shrank to the*

size of a peanut. It simply withered. Because of the cold, my body went into full retreat, and the tension, embarrassment and stress made it recede even more. I realized I couldn't play the scene this way, so I paced back and forth around the apartment stark naked, hoping for magic. I've always had a strong belief in the power of mind over matter, so I concentrated on my private parts, trying to will my penis and testicles to grow; I even spoke to them. But my mind failed me. I was humiliated, but not ready to surrender yet. I asked Bernardo to be patient and told the crew that I wasn't giving up. But after an hour I could tell from their faces that they had given up on me. I simply couldn't play the scene that way, so it was cut.

At one point, Bertolucci insisted that Marlon and Schneider have actual sex on film. Marlon objected to the command, claiming that, "We don't want our sexual organs to become characters in the film." Marlon recalled one scene of buggering, in which, "I used butter, but it was all ersatz sex."

Although Marlon refused to "fuck Maria on camera," author Norman Mailer felt that the director should have prevailed. Upon seeing the film, Mailer expressed his disappointment. "Brando's cock up Schneider's real vagina would have brought the history of cinema one huge march closer to the ultimate experience it has promised since its inception--that is, to embody life."

"SHE WAS A LITTLE LOLITA--ONLY MORE PERVERSE": Bertolucci told Maria Schneider, "Whether it's frontal nudity, masturbation, or sodomy, I will have a voyeuristic eye."

Bertolucci claimed that he considered one hundred actresses for the role before coming upon Maria Schneider. "I asked her to strip on camera for a screen test, and she did so without hesitation. It was her carefree attitude toward nudity that won her the role."

Marlon often seduced a fully nude Schneider on camera while he was partially dressed. When the film was released, women liberationists attacked *Last Tango* for concealing Marlon's genitals while exposing Schneider's charms. Although writing a very laudatory review, critic Pauline Kael said privately: "Do you really want to see a forty-seven-year old man, with a not perfect body, totally nude?"

Throughout the filming, Marlon had a hard time remembering his lines. He finally asked Bertolucci to scribble them on Schneider's naked derrière.

In *Last Tango*, Maria Schneider plays a twenty-year-old *petite bourgeoise* named Jeanne. Meeting Marlon while apartment hunting, she becomes involved with him in the throes of what Bertolucci labeled as "a vertical passion."

As the film depicts, Marlon and Schneider meet for three days in an abandoned apartment to act out their deepest sexual fantasies. Most of these fantasies are of a sadomasochistic variety.

Paul tells her he wants sex "stripped of romance and personality." He doesn't even want to know her name. Under Paul's spell, Schneider as Jeanne agrees to eat vomit for Paul, and even to allow a pig to fart in her face as she reaches orgasm.

All of Paris buzzed with the "news" that Marlon and Schneider were having a romance both on and off the camera. "Everybody knew that Daniel Gélin had fucked Marlon for years," said Roger Vadim. "Now he was going after the daughter." He smiled with a certain smugness.

"I guess if you like the father's ass, why not the daughter's?"

However, Schneider denied any romantic involvement with Marlon. "He was just a daddy to me. I never felt any sexual attraction to him. He's almost fifty, and he's only beautiful to his waist--certainly not below the waist. Not for me."

Promoting the film in New York, Schneider smoked a joint in front of a reporter from *The New York Times*. She told him, "I've had more men lovers than women."

LOVERS OR JUST GOOD FRIENDS?: Maria Schneider later shocked reporters when she claimed, "Bertolucci was in love with Marlon Brando, and that's what the movie was about. We were acting out Bernardo Bertolucci's sex problems--in effect, trying to transfer them to film."

Marlon, in a final reaction to the film, stated, "For the first time, I have felt the violation of my innermost self." Opening in the fall of 1972, the film earned forty-five million dollars, of which Marlon pocketed four million. For many viewers, the scenes in the *Last Tango* were hard to take. Dustin Hoffman, watching one scene, remembered getting up and hiding behind a pillar in the theater. In that scene, Paul excoriates Jeanne with a blistering diatribe. He informs her that "we are all alone until we look in the asshole of death." As a final act of sexual humiliation, he orders her to sodomize him with her hand.

"I thought I was watching a film scripted by Jean Genet," said Tennessee Williams, who put off for weeks going to see the film because he'd heard that Marlon, his beloved Stanley Kowalski, was appearing in hard core porno. "The ghost of Baudelaire hung over *Last Tango*," Tennessee claimed after sitting through the film twice. "I felt that all my reservoir as an artist had been depleted just by sitting through the movie. Of course, I saw it twice. Maybe that's the reason I'm so drained."

Mae West, who'd had a previous erotic encounter with Marlon herself, sent him a message. "It's good and dirty," she wrote. "But, of course, I'm easily shocked."

Rock Hudson, Mae's singing partner at the Academy Awards one time, expressed his disappointment in the film. "There was no oral sex. How could Bertolucci have made *Last Tango* without my favorite sport: fellatio?"

In Bertolucci's native Italy, censors at first prevented the release of *Last Tango*. The censors claimed it was "crude, repulsive, and even unnatural in its representation of the carnal union...accompanied off screen by sounds, sighs, and shrieks of climax pleasure."

Having turned down the Oscar for *The Godfather*, Marlon did not expect to be nominated again. But he was, as was Bertolucci for best director. Marlon lost that year to Jack Lemmon for *Save the Tiger*, with Bertolucci losing to George Roy Hill for *The Sting*.

597

MARLON IN WALLY WORLD: In Tahiti it was February 15, 1973. Marlon was in a different time zone but early morning listeners in California had awakened to hear that the comedian, Wally Cox, had been found dead at the age of forty-eight. After suffering from years of alcoholism, Wally had died on Rosacomare Road in Bel Air. His widow, Patricia Cox, had called the Bel Air Patrol to report the death at 7:30 that morning.

Was it suicide? The word spread like wildfire in Hollywood that it was. On a bedside table near Wally's body was found an empty bottle of Placidyl, a sleeping tablet. The day before and late into the night, Wally had been drinking heavily. His death brought renewed rumors that Wally and Marlon had engaged in homosexual relations ever since they were boys growing up together. Rumors of the famous photograph that Marlon had posed for, committing fellatio on Wally, were revived. "Wally was the big love of Marlon's life," said Stella Adler in New York, but only privately to friends.

Wally was heading downward in his career, reduced to flopping in Las Vegas, appearing on TV shows, and doing a comic bit as the "persnickety bird watcher," P. Casper Biddle, on two separate episodes of *The Beverly Hillbillies*. He had been cast in Marilyn Monroe's last film, *Something's Got to Give*, but she was murdered before its completion.

Wally was reduced to appearing on *Hollywood Squares* five days a week, "the last stop in a show business career." The producers kept him on because audiences found him hilarious, but they admitted that Wally always arrived "half bombed."

In the last months of his life, Wally claimed that "the only thing I have left in life to enjoy is to walk in the woods with Marlon." Assisted by Marlon and his girlfriend, Ursula Andress, Wally had created a taped recording of the entire King James version of the Bible, playing every devil and every saint. Copies of this project, tragically, have been lost.

Taking the next flight from Tahiti to Los Angeles, Marlon wanted to say a final good-bye to Wally. Arriving at his Mulholland Drive estate, he found a suicide note from Wally written two days previously. Marlon read the note and tore it up. His loyal friend, Sam Gilman, was at Marlon's side.

Marlon refused to divulge the contents of the note, telling Gilman that, "What Wally and I had was between the two of us. His final note wasn't meant for other eyes--just mine."

After an examination of the body, it was reported by Thomas Noguchi, the Los Angeles County Coroner, that the comedian had died of "severe coronary disease due to arteriosclerosis." But despite the official diagnosis, it was widely known that at the time of Wally's death, he had been despondant for months. His successful *Mr. Peepers* and its successor,

598

The Adventures of Hiram Holiday, were no longer being shown on TV. His book, *My Life as a Small Boy*, was published but attracted virtually no readers. In the last weeks of his life, his drinking had increased to what friends viewed as excessive.

Throughout his life, Wally denied ever having been Marlon's gay lover. But among their friends, the issue was debated. Actress Sondra Lee, who knew both men, insisted they were not lovers. Carlo Fiore and dozens of other intimates claimed that they were. Fiore went a step farther, charging that "Cox liked kinky sex--not just with Marlon but with hookers. He hired expensive hookers to service his needs. Modesty prevents me from going into details, but I can tell you that leather and whips were involved."

Since Wally despised funerals, his widow, Patricia Cox, decided to hold a wake for her late husband's friends, who included Vincent Price, Tom and Dick Smothers, Ernest Borgnine, and even Twiggy. Not wanting to see the other guests, Marlon slipped in through a bedroom window. He did not want to come out and greet the other mourners. "These assholes weren't Wally's friends," Marlon said. "I was the *only* friend Wally ever had."

Pat Cox recalled that Marlon "didn't want Wally to marry me. He was very possessive of Wally." But his widow refused to admit that her husband's death was a suicide. She did concede, however, that "Wally had been very depressed during recent months."

"If Wally didn't actually kill himself on the night in question," Sam Gilman said, "he did night after lonely night. He was drinking himself into oblivion. Marlon knew this and talked to me all the time about his concerns. I think Wally decided early one pre-dawn morning that life wasn't any fun anymore. I'm sure that he felt it was time for him to go."

Since Wally despised funerals, it was announced that his body would be cremated and his ashes tossed into the sea. That didn't happen. Marlon asked the widow for the ashes, claiming that he would spread them on the grounds around his Mulholland estate.

But in a bizarre twist, he concealed the ashes in his home. On nights when he was feeling lonely for Wally, he took them out of hiding and placed the urn on his dining table. There he would proceed to have "dinner with Wally," talking in his own voice but answering questions or making observations in Wally's voice. Marlon was always capable of doing a perfect imitation of his late friend.

In Tahiti, Marlon once talked to a journalist, Adrano Botta, of *L'Europeo*. Marlon was very candid, admitting that he'd had many women as "I insist on enjoying sex. Should sex and desire die in me, it would be the end." Then he candidly admitted that he'd "never been happy with a woman."

In the wake of Wally's death, Marlon admitted that he could no longer put any faith in friendship. "I only come through with deep wounds," he said, his eyes welling with tears at the loss of Wally. "I am deeply lonely. Alone without Wally." He noted that with the passing of Wally, he had death and old age to look forward to and to accept "with all feasible serenity. Here I am trying to save the world with all my noble causes, and I couldn't even save my best--my only--friend," Marlon said.

When Marlon himself died, two pictures were found in his bedroom--one of his mother, Dodie, the other of Wally. "He was my soulmate, the only person I've ever been able to really talk to," Marlon said. "I loved him as few men have ever loved another man. I'll miss him until the day I die. With him gone, there is no one left on earth for me to talk to. If Wally had been a woman, I would have married him, and we would have lived happily ever after."

MARLON IN DRAG: Teaming up with actor Jack Nicholson and director Arthur Penn, Marlon starred in *The Missouri Breaks*, released in 1976. Two of America's most acclaimed actors, including Marlon himself, and one of its most lauded directors couldn't save this turkey. Set in the foothills of the Tobacco Root Mountains, Montana, in the 1880s, *The Missouri Breaks*, if remembered at all today, is recalled for Marlon appearing in drag for no discernible reason. Instead of an attractive showgal, he looks like Old Mother Hubbard. The most famous scene is one depicting Marlon in his bath, being gazed upon by a gun-toting Nicholson. Marlon's sudsy body looks like a voluptuous nude as painted by Rubens. Flush from his Oscar-winning success in *One Flew Over the Cuckoo's Nest*, Nicholson overshadows Marlon as an actor. Russell Davies, in the *Observer*, noted: "This is one of the most extravagant displays of *grande-damerie* since Sarah Bernhardt." Fergus Cashin, in the *Sun,* wrote: "Marlon Brando at 52 has the sloppy belly of a 62-year-old, the white hair of a 72-year-old, and the total lack of discipline of a precious 12-year-old."

"BRANDO IS NEVER LESS THAN FAINTLY RIDICULOUS": So wrote Andrew Weiner in *New Society*. For this 1978 release, director Richard Donner, in what was viewed as an act of madness, cast Marlon Brando--yes, Brando of Stanley Kowalski and *Godfather* fame--as Jor-El, Superman's daddy. Knowing that Krypton was about to explode, Marlon with an English accent sends "my only son" to the planet Earth. This appalls his wife, as played by Susannah York. She has little respect for Earth, noting that, "They are primitives--thousands of years behind us."

In *Superman*, Marlon established a career pattern: Make a great deal of money in as short a period of time and with the least effort possible. Headlines about Marlon's salary made the world press. For twelve days filming, he received $3.7 million dollars. Not only that, but for such a brief appearance he got 11.3 percent of the domestic gross and 5.65 percent of foreign gross. All in all, he would be guaranteed a minimum of $1.7 million even if *Superman* failed at the box office, which it didn't. Slated for a tragic personal ending, the handsome, well-built twenty-four-year old Christopher Reeve garnered world attention, as he switched from Clark Kent to Superman. Marlon was asked if the studio could use footage shot from *Superman I* in *Superman II*. When he demanded his usual percentage--an outrageous demand, for sure--he was turned down.

"A PIECE OF HAM IN A FILM THAT IS RAW MEAT": So described Arthur Thirkell, in the *Daily Mirror*, about Marlon's appearance as a shaven-headed, bloated, and Buddha-like character in the 1979 release of *Apocalypse Now*. Based on Joseph Conrad's novella, *The Heart of Darkness*, the film about the moral dilemma of the Vietnam War teamed Marlon with his *Godfather* director, Francis Ford Coppola. Coppola cast Don Corleone this time as Kurtz, described as a "mad Minotaur in his murky labyrinth, waiting to be killed." Beset by troubles, including natural disasters such as typhoons raging through the Philippines, the film with an initial twelve million budget eventually ballooned to thirty million.

"SAM, I'VE GOT ANOTHER GIG AS A NAZI": Marlon's words to close friend Sam Gilman announced his latest role--not in the movies but in a TV series: *Roots: The Next Generation*, a TV mini-series broadcast in 1979. This was the second series of author Alex Haley's popular Roots series. The book was alleged to have traced the author's ancestors from 1882 to 1967. Much of the script has been questioned as to how authentic it was, and at one point, Haley was sued for plagiarism. Even so, Marlon made an appearance in Episode no. 7. This time he was not playing a German Nazi as he did in *The Young Lions*, but the American Nazi, George Lincoln Rockwell. Marlon's appearance in the TV series won him an Emmy. His scene was brief but he wanted it to be "villainous, a portrait of Evil," he told Haley. In his brief role, Marlon as

Rockwell is being interviewed by Haley for *Playboy* magazine. Marlon is seen sitting behind a large mahogany desk. He is framed by a portrait of Hitler and Nazi flags. As one critic said, "He radiated bigotry and paranoia." This was not one of his big money appearances. His fee went to charity. Marlon had come a long way since he'd appeared on this same stage, number 19, in Burbank. A quarter of a century before *Roots*, he'd arrived here to play Stanley Kowalski in *A Streetcar Named Desire*.

601

PATTON MEETS THE GODFATHER: The two stars of the 1980 release, *The Formula*, George C. Scott and Marlon, had turned down their respective Oscars, Scott for *Patton* and Marlon for *The Godfather*. For his brief appearance in *The Formula*, Marlon was granted an awesome salary of three million dollars for less than two weeks of work. He also demanded eleven percent of the worldwide gross. For his three scenes in the film, he'd earn an extra five-million dollars. "Not bad for a day's work," Marlon told Scott. In this so-called political thriller about oil tycoons and multi-national cartels, Marlon plays Steiffel, the chief of the OPEC cartel. Scott later said, "I think I played some washed-up son-of-a-bitch. But don't ask. I didn't wake up until shooting was over." Scott lauded Marlon's performance, perhaps out of kindness. "He goes beyond acting. He creates like an Impressionist painter." Marlon appeared with a hearing aid in the film. He wasn't actually losing his hearing, but wanted his aide to feed him his lines.

"THE MANTLE OF ORSON WELLES FALLS FROM HEAVEN ONTO MARLON BRANDO": Or so thought one critic of the outrageously obese Marlon when he appeared in the 1989 release of *A Dry White Season*. Directed by Euzhan Palci, the film co-starred Donald Sutherland. It was your standard anti-apartheid, propaganda film set in South Africa. Marlon was cast as a cynical, pot-bellied lawyer fighting apartheid, a far cry from his take as an American Nazi leader. Despite its status as a low-budget film, Marlon's agent originally got him an offer of $3.3 million, plus 11.3 of the world gross. "Look at Marlon's gut and you can see where the money is going," said a disgruntled cameraman. That was unfair. Unknown to the crew, Marlon had agreed to do the film for scale, and he donated "that paltry sum to charity if you don't mind my honking my own horn." He deplored his female director, calling her "an ama-

teur." He hated the final cut of the film and protested loudly to MGM. "I have never put more of myself into a film, never suffered more while doing it, and never received so little recompense of any kind in any motion picture over the last thirty-five years."

A FOND PARODY OF DON VITO CORLEONE: In 1990 a film was released called *The Freshman*. Marlon pronounced it "a stinker" until it started to do well at the box office, and then he withdrew his comment.

Directed by Andrew Bergman, it reteamed Marlon with Maximilian Schell (*The Young Lions*). Marlon also starred with baby-faced pretty boy, Matthew Broderick. Marlon brought his whale-like presence to the screen in this mob movie, where he seemed to be doing a take-off on his role in *The Godfather*.

The zany plot revolves around a Gourmet Club, at which the only dishes on the menu were endangered species. *The Freshman* in the movie is assigned the dangerous task of collecting and delivering a Komodo dragon--the famous giant lizard of Indonesia--to the kitchen of the club for slaughtering and cooking. Playing Buddha-boy again, Marlon and his mumbles had reached the point of inaudibility. For his appearance in the film, Marlon got a reported $3.3 million, plus 11 percent of the gross. During the shoot, Marlon appeared to be losing control. His longtime makeup man, Philip Rhodes, was treated with great hostility, although he'd been a loyal friend for years. "Eventually Marlon iced me out--wouldn't even speak to me," Rhodes said. "It was terrifying." Marlon was also coming up to people and making very indiscreet remarks. Sometimes the crew thought he might be jesting, but he looked very serious. He approached a cameraman when Broderick was doing a scene. "That's the most fuckable ass

I've ever seen," Marlon told the startled cameraman. "That's too bad he's straight. If I were a century younger, I'd like to reshoot *Last Tango in Paris* with a boy like young Matthew cast in Maria Schneider's part. I would demand that Matthew appear in full frontal nudity. This time, the fuck scenes in *Tango* would not be simulated. They would be real. Looking at that ass, well..I'd do the fucking picture for free!"

603

"THE MOST BEAUTIFUL, THE MOST INTELLIGENT, AND THE RICHEST GIRL IN TAHITI":
That's how Marlon's daughter, Cheyenne Brando, described herself in 1995, the same year, on April 16, when she hung herself at the Brando estate at Punaauia in Tahiti. At the time of her death at the age of twenty-five, this former model "with the perfect figure" had gained so much weight she was almost as corpulent as her famous movie star father.

Her life was short and tragic. She became the focal point of one of the most notorious murders in Hollywood history, based on events swirling around the night of May 16, 1990, when Marlon's 32-year-old son, Christian Devi Brando, Cheyenne's half-brother, shot 26-year-old, Dag Drollet, her Tahitian lover. Dag was the father of her future child.

Marlon's close friend, George Englund, accurately described Cheyenne: "She was a delicate riddle...luminously pretty, not large but with an almost aggressive beauty, black hair, dark eyes, and in those eyes an anima pulsing. In Marlon's female child, I was seeing the same penetrating stare, the offhand sexuality, the eyes that know--all the Brando hallmarks."

The story began in 1960 in Tahiti when Marlon met a beautiful Polynesian actress, Tarita Teriipaia, on the set of *Mutiny on the Bounty*. She would become his common law wife and the mother of his two children, beginning with a son, Teihotu, born May 30, 1963.

When Marlon told Tarita that he wanted another baby, to follow the birth of their son, he did not seduce her. Instead he took her to a medical specialist, and the baby was conceived by artificial insemination one hot afternoon in June of 1969. Following the birth of Cheyenne, it would take years for Marlon to officially recognize her and her older brother as his legitimate offspring.

Cheyenne's unusual name came about when Marlon flew Tarita and her baby girl to Washington D.C., for a reunion of American Indians. He'd already asked and had gained permission from the Cheyenne Indians to borrow their name for his newly born daughter. Taking the baby from its mother, who sat near the rear of the hall and who was until then unaware of what he had planned, Marlon carried his daughter to the stage, facing Indians assembled from all over the country. There, he raised his daughter "to the Great Spirit" and announced that henceforth she'd be called Cheyenne Brando in honor of the tribe whose rights he championed.

In the 1980s, growing up in Tahiti, Cheyenne was emerging as a beautiful girl with high hopes for her future. She was good in school and ambitious in her career plans--painter? doctor? actress? She was proud to be the daughter of Marlon Brando, remembering to send him presents on his birthday and on Father's Day, although she ignored her mother on those occassions. When she was old enough, she flew to Los Angeles to be with Marlon. At times he could

be extremely affectionate toward her, buying her presents. At other times he could be relatively indifferent as when he refused to pay her education bills.

No one knows for sure what happened to Cheyenne, but slowly and then more rapidly she seemed to undergo a major personality change, going from Dr. Jekyll to Mrs. Hyde.

One friend in Tahiti said that Cheyenne as a teenager became hooked on drugs, a dependency she'd maintain until the end of her life. "She went from being a sweet girl to a monster. Although I viewed myself as her best friend, I soon abandoned her. If I'd see her coming, I would cross over the street to avoid her."

One afternoon in Tahiti, Cheyenne was confronted with a "new sister," Petra, who had been flown in from Los Angeles. She was two years younger than Cheyenne and had been conceived by Marlon with one of his secretaries. Learning that she was on "equal footing" with Petra, Cheyenne exploded in an angry, violent outburst in which she went through the house breaking anything breakable. That afternoon would mark the beginning of violent outbursts that would continue throughout the rest of her short life, along with her drug abuse.

During one full-moon night in Tahiti--"fired up on angel dust"-- Cheyenne met Dag Drollet, a Polynesian man, then only twenty-three years old and very handsome. It was at a disco bordering the sea in Papeete. Spring had come to Tahiti that May of 1987. The coming together of Dag and Cheyenne would end tragically.

Their relationship quickly became passionate but stormy. Many of their fights were staged in public in Polynesian restaurants and dance clubs. One of their most violent confrontations occurred in August of 1989.

Fleeing from Dag, Cheyenne jumped into a Jeep belonging to Christian Brando. She roared down a night road at 100mph, but lost control of the car, crashing into a ditch. The impact broke her jaw, and part of her ear was ripped off. A section of her face "just caved in."

Marlon didn't want Cheyenne to be operated on by Tahitian surgeons, so he flew her to Los Angeles for better medical care. There, California surgeons put seven metal plates into her head. After a twelve-hour stint on the operating table, Cheyenne's face was saved "but what about her soul?" Tarita asked.

Flying back to Tahiti after her recovery, Cheyenne, according to her mother, Tarita, experienced a "degrading of personality." During one intense argument, Cheyenne tossed an ashtray at her mother, causing a severe facial injury.

At school, she physically attacked fellow students, even her teachers. Even though she'd

moved in with Dag and his mother, Lisette, Cheyenne claimed that Dag frequently beat her. Because of her heavy drug usage, Tarita suspected that her daughter might be hallucinating.

At one point in 1989, Cheyenne confronted her mother, claiming that she was pregnant with Dag's child. Seven years older than Cheyenne, Dag was already the father of another illegitimate child. During the early months of her pregnancy, Cheyenne became "uncontrollable and unpredictable"--slapping waiters in cafes and shops, even strangers on the street. "If my daughter had lived in a first world country," Tarita claimed, "she would have been judged as certifiably insane."

As Cheyenne's pregnancy deepened, Tarita's concerns grew. Cheyenne would often approach and then strike an innocent passerby. "The doctors told me that her pieced-together face was very fragile. If a stranger suffering an attack from Cheyenne were to strike her back, it might kill her, I was warned." When Tarita shared her concerns with Marlon, he responded, "My daughter is not sick."

Marlon wanted his grandson to be born in the United States, so he flew Tarita, Cheyenne, and Dag to his home on Mulholland Drive in Los Angeles. Dag (pictured below with Cheyenne) went along for the trip, although he planned to tell Cheyenne that even before their child was born that he was going to leave her. He could no longer stand her violence and her drug abuse.

At the time, police authorities in Tahiti wanted him to return there to face manslaughter charges. Driving drunk one night, he'd run over and killed an eight-year-old child getting out of a truck on a highway.

On hearing that his half-sister was in town, Christian called Cheyenne and invited her out to dinner at Frank & Musso, a restaurant in Hollywood. Dag was "invited" to remain behind and watch television in the den.

Driving back to Mulholland Drive, Christian stopped off at his girlfriend's house to retrieve an assault weapon, a Sig-Sauer .45--called "the Porsche of handguns." After the passage of California's ban on assault weapons, Marlon had demanded that his son bring the gun to Mulholland for safekeeping.

Reportedly, Christian arrived back at the house fuming in his anger at Dag's alleged assaults on his pregnant sister. With his assault weapon, Christian headed for the den. Although he would later claim that he struggled with Dag and the gun went off accidentally, in reality he may have shot Dag in the head without warning. He died instantly.

On the night of the murder, Tarita remembered waking up to the smell of smoke. She was immediately alarmed because she knew that her increasingly deranged daughter had taken up the habit of setting fires, including one recently in the laundry hamper. "She'd just sit back and watch the flames," Tarita said.

As Tarita wandered through the darkened house, where all the lights uncharacteristically had been turned off, she saw a flickering light coming from the TV room. With trepidation, she entered the room and saw a body sprawled on the sofa. "He was drenched in blood," Tarita said. "I checked to see if he were alive. There was blood everywhere. On my hands, my throat, all over the couch." She began to scream to awaken the household.

Rushing to Marlon's bedroom, she found that Christian was already there, confessing the murder to his father. "Their image was grave," she said. "Marlon ordered me to stop screaming. I fainted dead away."

When she was revived, she remembered the house filled with police officers. She saw two of those policemen leading Christian away in handcuffs.

At the time of the murder, a particularly shocking rumor emerged. Before leaving to have dinner with Christian, Cheyenne allegedly told Dag that the "baby growing in my stomach is not yours. It belongs to Christian."

Surveying the murder scene in the den were homicide detectives, A.R. Monsue and Lee Kingsford, who had been among the first police officers to examine Dag's six feet, five-inch dead body sprawled on the sofa. Barefoot, he was clad in a pair of gray surfer shorts. After a hurried examination, Monsue determined that the fatal bullet had entered Dag's left cheek.

Kingsford remembered that he was astonished when he questioned Marlon. Instead of answering questions about what he knew about the slaying, Marlon insisted that he'd tried to be a good father to Christian and Cheyenne. "I've tried to be a good father to all of my nine children," he said. "Four of them are adopted, incidentally."

On the phone "day and night" talking to lawyers, Marlon was also besieged by the press. Angrily, he addressed this invasion, and Tarita heard his words. "One of the things that's the most difficult to understand is that in the midst of all this chaos, all this anguish, we had to face the press. Men are trying to make money off our family tragedy. In normal times, the press can make you suicidal. But under these circumstances, they become completely impossible."

To defend his son, Marlon hired famed attorney, Robert Shapiro, who would later achieve notoriety during the O.J. Simpson trial.

In a preliminary court hearing, Christian testified that Cheyenne "went off on this bizarre tangent and kinda got me going. Knowing what I know now of her mental state, I doubt whether she was ever beaten by Drollet. I feel like a complete chump for believing her."

Christian was placed in jail for three months while lawyers tried to get him out on bail.

After the killing, Cheyenne flew back to Tahiti. Once on island, papers were delivered to her. The Drollet family was suing her as an "accessory" to the death of their son. In the days and weeks ahead, she made several suicide attempts. Marlon found that he too could not go

back to Tahiti. The Drollets case also named him as an accessory. Because of that, Marlon himself could be detained on Tahiti should he decide to fly back there.

Dag's father, Jacques Drollet, also filed a $100 million wrongful death suit against both Christian and Marlon while Drollet continued to press charges against Cheyenne in Papeete.

In Tahiti, Cheyenne was eight months pregnant and ready to have her baby when authorities in California wanted her there for questioning. On June 26, 1990, she gave birth to a baby boy named Tuki. A nurse told the local

607

press, "Tuki was born drug addicted. All during her pregnancy, Cheyenne Brando continued to take drugs. The kid could have been born with brain damage. He had to be sent to detox."

While still in detox, Cheyenne wandered into the ward where her child was asleep. With no security guard around, she picked him up and carried him into the bathroom where she plunged the infant under a cold water faucet trying to drown him. The nurses rushed in to retrieve the baby. Not able to prevent her from killing the infant, Cheyenne became violent and started to smash the furniture in her room. Her doctors committed her to the Vaiami Psychiatric Hospital. A doctor there told Tarita: "Don't worry about the baby. He's doing well in spite of his ordeal. Worry instead about the child's mother. She's the one who needs help."

On November 1, 1990, Cheyenne took a huge overdose of pills to kill herself. Only days before, a French judge in Tahiti, Max Gatti, had demanded that she not leave the country. She was to be tried in local courts as an accomplice to murder.

After having her stomach pumped, she survived that attempt on her own life. But on the night of November 14, she once again attempted suicide by tying a rope to a tree outside her bedroom window, the other to her neck. She then jumped. Miraculously, she also survived this attempt at hanging, although she remained in a coma for one week.

On February 26, 1991, Christian appeared at the Santa Monica Courthouse, telling his father, "I've been coming through these doors since I was a kid." He was referring, of course, to the vitriolic fights staged between Anna Kashfi, his mother, and Marlon over his custody. He pleaded guilty that day to a charge of voluntary manslaughter.

In what must be viewed as incredible understatement, Christian's psychiatrist, Dr. Saul Faerstein, testified: "Once an inquisitive and alert child, Christian has been damaged by his upbringing and chronic substance abuse. Despite the material advantages conferred by the Brando name, neither parent provided a stable, protective, and safe emotional environment for Christian to grow up in."

One of his probation officers took the stand to claim that Christian suffered "brain damage from alcohol and druge abuse as a youth. He was kidnapped several times by one or the other of his parents," the officer said. He also claimed that Christian was "molested by a hired kidnapper, and abused by his alcoholic, mentally ill mother.

608

Christian is unassuming, low-profile, low self-esteemed."

Marlon through his lawyers secured his release, but only after mortgaging his house to post two million dollars in bail money. It was at this point that Marlon walked over to his son in the courtroom and planted a kiss on his head, a picture which was flashed around the world.

Having already pleaded guilty to manslaughter, Christian's trial was set for January of 1991.

Taking the stand, Marlon delivered an Academy Award performance, saying, "You always tend to blame the other parent, but I know that I could have done better. I think perhaps I failed as a father, but I did the best I could."

In a bit of bizarre testimony, Marlon said, "As much as it may not be believed, I loved Dag. He was going to be the father of my grandchild. As they were carrying the boy out, I asked one of the officers to unzip the bag because I wanted to say good-bye to him properly. I kissed him and told him I loved him."

After seventy-five minutes of testimony from Marlon, Dag's father, Jacques Drollet, took the stand. He'd known Marlon for thirty years. "Brando is an actor," Drollet said. "He can cry and lie like a horse can run. He was acting up here on the stand. Does anyone believe a word of it?"

In spite of Marlon's plea for his son, Christian was sentenced to ten years in prison. Before his release, Christian would serve seven years of that sentence.

It is believed that Christian is living somewhere in the Northwest today.

In Tahiti on July 17, 1991, magistrate Max Gatti forced Cheyenne to testify for four hours. At the time, she said that her brother did not see her as a sister, "but as a young woman." The reference was clearly incestuous, which could establish a different motive for Dag's murder.

The judge found her completely irrational and unstable. Taking that into consideration, he granted Marlon's request to let her fly to the French mainland to enter a mental asylum in a western suburb of Paris. However, he ordered that she deposit her passport with the police station.

Once in France, Cheyenne underwent treatment for mental illness and in the weeks ahead showed some improvement.

Marlon flew to France and smuggled her out of the asylum, taking her to a friend's home in the French city of Orléans, even though this was against the court's orders.

Tarita, who had been assigned custody of Cheyenne's son, arrived in Orléans from Tahiti. Seeing her with her son after months of separation, Cheyenne reacted violently to her mother. She bit Tarita's finger, practically severing it. Tarita bit her back. When Marlon came into the room, he discovered "blood everywhere."

On October 27, 1991 a warrant was issued for Cheyenne's arrest. French police located her living with Marlon in Orléans and arrested her. Marlon was not charged, presumably because at the time, his reputation was so high in France, even greater than it was in America, that French authorities anticipated a public outcry if he were incarcerated. Under armed guard, Cheyenne was flown back on a French military aircraft to Tahiti.

Facing a hearing on April 15, 1992, Cheyenne made the astonishing and headline-screaming charge that, "I am sure that my father asked Christian to kill Dag." It was at this same hearing that she claimed she "detested" Marlon and reported his sexual advances toward her. According to Cheyenne, her father tried to get her to go with him to a sea-bordering hotel in Santa Monica so he could "spend hours making love to you," but she refused to go with him.

In spite of Marlon's efforts on her behalf, including trying to get treatment for her psychological disorders, Cheyenne constantly made indiscreet remarks to the press about her father. In one interview, she claimed, "Marlon Brando is the Godfather in the flesh, capable of manipulating others as he wants."

After endless dramas and international incidents worthy of a feature film, Judge Jean-Bernhard Taliercio, who had replaced Judge Gatti, dropped all charges against Cheyenne. The judge claimed they lacked merit.

With Christian in prison, Cheyenne no longer faced trouble with the Los Angeles police for fleeing to Tahiti. Marlon encouraged her to return to California. When she arrived, he placed her in a bleak mental asylum in San Francisco, where she languished for two full years before flying back to Tahiti in 1995.

Tarita, along with her son, Tuki, met her at the airport. But upon driving her back to Marlon's home, Cheyenne expressed undying hatred for her mother and threatened to kill her. She lunged at the wheel of the car and attempted to drive Tarita and her son off the autoroute and kill them. There was a lot of blood in the car, as Cheyenne bit Tarita and Tarita bit back.

When she finally managed to get Cheyenne home, Tarita called the police and reported the incident. The police came for Cheyenne and hauled her away to the local insane asylum.

But she escaped in April of 1995, returning to Marlon's house. In her bedroom, Cheyenne rigged a rope to a beam in her bedroom ceiling, climbed into a chair, put the noose around her neck, then kicked away the support.

Cheyenne was buried in a granite vault high on a hill overlooking Papeete. Her grave is at the end of a long, arrowhead shaped valley studded with mango trees and acacia. "Your soul is now in God's hands," said a priest in French over her grave.

Until the end of his life, Marlon claimed, "I'm being haunted." He was so convinced that he was being pursued by the ghost of Dag that close friends thought he might be cracking up. He spoke of "cold ghastly lips" that came in the middle of the night to plant the kiss of death on his own mouth. According to Marlon, the ghost kept whispering in his ear, "I should not have died."

"It's terrifying!" Marlon told his friends. "I know it's Dag's angry spirit."

Eight months after Marlon's death, Tarita burst onto the world scene, publishing in French her autobiography entitled, *Marlon, mon amour, ma déchirure (Marlon, My Love and My Torment)* To demonstrate that her former spouse was interested in teenage sex, she maintained that Marlon became her lover when she was very young. However, in her autobiography, she downplayed Marlon's sexual interest in her daughter.

However, Cheyenne left a diary whose passages were widely publicized after her death. In it, she wrote, "He (Marlon) used to like to massage me as if he wanted to pretend we were making love. He presented it as a game, but I was just a child and had no idea what he meant."

Cheyenne also claimed that her father fondled her breasts and "inserted his finger inside me," even when she was having regular intercourse with Dag. At no point did she ever maintain that there was penis/vaginal intercourse, although she claimed that her father discussed this possibility with her at length.

A friend in Tahiti, who did not want to be named, made the most bizarre charge of all. He said that Cheyenne told him that her father one night claimed that he wanted to become the father of "your next baby."

610

"BRANDO AS TORQUEMADA PHONES IN HIS PERFORMANCE": That terrible but poetically accurate putdown came from Anne Billson, of the *Sunday Telegraph* after having seen the 1992 release of *Christopher Columbus--The Discovery*, directed by John Glen, known for his James Bond movies. Although appearing only in a cameo role, Marlon got top billing, playing Torquemada (1420-98), the Inquisitor-General whose office used to adjoin a torture chamber. Producers Ilya and Alexander Salkind, who'd broken with Marlon on his percentage demands for *Superman II*, decided to take a chance with him again.

They also cast Tom Selleck as King Ferdinand of Spain and Rachel Ward as Queen Isabella. Marlon designed his own costume on the screen, a black skull cap and a mammoth black robe to hide his corpulent bulk. Throughout the film, he smiled enigmatically like the Mona Lisa.

Marlon insisted on rewriting the script to portray Columbus as the "cruel, ambitious man he was, a man who would stop at nothing, including exterminating the guileless Indians who offered him food and gold." But Alexander Salkind, Ilya's father, turned down Marlon's revision. Marlon was bitterly disappointed, claiming that Alexander stuck to the original story, which Marlon called "idiotic, untruthful, and uninteresting. It was a big mistake because the picture was a huge failure." He admitted that he just "walked through my part. I mumbled my way through the part and gave an embarrassingly bad performance." Marlon later said, "The pay wasn't bad, though: Five million dollars for five days' work."

"THE FILM HAS SERIOUS POTENTIAL TO BE THIRD RATE": Or so wrote Janet Maslin in *The New York Times* about *Don Juan DeMarco*, a film released in 1995 that starred Marlon and his admirer, Johnny Depp. The movie also brought Marlon and Faye Dunaway together on the screen for the first time, although their names had been romantically linked off screen years before. The plot has a psychiatrist, Dr. Jack Mickler, as played by Marlon, trying to treat a young patient (Depp), who presents himself as Don Juan, the greatest lover in the world. Even a bad

movie has one good scene, and it's the last in the film. Set on a beautiful tropical isle (shades of Tahiti), Marlon dances gracefully with his wife, Marilyn, as played by Dunaway. Depp only agreed to be in the film if Marlon were cast as the psychiatrist. To learn a Spanish accent, Depp watched a tape of *Fantasy Island* re-runs. "The hardest part of working with Brando was keeping a straight face," Depp later recalled.

611

"HE GIVES A GREAT IMITATION OF QUEEN ELIZA-BETH": Or so said a wag of Marlon's bizarre role as Dr. Moreau in *The Island of Dr. Moreau*, released in 1996. Cast opposite such actors as Val Kilmer, Marlon was directed by John Frankenheimer in this picture based on a novel by H.G. Wells. Through DNA experimentation, Dr. Moreau has upset the balance of nature by turning animals into humans. As the mad doctor, Marlon virtually appeared in drag, with red lipstick and Kabuki makeup, something his friend, Michael Jackson, might have done.

His appearance, riding through the jungle in a sedan chair as he surveys his hairy mutants, is startling--even alarming. Writing in the *Boston Globe*, critic Jay Carr said, "It's as if in this new celebrity age of genetic engineering, Brando is deconstructing the idea of actors sitting in for the gods."

The picture raised the question of "Whatever Happened to Marlon Brando?" In a seminal essay, Molly Haskell took a stab at answering that question. "What is the strength of his legend?" she asked. "How has it stayed alive in spite of so many dubious achievements? It is written in a word. Brando. Like Garbo. He is a force of nature. An element. Not a human being. There is only one Brando. Even when the actor plays his favorite role, that of the serious, socially committed anti-star, he is still one of the five or six greatest actors the cinema has produced."

"FOR TORTURING AND KILLING YOU, WE'LL GIVE YOU $50,000": New Hollywood was taking over old Hollywood. Rising star, Johnny Depp had purchased Bela Lugosi's old Los Angeles mansion for $2.3 million. Retiring to Lugosi's "Viper Room," Depp worked on the screenplay of *The Brave*, which he would direct and star in for its 1997 release. When not "surrounded by bimbos to wipe out his romantic sorrow," he read the novel by Gregory McDonald that told of a down-on-his-luck American Indian recently released from jail and offered the chance to "star" as victim in a snuff film. In the film, Depp is to be tortured and killed on camera for $50,000. He needs the money for his wife and kids. Marlon appeared only in the small role of McCarthy, but enjoyed the assignment, as he'd formed a friendship with Depp when they'd worked on *Don Juan DeMarco*. Depp later told Marlon that he was so deeply upset at the negative reviews he'd garnered when *The Brave* was shown at the Cannes Film Festival that he planned to refuse to show the film in the United States.

FREE MONEY OR BRANDO AS WALRUS?: In _Free Money_, released in 1998 and directed by Yves Simoneau, Marlon was cast once again opposite Donald Sutherland, with both Charlie and Martin Sheen in supporting roles. Playing "the Swede," Marlon in this slapstick comedy is an overprotective father to his ruthless son.

At this point in his career, critics were beginning to write about Marlon as if he were dead. Almost weekly, reports from so-called "friends" stated that Marlon might have only months to live. One article said that "Brando, hardly recognizable, is struggling to remain upbeat even though his last days are filled with sadness and regret over the tragedies of his life." Even though Marlon continued his work in films, reporters wrote about his "disappointment, regret and anger," claiming that "Marlon felt let down and abandoned by former wives, lovers, and children." One writer even claimed that, "Marlon Brando is haunted by the past and thoughts of dying."

MISS PIGGY BATTLES A GAY GODFATHER: In the 2001 release of _The Score_, a crime caper, director Frank Oz--much to his regret--cast Marlon Brando in the third lead of a picture starring Robert De Niro and Edward Norton. Two Hollywood veterans, 58-year-old De Niro and 77-year-old Marlon shared screen time together. Marlon plays an elderly gay cook orchestrating the biggest heist of his career; De

Niro a thief ready for retirement; and Norton an aspiring young thug. The film cost nearly $70 million, of which $3 million went to Marlon for three weeks of work in his last major film role.

Even more interesting than the film was what happened off camera. From the first, Marlon clashed with the director, Frank Oz. When he learned that Oz had been the voice of Miss Piggy in the Muppet Show, he constantly referred to him as "Miss Piggy." When Oz attempted to direct Marlon, he got a curt response of "Fuck you!" Defiantly, and despite (or perhaps because of) his heavy weight gain, Marlon frequently pulled off his pants and his underwear, appearing stark naked from the waist down. That forced the cameraman to shoot him from the waist up. Tensions between Oz and Marlon became so fierce that Marlon refused to appear on the set if his director were there. Marlon said he would take direction only from De Niro.

Before the film was released, Oz tried to play down any conflict he'd had with his star. "Movies can become all the better for off-screen conflict." Producer Gary Foster weighed in as well: "Everybody was trying to make the movie as great as it could be. When you have that kind of creative power, there is bound to be arguments. It's normal."

The reaction of critics was generally favorable. Roger Ebert in the _Chicago Sun-Times_ called it, "the best pure heist movie in recent years." Rita Kempley in the _Washington Post_ thought, _The Score_ was "smart, sleek, and sharply directed. Even if it stank, the volatile chemistry among Robert De Niro, Marlon Brando, and the dynamic Ed Norton would be worth the price of admission." Jay Carr of the _Boston Globe_ concluded that "What we've got in _The Score_ is three great actors kicking a caper movie around like a soccer ball."

For clever quips, the prize went to _Time_ magazine, which claimed that Marlon was made up "like Barbara Bush doing her best Truman Capote impression."

MARLON AND MICHAEL JACKSON--THE FINAL

EMBRACE: Back in the 1980s, Marlon was introduced to Michael Jackson through Quincy Jones. Their friendship grew slowly until the post-millennium when Marlon was proclaiming that "Michael is my best friend...at least the only loyal one. The others have betrayed me."

For nearly two decades Marlon's son, Miko, worked as a security guard at Jackson's Neverland Ranch. After his father's death, Miko told the press: "The last time my father left his house to go anywhere, to spend any kind of time, it was with Michael Jackson. He loved it. My father had a 24-hour chef, 24-hour security, 24-hour help, 24-hour kitchen, 24-hour maid service. Just *carte blanche*. Michael even bought a plasma TV screen for my father. When he moved the set to another room, Michael ordered him another." Miko also claimed that Jackson was the godfather to his daughter, Prudence.

While Jackson was filming a Pepsi Cola commercial in January of 1984, his hair caught fire. It was Miko, hired as his bodyguard, who saved him. Miko often drove Jackson to Mulholland Drive to spend evenings with Marlon. Marlon even worked on a screen treatment for Martin Scorsese. In the proposed scenario, Marlon cast himself as God, with Jackson playing the Devil.

One night Jackson, hoping to entice Marlon to lose weight, brought him fresh vegetables from his organic garden. But what made the evening rather bizzare was that Jackson arrived at Marlon's house dressed in a pink-and-chartreuse Pinocchio outfit, complete with a long nose.

Marlon, or so it was reported, had to use Jackson "as a bank," at one point borrowing one million dollars in cash from him.

Regardless of the stress Marlon faced, Jackson was there for Marlon. The singer was extremely generous to the actor he idolized. There were rumors that Jackson regarded Marlon as a father figure.

Marlon was a recipient of a million-dollar antique watch from Jackson and, in 2001, a milllion-dollar offer to appear at the singer's 30th anniversary concert at Madison Square Garden. In exchange for the cash, Marlon was to deliver a talk praising Jackson.

Marlon came out onto the stage and took a seat. He introduced himself by saying, "You may be thinking, who is that old fat fart sitting there." He then removed his watch and informed the packed crowd, "In the last minute, 100,000 children have been hacked to death with a machete." After that opening, Marlon started to ramble. After ten minutes of mumbling, he was booed off the stage.

By 2001, the world was no longer shocked by almost anything that Jackson or Marlon did. Therefore, the news that Marlon was going to appear in a Michael Jackson video, his latest single, "You Rock My World," didn't cause any shock waves. Marlon was depicted sitting in a chair smoking a cigar, watching, along with a group of mobsters, Jackson dance. Marlon's henchmen appeared poised to beat Jackson up for flirting with Marlon's girl.

In 2002, Marlon was holding private, invitation-only acting workshops for VIPs in Hollywood, everyone from Sean Penn to Johnny Depp. Even Jackson showed up to see an actor almost as eccentric as he was. Before the class, a curtain opened to reveal a corpulent Marlon dressed as a woman under a long blonde wig and wearing a dress of red and purple polka dots with so-called "Joan Crawford fuck-me high heels." He'd slashed his mouth with scarlet red lipstick like Tallulah Bankhead used to wear.

In return for Jackson's kindness, Marlon promised the singer that if any of "those child molestation charges" ever stick to you, I'll get you out of the country and get you to a safe refuge in Tahiti. Don't worry. I can do it!"

614

EPILOGUE

After a life of success, failure, and excess, Marlon Brando died on July 1, 2004. He was 80 years old. New York's *Daily News* screamed in a "secondcoming" banner: THE DON IS DEAD.

According to his wishes, Marlon was cremated. When the ashes were returned to Marlon's home on Mulholland Drive, three vehicles set out heading for Death Valley. The cars contained some of the last remnants of Marlon's dysfunctional family, including Tarita who remembered that the heat was so intense that she could hardly breathe.

As indicated in Marlon's will, family members were taking his ashes here. Before leaving home, they had been mixing his ashes with those of Wally Cox, his longtime companion who had died "so long ago," as Marlon often said.

Facing the scorching sun and biting desert winds, family members tossed half of the combined ashes "into the elements."

The other half of the ashes of both Wally and Marlon were flown to Tetiaroa, his beloved Shangri-La in the South Pacific. There, only Tahitian members of Marlon's family, including Tarita once again, were present as the ashes "committed suicide in the winds."

On the way home from Marlon's Tahitian funeral, Tarita wondered why she, too, couldn't fly away like the birds of Tetiaroa. "Out and up, away into the shadows of the sunset," she pondered. "Like the ashes of Marlon Brando, never to return to this earth."

ADIEUX

AUTHOR'S ACKNOWLEDGMENTS

My mother used to work as the "Girl Friday" (now a politically incorrect term, of course) for that fabulous cabaret entertainer, Sophie Tucker, "The Last of the Red Hot Mammas." Growing up on Miami Beach, I was dazzled by the film and theatrical stars who came to call on Madame Tucker. Ronald Reagan, Jackie Gleason, Bob Hope, Tony Martin, Judy Garland (who knew me by name), and Frank Sinatra, who always gave me a ten-dollar bill (a lot of money for a kid back then). Lena Horne even offered me a glass of champagne. Well, not really. I sipped from her glass when she went to the powder room.

When Ms. Tucker sent my mother to New York with some of her wardrobe concerns, my mother used the opportunity to see a Broadway play. Everybody was talking about the sensational Marlon Brando appearing at the time in Tennessee Williams' *A Streetcar Named Desire.* When she returned to Miami Beach, she told me, "Marlon Brando is the only man I'd ever leave your father for."

This was my first exposure to the mesmerizing influence Marlon had on women. She couldn't stop talking about him, and became one of his most obsessive fans.

When the film version of *Streetcar* opened in Miami, I was the first in line for the twelve o'clock showing. I even stayed glued to my seat for the day's second showing as well. To do this, I had to skip school. That night over dinner, after my mother asked me how my school day went, she invited me to accompany her to the eight o'clock showing of *Streetcar.* That night I saw the movie for the third time. Since then, I long ago lost count of how many stage versions of the play I've seen, how many Stanleys, how many Blanches. There was even a disastrous performance by Tallulah Bankhead as Blanche.

Throughout the 1950s, my classmates and I grew up with Marlon Brando. Movie debates often focused on the question, "who is you favorite actor?" It was always Marlon Brando, James Dean, or Montgomery Clift. When Marlon came charging onto the screen on his motorcycle in *The Wild One*, we abandoned our preconceptions about dress codes and adopted his style.

After my university education, to my surprise, and despite my youth, *The Miami Herald* sent me to Key West as its bureau chief. In those coincidences of life, my next door neighbors turned out to be Tennessee Williams and his longtime companion, Frank Merlo. In no time at all, I was going over there almost nightly for dinners, enjoying Frank's marvelous Italian cooking. In the years to come, I'd reciprocate those dinners both at my home in Key West and in New York.

When Tennessee kicked Frankie out, he came to stay with me in New York. It was there that he started to dictate his memoirs to me. They were mainly revelations about Tennessee, but they also included a number of stories about Marlon. Frankie eventually reconciled with Tennessee, but then died of lung cancer before those memoirs could ever be completed.

I would continue my friendship with Tennessee until his death, hanging out with him in Key West, New York, London, Rome, Los Angeles, and, on one occasion, in Madrid. That was easy and convenient for me to do since I wrote travel books to each of those destinations.

Once when I was living there, Marlon slipped into Key West for a nine-day visit. Since Tennessee was busy writing during the day, his companion and I had Marlon all to ourselves during the day. At night, Marlon had more important things to do. During that brief time, we learned more about Marlon than we ever thought possible.

Over the years Tennessee introduced me to his friends, who sometimes introduced me to their friends. Many of these same friends also knew Marlon, and, if they knew Marlon, if only slightly, they had stories to tell. In fairness to many of the persons I've talked to over the years, no one necessarily knew at the time that they were being "interviewed." Some of them might have been horrified to learn that their comments would one day appear in a book. But, as Tennessee's friend, Truman Capote, once said, "Never trust a writer."

He too arrived in Key West to visit Tennessee and to pursue nocturnal adventures. He not only had scandalous stories about Marlon to entertain us with, but many indiscretions to report. His subjects were just as fascinating as he was: Marilyn Monroe, Jacqueline Kennedy, Montgomery Clift, and, among others, John F. Kennedy.

It was through Tennessee that James Leo Herlihy (the author of *Midnight Cowboy*) and I first met the director Elia Kazan. Although he wrote about Marlon in his autobiography, Kazan saved the most risqué of his tidbits to report in private to intimates.

It was in Rome that Tennessee introduced me to his close friend, Anna Magnani. We made several visits to her apartment, which was always followed by dinner. Ms. Magnani had plenty to say about Marlon. Nothing good.

I was also allowed to visit with Tennessee and Ms. Magnani during the shooting of *The Rose Tattoo*.

One night in Rome, her favorite director, Vittorio De Sica, joined us at table. He had a number of stories to tell about "early Brando," including details about Marlon's involvement with Pier Angeli.

A special thank you goes to Walter Starcke, whom I met in Key West in the late 1950s. This well-known producer collaborated with the playwright-director, John Van Druten, on his play, *Bell Book and Candle*. Later, he became Van Druten's assistant director on the original Broadway production of *The King and I*, and he was privy to the most private details in the life of Van Druten as well as his close friends Noël Coward and Cole Porter. Marlon appeared in the Van Druten play , *I Remember Mama*, long before *Streetcar*.

Through Jim Herlihy, I met Tallulah Bankhead, who was resting in Key West after touring in his play *Crazy October*, which was produced by Walter Starcke. Tallulah had many stories to tell about Marlon—none of them flattering—as well as revelations about virtually everyone else.

In New York, I met Edith Van Cleve, one of Tallulah's closest friends. She was Marlon's theatrical agent, and in time provided priceless information about his early days in theater. She also related enlightening and amusing stories about the famous actresses who appeared backstage to seduce Marlon when he was appearing in *Streetcar*. Shelley Winters first exposed these "string of seductions" in her autobiography, but didn't name names, much less relate details about specific incidents. But Edith did. Normally, Marlon wouldn't have told her so much, but he quickly realized that she was "salivating at the mouth for red meat."

Some of these famous actresses I would eventually meet and know on my own, although Edith's stories were invaluable. I had first met Veronica Lake when I was just a kid. My mother had worked on her picture, *Slattery's Hurricane,* which was shot in Miami.

Tamara Geva introduced me to her best friend, Anne Baxter, who I came to know near the end of her life. The famous literary agent, Jay Garon, threw a party for his client, Hedy Lamarr, and invited me. During the first of several evenings together, she told me, much to my surprise, of her "encounter" with Marlon.

Nearing the end of her life, Ingrid Bergman allowed me to visit her summer home off the western coast of Sweden where she fed me a large beet for lunch. Freed of the pressures of Hollywood and its hype, she talked freely, even telling of many directors who had tried to bring Marlon and her together on the same picture, although she'd met him privately long before.

In Fort Lauderdale, Peter Pell, one-time secretary to Susan Hayward, introduced me to his friend and former employer. Her comments were candid, sizzling, and often testy. Flying to Chicago to see *The Night of the Iguana*,

I was introduced to the play's star, Bette Davis, by Tennessee.

In the years to come, I spent many evenings with her, as I would with her nemesis, Joan Crawford, whom I met when my partner, Stanley Haggart, worked as the art director for some of the Pepsi Cola advertising campaigns. I even spent an evening with Miriam Hopkins off Sheridan Square in New York's Greenwich Village when she was trying to mount a play called *Damn You, Scarlett O'Hara.*

A few years before his death, Maynard Morris, Edith's fellow theatrical agent, entered my life. He was filled with wonderful anecdotes about his clients, Marlon and Monty Clift in the 1940s, including his own chance meeting with Marlon in Paris.

No one hooked me up with more people than Stanley Haggart, who seemed to know everybody in the dance, movie, and theater world. He'd arrived in Hollywood back in the days when you could actually get to know people such as Charlie Chaplin and Mary Pickford. Stanley was a longtime friend of Cary Grant and Randolph Scott.

One of the early boosters of the Katherine Dunham dance troupe, Stanley provided many private details about Marlon's days of "going tribal" when he joined the group. Stanley was also a close friend of Jimmy Donahue, the Woolworth heir, who revealed the juicy details about Marlon's involvement with the tobacco heiress, Doris Duke.

Stanley also had a close friend, Brooks Clift, who worked with him in advertising. Brooks also became my friend, showing up for dinner either alone or, more often, with his famous brother, Monty.

Sometimes he'd bring his mistress, Kim Stanley, the brilliant actress. I eventually learned of Kim's own early involvement with Marlon. Back in Key West, Tennessee also introduced me to Kim's rival, Geraldine Page, an equally brilliant actress, who contributed a marvelous story to this book.

I am also grateful to the Viennese *chanteuse,* Greta Keller, for sharing stories about Marlon's close encounters with Noël Coward and his lover, Jack Wilson.

At TV Graphics, a New York studio that filmed commercials, I encountered a fellow employee, Minnesota-born Steve Gilmore, who provided me with heretofore unknown and behind-the-scenes information about Marlon's days at the Shattuck Military Academy and his own involvements with Marlon. Later in life, Steve's love for Marlon turned bitter when he was abruptly cut off from his idol.

During my first summer in New York, I headed for a holiday in Provincetown. Once there, I immediately encountered Jesse Steele, longtime resident. Back in the 1940s, he knew what was happening in every bedroom at this bohemian resort back. He provided rich anecdotes not only about

Marlon's visits, but about Tennessee's link to the resort as well. In Key West, Tennessee also shared his insights into P-town with me.

I will be forever grateful for the young actor, Howard Bennett, for introducing me to Bobby Lewis, famous for his association with the Actors Studio, and for Bobby allowing me to be ushered into the august presence of Stella Adler. Both of these brilliant people were filled with insights into the life of Marlon in the New York theater during the 1940s. Bobby told me that he was a "voyeur to Marlon in the 1940s. I knew everything going on...well, in Marlon's case, I'd better say 'almost everything.'"

The producer, Harold Clurman, husband of Stella Adler, was a font of information about New York theater in the 40s, and about Marlon in particular. He both admired Marlon's talent and at times "despised the young man."

To actress Ruth Warrick (remember her in *Citizen Kane?*) and Greta Keller, my thanks for confirming what had been rumored for decades—that Marlon worked briefly as a "gentleman escort" in New York during the mid-1940s.

Ted Hook, Tallulah's "secretary," brought that veteran character actress, Mildred Natwick, into my life. Almost immediately, we "bonded at the hip." She told me many stories about the "lavender marriage" of Guthrie McClintic and Katharine Cornell, and she also had a front row seat during the brief affair between Marlon and the bisexual actor, Sir Laurence Olivier.

During her Broadway performance in *Midgie Purvis,* Tallulah introduced me to her director, actor Burgess Meredith. He richly contributed many anecdotes to this book, especially about the theater world of the 1940s, as well as many stories about Marlon. Theresa Helburn, of the Theater Guild and a close friend of Katharine Hepburn, was also a rich contributor, providing insights into Marlon's relationship with his muse, Stella Adler.

It was during Tallulah's very short run in *Midgie Purvis* that I also encountered actor William Redfield. Once a friend of Marlon's, he told me of his own involvement with Marlon, when they both ventured forth in summer stock. Years later, he also provided revelations about his work with Marlon during the 1965 filming of *The Saboteur: Code Name, Morituri.* His comments about Marlon and Yul Brynner were particularly enlightening.

When I was seeing a lot of Susan Strasberg, I met Lee Strasberg, who contributed his own version of events centering around Marlon, Stella Adler, and Method acting. He was not a great admirer of either Stella or Marlon.

It wasn't Tennessee, but the composer Bart Howard ("Fly Me to the Moon") who introduced me to his neighbors, Jessica Tandy and Hume Cronyn. In the months that followed, I spent many evenings with them, as they shared memories of *Streetcar* with me and gave me enough additional material to fill a book on the theater, if I had wished. Their friend, Kim

Hunter, once their guest, also shared her memories of working with Marlon and Jessica for Elia Kazan.

Tennessee also introduced me to his onetime producer, Irene Mayer Selznick, who provided information, not only about the launch of *Streetcar,* but about her father, Louis B. Mayer, and the early days of MGM.

In the 1960s, I frequently encountered author James Baldwin, who had many "delicious tidbits" to tell about Marlon and his other experiences as well. Baldwin contributed the incident about where Marlon met Norman Mailer and himself in a Greenwich Village cafeteria.

Tom Ewell appeared in his last film, *The Last Resort,* based on a novel I'd written, *Butterflies in Heat.* Nearing the end of his life, Ewell was in a confessional mood. Night after night in Key West, where the film was shot, he spoke about his life, with marvelous stories about Marlon during the Forties in New York, as well as anecdotes about Katharine Hepburn and Marilyn Monroe, with whom he'd appeared in films. Barbara Baxley, also starring in *The Last Resort,* had keen insights to offer about two of her former best friends, Marlon Brando and James Dean. Both Tom Ewell and Dorothy Raymer, a columnist for the *Key West Citizen,* contributed insights into the brief Leonard Bernstein/Brando affair.

Stanley Haggart had a friend, the TV producer, Rogers Brackett, who had virtually launched James Dean in New York. Stanley and another friend, the composer Alec Wilder, shared many Marlon/Dean stories with me, although not for publication.

Jane Sinclair, whom I'd first met in California and then later called upon at her home in Paris, had been a close friend of Rita Hayworth. She knew about Marlon's own involvement with the love goddess and spoke freely about this. Jane was also a friend of Marlon's two longtime French lovers, Christian Marquand and Daniel Gélin. She provided many insights into Marlon's controversial relationships with these two handsome French actors, and she also knew of Marlon's days with Roger Vadim and his "sex kitten," Brigitte Bardot. But no one helped me more than Jane's friend, Jacques Viale, who at one time had entertained the idea of writing a memoir about Marlon's early days in Paris and his involvements with the cultural elite there.

During the course of my decades in California, I often sought out movie producers such as Stanley Kramer and Fred Zinnemann to talk to about movies and their careers in general—and often about Marlon specifically. Edward Dmytryk also had much insiderish information to tell about directing Monty Clift and Marlon in *The Young Lions.*

None of these august men were as articulate and as charming as the director, Joseph Mankiewicz. I met him at a party that Lucille Lortel threw for him at her suite in New York's Sherry-Netherland Hotel. Nearing the end of his life, he was most willing in the weeks ahead to share his memories, especially those that involved his direction of Marlon in both *Julius Caesar* and *Guys and Dolls,* and what was going on behind the scenes.

No one helped me more than Carlo Fiore, for decades Marlon's best friend, until Marlon turned on him. I met Carlo when he was working for my dear friend, the California-based tycoon, Gordon Howard. Over the years, I spent much time with Carlo, listening to his stories about Marlon, only a few of which he related within his book, *Bud: The Brando I Knew.*

Marlon was furious at Carlo for writing a book about him after their friendship had ended. Carlo thought that his former friend was completely unfair. "Since I could have told so much more—I knew where all the bodies were buried." At any rate, Marlon never forgave Carlo, who grew increasingly bitter after Marlon denounced him. Without Carlo, I would not have had a book with such rich "insider" details.

Gordon Howard himself, a Westerner of charm, grace, and sophistication, collected old cars once owned by movie stars during the 1920s, and restored them to running order. "I know everybody in California worth knowing," he often boasted to me. Sometimes I put him to the test, as on the weekend we drove out to see "my dear friend," Louis L'Amour, the famous Western writer. At the time, I had no idea that L'Amour even knew Marlon, but immediately following Marlon's marriage to Anna Kashfi, he spent his honeymoon week with the L'Amours.

L'Amour, to hear him tell it, let a life that was far more interesting that anything he ever put on paper.

Sam Gilman replaced Carlo Fiore as Marlon's best friend. Except for one break, Marlon and Sam became "friends for life." However, during that break, Gilman was so infuriated at Marlon that he contacted Jay Garon, the literary agent in New York who specialized in celebrity exposés, and poured out much of what he knew about Marlon. However, when Marlon learned that yet another book was coming out about his private life, in the wake of the publication of *Bud* by Carlo Fiore, he called Gilman. The two friends reconciled, and Marlon even arranged for future acting work for Gilman. Gilman withdrew his proposed memoirs from circulation, but not before some of his most personal revelations about Marlon made the rounds of New York publishers.

In half a century, I heard and recorded hundreds of stories about Marlon. To write this portrait, I had to toss out enough material for a dozen other books about Marlon. It was all too much, the life too rich. But for all the many people over the years who contributed even the smallest detail, a paragraph or less, I am deeply grateful.

The author wishes to thank **Monica Dunn** for her ongoing assistance with editorial aspects of this book.

My gratitude is also extended to my courageous publisher, **Danforth Prince**, who labored long and diligently to get this book onto the shelves of bookstores. He reviewed my sources, perused my notes (many of them withered with age), and sharpened and focused this book's presentation. Without undue drama, he handled zillions of problems, and aggressively promoted this book in most of the countries of the English-speaking world. To Dan, and to Blood Moon Productions, heartfelt thanks.

Author's Final Note

Within the pages of this book, the source of each individual piece of information is positioned very close to the spot where the information actually appears.

Also within the pages, direct quotations have been transcribed "as they were remembered" by the people who originally heard the remarks. They're presented in the same format, using the same phraseologies, that were used when those remarks were originally transmitted to me. If the exact wording and phraseologies of any individual quotation are *not* accurately presented, the author hopes that the points being made, and the impressions being relayed, have nonetheless been rendered and repeated as accurately as possible.

Throughout this biography, I sincerely hope that I have transmitted and preserved the essence of once-fabled lives, including that of Mr. Brando himself.

To each of the sources noted above—dead or alive—and to the countless others not mentioned, I extend my heartfelt thanks for unveiling an American original, Marlon Brando Jr.

Darwin Porter
New York City
October, 2005

INDEX

If you've enjoyed this book,

Please consider these other fine works by
Darwin Porter

from

Biographies that change the way America
interprets its cinematic past.

www.BloodMoonProductions.com

The Secret Life of
HUMPHREY BOGART
The Early Years (1899-1931)

by Darwin Porter

When it was released in June of 2003, this book ignited a firestorm of media controversy that spilled immediately from the tabloids into mainstream newspapers, magazines, and talk shows.

This is the best, most controversial, and most revealing book ever written about the movie stars of the Golden Age.

The Secret Life of
Humphrey Bogart
The Early Years
(1899 - 1931)
Darwin Porter

This myth-shattering biography gives a controversial CLOSEUP of a young, hot and horny Bogart pre-Casablanca, pre-Bacall, pre-African Queen Revealing for the first time what was under the trench coat of history's most famous movie star

"Humphrey Bogart was one of Hollywood's most celebrated lovers, his romance with Lauren Bacall hailed as one of the greatest love stories of the 20th century. But before they met, he was a drug-taking womanizer, racking up a string of failed marriages and broken relationships with some of the world's most beautiful women. In this extraordinary biography, drawing on a wealth of previously unseen material, veteran showbusiness writer Darwin Porter, author of *Hollywood's Silent Closet,* reveals the truth about Bogart's shady past."

As reported by London's *Mail on Sunday* in June of 2003

From The Georgia Literary Association
(an affiliate of Blood Moon Productions)
ISBN 0966-8030-5-1
528 pages, plus 64 photos. $16.95

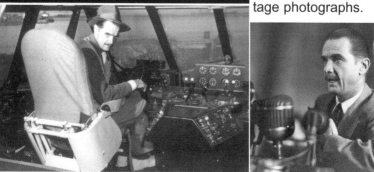

WHAT THE CRITICS SAID:

"Thanks to Darwin Porter's biography of Howard Hughes, we'll never be able to look at the old pin-ups in quite the same way"

THE LONDON TIMES,
March 30, 2005

"Darwin Porter grew up in the midst of Hollywood Royalty. His access to film industy insiders and other Hughes confidantes supplied him with the resources he needed to create a portrait that both corroborates what other Hughes biographies have divulged and go them one better."

CAROL HAGGAS, WRITING FOR FOREWORD
MAGAZINE, JULY, 2005

"According to a new biography by Darwin Porter, Hughes's attitude toward sex, like the Emperor Caligula, was selfish at best and at its worst, sadistic. He was obsessed with controlling his lovers and, although he had a pathological fear of relationships and marriage, he proposed to countless women, often at the same time. Only three people successfully resisted Hughes's persistent advances: Elizabeth Taylor, Jean Simmons, and Joan Crawford. Of the three, it was Crawford who most succinctly revealed her reasons for refusing Hughes's advances, "I adore homosexuals, but not in my bed after midnight."

LONDON's SUNDAY EXPRESS,
MARCH 20, 2005